Julius Heise
Securitising Decolonisation

Postcolonial Studies | Volume 51

Die freie Verfügbarkeit der E-Book-Ausgabe dieser Publikation wurde ermöglicht durch
Pollux – Informationsdienst Politikwissenschaft

und die Open Library Community Politik 2024 – einem Netzwerk wissenschaftlicher Bibliotheken zur Förderung von Open Access in den Sozial- und Geisteswissenschaften:

Vollsponsoren: Technische Universität Braunschweig | Carl von Ossietzky-Universität Oldenburg | Eberhard-Karls Universität Tübingen | Freie Universität Berlin – Universitätsbibliothek | Niedersächsische Staats- und Universitätsbibliothek Göttingen | Goethe-Universität Frankfurt am Main | Gottfried Wilhelm Leibniz Bibliothek – Niedersächsische Landesbibliothek | TIB – Leibniz-Informationszentrum Technik und Naturwissenschaften und Universitätsbibliothek | Humboldt-Universität zu Berlin | Justus-Liebig-Universität Gießen | Universitätsbibliothek Eichstätt-Ingolstadt | Ludwig-Maximilians-Universität München | Max Planck Digital Library (MPDL) | Rheinische Friedrich-Wilhelms-Universität Bonn | Ruhr-Universität Bochum | Staats- und Universitätsbibliothek Carl von Ossietzky, Hamburg | SLUB Dresden | Staatsbibliothek zu Berlin | Bibliothek der Technischen Universität Chemnitz | Universitäts- und Landesbibliothek Darmstadt | Universitätsbibliothek „Georgius Agricola" der TU Bergakademie Freiberg | Universitätsbibliothek Kiel (CAU) | Universitätsbibliothek Leipzig | Universitäts- und Landesbibliothek Düsseldorf | Universitäts- und Landesbibliothek Münster | Universitäts- und Stadtbibliothek Köln | Universitätsbibliothek Bielefeld | Universitätsbibliothek Erfurt | Universitätsbibliothek der FernUniversität in Hagen | Universitätsbibliothek Kaiserslautern-Landau | Universitätsbibliothek Kassel | Universitätsbibliothek Osnabrück | Universität Potsdam | Universitätsbibliothek St. Gallen | Universitätsbibliothek Vechta | Zentralbibliothek Zürich

Sponsoring Light: Bundesministerium der Verteidigung | Bibliothek der Hochschule für Technik und Wirtschaft Dresden | Bibliothek der Hochschule für Technik, Wirtschaft und Kultur Leipzig | Bibliothek der Westsächsischen Hochschule Zwickau | Bibliothek der Hochschule Zittau/Görlitz, Hochschulbibliothek | Hochschulbibliothek der Hochschule Mittweida | Institut für Auslandsbeziehungen (IfA) | Landesbibliothek Oldenburg | Österreichische Parlamentsbibliothek

Mikrosponsoring: Bibliothek der Berufsakademie Sachsen | Bibliothek der Evangelische Hochschule Dresden | Bibliothek der Hochschule für Musik und Theater „Felix Mendelssohn Bartholdy" Leipzig | Bibliothek der Hochschule für Bildende Künste Dresden | Bibliothek der Hochschule für Musik „Carl Maria von Weber" Dresden | Bibliothek der Hochschule für Grafik und Buchkunst Leipzig | Bibliothek der Palucca-Hochschule für Tanz Dresden | Leibniz-Institut für Europäische Geschichte | Stiftung Wissenschaft und Politik (SWP) – Deutsches Institut für Internationale Politik und Sicherheit

Julius Heise

Securitising Decolonisation

The Silencing of Ewe and Togoland Unification
under United Nations Trusteeship, 1945-1960

[transcript]

This publication constitutes a shortened version of the doctoral dissertation "'Give Unification or We Perish': The (failed) Securitisation of Ewe and Togoland Unification under United Nations Trusteeship" submitted to the Department of Social Sciences and Philosophoy at the University of Marburg.

The research was funded by the Deutsche Forschungsgemeinschaft (DFG, German Research Foundation) – project number 227068724. Open access funding provided by the Open Access Publishing Fund of Philipps-Universität Marburg with support of the Deutsche Forschungsgemeinschaft (DFG, German Research Foundation).

Bibliographic information published by the Deutsche Nationalbibliothek
The Deutsche Nationalbibliothek lists this publication in the Deutsche Nationalbibliografie; detailed bibliographic data are available in the Internet at https://dnb.dnb.de/

This work is licensed under the Creative Commons Attribution 4.0 (BY) license, which means that the text may be remixed, transformed and built upon and be copied and redistributed in any medium or format even commercially, provided credit is given to the author.
https://creativecommons.org/licenses/by/4.0/
Creative Commons license terms for re-use do not apply to any content (such as graphs, figures, photos, excerpts, etc.) not original to the Open Access publication and further permission may be required from the rights holder. The obligation to research and clear permission lies solely with the party re-using the material.

First published in 2024 by transcript Verlag, Bielefeld
© Julius Heise

Cover layout: Maria Arndt, Bielefeld
Cover illustration: UN Photo / Lomé, French Togoland, natives manifest for Unification of Eweland during visit of the Mission to West Africa
Printed by: Majuskel Medienproduktion GmbH, Wetzlar
https://doi.org/10.14361/9783839473061
Print-ISBN: 978-3-8376-7306-7
PDF-ISBN: 978-3-8394-7306-1
EPUB-ISBN: 978-3-7328-7306-7
ISSN of series: 2703-1233
eISSN of series: 2703-1241

Printed on permanent acid-free text paper.

Contents

List of Photographs, Figures, and Maps 9

List of Tables 11

List of Abbreviations 13

Acknowledgements 15

1. **Introduction** 17
1.1 Secessionist Conflict in "Western Togoland" 17
1.2 Research Puzzle & Goal 32
1.3 Argument & Approach 33
1.4 Relevance & Contribution 35
1.5 Outline 35

2. **State of the Art** 37
2.1 Neo-Trusteeship & (In)Security 37
    2.1.1 Antecedents: From Transitional to Structural Problems (1960-1970s) 38
    2.1.2 The 1st Generation: Of 'Quasi' & 'Failed States' 38
    2.1.3 The 2nd Generation: From Peace-*Keeping* to State-*Building* 45
    2.1.4 The 3rd Generation: Colonial Reminiscence 48
    2.1.5 The 4th Generation: The Local Turn 57
    2.1.6 The 5th Generation? Decolonising State-Building 59
    2.1.7 Postcolonial Security Studies 61
2.2 Trusteeship & (De)Colonisation 67
    2.2.1 Origins of Trusteeship 67
    2.2.2 The United Nations Trusteeship System & Security 72
2.3 Togoland 79
    2.3.1 State- & Nationhood 79
    2.3.2 Security 87
2.4 Situating the Research Agenda 91

3. Theoretical Framework ... 93
3.1 Copenhagen School ... 94
3.1.1 Internalist vs. Externalist Understanding ... 97
3.1.2 The Audience's Agency ... 98
3.1.3 Securitisation *Theory*? Or: How to Predict the Present ... 100
3.1.4 Historicisation of Security & Securitisation of History ... 102
3.1.5 Securitisation in a Postcolonial Reading ... 105
3.2 Paris School ... 110
3.3 Research Perspective ... 112

4. Methods ... 115
4.1 Research Design ... 115
4.1.1 A Constructivist Study ... 115
4.1.2 A Qualitative & Comparative Study ... 117
4.2 Archival Research ... 118
4.2.1 Archives Visited ... 121
4.2.2 Challenge of Access & Supplementary Sources ... 124
4.2.3 Research Procedure & Evaluation ... 128

5. Historical Background: From Slave Coast to Mandate Territory ... 131
5.1 Precolonial Era & Introduction of European Rule ... 132
5.1.1 From 'Gold Coast' to 'Slave Coast' ... 132
5.1.2 Ewe Heterogeneity ... 133
5.1.3 The Emergence of 'Eweness' ... 135
5.2 The 'Schutzgebiet Togoland' ... 137
5.2.1 Drawing Borders & Conquest of the Hinterland ... 139
5.2.2 Exploitation & Modernization ... 141
5.2.3 Petitions as Anticolonial Resistance ... 143
5.3 Togoland under Mandate ... 145
5.3.1 Creation of the Mandates System ... 145
5.3.2 French & British Togoland under Mandate ... 158

6. The Securitisation of Ewe & Togoland Unification before the United Nations ... 167
6.1 Bringing Togoland under United Nations Trusteeship ... 167
6.1.1 Establishment of the United Nations Trusteeship System ... 169
6.1.2 The Instruments of International Supervision ... 172
6.2 The All-Ewe-Conference & First Petitions under Trusteeship ... 179
6.2.1 Formation of the 'Ewe Parties' ... 179
6.2.2 Establishment of the Petition Procedure ... 182
6.3 Security Matters: Trouble in Accra & Abidjan (1948-1951) ... 194
6.3.1 The Accra Riots & the Special Branch ... 194
6.3.2 The Abidjan Troubles & the Service de Sûreté ... 202
6.4 Securitising Petitions I: Trusteeship Council (1949-1951) ... 204
6.4.1 New Restrictions for Petitions & Visiting Missions (1949) ... 204
6.4.2 The Anglo-French "Master Stroke" (1950) ... 217

  6.4.3 From Ewe to Togoland Unification (1951).. 226
6.5 Securitising Petitions II: The General Assembly (1951-1955)................................ 237
  6.5.1 After Vogan: Double Standard for Examining Petitions (1951)........................ 239
  6.5.2 Political Development under Security Surveillance (1952) 245
  6.5.3 Securitising the French "Reign of Terror" (1952) 253
  6.5.4 A Spectre haunts Africa – the Spectre of the "Red Menace" (1953) 262
6.6 Turning the Tides I: British Togoland (1954-1957).. 275
  6.6.1 "A New Type of Threat" (1954).. 278
  6.6.2 Action Plan & Internal Security Updates (1955) 290
  6.6.3 The 3rd Visiting Mission (1955) 293
  6.6.4 Anglo-French Arrangements for the Togoland Referenda (1955) 296
  6.6.5 The British Togoland Referendum (1956) 301
6.7 Turning the Tides II: French Togoland (1956-1960) 304
  6.7.1 Loi-Cadre & the Autonomous Republic of Togoland (1956) 304
  6.7.2 The French Togoland Referendum (1956) 308
6.8 The Independence of British & French Togoland 320
  6.8.1 Securitising the Independence of French Togoland (1957).......................... 326
  6.8.2 The Parliamentary Election in French Togoland (1958) 338
  6.8.3 Termination of Trusteeship & Independence 344
6.9 Post-Independence Conflict.. 347
  6.9.1 Repressive Tit-For-Tat (1960-1962) 354
  6.9.2 Assassination of Olympio (1963).. 362
  6.9.3 Aftermath: Rise & Demise of The Togoland Liberation Movement 365

7. Conclusion.. 367
7.1 General Summary.. 367
7.2 Key Findings and Conclusion 369
  7.2.1 Sub-Question 1: (In)Securitisation by the Administering Authorities 369
  7.2.2 Sub-Question 2: Securitisation by the Petitioners 373
  7.2.3 Sub-Question 3: The United Nations as an Audience of Securitisation 375
  7.2.4 General Conclusion 377
7.3 Potentials, Limits, Outlook 380

Bibliography 383

List of Photographs, Figures, and Maps

Map 1:	"Western Togoland"	18
Map 2:	Ewe Settlements & Togoland under UN Trusteeship (1946-1957)	19
Map 3:	Reorganization of the Volta Region	23
Map 4:	Ewe Settlements	134
Photo 1:	Schutztruppe in German Togoland	139
Map 5:	German Togoland (1885-1915)	140
Map 6:	Simon-Milner Boundary Accords (1920)	150
Map 7:	Border Demarcation across Eweland (1920-1956)	151
Figure 1:	Distribution of the Ewe-speaking population (1947)	151
Photo 2:	Meeting of the Togobund, Accra (26 July 1931)	154
Figure 2:	Structure of the Trusteeship System	171
Photo 3:	Sylvanus Olympio & Ralph Bunche, Lake Success (8 December 1947)	188
Photo 4:	Olympio addressing a crowd at Hotel Tonyeviadji, Lomé (4 January 1948)	190
Photo 5:	CUT Meeting after Olympio's return, Lomé (4 January 1948)	191
Photo 6a & 6b:	AEC Meeting after Olympio's return, Ho (11 January 1948)	191
Figure 3:	Police Force in British Togoland (1947-1955)	198
Photo 7:	Ewe Unificationist awaiting the Visiting Mission, Lomé (December 1949)	210
Photo 8:	Amu, Simpson & Olympio at Palais de Nations, Geneva (20 March 1950)	215
Photo 9:	Asare, Antor & Olympio before Hearing, Lake Success (11 July 1950)	218
Photo 10:	Ayeva & Olympio before Council Hearing, Lake Success (11 July 1950)	219
Figure 4:	Written Petitions from Togoland handled by the Council (1947-1959)	223
Photo 11:	Enlarged Consultative Commission (7 November 1950)	225
Figure 5:	Written Petitions on the Trusteeship Council's Agenda (1954-1957)	244
Figure 6:	Trusteeship Council Resolutions on Petitions (1952-1956)	245
Photo 12:	Chairman of the 1952 UN Visiting Mission (2 September 1952)	250
Photo 13:	Olympio & Antor conversing with Ralph Bunche (1 December 1952)	255
Photo 14:	Robert Ajavon addressing the 4th Committee (12 December 1952)	258
Photo 15:	Odame, Olympio & Kpodar before 4th Committee (15 December 1952)	259
Photo 16:	Petitioners of Togoland Congress (17 November 1953)	272
Photo 17:	Oral Hearing of Integrationists (1 March 1954)	277
Photo 18:	15 Togoland Petitioners before the 4th Committee (1 December 1954)	284

Figure 7:	Number of Petitioners before the 4th Committee (1951-1957)	287
Map 8:	Voting Districts as Recommended by Visiting Mission (1955)	295
Photo 19:	Togoland Unificationists before 4th Committee (1 December 1955)	298
Photo 20:	Voting Campaign in Southern Togoland (April 1956)	301
Photo 21:	March organised by Togoland Congress, Ho (6 May 1956)	302
Photo 22:	Alex Odame addressing a gathering, Jasikan (April 1956)	302
Photo 23:	Referendum Day, Logba Adzakoe (9 May 1956)	302
Map 9:	British Togoland Referendum (1956)	303
Photo 24:	Togoland Congress and CPP before 4th Committee (ca. November 1956)	311
Photo 25:	Pro-French Counter-Petitioners before 4th Committee (3 January 1957)	316
Photo 26:	Akakpo, Santos & Olympio before 4th Committee (03 January 1957)	317
Photo 27:	The "King-Commission" (3 May 1957)	319
Photo 28:	Sylvanus Olympio before Trusteeship Council (17 April 1957)	327
Photo 29:	Apedo-Amah & Koscziusko-Morizet (12 September 1957)	332
Photo 30:	Akakpo & Ohin before 4th Committee (8 November 1957)	333
Photo 31:	Santos & Olympio before 4th Committee (8 November 1957)	335
Photo 32:	Bureau of UN Observation Mission (25 March 1958)	338
Photo 33:	Emergency registration, Hall of Justice, Lomé (7 April 1958)	339
Photo 34:	Line-up during election day, Agabadelogan (27 April 1958)	341
Photo 35:	CUT and Juvento supporters celebrating, Lomé (1 May 1958)	342
Map 10:	French Togoland Parliamentary Elections (1958)	343
Photo 36:	Juventists singing party song on election eve (26 April 1958)	344
Photo 37:	Olympio (with nameplate of France), 4th Committee (3 November 1958)	346
Photo 38:	Prime Ministers Olympio & Nkrumah, Lomé (11 June 1960)	355
Photo 39:	March for the re-unification of Togoland, Lomé (23 September 1961)	357
Photo 40:	"The Togo that we want," Lomé (23 September 196)	357

List of Tables

Table 1: Silence Dilemma & Three Wise Monkeys 107
Table 2: Securitisation's Silence Dilemma resulting from..... 108
Table 3: Results Togolese Assembly, Elections (1946-1952) 246
Table 4: 1954 General Elections' results in British Togoland (South) 281
Table 5: Togolese Security Personnel after Independence 353

List of Abbreviations

AFP	Agence France-Presse
ANOM	Archives Nationales d'Outre-Mer (Aix-en-Provence)
ANF	Archives Nationales de France (Pierrefitte-sur-Seine)
ANT	Archives Nationales du Togo (Lomé)
AOF	Afrique Occidentale Français
BNI	Bureau of National Investigation (Ghana)
CenSeC	Central Security Committee (Gold Coast)
CFA	Franc des Colonies Françaises d'Afrique
CPP	Convention People's Party
CSS	Critical Security Studies
CUT	Comité de l'Unité Togolaise
DisSeC	District Security Council
GAOR	General Assembly Official Records
HMG	Her/His Majesty's Government
HSGF	Homeland Study Group Foundation
ILRM	International League for the Rights of Man
Juvento	Mouvement de la Jeunesse Togolaise
LIC	Local Intelligence Committee (Gold Coast)
MAE	Archives Diplomatiques du Ministère des Affaires Étrangères (La Courneuve)
MI5	Military Intelligence 5
MPT	Mouvement Populaire Togolais
NIB	National Intelligence Bureau (Ghana)
NSC	National Security Council (Ghana)
NSGTs	Non-Self-Governing Territories
PTP	Parti Togolais du Progrès

R2P	Responsibility to Protect
RDA	Rassemblement Démocratique Africain
RegSeC	Regional Security Council
PMC	Permanent Mandates Commission
PRAAD	Public Records and Archives Administration Department (Accra & Ho)
PUT	Parti de l'Unité Togolaise
SB	Special Branch
SCRBC	Schomburg Center for Research in Black Culture (New York)
SDECE	Service de Documentation et de Contre-Espionage
SLO	Security Liaison Officer
TCOR	Trusteeship Council Official Records
TNA	The National Archive (London)
TOLIMO	Togoland Liberation Movement
UCPN	Union des Chefs et des Population du Nord
UDPT	Union Démocratique des Peuples Togolais
UN	United Nations
UN	ARMS United Nations Archives and Records Management
UNPO	Unrepresented Nations and Peoples Organization
USA	United States of America
USSR	Union of Soviet Socialist Republics

Acknowledgements

A project of this size and scope is a product of rewarding friendships and rich collegial exchanges that accumulated many intellectual, personal, and financial debts.

Thorsten Bonacker, under whose supervision this dissertation was written, first drafted the cornerstones of this project. Above all, I thank him for "entrusting" me with the investigation of this case as a research fellow. Special gratitude goes to the circle of colleagues in the research project: Werner Distler and Maria Ketzmerick have contributed to this study with their own research on the UN Trusteeship System and showed me the way around the vagaries of the German university system and academia in general. Our research project could not have been what it was without the work of our student assistants: Karoline Möller, Lea Stromowski, Luisa Seutter, Laura Kotzur, Theresa Bachmann, and Leonie Disselkamp. Special gratitude must go the latter for supporting my work with her incredible dedication and with in-depth office conversations that kept me on the toes. I am grateful to have enjoyed the collegial companionship of the staff at the Center for Conflict Studies (CCS): Susanne Buckley-Zistel, Stéphane Voell, Philipp Lottholz, Alina Giesen, Miriam Tekath, Tareq Sydiq, Joana Amaral, Stephen Foose, Alexandra Engelsdorfer, and Astrid Juckenack.

I would also like to thank my colleagues from the SFB/TRR 138 "Dynamics of Security," especially Marina Kraft and Angela Marciniak for their supportive work, but also the other doctoral students, through the unifying awareness that we were all in the same boat. I also benefited immensely from the collegial exchange with the members of the project group *Intersectionality and Difference*. Gratitude goes to Sigrid Ruby for willingly steering the group over the four years and to Huub van Baar for the many helpful comments.

In my research, I benefited from the expertise and guidance of the staff of several archival institutions to whom I am grateful for allowing me to consult documents and other works in their possession. Among those I would like to mention the reading room staff the *Archives Nationales du Togo* (ANT) and the *Bibliothèque Nationale du Togo* in Lomé; the *Public Records and Archives Administration Department* (PRAAD) in Accra and the regional branch in Ho (special gratitude goes to Augustine Julius Gede, who with tremendous kindness helped me immensely in finding delicate source material); Kathryn of the *United Nations Records Management Section* (UN ARMS) in New York, the staff at the *Archives Nationales de France* (ANF) in Pierfitte-sûr-Seine, Paris; the staff of *The National Archive* (TNA) in London; the *Archives Nationales d'Outre Mer* (ANOM) in Aix-en-Provence; and the *Archives Diplomatiques du Ministère des Affaires Étrangères* (MAE) in La Courneuve, Paris.

I am grateful for the research tips of the following scholars who pointed me to source material and initiated further contacts: Joël Glassman, Kokou Azamade, Emmanuel K. Noglo, Adovi Michel Goeh-Akue, and Alexander Keese.

I am also grateful to all the anonymous reviewers of the research papers, who cannot be named here. Although not always easy to deal with the anonymised criticism, the comments have nonetheless improved the argumentation of this dissertation.

In Togo and Ghana, I was fortunate to have many friends and an incredibly supportive host-family. Special thanks to the Ahli family who hosted me so long ago, who endeavoured to stay connected and who hosted me again without further ado. Especially I would like to thank my host mother, Lucie Ahli and my *fofoga* Albert Yao Ahli. You were the most patient and loyal company I had during my stays in Togo. I would like to thank my long friend Alfred Kokou Gbidi, who provided me access to Emmanuel Go-Konu at the *Université de Lomé*.

The best should be saved for last. Above all, I would like to thank my family: my lovely daughter, without whom this project would certainly have been completed a year earlier, and my wife, Alina. This project has benefited in so many ways from her help, whether academically, linguistically, organisationally, emotionally, or financially. You always had my back.

Thank you. To all of you.

1. Introduction

> "We live in an illusion of security in this country without recourse to the lessons of the past."[1]

1.1 Secessionist Conflict in "Western Togoland"

On 6 March 2017, during Ghana's 60-year independence celebrations, Ghanaian security forces arrested the leadership of the *Homeland Study Group Foundation* (HSGF),[2] including its then 84-year-old founder, Charles Kwame Kudzordzi. Shortly after Ghana returned to democratic rule in 1992, the former educationist and self-proclaimed Ewe-historian founded the HSGF in 1994 to openly advocate for the secession of parts of Ghana's Northern, Upper East, and Volta Region to form the state of "Western Togoland" (see Map 1).[3]

When members of the HSGF were spotted wearing T-shirts reading "9 May 2017 is OUR DAY Western Togoland" Ghanaian security agencies suspected the group to make a declaration of independence and thus arrested its leadership.[4] Apart from the suspiciously deliberate decision of the Ghanaian security forces to arrest the group on 6 March, thereby producing a nationalist statement during Ghana's 60th independence celebration, the HSGF's allusion to "9 May" was a reference to another symbolic date – in Ghana's national history and the history of decolonisation at large.

---

1   Samuel Adjei Sarfo, "The Secession of the Togolanders," *GhanaWeb*, 26 September 2020.
2   A. B. Kafui Kanyi, "Police Arrest Volta Secessionist Group Leaders," *Modern Ghana*, 08 March 2017.
3   Leticia Osei, "Police to Charge Volta 'Separatist' Group Members with Treason," *Ultimate FM online*, 08 March 2017.
4   Tim Dzamboe, "Group to Declare 'Volta Region' Independence on May 9, 2017," *Graphic Online*, 17 August 2016.

Map 1: "Western Togoland"

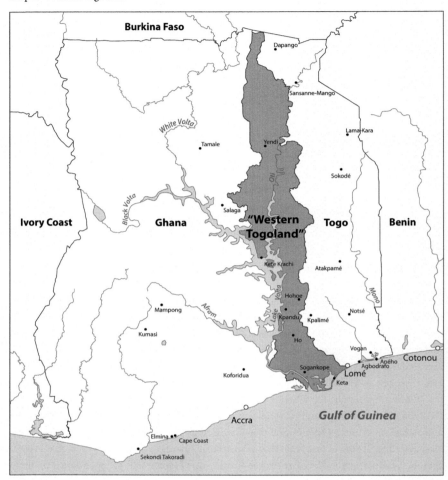

Source: Own creation.

The Division of Togoland

After World War I, the former colony of German Togoland was divided among France and Britain as spoils of war: "Eastern" Togoland became a League of Nations mandate territory under French administration and "Western" Togoland became a mandate territory under British administration. However, the new colonial border demarcation cut through the settlement area of the Ewe people(s),[5] the majority of which found itself split among three territories: French mandated Togoland, British mandated Togoland, and the "Volta Triangle" of the British Gold Coast Colony (see Map 2).

---

5   The plurality-s aims to indicate the commonly held understanding that the Ewe-speaking people in the region neither ethnically nor politically formed a homogeneous unit in the pre-colonial period.

Map 2: Ewe Settlements & Togoland under UN Trusteeship (1946–1957)

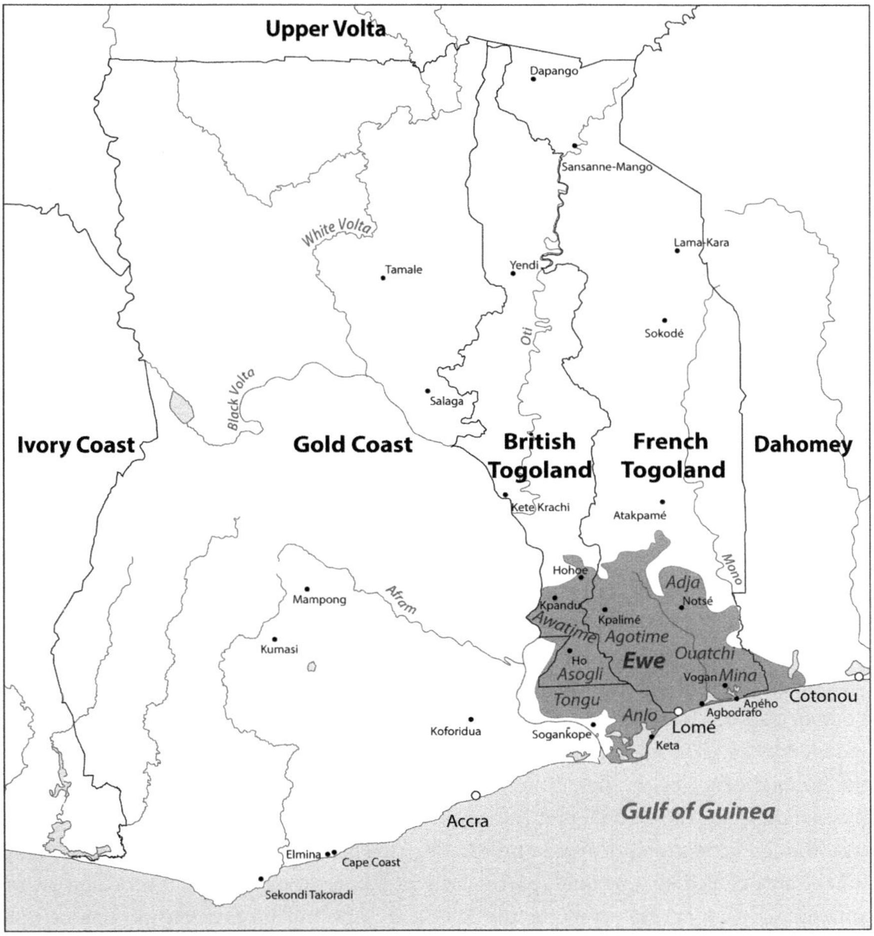

Source: Own creation.

After World War II, the League of Nations Mandates System was transformed into the United Nations Trusteeship System and oversight of Togoland's path to self-determination developed a dynamic of its own: the division of the territory led to the formation of a unification movement, which at first campaigned for the unification of 'Eweland' and later for the reunification of French and British Togoland within its former 'German' borders. The unification movement petitioned the United Nations – a right which hardly any other dependent people had dreamed of having recourse to. By using the *right to petition* the unification movement soon turned into something like a "star turn"[6] of the United

---

6   TNA (London), FO 371/138270, *Foreign policy of Togoland*, 1959, A.T. Oldham to H.F.T. Smith [Confidential Letter No. 5110/59], 24 April 1959.

Nations, where it regularly pointed out violations of the Trusteeship Agreements and human rights, discrediting the rule and prestige of France and Britain.

For these two colonial powers, the unificationists' campaign represented a concrete threat to the unity and integrity of their post-colonial associations of states: France wanted to keep French ("Eastern") Togoland in the French Union and Britain wanted to integrate British ("Western") Togoland into the Gold Coast, thereby keeping it within the British Commonwealth of Nations. Even though human rights gained international recognition and France and Britain were *de jure* the United Nations' "Administering Authorities" and not colonial powers, both powers ostracized the Ewe and Togoland unification movement, presenting unification as a minority demand that was unfeasible, unpractical, and overall, a serious threat that could set a potential precedent for the 'balkanisation' of the African continent at large.

In the end, after years of negotiations before the venues of the United Nations as well as political campaigns and colonial repression in the trusteeship territories themselves, the movement's *Dream of Unity*[7] failed to materialise: On 9 May 1956, the United Nations supervised for the first time in its history an independence referendum, which eventually sealed the incorporation of the trusteeship territory of British ("Western") Togoland into the neighbouring colony of the British Gold Coast. Consequently, the referendum sealed the definitive separation of the trusteeship territory of British ("Western") Togoland from the trusteeship territory of French ("Eastern") Togoland and thereby put an end to the decade-long debate at the United Nations on the demand for the unification of the Ewe people and the two Togolands.

Under the leadership of Kwame Nkrumah, British Togoland and the Gold Coast merged to form a new state, Ghana, which became the first African colony to gain independence on 6 March 1957. Ghana's independence, thus, encompassed not only the independence of the first colony in sub-Saharan Africa but at the same time the independence of the first United Nations trusteeship territory. Ghana's independence on 6 March 1957 is widely deemed a milestone in the history of decolonisation.[8] For many inhabitants of British Togoland, particularly in its northern regions, it represented an anticolonial victory. However, for the Ewe and Togoland unification movement, the referendum on 9 May 1956 was tantamount to an anticolonial defeat. Especially many Ewes criticised the integration because it degraded them to an ethnic minority within the Akan-dominated state of Ghana and further removed them from the Ewes in neighbouring French Togoland. Thus, until today, 9 May 1956 and 6 March 1957 respectively, symbolize the tension between two contesting nationalist visions for the region.

A Reawakened Western Togoland Nationalism

Although the HSGF is calling for neither the unification of the Ewe people nor of the two former Togolands anymore, its followers still embrace a territorial 'Western Togoland'

---

7 Claude E. Welch, *Dream of Unity: Pan-Africanism and Political Unification in West Africa* (Ithaca: Cornell University Press, 1967).

8 Adom Getachew, *Worldmaking after empire: The rise and fall of self-determination* (Princeton: Princeton University Press, 2019).

identity,⁹ similar to the unification movement of the trusteeship era. In fact, the formation of the HSGF represented a direct revival of a territory-based Togoland-nationalism under Ewe leadership that since the partition of German Togoland has been propagated by the ('Western') Togoland Liberation Movement (TOLIMO) in the 1970s, itself a successor to the Togoland Congress of the 1950s, the Togoland Union of the 1940s and the *Bund der deutschen Togoländer* (Togobund) of the 1920/30s.¹⁰ At the same time, many HSGF followers embrace an ethnic Ewe identity,¹¹ for in the HSGF-produced maps of 'Western Togoland,' which are printed on T-Shirts and banners or distributed digitally on social media, the HSGF also lays claim to the Ewe-populated areas such, as Tongu or Anlo, that fall in the area of the former "Volta Triangle" of the British Cold Coast Colony, which historically never belonged to Togoland (see Map 2).

Since the HSGF's founding in 1994, Charles Kwame Kudzordzi and his followers claimed that the 1956 UN-supervised referendum was rigged and 'Western Togoland' was therefore illegally integrated into Ghana.¹² Besides the alleged invalidity of the referendum, according to the HSGF, UN Secretary-General Dag Hammarskjöld and Queen Elisabeth II allegedly tied the referendum's result to a moratorium, which required an approval of the 'union' between the Gold Coast and British ("Western") Togoland within 50 years; otherwise, the union would be void.¹³ As long as the 'union' was not approved, the people of 'Western Togoland' were merely "plebiscite citizens in Ghana."¹⁴ Ghanaian historians were alarmed by the HSGF's "bogus and unsubstantiated claims about the scope and import of the plebiscite,"¹⁵ stressing "the legality of the integration of British Togoland into Ghana."¹⁶ When in 2007 the alleged 'union document' could not be produced, the HSGF contrived a narrative that Kwame Nkrumah, the figurehead of Ghanaian independence, probably made said document disappear. Losing much of its credibility, public interest in the HSGF dwindled – at least until the arrest of its leadership during the 60-year independence celebrations on 6 March 2017.

Kudzordzi and two of his comrades-in-arms were charged with treason. However, the Attorney-General dropped the charges due to their advanced age. Kudzordzi was cautioned and dismissed after signing a pledge of good behaviour along with a docu-

---

9   Charles Kwami Kudzordzi, *A Stolen Nation and Her Deprived Nationals: (Franco-British Atrocities in Togoland). An Irredentist Nationalism* (Ho: Win I.C.T. Centre, 2016).
10 For his part, Kudzordzi makes no secret of his Germanophilia and glorification of the *Deutsch Togobund* as the national boundaries of the longed-for state of "Western Togoland" are based on the borders drawn first by German colonial officials.
11 Charles Kwami Kudzordzi, *A history of Eweland: A Resource Document for Ewe Socio-Political Studies* (Ho: E.P. Church Publishing Ltd., n.d.).
12 Charles Kwami Kudzordzi, interview by Julius Heise, 19 November 2018, Ho, Ghana.
13 Charles Kwami Kudzordzi, interview by Julius Heise, 21 November 2018, Ho, Ghana.
14 Dzamboe, "Group to declare 'Volta region' independence on May 9, 2017."
15 D. E. K. Amenumey, "The Brouhaha over Togoland Plebiscite. The Historical Fact," *GhanaWeb*, 03 September 2016.
16 Obed Y. Asamoah, *The political history of Ghana (1950–2013): The experience of a non-conformist* (Bloomington, IN, USA: AuthorHouse, 2014), p. 23.

ment acknowledging that the continuation of the HSGF's secessionist activities is likely to pose a "threat to national security."[17]

The Division of the Volta Region

To understand why the Ghanaian Attorney-General attorney found compelled to threaten the three elderly HSGF leaders with imprisonment unless they give up their activities, it is important to note that the HSGF's demand for secession not only posed a threat to Ghana's one-nation-agenda but at the same time exacerbated a dilemma for the newly elected Ghanaian government.

A couple of months earlier, during the 2016 parliamentary elections,[18] the presidential candidate of the conservative *New Patriotic Party* (NPP), Nana Akufo-Addo, won against the *National Democratic Congress* (NDC) of incumbent President John Mahama. Akufo-Addo's victory was in part due to the campaign promise to representatives of various ethnic groups that Ghana's intrastate boundaries would be redrawn to create new regions. In January 2017, barely a month after the elections, Akufo-Addo ordered the creation of the *Ministry of Regional Reorganisation and Development*. In the northern part of the Volta Region, the *Joint Consultative Committee* (JCC), composed mainly of chiefs from the Guan ethnic sub-group, petitioned to President Akufo-Addo on 6 June 2017 calling for the creation of a separate region from the existing Volta Region: the Oti Region (see Map 3).[19]

A government-appointed commission of enquiry subsequently determined that there was a need and necessity in Ghana for a *New Regions Referendum* to decide on the division of four regions to create six new regions. While the report of the government-appointed commission argued that the regional reorganization was "for enhanced socio-economic development and not based on ethnic, cultural and religious issues,"[20] the proposed new regional lines and support for them fell on an almost perfect parallel to where the new Oti Region would separate the Guans in the north from the Ewes in the south (compare Map 2 and Map 3).

The ruling NPP-government was in a predicament: Since it had to support the one-nation-agenda vis-à-vis the secessionist HSGF, at the same time it could not afford the impression that it was bowing to the pressure of ethnic appeasement. Soon voices were raised that the referendum on the redrawing of the internal border was an unconstitutional attempt at ethnic appeasement, representing a first step towards a possible descent into the 'balkanisation' of the Volta Region and a fragmenting "one-dialect-one-

---

17   Tim Dzamboe, "Western Togoland "Secessionists" Discharged, Bonded," *Graphic Online*, 20 July 2017; Osei, "Police to charge Volta 'separatist' group members with Treason"; "Member Profile: Western Togoland," UNPO, accessed 09 July 2020, available from https://unpo.org/downloads/2363.pdf.

18   Nathalie Raunet Robert-Nicoud, "Elections and Borderlands in Ghana," *African Affairs* 118, no. 473 (2019), https://doi.org/10.1093/afraf/adz002.

19   Government of Ghana, "Report of the Commission of Inquiry into the Creation of New Regions: Equitable Distribution of National Resources for Balanced Development" (2018), p. 91.

20   Government of Ghana, "Report of the Commission of Inquiry into the Creation of New Regions: Equitable Distribution of National Resources for Balanced Development" (2018), p. 24.

region" system.²¹ Particularly in the Ewe-dominated southern part of the Volta Region, complaints were raised that voting was only allowed in the areas of the proposed Oti Region – a provision, which would prejudge the outcome of the referendum.²²

Map 3: Reorganization of the Volta Region

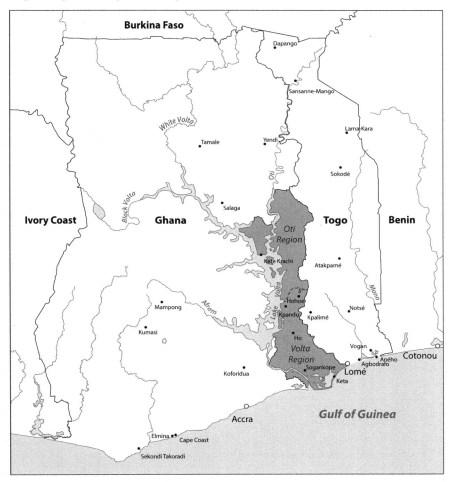

Source: Own creation.

In 2018, this prompted the US-based *Association of Volta Youth* to petition UN Secretary-General, Antonio Guterres, to intervene. The petition likened the *New Regions Referendum* to the British Togoland referendum of 1956, condemning it as "yet another

---

21   Komla Dzigbodi-Adjimah, "Oti Region," *Gbi Voice*, 22 March 2017.
22   Nii L. Lartey, "Ohene, Elizabeth Asks: Who Speaks for Ewes?," *Citi Newsroom*, 02 November 2018.

fraudulent plebiscite."²³ Desiring to secede the entire region from Ghana, Kudzordzi opposed the fragmentation of the region, which before Ghana's independence, as Kudzordzi pointed out, was called Trans-Volta-Togoland: "A trusteeship territory – it's an aggression to divide it!"²⁴ Kudzordzi regarded the *New Regions Referendum* as yet another weaponization of a popular consultation by the government in Accra against the traditional inhabitants of the Volta Region, particularly the Ewes, who over the last 150 years have seen the borders around them constantly change due to foreign interests.²⁵ For Kudzordzi, the division of the Volta Region was just another item on the growing list of Ewe indignities in an Akan-dominated Ghana. Instances, such as the 2007 forcible eviction of hundreds of residents from Dudzorme Island in Lake Volta's Digya National Park, during which more than 100 of the forcibly evicted died when a ferry capsized,²⁶ or when the NPP-MP Kennedy Agyapong's held his "Kill all the Ewes" hate speech in 2012,²⁷ led Kudzordzi to the conclusion: "Today we are not safe. Insecurity is in our land."²⁸ Accordingly, the HSGF has...

> "...decided to use force and leave. Yet, we are afraid. The nations of this world who will say 'No. Why should you go by means of force? You must go democratically.' What is the meaning of democracy? Does it not affect us as human beings too? This is the stage we have reached. And we are deciding now strongly, firmly to go, even if the United Nations, even if Britain would assist Ghana to commit genocide to all of us in the land, they could do so. They could decide to do so..."²⁹

Similarly, when opposing youth groups clashed violently at a hearing in the run-up to the *New Regions Referendum*,³⁰ the Asogli State Council, a representation of Ewe chiefs from the capital city of the Volta Region, Ho, voiced its opposition to the referendum as it represented apparently "a threat to the cherished peace we have enjoyed over the years in the Volta Region."³¹ These statements were taken seriously: In the run-up to the ballot, 1,000 extra security personnel were deployed to the then still northern part of the Volta

---

23   Association of Volta Youth, "Petition," accessed 22 March 2021, available from https://www.modernghana.com/news/828252/volta-group-in-the-usa-petitions-un-over-split.html.
24   Charles Kwami Kudzordzi, interview by Julius Heise, 19 November 2018, Ho, Ghana.
25   Vincent Djokoto, "Eeto and the Partitions of Eenyigba," *My Joy Online*, 30 April 2020.
26   Amnesty International, "Ghana: Forced Evictions in the Digya National Park Area Must Stop," news release, 19 April 2006, accessed 10 June 2019, available from https://www.amnesty.org/download/Documents/68000/afr280012006en.pdf.
27   *GhanaWeb*, "Kill All Ewes in the Ashanti Region – Kennedy Agyapong," 16 April 2012.
28   Charles Kwami Kudzordzi, interview by Julius Heise, 21 November 2018, Ho, Ghana.
29   Charles Kwami Kudzordzi, interview by Julius Heise, 19 November 2018, Ho, Ghana.
30   Samuel Akumatey, "Hohoe and Buem Youth Clash at Hearing on New Region," *Ghana News Agency*, 20 January 2018.
31   Asogli State Council, "Oti Region Referendum: Entire Region Must Vote," news release, 03 October 2018, accessed 24 February 2020, available from https://starrfm.com.gh/2018/10/oti-region-referendum-entire-region-must-vote-asogli-state/.

Region.³² Journalists were banned.³³ In the end, in December 2018, according to official figures, an astonishing 99% voted in favour of becoming part of the new Oti Region.³⁴

Six months after the *New Regions Referendum*, on 5 May 2019, that is, again just before the symbolic 9 May anniversary of the 1956 British Togoland referendum, the HSGF protested with T-shirts reading "Independence for Western Togoland – No Division of Volta."³⁵ Again, eight members, including Kudzordzi, were arrested by the Ghanaian security forces. Once more, the scale of the swoop was a national statement by the Ghanaian state that provided some bizarre imagery: described as a "Rambo-style" operation,³⁶ 26 armed police officers, 20 armed military personnel and some Bureau of National Investigation operatives whisked the eight arrested HSGF members to the 66 Artillery Regiment in Ho, where a waiting helicopter airlifted them to Accra. Video footage of the arrest shows the armed military personnel surrounding the by-then frail Kudzordzi, who approached the helicopter on a cane only with difficulty.³⁷ However, when the court hearings began two months later, as before, on the government's instructions, the Attorney-General withdrew the charges due to Kudzordzi's advanced age and general health conditions. The defendants were cautioned and released by July 2019.

Securitising "Western Togoland" Secessionism

Despite the previous arrests and judicial caveats, Kudzordzi could not be deterred in his determination: On 16 November 2019, he gathered his supporters at a rally, which was disguised as a funeral procession to elude the Ghanaian intelligence services, and publicly declared the secession and independence of 'Western Togoland'.³⁸ Broadcasted via social media platforms, the livestream showed a crowd raging with joy and Kudzordzi being driven from the scene.³⁹ Soon after the declaration, pictures circulated on social media platforms, showing the supposed new country's armed forces at the *Western Togoland Gorilla Army* training camp.⁴⁰

---

32 Abu Mubarik, "Over 1000 Security Personnel Deployed for Oti Region Referendum," *Pulse GH*, 26 December 2018.
33 *Starr FM Online*, "Journalists Barred from Covering Oti Referendum," 27 December 2018.
34 Jude Duncan, "Referendum: Oti Residents Okay New Region with 99% YES Vote," *Citi Newsroom*, 26 February 2020.
35 Jonas Nyabor, "Eight Arrested for Trying to Declare Volta Region an Independent State," *Citi Newsroom*, 06 May 2019.
36 Rockson-Nelson E. Dafeamekpor, "Rambo-Style Arrest of 'Western Togoland' Separatists Worrying – MP," news release, 07 May 2019, accessed 23 November 2021, available from https://www.ghanaweb.com/GhanaHomePage/NewsArchive/Rambo-style-arrest-of-Western-Togoland-separatists-worrying-MP-744471.
37 Mary Mensah, "Suspected Secessionists Charged for Conspiring to Commit Treason Felony," *Graphic Online*, 08 May 2019.
38 Peter Atsu Ahianyo, "Secessionist Armed Conflict Looms in Ghana as the World Is Silent," *Modern Ghana*, 23 December 2019; A. R. Gomda, "Manhunt for Papavi as New Group Emerges," *Daily Guide Network*, 22 November 2019; Benjamin Aklama, "Separatist Movement Declares Independence for Western Togoland," *Citi Newsroom*, 17 November 2019.
39 *Western Togoland Independence Declaration* (Ewe TV Online, 2019), YouTube, accessed 26 November 2021, available from https://www.youtube.com/watch?v=3J8Le-8hphI.
40 Emmanuel Ayamga, "National Security Confirms Operations of Western Togoland Militia Group; Goes After Them," *Pulse GH*, 18 December 2019; "New Photos Revealing 'Military Opera-

From this moment on, various Ghanaian security analysts were alarmed and publicly called out the apparent lapsus by Ghanaian intelligence agencies,[41] raising concerns that the aspirations of the Western Togoland secessionists could take on violent dimensions such as that of the Anglophone crisis in Cameroon.[42] Numerous newspaper commentators and established security experts made appeals for a harsh and rapid crackdown:[43] "Now that the issue is becoming an *existential threat* to the Volta Region and Ghana, stakeholders including chiefs, politicians and duty bearers from the region must be seen and heard doing *something to contain the threat*."[44] Some analysts considered "the stability of the entire country and, perhaps, even the entire West African sub-region" at risk.[45] Others cautioned that the secession campaign by the HSGF might cause "tribal war."[46] Public calls were made to increase police presence in the Volta Region.[47]

Endorsed by such calls, the Ghanaian security agencies launched a crackdown and fugitive hunt for Kudzordzi as well as members and suspected sympathisers of the HSGF. In the following two weeks some thirty people were arrested.[48] In a video message from his hiding place, Kudzordzi expounded that the Ghanaian authorities had forced the HSGF into exile and that those arrested had been put in prisons without trial and many people had disappeared. Kudzordzi called upon his supporters to remain peaceful in the face of antagonism from the Ghanaian security agencies. Yet, he reiterated his stance on secession by calling on international support: "I do appeal to the international world, those in the corridors of peace […] to come here, to put the situation under control, [and] to avoid any possible mayhem."[49] From his hide-out, Kudzordzi liaised with the Belgium-based *Unrepresented Nations and Peoples Organization* (UNPO), which in January 2022

---

tions' of Western Togolanders Pop up," GhanaWeb, accessed 18 December 2019, available from https://www.ghanaweb.com/GhanaHomePage/NewsArchive/New-photos-revealing-milita ry-operations-of-Western-Togolanders-pop-up-818080.

41 Jonas Nyabor, "Clamp down on Western Togoland 'Militia Group' – Security Analyst to Government," *Citi Newsroom*, 18 December 2019; Gomda, "Manhunt for Papavi as new group emerges."

42 Atsu Ahianyo, "Secessionist Armed Conflict Looms In Ghana As The World Is Silent"; Maria Ketzmerick, *Staat, Sicherheit und Gewalt in Kamerun: Postkoloniale Perspektiven auf den Dekolonisierungsprozess unter französischer UN-Treuhandverwaltung*, Postcolonial studies 36 (Bielefeld: transcript, 2019).

43 Kwame Acheampong, "Deal with Western Togoland Security 'Training' Reports – Adam Bonaa to Akufo-Addo," *Starr FM Online*, 18 December 2019.

44 Nicholas Mawunyah, "The Complexities of the Western Togoland Problem," *My Joy Online*, 26 September 2020, authors emphasis.

45 Kwame Okoampa-Ahoofe, JR., "Let Us Settle the Western Togoland Problem Once and for All," *Modern Ghana*, 08 December 2019.

46 Felix Anim-Appau, "Western Togoland Brouhaha Is Recipe for Tribal War – Antwi-Danso Warns," *My Joy Online*, 26 November 2019; Kabu Nartey, "Our Independence Is Not Complete Without Western Togoland," *My Joy Online*, 04 December 2019.

47 Edward Williams, ""We Have No Support for Secessionist Activities"-Fodome Traditional Council," *Ghana News Agency*, 16 January 2020.

48 "Western Togoland: Members of HSGF Systematically Persecuted by Ghanaian Authorities," UNPO, accessed 09 July 2020, available from https://unpo.org/article/21783.

49 Charles Kwami Kudzordzi, *Founder of Western Togoland Papavi sends "Love Note" to President Akufo-Addo* (GhanaNews TV, 2019), YouTube, accessed 15 June 2021, available from https://www.youtube.com/watch?v=P5phVqGsO9A.

brought the matter officially to the attention to of the UN, when it filed a complaint to the UN's *Working Group on Arbitrary Detention*, alleging that the government of Ghana was systematically misusing the criminal justice system to target the HSGF.⁵⁰ In June 2022, the UNPO followed up with a submission of a *Universal Periodic Review* to the UN Human Rights Council on the subject of Ghana's crackdown on members of the HSGF.⁵¹

In the meantime, Ghanaian media outlets hotly debated the influence and legacy of these very 'international corridors of peace' invoked by Kudzordzi. Journalists dug up 60-year-old UN documents, strongly arguing for and against the historical (il)legality of the integration of British Togoland into the Gold Coast.⁵² In the course of the debate some notions of the United Nations' colonial complicity were expressed: "Ghana's rule over Western Togoland is […] an injustice, a trespass, a tyranny, worse than colonialism. […] that annexation of Western Togoland by Ghana for the purposes of expansionism or preponderance have been allowed, questioned the sacredness of the UN trust."⁵³ After a radio anchor in Sogakofe, South Tongu, criticised the Volta Regional Minister, Archibald Yao Letsa, for the heavy-handed crackdown, the later responded that "some media houses have become mouthpieces for the group whose activities threaten the peace and security of the country. But […] they will be held liable if national security takes action against the group."⁵⁴ The Ghanaian Bureau of National Investigation arrested the radio's director and shut the radio station down on grounds of national security concerns,⁵⁵ which caused a massive backlash by press and NGOs.⁵⁶

Eventually, the training camp of the *Western Togoland Gorilla Army* was located at Wli Todzi, near Hohoe, at the Togo-Ghana border. Two separate counter-insurgency operations by the Ho-based 66 Artillery Regiment and the Ghana Police Service led to over 70

---

50   "UNPO Submits Complaint to UN on Detention of Western Togoland Activists," UNPO, accessed 02 August 2022, available from https://www.unpo.org/article/22183.
51   "Western Togoland," UNPO, accessed 02 August 2022, available from https://unpo.org/article/22222.
52   Enimil Ashon, "Western Togoland: Blame UK and UN, Not Ghana," *Graphic Online*, 22 November 2019; Cameron Duodu, "The 'Western Togoland' Issue," *Peace FM Online*, 28 November 2019; Appiah Brobbey, "Opinion: History of Trans Volta Togoland," *My Joy Online*, 28 November 2019; Richard Amoako Bahh, "The UN Document on the Ghana and 'Western Togoland' Unionization," *GhanaWeb*, 06 October 2020; Mawunyah, "The complexities of the Western Togoland problem."
53   Not to be mistaken with the UN Trusteeship System; Seth Mifetu, "Why Western Togoland Restoration Struggle Is Lawful," *Modern Ghana*, 27 November 2019.
54   *Daily Guide Network*, "Letsa Warns Media Promoting Secessionists," 10 January 2020.
55   Nii L. Lartey, "NCA Shuts down Radio Tongu over National Security Concerns," *Citi Newsroom*, 12 February 2020.
56   *Committee to Protect Journalists*, "Radio Tongu Broadcaster Suspended, Director Arrested in Ghana," 11 March 2020.

arrests by May 2020.[57] However, many of the suspected secessionists were discharged in subsequent court hearings.[58]

Yet, despite the military-aided crackdown, more separatist groups, such as the *Peoples' Liberation Council of Western Togoland*,[59] the *United Freedom Fighters*,[60] the *Association of Western Togoland Youths*,[61] or the *Concerned Citizens of Western Togoland* made themselves publicly known.[62] The latter claimed, given that Western Togolander's "fundamental human rights always have been abused, they have come to the point of no return in becoming a state on its own."[63] A former MP from the Volta Region, Kosi Kedem, who has been echoing the HSGF's thesis of the absent union document,[64] argued that Ghana did not legally exist.[65] While President Akufo-Addo, for his part, invoked Ghana's national cohesion, he contended that the Western Togoland secessionists "do not understand nation-building."[66]

In the meanwhile, some analysts opposed the hardliners that called for the heavy-handed crackdown, pleading that "government overreaction […] should not escalate into full blown destructive wars."[67] Especially John Mahama, presidential candidate of the oppositional NDC, which maintains a stronghold in the Volta Region, condemned the ruling NPP for the deployment of military and security agencies in the Volta Region as a strategy to intimidate people ahead of the voter registration for the parliamentary elections in December 2020:[68] "The military siege of the Volta Region and other locations during the [voters] registration exercise created an intimidatory atmosphere akin to a

---

57   *My Joy Online*, "17 Members of Separatist Group Rounded up in Dawn Swoop," 24 December 2019; Mohammed Alabira, "18 Suspected Western Togoland Separatists Arrested in Bimbilla," *Citi Newsroom*, 30 December 2019; Fred Q. Asare, "Update: Military Invades 'Secessionist' Training Camp, Arrests 21 Trainees," *My Joy Online*, 17 February 2020; Fred Q. Asare, "Western Togoland: 14 Suspected Secessionists Arrested at Kpando Aziavi," *My Joy Online*, 30 May 2020.

58   Justice Agbenorsi, "Court Discharges 20 Suspected Western Togoland Secessionists," *Graphic Online*, 04 April 2020.

59   Seth Mifetu, "How Divine Odonkor Saved Ghana from Torrential Encumbrances," *Modern Ghana*, 08 August 2020.

60   Peter Atsu Ahianyo, "New Separatist Group Pops-up in Volta Region," *Modern Ghana*, 19 August 2019.

61   Enimil Ashon, "West Togoland: Let's Go to UN," *My Joy Online*, 05 October 2020.

62   Gomda, "Manhunt for Papavi as new group emerges."

63   *Rainbow Radio*, "No Amount of Arrest Will Stop Us – Citizens of Western Togoland," 18 September 2020.

64   Amoako Bahh, "The UN document on the Ghana and 'Western Togoland' unionization"; Kate Skinner has previously discussed Kedem's stance on the status of Western Togoland, Kate Skinner, "Local Historians and Strangers with Big Eyes," *History in Africa* 37 (2010), https://doi.org/10.1353/hia.2010.0022.

65   *GhanaWeb*, "Ghana Doesn't Legally Exist – Kosi Kedem," 30 September 2020.

66   *Modern Ghana*, "Attempts to Cede Volta Region from Ghana Misguided – Prez Akufo-Addo," 09 June 2021.

67   Andy C. Kwawukume, "Revisiting the Road to Secession Agitation in the Volta Region," *Modern Ghana*, 08 December 2019.

68   Andres Atta-Asamoah, "Are Africa's Borders Sacrosanct? Ghana's Western Togoland Crisis," Institute for Security Studies (ISS), accessed 11 December 2020, available from https://issafrica.org/iss-today/are-africas-borders-sacrosanct-ghanas-western-togoland-crisis; *Starr FM Online*, "Separatist Movement Intended to Destabilize Volta Reg. Ahead of Polls – MP," 30 September 2020.

nation at war."[69] Unsurprisingly the NDC's founder and Ghana's former Ewe-born president, John Rawlings, put his political weight into the balance, condemning that the "deployment of the military and other security agencies in some parts of the Volta and Oti Regions is generating animosity especially amongst innocent citizens."[70]

While Ghana's Minister of National Security, Albert Kan-Dapaah, justified the use of military personnel by claiming that the Ghana Police Service was at times not up to the task when it comes to the level of security equipment required, several of Ghana's prominent security analysts called for his removal saying that events in the Volta Region apparently vindicated that "the practice of 'civilianising' the military cannot be justified, cautioning that the military may lose its relevance and respect."[71] A media commentator's historical analysis of Ghana's security personnel concluded that Ghana's security system is not fit for the separatists anyway, concluding that "at first gunshot emanating from these Western Togolanders, every one of them will run into the bush."[72] And shots were fired.

On 25 September 2020, events came thick and fast: militants of the previously unknown *Western Togoland Restoration Front* (WTRF) blocked several streets into the Volta Region, stormed two police stations, freed inmates, kidnapped three officers, stole two vehicles and a dozen or so machine guns from the armoury. During an exchange of gunfire, a member of the WTRF and the Chief Superintendent were shot.[73] The WTRF subsequently issued a press release regarding their attempt to "assert their sovereignty on the Volta Region,"[74] and called on the Ghanaian government to negotiate a ban on all its political activities including the withdrawal of all security forces from the Volta Region. By October 2020, another militia faction calling itself the *Dragons of Western Togoland Military Army* sent a note of caution to the Regional Minister, Letsa, claiming that "4,000-plus persons have been trained in another country to rescue their motherland" within 3 weeks.[75] This claim has not materialised and operations by the Ghanaian security forces have had some success in containing the situation.

The ensuing media discussion was in full swing, and the spotlight was on historians and security analysts who offered different assessments of the causes *of* and possible responses *to* the secessionist threat.[76] Security analysts engaged in an exchange of blows

---

69 *GhanaWeb*, "Election 2020: 'Military Siege' of Volta Region Creates Atmosphere of Fear – Mahama," 04 December 2020.
70 Kobina A. Amoakwa, "Statement by Former President Rawlings on Deployment of Security Agencies in Volta, Oti Regions," news release, 29 July 2020, accessed 27 October 2021, available from https://twitter.com/officeofJJR/status/1277480313070006272/photo/1.
71 *My Joy Online*, "Kan Dapaah's Attack on Security Analysts Laughable – Adib Saani," 12 February 2020.
72 Adjei Sarfo, "The secession of the Togolanders."
73 *GhanaWeb*, "Detailed Account of How Western Togoland Group Staged Successful Attacks in Volta Region," 04 October 2020.
74 *Ghana News Agency*, "Deal with Secessionist Group-Awoamefia," 27 September 2020.
75 *Class FM online*, "Our 4000-Man Army Dragons'll Re-Claim 'The Motherland' in 21 Days – Togolanders Warn Amewu, Letsa, Ablakwa," 14 October 2020.
76 Listing the news articles here would go beyond the scope of this chapter. The news outlet *GhanaWeb* has compiled a dossier on the debate: https://www.ghanaweb.com/GhanaHomePage/NewsArchive/dossier.php?ID=605.

with the Minister of National Security, again calling for his removal over the failure of intelligence and security agencies.[77]

Indeed, the events and public debate had an effect as it eventually prompted a whole series of reforms addressing Ghana's national security challenges.[78] In the following, Ghana's 25-year-old *Security and Intelligence Act* was reformed,[79] transforming the Bureau of National Investigation into a National *Intelligence* Bureau (NIB), thereby conflating core competencies of policing and criminal investigation with increased intelligence-driven activities.[80] The reform furthermore updated Ghana's pyramidal security architecture, rooted in the colonial period,[81] and created additional committees for the National Security Council (NSC). Furthermore, memberships of the Regional Security Councils (RegSeCs) and District Security Councils (DisSeCs) were expanded to include community leaders with expertise in human security. To encourage public vigilantism as a direct reaction to the violence by the Western Togoland secessionists in the Volta Region, in June 2020, the Ministry of National Security and the *National Commission for Civic Education* (NCCE)[82] launched a workshop campaign with representatives of civil society and religious communities, as well as district directors of the police and the newly created NIB.[83] Finally, under the directive of President Akufo-Addo, a comprehensive *National Framework for Preventing and Countering Violent Extremism and Terrorism* has been introduced – the first document of this kind in Ghana's history.[84]

---

77   *Starr FM Online*, "Western Togoland: There Was No Intelligence Failure – Govt," 27 September 2020; *Happy Ghana*, "Keep Quiet and Let Experts Speak – Information Minister Chided over Western Togoland Comments," 30 September 2020; *Happy Ghana*, "Kan Dapaah Must Resign – Adib Sani on Western Togoland Brouhaha," 29 September 2020.

78   *Ghana News Agency*, "It Is Our Responsibility to Prevent Violent Extremism – National Security," 01 September 2021.

79   *Ghana News Agency*, "Parliament Discusses Security and Intelligence Agencies Bill, 2020," 12 August 2020; After Jerry Rawlings came to power in a 1981 coup d'état and he put Ghana back on the path of multiparty democracy through the 1992 referendum. The Security and Intelligence Act of 1996 (Act 526 – a security sector reform) was the first law passed after Rawlings' election victory in December 1996. See Avinash Paliwal, "Ghana's National Security Ministry Ignites Old Fears After Fracas over Photos," *The Conversation*, 30 May 2021.

80   *Ghana News Agency*, "Parliament discusses Security and Intelligence Agencies Bill, 2020."

81   Obuobi provides a good overview for Ghana's security and intelligence architecture before the reform: Patrick P. Obuobi, "Evaluating Ghana's Intelligence Oversight Regime," *International Journal of Intelligence and CounterIntelligence* 31, no. 2 (2018), https://doi.org/10.1080/08850607.2017.13758 41.

82   *Business Ghana*, "NCCE Calls for Peaceful Co-Existence," 24.082021; *Ghana News Agency*, "NCCE Cautions Security Against Threats of Vigilantism, Fundamentalism and Secessionism," 09 May 2021.

83   Per the Constitution of Ghana implement and oversee programs intended to inculcate in the citizens of Ghana awareness of their civic responsibilities and maintain with the community the sense of the principles and objectives of the Constitution of the Republic of Ghana.

84   European Commission, "Commission Decision: on the financing of the Annual Action Programme 2020 in favour of the Republic of Ghana" (Annex, 2020), available from https://ec.europa.eu/international-partnerships/system/files/ghana_aap_2020-annex.pdf, p. 7.

Final Act?

These measures soon paid off: the figurehead of the secessionist movement, Kudzordzi, was tracked down by the Ghanaian intelligence services at his hideout near Ho and arrested on 28 July 2021.[85] Due to health reasons, the trial against Kudzordzi had to be postponed several times and was finally scheduled to begin on 22 October 2021. In a final media interview, Kudzordzi presented himself combative: "I'll be angry with God if my dream for Western Togoland is not realized."[86] Yet, after being released from custody to seek medical treatment, Kudzordzi passed away at St. Paul Hospital in Aksthi South, Volta Region, on 15 October 2021, at the age of 88.[87]

Expectedly, Kudzordzi's passing was not the end of the story as even his funeral polarised the Ghanaian society: the MP for Volta Region's district of North Tongu, Samuel Okudzeto Ablakwa, called on President Akufo-Addo to pay Kudzordzi the honour of a state funeral, whereas security analysts, on the other hand, pointed to the still lingering threat posed by Kudzordzi's ideas for which he should be buried in an unmarked grave so as not to create a place of pilgrimage for a martyr.[88] On 29 October 2022, Kudzordzi was finally laid to rest in his hometown Xavi, in the south of the Volta Region, with tributes paid by HSGF comrades and amidst heavy presence of state security personnel.[89]

A month later, in November 2022, by order of the Ministry for National Security, Ghana's National Peace Council had undertaking consultations with stakeholders in the Volta and Oti Regions regarding alleged ethnic identity-based discrimination and marginalization raised by people of Ewe origin and put together a report including recommendations, which would serve in addressing the concerns. Ironically, speaking on behalf of the Minister of National Security was the National Coordinator of the Ghana Boundary Commission, Major General Emmanuel Kotia, that is, head of the very state institution that for the HSGF was the starting point of the most recent bloodshed over 'Western Togoland.' This context was not sidestepped by the Volta Regional Minister, Archibald Letsa, who reminded at the event that "the alleged marginalization of the Ewe ethnic group dates back to 1956, following the plebiscite which saw the unification of the then Western Togoland and other territories to form Ghana."[90]

In January 2023, the United Nations *Working Group on Arbitrary Detention* (WGAD) finally delivered its verdict in the case of arrested Western Togoland secessionists, concluding that the Ghanaian government had violated their rights by detaining them for

---

85 *GhanaWeb*, "Western Togoland Founder Papavi Arrested After Months of Hiding," 29 July 2021.
86 *MyNewsGH*, "I'll Be Angry with God If My Dream for Western Togoland Is Not Realized – Papavi," 26 September 2021.
87 "Charles Kormi Kudzorzi, Leading Figure of Western Togoland's Self-Determination Movement, Passes Away Aged 88," UNPO, accessed 20 October 2021, available from https://unpo.org/article/22162.
88 *GhanaWeb*, "Papavi's Death Should Not Be Viewed as End of Western Togoland Separatists – Security Analyst Warns," 18 October 2021.
89 *GhanaWeb*, "Western Togoland Leader 'Papavi Hogbedetor' Laid to Rest at Xavi," 31.10.2022.
90 Fred Q. Asare, "Peace Council Moves to Address Allegations of Ethnic Identity-Based Discrimination, Marginalization by Ewes," *My Joy Online*, 30.11.20222.

sedition.[91] Two months later, on 21 March 2023, the Accra High Court finally convicted the five arrested in the aftermath of the September 2020 attacks.[92] Although the trial implicated the accused in the attacks, they were not charged for the attack and the policeman's murder *per se*, but each received the maximum sentence of five years in prison in hard labour for violations of the *Prohibited Organisations Act*. Although the WTRF was unknown until the attacks, the *Prohibited Organisations Act* (which was passed in 1976 when Ghana was under military rule) banned the National Liberation Movement of Western Togoland (Tolimo) and thus also "any other organisation howsoever called, whose objects include advocating and promoting the succession from Ghana of the former British mandated territory of Togoland or part thereof."[93]

1.2 Research Puzzle & Goal

The events and debates following the declaration of independence of 'Western Togoland' are exemplary of many speech-acts collected in the course of this work, demonstrating that the conflicts once considered resolved after the termination of United Nations trusteeship over Togoland are flaring up again. By reviving a language of threat and security in the conflict over 'Western Togoland,' the Ghanaian state and the secessionists entered a discursive exchange of blows in which one side is portrayed as an existential threat for the other – a dynamic which eventually led to bloodshed. Inspired by this empirical observation, this dissertation traces the history of Togoland's internationally supervised decolonisation process to solve the puzzle of how (re)awakenings of a dormant Ewe and ("Western") Togoland nationalism became a matter of security.

Over 60 years ago, 'Western Togoland' was hailed as the first territory to achieve independence under the international supervision of the United Nations Trusteeship System. Against the backdrop of the internationalisation of global governance, an emerging anti-colonialism as well as a right for the inhabitants of trusteeship territories to petition directly to the United Nations, Ewe and Togoland unificationists continuously petitioned against French and British rule and for sovereign statehood before United Nations venues. Their claims for unification, self-determination, statehood, and independence were similarly negotiated through a language of threat and security, influencing international opinion in a way that hardly any other independence movement in Africa had managed before. Yet, as Claude Welch put it in 1967,[94] the institutions of international

---

91 United Nations, "Opinion No. 47/2022 concerning George Nyakpo (Ghana)" A/HRC/WGAD/2022/47 (Human Rights Council, 2023), available from https://www.ohchr.org/sites/default/files/documents/issues/detention-wg/opinions/session94/2023-01-30/A-HRC-WGAD-2022-47-Ghana-ADVANCE-EDITED-VERSION.pdf.

92 *GhanaWeb*, "Western Togoland Case: High Court Sentences 5 Secessionists to a Total of 25 Years in Prison," 22 March 2023; *GhanaWeb*, "Western Togoland Attacks: Five More Arrested for Stealing AK 47 Rifles," 04 October 2020.

93 Prohibited Organisations Act, Supreme Military Council Decree 20 at Section 1(1)(b) (1976), accessed 22 March 2023, available from https://lawsghana.com/pre_1992_legislation/SMC%20Decree/PROHIBITED%20ORGANISATIONS%20ACT,%201976%20(SMCD%2020)/118.

94 Welch, *Dream of Unity*.

governance did not grant the unificationists their *Dream of Unity*, thus allowing the seeds of conflict to grow. The question arises why, despite all these favourable conditions, did the unificationists not have the upper hand in deciding the shaping of their future statehood? An answer to this question, which at first glance seems to be purely historical and only about Ghana, touches on broader, intersecting themes of decolonisation history, such as debates on national belonging, statehood, self-determination, but also international responses to security threats – in short, it informs current debates of international concern from a historical perspective.

To this end, the dissertation analyses a security-specific mode of communication from a historicising state-building perspective in the context of the United Nations trusteeship over Togoland under British and French administration (1947–1960). With a research agenda that looks at discursively negotiated constructions of threat and security, the research is guided by the question: "How have constructions of threat and (in)security influenced the decolonisation of Togoland, and to what extent is the recent conflict over the attempted secession of 'Western Togoland' rooted in these constructions?" This question will be broken down into three sub-questions, each focussing on a specific actor within the trilateral constellation of the United Nations Trusteeship System:

1. How did the French and British trustees (de)securitise their administration over French and British Togoland?
2. How did the unificationist petitioners securitise the trusteeship administration in Togoland, what agency is revealed in relation to it, and why did their attempts to securitise the (re)unification of Ewe- and Togoland not succeed?
3. What role did the United Nations, and the influence of world opinion more broadly, have in this dynamic of security constructions?

1.3 Argument & Approach

Security plays a significant role in international administrations as it is one of the core tasks named in the respective mandate agreements, thus representing a key point of reference for the legitimisation of international rule. In the introductory account of events, security emerged, on the one hand, as an object of conflict: the central purpose of state intervention is to ensure security and prevent serious threats, both internal and external, regarding previous violent conflicts or foreign domination. On the other hand, the events demonstrate that security also turned out to be a strategic mode of communication by which actors tried to make their political decisions, opposition, or resistance plausible to an audience and thus influenced a contested attempt at secession. Security communication can thus paradoxically not only ensure peace and public order, but also suppress oppositional forces.[95]

---

95 Thorsten Bonacker, "Internationales Statebuilding Und Die Liberale Politik Des Schutzes," in *Vorsicht Sicherheit! Legitimationsprobleme der Ordnung von Freiheit*, ed. Gabriele Abels, Nomos eLibrary Politikwissenschaft (Baden-Baden: Nomos, 2016).

The research explores security constructions in and around decolonisation. Using Togoland as a case study, it delves into security dynamics under French and British administration, examining conflicts around the Ewe and Togoland unification movement. The study identifies threat constructions, analyses argumentation patterns, and explains mechanisms of action. Overarching all of this lingers the political science question of how to decide what security threats do and, what it says about the actors involved.

Drawing from Critical Security Studies (CSS),95F[96] the struggle over Togoland's decolonisation will be decoded primarily via a postcolonial reading of CSS' *securitisation* framework. This framework explains how 'security issues' are an important vehicle for negotiating political power. Securitisation conceptualises security as a social process that classifies an issue as so significant that it is lifted out of normal everyday politics and makes extraordinary measures possible. Thus, at the centre of a securitisation process is a speech act, that is, an empirical object, which is not a threat *per se* but is only discursively made into one.

With approaches to securitisation, it is possible to address security speech acts and threat communication as well as macro-constellations, which link the international scene with local events in the territories themselves. This is what is special about Togoland's internationally supervised decolonisation process, where a conflict developed over the conditions of independence. Petitioners from Togoland agitated before the United Nations Trusteeship Council and General Assembly for the reunification of once colonially divided territories. In doing so, they took on the role of anti-colonial securitising actors. In the case of Togoland, France and Britain assumed responsibility for the administration in the trusteeship territories, and in doing so, they fulfilled virtually all government functions. The trustees were monitored through the Trusteeship Council and General Assembly, with regular debates, reporting, and Visiting Missions to the trusteeship territories. This distinguished trusteeship *de jure* from colonial rule, yet *de facto* Togoland and other trusteeship territories were still under control of colonial powers. The ruling trusteeship powers, so-called Administering Authorities, demonstrated this through a continuity in colonial practice and discourse, enacting before the UN *disabling frames* to thwart the Ewe and Togoland unificationists' securitising moves. Ultimately, their *Dream of Unity*[97] failed to materialise because the structures supposed to ensure the "just treatment,"[98] "well-being,"[99] and "freely expressed wishes of the peoples concerned,"[100] were used to limit the scope for protest. Thus, the failure of the Togolese petitioners was due to silencing effects originating from the colonial constellation of international supervision.

This study analyses these actors' constructions of security and threat perceptions, their ruptures, and dilemmas in a historical perspective. This historical study of the de-

---

96   The term originally referred to the approach of Ken Booth. However, the term has come to refer to security research that simply distinguishes itself from realism; see Columba Peoples and Nick Vaughan-Williams, *Critical Security Studies: An Introduction* (London: Routledge, 2010), p. 18..
97   Welch, *Dream of Unity*.
98   League of Nations, Covenant, Art. 22.
99   United Nations, Charter, Art. 73.
100   United Nations, Charter, Art. 77.

bates around the trusteeship territories of British and French Togoland addresses the tripartite constellation of African, colonial, and UN actors, that is, the various levels of influence that legitimised political measures and interests during the period of decolonisation. The empirical analysis will show that constructions of (in)security were influential for the negotiation of trusteeship rule.

1.4 Relevance & Contribution

The study aims to contribute to literature in three key areas: historical Togoland research, statebuilding literature, and postcolonial perspectives in International Relations.

Regarding Togoland, the research delves into its significance as a site of historical precedents for postcolonial African states, such as being the location of the first UN-led independence referendum.[101] The study emphasizes the lack of comprehensive theory-driven perspectives on Togoland's decolonisation, highlighting its unique circumstances and the role it played in the international spotlight due to the reunification movement. In the realm of statebuilding literature, the research critiques the prevailing notion that deficits in statehood, often observed in postcolonial African states, pose direct threats to international security. It challenges the colonial continuity in contemporary statebuilding missions and emphasizes the need for a nuanced examination of securitisation moves and accountability bottlenecks in international statebuilding.

From a postcolonial perspective on International Relations and Critical Security Studies, the study explores the historical context of the UN Trusteeship System within 20th-century decolonisation. It advocates for incorporating postcolonial theory into Critical Security Studies, examining the conditions for success and failure in securitization moves and addressing the colonial legacy in the Togo-Ghana region. The study aims to bridge the gap between discourse approaches and sociological practices by analysing articulations of colonial fears and threat constructions in both public and behind-the-scenes forums. As this work is ultimately about a history of exclusion, it draws on guidance on how to promote more inclusion, both in ways that would expand the circle of who is speaking International Relations and Critical Security Studies,[102] as well as the inclusion of marginalized security speech.[103]

1.5 Outline

The work is structured as follows: After this introduction, Chapter 2 outlines not only the current state of research *on* but also the course *of* the academic debate on state- and peacebuilding as well as Critical Security Studies. This is followed by the state of research

---

[101] Julius Heise, "United Nations Colonial Complicity in Decolonization Referenda," *Topos*, no. 1 (2021), available from journals.ehu.lt/index.php/topos/article/view/1048.

[102] Meera Sabaratnam, "IR in Dialogue … but Can We Change the Subjects?," *Millennium: Journal of International Studies* 39, no. 3 (2011), https://doi.org/10.1177/0305829811404270.

[103] Sarah Bertrand, "Can the Subaltern Securitize?," *European Journal of International Security* 3, no. 03 (2018), https://doi.org/10.1017/eis.2018.3.

on historical trusteeship and finally the research on security as well as nation- and statehood in Togoland. Chapter 3 engages the Copenhagen and Paris School of Critical Security Studies and presents the research approach of a post-colonially informed securitisation framework. Chapter 4 presents the methodological approach, explaining the research design and operationalisation of archival sources, including considerations that will address postcolonial sensitivities. Chapter 5 provides the historical context for the main analytical chapter. Although this is not the main chapter, the analytical framework comes into play to some extent in the presentation. Chapter 6 is the main empirical chapter, which contextually examines how Ewe and Togoland unification were securitised in the decolonisation process. An attempt was made to present the development of events and thus the context for the articulations of (in)security as chronologically as possible. On the one hand, this is deliberately done so as not to take securitisation moves out of their context and, on the other hand, because earlier works tended to separate their analyses of British Togoland and French Togoland for the sake of clarity.[104] Such an approach was decidedly not applied in the present work to emphasise the interconnectedness and simultaneity of events from the anti-colonial actor's point of view. Finally, Chapter 7 summarizes the findings and situates them in the context of the academic debate. A reflection on the potentials and limitations of the research approach aim to provide an outlook on remaining research desiderata.

---

[104] Most notably D. E. K. Amenumey, *The Ewe Unification Movement: A political history* (Accra: Ghana University Press, 1989), Ph.D. Thesis; George Thullen, *Problems of the Trusteeship System: A Study of Political Behavior in the United Nations*, Travaux de droit d'économie, de sociologie et de sciences politiques 24 (Genève: E. Droz, 1964).

2. State of the Art

> "Bunche would be rolling over in his grave if he saw that."[1]

Several developments that inform this study emerged in the 1990s: the heightened interventionism and neo-trusteeship models following the failed states debate, the advent of Critical Security Studies in response to the conclusion of the Cold War, and the ascent of post- and decolonial scholarship. To contextualise the present research, these strands of literature are brought together:[2] Chapter 2.1 traces the evolution of interventionism and statebuilding practices, closely examining their rationale, particularly the asserted prevention of 'fragile states' from threatening international security. This exploration concludes by delving into the realm of emerging decolonial approaches within statebuilding research and expands into the field of postcolonial security research. Chapter 2.2. addresses the gap in statebuilding scholarship, emphasizing the inadequate attention given to historical predecessor institutions. It reviews the still limited contributions to historic trusteeship and decolonisation. In this context, Chapter 2.3 presents specific literature on Togoland, exploring scholarly contributions to its state- and nationhood as well as its security institutions.

2.1 Neo-Trusteeship & (In)Security

After the end of the Cold War, there has been a considerable increase in peacekeeping missions, particularly by the United Nations, with varying duration and intensity of intervention, replacing traditional conceptions of *nation-building* by *state-building*. Characterizing the relationship between the Global South and the Global North, this 'new' form of intervention was justified by the apparent fragility of statehood in the Global South,

---

1   Robert Vitalis, *White world order, black power politics: The birth of American international relations*, The United States in the World (Ithaca: Cornell University Press, 2015), p. 229.
2   The arrangement of the sub-chapters does not correspond to the actual chronological progression of research literature. This was deliberately done to illustrate how the course of the academic debate on state-building over the last 30 years has led to a research desideratum for the study of security in historical cases of trusteeship.

which was frequently considered a potential security threat to the Global North. While critics find fault with the quasi-colonial structures of the top-down processes in the societies concerned and conclude that interventions are controversial and problematic in themselves, in practice they are often employed as a necessary evil driven by security considerations. In the following, it will be established that scholarship on the new interventionism since the 1990s, although not clearly distinguishable from each other chronologically, can be divided into five cohorts or 'generations.'[3]

2.1.1 Antecedents: From Transitional to Structural Problems (1960-1970s)

The year 1960 was the "Year of Africa," when seventeen African states, including French Togoland, gained their independence. During the first wave of decolonisation between 1945 and 1970, it was modernisation theory, which postulated that the 'underdeveloped countries of the Third World' were simply on their way to catch up with the West. Under modernisation theory's paradigm, neither the foreign policy of Western powers nor the United Nations were too keen on interfering in the internal affairs of the so-called developing countries. As promising as the post-colonial future of these new, sovereign states seemed, disillusionment quickly spread in the face of the continuity of global inequality, insecure statehood, economic dependency, and especially the increasing number of autocracies, including in Togo, where after an initial coup d'état in 1963, Gnassingbé Eyadéma finally seized absolute power in 1967.

Thus, in the early 1970s, perspectives from dependency theory, particular by André Gunder Frank and Immanuel Wallerstein, rallied against modernisation theory by arguing that the problems in the so-called 'Third World' were not transitional but structural.[4] In the early 1980s, despite decades of aid and technical assistance, the deteriorating economic performance of many countries in the 'Third World' ended the relative neglect by the West, which focused attention on domestic economic structures.

2.1.2 The 1st Generation: Of 'Quasi' & 'Failed States'

With modernization theory going into deep eclipse and the West taking renewed interest in the internal affairs of formerly colonized countries, in the early 1980s the idea of the "liberal peace" made the rounds in International Relations, that is, the conviction that liberal democracies do not wage war against each other,[5] and therefore the spread of this particular form of government is a prerequisite for peace. Drawing on Immanuel Kant's theory of eternal peace, it was particularly Michael Doyle, who argued that democracy,

---

3   Jahn, Beate. "Liberal Internationalism." In Richmond; Visoka, *The Oxford Handbook of Peacebuilding, Statebuilding, and Peace Formation*, 31-41.
4   Michael S. Wesley, "The state of the art on the art of state building," *Global Governance* 14, no. 3 (2008): 370; Immanuel Wallerstein, *The modern world-system I: The capitalist agriculture and the origins of the European world-economy in the sixteenth century*, Studies in social discontinuity (San Diego: Academic Press, 1974); Andre Gunder Frank, *Capitalism and Underdevelopment in Latin America: Historical Studies of Chile and Brazil*, The Pelican Latin American library (Harmonsworth: Penguin, 1971).
5   Vivienne Jabri and Oliver P. Richmond, "Critical Theory and the Politics of Peace," in Richmond; Visoka, *The Oxford Handbook of Peacebuilding, Statebuilding, and Peace Formation*, Vol, p. 97.

trade-interdependence, and membership in more intergovernmental organisations constituted the basic prerequisites for sustainable development and peace.[6] Thus, the spotlight of critique shifted from dependency-theory-based explanations to growing concerns about the capacity of 'good governance' of developing countries.

In this respect, Robert Jackson and Carl Rosberg's analysis attributed the pervasive underdevelopment paradigm of 1980s to the weakness of the 'African state.'[7] The debate of the 1980s was trailblazing for the transition from advice and requests for assistance to the direct physical intervention in the 1990s. Especially the notion of liberal peace would serve as a guiding principle for the United Nations concept of peace developed in the early 1990s. Thus, in the 1980s, the 'developed world' became more interventionist in its responses. Following the emergence of state-led development strategies in the post-war period, such as the International Monetary Fund and the World Bank, which emphasised the problem of market failure that needed to be corrected through state intervention, the *Washington Consensus*, that is, the paradigm of neoliberal economic doctrine was soon applied to development economics. As the internal economic policies and institutions of developing countries came under scrutiny, with particular focus on state intervention in the economy, corruption, and distributional inefficiencies, the World Bank, the International Monetary Fund, and individual states began to advocate a mix of structural adjustment programmes, macro-stability, liberalisation, and privatisation for the economic policies of developing countries.

In the early period after the Cold War, Amitav Acharya identified that most of the wars fought in the so-called 'Third World' were intrastate wars.[8] Primarily Western scholars and policymakers attributed this state of affairs to what in the 1980s Jackson and Rosberg called "weak" or "quasi" states.[9] By the early 1990s, these came to be commonly known under the term "failed states" – a nomenclature which described regions where organized government has collapsed. Moreover, Saddam Hussein's attack on Kuwait in 1991 and the fear of yet another international oil crisis were taken as indication that out-of-control autocracies did not only pose a threat to their own populations but to the fabric of international, that is, western, dominated economy and security at large.[10] Yet, driven by the writings of Jackson and Rosberg or Jean-François Bayart's *Politics of the Belly*,[11] state failure was commonly associated with African states.

---

6   Michael W. Doyle, "Kant, Liberal Legacies, and Foreign Affairs," *Philosophy & Public Affairs* 12, no. 3 (1983), available from https://www.jstor.org/stable/2265298.

7   Robert H. Jackson and Carl G. Rosberg, "Why Africa's Weak States Persist," *World Politics* 35, no. 1 (1982), available from https://www.jstor.org/stable/2010277; Robert H. Jackson and Carl G. Rosberg, "Sovereignty and Underdevelopment," *The Journal of Modern African Studies* 24, no. 1 (1986), available from https://www.jstor.org/stable/160511; Robert H. Jackson, *Quasi-states: Sovereignty, international relations, and the Third World*, Cambridge studies in international relations 12 (Cambridge: Cambridge University Press, 1990).

8   Amitav Acharya, "The Periphery as the Core," in Krause; Williams, *Critical Security Studies*, Vol, pp. 300–301.

9   Jackson and Rosberg, "Why Africa's Weak States Persist."

10 Stephen M. de Luca, "The Gulf Crisis and Collective Security Under the United Nations Charter," 3, no. 1 (1991); Acharya, "The Periphery as the Core," p. 309.

11 Jean-François Bayart, *L'État en Afrique: La politique du ventre*, L'espace du politique (Paris: Fayard, 1989).

The idea of state failure found much resonance in the West: the debate on the West's new role certainly rode within the slipstream of Francis Fukuyama's widespread *end of history* thesis,[12] that is, the conviction that the end of the Cold War cleared the way for the principles of Western liberalism in the form of market economy, democracy, and human rights, to finally prevail everywhere. Thus, the argument for increased interventionist commitment of the West seemed compelling: from early on Peter Lyon, Gerald Helman and Steven Ratner sparked the idea of "international trusteeship" as a possible means of coping with the problem of so-called "failed states."[13] This prompted voices within the scholarly debate and Western press calling for the West to return for a 'new' kind of "benign colonization."[14]

A common feature of many of these proposals was (and still is) the idea that decolonisation came too quickly: Expressing criticism that decolonisation was too hastily pursued, Jackson speaks of "negative sovereignty,"[15] that is, the new post-colonial states were assured of their sovereignty at the international level, regardless of their ability to govern their population and territory as a viable state entity. Similarly, William Pfaff argued that "Colonialism lasted long enough to destroy the pre-existing social and political institutions, but not long enough to put anything solid and lasting in its place."[16] Tom Parker concluded that because of the "rush to self-government little thought was given to their long-term survivability. [...] Against a majority in the General Assembly eager to consign all vestiges colonialism to the 'dustbin of history' even the Trusteeship System could not protect territories from premature statehood."[17] Parker argues that independence, and its central assumption of self-determination as an indispensable prerequisite of peace, security, and welfare, have been turned on its head, insinuating that the hazards of premature independence constituted state failure.

Even disapproving scholarly interventions, such as Mohammed Ayoob's "subaltern realism,"[18] did not escape the state-centric arguments of the 'failed states' maelstrom. In the end, the fragility of statehood, identified primarily in the Global South, resulted in a new form of intervention after the end of the Cold War to prevent 'fragile states' from compromising global and regional security.[19]

---

12 Francis Fukuyama, *The end of history and the last man* (New York: Free Press, 1992).
13 Gerald B. Helman and Steven R. Ratner, "Saving Failed States," *Foreign Policy*, no. 89 (1992); Peter Lyon, "The Rise and Fall and Possible Revival of International Trusteeship," *The Journal of Commonwealth & Comparative Politics* 31, no. 1 (1993), https://doi.org/10.1080/14662049308447651.
14 Ali Mazrui, "Decaying Parts of Africa Need Benign Colonization," *International Herald Tribune*, 04 August 1994; Charles Krauthammer, "Trusteeship for Somalia: An Old-Colonial-Idea Whose Time Has Come Again," *Washington Post*, 09 October 1992; William Pfaff, "A New Colonialism?," *Foreign Affairs* 74, no. 1 (1995), https://doi.org/10.2307/20047013.
15 Jackson, *Quasi-states*, 26, 95–101.
16 Pfaff, "A New Colonialism?," p. 361.
17 Tom Parker, *The Ultimate Intervention: Revitalising the UN Trusteeship Council for the 21st Century* (Sandvika, 2003), accessed 29 July 2019, available from www.bi.edu/globalassets/forskning/centre-for-european-and-asian-studies/pdf/03-03the_ultimate_intervention.pdf, pp. 31–32.
18 Mohammed Ayoob, "Defining Security," in Krause; Williams, *Critical Security Studies*, Vol:
19 Mark Duffield and Nicholas Waddell, "Securing Humans in a Dangerous World," *International Politics* 43, no. 1 (2006), https://doi.org/10.1057/palgrave.ip.8800129., Duffield and Wadell discuss how the War on Terror refocusses human security approaches to issues regarded as important for

Human Security & the Responsibility to Protect

The first wave of 'failed state scholars' turned some of the central assumptions of traditional security studies on their head: while in the context of the Cold War, realism's state-centrism preached primarily security measures directed to safeguard the integrity of the state, the state was now conceptualized as a potential source of insecurity for its own population and (only as a consequence of this) to the international community.[20] As such, the concept of security of the *state* (national security) expanded to the notion of security of the *people*.[21] This shift was most clearly illustrated by the 1994 UNDP report introducing the concept of *human security*:

> "It will not be possible for the community of nations to achieve any of its major goals – not peace, environmental protection, not human rights, not democratization, not fertility reduction, not social integration – except in the context of sustainable development that leads to *human security*."[22]

The concept of human security extended the traditional understanding of security as "freedom from fear" to include the Western individual-centred components of "freedom from want," which encompassed economic, food, health, environmental, personal, community, and political security. Though not entirely novel,[23] the 1994 UNDP report clearly placed "human security" in the development context,[24] which the literature discussed as the *Security-Development-Nexus*.[25] Besides the UNDP report, five additional UN reports, namely the UN Secretary-General's Boutros-Ghali's 1992 *Agenda for Peace*,[26] the 1995 *Supplement to* An Agenda for Peace,[27] the 2000 *Report of the Panel on United Nations Peace Opera-*

---

homeland security; Jeremy Weinstein, Stuart E. Eizenstat, and John E. Porter, "Rebuilding Weak States," *Foreign Affairs*, 2005, accessed 30 November 2021, available from https://www.foreignaff airs.com/articles/2005-01-01/rebuilding-weak-states.

20 Acharya, "The Periphery as the Core."
21 Ole Wæver, "Securitization and Desecuritization," in *On security*, ed. Ronnie D. Lipschutz, New directions in world politics (New York: Columbia University Press, 1995); An allusion to this is also the title of the book by Simon Chesterman, *You, the people: The United Nations, transitional administration, and state-building*, Project of the International Peace Academy (Oxford, New York: Oxford University Press, 2004).
22 UNDP, "Human Development Report" (New York, 1994), emphasis added.
23 See discussion of Truman's speech of 1949 below.
24 Eckart Conze, *Geschichte der Sicherheit: Entwicklung – Themen – Perspektiven*, V&R Academic (Göttingen: Vandenhoeck & Ruprecht, 2018), p. 64; Meera Sabaratnam, *Decolonising intervention: International statebuilding in Mozambique*, Kilombo: International Relations and Colonial Questions (London, Lanham, Maryland: Rowman & Littlefield, 2017), p. 18.
25 Lars Buur, Steffen Jensen and Finn Stepputat, *The security-development nexus: Expressions of sovereignty and securitization in Southern Africa* (Uppsala, Cape Town: Nordiska Afrikainstitutet; HSRC, 2007); Mark Duffield, *Global governance and the new wars: The merging of development and security*, Critique, Influence, Change (London: Zed Books, 2001); Paul Jackson, ed., *Handbook of International Security and Development* (Cheltenham: Edward Elgar Publishing, 2015).
26 Boutrous Boutros-Ghali, "An Agenda for Peace: Preventive Diplomacy, Peacemaking and Peace-Keeping" (New York, 1992).
27 Boutrous Boutros-Ghali, "Supplement to An Agenda for Peace" (New York, 1995).

tions, the so-called *Brahimi report*,[28] the 2001 *Report of the International Commission on Intervention and State Sovereignty*[29] and the Kofi Annan's 2005 report *In larger freedom: towards development, security and human rights for all*,[30] have identified defective states or even total state failure as the causes of war, arguing that the only way to achieve lasting peace was to address state deficiencies that led to war and collapse in the first place.

Although the *International Commission on Intervention and State Sovereignty*, a UN ad-hoc committee, proposed to turn away from a policy of 'humanitarian intervention,' it advanced at the same time the infamous *responsibility to protect* (R2P) concept: Should a state fail to live up to this responsibility, then "human security" was a normative claim and subsidiary right for the international community to intervene.[31] If a state proved to be insufficiently functional to ensure order and stability, international administrations take over the maintenance of peace and security for a transitional period, sometimes by means of military intervention. At its core, R2P changed the long-held principle of state sovereignty and non-interference. While the UN's sovereignty paradigm previously postulated non-interference into the affairs of a state, R2P made a state's responsibility for the "human security" of its citizens a condition of sovereignty – a general shift, which failed state scholars such as Dominik Zaum coined approvingly as "sovereignty as responsibility."[32] A whole series of states, particularly African states, have taken a critical stance on human security and R2P as the basis of a new intervention policy under the umbrella of the United Nations, not least because they have experienced Western interventions in some form in their colonial past.[33]

In the late 1980s and early 1990s, the first generation of UN observation and verification missions administered elections and plebiscites, such as in Angola, monitored ceasefire agreements and the long-term commitments of the parties, such as in Guatemala and El Salvador. In the mid-1990s, the humanitarian debacles in Somalia, Rwanda, Cambodia, Liberia, Haiti, and Yugoslavia, gave rise to a significant increase in UN peace-keeping missions. These missions initially intervened to *enforce* peace with the aim of preserving the existing state and containing the conflicts by strengthening state institutions. To facilitate political reconstruction, these administrations took over the monopoly of violence, including the main functions of a state (including financing and administration). The execution of these mandates was a multi-stage process: the first stage focused on security, order, and the provision of humanitarian aid. The second stage focuses on (re)building institutions and public administration. The third stage

---

28   United Nations, "Report of the Panel on United Nations Peace Operations" A/55/405-S/2000/809 (New York, 2000).

29   ICISS, *The responsibility to protect: Report of the International Commission on Intervention and State Sovereignty* (Ottawa: International Development Research Centre, 2001).

30   Kofi Annan, "In larger freedom: towards development, security and human rights for all" A/59/2005 (2005).

31   Conze, *Geschichte der Sicherheit*, p. 64.

32   Dominik Zaum, *The sovereignty paradox: The norms and politics of international statebuilding* (Oxford: Oxford University Press, 2007). https://doi.org/10.1093/acprof:oso/9780199207435.001.0001.

33   Thorsten Bonacker, "'Wann Werden Die Vereinten Nationen Truppen Nach Kalifornien Senden?'," in *Menschliche Sicherheit und gerechter Frieden*, ed. Ines-Jacqueline Werkner and Bernd Oberdorfer, Gerechter Frieden Politisch-ethische Herausforderungen 4 (Wiesbaden: Springer, 2019), p. 58.

was concerned with the rule of law, the promotion of democratic processes and the economy.[34]

The UN missions in Somalia (UNOSOM, 1993–5), Cambodia (UNAMIC & UNTAC, 1992–3), Rwanda (UNAMIR, 1993–6), Liberia (UNOMIL, 1993–7), Haiti (UNMIH, 1993–6) and the Office of the High Representative (OHR) in Bosnia and Herzegovina (1996-today) already exercised *partial* administrative functions, which were representative for this first "limited" approach of UN peace-*keeping* missions.

Reactivating the Trusteeship Council?

In the slipstream of the 'failed states' and 'human security' debate, many scholarly proposals had emerged that either the Trusteeship Council, other UN bodies, or regional organizations should be partially or even fully entrusted with the administration of the affairs and supervisory functions of complex UN missions.[35]

Inactive since 1994, when Palau (the last remaining trusteeship territory) was released into independence, the Trusteeship Council has been regularly described as a success story in the history of the United Nations.[36] In 2004, Secretary-General Kofi Anan's Director of Communications, Edward Mortimer, suggested to "revive and reform the Trusteeship Council, using it as a mechanism through which the community of nations could effectively exercise its tutelage and responsibility for the interests of those unfortunate peoples who may from time to time find themselves in need of international protection."[37] Still by 2013, UN Secretary-General, Ban Ki-Moon, praised that although trusteeship might seem old-fashioned "It testifies to the great success of the United Nations. I wish other UN bodies could finish their business with the same effectiveness of the Trusteeship Council."[38]

Although the UN Charter does not even allow for the placement of its member states under the former Trusteeship System, the idea of trusteeship had three core elements:

---

34   Wesley, "The state of the art on the art of state building," p. 373.
35   Tom Parker, *The Ultimate Intervention: Revitalising the UN Trusteeship Council for the 21st Century* (Sandvika, 2003), accessed 29 July 2019, available from www.bi.edu/globalassets/forskning/centre-for-european-and-asian-studies/pdf/03-03the_ultimate_intervention.pdf; Lyon, "The rise and fall and possible revival of international trusteeship"; Henry H. Perritt, "Structures and Standards for Political Trusteeship," *Journal of International Law and Foreign Affairs* 8, no. 2 (2003); Henry H. Perritt, "Providing Judicial Review for Decisions by Political Trustees," *Duke Journal of Comparative & International Law* 15, no. 1 (2004); Gerard Kreijen, *State failure, sovereignty and effectiveness: Legal lessons from the decolonization of Sub-Saharan Africa* (Leiden, Great Britain: Martinus Nijhoff Publishers, 2004); Richard Caplan, *A New Trusteeship? The International Administration of War-torn Territories* (Oxford: Oxford University Press, 2002); Edward Mortimer, "The Politics of International Administration," *Global Governance* 10, no. 1 (2004), available from https://www.jstor.org/stable/27800505.
36   A. J. R. Groom, "The Trusteeship Council," in *The United Nations at the millennium: The principal organs*, ed. Paul Taylor and A. J. R. Groom, 1st ed. (London: Continuum, 2000); The question that Groom does not ask is, of course, "Successful for whom?
37   Mortimer, "The Politics of International Administration," p. 13.
38   *UN News*, "UN Trusteeship Council Chamber Reopens with New Hopes for the Future, Ban Says," 26 April 2013.

legal accountability of the trustee to third parties, that is, that they report to someone besides themselves; a commitment to improve the conditions of the people under trusteeship; and respect for the ability of the people eventually shape their own lives.

Yet, these proposals were criticised in particular for their "neo-colonialist notion," disavowing them as an "ultimate intervention."[39] Steven Ratner, for his part, rejected the 'colonial' tag for international territorial administration,[40] but the criticism stuck that reactivation of the Trusteeship Council implicitly hierarchized the security challenges in the world: while acute threats to (international) security were to be brought before the Security Council in the first instance, the administration of threatened (and threatening) regions (the majority of which were in the Global South) was to be transferred to a subsidiary body, so to speak, that is, the Trusteeship Council.

In the early years of the "failed states" debate, William Bain was the first to discuss theoretically the idea of trusteeship as a security arrangement, suggesting that historical manifestations of trusteeship have always been linked to the idea of security. In fact, Bain considers Kosovo "an international protectorate not substantially unlike the protectorates that were established in nineteenth century Africa."[41] Bain argues that it is a mistake to assume that "institutionalized forms of trusteeship subordinate the well-being of dependent peoples to the argument of national or international security."[42] He holds that trusteeship as an *arrangement of security* is "concerned with the general welfare of certain people, rather than in […] motives and actions that are in so many ways elusive, contested, and unsettled."[43]

Nonetheless, although Bain subscribes to the failed states argument, he considers trusteeship to be an "unpromising arrangement of security,"[44] since "in exchange for security, advocates of trusteeship must accept the proposition that some people do not fully understand the responsibilities of liberty and that they are consequently unfit to rule themselves. Indeed, they must be prepared to overturn the normative settlement that emerged out of decolonization."[45] Bain cautions that trusteeship always implies some form of non-consensual coercion:

> "A trustee is someone who acts on behalf of someone else who is thought to be incapable of navigating the responsibilities of ordinary life, just as a parent acts on behalf of a child who is not yet ready to take on the responsibilities of adulthood. Indeed, it makes no sense whatsoever to speak of trusteeship if a state can consent to being a

---

39 Henry J. Richardson, ""Failed States," Self-Determination, and Preventive Diplomacy," *Temple international and comparative law journal*, 1996; Ruth E. Gordon, "Some Legal Problems with Trusteeship," *Cornell international law journal*, 1995; Ruth E. Gordon, "Saving Failed States," *The American University journal of international law and policy*, 1997.
40 Ralph Wilde, *International territorial administration: How trusteeship and the civilizing mission never went away* (Oxford: Oxford University Press, 2008), p. 384.
41 William Bain, "Saving Failed States," in *The empire of security and the safety of the people*, ed. William Bain, Routledge advances in international relations and global politics 45 (London, New York: Routledge, 2006), p. 199.
42 Bain, "Saving failed states," p. 196.
43 Bain, "Saving failed states," p. 197.
44 Bain, "Saving failed states," p. 188.
45 Bain, "Saving failed states," p. 203.

ward and, at the same time, possess the authority to terminate that status at its own choosing."⁴⁶

Grasping the international system from the perspective of the English School, Bain essentially concludes that the application of a trusteeship principle may only find a place in a *universitas* of states, that is, states united around a common purpose, in pursuit of a recognised material objective, or in furtherance of a particular enduring interest. Yet given that some states rather resemble 'a state of nature,' Bain doubts their worth as arrangements of security.⁴⁷ In contrast, a *societas* of states, that is, states united in recognition of their mutual authority rather than the pursuit of a common substantive purpose (which according to Bain is where world affairs are more likely to be at present), offers little room for the application of the trusteeship principle *per se*. Therewith, Bain indirectly critiques the English School, including the Aberystwyth School's conception of 'security as emancipation' and its associated responsibility of the community of states, as he concludes: "in a world where the fundamental ends of life remain unsettled, persons who are determined to act as if international society consists in a *universitas* of states are more likely to engender the insecurity that all too often accompanies moral crusading rather than lasting peace."⁴⁸

2.1.3 The 2ⁿᵈ Generation: From Peace-*Keeping* to State-*Building*

The literature of the early 2000s notes that the first generation of UN missions in the 1990s was generally successful in terms of peace-*keeping*,⁴⁹ yet largely failed to achieve their goal of successfully transforming state institutions, which were hoped to ensure building *lasting* peace.⁵⁰ Furthermore, the debate gained momentum with the 9/11 attacks and the subsequent *War on Terror*, shifting the focus on 'failed' or even 'rouge' states as source for insecurity.⁵¹ The 9/11 attacks reinforced the underlying perception that poorly governed states constituted weaknesses in the fabric of international society. The 'failed state' shifted security thinking from focusing on concentrations of state power to

---

46   Bain, "Saving failed states," p. 201.
47   Bain, "Saving failed states," p. 198.
48   Bain, "Saving failed states," pp. 203–4.
49   Virginia Page Fortna, *Does peacekeeping work? Shaping belligerents' choices after civil war* (Princeton, NJ: Princeton Univ. Press, 2008); Michael J. Gilligan and Ernest J. Sergenti, "Do UN Interventions Cause Peace?," *Quarterly Journal of Political Science* 3, no. 2 (2008), https://doi.org/10.1561/100.00007051; Michael W. Doyle and Nicholas Sambanis, *Making War and Building Peace: United Nations Peace Operations* (Princeton: Princeton University Press, 2011).
50   Roland Paris, *At war's end: Building peace after civil conflict* (Cambridge: Cambridge University Press, 2004). https://doi.org/10.1017/CBO9780511790836; Larry Diamond, "Is the Third Wave over?," *Journal of Democracy* 7, no. 3 (1996).
51   Holger Stritzel and Sean C. Chang, "Securitization and Counter-Securitization in Afghanistan," *Security Dialogue* 46, no. 6 (2015), https://doi.org/10.1177/0967010615588725; Stephen D. Krasner and Carlos Pascual, "Addressing State Failure," *Foreign Affairs*, July/August (2005); Stephen van Evera, "Bush Administration, Weak on Terror," *Middle East Policy* 13, no. 4 (2006), https://doi.org/10.1111/j.1475-4967.2006.00268.x; Michael Wesley, "Toward a Realist Ethics of Intervention," *Ethics & International Affairs* 19, no. 2 (2005), https://doi.org/10.1111/j.1747-7093.2005.tb00500.x.

worrying about zones of state powerlessness, so-called "areas of limited statehood,"[52] where threats such as transnational terrorism can incubate, transit, and exploit the interdependence of a globalized world for attacks.

According to Paul Roe, there was a need for ever greater engagement and expansion of the UN mission from limited peace-*keeping* missions to comprehensive peace-*building* interventions. This was based on the notion of the *internal security dilemma*,[53] that is, if peace-*keeping* missions failed, it was likely that former conflict parties (due to the mutual uncertainty about motivations) were likely to relapse into violent confrontation.[54]

Roland Paris noted that in Angola, Rwanda, Cambodia, Liberia, or Bosnia, the rapid introduction of democratic elections either exacerbated old or sparked new conflicts. He noted, on the one hand, that the end of the conflicts in Croatia and Namibia was not brought about by the introduction of liberal institutions but by the withdrawal of Serbia and South Africa, respectively. On the other hand, in Latin America, such as in Guatemala, Nicaragua, or El Salvador, discontent grew as the economic liberalisation programme of the Bretton Woods institutions led to more poverty and inequality, thus reproducing the causes of the original conflict.[55]

Overall, these setbacks were not attributed to intervention being the wrong approach *per se*, but to corruption or an overly traditionalist society hindering the preconditions for a functioning market democracy, such as good governance, a stable social and political order, the rule of law, accountability, a vibrant civil society, and responsible political parties.[56] In short, scholars and policymakers put it down to the fact that the conflict-ridden societies were much less "developed" than their Western role models.[57]

This 'insight' led a second wave of failed states scholars, such as Roland Paris or Francis Fukuyama, to conclude the "Imperative of State-Building,"[58] that is, these conflict-ridden societies needed a more comprehensive approach to reconstruction. As the primary objective, international interventions still had to provide security, some degree of transitional justice via war crime tribunals and truth commissions, but after all they had to build robust administrative governance structures, mobilise civil society, provide justice and reconciliation, fight corruption, change political culture – basically, produce a completely new society. The state-*building* concept of this second generation carried two assumptions that, on the one hand, all states are ultimately functioning in the same way and, on the other hand, that an accomplished state would somewhat resemble the Western role models.

---

52   Thomas Risse, *Governance Without a State: Policies and Politics in Areas of Limited Statehood* (New York: Columbia University Press, 2011).
53   Heather Marquette and Danielle Beswick, "State Building, Security and Development," *Third World Quarterly* 32, no. 10 (2011), https://doi.org/10.1080/01436597.2011.610565.
54   Paul Roe, "The Intrastate Security Dilemma," *Journal of Peace Research* 36, no. 2 (1999).
55   Paris, *At war's end*, pp. 63–147.
56   Paris, *At war's end*; Diamond, "Is the Third Wave Over?."
57   Roland Paris, "Saving Liberal Peacebuilding," *Review of International Studies* 36, no. 2 (2010), https://doi.org/10.1017/S0260210510000057.
58   Francis Fukuyama, "The Imperative of State-Building," *Journal of Democracy* 15, no. 2 (2004), https://doi.org/10.1353/jod.2004.0026.

To achieve those goals, Fukuyama argued that the order of peace-building had to be reversed: economic development and state structures had to be promoted first before political freedom could be introduced. Peacebuilders had "to abandon liberalization as a core element of peacebuilding in favour of establishing authoritarian regimes with international military and financial backing" and suppress "certain forms of political expression" in the target countries.[59] Thus, peace-*keeping* missions soon turned into state-*building* missions, which were understood to be more comprehensive: the growing conviction to transform state institutions, building stable political institutions of failed states were conceptualised as an Weberian approach,[60] relating to the "essence of stateness as the monopoly of the means of legitimate violence."[61] While earlier peace-*keeping* missions were regularly described as occurring on an ad hoc basis,[62] the comprehensive transformation programmes for peace- and state-*building* required a much longer-term commitment than was envisaged for the first-generation of UN peace-*keeping* missions.[63]

Moreover, the argument for more engagement seemed to be a simple solution to the debate on whether too much or too little state threatens human security: on the one hand, it was argued that a *deficit of statehood*, that is the collapse of state and controlling institutions would directly lead to insecurity in form of threats to the 'human security' of domestic populations and potentially to the security of the international community. On the other hand, it was argued that 'too much state,' in the form of power concentration in the hands of (semi-)authoritarian regimes with a lack of term limits and the absence of a functioning civil society would lead to threatening human security. Both perspectives, that is, whether too much and too little state was the cause, were based on the same underlying assumption: they deviated from its Western role model.

The 'lessons learned' of the second generation were applied to peace-building missions, such as the United Nations Transitional Administration for Eastern Slavonia, Baranja and Western Sirmium (UNTAES, 1996–1998), the United Nations Interim Administration Mission in Kosovo (UNMIK, 1999-today), and the United Nations Transitional Administration in East Timor (UNTAET, 1999–2002), all of which exercised *full* administration functions. The new approach in these three transition missions was furthermore fundamental to the elaboration of Security Sector Reform (SSR), which was based on the belief that the necessary preconditions for human security are a

---

59 Paris, At war's end, 180, 209.
60 Jahn, "Liberal Internationalism," p. 34. Nicolas Lemay-Hébert, "Rethinking Weberian Approaches to Statebuilding," in Chandler; Sisk, *Routledge Handbook of International Statebuilding*, Vol, p. 10.
61 Wesley, "The state of the art on the art of state building," p. 377.
62 Neta Crawford, "Decolonization Through Trusteeship," in *Trustee for the Human Community: Ralph J. Bunche, the United Nations, and the Decolonization of Africa*, ed. Robert A. Hill and Edmond J. Keller (Athens, OH: Ohio University Press, 2010), p. 109; Tom Parker, *The Ultimate Intervention: Revitalising the UN Trusteeship Council for the 21st Century* (Sandvika, 2003), accessed 29 July 2019, available from www.bi.edu/globalassets/forskning/centre-for-european-and-asian-studies/pdf/03-03the_ultimate_intervention.pdf, p. 3; James Crawford, *The creation of states in international law*, 2nd ed. (Oxford: Clarendon Press, 2010), p. 601.
63 Paris, At war's end, p. 177.

functioning state and accountable institutions.[64] At the same time, SSR suggested that security is after all a political interdependent process that goes beyond the traditional spheres of security such as the military and the police. Thus, what had begun as a series of UN peace-*keeping* operations turned into a debate on peace-*building*, only to become a discussion on market- and *state*-building missions,[65] in the belief that a strong civil society and a developed economy was the path to stability.[66] Though state-building interventions (both as a principle and as a means to achieve their goals) remained highly controversial, in practice, they were considered a necessity without an alternative.[67]

2.1.4 The 3rd Generation: Colonial Reminiscence

The hope that state-building missions would lead to a permanent transition to market democracy and, consequently, establish enduring peace ultimately proved to be a disappointment. Barnett Rubin noted that even long-term commitments such as in Afghanistan never managed to put an end to insurgency to establish sustainable market democracies or hamper the influence of the Taliban.[68] Similarly, the intervention in Iraq led to insurgency, increased crime and insecurity, and political instability – not only in the domestic sphere but for the entire region.[69] Similarly, David Lake holds that interventions neither led to an increase in state capacity,[70] nor in the durability of those states in the future.[71] In the mid-2000s, this insight was the focus of a third generation of scholars and policymakers, whose criticism was directed at the Western-centric normativity of interventions.

Post-Liberal Critique

The United Nations' guiding principles, which served as a blueprint for a wave of peace- and state-building missions in the late 1990s and early 2000s, received much criticism

---

64 See Paris' review of the literature at Roland Paris, "Human Security," *International Security* 26, no. 2 (2001): 91.
65 Oliver P. Richmond, "Rescuing Peacebuilding? Anthropology and Peace Formation," *Global Society* 32, no. 2 (2018): 224, https://doi.org/10.1080/13600826.2018.1451828.
66 Crawford, "Decolonization through Trusteeship," pp. 106–7.
67 Roland Paris and Timothy D. Sisk, eds., *The dilemmas of statebuilding: Confronting the contradictions of postwar peace operations*, Security and governance series (London: Routledge, 2010).
68 Barnett Rubin, "Peace Building and State-Building in Afghanistan," *Third World Quarterly* 27, no. 1 (2006).
69 Robert I. Rotberg, "Failed States in a World of Terror," *Foreign Affairs* 81, no. 4 (2002), https://doi.org/10.2307/20033245; Jennifer Milliken, ed., *State failure, collapse and reconstruction*, Development and change book series (Malden, MA: Blackwell, 2003); Bain, "Saving failed states."
70 David A. Lake and Christopher J. Fariss, "Why International Trusteeship Fails," *Governance* 27, no. 4 (2014), https://doi.org/10.1111/gove.12066.
71 David A. Lake, "Coercion and Trusteeship," in *The Oxford handbook of governance and limited statehood*, ed. Thomas Risse, Tanja A. Börzel and Anke Draude, 1st ed., Oxford handbooks (Oxford, New York: Oxford University Press, 2018), p. 304; Lisa Hultman, Kathman Jacob D., and Megan Shannon, "United Nations Peacekeeping Dynamics and the Duration of Post-Civil Conflict Peace," *Conflict Management and Peace Science* 33, no. 3 (2016).

from the early-2000s onwards.[72] Coining the second-generation approach as the "liberal peace,"[73] Mark Duffield argued that the emerging strategic complex of humanitarian, military, and development actors engaged the Global South through the *security-development-nexus*, whilst the relations of liberal governance and global economic processes increasingly excluded the Global South from production and investment prospects. Several authors increasingly stressed the liberal peace's *neo*-liberal character, which entailed a mimicry of Western institutions, the downsizing of the public sector, and integration into the global market economy.[74] They criticised that the states that have emerged in such internationalised processes lack sovereignty, legitimacy,[75] social penetration, and thus societal validity.[76] The critique pointed to the inherent contradiction of Western values such as self-determination, sovereignty and democratic decision-making, as the societies where intervention took place could not achieve them as long as they were dictated by the interveners.

By the late 2000s, a wide arrange of scholars problematised overall limitations of externally induced reforms,[77] and the notion of 'recipe-like' state-building approaches,[78] which had been advocated mostly by Western actors.[79] Critique was directed against the top-down and one-size-fits-all approach that considered the state as an independent variable and a sphere separate from politics and economics. In their view, the state- and peace-building operations' quasi-governmental policies (including electoral assistance, human rights, rule of law assistance, institutional or Security Sector Reform)[80] tended to

---

72 Roland Paris, "Peacebuilding and the Limits of Liberal Internationalism," *International Security* 22, no. 2 (1997), https://doi.org/10.2307/2539367; Michael Dillon and Julian Reid, *Global governance, liberal peace, and complex emergency*, Contemporary welfare and society (2000).

73 Duffield, *Global governance and the new wars*, p. 9.

74 David Chandler and Timothy D. Sisk, eds., *Routledge handbook of international statebuilding*, Routledge handbooks (London: Routledge, 2013).

75 Bernhard Knoll, "Legitimacy and UN-Administration of Territory," *German Law Journal* 8, no. 1 (2007), https://doi.org/10.1017/S207183220000540X.

76 Wesley, "Toward a Realist Ethics of Intervention," p. 57.

77 Risse, *Governance Without a State*; Paris and Sisk, *The dilemmas of statebuilding*; Bryn W. Hughes, Charles T. Hunt and Boris Kondoch, eds., *Making sense of peace and capacity-building operations: Rethinking policing and beyond* (Leiden: Martinus Nijhoff Publishers, 2010)..

78 Berit Bliesemann de Guevara, *Statebuilding and state-formation: The political sociology of intervention*, Routledge studies in intervention and statebuilding (Abingdon, Oxon, New York: Routledge, 2012); Berit Bliesemann de Guevara and Florian P. Kühn, *Illusion Statebuilding: Warum sich der westliche Staat so schwer exportieren lässt* (Hamburg: Ed. Körber-Stiftung, 2010); Meera Sabaratnam, "History Repeating?," in Chandler; Sisk, *Routledge Handbook of International Statebuilding*, Vol.:; Kai Koddenbrock, "Recipes for Intervention," *International Peacekeeping* 19, no. 5 (2012), https://doi.org/10.1080/13533312.2012.721987; Michael Pugh, Neil Cooper and Mandy Turner, *Whose Peace? Critical Perspectives on the Political Economy of Peacebuilding*, New Security Challenges (London: Palgrave Macmillan, 2008). https://doi.org/10.1057/9780230228740; Oliver P. Richmond, *Failed statebuilding: Intervention, the state, and the dynamics of peace formation* (New Haven: Yale University Press, 2014), http://search.ebscohost.com/login.aspx?direct=true&scope=site&db=nlebk&db=nlabk&AN=861313.

79 James Dobbins et al., *The beginner's guide to nation-building* (Santa Monica: Rand, 2007).

80 Chesterman, *You, the people*, p. 5.

take on a technical management character,[81] that evaded their actual political nature.[82] Andersen and Zaum independently pointed out that international staff members meanwhile often endeavoured to define themselves as neutral, apolitical actors.[83] Bliesemann de Guevara and Kühn criticised the so-called Weberian approaches of the second generation as an "illusion of statebuilding,"[84] because these missions aimed to meet solely the technical expectations of statehood, but not the underlying social relations, which seemed to follow other structures, patterns, and logics. Because of this, the to-be-built states lack recognition and legitimacy in the recipient societies. Since these states did not penetrate society, they were unable to implement political goals, even if institutions appeared to be functional from an external perspective.[85]

Accountability Deficit

Beyond the question to what extent the prospects of success of international administrations were limited, since the mid-2000s critics such as Michael Pugh,[86] Outi Korhonen,[87] David Chandler,[88] and Anne Orford,[89] have highlighted what might be called the 'dark sides' of state-building missions. Beyond the fixation with neoliberal economic reforms, these authors emphasised the tendentious authoritarian character of the top-down approaches. In fact, numerous scholars have assessed and critiqued the human rights record of different international administrations.[90] Most notably, Krempel, Friesendorf, and Jackson identified an increasing tendency towards militarisation

---

81   Richmond, *Failed statebuilding*.
82   Mats Berdal and Richard Caplan, "The Politics of International Administration," *Global Governance* 10, no. 1 (2004).
83   Louise Andersen, "Outsiders Inside the State," *Journal of Intervention and Statebuilding* 4, no. 2 (2010), https://doi.org/10.1080/17502970903533660; Zaum, *The sovereignty paradox*; Christof P. Kurz, "What You See Is What You Get: Analytical Lenses and the Limitations of Post-Conflict Statebuilding in Sierra Leone," *Journal of Intervention and Statebuilding* 4, no. 2 (2010), https://doi.org/10.1080/17502970903533702.
84   Bliesemann de Guevara and Kühn, *Illusion Statebuilding*.
85   Bliesemann de Guevara and Kühn, *Illusion Statebuilding*, p. 10.
86   Michael Pugh, "The Political Economy of Peacebuilding," *International Journal of Peace Studies* 10, no. 2 (2005), accessed 08 February 2022, available from https://www.jstor.org/stable/41852928.
87   Outi Korhonen, "'Post' as Justification: International Law and Democracy-Building After Iraq," *German Law Journal* 4, no. 7 (2003), https://doi.org/10.1017/S2071832200016357.
88   David Chandler, "The Uncritical Critique of 'Liberal Peace'," *Review of International Studies* 36, S1 (2010), https://doi.org/10.1017/S0260210510000823.
89   Anne Orford, *International Authority and the Responsibility to Protect* (Cambridge: Cambridge University Press, 2011). https://doi.org/10.1017/CBO9780511973574.
90   Annemarie Devereux, "Searching for Clarity," in *The UN, human rights and post-conflict situations*, ed. Nigel D. White and Dirk Klaaasen (Manchester: Manchester University Press, 2005); Remzije Istrefi, "Should the United Nations Create an Independent Human Rights Body in a Transitional Administration?," in *Accountability for human rights violations by international organisations*, ed. Jan Wouters et al. (Antwerpen: Intersentia, 2010); Ralph Wilde, "Accountability and International Actors in Bosnia and Herzegovina, Kosovo and East Timor," *ILSA Journal of International and Comparative Law* 7, no. 2 (2001).

of the police structure as part of the state-building efforts.[91] Using the examples of the international administrations in Kosovo and East Timor, Frédéric Mégret and Florian Hoffman have argued that it is necessary to start considering the United Nations as a potential violator of human rights.[92] Joel Beauvais showed that the administration in East Timor tended towards a paternalistic, authoritarian style of government with little regard for local political actors.[93] Similarly, Jarat Chopra referred to UNTAET as "the UN's Kingdom of East Timor."[94] Therefore, Oliver Richmond pointed out that 'liberal' top-down peace- and state-building approaches paradoxically undermined their own promises associated with the broader understanding of human security and R2P.[95]

Scholars addressed the lack of accountability on the part of security actors, the strengthening of autocratic rule, or an overemphasis on security at the expense of socio-economic development.[96] Although the scope of accountability mechanisms has expanded through the stricter imposition in human rights treaties, such as the petition procedure of the United Nations Human Rights Council, this progress has paradoxically not applied to UN peace- and state-building missions. In fact, in 2004, Secretary-General Kofi Anan's Director of Communications, Edward Mortimer, who proposed the reactivation of the Trusteeship Council, based his proposal on the argument that without proper accountability, international territorial administrations have a potential for abuse,[97] since, unlike in the case of mandate and trusteeship territories, the UN Charter does not provide a specific framework of accountability mechanisms for contemporary peace- and state-building missions.

Securitisation of Failed States

Several scholars argued that the securitising rhetoric about 'rogue' or 'failed states,' which allegedly jeopardise global order, international peace, and security, has overturned the universal principle of sovereign equality in the postcolonial context. This postulate of inequality allegedly legitimised military interventions and enabled the introduction of

---

91 Cornelius Friesendorf and Jörg Krempel, *Militarized versus civilian policing: Problems of reforming the Afghan National Police*, PRIF reports in English 102 (Frankfurt am Main: Peace Research Institute Frankfurt (PRIF), 2011); Paul Jackson, *Reconstructing security after conflict: Security sector reform in Sierra Leone*, New security challenges series (Basingstoke, England: Palgrave Macmillan, 2011), http://site.ebrary.com/lib/alltitles/docDetail.action?docID=10445769.

92 Frédéric Mégret and Florian Hoffmann, "The UN as a Human Rights Violator?," *Human Rights Quarterly* 25, no. 2 (2003).

93 Joel C. Beauvais, "Benevolent Despotism," *New York University Journal of International Law and Politics*, no. 33 (2001).

94 Jarat Chopra, "The UN's Kingdom of East Timor," *Survival* 42, no. 3 (2000), https://doi.org/10.1093/survival/42.3.27.

95 Oliver P. Richmond, "A Post-Liberal Peace," *Review of International Studies* 35, no. 3 (2009), https://doi.org/10.1017/S0260210509008651.

96 Christopher Daase and Cornelius Friesendorf, eds., *Rethinking security governance: The problem of unintended consequences*, Contemporary security studies (London: Routledge, 2012); Jackson, *Reconstructing security after conflict*; Rubin, "Peace Building and State-Building in Afghanistan"; Aleksandar Momirov, *Accountability of International Territorial Administrations: A Public Law Approach* (The Hague: Eleven International Publishing).

97 Mortimer, "The Politics of International Administration," p. 13.

Weberian-style trusteeship administrations for state-building.[98] Oliver Richmond attributes this to the unwillingness of the West to let go of "a paternalistic discourse of trusteeship, or a focus on counterfactual securitisation, that is, the security threats that might arise if intervention does not occur."[99] David Lake holds that military interventions in 'failed states' represent "the most aggressive mode of trusteeship and state-building" and argued that interveners will almost certainly have interests of their own in the client-states.[100] Jaap de Wilde illustrated that while the Global South is primarily the target of international interventions, similarly precarious security conditions in parts of the Global North are largely neglected.[101] De Wilde argues that from a human security perspective, "the homicide rate in California needs to be treated with the same concern and urgency as the killings in Liberia. But when will the UN send troops to California?"[102] Wilde contends that the idea of the 'white man's burden' is thus simply continued, now under the banner of the struggle against human *in*-security.[103] Alison Howell and Melanie Richter-Montpetit argue in a similar direction that in "'failed states' securitization runs amok" as "Discourses of state failure [...] operate within a lineage of racial discourse that emerged to justify colonialism and continuing trusteeship."[104] An illustrative example of this discursive shift is Bridget Coggins' analysis of the *Failed States Index*, established in 2005 by the American *Fund for Peace*. Coggins identified major flaws with the index' measurement criteria, as well as the lack of transparency surrounding its data base, accusing the index of being instrumental in the discursive construction of failed states by establishing a false binary between salvageable and non-salvageable states.[105] Furthermore, Coggins' analysis hints towards the dilution of terminology: What has been described as "quasi" states in the 1980,[106] became "failed" states in the 1990, then "weak" states in the 2000s,[107] to result in "fragile" states in the 2010s.[108]

---

98   Wilde, *International territorial administration*; Marta Silva, "Securitization as a Nation-Building Instrument," *Politikon: IAPSS Journal of Political Science* 29 (2016), https://doi.org/10.22151/politikon.29.12; Sabaratnam, *Decolonising intervention*; K. P. O'Reilly, "Perceiving Rogue States," *Foreign Policy Analysis* 3, no. 4 (2007), https://doi.org/10.1111/j.1743-8594.2007.00052.x.
99   Richmond, *Failed statebuilding*.
100 David A. Lake, *The Statebuilder's Dilemma* (Cornell University Press, 2016). https://doi.org/10.7591/9781501703836.
101 Jaap de Wilde, "Speaking or Doing Human Security?," in *The viability of human security*, ed. Monica den Boer and Jaap d. Wilde (Amsterdam: Amsterdam University Press, 2008).
102 de Wilde, "Speaking or Doing Human Security?," p. 237.
103 Wilde, *International territorial administration*.
104 Alison Howell and Melanie Richter-Montpetit, "Is Securitization Theory Racist?," *Security Dialogue* 26, no. 22 (2019): 8.
105 Bridget L. Coggins, "Fragile Is the New Failure," *Political Violence at a Glance*, 27 June 2014.
106 Roxanne Lynn Doty, *Imperial encounters: The politics of representation in North-South relations*, Borderlines 5 (Minneapolis: University of Minnesota Press, 1996), p. 150.
107 James D. Fearon and David D. Laitin, "Neotrusteeship and the Problem of Weak States," *International Security* 28, no. 4 (2004).
108 Coggins, "Fragile is the New Failure."

Colonial Reminiscence

The third generation of intervention scholars emphasized that state-building was predominantly influenced by policymakers, who drew on conceptions of security and the state based on discourses and experiences of the Global North. They criticized that through the securitisation of failed states, which allegedly threatened global security, those states were constructed by Western 'experts' as inferior Others and they produced knowledge that was adopted without alternative into the state-building canon. For Duffield this is particularly evident in the maintenance of colonial patterns of interpretation, such as the distinction between developed and underdeveloped countries, or between a civilised North and a dangerous South.[109] Reading state-building practices as a of form liberal power, Duffield noted the growing influence of Western biopolitical governance, identifying it as a "new imperialism."[110] Neta Crawford argued that transitional administrations were increasingly comprehensive and come to function like colonial trusteeships.[111] Michael Ignatieff attributed the technocratic turn in state-building mission to the "desire to imprint our values, civilisation and achievements on the souls, bodies and institutions of other people,"[112] without invoking the spectre of neo-colonial appearance.[113] Similarly, Robert Rubinstein has argued that an essential characteristic of contemporary peacekeeping is the risk "to incorporate a troubled region into an economic and moral order imposed from outside."[114]

Thus, the observation became common ground that mainly industrialised countries intervene in the Global South. As the historical context of colonialism and decolonisation makes any intervention suspect,[115] the similarities between the "new interventionism"[116] and decolonisation administrations were judged as a continuity of colonial logics.[117] Thus, the 'new interventionism' after the Cold War was frequently referred to as neo-trusteeship or postmodern imperialism, meant highlight the continuation of colonial logics. A common critique of the third generation was to term the period after the

---

109 Duffield and Waddell, "Securing Humans in a Dangerous World."
110 Duffield, *Global governance and the new wars*, pp. 31–34.
111 Crawford, "Decolonization through Trusteeship," p. 108.
112 Michael Ignatieff, "Empire Lite," *Prospect*, 2003, p. 42.
113 Wesley, "The state of the art on the art of state building," p. 373.
114 Robert A. Rubinstein, "Peacekeeping and the Return of Imperial Policing," *International Peacekeeping* 17, no. 4 (2010): 468, https://doi.org/10.1080/13533312.2010.516652.
115 Neta Crawford, *Argument and change in world politics: Ethics, decolonization, and humanitarian intervention*, Cambridge studies in international relations 81 (Cambridge: Cambridge University Press, 2002), https://doi.org/10.1017/CBO9780511491306, p. 427.
116 Doyle and Sambanis, *Making War and Building Peace*, p. 6.
117 Werner Distler, "Breaking with the Past?," in *United Nations Trusteeship System: Legacies, continuities, and change*, ed. Jan Lüdert, Maria Ketzmerick and Julius Heise, Global Institutions (London: Routledge, 2022).

Cold War, for example, *new interventionism*,[118] *Empire-lite*,[119] *Neo-Trusteeship*,[120] *postmodern imperialism*,[121] *new protectorate*,[122] or simply *tacit trusteeship*.[123]

Historical Scholarship

Bain, Chesterman, Wesely, Fearon and Laitin, pointed out that after the end of the Cold War the academic debates and policies on peace- and state-building in post-conflict societies did not engage with the historical cases of decolonisation or trusteeship,[124] probably out of fear to strike "neo-colonial overtones."[125] Given this context, there were hardly any empirical-comparative studies between the historic UN Trusteeship System and what some scholars call the "neo-trusteeships" after 1990.[126] It is one of the reasons why international administrations were initially branded as 'novel' or 'unique.' This levelled criticism above all regarding the ahistorical nature of the second-generation state-building approaches.[127]

A series of postcolonial scholars accused the *liberal peace* of Eurocentrism because it overlooked the Global North's responsibility in the historical conditions of postcolonial statehood in the Global South.[128] Kai Koddenbrock criticizes the neglect of the specific historical context in which African states emerged, as well as the application of universal standards to Africa and the self-evidence of intervention logic.[129] Also Laura Appeltshauser demands to historicise African insecurity and points out that Critical Security Studies has neglected this complexity.[130] According to Rubinstein "peacekeeping has been sliding toward recreating earlier practices of imperial policing by placing the concerns of international actors ahead of those of the local communities in which peace operations take place."[131] Heonik Kwon holds that "it appears that cold war history has a

---

118 Doyle and Sambanis, *Making War and Building Peace*, p. 6.
119 Ignatieff, "Empire lite"
120 Richard Caplan, "From Collapsing States to Neo-Trusteeship," *Third World Quarterly* 28, no. 2 (2007), https://doi.org/10.1080/01436590601153622.
121 Fearon and Laitin, "Neotrusteeship and the problem of weak states."
122 Michael Pugh, "Protectorates and Spoils of Peace," in *Shadow globalization, ethnic conflicts and new wars: A political economy of intra-state war*, ed. Dietrich Jung, The new international relations series (London: Routledge, 2003); James Mayall and Ricardo Soares de Oliveira, *The new protectorates: International tutelage and the making of liberal states* (New York: Columbia University Press, 2011).
123 Andersen, "Outsiders Inside the State."
124 William Bain, *Between anarchy and society: Trusteeship and the obligations of power* (Oxford: Oxford University Press, 2003); Fearon and Laitin, "Neotrusteeship and the problem of weak states"; Chesterman, *You, the people*; Wesley, "The state of the art on the art of state building," p. 375.
125 Caplan, "From collapsing states to neo-trusteeship," p. 242.
126 Wilde, *International territorial administration*; Chesterman, *You, the people*.
127 Chesterman, *You, the people*, p. 11; Bain, *Between anarchy and society*, pp. 145–46.
128 Phillip Darby, "Rolling Back the Frontiers of Empire: Practising the Postcolonial," *International Peacekeeping* 16, no. 5 (2009), https://doi.org/10.1080/13533310903303347.
129 Koddenbrock, "Recipes for intervention."
130 Laura Appeltshauser, "African In/Security and Colonial Rule: Security Studies' Neglect of Complexity," in *Globalizing International Relations*, ed. Ingo Peters and Wiebke Wemheuer-Vogelaar (London: Palgrave Macmillan, 2016).
131 Rubinstein, "Peacekeeping and the Return of Imperial Policing," pp. 457–58.

concentric conceptual organization, consisting of a 'formal' history of relative peace in the center and 'informal' violence in the periphery."[132]

In the mid-2000s, a series of relevant historical analyses on international territorial administration appeared, focussing on the similarities between historical examples of imperialism and current practices of statebuilding. Edward Newman points out that historically, the formation of states has usually been violent and conflictual, and that this dynamic is unlikely to change in the context of contemporary peacebuilding efforts.[133] Charles Tilly serves as a key reference for such studies on violence, contending that the state is a historical byproduct of warfare, wherein monopolizing violence and extracting resources arise to enhance the state's war capabilities.[134] Tilly examines the violent nature of European state-building,[135] distinguishing between state-building and state-formation—highlighting the latter as an unconscious historical process and the former as a conscious effort.[136] However, Julian Go criticizes Tilly for bifurcating European states from their colonial empires, suggesting a need for more nuanced approaches to interconnected histories.[137] Indeed, there are now other approaches to entangled multiple histories and modernities.[138] Likewise, Philipp Lottholz and Nicolas Lemay-Hébert contend that Tilly's work on the emergence of European statehood still represents a pivotal point of criticism for neo-Weberian approaches of statebuilding.[139]

Due to the structural similarities between decolonisation administrations and international administrations, Marauhn and Bothe pointed to a continuity of intervention logics, comparing the UN interventions in Kosovo and East Timor to "Security Council-Mandated Trusteeship Administrations."[140] Anne Orford argued that the R2P grew

---

132 Heonik Kwon, *The other Cold War*, Columbia studies in international and global history (New York: Columbia University Press, 2010), https://search.ebscohost.com/login.aspx?direct=true&scope=site&db=nlebk&db=nlabk&AN=982234, pp. 154–55.

133 Edward Newman, "The Violence of Statebuilding in Historical Perspective," *Peacebuilding* 1, no. 1 (2013), https://doi.org/10.1080/21647259.2013.756281.

134 Charles Tilly, ed., *The formation of national states in Western Europe*, Studies in political development 8 (Princeton, N.J.: Princeton University Press, 1975).

135 Tilly, *The formation of national states in Western Europe*; Charles Tilly, *Coercion, capital, and European states, AD 990–1990*, Studies in social discontinuity (Cambridge, MA: Blackwell, 1990).

136 Thorsten Bonacker, Maria Ketzmerick, and Werner Distler, "Introduction: Securitization in Statebuilding and Intervention," in Bonacker; Distler; Ketzmerick, *Securitization in Statebuilding and Intervention*, Vol, p. 13.

137 Julian Go, ed., *Postcolonial sociology*, 1st ed., Political power and social theory (Bingley: Emerald, 2013).

138 Richard Rathbone, "West Africa," in *African modernities entangled meanings in current debate*, ed. Heike Schmidt and Jan-Georg Deutsch (Portsmouth, NH: Heinemann, 2002); Robert A. Schneider, ed., "AHR Forum," special issue, *The American Historical Review* 112, no. 3 (2007), available from https://www.jstor.org/stable/i40000361.

139 Philipp Lottholz and Nicolas Lemay-Hébert, "Re-Reading Weber, Re-Conceptualizing State-Building: From Neo-Weberian to Post-Weberian Approaches to State, Legitimacy and State-Building," *Cambridge Review of International Affairs* 29, no. 4 (2016), https://doi.org/10.1080/09557571.2016.1230588.

140 Thilo Marauhn and Michael Bothe, "UN Administration of Kosovo and East Timor: Concept, Legality and Limitations of Security Council-Mandated Trusteeship Administration," in *Kosovo and*

out of the UN's practices of executive rule, which once arose in response to decolonisation.[141] Focussing on South Africa, Buur, Jensen and Stepputat show that the much-debated nexus of security and development is by no means a recent invention.[142] Rather, the security-development linkage has been a principal element of the state policies of colonial as well as post-colonial regimes during the Cold War, and it seems to be prospering in new configurations under the present wave of democratic transitions. Alex Veit compares the intervention with one of the core ideas of Frederick Lugard, the architect of 19th and 20th century British imperialism, namely *indirect rule*, and points out that the history of colonial, external rule determines the understanding and development of statehood in societies today.[143] Bain examined similarities and differences between trusteeships and neo-trusteeships by comparing imperial possessions of the British Empire to international engagement in East Timor and Kosovo.[144] Ralph Wilde argues that the existence of international administrations raises the possibility that colonial ideas live on today in practices that operate in the same manner as colonial trusteeship, the only difference being in the identity of the administering actor.[145] Chesterman's historic analysis of past UN state-building missions focuses on the tensions between the idealistic goals of international territorial administrations and the less ideal means of achieving them.[146] Though peace and security are the core drivers of transitional administrations, with the UN playing the role of the administering government attempting to build justice and economic structures, Chesterman points to the lasting significance and legacy of the era of decolonisation. To this day, decolonisation legacy left an organisational imprint in the UN's peacebuilding operations since the Decolonisation Unit is part of the *Department of Political and Peacebuilding Affairs*. Ivarsson and Rud note that many of the states that are considered failed also have a colonial past. It should therefore come as no surprise that the colonial states from which they emerged would be no less considered failures by today's standards.[147] A first criterion for comparison would be the similar tendency towards the use of coercive state power. Secondly, colonial states and today's neo-trusteeships were similarly dependent on metropolitan states. Finally, the colonial state and failed states are at times not recognised as stakeholders with voting rights on the international stage. Although the establishment of the League of Nations Mandates System enshrined the specific colonial state in international law, neither the local population nor the colonial state itself enjoyed its own representation in the governing bodies of international organisations; only metropolitan states 'spoke' for the territories under their

---

the international community: A legal assessment, ed. Christian Tomuschat (The Hague: Den Haag; Kluwer Law International, 2002).

141 Orford, *International Authority and the Responsibility to Protect*, pp. 3–6.
142 Buur, Jensen and Stepputat, *The security-development nexus*.
143 Alex Veit, *Intervention as indirect rule: Civil war and statebuilding in the Democratic Republic of Congo*, Mikropolitik der Gewalt 3 (Frankfurt/Main: Campus, 2010).
144 Bain, *Between anarchy and society*.
145 Wilde, *International territorial administration*, p. 297.
146 Chesterman, *You, the people*.
147 Søren Ivarsson and Søren Rud, "Rethinking the Colonial State," in *Rethinking the colonial state*, ed. Søren Rud and Søren Ivarsson, Political power and social theory 33 (Bingley: Emerald Publishing, 2017), p. 3.

jurisdiction. Aleksander Momirov has shown that some of the safeguards associated with the Mandates System are absent in transitional administrations, that is, accountability is less institutionalized within contemporary international administrations than in historical trusteeship.[148] He insinuates the fact that today's peacebuilding missions have an accountability deficit is also due to the mandate period: Colonial powers were actively involved in truncating petition mechanisms. In consequence, comparable accountability mechanisms are no longer to be found in contemporary peace- and state-building mission agreements.

These historic works suggest that by all contemporary standards of sovereignty and democratic principles, contemporary transitional administrations are a step backward. These authors certainly agree that colonial trusteeship and neo-trusteeships differ since the historical constellations in the era of decolonisation are different from international constellations of the last decades. Yet, they note that the latter encompass colonial continuities. Comparing the UN administrations of the post-Cold War era with the trusteeship administrations after World War II, it becomes apparent that both were subject to similar challenges: The former had to deliver a quick peace dividend and the latter was under pressure to accelerate decolonisation. Inherent in both were attempts of internationally mandated and monitored actors to establish state and security administrations, keep violence/riots at bay, and create" sovereign states in enormously complex and hierarchical settings of practices and discourses of statehood.[149] The self-evident distinction between trusteeship administrations for decolonisation and UN administrations is, therefore, too narrow. They are connected by a history of foreign rule, which ranges from colonial subjugation to the recent intervention.

2.1.5 The 4th Generation: The Local Turn

Since the early 2010s, criticism of the top-down approach and the legitimacy deficit of international statebuilding administrations led to the emergence of academic scholarship, which Oliver Richmond identified as peacebuilding's "fourth generation."[150] This generation is characterized by a "local turn,"[151] which refocuses attention on grassroots

---

148 Aleksandar Momirov, "The Individual Right to Petition in Internationalized Territories," *Journal of the History of International Law* 9, no. 2 (2007): 227, https://doi.org/10.1163/138819907X237174; Momirov, *Accountability of International Territorial Administrations*.
149 Wilde, *International territorial administration*; Thorsten Bonacker, Werner Distler, and Maria Ketzmerick, "Securitisation and Desecuritisation of Violence in Trusteeship Statebuilding," *Civil Wars* 20, no. 4 (2018), https://doi.org/10.1080/13698249.2018.1525675.
150 Oliver P. Richmond, *A post-liberal peace*, Routledge studies in peace and conflict resolution (London: Routledge, 2011), p. 15.
151 Roger Mac Ginty and Oliver P. Richmond, "The Local Turn in Peace Building," *Third World Quarterly* 34, no. 5 (2013), https://doi.org/10.1080/01436597.2013.800750.

actors, local resistances,[152] and so-called hybrid,[153] post-liberal,[154] or post-Westphalian approaches.[155] Even conservative statebuilding scholars, such as Ashraf Ghani and Clare Lockhart, advocated this "citizen-based approach to state building."[156]

The local turn influenced academic debates on international intervention as much as on security and statehood. Tobias Hagmann and Didier Péclard contrast the technocratic approach to state formation in Africa with a framework that understands statehood as the subject of a negotiation process. In doing so, they bring to the fore the historicity of the state, the social embeddedness of its bureaucratic organisations, the symbolic and material dimensions of statehood and the significance of its legitimacy.[157] Similarly, Klaus Schlichte draws attention to contentious understandings of statehood and the hitherto under-researched "rule of the intermediary."[158] Aning and Danso note that the North-South power imbalance has had implications for policy articulation and ownership in Africa. The security policy around issues, such as Security Sector Reform, disarmament, demobilization, reintegration, and counter-insurgency, has often been informed by knowledge generated by scholars from the Global North.[159] They urge that *hybrid security approaches*, in particular African experiences, must be given greater consideration in theorizing about security,[160] championing the "episteme of alternativity that takes cognizance of the context of hybridity in which a vast array of state and non-state actors outside the formal arena interact to shape the security realities of people in Africa."[161] Bagayoko, Hutchful, and Luckham suggest that hybrid systems, that integrate 'traditional' and standard state-focused institutions of security, are similarly embedded

---

152   Roger Mac Ginty, *International peacebuilding and local resistance: Hybrid forms of peace*, Rethinking peace and conflict studies (New York: Palgrave Macmillan, 2011), http://site.ebrary.com/lib/alltitles/docDetail.action?docID=10481693.

153   Oliver P. P. Richmond, *Hybrid Forms of Peace: From Everyday Agency to Post-Liberalism*, Rethinking peace and conflict studies (Basingstoke: Palgrave Macmillan, 2011), http://gbv.eblib.com/patron/FullRecord.aspx?p=931736; Olivier Nay, "Fragile and Failed States: Critical Perspectives on Conceptual Hybrids," *International Political Science Review* 34, no. 3 (2013), https://doi.org/10.1177/0192512113480054.

154   Richmond, "A post-liberal peace."

155   Mac Ginty, *International peacebuilding and local resistance*.

156   Ashraf Ghani and Clare Lockhart, *Fixing failed states: A framework for rebuilding a fractured world*, 1st ed. (Oxford: Oxford University Press, 2009), p. 7.

157   Tobias Hagmann and Didier Péclard, eds., *Negotiating Statehood: Dynamics of Power and Domination in Africa* (New York, NY: John Wiley & Sons, 2013).

158   Klaus Schlichte, *Der Staat in der Weltgesellschaft: Politische Herrschaft in Asien, Afrika und Lateinamerika* (Frankfurt/Main, New York: Campus, 2005), p. 292; For Ewe and Togoland nationalism, see also Benjamin N. Lawrance, Emily L. Osborn and Richard L. Roberts, eds., *Intermediaries, interpreters, and clerks: African employees in the making of colonial Africa*, Africa and the diaspora: history, politics, culture (Madison: University of Wisconsin Press, 2006).

159   Kwaku Danso and Kwesi Aning, "African Experiences and Alternativity in International Relations Theorizing About Security," *International Affairs* 98, no. 1 (2022): 75, https://doi.org/10.1093/ia/iiab204.

160   Danso and Aning, "African experiences and alternativity in International Relations theorizing about security."

161   Danso and Aning, "African experiences and alternativity in International Relations theorizing about security," p. 68.

in their own power hierarchies.¹⁶² Kwaku Osei-Hwedie and Morena Rankopo, examined the conflict resolution process of the Akans in Ghana and the Tswana of Botswana and conclude that "most individuals, families and communities still prefer indigenous conflict resolution processes [...] because they are based on cultural concepts, values, and procedures that are understood and accepted."¹⁶³

2.1.6 The 5th Generation? Decolonising State-Building

Since the emergence of postcolonial scholarship, there have also been efforts in International Relations to decolonise the subject and discipline in order to make research approaches more global.¹⁶⁴ This interest has led to researchers increasingly foregrounding experiences from the Global South. The fourth generation's local actor- and recipient-oriented perspective inevitably brought decolonial concerns to the forefront, indicating since the mid-2010s the emergence of a 'fifth generation' that aspires to live up to the trend of decolonisation in questions of peace and state-building as well. There are now several scholars working explicitly on decolonial approaches to research,¹⁶⁵ while work has also emerged that seeks to mediate between International Relations and post/decolonial concepts.¹⁶⁶

Robert Vitalis' *White World Order, Black Power Politics* revisits the arguments of a group of African-American professors at Howard University, including Ralph Bunche, who played a major role in shaping the UN Trusteeship System. Vitalis responds to Jeffrey Pugh, who interpreted that the originators of the UN Trusteeship System somewhat foresaw the administration of 'failed states' under the aegis of the UN, a great power state or group of states. In a tragically humorous way Vitalis commented that "Bunche would be rolling over in his grave if he saw that."¹⁶⁷ Vitalis concludes that for some state-building scholars...

> "refitting the trusteeship system is the answer to the problem of 'rogue states' and 'state failures' in Cambodia, East Timor, Kosovo, Sierra Leone, and elsewhere. For others, it is a humane alternative to the destruction the United States wrought in Iraq in 2003. All these advocates of 'neo-trusteeship,' though, conjure a past that never actually existed."¹⁶⁸

---

162 Niagale Bagayoko, Eboe Hutchful, and Robin Luckham, "Hybrid Security Governance in Africa," *Conflict, Security & Development* 16, no. 1 (2016), https://doi.org/10.1080/14678802.2016.1136137.
163 Kwaku Osei-Hwedie, T. Galvin and H. Shinoda, eds., *Indigenous methods of peacebuilding* (Hiroshima: Institute for Peace Science Hiroshima University, 2012), p. 47.
164 Branwen Gruffydd Jones, ed., *Decolonizing International Relations* (Lanham: Rowman & Littlefield, 2010).
165 Sabaratnam, *Decolonising intervention*.
166 Robbie Shilliam, *International relations and non-Western thought: Imperialism, colonialism and investigations of global modernity* (London: Routledge, 2012); Geeta Chowdhry, "Edward Said and Contrapuntal Reading," *Millennium: Journal of International Studies* 36, no. 1 (2007), https://doi.org/10.1177/03058298070360010701.
167 Vitalis, *White world order, black power politics*, p. 229.
168 Vitalis, *White world order, black power politics*, p. 172.

Another noteworthy contribution is Meera Sabaratnam's work on Mozambique and her concern to decolonise the intervention through three strategies: reappraising the historical conditions of the recipients, examining their political consciousness, and appreciating the material conditions under which they work. Sabaratnam, too, concludes that "we must think historically about statebuilding," because "dynamics of statebuilding are embedded substantially in particular dynamics that long pre-date the past 20 years."[169] Sabaratnam shows that it is analytically important to mark the continuities of colonial patterns in power and authority configurations in order to be able to recognise patterns of external domination.[170] Also, Dauda Abubakar argues that the 'failed state' debate and the resulting liberal interventionism, with its various security measures, has not traced Africa's historical encounter with Europe through colonial rule. It overlooked the unintended consequences, such as the displacement of people, the radicalisation of youth, and structural violence, which ultimately undermine state-building projects. In conclusion, Abubakar asserts that the African political space and economic sphere need to decolonise in order to ensure development and human security.[171]

Getachew's *Worldmaking after Empire* critiques that scholars have typically viewed the post-1945 decolonisation movement as a history of nation-building, according to which postcolonial leaders in Africa and Asia adopted Western norms of nationhood, sovereignty, and self-determination seemingly without question. Allegedly, colonised peoples did not overthrow European ideas of tutelage and trusteeship, but rather fulfilled them.[172] Pushing for a research programme of "decolonizing decolonization,"[173] Getachew looks in depth at political figures such as W.E.B. DuBois, George Padmore, but especially Kwame Nkrumah, in whose ideas she identifies a more revolutionary project to steer the world in a more egalitarian and anti-imperial direction. Adopting the term of "worldmaking," which Mazower used to describe the emergence of the development-paradigm,[174] Getachew considers that decolonisation meant more than just the full participation of post-colonial nations in the world system of European imperialism because they were already fully integrated into that system as colonies. Getachew identifies several pushes for self-determination at the United Nations (focusing on the *Declaration on the Granting of Independence to Colonial Countries and Peoples*),[175] the building of postcolonial regional federations, such as Kwame Nkrumah's Pan-Africanism, and the calls for the adoption of a New International Economic Order. However, as Cristopher Lee has noted, Getachew's approach to *worldmaking* leaves open thorny questions about aspects

---

169 Sabaratnam, "History repeating?," p. 115.
170 Sabaratnam, "History repeating?."
171 Dauda Abubakar, "The Role of Foreign Actors in African Security," in *African Security in the Anthropocene*, ed. Hussein Solomon and Jude Cocodia, The Anthropocene: Politik—Economics—Society—Science (Cham: Springer Nature Switzerland, 2023).
172 Getachew, *Worldmaking after empire*.
173 Andrew Zimmerman, "Decolonizing Decolonization," accessed 08 November 2021, available from https://www.boundary2.org/2020/06/zimmerman-decolonizing-decolonization-review-of-adom-getachews-worldmaking-after-empire/.
174 Mark Mazower, *Governing the world: The history of an idea* (London: Lane, 2012), Chapter 10.
175 General Assembly Resolution 1514, *Declaration on the Granting of Independence to Colonial Countries and Peoples*, A/RES/1514(XV) (14 December 1960).

that could be described as the dark side of postcolonial worldmaking. These include, for example, Nkrumah's authoritarian measures at the height of the decolonisation wave, such as the imprisonment of political opponents, who positioned themselves against his call for Pan-Africanism. In fact, what Getachew calls "worldmaking" often has been portrayed by the Ewe and Togoland unificationists as a Nkrumah's continuation of "black imperialism,"[176] which is discussed here and elsewhere.[177]

These research approaches unite the conceptual inclusion of different historical experiences, including colonial experiences so as to narrow the dividing line between North and South. According to Julian Go, in doing so, they unite the following insight: "[F]or it to be truly postcolonial, it must move beyond colonial knowledge structures entirely, hence it must strive to transcend the very opposition between Europe and the Rest, or the West and the Rest, which colonialism inscribed in our theories."[178] Postcolonial-inspired historical research must not stop at a mere description of the subject matter but must engage with its object on an analytical level. Therefore, this present thesis endeavours to undertake a theory-driven analysis.

2.1.7 Postcolonial Security Studies

International Relations has been criticised for being overly ahistorical, especially from post- and decolonial scholars.[179] Much of this criticism draws from Dipesh Chakrabarty, who first claimed that the very idea of historicization, which invokes 'disenchanted spaces,' 'secular time' or 'sovereignty,' implies fundamentally Eurocentric assumptions that Europe is the principal subject of world history and therefore needs to be provincialized.[180] More recently, Meera Sabaratnam contended that International Relations "has been trying to transcend its imperial, colonial and racist roots,"[181] yet she noted that it fails to do so since it is "constructed around the exclusionary premise of an imagined Western subject of world politics."[182] Therefore, Sabaratnam champions "to challenge the exceptionalist presumption of the West as the primary subject of modern world

---

176 TNA (London), CO 554/667, *Togoland Administration*, 1953, W.A.C. Mathieson to British UN delegation.
177 Kate Skinner, *The Fruits of Freedom in British Togoland: Literacy, Politics and Nationalism, 1914–2014*, African Studies 132 (New York: Cambridge University Press, 2015), pp. 168–207.
178 Julian Go, "Introduction," in *Postcolonial sociology*, ed. Julian Go, 1st ed., Political power and social theory (Bingley: Emerald, 2013), p. 9.
179 Shilliam, *International relations and non-Western thought*; Gruffydd Jones, *Decolonizing International Relations*; John M. Hobson, *The Eurocentric conception of world politics: Western international theory, 1760–2010* (Cambridge: Cambridge University Press, 2012); John M. Hobson, "Unmasking the Racism of Orthodox International Relations/international Political Economy Theory," *Security Dialogue* 53, no. 1 (2022), https://doi.org/10.1177/09670106211061084; Gurminder K. Bhambra et al., "Why Is Mainstream International Relations Blind to Racism?," *Foreign Policy*, 03 July 2020.
180 Dipesh Chakrabarty, *Provincializing Europe: postcolonial thought and historical difference* (Princeton: Princeton University Press, 2000).
181 Sabaratnam, *Decolonising intervention*, p. 4.
182 Sabaratnam, "IR in Dialogue … but Can We Change the Subjects?," p. 785.

history and international relations."[183] Barry Buzan tried to address such objections.[184] Yet, Buzan's continued use of problematic terms such as "Third World" and thoughts on the "conflictual anarchy of the non-West"[185] continue to be emblematic for the discipline at large.

Regarding International Relation's subfield at hand, that is, Critical Security Studies, Pinar Bilgin criticised that "'historical absence' from security studies of non-Western insecurities and approaches has been a 'constitutive practice' that has shaped (and continues to shape) both the discipline and subjects and objects of security in different parts of the world."[186] Jana Hönke and Markus Müller pose that Critical Security Studies generally suffers from a West-centrism, that is, it has "arguably limited empirical and political relevance for major parts of the non-western world."[187] Amidst these critiques, Tarak Barkawi and Mark Laffey demanded a departure towards a "non-eurocentric security studies."[188] Since the answer to the debate about *what* or rather *who* constitutes security ultimately determines which actors receive analytical attention, they find that an erasure of agency has been untenably ignored. Therefore, Claudia Aradau finds that Critical Security Studies consequently "hid more than helped us to see."[189] Ironically, the demand for a non-eurocentric Critical Security Studies has been much more vocal than its actual development. To this date, there are only few works addressing the *postcolonial moment* within security studies,[190] making analytical use of postcolonial theories or adopting a non-western historical perspective on security.

In the 1990s, as a rebuttal to the Aberystwyth School's conflation of security and emancipation, Mohammed Ayoob promoted the idea of "subaltern realism," which in the maelstrom of the failed states debate considered that the states of the so-called 'Third World' were weak states and therefore had necessarily security needs that differed from countries in the 'developed' world. But while the 'realism' part was based on Ayoob's assumption that the state still plays a central role in security issues, Ayoob himself admits that the 'subaltern' part of his proposition had little to do with the Subaltern Studies Collective, [191] which had formed a decade prior using post-colonial theory to study 'history from below.'

---

183   Sabaratnam, "IR in Dialogue ... but Can We Change the Subjects?," pp. 785–86.
184   Amitav Acharya and Barry Buzan, "Why Is There No Non-Western International Relations Theory?," *International Relations of the Asia-Pacific* 7, no. 3 (2007), https://doi.org/10.1093/irap/lcm012.
185   Acharya and Buzan, "Why is there no non-Western international relations theory?," p. 288.
186   Pinar Bilgin, "The 'Western-Centrism' of Security Studies," *Security Dialogue* 41, no. 6 (2010): 615, https://doi.org/10.1177/0967010610388208.
187   Jana Hönke and Markus-Michael Müller, "Governing (In)Security in a Postcolonial World," *Security Dialogue* 43, no. 5 (2012): 384, https://doi.org/10.1177/0967010612458337.
188   Tarak Barkawi and Mark Laffey, "The Postcolonial Moment in Security Studies," *Review of International Studies* 32, no. 02 (2006): 330, https://doi.org/10.1017/S0260210506007054.
189   Claudia Aradau, "From Securitization Theory to Critical Approaches to (In)Security," *European Journal of International Security* 3, no. 3 (2018): 300, https://doi.org/10.1017/eis.2018.14.
190   Barkawi and Laffey, "The postcolonial moment in security studies."
191   Ayoob, "Defining Security," p. 141.

This necessary step was undertaken by Julian Go through the idea of the *imperial* and *subaltern standpoint*,[192] arguing that there is no global absolute sense of security, rather the sense of security is always relational and dependent on one's point of view. Drawing on Judith Ann Tickner's feminist standpoint theory,[193] which takes feminists' perspectives and experiences in global politics as a basis for theorising global security relations, Julian Go's subaltern standpoint theory reveals how security constructions affect actors of different positionality, especially marginalised groups.

Jana Hönke and Markus-Michael Müller, who focus on contemporary examples of policing worldwide,[194] argue that "taking historical sociology seriously is indispensable for a postcolonial security studies research programme."[195] As a possible approach they propose to recentre the „entangled histories of (in)security governance."[196] One such example is Tarak Barkawi and Mark Laffey proposition of a historicized reading of what they call the "Imperial Peace," highlighting that zones of war and peace have a mutually constitutive character.[197] A similar take is Connor Woodman's study of the "colonial boomerang effect,"[198] which argues that colonies were a fundamental "laboratories of modernity,"[199] particularly when it comes to such security and surveillance practices, which were primarily developed to manage subject populations. Woodman argues that much of what earlier scholarship understood as endogenously Western derives from practices invented in the colonies. This boomerang effect had considerable impact "on the mechanisms of power in the West, and on the apparatuses, institutions, and techniques of power. A whole series of colonial models was brought back to the West, and the result was that the West could practice something resembling colonization, or an internal colonialism, on itself."[200] Hönke and Müller therefore conclude that the evolution of colonial security/police practices was not a unidirectional processes in which "seemingly all-powerful 'Western' actors and interests simply impose their will and 'domestic' institutions upon 'the rest'."[201] Instead, the emergence of modern police forces in Europe was in part a result of an entangled 'cross-fertilization' of metropolitan

---

192   On the imperial standpoint see Go, "Introduction"; on the subaltern standpoint see Julian Go, *Postcolonial thought and social theory* (New York: Oxford University Press, 2016).
193   Judith Ann Tickner, *Gender in international relations: Feminist perspectives on achieving global security*, New directions in world politics (New York, NY: Columbia Univ. Press, 1992).
194   Jana Hönke and Markus-Michael Müller, eds., *The global making of policing: Postcolonial perspectives*, Interventions (London, New York: Routledge, 2016).
195   Hönke and Müller, "Governing (in)security in a postcolonial world," p. 390.
196   Hönke and Müller, "Governing (in)security in a postcolonial world," p. 391.
197   Tarak Barkawi and Mark Laffey, "The Imperial Peace," *European Journal of International Relations* 5, no. 4 (1999), https://doi.org/10.1177/1354066199005004001.
198   Connor Woodman, "How British Police and Intelligence Are a Product of the Imperial Boomerang Effect," accessed 25 May 2021, available from https://www.versobooks.com/blogs/4390-how-british-police-and-intelligence-are-a-product-of-the-imperial-boomerang-effect.
199   Frederick Cooper and Ann L. Stoler, eds., *Tensions of empire: Colonial cultures in a bourgeois world* (Berkeley, Calif.: University of California Press, 1997), p. 5.
200   Michel Foucault, *Society must be defended: lectures at the Collège de France, 1975–1976*, ed. Mauro Bertani and Alessandro Fontana, Lectures at the Collège de France 3 (New York: Picador, 2003), p. 103.
201   Hönke and Müller, "Governing (in)security in a postcolonial world," p. 388.

and colonial police forces. Thus, practices developed and refined in the colonies were not merely applied during late colonialism but ultimately travelled back to the metropole.[202] With thematically very heterogeneous contributions, Ruby et al. strive through a diverse array of theoretical references for a historical consideration of security in connection with (intersectional) categories of difference.[203]

Postcolonialism & Securitisation

The Copenhagen School has been subject of postcolonial critique, too. Lene Hansen first highlighted its inbuilt silence problem,[204] which Ken Booth took as an opportunity to critique that "Those without discourse making power are disenfranchised and therefore unable to join the securitization game."[205] Since then a whole series critics (post- and decolonial ones in particular) claimed that that Copenhagen School struggles to outgrow its reliance on Western conceptualizations of normal politics,[206] epistemically underrepresents non-white/western experiences, is politically passive,[207] conservative, statist, elite- and Eurocentric, and neither progressive nor radical.[208] Vuori applies securitisation to non-democratic/non-Western contexts and argues that even autocratic regimes, such as in China, need to resort to continuous securitisation in order to legitimise themselves, thereby arguing that the Copenhagen School on normal politics is too narrow.[209] Looking at the Egyptian revolution in the context of the Arab spring, Ole Wæver himself admits this, by noting that such an exceptional context challenges the 'theory' due to its possible Western bias.[210] Wæver suggested a link between (macro-)securitisation and colonial metanarratives of Western modernity. Similarly, Barry Buzan and Ole Wæver point to this connection in a discussion of the War on Terror, which brings "the history

---

202 Yael Berda, "Managing Dangerous Populations," *Sociological Form* 28, no. 3 (2013): 628, available from https://www.jstor.org/stable/43653901.
203 Sigrid Ruby and Anja Krause, eds., *Sicherheit und Differenz in historischer Perspektive*, 1st edition, Politiken der Sicherheit 10 (Baden-Baden: Nomos, 2022).
204 Lene Hansen, "The Little Mermaid's Silent Security Dilemma and the Absence of Gender in the Copenhagen School," *Journal of International Studies* 29, no. 2 (2000).
205 Ken Booth, *Theory of world security* (Cambridge: Cambridge University Press, 2007), p. 166.
206 C.A.S.E. Collective, "Critical Approaches to Security in Europe," *Security Dialogue* 37, no. 4 (2006): 455, https://doi.org/10.1177/0967010606073085; Martin Holbraad and Morten A. Pedersen, "Revolutionary Securitization: An Anthropological Extension of Securitization Theory," *International Theory* 4, no. 2 (2012), https://doi.org/10.1017/S1752971912000061.
207 Bertrand, "Can the subaltern securitize?"; Booth, *Theory of world security*; Bilgin, "The 'Western-Centrism' of Security Studies"; Pinar Bilgin, "The Politics of Studying Securitization?," *Security Dialogue* 42, 4–5 (2011), https://doi.org/10.1177/0967010611418711; Claire Wilkinson, "The Copenhagen School on Tour in Kyrgyzstan," *Security Dialogue* 38, no. 1 (2007), https://doi.org/10.1177/09670106070 75964; David Moffette and Shaira Vadasaria, "Uninhibited Violence," *Critical Studies on Security* 4, no. 3 (2016), https://doi.org/10.1080/21624887.2016.1256365; Saloni Kapur and Simon Mabon, "The Copenhagen School Goes Global," *Global Discourse* 8, no. 1 (2018), https://doi.org/10.1080/23 269995.2018.1424686.
208 Booth, *Theory of world security*, pp. 163–69.
209 Juha A. Vuori, *How to do security with words: A grammar of securitisation in the People's Republic of China*, Turun yliopiston julkaisuja. Sarja B, Humaniora 336 (Turku: University of Turku, 2011).
210 Maja T. Greenwood and Ole Wæver, "Copenhagen–Cairo on a Roundtrip: A Security Theory Meets the Revolution," *Security Dialogue* 44, 5–6 (2013), https://doi.org/10.1177/0967010613502573.

of macrosecuritisation full circle, with the Manichean, zero-sum, rhetoric of the [global War on Terror] resurrecting the civilised vs. barbarian themes of both pre-modern and colonial times."[211]

In 2018, this prompted a Special Issue bringing together the application of securitisation in multiple non-Western contexts.[212] In it, Edwin Ezeokafor and Christian Kaunert argue that the audience within the securitisation framework, especially in the context outside the West is undertheorized.[213] Conceptualizing a securitisation-neo-patrimonialism nexus in Africa, Ezeokafor and Kaunert attempt to make the securitisation framework fruitful for the African context, however, by stating that "patrimonialism in Africa has been practiced in an extreme form, thereby undermining the benefits of the system" they also can't pull it off without a relapse into the discourse that draws on the shortcomings of the continent.[214]

Sarah Bertrand took the critique of securitisation's under-theorisation of the audience as an impetus to subject it to a postcolonial reading, shifting the focus from the muteness of the speaker to the power of the audience to silence and exclude.[215] By combining Fanonian decolonial theory of emancipatory violence with securitisation, Akinbode Fasakin argues that the subaltern is indeed able to securitise, when resorting to protest and violence.[216] In his conceptualisation of subaltern securitisation, Fasakin is careful not to conflate Fanon's idea of emancipatory and cathartic violence with Ken Booth's emancipatory concept of security. Unlike Maria Ketzmerick, who considers the Aberystwyth School connectable to postcolonial theories and the empirical object of decolonisation.[217] Ketzmerick strives to make the connection between securitisation and postcolonial theories fruitful, for example, by understanding the securitisation audience in terms of Homi Bhabha's third space.[218]

In 2020, Alison Howell and Melanie Richter-Montpetit fundamentally accused 'Securitization Theory' of a general "civilizationism, methodological whiteness, and anti-black racism."[219] Howell and Richter-Montpetit critiqued that when securitisation scholars draw on historical instances of speech acts, they omit instances of colonial nature and therefore consider that "Securitization theory *refuses* to seriously consider the role of

---

211   Barry Buzan and Ole Wæver, "Macrosecuritisation and Security Constellations," *Review of International Studies* 35, no. 02 (2009): 272.
212   Kapur and Mabon, "The Copenhagen School goes global."
213   S. Leonard and Christian Kaunert, "Reconceptualising the Audience in Securitization Theory," in *How Security Problems Emerge and Dissolve*, ed. Thierry Balzacq (London: Routledge, 2011); Edwin Ezeokafor and Christian Kaunert, "Securitization Outside of the West," *Global Discourse* 8, no. 1 (2018), https://doi.org/10.1080/23269995.2017.1412619.
214   Ezeokafor and Kaunert, "Securitization outside of the West," p. 90.
215   Bertrand, "Can the subaltern securitize?."
216   Akinbode Fasakin, *Subaltern Securitization: The Use of Protest and Violence in Postcolonial Nigeria*, Stockholm Studies in International Relations 2 (Stockholm: Department of Economic History and International Relations, Stockholm University, 2022).
217   Ketzmerick, *Staat, Sicherheit und Gewalt in Kamerun*, p. 70.
218   Ketzmerick, *Staat, Sicherheit und Gewalt in Kamerun*, p. 160.
219   Dan Nexon and Patrick T. Jackson, writers, "It Isn't Just About Wæver and Buzan," aired May 27, 2020, available from https://www.duckofminerva.com/2020/05/it-isnt-just-about-waever-and-buzan.html.

modern colonialism and ongoing imperial warfare in 'failed states.'"[220] Coinciding with the heights of the 2020 Black Lives Matter protests, this controversy found much resonance. A special issue of *Security Dialogue* addressed the debate with contributions on the role of race and white privilege in International Relations and humanitarianism as a Eurocentric practice.[221]

Whilst these interventions do not necessarily invalidate the Copenhagen Schools explanatory capacity, the controversy is a reminder to consider the broader historical context of relations between the Global North and the Global South and include those voices in our analysis that have been and still are marginalized. Eloquently put, Sabaratnam holds that "traditions of critical thinking in [International Relations] – broadly put, liberal, Marxist, Foucauldian and constructivist [...] can all contribute to project of global justice, without serious attention to the people in whose name justice is being pursued as political subjects and not *mute* objects, they are likely to remain constrained in their vision and analysis."[222]

In her securitisation analysis of Cameroon's decolonisation, Ketzmerick deliberately refrains from incorporating Hansen's and Bertrand's critique in her postcolonial reading of the Copenhagen School since she does not view the *Union Démocratique du Cameroon* (UPC) as a subaltern securitising actor because, so she reasons, the UPC cannot be considered a subaltern actor because it is capable of speaking.[223] By attributing subaltern status to an actor merely based on their silence, and conversely defining them as mute due to their perceived subaltern position, she engages in a form of reasoning that is circular in nature. Put differently: If subalternity was defined only by the ability to speak, then the answer to Spivak's "Can the subaltern speak?" would have been "No" by definition and not by her discursive interrogation of 'sati.' Yet, Ketzmerick sidesteps that Bertrand draws precisely from Spivak's critique that an actor is silenced even though they raise their voice. Bertrand specifically pointed out that "one can be silent while screaming loudly."[224] On the one hand, one reason for this lies in Ketzmerick's focus on the *grammar of security*, that is, a functions-focused analysis of securitisation. Although she avowedly seeks to include decolonisation through a contextual reading, the functions-focused analysis of securitisation moves becomes clear in that, like Meridith Terretta before her, she analyses the grievances expressed in the Cameroonian petitions in terms of what discourses they mobilise, what they say about the author and the addressee, but not how they were received. Behind this conceptual choice lies certainly the intention to emphasize the anti-colonial agency and the valorisation of her research's protagonists, that is, the UPC and its most prominent spokesman, Ruben Um Nyobe. Yet, due to the theoretical reluctance to situate the UPC in a subaltern subject position, Ketzmerick sidesteps a theory-driven interrogation of the silencing effects within the Trusteeship System vis-à-vis the UPC and moves rather away from Julian Go's *subaltern standpoint theory*, which

---

220 Howell and Richter-Montpetit, "Is securitization theory racist?," 8.
221 "Forum on Race and Racism in Critical Security Studies," *Security Dialogue* 52, 1S (2021).
222 Sabaratnam, *Decolonising intervention*, p. 8.
223 Ketzmerick, *Staat, Sicherheit und Gewalt in Kamerun*, p. 80.
224 Sarah Bertrand, "Can the Subaltern (In)Securitize?," *European Journal of International Security* 3, no. 03 (2018): 308, https://doi.org/10.1017/eis.2018.15.

Ketzmerick avowedly endeavours to integrate into her post-colonially-informed securitisation perspective.

2.2 Trusteeship & (De)Colonisation

The idea of imperial tutelage, that is, viewing external rule as a form of 'trusteeship' in which (colonial) powers act as 'trustee' exercising political power for the 'benefit' of their subjects, has a long genealogy, written down in resolutions such as the Valladolid Dispute, the General Act of the Berlin Congo Conference, the League of Nations Covenant, and the United Nations Charter.[225] The following literature review will illustrate that historically, the self-authorisation of (colonial) trusteeship was consistently legitimised by varying forms of security speech. In short, trusteeship and security speech have historically always been two sides of the same coin.

2.2.1 Origins of Trusteeship

Bain and Chowdhuri emphasise that the first colonial encounters were central to the emergence of the trusteeship principle.[226] The earliest references date back to the 16th century Conquista and writings by the Spanish theologians Francisco de Vitoria and Bartolomé de las Casas on the moral obligation of the Christian world to assume the role of a "trustee of civilization."[227] De Vitoria claimed that Native Americans were childlike, unfit of running their own affairs, and over whom it would therefore be perfectly lawful and proper for European Christians to exercise authority, but only as long as "everything is done *for the benefit and good of the barbarians, and not merely for the profit of the Spaniards.*"[228] This doctrine was also at the heart of the Valladolid Dispute between Bartolomé del Las Casas and Juan Ginés de Sepúlveda over the question of whether Native Americans possessed a soul, which in consequence would have prohibited their enslavement. If they had no soul, so the reasoning went, they would be equal to animals and therefore their enslavement would be perfectly lawful. If, however, they had a soul, the Catholic Church would be obliged to the indigenous people to save them from purgatory.

However, according to Chowdhuri, Edmund Burke, the British conservative theorist and politician, can be credited as being the first to widely popularize the concept and to coin the phrase "sacred trust" in his famous speech in the House of Commons, on 15 February 1788, during the impeachment of Warren Hastings, the first Governor-General of Bengal.[229] Accusing Hastings of misconduct during his time in Calcutta, particularly

---

225 Wilde, *International territorial administration*, p. 326.
226 Bain, *Between anarchy and society*, pp. 15–16; Ramendra Nath Chowdhuri, *International Mandates and Trusteeship Systems: A Comparative Study* (Dordrecht: Springer, 1955), p. 13.
227 Chowdhuri, *International Mandates and Trusteeship Systems*, p. 13. Bain, "Saving failed states," p. 189.
228 Emphasis in original, Francisco de Vitoria, "On the American Indians," in *Political writings*, ed. Anthony Pagden and Jeremy Lawrance, Cambridge texts in the history of political thought (Cambridge: Cambridge University Press, 1991), Vol. .
229 Chowdhuri, *International Mandates and Trusteeship Systems*, pp. 13–14.

relating to mismanagement and personal corruption, the impeachment prosecution became a wider debate on British rule in India and the role of the British East India Company.

It is worth highlighting that Burke was convinced that the affairs in British India had to be placed under parliamentary control since it is "the very essence of every trust to be rendered *accountable*, – and even totally to *cease*, when it substantially varies from the purposes for which alone it could have a lawful existence."[230] For Burke, describing the rights and privileges of *rule as a trust* implied for that "all political power which is set over men [...] ought to be some way or other exercised ultimately for their benefit."[231] As such, Burke's idea of trusteeship was to replace the exploitative forms of colonialism, such as private ventures and corporations like the British East India Company, which were generally understood as a failure in terms of neglect, exploitation, profit, and general irresponsibility. Ralph Wilde holds that Burke hoped to humanize colonialism through the concept of trusteeship, whereas the tenets of Enlightenment provided imperial rule with the 'obligation' of colonial trusteeship for the 'benefit' of its subjects.[232]

While Burke coined the 'sacred trust' expression to argue for limitations on imperial rule, Bain argues that by the late 19th century this language was redeployed in the General Act of the Berlin Conference, with its obligation to 'watch over' and 'care for … improvement'.[233] Wilde emphasizes that this language, coupled with the principle of trusteeship, was incorporated into the Covenant of the League of Nations.[234] Article 22 of the League's Covenant articulates the 'sacred trust of civilization' forming the basis for the Mandate arrangements in terms of the 'well-being and development' of the people in mandated territories.[235] The provisions of the UN Charter concerning Non-Self-Governing Territories (NSGTs) and trusteeship territories are similarly concerned with ideas of both care and advancement.

Non-European voices were prevented from taking part in the conversation of trusteeship on account of their presumed ignorance and immaturity. According to Bain, they were no more than objects, because they could be no more than objects in a conversation that was concerned with the conditions of their 'true' happiness.[236]

"A *Sacred* Trust"? Petitioning and Accountability

As already stated, Edmund Burke held that "the essence of any trust [is] to be rendered *accountable*."[237] Petitions were not only characteristic but for a long time the only accountability mechanism under the trusteeship principle. Since the Middle Ages English law

---

230 Edmund Burke, *The Works of the Right Honourable Edmund Burke* 2 (Boston: Little, Brown, and Company, 1899), p. 439., emphasis in original
231 Edmund Burke, *Miscellaneous writings*, ed. Francis Canavan, Select works of Edmund Burke a new imprint of the Payne edition 4 (Indianapolis, Ind.: Liberty Fund, 1999), p. 101.
232 Wilde, *International territorial administration*, pp. 320–21.
233 Bain, "Saving failed states," p. 194.
234 Wilde, *International territorial administration*, p. 322.
235 League of Nations, Covenant at Art. 22 (1919), available from avalon.law.yale.edu/20th-century/leagcov.asp.
236 Bain, *Between anarchy and society*, p. 11.
237 Burke, *The Works of the Right Honourable Edmund Burke*, p. 439.

provided the right to petition the Crown,[238] and as one of the earliest studies on the Mandates and the Trusteeship System, Duncan Hall notes that this right "extended automatically to all British subjects in British dependencies and colonies."[239] Although not yet internationally legalized, petitioning was a widespread practice in almost all colonial empires.

While a successful lawsuit, through the weary detours of the judiciary, may well have guaranteed certain political actions, petitions aimed to intervene directly into the executive, albeit with the drawback that compliance to petitions is left to the discretion of the political decision-makers. In fact, unlike lawsuits, this 'ignorability' is indeed the decisive distinguishing criterion of petitions. Petitioners could not appeal to the government to judge their complaints on their own merit but had to fit them in to the conceptual schemes of the colonizers. For example, petitioners who opposed corporal punishment, had to argue that whipping went against *European* notions of morality, civilization, and law.[240] Trevor Getz and Heather Streets-Salter therefore argue that by submitting petitions, petitioners accommodated or even cooperated with the colonial system. Furthermore, whether a presentation of grievances constituted a petition or not, had of course less to do with the intention of the author, but its fate was decided ultimately by the receiving agency that classified and examined it as such. In fact, as Getz and Streets-Salter argue, "Petitions were seen as a useful means of control because in order to submit them, individuals and groups not only had to accept the power of the officials that received them but also to mimic the language and forms of colonial authority."[241] The very fact that petitioners addressed colonial governments, the Permanent Mandates Commission, or the Trusteeship Council, indicated that they "acknowledged the overwhelming power of the colonial system."[242] As such, petitions were a recognition of the *de facto* colonial rule.

After World War I, the League of Nations had not yet legally introduced the right to petition, yet it recognized the practice by introducing an examination procedure for written petitions. As John Groom framed it: "The genie of international accountability could not be put back into the bottle of untrammelled colonial possession."[243] Since the 1990s, a whole series of studies has dealt extensively with the petition scheme of the Mandates System. On a quantitative level, Antonia van Ginniken's doctoral thesis meticulously researched the petitions statistically.[244] Michael Callahan has dealt in particular

---

238 Paul Brand, "Petitions and Parliament in the Reign of Edward I," *Parliamentary History* 23, no. 1 (2004), https://doi.org/10.1111/j.1750-0206.2004.tb00718.x.
239 H. Duncan Hall, *Mandates, Dependencies and Trusteeship*, Studies in the administration of international law and organization 9 (Washington: Carnegie Endowment for International Peace, 1948), p. 198.
240 Peter Sebald, *Togo 1884–1914. Eine Geschichte der deutschen „Musterkolonie" auf der Grundlage amtlicher Quellen* (De Gruyter, 1987). https://doi.org/10.1515/9783112472583, pp. 539–80.
241 Heather Streets-Salter and Trevor R. Getz, *Empires and colonies in the modern world: A global perspective* (New York: Oxford University Press, 2016), p. 412.
242 Streets-Salter and Getz, *Empires and colonies in the modern world*, p. 412.
243 Groom, "The Trusteeship Council," pp. 145–46.
244 Antonia H. M. van Ginneken, "Volkenbondsvoogdij: Het toezicht van de Volkenbond op het bestuur in mandaatgebieden, 1919–1940" [The League of Nations: The supervision of mandatory authority by the League of Nations 1919–1940] (PhD Dissertation, University of Utrecht, 1992), pp. 211–18.

with petitions from the Duala or the *Bund der deutschen Togoländer* on a more qualitative level.[245] Aleksander Momirov shows how the League's petitions procedure practically functioned to remove unwanted petitions from circulation.[246] Jane Cowan has been particularly concerned with admissibility rules regarding the use of "violent language."[247] The most comprehensive study on the Mandates System's petition regime among the recent publications, however, is by Susan Pedersen, highlighting the absurdity that the League's petition procedure, which the European public believed provided possible channels for protests and complaints "contributed significantly to containing and delegitimizing pressure and protests from below."[248]

After World War II, the UN Charter established for the first time the *right to petition*, yet exclusively for residents of UN Trusteeship Territories – a right which hardly any other dependent people had dreamed of having recourse to. Yet, dissatisfied with the colonial powers' "stranglehold on the Trusteeship Council,"[249] in the 1950s, petitioners, especially from Togoland and Cameroon, increasingly addressed the General Assembly directly through oral hearings convened by its Fourth Committee. Although the requests of just a very few petitions were granted, petitions at least forced generally the Administering Authorities to clearly state their position in such cases. Meridith Terretta has written extensively about the petition campaign of the Duala and *Union des Peuples Camerounais* (UPC) from the trusteeship territory of Cameroon.[250] Terretta takes issue with Roland Burke's analysis of the petition system of the UN Third Committee on Human Rights for completely ignoring the impact of the petition system on the previously established Trusteeship System,[251] only to inadequately contextualize herself the qualitative content analysis of the Cameroonian petitions in terms of their impact. Like others, she confidently highlights the overwhelming number of 45,000 Cameroonian petitions in 1956 alone, while failing to emphasize that quantity was only as high because the counting method and statistical recording of the Trusteeship Council's Standing Commission on Petition changed in that same year. Had the procedure changed a few years earlier, the

---

245 Michael Dennis Callahan, *A sacred trust: The League of Nations and Africa, 1929–1946* (Brighton: Sussex Academic Press, 2004), pp. 48–52.

246 Momirov, "The Individual Right to Petition in Internationalized Territories"; Susan Pedersen, *The guardians: The League of Nations and the crisis of empire* (New York, NY: Oxford University Press, 2015), pp. 77–95.

247 Jane K. Cowan, "Who's Afraid of Violent Language?," *Anthropological Theory* 3, no. 3 (2003), https://doi.org/10.1177/14634996030033002.

248 Pedersen, *The guardians*, p. 93.

249 GAOR, "6th Session: 4th Committee" (1951), p. 180.

250 Meredith Terretta, "'We Had Been Fooled into Thinking That the UN Watches over the Entire World'," *Human Rights Quarterly* 34, no. 2 (2012), https://doi.org/10.1353/hrq.2012.0022 ; Meredith Terretta, *Nation of outlaws, state of violence: Nationalism, Grassfields tradition, and state building in Cameroon*, New African histories (Athens, Ohio: Ohio University Press, 2014); Meredith Terretta, *Petitioning for our rights, fighting for our nation: The history of the Democratic Union of Cameroonian Women, 1949–1960* (Bamenda, Cameroon: Langaa Research & Publishing, 2013), URL http://afrika.proxy.fid-lizenzen.de/fid/abc-ebooks/publikationen.ub.uni-frankfurt.de/frontdoor/index/index/docId/60341

251 Terretta, "'We Had Been Fooled into Thinking that the UN Watches over the Entire World'," p. 331.

200,000 Togolese petitions to the 1952 Visiting Mission would have would have overshadowed the petition campaign of any other trusteeship territory. Thus, while Terretta deals qualitatively with the mobilized discourses and demands in the petitions, she sidesteps how they were actually examined, that is, they were barely read. Ullrich Lohrmann's study of the trusteeship territory of Tanganyika, on the other hand, addresses this aspect of the petition system,[252] but relies mainly on Shirley B. Smith's excellent 1957 master's thesis on the trusteeship petition system (with some passages incredibly close to Smith's work) without citing her however.[253]

Yet, as numerous trusteeship territories were released into independence in the 1960, the debate on the Trusteeship System's petition scheme, including the right to petition, moved increasingly into the background. In the early 1960s, an increasing number of independent African and Asian UN member states sought to bypass the Trusteeship Council and its restrictive *rules of procedure*, to extend the right to petition to all colonial territories, giving rise to petitioning schemes in the UN's *Special Committee on Decolonization*[254] and the *Commission on Human Rights*.[255] However, as Roland Burke shows, these had no Charter status and their advocates were careful to establish procedures that could be directed against colonial powers, yet, which ran negligible risk of being used against themselves.[256]

In 1994, the Charter provision for petitioning practically ceased to exist when the UN Trusteeship Council suspended its operations. Cesare Scartozzi holds that today's oral hearings before the Fourth Committee of the General Assembly are merely an uncodified, customary, and inefficient practice, open only to the 17 remaining Non-Self-Governing Territories (NSGTs).[257] Contemporary UN peace- and state-building missions operate under Security Council resolutions, which do not provide petitioning or other comparable mechanisms that would reduce their long-criticized accountability deficit[258] – a state of affairs which Chopra likens to be "comparable with that of a pre-constitutional monarch in a sovereign kingdom."[259] In sum, the perpetuated colonial legacy has undermined the *right to petition* of peoples under international rule.

---

252 Ullrich Lohrmann, *Voices from Tanganyika: Great Britain, the United Nations and the decolonization of a Trust Territory, 1946–1961*, Europa-Übersee 16 (Berlin, London: Lit; Global, 2008), pp. 27–37.
253 Shirley B. Smith, "The formation and functioning of the Trusteeship Council procedure for examining petitions" (Master's Thesis, Boston University, 1957), accessed 03 February 2020, available from hdl.handle.net/2144/22520.
254 By General Assembly Resolution 1514 (XV), 1962, the Special Committee on Decolonization (or C-24) was to supervise the implementation of the Declaration on the Granting of Independence to Colonial Countries and Peoples.
255 Marc Limon, *Reform of the UN Human Rights Petitions System: An assessment of the UN human rights communications procedures and proposals for a single integrated system* (2018).
256 Roland Burke, *Decolonization and the evolution of international human rights*, Pennsylvania studies in human rights (Philadelphia: University of Pennsylvania Press, 2010).
257 Cesare M. Scartozzi, "Decolonizing One Petition at the Time," *Politikon: IAPSS Journal of Political Science* 34 (2017), https://doi.org/10.22151/politikon.34.4.
258 Momirov, "The Individual Right to Petition in Internationalized Territories"
259 Chopra, "The UN's Kingdom of East Timor," p. 29.

2.2.2 The United Nations Trusteeship System & Security

Following the atrocities of World War II, the maintenance of world peace and global security was the main impetus for the creation of the United Nations. The Trusteeship System, like the Mandates System before it, was a by-product of the preceding World War. Just as the League of Nations did before, the UN consequently integrated an institutional framework reflecting the existing balance of power, peacekeeping, and administrative organisation.

Colonialism & the Advent of the United Nations

Analysing the main debates at *United Nations Conference on International Organization* (UNCIO) outlined in the Dumbarton Oaks and Yalta proposals, Sylvanna Falcón follows African-American leaders who linked struggles against colonialism and racism, concluding that the UN was being created as a racializing and gender-specific institution, whilst its most prominent organ, the Security Council, is essentially undemocratic.[260] Although the UNCIO failed to bring all colonial territories under the umbrella of international trusteeship, the very threat of expanding international oversight shaped the relationship between colonial governments and international organizations.

The volume edited by Nicole Eggers, Jessica Lynne Pearson, and Aurora Almada e Santos examines how on the one hand, the United Nations was conceived as a tool to advance colonial interests, while, on the other hand, emphasizing its influence in facilitating the self-determination of dependent territories. Significantly, the volume explores the effect of the eleven territories within the Trusteeship System on the much larger list of 72 Non-Self-Governing Territories (NSGTs).[261] Pearson argues that while *de jure* the UN Special Committee on NSGTs was not a monitoring system for dependent territories, it has become one *de facto*, which is why colonial powers banded together to defend colonialism at the United Nations, arguing that subject populations living in independent territories often endured worse conditions than those living in formal overseas empires.[262]

The 'Colonial Question' & Global Security

Comprehensive studies on the UN Trusteeship System all locate security at the heart of the trusteeship principle.[263] The Trusteeship Council, alongside the General Assembly and the Security Council, was one of the six main organs of the UN. Whilst the Security Council was the central response to global insecurity, the Trusteeship Council at this time

---

260 Sylvanna M. Falcón, *Power interrupted: Antiracist and feminist activism inside the United Nations*, Decolonizing feminisms (Seattle: University of Washington Press, 2016), p. 33.
261 Nicole Eggers, Jessica L. Pearson and Aurora Almada e Santos, eds., *The United Nations and decolonization*, Routledge studies in modern history 69 (Abingdon, Oxon, New York, NY: Routledge, 2020).
262 Jessica L. Pearson, "Defending Empire at the United Nations," *The Journal of Imperial and Commonwealth History* 45, no. 3 (2017), https://doi.org/10.1080/03086534.2017.1332133.
263 H. D. Hall, "The British Commonwealth and Trusteeship," *International Affairs* 22, no. 2 (1946); Hall, *Mandates, Dependencies and Trusteeship*; Chowdhuri, *International Mandates and Trusteeship Systems*; Thullen, *Problems of the Trusteeship System*.

stood like no other UN organ for the question of decolonisation – a major ideational, material, and geopolitical transformation for years to come.

Duncan Hall, who due to his study's early nature could only compare the ending Mandates System with the beginning of the Trusteeship System, discussed the centrality of security and the 'sacred trust,' concluding "The dilemma of the Dominions at Paris was thus that of the United States at San Francisco: either make certain now of your strategic frontier or risk it becoming in other hands a threat to national security."[264] Security consideration are one of the aspects why Hall argues from a realist perspective that historians have exaggerated the extent to which humanitarianism and liberal idealism account for the establishment of mandates and trusteeship territories. He argues that they are "largely byproducts of the working of the state system of the world, of the political relations of the powers, and thus factors in the balance of power."[265] A similar argument is made by Susan Pedersen's study on the Permanent Mandate Commission. Her core argument is: "The League helped make the end of empire imaginable, and normative statehood possible, not because the empires willed it so, or the Covenant prescribed it, but because that dynamic of internationalization changed everything."[266] Mazower concluded that the League's Mandates System, as well as the United Nations Trusteeship System after it, was rather designed to defuse imperial rivalries and therefore "started out life not as the instrument to end colonialism, but rather [...] as the means to preserve it."[267] According to Gustavo Esteva, the post-World War II paradigm of "underdevelopment" began with American President Harry Truman's inaugural address in 1949, which revealed the apparent discovery of large-scale poverty in the "underdeveloped regions" of the world. Truman's inaugural address set out a vision for the post-war global order in a four-point agenda: first, the support and expansion of the UN; second, the continuation of the reconstruction of Europe; third, the establishment of NATO – Truman's fourth point, dealing with the rest of the world, was particularly illustrative:

> "we must embark on a bold new program for making the benefits of our scientific advances and industrial progress available for the improvement and growth of *underdeveloped areas*. [...] This should be a cooperative enterprise in which all nations work together through the United Nations and its specialized agencies whenever practicable. It must be a worldwide effort for the achievement of peace, plenty, and freedom. [...] The old imperialism – exploitation for foreign profit – has no place in our plans. [...] Slowly but surely we are weaving a world fabric of international security and growing prosperity."[268]

Post-development scholars, such as Esteva or Aram Ziai, assert that Truman's speech marked the "invention of the concept of underdevelopment," whereupon virtually

---

264 Hall, *Mandates, Dependencies and Trusteeship*, p. 122.
265 Hall, *Mandates, Dependencies and Trusteeship*, p. 8.
266 Pedersen, *The guardians*, p. 406.
267 Mark Mazower, *No Enchanted Palace: The End of Empire and the Ideological Origins of the United Nations*, Lawrence Stone lectures (Princeton: Princeton University Press, 2009), p. 31.
268 Harry Trumann, "Inaugural Address," available from https://www.presidency.ucsb.edu/documents/inaugural-address-4.

overnight "two billion people became underdeveloped."[269] Truman's reference to "old imperialism," acknowledged that the apparent underdevelopment was not self-inflicted but a result of colonialism. But Truman did not use underdevelopment solely to call upon the West's altruism: the problem of underdevelopment was linked to a promise of *security* for the American nation and the international community. This promise was made in the context of a growing expansion of Soviet influence. Mark Mazower also hinted at a link between these larger trustee-like missions and notions of security: "The idea that America had a special mission to transform societies across the world was an integral part of this new conception of its role. In the great ideological confrontation with Soviet communism, the Truman administration believed it had to demonstrate that capitalism had the better tools for improving the lives of the world's poor and underprivileged."[270] Post-development scholars widely overlook this discursive security-relation, and in fact, the even critical state-building contributions, such as by Mark Duffield, in turn often present the *security-development nexus* as "new" development.[271] However, the development-security-nexus preceded the state-building debate as early as 1945, that is, at the very beginning of the concomitant decolonisation and Cold War era.

Black American scholars, such as Rayford Logan, who was the former mentor of the Trusteeship Division's Director-General, Ralph Bunche, found the submissiveness to the administering powers' security interests particularly worrying.[272] Chowdhuri takes a somewhat milder stance, concluding simply that "considerations of national security in this atomic age also demand the retention of dependent territories."[273] Thullen devotes considerable space to the discussion of American security arrangements in the emerging Trusteeship System, arguing that these American security considerations diluted the Trusteeship System and failed to provide a robust institutional framework for anti-colonialism.[274]

> "Within relatively few years *anti-colonialism nearly eclipsed security issues as the center of United Nations attention*, a development with considerable repercussions on the trusteeship system. The system was designed to deal with an aspect of the colonial question; yet, its form and purpose were determined during the earlier, *security-obsessed period*. These changes in the international environment make it clear that a study of the trusteeship system merely in terms of its established goals would evade the central thread determining its nature and development."[275]

---

269 Gustavo Esteva, Salvatore J. Babones and Philipp Babcicky, *Future of development: A radical manifesto* (Britsol: Policy Press, 2013), p. 7; Aram Ziai, *Development Discourse and Global History: From colonialism to the sustainable development goals* (Hoboken: Taylor and Francis, 2015).
270 Mazower, *Governing the world*, p. 273.
271 Duffield, *Global governance and the new wars*.
272 Rayford Logan, "The System of International Trusteeship," *The Journal of Negro Education* 15, no. 3 (1946)
273 Chowdhuri, *International Mandates and Trusteeship Systems*, p. 303.
274 Thullen, *Problems of the Trusteeship System*, pp. 23–55.
275 Thullen, *Problems of the Trusteeship System*, p. 13.

Thullen remarks that while the League's Mandates System was designed to mitigate imperial rivalries, ensuring peace through idealistic and passive peacekeeping provisions, such as disarmament and non-militarisation, the Trusteeship System was imbued with emergent Cold War real-political considerations and active peacekeeping provisions, such as the authorisation of military bases and the introduction of strategic trusteeship territories. To put it differently, the ideological conflict dynamics of the Cold War equally found their expression in the UN Trusteeship System.

The 'Colonial Question' & the Cold War

Considering the broader context of the Cold War, Gordon Morell holds that the Trusteeship Council was criticised not least as a formal bulwark against Soviet influence in the former colonial territories.[276] John Hobson holds that the characterisation of the 1947–1989 era as that of the *Cold* War diverts attention from the struggle for decolonisation in the Global South.[277] In fact, for some states in the Global South the '*Cold* War' was not so cold after all, which for Hobson establishes "the racist decision by the superpowers to outsource war to the 'inferior' and expendable 'wastelands' of the Global South."[278] Similarly, Trevor Getz establishes that in the period from 1945 to 1975, for many movements, the Cold War and decolonisation (due to their simultaneity and interconnectedness) were one experience rather than two.[279]

The Soviet Union boycotted the Trusteeship Council in its founding phase, accusing it of being an imperial institution. State representatives of the Soviet bloc hardly missed an opportunity to denounce the exploitation endemic to Western colonialism, inadequate health provisions, lack of access to education and other social services in the trusteeship areas, and most critically, vehemently opposed the distinction made between trusteeship territories and NSGTs. Being forced at San Francisco to accept a limited Trusteeship System rather than having none at all, the Soviets endeavoured to revise the rules underlying the Trusteeship System, extending them to NSGTs.[280] Thus, alongside the Bandung states, the Soviet Union also took the lead in introducing what became the *Declaration on the Granting of Independence to Colonial Countries and Peoples*.[281]

---

276 W. G. Morrell, "A Higher Stage of Imperialism? The Big Three, the UN Trusteeship Council, and the Early Cold War," in *Imperialism on trial: International oversight of colonial rule in historical perspective*, ed. R. M. Douglas, Michael D. Callahan and Elizabeth Bishop (Lanham, Md.: Lexington Books, 2006), p. 112.

277 John M. Hobson, "Un-Veiling the Racist Foundations of Modern Realist and Liberal IR Theory," in *Globalizing International Theory: The Problem with Western IR Theory and How to Overcome It*, ed. A. Layug and John M. Hobson, Worlding Beyond the West Ser (Milton: Taylor & Francis Group, 2022), p. 58.

278 Hobson, "Unmasking the racism of orthodox international relations/international political economy theory," p. 13.

279 Trevor R. Getz, "Connecting Decolonization and the Cold War," 820L Khan Academy, accessed 27 December 2023, available from https://www.oerproject.com/-/media/WHP-1200/PDF/Unit8/WHP-1200-8-1-9-Read---Connecting-Decolonization-and-the-Cold-War---820L.ashx.

280 Morrell, "A Higher Stage of Imperialism? The Big Three, the UN Trusteeship Council, and the Early Cold War," p. 118.

281 General Assembly Resolution 1514, *Declaration on the Granting of Independence to Colonial Countries and Peoples*, A/RES/1514(XV) (14 December 1960).

On the other side, by responding with counterattacks on human rights abuse and economic exploitation in the Soviet Union and its quasi-colonial satellite states, colonial powers joined the US in a campaign to invalidate Soviet efforts to gain legitimacy as leaders of the anti-colonial cause. In the trusteeship territories themselves, the Administering Authorities feared the fusion of nationalism and communism into an ideologically stronger anti-imperialism.[282] Communist activity was feared not only where there was an organised communist party or obvious overseas contacts, but especially within nationalist independence movements. In retrospect, what colonial powers constructed as a 'red menace' emanating from nationalist movements, in many cases turned out to be more the desire for independence from colonial rule than an affiliation with the Soviet camp. An issue which can be traced in the emergence of the non-aligned movement at the Bandung conference by which newly independent states sought to create a neutral ground and alliance structure outside of US-Soviet tensions.[283] Indeed both anticolonialism as well as anti-communism, can be traced in Trusteeship Council deliberations.

Anti-colonial movements sought assistance either from the United States, proclaiming democracy and the economic prospects of free markets, or the Soviet Union, promising to break capitalist and imperial rule (or both).[284] As the US was allied with the major imperial powers, many decolonisation movements sought the support of the Soviet Union, while more conservative independence leaders sought the support of the United States by promising to stop the spread of communism in their region. While the influence of the Soviet Union in the NSGTs would initially be a matter of bilateral relations, the trusteeship status protected against direct unilateral influence by the Soviet Union.

Yet, while both superpowers declared themselves as anti-imperial in the debates of the Fourth Committee and the Trusteeship Council, they expanded their global dominance in an imperial fashion: the Soviet Union treated its satellite states almost like colonies and the United States replaced undesirable leaders in its 'backyard.' In fact, anti-colonial as well as colonial delegates argued with the *saltwater thesis* that the system set out in the UN Charter had failed to hold contiguous land empires, such as those of the USA or the USSR, to the same standards of accountability as colonial empires made up of overseas territories. In trying to be 'non-aligned,' the Afro-Asian bloc refused to be drawn into the logic of the Cold War and insisted on separating decolonisation from the East-West confrontation. At times, the colonial powers often found the criticism of the Afro-Asian bloc more dangerous than that of the Soviets. Yet, confronted with either Soviet or American interference in their struggle for independence, many decolonisation movements were forced to enlist the help of the other power and thus inevitably got caught up in the maelstrom of the Cold War. Thus, amid the geopolitical context of the Cold War, Western powers limited themselves merely to regime change when they perceived the threat that the foreign policy of a particular post-colonial state overly aligned with that

---

282 Crawford Young, *The African Colonial State in Comparative Perspective* (New Haven, CT: Yale University Press, 1994). https://doi.org/10.12987/9780300164473, https://www.degruyter.com/isbn/9780300164473, p. 32.
283 Morrell, "A Higher Stage of Imperialism? The Big Three, the UN Trusteeship Council, and the Early Cold War," p. 130.
284 Getz, "Connecting Decolonization and the Cold War."

of the Eastern bloc.[285] The coexistence of modernisation theory and realism, postulated that as long as the states did not pose a threat to each other in the international system of states, internal affairs simply remained internal affairs.

Decolonisation & Nation-State-Building

Latham argues that American foreign policy during the Kennedy administration was significantly shaped by modernisation theory in order to contain communism in the developing world and recast older Marxist and imperialist ideologies of "nation building."[286] The colonial powers were primarily concerned with nation-building, to unite the linguistically, culturally and ethnically diverse populations of their colonies by creating higher national-territorial loyalties in order to link them in turn with the metropolitan regions created in confederations such as the British Commonwealth of Nations or the French Union. Yet, although the nation-state was a European export, which has been situated within the Enlightenment era,[287] it was feared as a vehicle for decolonisation because national consciousness and sovereignty could not be reconciled with colonial foreign domination.[288]

Mark Berger emphasis that the policies such as those of the two major colonial powers, France and Britain, which were reluctant to release their colonial territories into independence, was less one of "state-building" than of "nation-building."[289] Their goal was to integrate the ethnic, cultural, linguistical fragmentation of their colonial possessions into superordinate territorial loyalties. Before World War II, colonial powers were engaged in nation-building in colonies that were heterogeneous in terms of population. It was only with the end of World War II that there was a gradual shift from nation-building to state-building. While the strategy of nation-building in the decolonisation period still counted on the development of shared notions of political order and a collective sense of belonging, contemporary understandings of state-building are increasingly technocratic, as they focus on building legitimate state institutions such as bureaucracy and security structures to enable positive development of the economy, society, and political life. Though there is an obvious shift, Lemay-Hébert contends that it is impossible to conceive of state-building as a process separate from nation-building.[290]

Thus, overall, the principle of state sovereignty and non-interference established by the United Nations was used by the old powers and was upheld accordingly. The rationale

---

285 Examples include Cuba, North Korea, Congo, and the Vietnam War. Wesley, "The state of the art on the art of state building," p. 370.
286 Michael E. Latham, *Modernization as ideology: American social science and "nation building" in the Kennedy era*, 2nd impr, The new Cold War history (Chapel Hill: University of North Carolina Press, 2006).
287 Benedict Anderson, *Imagined Communities: Reflections on the Origin and Spread of Nationalism* (London, New York: Verso, [1983] 2006), http://hdl.handle.net/2027/heb.01609.0001.001
288 John D. Kelly and Martha Kaplan, "Nation and Decolonization," *Anthropological Theory* 1, no. 4 (2001), https://doi.org/10.1177/14634990122228818.
289 See Mark T. Berger, *From Nation-Building to State-Building*, Third Worlds (Hoboken: Taylor and Francis, 2013).
290 Nicolas Lemay-Hébert, "Statebuilding Without Nation-Building?," *Journal of Intervention and Statebuilding* 3, no. 1 (2009), https://doi.org/10.1080/17502970802608159.

and antecedent for UN peacekeeping interventions remained limited: UN Secretary-General Dag Hammarskjöld introduced the framework for "preventative diplomacy" in the 1950s, as a procedure for future UN mission aimed at preventing potential disputes between the parties.[291] Notable examples were the United Nations Operation in the Congo (ONUC, 1960–1964) and the United Nations Security Force in West New Guinea (UNSF, 1962–1963).

One exception to this paradigm was France, which continued to intervene unrestrained in its former colonies, especially in West Africa. Tony Chafer establishes that the decolonisation of French West Africa was by no means trouble-free, and due to France's colonial policy of *assimilation*, was rather treated as a 'development internal to the French Union,' which prevented actual decolonisation. One indication is that since 1960, France has conducted over fifty military interventions in its former African colonies.[292] It is noteworthy, that France's military presence in Africa was based on the weak-states argument,[293] some 20 years prior to its surge in the 1990s and popularised in France by Jean-François Bayart's *politics of the belly*.[294] Lelouche und Moisi, for example, cite a 1976 speech by French President Valéry Giscard d'Estaing (1974–1981), in which he considered that France's security is inextricably linked to North-South relations: "Our world is an over-armed world in a case of an East-West conflict and a world which is looking for a North-South balance. On the other hand, it is a very unstable world regionally for a series of reasons ranging from ideology to under-development, which explains that everywhere we witness a general destabilization of security."[295] According to Nathaniel Powell, three motives guided French interventionism: the safeguarding of economic interests, the containment of a (miscalculated) threat of communist and rebel groups, and the spread of Anglo-Saxon imperialism.

In 1998, François-Xavier Verschave described this exceptional relationship of France to its former colonies under the contraction *Françafrique* to criticise the alleged corrupt and clandestine activities of various Franco-African political, economic, and military networks.[296] In the same work, Verschave propagated the already standing thesis that France was behind the assassination of the first head of state in postcolonial Africa: Togo's president, Sylvanus Olympio. According to Verschave, as Olympio wanted to lead Togo out of the franc zone and make his country independent of the former tutelary power, the General-Secretary for African and Malagasy Affairs, Jacques Foccart,

---

291 Luc Reychler, "Peacemaking, Peacekeeping, and Peacebuilding," *Oxford Research Encyclopedia of International Studies*, 2017, p. 6, accessed 12 October 2021, https://doi.org/10.1093/acrefore/9780190 846626.013.274, available from https://oxfordre.com/internationalstudies/view/10.1093/acrefore /9780190846626.001.0001/acrefore-9780190846626-e-274.

292 Commission des Affaires Étrangères, "Engagement et diplomatie: quelle doctrine pour nos interventions militaires?," Rapport d'Information 2777 (Assemblée Nationale, 2015), available from https://www.assemblee-nationale.fr/14/rap-info/i2777.asp#P830_305195, pp. 115–33.

293 Nathaniel K. Powell, "Battling Instability?," *African Security* 10, no. 1 (2017): 52–54, https://doi.org/10.1080/19392206.2016.1270141.

294 Bayart, *L'État en Afrique*.

295 As cited in Pierre Lellouche and Dominique Moisi, "French Policy in Africa," *International Security* 3, no. 4 (1979): 121, https://doi.org/10.2307/2626765.

296 François-Xavier Verschave, *La Françafrique: le plus long scandale de la République* (Paris: Stock, 1998).

purportedly turned on him, commissioning the French Commander of the Togolese Gendarmerie, Georges Maîtrier, to initiate the plot. After the meeting that prepared the coup, Maîtrier is said to have taken Eyadéma aside and asked him to shoot Olympio for 300,000 CFA francs (6,000 French francs).[297] After learning from Ambassador Henri Mazoyer on the night of the 12–13 January 1963 that Olympio was hiding in the courtyard of the US Embassy, Maîtrier reportedly informed the coup plotters and encouraged them "to complete the work that has already begun."[298]

2.3 Togoland

In contrast to many other decolonisation processes, the independence of Togoland was granted under UN trusteeship. Although not as violent as the case of the trust territory of Cameroon, for example, the case of Togoland attracted enormous international attention. There are many detailed scholarly perspectives on the colonial history of French or British Togoland. The main strands of literature that have been included concern the rise and fall of (colonial) statehood and nationalism, particularly around the demand of Ewe and Togoland unification as well as contributions on colonial policing and security.

2.3.1 State- & Nationhood

German Togoland

Compared to other territories formerly under German colonial rule, literature on the German colonisation of Togoland is not very extensive and although Germany's colonisation of Togoland preceded the French and British mandate era, the literature on this period is less extensive than on the mandate period.

A handful of monographs are devoted to the study of the colonial state and administration in German Togoland, yet, in which Togolese themselves hardly make an appearance.[299] Literature that examines, with varying degrees of historical emphasis, the web of colonial relations between the German administration, its colonial crimes, indigenous resistance, and its aftermath is of rather recent nature.[300]

---

297 Verschave, *La Françafrique*, 117–119.
298 Verschave, *La Françafrique*, p. 114.
299 Arthur J. Knoll, *Togo under Imperial Germany 1884–1914: a case study in colonial rule*, Hoover colonial studies 190 (Stanford: Hoover Inst. Press, 1978); Ralph Erbar, *Ein" Platz an der Sonne"? Die Verwaltungs- und Wirtschaftsgeschichte der deutschen Kolonie Togo 1884–1914*, Beiträge zur Kolonial- und Überseegeschichte 51 (Stuttgart: Steiner, 1991); Trutz von Trotha, *Koloniale Herrschaft: Zur soziologischen Theorie der Staatsentstehung am Beispiel des "Schutzgebietes Togo"* (Tübingen: Mohr, 1994); Dennis Laumann, "A Historiography of German Togoland, or the Rise and Fall of a "Model Colony"," *History in Africa* 30 (2003); Bettina Zurstrassen, *"Ein Stück deutscher Erde schaffen": Koloniale Beamte in Togo 1884–1914*, Campus Forschung 931 (Frankfurt/Main, New York: Campus, 2008).
300 Peter Sebald, *Die deutsche Kolonie Togo 1884–1914: Auswirkungen einer Fremdherrschaft*, Schlaglichter der Kolonialgeschichte 14 (Berlin: Links, 2013); Rebekka Habermas, *Skandal in Togo: Ein Kapitel deutscher Kolonialherrschaft* (Frankfurt/Main: S. Fischer, 2016); Trotha, *Koloniale Herrschaft*.

Although Sebald's chronicle is rather descriptive, it ranks with some authority in the literature on German Togoland. Sebald highlights that in the mere three decades of German rule over the narrow territory, the German colonisers made use of all the typical means of European colonial rule.[301] By restoring large parts of the archival holdings left behind by the German colonial administration in Togo, Sebald thus compiled source material as a basis for subsequent historical works, debunking the myth of a self-sustaining "model colony" that never applied to the perspective of the colony's inhabitants anyway.[302] Among German historian, he was one of the first to turn to anti-colonial resistance in Togoland, identifying petitioning as a central form of resistance.[303]

Departing from rather historical-descriptive contribution, Trotha draws on Heinrich Popitz' sociological aspects of rule to develop a general sociological theory of state-formation in Africa based on the German colonisation of Togoland. According to him state-formation took place in three steps: in a first step, the (German) colonizers concealed their numerical inferiority through a policy of selective terror to achieve maximum intimidation with minimum use of resources.[304] Although still in possession of the despotic instrument of violent oppression, in a second step, colonial rule was transformed into bureaucratic rule. In addition to the already existing monopoly of violence, in a third step the colonial state gained a monopoly on knowledge: educational institutions, literacy and statistics were introduced, and the capabilities of the colonial headquarters were strengthened by technical inventions such as the telegraph. Eckert assesses that Trotha accounted well for the ambiguity of the bureaucratic colonial state, yet, due to the lack of a comparative perspective Trotha erroneously assumes that state formation in Africa was only initiated by European colonisation. In doing so, he hastily adopts the *failed states* motif of the 1990s, which invokes the "incompleteness" of colonial state-building as the reason for the preponderance of military regimes in the post-colonial period.[305]

Habermas' study is a microhistory of a colonial scandal that was caused by the abuse of an African minor through which she traces the broad lines of the colonial imagination, such as colonial gender relations, the violent economic exploitation on the cotton plantations, the relationship between the German colonial administration, German missionary schools and metropolitan Germany. Though Togolese under German rule regularly petitioned the governor or the Reichstag to draw attention to abuses of power, Habermas characterizes their reception as "eloquent silence," because the treatment these petitions received mobilized stereotypical rather than realistic images of Africa and Europe and thereby concealed more than it brought to the fore.[306]

---

301 Sebald, *Die deutsche Kolonie Togo 1884–1914*.
302 Laumann, "A historiography of German Togoland, or the rise and fall of a "model colony"".
303 Sebald, *Die deutsche Kolonie Togo 1884–1914*, p. 170.
304 Trotha, *Koloniale Herrschaft*, p. 37.
305 Andreas Eckert, "Theories of Colonial Rule," *The Journal of African History* 38, no. 2 (1997): 17, https://doi.org/10.1017/S0021853797377019.
306 Habermas, *Skandal in Togo*, 17, 130–138.

Early Post-Independence Works

The political developments in the trusteeship territories and protracted discussion on the Ewe and Togoland unification at the United Nations inspired a whole series of writings on various aspects of the issue in the late 1950s and early 1960s. The earliest comprehensive works on the history of Togoland are by François Luchaire,[307] Robert Cornevin,[308] and Jean-Claude Pauvert.[309] Yet, since they speak only rudimentarily about the Ewe and Togoland reunification movement and foreground France's accomplishment, the works by Cornevin and Luchaire can be regarded as justifying French policy in Togo.[310] Similarly, Alan Burns, former governor of the Gold Coast and British Togoland who was later the British permanent representative on the Trusteeship Council, justified British policy in Togoland.[311] In fact, Charles Arden-Clarke, late governor of the Gold Coast and British Togoland argued:

> "It seemed to all of us out there that the natural destiny of Togoland under United Kingdom Trusteeship was to become an integral part of the Gold Coast [...] in the case of Togoland there seemed to be quite a lot of Gold Coast imperialism and imperialism was not necessarily a bad thing! I am glad to say that Gold Coast imperialism has won the day and that British Togoland is now an integral part of independent Ghana."[312]

The first widely cited scholarly contribution was James Coleman's *Togoland*, who chiefly accused the Ewe and Togoland unification movement essentially of running a smear campaign against the Administering Authorities and accused the UN General Assembly of tending toward irrationality on the unification question.[313] In fact, Coleman argued that by providing the unificationists with a platform, the United Nations effectively created the unification problem in the first place. While Dennis Austin holds that trusteeship powers had a more stabilizing effect on the dynamics on the Togo-Ghana border than postcolonial Togo and Ghana,[314] Franz Ansprenger's study of Togolese po-

---

307 As professor of French Public Law, François Luchaire was co-author of the *loi-cadre* and as such a co-architect for the plans to integrate postcolonial French Africa into the French Union. François Luchaire, *Du Togo français sous tutelle à la République autonome du Togo* (Paris: Librairie générale de droit et de jurisprudence, 1957).
308 Robert Cornevin, who was stationed as colonial administrator in French Togoland from 1948 to 1956, can certainly be considered an expert on the country and its history. Although he did not call Togo a "model colony," he also took up the rhetoric once invented by the Germans and praised France's achievement by celebrating Togo as a "nation-pilot" after its independence: Robert Cornevin, *Histoire du Togo* (Paris: Berger-Levrault, 1959); Robert Cornevin, *Le Togo: Nation-Pilote*, Collection Survol du monde (Paris: Nouvelles Éditions latines, 1963).
309 Jean-Claude Pauvert, "L'évolution Politique Des Ewés," *Cahiers d'études africaines*, no. 2 (1960)
310 See preface in Amenumey, *The Ewe Unification Movement*.
311 Alan Burns, *In defence of colonies: British colonial territories in international affairs* (London: Allen & Unwin, 1957).
312 Charles Arden-Clarke, "Gold Coast into Ghana," *International Affairs* 34, no. 1 (1958): 54
313 James S. Coleman, *Togoland*, International Conciliaton 509 (New York: Carnegie Endowment for International Peace, 1956), p. 60.
314 Dennis Austin, "The Uncertain Frontier," 1, no. 2 (1963), accessed 13 December 2019, available from https://www.jstor.org/stable/159025.

litical parties was the first of the European contributions to take a more critical stance, especially towards the French trusteeship administration.³¹⁵

The Ewe and Togoland unification question also formed the empirical case in the studies by Iwuoha Aligwekwe on the *Paradoxes and Problems of Political Transition in West Africa*,³¹⁶ and by George Thullen on *The Problems of the Trusteeship System*.³¹⁷ Yet, as Amenumey pointed out, both dissertations relied heavily on Coleman's tendentious sympathetic stance toward the colonial powers, and his inadequate knowledge of Ewe history. Thus, one of Aligwekwe's hypotheses, along with Coleman's Eurocentrism, is strikingly reminiscent of the recent securitisation of secessionists in Western Togoland:

> "The present [1960] political and demographic or ethnographic picture of Togoland and West Africa embody the danger of tribal or ethnic unification and irredentist movements which can pose threats to the peace and security of the whole region or at best leave it a mere potential area of crisis; and this has been made more so by the development of a trans-territorial nationalism in the region."³¹⁸

Thullen, on the other hand, who apart from Chowdhuri can be considered the only notable comprehensive study of the Trusteeship System. The inability to conduct fieldwork in the study area or access unofficial records led to Thullen's uncritical acceptance of Coleman's leniency toward the colonial powers. This is evidenced by assessments such as that anti-colonial state representatives at the UN "were prepared to sacrifice the further search of objectivity"³¹⁹ or that "[m]ost petitioners [were] *not understanding* the constitutional limitations on what the United Nations could do for them."³²⁰

The dissertation by Ghanaian Ewe historian D.E.K. Amenumey is probably the most comprehensive work on the political run-up to Togoland's independence. Amenumey's dissertation draws on Thullen's work,³²¹ especially regarding the discussions at the UN, but distances itself from the administration-lenient perspective which Thullen adopted from Coleman. Amenumey brings the anti-colonial actors back to the centre of historiography by situating the historical developments based on the activities of the unification movement in the territory itself, thereby filling in the previous gaps in the historiography. Amenumey, however concedes that the very core period of his study falls into the "closed" period for which records were inaccessible at the time.³²²

---

315 Franz Ansprenger, *Politik im Schwarzen Afrika: Die modernen politischen Bewegungen im Afrika französischer Prägung* (Wiesbaden: Verlag für Sozialwissenschaften, 1961). https://doi.org/10.1007/978-3-322-98464-7
316 Iwuoha E. Aligwekwe, "The Ewe and Togoland problem: a case study in the paradoxes and problems of political transition in West Africa" (Dissertation, Ohio State University, 1960), accessed 07 June 2021, available from http://rave.ohiolink.edu/etdc/view?acc_num=osu1486478713870084.
317 Thullen, *Problems of the Trusteeship System*.
318 Aligwekwe, "The Ewe and Togoland problem," p. 33.
319 Thullen, *Problems of the Trusteeship System*, p. 180.
320 Emphasis added, Thullen, *Problems of the Trusteeship System*, p. 77.
321 Compare Amenumey, *The Ewe Unification Movement*, p. 210; Thullen, *Problems of the Trusteeship System*, p. 145.
322 Amenumey, *The Ewe Unification Movement*, preface.

Constructed Nationalisms: Togoland & Ewe Nationalism

Claude Welch's dissertation on Pan-Africanism and political unification in West Africa, later published as *Dream of Unity*,[323] included a study of the unsuccessful Ewe unification movement. Welch's study is a central reference point to a series of studies on Ewe and Togoland nationalism that would appear from the 1980s onwards. Drawing on Welch, Hodder tried to pin "Eweness", estimating the population size of the Ewe and pointed out the tendency to exaggerate the homogeneity of so-called ethnic and tribal groups. In any case, Hodder argued, "the desire for unification among the Ewe – an idea of Eweland as a distinct and homogeneous unit – is in reality of European origin."[324]

In the absence of a politically unifying Ewe or Togolese identity in precolonial times, subsequent studies by and large adopted the constructivist thesis of *imagined communities*,[325] arguing that both Ewe ethnic-nationalism and Togoland territorial-nationalism are products of colonial inventions. David Brown wrote about the post-independence struggle of the Ewe and the *National Liberation Movement of Western Togoland* (better known as the "Togoland Liberation Movement" or TOLIMO) against the central government after Ghana's independence in 1957. Yet, Brown attested the demise of TOLIMO in the late 1970s,[326] particularly due to "the propagation by incumbent elites of an 'ethnic rivalry' view of politics and an 'ethnic plot' threat to stability" that operates along an "Ewe *versus* Akan" factionalism.[327]

Providing perhaps the most comprehensive account of the emergence and growth of the Ewe unification movement, D.E.K. Amenumey extended Thullen's analysis of the UN debates by additionally examining what was happening on the ground within the Ewe unification movement. Amenumey credited the development of the Ewe Presbyterian Church prompted by German Christian missionaries and the standardisation of the Ewe language as the birth point of Ewe nationalism.[328] Similarly, Sandra Greene argues that 'Eweness' stems from religious and mythical identifications.[329] While Amenumey mainly focuses his analyses on the political struggle of the Ewe unification movement and its suppression by the British and French authorities, John Kent concludes that it was not African nationalism but Anglo-French intergovernmental as well as international considerations that determined British and French policy towards the movement.[330] Although his archival work should not be discounted, Kent thus echoed a number of his contemporaries that decolonisation was bequeathed by the merciful hand of the benevolent West and not won by the nationalist movements against the resistance of the colonial powers.

---

323 Welch, *Dream of Unity*.
324 Bramwell W. Hodder, "The Ewe Problem," in *Essays in Political Geography*, ed. Charles A. Fisher (London: Methuen, 1968), p. 281.
325 Anderson, *Imagined Communities*.
326 David Brown, "Borderline Politics in Ghana," *The Journal of Modern African Studies* 18, no. 4 (1980)
327 David Brown, "Sieges and Scapegoats," *The Journal of Modern African Studies* 21, no. 3 (1983): 458
328 Amenumey, *The Ewe Unification Movement*, p. 28.
329 Sandra E. Greene, "Notsie Narratives," *South Atlantic Quarterly* 101, no. 4 (2002), https://doi.org/10.1215/00382876-101-4-1015.
330 John Kent, "The Ewe Question 1945–56," in *Imperialism, the State, and the Third World*, ed. Michael Twaddle (London: British Academic Press, 1992), p. 202.

At the same time, increasingly more French-language works were being written again, both in France and in Togo, to critically examine the period of Togoland under French trusteeship. Wen'saa Ogma Yagla emphasised the ethnic divisions of the short period of the post-independence Olympio government, and the perception of bias towards the Ewe-speakers of the south, thereby offering an implicit justification for the *coup d'état* that brought Gnassingbé Eyadéma to power in 1967 and ushered in Africa's longest single-party regime.[331] Marc Michel concluded that France certainly did not establish a *"nation pilote,"* as the ex-colonial officer Robert Cornevin tried to establish in the 1960s.[332] Addressing the question why Togoland remained peaceful while other French territories such as Côte d'Ivoire or the trusteeship territory of Cameroon experienced violence, Michel dismisses that this was due to less repression by the French authorities, mass mobilisation, or class conflict. Rather, it was the unification movement's early and sustained intervention at international venues that gave peaceful measures a chance.[333] Since the 1990s Togolese historians under the leadership of Nicoué Lodjoudie Gayibor have continuously published on the period in question in the series titled *Histoire des Togolais : des origines aux années 1960*, that comprises four volumes to this date. With the explicit aim of promoting the democratisation of Togo and overcoming the often politically manipulated regional differences between the ethnic groups of the north and the south.[334]

The debate on the origin of Ewe and Togoland nationalism was continued Paul Nugent, who recasts Amenumey's thesis of German missionaries as the cradle for Ewe and Togoland nationalism as it does not explain why individuals, that were educated in the same institutions and ethos, ended up mobilising behind opposing political projects (that is, on the one side, the integration of British Togoland into Ghana and the accommodation of French Togoland within the French Union versus the complete independence of a reunified Togoland, on the other side).[335] Somewhat novel within in African Studies, Nugent rather advances spatial theoretical approaches to explain the identarian dynamics in the border region of nowadays Togo and Ghana.[336] Nugent concurs that an overarching Ewe identity did not exist before colonial partition and

---

331 Wen'saa Ogma Yagla, *L'édification de la Nation Togolaise: Naissance d'une conscience nationale dans un pays africain* (Paris: Harmattan, 1978).

332 Cornevin, *Le Togo*.

333 Marc Michel, "The Independence of Togo," in *Decolonization and African Independence: The transfer of power, 1960–1980*, ed. Prosser Gifford (New Haven: Yale University Press, 1988)

334 Nicoué L. Gayibor, ed., *de l'histoire des origines à l'histoire des peuplements*, 4 vols., Histoire des Togolais. Des origines aux années 1960 1 (Paris, Lomé: Karthala; Presses de l'Université de Lomé, 2011); Nicoué L. Gayibor, ed., *du XVIe siècle à l'occupation colonaiale*, 4 vols., Histoire des Togolais. Des origines aux années 1960 2 (Paris, Lomé: Karthala; Presses de l'Université de Lomé, 2011); Nicoué L. Gayibor, ed., *Le Togo sous administration coloniale*, 4 vols., Histoire des Togolais. Des origines aux années 1960 3 (Paris, Lomé: Karthala; Presses de l'Université de Lomé, 2011); Nicoué L. Gayibor, ed., *Le refus de l'ordre colonial*, 4 vols., Histoire des Togolais. Des origines aux années 1960 4 (Paris, Lomé: Karthala; Presses de l'Université de Lomé, 2011).

335 Paul Nugent and Carola Lentz, eds., *Ethnicity in Ghana: The Limits of Invention* (London: Palgrave Macmillan, 2016).

336 Paul Nugent, *Smugglers, secessionists & loyal citizens on the Ghana-Togo frontier: The lie of the borderlands since 1914*, Western African studies (Athens: Ohio University Press, 2002); Paul Nugent,

developed only in response to European domination. However, different from Amenumey, Nugent does not assume the borders of colonial states were simply invented at the Berlin Conference of 1884/5, but that the Ewe, not the Europeans, gave meaning to the border. The boundaries of colonial entities were shaped by deeper spatial logics as colonial states were superimposed on pre-existing political formations. For Nugent, these borders were central to processes of state-formation. Although Nugent's theory of the emergence of (colonial) states is rooted in European political theory, he tries to avoid "conceptual Eurocentrism" by emphasising that during the colonial period, local problems, and the persistence of cross-border trade (especially smuggling) provided for, on the one hand, the impetus for the emergence of the Ewe question and, on the other, its inevitable end. Yet, because of these considerations, Nugent prematurely echoes Brown in that desires of Ewe unification and TOLIMO's Western Togoland secessionism are all but extinguished as a Volta Region identity amongst Ghanaian citizenship has emerged trump. Understandably, as before 2006 the Western Togoland separatists hardly managed to gain media attention.

Subsequently adopting a similar spatial perspective, Lawrance argues that the Ewe ethno-nationalist struggle was doomed from the outset because the Ewe never constituted a coherent, self-conscious ethnic group capable of pushing a political agenda.[337] Analysing the emergence of a "proto-nationalism" in the interwar period, Lawrance is particularly critical of the fact that the role of urban elites was overstated and the strategic place of the rural electorate (so-called *dokuwo*) was underestimated. Lawrance argues that historians are far too infatuated with the elites of the unificationist movement such as Sylvanus Olympio. It is just as important, if not more so, to look at the "local" population (those who make up the nation beyond the elites). Lawrance tries to capture the local population through the various Ewe Newspapers such as the *Ewe Newsletter*, the *Guide du Togo*, and the *Gold Coast Leader*. Uniting the urban and rural experiences of colonialism after World War I, Lawrance documents the contributions of rural people to anti-colonial struggles against what he calls 'periurban colonialism.'

Digre intended to refocus the debate on the unification movement towards the role of the UN-monitored referenda. On the one hand, he compares the 1956 UN-supervised referendum on the integration of British Togoland into the Gold Coast with the 1956 referendum in French Togoland on the admission of French Togoland into the French Union.[338] In doing so, he points out that (as is too often forgotten today) a consideration of the referendum in British Togoland without reference to the referendum in French Togoland would be incoherent, as their interactions were part of a concerted Anglo-French strategy. Furthermore, Digre elaborates the different imperial strategies of France and Britain on the issue of ethnic mobilisation in a comparison of the UN-supervision in the 1956

Boundaries, communities, and state-making in West Africa: The centrality of the margins, African Studies 144 (Cambridge, United Kingdom, New York: Cambridge University Press, 2019).
337 Benjamin Nicholas Lawrance, *Locality, Mobility, and "Nation": Periurban colonialism in Togo's Eweland, 1900–1960*, Rochester studies in African history and the diaspora (Rochester, NY: University of Rochester Press, 2007).
338 Brian K. Digre, "The United Nations, France, and African Independence," *French Colonial History* 5, no. 1 (2004), https://doi.org/10.1353/fch.2004.0003.

Togoland referendum with the 1961 referendum in Cameroon.[339] Digre again brings into focus the special role of UN observation, which he advocates despite its pitfalls because generally UN-led trusteeship led to peaceful outcomes.

Similarly, Ashley Bulgarelli juxtaposes the 1956 British-Togoland referendum with the 2018 New Regions Referendum, identifying the revival of three competing nationalisms in the Volta Region: ethnicity-based Ewe nationalism, territory-based Western Togoland nationalism and a forming Voltarian identity, the latter of which he advocates as the only inclusive identity.[340]

Like Nugent, Kate Skinner is wary of mission-centric narratives of Ewe nationalism yet relocates the history of its emergence within educationist institutions and literacy frameworks.[341] Moreover, while concurring with the insufficient nationalist mobilisation in the late colonial period, Skinner overall challenges the supposed end of the Ewe and Western Togoland movements with reference to the position of Kosi Kedem, a former parliamentarian of the Volta Region. As of 2022, Kedem advocates integrating 'Western Togoland' more closely into Ghana while preserving its distinct national identity.[342]

Alexander Keese interrogates the mobilisation of Ewe ethnic identity as an anti-colonial weapon between the late 19th century and the 1960s.[343] Unwittingly adapting the ideas of Leibnitz, Humboldt, and Tilly on the interplay of state formation and external as well as internal security,[344] Keese argues that in those pre-colonial societies that possessed functioning state structures, that is, where the population enjoyed some protection from external and internal attacks, ethnic mobilisation was normally *not* regarded as a necessary strategy. Ethnicity was mainly used as a basis for group solidarity and political claims where, as in the case of the pre-colonial Ewe territories, pre-colonial state structures were either weak or non-existent. According to Keese, in the colonial period the differences in the mobilisation of Ewe ethnicity, among others, are not so much the result of often inflated differences between British 'indirect' and French 'direct' traditions in colonial administration, but rather the result of local experiences of statehood: "if the structures of states and administrations provide a reasonably reliable set of rules, 'ethnicity' is not usually needed as a factor in group mobilisation."[345]

---

339   Brian K. Digre, "Ethnic Loyalties, National Choices, and International Oversight," in *The Histories, Languages, and Cultures of West Africa: Interdisciplinary Essays*, ed. Akua Sarr (Lewiston, NY: Edwin Mellen Press, 2006)
340   Ashley Bulgarelli, "Togoland's Lingering Legacy," *Australasian Review of African Studies* 39, no. 2 (2018), https://doi.org/10.22160/22035184/ARAS-2018-39-2/222-238.
341   Skinner, "Local Historians and Strangers with Big Eyes"; Skinner, *The Fruits of Freedom in British Togoland*.
342   GhanaWeb, "Ghana doesn't legally exist – Kosi Kedem"; Kosi Kedem, "Why There Is Urgent Need to Talk About the British Togoland Question," *Ghanaian Times*, 15 June 2022
343   Alexander Keese, *Ethnicity and the Colonial State*, Studies in global social history 22 (Boston: Brill, 2016). https://doi.org/10.1163/9789004307353
344   For a discussion on security in a historical perspective see Conze, *Geschichte der Sicherheit*, pp. 24–30.
345   Keese, *Ethnicity and the Colonial State*, 308, 311.

2.3.2 Security

Although most of the contributions on Togoland discussed so far deal with the repression and resistance against the colonial state, they only analyse the colonial security apparatus and its legacies to a limited extent. The decolonisation of British and French Togoland represents a special case of decolonisation since their path to statehood and independence was subject to international supervision. The significance of security for decolonisation contexts and postcolonial statebuilding processes has hardly been studied in a historical perspective. Only recently, Marco Wyss contributed to the importance of security for decolonisation contexts, by analysing the discrepancy between Britain and France's post-colonial security roles in Nigeria and Côte d'Ivoire.[346] Wyss argues that while France remains a major neo-colonial actor in Africa, Britain purportedly 'decolonised' its foreign policy vis-à-vis its previous colonies for the most part. Contrary to what CSS or scholars of postcolonial theory might expect from the title, Wyss' work is unfortunately not theory-driven but provides a purely historiographical appraisal of African post-independence security relations with the metropolis. Nonetheless, by bringing the role of two African leaders in shaping the security relationships in the Cold War era into the limelight, he highlights the African agency in the within the emergent global security architecture.

As for German Togoland, Trotha and Morlang provide ethnographic historical studies of the colonial law enforcement forces,[347] whilst Sebald and Habermas focus mainly on the resistance of African actors.[348] After the partition of German Togoland, British Togoland was administered from the Gold Coast. Therefore, the literature on colonial policing in British Togoland tends to focus on the Gold Coast rather than British Togoland separately.

British Togoland

It was not until the late 1980s and early 1990s that several works by British authors critically examined the origins of colonial policing on the Gold Coast.[349] Deflem takes a mostly comparative look at colonial policing in relations to the general characteristics of British colonialism.[350] Baynham analyses the security forces in the period of the transfer of sovereignty and refers to the colonial continuities after Ghana's independence (including British Togoland), pointing to the vital role of security forces in identity and nation-building, for example, by performing the state through marches at independence celebrations. He argues that the departure of the British officers, forced Nkrumah to adopt the British format of control by organizationally neutralizing threats within the

---

346 Marco Wyss, *Postcolonial security: Britain, France, and West Africa's Cold War*, First edition (Oxford, New York, NY: Oxford University Press, 2021).
347 Trotha, *Koloniale Herrschaft*; Thomas Morlang, *Askari und Fitafita: "Farbige" Söldner in den deutschen Kolonien* (Berlin: Ch. Links, 2008).
348 Habermas, *Skandal in Togo*; Sebald, *Die deutsche Kolonie Togo 1884–1914*.
349 Joël Glasman, *Les corps habillés au Togo: Genèse coloniale des métiers de police* (Paris: Karthala, 2015), p. 30.
350 Mathieu Deflem, "Law Enforcement in British Colonial Africa," *Police Studies* 17, no. 1 (1994)

security forces.[351] Similarly, Brogden argued that British police work in particular and colonial policework in general perhaps was pre-eminently missionary work to legitimize foreign rule.[352] Killingray, on the other hand, argues that ex-service men, in fact, had little to no economic or political influence on the nationalist mobilisation of the Gold Coast.[353] Richard Rathbone argued that there was nothing natural about the fact that the British administration kept a tight grip on the Gold Coast security sector until the last moment.[354]

However, in the absence of archival material, little has been published on the Gold Coast security and intelligence apparatus since the 1980s. This changed after the British government lifted its embargo on colonial security papers in 2011 and the publication of Calder Walton's *Empire of Secrets*.[355] Chase Arnold's analysis of the early post-war activities of the Special Branch builds on Walton's work.[356] Walton and Arnold provide a detailed look at the workings of the MI5 in the Gold Coast and highlight the differences of opinion between London, the governor, and the intelligence officers. Yet, unfortunately, both focus on the spying on the likes of Kwame Nkrumah – a pattern that historians are still too infatuated with the great figures of history, while little attention is given on the day-by-day spying on grass-roots activists.

Among the more recent works, Paliwal illustrates that entangled histories not only took place between the metropolis and the colony, but also in South-South relations, for example between India and post-independence Ghana.[357] It was Indian security agents who helped Nkrumah develop Ghana's security and intelligence apparatus, which was used to persecute his political opponents such as the members of the oppositional Togoland Congress. Paliwal argues that it was Nkrumah's authoritarianism, which politicised Ghana's security establishment, thereby forestalling democratic progress.[358] Patrick Obuobi, evaluates Ghana's oversight regime over its intelligence services as lacking – a circumstance, which, among other things, he attributes to Ghana's pyramidal organisational principles, stemming from its colonial period and which have hardly been reformed ever since.[359]

---

351 Simon Baynham, "Quis Custodiet Ipsos Custodes?," *The Journal of Modern African Studies* 23, no. 1 (1985), available from https://www.jstor.org/stable/160465.

352 Mike Brogden, "The Emergence of the Police," *British Journal of Criminology* 27, no. 1 (1987): 9

353 David Killingray, "Soldiers, Ex-Servicemen, and Politics in the Gold Coast, 1939–50," *The Journal of Modern African Studies* 21, no. 3 (1983); David Killingray, "Guarding the Extending Frontier," in *Policing the empire: Government, authority and control, 1830–1940*, ed. David Anderson and David Killingray, Studies in imperialism (Manchester: Manchester University Press, 1991)

354 Richard Rathbone, "Police Intelligence in Ghana in the Late 1940s and 1950s," *The Journal of Imperial and Commonwealth History* 21, no. 3 (1993), https://doi.org/10.1080/03086539308582909.

355 Calder Walton, *Empire of Secrets: British Intelligence, the Cold War, and the Twilight of Empire* (New York: ABRAMS Books, 2014).

356 Chase Arnold, ""The Cat's Paw of Dictatorship": Police Intelligence and Self-Rule in the Gold Coast, 1948–1952," *The Journal of the Middle East and Africa* 11, no. 2 (2020), https://doi.org/10.1080/21520844.2020.1756604.

357 Avinash Paliwal, "Colonial Sinews of Postcolonial Espionage," *The International History Review*, 2021, https://doi.org/10.1080/07075332.2021.1888768.

358 Paliwal, "Ghana's national security ministry ignites old fears after fracas over photos."

359 Obuobi, "Evaluating Ghana's Intelligence Oversight Regime"

In broader terms, Georgina Sinclair argues that the emergence of the London Metropolitan Police in 1829, often referred to as the world's first "modern" police force, was inextricably linked to the production of knowledge and practices of managing (in)security, political order, "native subjects" and "dangerous classes" in the British colonies. Throughout the 20th century, this "cross-fertilisation" between colonial and native policing practices and knowledge informed British policing.[360]

French Togoland

Among the earliest mentions on security in French Togoland is Quincy Wright's study of the Mandates System, who evaluates the provision of security as one of the primary achievements by the Mandates System, opening with the presumptuous notion that "From the native point of view, security means the continuation of traditional customs, and these are frequently opposed to economic and political development."[361] Thus, as the colonial *Zeitgeist* demanded at the time, Quincy advocates that the mandatory powers had to strive for the eradication of the native's notion of security. Wright praises the economic efficiency maintained by the mandated powers:

> "The existence of general security is hardly susceptible of statistical measurement, but the Mandates Commission's policy [of] elimination of conscription except for police purposes, would seem to promote it. In the latter respect a marked contrast seems to exist between the French mandated territories and the French colonies of West Africa. The cost of the local militia in Togoland and Cameroons is much less than was the military cost under German rule, and even less than the British military expenses in Tanganyika."[362]

Regarding recent research, Blanchard offers a general overview of colonial policing across the French colonial empire.[363] Similar to Woodman and Sinclair, Martin Thomas holds that French colonial policing emerged as "an interactive process between the empire and mainland France," a process in and through which ideas of urban planning, as well as practices of legal and social control, permanently travelled back and forth between colony and metropole, thereby converting French colonies into "laboratories for organized violence, where new forms of suppression, punishment, and political control were practiced and refined."[364] Thomas traces the anti-colonial resistance and its repression by police forces primarily back to the order of the economic exploitation system of colonial rule. The economic situation after World War I, with its new forms

---

360   Georgina Sinclair and Chris A. Williams, "'Home and Away'," *The Journal of Imperial and Commonwealth History* 35, no. 2 (2007), https://doi.org/10.1080/03086530701337567.
361   Quincy Wright, *Mandates under the League of Nations* (Chicago, Ill.: University of Chicago Press, 1930), p. 563.
362   Wright, *Mandates under the League of Nations*, pp. 563–64.
363   Emmanuel Blanchard, "French Colonial Police," in *Encyclopedia of Criminology and Criminal Justice*, ed. Gerben Bruinsma and David Weisburd (New York, NY: Springer, 2014).
364   Martin Thomas, ed., *The French Colonial Mind: Mental Maps of Empire and Colonial Encounters*, 2 vols., France Overseas: Studies in Empire and Decolonization Series 1 (Lincoln: University of Nebraska Press, 2011), pp. xxii–xxiii.

of wage labour and additional taxation, led to spontaneous protests and strikes. Since the respective colonial police forces were understaffed and viewed with constant suspicion by the authorities due to their mostly multi-ethnic composition, this resulted in police reforms that led to a more paramilitary- and intelligence-driven orientation of the police forces, whose main task was to secure production processes and containing demonstrations.[365]

Other works challenge the supposedly stable colonial dichotomies between the exploiting coloniser and the exploited colonised, white and black, collaborators and resisters. Focus is put on the hitherto under-researched "rule of the intermediary,"[366] that is, African employees of the colonial period such as traditional chiefs, interpreters, postal workers, but also police forces. One such study is Joël Glasman's work on the genesis of the police profession in French-mandated Togoland, which is a socio- and microhistory of law enforcement agents' daily practices within the context of the colonial state. According to Glasman, the creation of the *Service de Police et de Sûreté* was a response to the 1933 tax revolt in Lomé and initiated a process of bureaucratization of police services that shifted the focus of police work from the military camp to the police station. Not the military presence in the streets, but the growing importance of paper, such as verbatim records or informant reports, highlighted a new form of "remote control."[367] The physical and brutal punishments of the early days of colonization were replaced by more diffuse administrative controls – not meaning that these "softer means" of bureaucratization immediately meant a pacification, which side-lined the repressive practices of criminal prosecution. The new law enforcement practices, both in their relations with the population and internally, demonstrated that "It was no longer just a question of being seen, but, more and more, of seeing."[368] Although the core period of his investigation falls in the period of the Mandates System, Glassman also provides some important statistics on the size and spending on security forces in French Togoland during the trusteeship period up until the assassination of Sylvanus Olympio in 1963. Although the trusteeship period indicates that security was a core policy of French colonial administration as spending on the police forces was increased more than tenfold and staffing virtually doubled, the French administration remained a minimal state.

France, as Togo's previous protecting power, has come under criticism for bearing partial responsibility in the assassination of President Sylvanus Olympio in 1963 by Togolese veterans who had fought for France in Algeria and Indochina. Though not endorsing the assassination, Robert Cornevin and to some extent even the Olympio-friendly journalist Russel Warren Howe, effectively exonerated the ex-combatants at the time by showing comprehension of the ex-combatants' motifs.[369] For Cornevin, it was

---

365 Martin Thomas, *Violence and colonial order: Police, workers and protest in the European colonial empires, 1918–1940*, 1st ed., Critical perspectives on empire (Cambridge: Cambridge University Press, 2012), p. 300.
366 Schlichte, *Der Staat in der Weltgesellschaft*, p. 292; For Ewe and Togoland nationalism, see also Lawrance, Osborn and Roberts, *Intermediaries, interpreters, and clerks*.
367 Glasman, *Les corps habillés au Togo*, p. 217.
368 Glasman, *Les corps habillés au Togo*, p. 224.
369 Robert Cornevin, "Les Militaires Au Dahomey Et Au Togo," *Revue française d'études politiques africaines*, 1968; Russell Warren Howe, "Togo: Four Years of Military Rule," *Africa Report* 12, no. 5 (1967)

not the conspirators who provoked Olympio's assassination, but Olympio himself, who "longed for undivided and uncontrolled power."³⁷⁰ Around the same time, Scott Thompson was the first academic to suggest that Nkrumah-led Ghana was behind Olympio's assassination.³⁷¹ Another thesis is that of *Françafrique* put forward by François-Xavier Verschave, according to which the French commander of the Togolese gendarmerie, Georges Maîtrier, instigated the coup.³⁷² Tété-Adjalogo picked up on Verschave's thesis, arguing that Olympio's plans to take Togo out of the franc zone were practically the last straw that broke the (French) camel's back.³⁷³ Discussing all these three theories, Skinner argues that none was more valid or accurate than the other, yet, the 'unideological military/security-forces-explanation,' was more convenient for political actors during the further development of events, and therefore prevailed.³⁷⁴ The 1963 coup and Eyadema's seizure of power in 1967 set in motion a remarkable development, as Togo had only about 1.000 police officers and no military forces at the time of its independence,³⁷⁵ but has risen to become "one of the most militarised countries in Africa."³⁷⁶

2.4 Situating the Research Agenda

The preceding review of the research literature demonstrates that the research drive originates primarily from the field of International Relations. It has been shown that since the emergence of the failed states debate, questions of state-building have been closely linked to an *evolving* understanding of security, while postcolonial and decolonial scholarship, which has been critical of this evolution and the emerging 'new interventionism,' formulated a desideratum of historical case studies. However, although the importance and implications of the historical perspective are often emphasised, only very few studies have been addressing the historicity of the state-building-security nexus.³⁷⁷ The objective of this study is to fill this research gap by developing a research perspective that underpins the theories and assumptions of Critical Security Studies with a postcolonial perspective. While the importance of historicising and decolonising scholarly concepts is recently gaining traction within International Relations, especially in the literature on statebuilding and security studies, this research project originally started out with the aim to decolonise the concept of security. However, scholars such

---

370 Mathurin C. Houngnikpo, "The Military and Democratization in Africa," *Journal of Political and Military Sociology* 28, no. 2 (2000): 219
371 Willard Scott Thompson, *Ghana's Foreign Policy, 1957–1966: Diplomacy Ideology, and the New State*, Princeton Legacy Library (Princeton: Princeton University Press, 1969), p. 313.
372 Verschave, *La Françafrique*.
373 Têtêvi Godwin Tété-Adjalogo, *Histoire du Togo: Le regime et l'assassinat de Sylavanus Olympio 1960–1963*, Histoire du Togo 3 (Paris: NM7 Editions, 2002), p. 111.
374 Kate Skinner, "West Africa's First Coup," *African Studies Review* 63, no. 2 (2019), https://doi.org/10.1017/asr.2019.39.
375 Houngnikpo, "The military and democratization in Africa," p. 219.
376 Comi M. Toulabor, "Togo," in *Challenges of security sector governance in West Africa*, ed. Alan Bryden, Boubacar N'Diaye and Funmi Olonisakin (Wien, Zürich, Berlin, Münster: Lit, 2008), p. 304.
377 Ketzmerick, *Staat, Sicherheit und Gewalt in Kamerun*.

as Fiona Adamson put an unignorable question mark behind this aim, concluding that meaningful decolonisation would mean transforming structures, rather than diversifying them.[378] Yet, the later seems to be the trend. Similarly, Christopher Murray criticizes that decolonial approaches, in their efforts to break away from Eurocentric universalisms, run into the problem of precisely reproducing the colonial binary of Western and non-Western worlds, rather than overcoming it.[379] Though still sympathetic to the decolonial programme, out of consideration of positionality, this present work abandoned the presumption to 'decolonise security.' As the next best thing, so to say, postcolonial critique to Critical Security Studies is used to show the potential of linking postcolonial theory and critical security research, thus tracing the changes, and contested nature of security from different positionalities.

By incorporating a theory-driven framework into historical research, it is hoped to open new perspectives for research on international organisations. In doing so, it is assumed that studying the origins of the recent secessionist conflict surrounding "Western Togoland" requires a combination of constructivist understandings of security (Copenhagen School) as well as procedural security practices (Paris School), whereby postcolonial theories are considered as a bridge between the historical contextual factors of the decolonisation processes and the concepts of social science research.

---

378   Fiona B. Adamson, "Pushing the Boundaries: Can We "Decolonize" Security Studies?," *Journal of Global Security Studies* 5, no. 1 (2020): 132, https://doi.org/10.1093/jogss/ogz057.
379   Christopher Murray, "Imperial Dialectics and Epistemic Mapping: From Decolonisation to Anti-Eurocentric IR," *European Journal of International Relations* 26, no. 2 (2020), https://doi.org/10.1177/1354066119873030.

3. Theoretical Framework

> "But if thought corrupts language, language can also corrupt thought."[1]

This study will apply a theory-driven analysis to examine historically the international supervision of Togoland's decolonisation process. The special role that trusteeship territories played in the history of decolonisation vis-à-vis the much larger group of colonies, the euphemistically called Non-Self-Governing Territories (NSGTs), offered inhabitants of the trusteeship territories scope for action that other independence and liberation movements hardly dreamed of having recourse to. This study stipulates that this leeway was facilitated, negotiated, and occupied through a strategic mode of communication about (in)security, with which colonial and anti-colonial actors alike attempted to make their political decisions, opposition, or resistance around certain issues in the decolonisation process plausible to an international audience. Security-centred speech was crucial for handing over the monopoly of violence, the legitimisation of power, and claims to rule in the future state. To unravel the intricacies of Togoland's decolonisation, this chapter introduces two important strands of research within Critical Security Studies (CSS). Chapter 3.1. is dedicated to the influential Copenhagen School and its postcolonial interpretation with the aim of elucidating securitisation dynamics at the United Nations. Chapter 3.2. is dedicated to the Paris School, which captures security routines and the emergence of security actors, structures, and practices to analyse the administrations of the trusteeship territories themselves. The particular concern is whether and how these so-called *in*securitisations or automatisms of security-thinking influenced the negotiations at the United Nations.

---

1   George Orwell, *Politics and the English Language* (London: Penguin Books UK, 2013 [1946]), p. 16.

In response to a frequently expressed demand to historise security,[2] it is assumed that these theories of International Relations will benefit from the introduction of historicising approaches just as historical research will benefit by the introduction of theories of International Relations. However, this should be pursued with caution. For example, the present work decidedly averted the Aberystwyth's or Welsh School's concept of *security as emancipation*. Although at first glance an emancipatory concept of security seems to be an obvious choice in a historical study of security practices and discourses during decolonisation, the view is shared that the Aberystwyth School's theoretic contributions underpin the very interventionist politics that postcolonial critics decry as a revival of colonial trusteeship.[3]

3.1 Copenhagen School

The concept of securitisation is considered to have been developed by Ole Wæver, who first introduced the term in 1989 in a working paper,[4] further developed the concept in an article in 1995,[5] and in 1998, together with Barry Buzan and Jaap de Wilde, introduced a whole new field of research by publishing the book *Security: A New Framework for Analysis*.[6] With securitisation, Wæver joined the advent of constructivism within International Relations, which was initiated by Alexander Wendt to explain the relatively peaceful end of the Cold War.[7] Coined by McSweeney as the "Copenhagen School" of International Relations,[8] securitisation, thus, represented a constructivist departure from traditional, that is, realist and liberal approaches to security.

Securitisation has undisputedly become one of most well-established research approaches within Critical Security Studies. On the one hand, securitisation accounted for the *broadening* of the security agenda, that is, the moving away from realism's narrow focus on the military sector to analysing issues in other sectors such as the environmental, economic, political, and societal spheres. As Wæver puts it:

---

2   Ketzmerick, *Staat, Sicherheit und Gewalt in Kamerun*, p. 198; Eckart Conze, "Securitization," *Geschichte und Gesellschaft* 38, no. 3 (2012), https://doi.org/10.13109/gege.2012.38.3.453; Stefano Guzzini and Dietrich Jung, eds., *Contemporary security analysis and Copenhagen peace research*, The new international relations (London, New York: Routledge, 2004); Barry Buzan and George Lawson, *The global transformation: History, modernity and the making of international relations*, Cambridge studies in international relations (Cambridge: Cambridge University Press, 2015). https://doi.org/10.1017/CBO9781139565073
3   Sergen Bahceci, "Universal Security/Emancipation," *E-International Relations*, 23.03.2015, accessed 13 December 2020, available from https://www.e-ir.info/2015/03/23/universal-securityemancipation-a-critique-of-ken-booth/.
4   Ole Wæver, *Security, the Speech Act: Analysing the Politics of a Word* (Jerusalem/Tel Aviv, 1989); 2nd Draft
5   Wæver, "Securitization and Desecuritization"
6   Barry Buzan, Ole Wæver and Jaap de Wilde, *Security: A new framework for analysis* (Boulder, London: Lynne Rienner Publishers, 1998).
7   Alexander Wendt, "Anarchy Is What States Make of It," *International Organization* 46, no. 2 (1992)
8   Bill McSweeney, "Identity and Security," *Review of International Studies* 22, no. 1 (1996), available from https://www.jstor.org/stable/20097432.

"Military threats have been primary in the past because they emerged 'very swiftly' and with 'a sense of outrage at unfair play'; if defeated, a state would find itself laid bare to imposition of the conqueror's will. Such outcomes used to characterize the military sector. But, if the same overturning of the political order can be accomplished by economic or political methods, these, too, will constitute security problems."495F[9]

On the other hand, securitisation also contributed to the *deepening* of security, that is, mowing away from considering the state as the sole referent object. Other than realism or the more liberal Aberystwyth School, both of which understand security ontologically as a *state of being* in which something or someone is in, securitisation describes a social and referential *process* in which an actor presents a referent object – tangible or abstract – to be existentially threatened to such an extent that, in order to protect the referent object, a relevant audience approves extraordinary measures (though, neither does the existential threat have to be 'true' nor the measure need to be taken).

Drawing from John Austin's seminal work "How to *do* things with words,"[10] utterances of (in)security, thus, mean more than saying or describing something factually; the communication of security rather aims to invoke (extraordinary) measures. Securitisation, thus, shifted the focus from what security *is* to what the invocation of insecurity *does*. In the words of Buzan, Wæver, and Wilde securitisation, thus, means…

> "the move that takes politics beyond the established rule of the game and frames the issue either as a special kind of politics or as above politics. Securitization can thus be seen as a more extreme version of politicization. In theory, any public issue can be located on the spectrum ranging from non-politicized (meaning the state does not deal with it and it is not in any other way made an issue of public debate and decision) through politicized (meaning the issue is part of public policy, requiring government decision and resource allocations or, more rarely, some other form of communal governance) to securitized (meaning the issue is presented as an existential threat, requiring emergency measures and justifying actions outside the normal bounds of political procedure)."[11]

However, Wæver argued from early on for the normative preference of the opposite, that is, *de*-securitisation, which describes the return of a securitised topic to the sphere of "normal" politics and diplomacy.[12] At the end of the Cold War, this normative aspiration of the securitisation approach was certainly programmatic as it intended to counter the theoretical preponderance of the realist school of thought with its inherent logics of armament and deterrence.[13] In presenting security as a speech act, the Copenhagen School thus represented a scholarly critique of and departure from realist ethics, "presenting a

---

9 Wæver, "Securitization and Desecuritization," p. 52.
10 Emphasis in original: John Langshaw Austin, *How to do things with words* (London: Oxford University Press, 1962).
11 Buzan, Wæver and Wilde, *Security*, pp. 23–24.
12 Wæver, "Securitization and Desecuritization"
13 Stefano Guzzini, "A Dual History of Securitization," *DIIS Working Paper*, no. 2 (2015), available from https://www.files.ethz.ch/isn/192491/DIIS_WP_2015_02_A_dual_history_of_Securitisation.pdf.

political ethic of communicative action and discursive ethics,"[14] though, as Huysmans and Hansen would later point out, "the preference for desecuritisation is technical, managerial and instrumental, rather than genuine political or ethical."[15]

The Copenhagen School assumes that (apart from exceptional cases) the particular mode of communication of a successful securitising move leads to a break with the rules of normal politics. Drawing on linguistic concepts, the particular epistemological interest of the Copenhagen School's early scholars attempted to decode the communicative structure of the securitisation process, that is, the *grammar of security*, that forms the linguistic framework and universal set of rules that exist underneath the variously distinct "security dialects" of society's different sectors, such as identity in the social sector, recognition and sovereignty in the political sector, sustainability in the ecological sector, etc.[16]

From the Copenhagen School's constructivist perspective, an empirical object is not a threat by itself. Rather, threats and (in)security are discursive social constructions. To lay a foundation for this consideration, Wæver drew on Austin's speech act theory, according to which certain propositions do more than simply describe, or state a given reality.[17] Whereas earlier positivist perspectives reductively described sentences simply as 'false' or 'true,' Austin emphasises that they are also performative, that is, they *do* things.

For example, the phrase *"Do we have any salt?"* can convey three types of acts, the combination of which constitutes the total speech act:

i. The *locutionary* act captures the utterance 'in the full normal sense' and its *apparent* verbal, social and rhetorical meaning (e.g., the apparent question: "Is there any salt present at the table?"),
ii. The *illocutionary* act captures the non-uttered intention of the speaker in its explicitly performative character (e.g., an implied order: "Pass me the salt!"),
iii. The *perlocutionary* act captures the 'consequential effects' of the locutionary and illocutionary acts, which aimed at evoking the feelings, beliefs, thoughts, or actions of the target audience (e.g., the listener feels called upon to pass the salt).

While the *locutionary* act still captures the preceding positivist perspective (from which Austin intents to part), the *illocutionary* and *perlocutionary* act form the innovation and interest of speech act theory.

---

14 Michael C. Williams, "Words, Images, Enemies," *International Studies Quarterly* 47, no. 4 (2003): 524, https://doi.org/10.1046/j.0020-8833.2003.00277.x; see also Wesley, "Toward a Realist Ethics of Intervention"
15 Lene Hansen, "Reconstructing Desecuritisation," *Review of International Studies* 38, no. 03 (2012): 527, https://doi.org/10.1017/S0260210511000581.
16 Buzan, Wæver and Wilde, *Security*, p. 33.
17 Austin, *How to do things with words*.

3.1.1 Internalist vs. Externalist Understanding

In the further development of this classical concept, two strands have emerged: An internalist approach focuses on the functions or intentions of a securitising move itself, while an externalist approach focuses on the context and consequences.

Internalist Understanding: Focus on the Speech Act

Drawing from Austin's speech act theory, Wæver insists on "analysing securitization as an illocutionary and not a perlocutionary act in order to organize the theory around the constitutive, transformative event of actors [...] rather than seeing an external cause–effect relationship between speech and effects."[18] Representatives of this analytical approach attempt to decode the *grammar of security*. Presumably drawing inspiration from speech act theory and leveraging linguistic vocabulary, Wæver, Buzan, and de Wilde introduced the term *grammar of security*. Interestingly, they associated its meaning with the construction of a plot rather than a universal set of rules and constraints, like scholars such as Vuori, who taxonomized general functions of securitisation speech acts.[19] Again, securitisation, does not seek to grasp what (in)security *is* but what constructions of (in)security *do*, that is, they do not have to be 'true' in order to be effective.

While the focus on the *illocutionary act*, that is, the intention or function of the speech act, focuses on a temporal snapshot in analysis, the *perlocutionary act*, that is, the effect and consequence of the speech act, involves a temporal frame that goes beyond the utterance itself. Moreover, Austin already noted that the *perlocution* is "specific to the *circumstances* of issuance and is therefore not conventionally achieved just by uttering particular utterances, and includes all those effects, intended or unintended, often indeterminate, that some particular utterances *in a particular situation* may cause."[20] In other words: context matters.

For a second generation of securitisation scholars, this was the starting point to critique various aspects of the use of speech acts,[21] which eventually led to more contextualist readings of securitisation. Holger Stritzel notes that since the internalist understanding of securitisation does not convincingly explain why some securitisations are successful and while others fail, it is of limited use for empirical research.[22] An internalist understanding could only point to the rhetoric, which must be persuasive by nature. Due to this explanatory weakness, a more externalist understanding developed, which focuses on the context of a speech act.

---

18 Ole Wæver, "The Theory Act: Responsibility and Exactitude as Seen from Securitization," *International Relations* 29, no. 1 (2015): 122–23
19 Vuori, *How to do security with words*.
20 Emphasis added, Austin, *How to do things with words*, pp. 14–15.
21 Thierry Balzacq, ed., *Securitization theory: How security problems emerge and dissolve*, PRIO new security studies (New York: Routledge, 2011); Stritzel and Chang, "Securitization and counter-securitization in Afghanistan"; Hansen, "The Little Mermaid's Silent Security Dilemma and the Absence of Gender in the Copenhagen School"; Howell and Richter-Montpetit, "Is securitization theory racist?"; Bertrand, "Can the subaltern securitize?"
22 Holger Stritzel, "Towards a Theory of Securitization," *European Journal of International Relations* 13, no. 3 (2007): 362, https://doi.org/10.1177/1354066107080128.

Externalist Understanding: Focus on the Context

Asking why some securitisation moves succeed while others fail, and what the political consequences are, Balzacq's shift to focus on the *perlocutionary act* brought contextual factors into the centre of the analysis.[23] While prioritizing the *illocutionary act* allows for an analysis of a context-independent *grammar of security*, that is, the intended functions of security speech acts in any given society, prioritizing the *perlocutionary act* has allowed for the emergence of a diverse body of scholarly work that has focused on specific kinds of context, for instance the regional context,[24] international context,[25] political-historical context,[26] or gendered context.[27] In other words, the focus shifted from the 'grammar of security' to the 'dialects of security.'

In their different facets, these dialects focus on the social, political, and cultural contexts in which threats are constructed. Contextual factors are non-exhaustive and include, for example, the symbolic and social capital of the securitising actor, the cultural or historical disposition of the audience, power relations between securitising actor and audience,[28] etc. Context is not a purely independent variable, though, because agents can also bring about or prevent certain contexts. In this regard, Bonacker points out that this contextualist reading of securitisation theory is analytically unsatisfactory, as it has not yet been clarified from a methodological point of view what is meant by a "context."[29] But the *methodological situationism* that he proposes to replace 'context' suffers from the logical fallacy that he defines situations *idem per idem* as "interactional *contexts* in which social order is first produced."[30] Nonetheless, he draws attention to the fact that if context is emphasized too much in the *perlocutionary-/*context-focused strand of securitisation analysis, its validity degenerates into 'everything depends on context' and thus loses analytical sharpness.

3.1.2 The Audience's Agency

Already in 1998, the representatives of the Copenhagen School assessed that in the *grammar of security* the audience represented the *conditio sine qua non* because an "issue is secu-

---

[23] Thierry Balzacq, "The Three Faces of Securitization," *European Journal of International Relations* 11, no. 2 (2005), https://doi.org/10.1177/1354066105052960.

[24] Nergis Canefe, "Turkish Nationalism and the Kurdish Question," *South European Society & Politics*, no. 3 (2013)

[25] Nicole J. Jackson, "International Organizations, Security Dichotomies and the Trafficking of Persons and Narcotics in Post-Soviet Central Asia," *Security Dialogue*, 2006.

[26] Jef Huysmans, *The European Union and the securitization of migration* (2000); Jef Huysmans, "Agency and the Politics of Protection," in *The politics of protection: Sites of insecurity and political agency*, ed. Jef Huysmans, Andrew Dobson and Raia Prokhovnik, 1st ed., Routledge advances in international relations and global politics (New York, N.Y: Routledge, 2006)

[27] Hakan Seckinelgin and Joseph Bigirumwami, "Securitization of HIV/AIDS in Context," *Security Dialogue* 41, no. 5 (2010)

[28] Silva, "Securitization as a nation-building instrument"

[29] Thorsten Bonacker, "Situierte Sicherheit," *Zeitschrift für Internationale Beziehungen* 28, no. 1 (2021), https://doi.org/10.5771/0946-7165-2021-1-5.

[30] Emphasis added, Bonacker, "Situierte Sicherheit," p. 7.

ritized only if and when the audience accepts is as such."³¹ A discourse that takes the form of presenting something as an existential threat to a referent object does not itself create securitisation – this is merely the securitising move.³² Legitimacy for extraordinary measures must be argued somehow and cannot be forced.³³ Thus, securitisation is not a goal of an interaction whereby securitising actors present themselves and the extraordinary measures as legitimate, but rather legitimacy is the goal of a process of securitisation. Thus, a threat is not only accepted or rejected, but negotiated between the securitising actor and the audience.³⁴ As Ezeokafor and Kaunert put it, the securitising actor must find a "line of argument that will effectively resonate with or swing the audience in full of support of the intended line of action."³⁵ The analytical focus must therefore be directed towards the intersubjective negotiation process.

Between the internalist and externalist strands of securitisation there has been a divergence of what or who constitutes the audience. Vuori, although decidedly studying securitisation in non-democratic contexts, leans toward the *internalist/illocutionary* strand of securitisation, arguing that the audience's receptibility of a securitisation move depends on the socio-historic contexts, thereby rendering any fixed *perlocution*-centred definition of an audience non-sensical.³⁶ Therefore he holds that "audiences depend on the *function* the securitization act is intended to serve."³⁷ Vuori sees an advantage in define audiences by their "ability to provide the securitizing actor with whatever s/he is seeking to *accomplish* with the securitization."³⁸

Balzacq, as a representative of the *perlocutionary* and context-centred strand, stresses that securitisation is not a one-way process but that both the speaker and the audience bring agency into the interaction.³⁹ Balzacq et al. emphasize the notion of an 'enabling' or 'formal' audience that "empowers the securitizing actor [...] to act."⁴⁰ Adam Côte, who characterises earlier definitions of the audience as "agents without agency"⁴¹ emphasizes that these definitions represent important departures from previous ones, as they define audiences by what they contribute to the securitisation process rather than by a task or characteristic. Michael Williams stipulates that "this raises questions about who counts as a 'significant audience' and how this idea should be applied to states or organizations that do not boast a functioning public sphere,"⁴² while Vibeke Tjalve underscores that it is

---

31 Buzan, Wæver and Wilde, Security, p. 25.
32 Buzan, Wæver and Wilde, Security, p. 25.
33 Wæver, "Securitization and Desecuritization"
34 Stritzel, "Towards a Theory of Securitization," p. 363.
35 Ezeokafor and Kaunert, "Securitization outside of the West," p. 88.
36 Juha A. Vuori, "Illocutionary Logic and Strands of Securitization," *European Journal of International Relations* 14, no. 1 (2008), https://doi.org/10.1177/1354066107087767.
37 Vuori, "Illocutionary Logic and Strands of Securitization," p. 72.
38 Emphasis added, Vuori, "Illocutionary Logic and Strands of Securitization," p. 72.
39 Balzacq, "The Three Faces of Securitization," p. 172.
40 Thierry Balzacq and Stefano Guzzini, "Introduction: 'What Kind of Theory – If Any– Is Securitization?,'" in Balzacq et al., *What Kind of Theory – If Any – Is Securitization?*, Vol, p. 7.
41 Adam Côté, "Agents Without Agency," *Security Dialogue* 47, no. 6 (2016), https://doi.org/10.1177/0967010616672150.
42 Williams, "Words, Images, Enemies," p. 517.

quite difficult to define term "the public," which many studies adopt prematurely within the securitisation framework.⁴³

3.1.3 Securitisation *Theory*? Or: How to Predict the Present

Attentive readers will not have failed to notice that the present study has so far been careful not to speak of securitisation *theory* but only of the securitisation *framework* or *concept*. On the one hand, one of the great attractions of securitisation and a major reason for its success is its usefulness as an analytical framework capable of practical application and empirical enquiry. On the other hand, it has been criticised for being more of an interesting observation than a theory that has a practical purpose for political actors. This ambivalence, that is, the symptomatic lack of theoricity has been subject of the 2014 forum "What kind of theory (if any) is securitization theory?"⁴⁴

The "(if any)" in the forum's title was a suggestive reference to the doubts harboured by some of the most prominent securitisation scholars. Their choice of words was telling about their implicit understanding of theoricity and consequently their answer to the question in the title of the forum. While Thierry Balzacq and Stefano Guzzini, both representatives of the context-centred *perlocutionary* strand, largely avoided the combined term 'securitisation *theory*' and speak simply of 'securitisation' or 'the concept of securitisation,'⁴⁵ Wæver, after begging the question "*what* is politics, theory, sociology and philosophy,"⁴⁶ simply continues to refer to securitisation as 'the theory.'

Yet, whether and to what extent securitisation constitutes a theory was not explored in depth by Wæver and though he admitted that "the specific meta-theoretical explications were not available at the time, but probably present implicitly," Wæver concludes confidently:

> "Many references [to securitisation] are to the 'idea' or the 'slogan'. However, numerous dissertations and other studies have been made with this 'framework for analysis', so it seems that more than the concept has proven useful. [...] The critical question is rather whether it has been *too much* of a theory – whether it is necessary and/or helpful to play the theory card that hard or more is gained by a 'less theoretical' approach such as, for example, the so-called 'sociological' version. To assess this, the discipline needs to cultivate a more elaborate terminology and publication format for assessing *how* a theory participates in specific studies – what exactly does it do."⁴⁷

Since the theoretical framework of this present 'theory-driven' historical study draws in large part on securitisation, the substance of this assertion should be addressed.

---

43 Vibeke Schou Tjalve, "Designing (De)Security," *Security Dialogue* 42, 4–5 (2011), https://doi.org/10.1177/0967010611418715.
44 Thierry Balzacq et al., eds., *What kind of theory – if any – is securitization?* 29 (2015).
45 Balzacq and Guzzini, "Introduction: 'What Kind of Theory – If Any– Is Securitization?'"
46 Balzacq et al., *What kind of theory – if any – is securitization?*, p. 26.
47 Ole Wæver, "The Theory Act," in Balzacq et al., *What Kind of Theory – If Any – Is Securitization?*, Vol, p. 31., emphasis in the original

Rachel Suissa has cautioned that theories of the "New Security Studies" must pass the test of falsifiability in order to distinguish themselves from pseudo-science.[48] She contends that analogous to Popper's critique of Freud's psychoanalysis,[49] securitisation seems to be able to explain any outcome by putting any empirical observation to work in its service: securitisation can be used to explain why a certain referent object was successfully securitised, but may also explain the opposite case, that is, why the securitisation of the very same referent object failed. Securitisation analysis thus runs the risk of its use becoming self-fulfilling: any analysis that announces its use in the introduction would automatically imply its endorsement in the conclusion. This type of theoricity problem stems from the fact that every outcome of a securitising move lies within the limits of what is permissible and possible, including successful securitisation and successful desecuritisation, yet as Ruzicka showed,[50] also *failed* securitisation and *failed* desecuritisation including all the consequences of the 'in-betweens' of these four types.

Furthermore, according to Ruzicka, securitisation scholars have been too infatuated with facilitating conditions but largely neglected much thought on hindering conditions, which may include that the securitising actor is unable to securitise in a specific context,[51] may not have sufficient authority or social capital, the threat is unsuitable for securitisation or simply the audiences refuse to grant the extraordinary measure because it does not deem the referent object worthy to be saved.[52]

In any case, pointing out the irrationality of successfully securitising a referent object does little to change the political dynamic. Even despite scholarly analysis, political actors cannot escape a securitised event and are still forced to deal with (de)securitised issues in the same (de)securitised way. Thus, analysing a (de)securitising move has a lot of explanatory potential but little predictive potential because the contextual factors represent myriad tweakable variables, which are incidentally non-exhaustive.

Yet, according to Popper's demarcation criterion, theory needs to be prohibitive and make risky prediction about the future of states of affairs. Since Megan MacKenzie showed that the Copenhagen School's normative preference for desecuritisation is not always favourable in terms of gender-equality,[53] Suissa stresses that the falsifiability of securitisation is not just a theoretical argument but one of direct practical relevance:

> "In order to protect against potential terrorist threats, it may be legitimate to take preventive measures when there is a valid threat, yet insufficient evidence of an im-

---

48 Rachel Suissa, "The Scientific Status of New Security Studies: A Critical Search for Epistemic Identity of Homeland and Civil Security Research," in *Cross-disciplinary Perspectives on Homeland and Civil Security: A Research-Based Introduction*, ed. Alexander Siedschlag (New York: Peter Lang Inc., International Academic Publishers, 2016), p. 233.
49 Karl R. Popper, *Conjectures and Refutations: The growth of scientific knowledge* (London: Routledge, 1963).
50 Jan Ruzicka, "Failed Securitization," *Polity* 51, no. 2 (2019), https://doi.org/10.1086/702213.
51 It should be borne in mind that the issue with context is also that what facilitates securitisation may but not necessarily will hinder (de)securitisation.
52 Ruzicka, "Failed Securitization," p. 373.
53 Megan H. MacKenzie, *Female soldiers in Sierra Leone: Sex, security, and post-conflict development*, Gender and political violence series (New York: New York University Press, 2016).

pending terrorist attack. This must be distinguished from taking measures against an alleged terrorist threat that may be a theoretical possibility, but for which there is no valid evidence present. Therefore, decision-makers in homeland security must be able to distinguish between scientific and pseudoscientific claims."[54]

In contrast, essential understandings of security, such as the Aberystwyth School's, provide a basis for how to conduct international diplomacy. Yet, as outlined above, these are problematic in another way. Thus, though this study draws from securitisation, it is careful not to call it a 'theory' because its state of 'theoricity,' as seen by Popper, is controversial.

However, the argument at hand is not to revive the positivism controversy of the 1960s – on the contrary, as described at the beginning of the chapter, the merit of constructivism is to elaborate the processualism of security – but, to put it succinctly, the argument at hand is that studies using securitisation tend to analyse past events to 'predict the present.' For example, Vuori pointed out that securitising moves are frequently used to legitimise past events.[55] In consequence, securitisation seems to be a mainly backward-looking framework that should be well-suited for historical analysis. Ironically, however, applying securitisation to historical analysis has only been a case of the recent past.

3.1.4 Historicisation of Security & Securitisation of History

A common criticism directed toward International Relations concerns its ahistorical tendencies since it focuses its attention predominantly on the immediate political context of direct-physical and directly observable violent events. Securitisation is also frequently subject to the same criticism, that is, concrete structures and practices of governance (as well as the possibility of mobilising opposition and resistance against them) are commonly regarded to be more decisive for the emergence and course of (de)securitisation dynamics than the historical constellation.[56]

Aglaya Snetkov noted that for this reason there are only few long-term perspectives for securitisation so far. Snetkov, who understands issues of security not as isolated, self-contained events, but as simultaneous processes that are part of a larger dynamic and therefore only become visible in a long-term perspective, contends that "Little empirical work has been conducted on the way in which securitizations, initially constructed across multiple spatially bounded referent objects, subsequently evolved over the full life cycle of (de)securitization processes and the political effect this has had on security politics."[57] Considering this with the aforementioned, this observation seems surpris-

---

54 Suissa, "The Scientific Status of New Security Studies: A Critical Search for Epistemic Identity of Homeland and Civil Security Research," p. 233.
55 Vuori, "Illocutionary Logic and Strands of Securitization," p. 83.
56 Ketzmerick, Maria, and Werner Distler, "The 'Politics of Protection' and Elections in Trusteeship and International Administration. The Cases of Cameroun and Kosovo." In Bonacker; Distler; Ketzmerick, *Securitization in Statebuilding and Intervention*, 127-54.
57 Aglaya Snetkov, "Theories, Methods and Practices," *Security Dialogue* 48, no. 3 (2017): 260, https://doi.org/10.1177/0967010617701676.

ing, since Wilde, Buzan and Wæver even underline in their seminal work *Security: A New Framework for Analysis*:

> "The major new opening is probably an ability to historicize security, to study transformations in the units of security affairs. Traditional security studies defines the units (states) and the instruments (military) that by definition make any security phenomena elsewhere invisible."543F[58]

Therefore, it is important not to understand the activity of writing history of security as examining, understanding, and judging the past with reference to the standards of the present. In this sense, history would be reduced to a ratification of the present. The quest to historicise security involves examining the changes of its meaning in relation to the historical context.[59] Providing an illustrative example, Stefano Guzzini holds that…

> "the understanding of (de)securitization is historical. The strong emphasis on an allegedly realist reading of security (connected to war, exceptional measures, done by foreign policy elites, etc.) is not to be understood as the 'essence' of security, but rather as the effect of a historical development in which certain actors have come to be authorized to talk and effect war and peace in a 'realist' way."[60]

Thus, the advantage of the securitisation is its capacity to function as a historical metaexplanation, that is, by analysing security speech acts and identifying moments of change, continuity and discontinuity in history, securitisation allows to explain other understandings of security as derived concepts, such as realist understanding of security located within the specific historical post-war constellation of the Cold War.

Indeed, today it is commonplace that conceptions of security "derive from different underlying understandings of the character and purpose of politics."546F[61] Thus, as with other such 'derivate concepts', understandings of security depend on one's political outlook and philosophical worldview.547F[62] Securitisation's emphasis on the mutability of security discourses and practices, underscore that contemporary understandings of security are rather the product of historical contingencies and thus not hardwired. Therefore, in this study, security will be treated as a historically contingent social construction.

While an important innovation of the securitisation approach is probably the ability to historicise security, that is, to study the historical transformations of affairs of security concern, history in itself may constitute a facilitating or hindering condition for securitisation moves in the present. Matti Jutila pointed out that history, or a certain interpretation of it, can be the reference object of securitisation or a facilitating condition

---

58   Emphasis added, Buzan, Wæver and Wilde, *Security*, p. 206.
59   Ketzmerick, *Staat, Sicherheit und Gewalt in Kamerun*, p. 84.
60   Stefano Guzzini, "Securitization as a Causal Mechanism," *Security Dialogue* 42, 4–5 (2011): 335, https://doi.org/10.1177/0967010611419000.
61   Emphasis added, Booth, *Theory of world security*, p. 119.
62   Booth, *Theory of world security*, p. 150.

for it,[63] since securitisation moves almost inevitably mobilise references to the past. This is the advantage of securitisation: even abstract referent objects such as history or interpretations thereof can be securitised. Past violent conflicts can facilitate current securitisation moves, for example. But, for history to be a facilitating condition, it must be assumed that audience and securitising actor share the same historical frame of reference. History may become a hindering condition when two interpretations of history clash: "Sometimes particular interpretations of history are so deeply embedded in politics that an interpretation becomes a referent object in its own right; defending it might seem to justify measures that are extraordinary in the academic field or popular history."[64] Therefore Jutila cautions to securitise history:

> "Academic history writing and education have been key mediums of this transmission. Historians were often involved in various 'national awakenings' writing Whig histories of how we came to be who we are. When nations were imagined, history had to be imagined anew. 'National memory' is preserved through history writing and other presentations of history."[65]

This points toward the particular sensitivity that historians using securitisation must consider the longevity of historical securitisation. For example, a historian who argues that a historical actor had 'good reasons' to securitise a past danger, which eventually did not materialise, unwittingly reproduces the legitimacy of extraordinary measures. The historian's dilemma is that this also applies to the reverse case, in which threats that were desecuritised eventually turned out to be true.

Furthermore, Jutila points out that at times, certain groups hope to purge the historical inventory of thinkers they deem for example too racist to consider. An illustrative example is the outcry to 'erase history' when statues of historical figures are demolished or names of institutions or streets are changed, though not least it is often the subaltern's experience of insecurity that is excluded from history.[66] Ironically, because of its recourse to Arendt or Carl Schmitt, the Copenhagen School itself became the victim of such controversy,[67] underscoring the leading role of the securitisation of history in the current debate on identity politics.[68]

---

63 Matti Jutila, "Securitization, History, and Identity," *Nationalities Papers* 43, no. 6 (2015), https://doi.org/10.1080/00905992.2015.1065402.
64 Jutila, "Securitization, history, and identity," p. 933.
65 Jutila, "Securitization, history, and identity," p. 936.
66 Jutila, "Securitization, history, and identity," p. 938; Gayatri C. Spivak, "Can the Subaltern Speak?," in *Colonial discourse and post-colonial theory: A reader*, ed. Patrick Williams (New York, NY: Harvester Wheatsheaf, 1993), http://planetarities.web.unc.edu/files/2015/01/spivak-subaltern-speak.pdf
67 Howell and Richter-Montpetit, "Is securitization theory racist?"; Lene Hansen, "Are 'Core' Feminist Critiques of Securitization Theory Racist?," *Security Dialogue*, 2020, https://doi.org/10.1177/0967010620907198; Ole Wæver and Barry Buzan, "Racism and Responsibility," *Security Dialogue* 51, no. 4 (2020), https://doi.org/10.1177/0967010620916153.
68 Christopher S. Browning and Pertti Joenniemi, "Ontological Security, Self-Articulation and the Securitization of Identity," *Cooperation and Conflict* 52, no. 1 (2017), https://doi.org/10.1177/0010836716653161; Uliana Hellberg, "Securitization as a Modern Strategy of Constructing Identity 'Negative

Discussing Wæver's conceptualisation of *societal security*,[69] which actually preceded the development of securitisation, Jutila also raises awareness to the distinct role, which history plays in the securitisation of national identities, and respectively, in the securitisation of history to consolidate national identities. Usually, history and myths, which are not infrequently collective traumas, are mobilised by securitising actors to construct or reinforce identity or to point to historic narratives to identify threats to this identity.[70] In times of uncertainty, family history can serve as a coping mechanism and politicians often invoke a nation's history to reinforce a country's national identity. But Jutila cautions that a security-centred history of identity is only a short way from othering and producing divisions into friends and enemies, which might transform "pluralist communities into two opposing camps: 'If you're not for us, you're against us!'."[71] As a possible form of resistance to such a securitisation of national identities, Jutila bets on 'responsible studies of history' that lead to a complex and nuanced picture of the past that is ill-suited for nationalist purposes. In other words, it is the responsibility of the historian not to render history itself a repertoire against a securitised Other. Because of this inherent relationship between othering and securitisation of history, postcolonial critique is not far away.

3.1.5 Securitisation in a Postcolonial Reading

Silence Dilemma

In principle, post- and decolonial historiographies drew attention to two types of silence: on the one hand, attention is drawn to those narratives of the past that did not correspond to the scope of action imaginable at the time and which now must be laboriously excavated or else be lost forever. On the other hand, attention is drawn to the silencing of contemporary, yet marginalized interpretations of history.

Lene Hansen referenced first to the silence problem within the securitisation framework, by dealing with the dilemma of Pakistani women who are prevented from publicly speaking about the threats they face (e.g., rape, honour killings, etc.) because if they did, they would provoke the very threats they try to address in the first place. Thus, the women are forced to remain silent. Ken Booth critiqued this blind spot of securitisation concisely: "If security is always a speech act, insecurity is frequently a zipped lip."[72]

Sarah Bertrand extends Hansen's notion of the silence dilemma by shifting attention to the audience. Bertrand shows that silence, and hence insecurity, is not exclusively due to the muteness of the subaltern but also due to the audience. In the Copenhagen School, or more specifically, within the dramaturgy of the *grammar of security*, the success or failure of a securitising move ultimately depends on the audience. However, the

---

Proof Identity' in the European Union," Malmö University Electronic Publishing, available from http://muep.mau.se/handle/2043/14368.
69 Ole Wæver, "Identity, Integration and Security," *Journal of International Affairs* 48, no. 2 (1995), available from https://www.jstor.org/stable/24357597.
70 Ketzmerick, *Staat, Sicherheit und Gewalt in Kamerun*, p. 199; Jutila, "Securitization, history, and identity," p. 927.
71 Jutila, "Securitization, history, and identity," p. 938.
72 Booth, *Theory of world security*, p. 168.

conceptual involvement of the audience is passive, that is, the audience's participation is limited to either granting or not granting extraordinary measures. The audience is not conceptualized as an actor with its own agenda. Adam Côté speaks in this regard of "agents without agency."[73] Drawing on Spivak,[74] Bertrand reorients the analytical focus from the speaker's muteness to the audience's power to silence and exclude. Bertrand emphasizes that any securitising actor, who occupies a subaltern subject position, can similarly also not be listened to (*illocutionary frustration*) or not be heard or understood (*illocutionary disablement*), regardless of the persuasiveness of the securitising argument.

Illocutionary frustration involves the unwillingness of an audience to agree to the securitising move. It describes the situations in which actors can certainly speak, but do not have the power to make an audience listen and are thus also excluded from the production of security, or the audience very much acknowledges the existential threat to the referent object but is not willing to confront the threat. This occurs when an audience does not see itself as the competent body or when it has an agenda of its own (be it due to personal benefits or ideology). Ken Booth commented on this aspect, noting that…

> "we all know that in politics as in life in general, there are none so deaf as those who do not want to hear. Audiences with agenda-making power can choose not to be an 'audience,' as happened with the UN Security Council (UNSC) during the Rwandan genocide in 1994."[75]

Illocutionary disablement describes an audience's inability to understand the intended meaning of a message due to 'disabling frames.' Banal examples would be when an audience does not speak the same language or interference distorts a radio distress signal beyond recognition. Bertrand points out that also certain forms of repetition can also act as 'disabling frames.' Shouting 'help' just for fun is commonly discouraged, since actual calls for help might therefore probably be understood differently over time and will not trigger a reaction even in the case of real danger.[76]

Yet, drawing on Spivak's concept of discursive or *epistemic violence*, Bertrand specifically refers to *epistemic* disabling frames, which have a cognitive or epistemic impact on the audience. Bertrand provides the illustrative example of a theatre actor trying to warn an audience about a fire, but who tragically fails to do so because the audience takes the warnings to be part of the play. Thierry Balzacq already thought about this as the "relevant aspects of the *Zeitgeist* that influence the listener,"[77] whereas other works circumscribe this aspect as a form of "security heuristics."[78] Yet, in certain power constellations, especially colonial ones, *illocutionary disablement* may distort securitising speech acts to the point of incomprehensibility. Similar to what Walter Mignolo analogously termed

---

73 Côté, "Agents without agency"
74 Spivak, "Can the subaltern speak?"
75 Booth, *Theory of world security*, pp. 167–68.
76 Bertrand, "Can the subaltern securitize?," p. 285.
77 Balzacq, "The Three Faces of Securitization," p. 192.
78 Bonacker, "Situierte Sicherheit"

the "colonial matrix of power,"[79] *illocutionary disablement*, thus, describes epistemic operations of power, such as racism or patriarchy, that filter and shape an audience's view of reality, whereby the "subaltern are silenced by the epistemic violence of essentialisation."[80] While Bertrand argues that the category of *perlocutionary frustration* is inapplicable to securitisation, her creation of the category *illocutionary frustration* also captures the active part played by the audience in producing silence that the category *perlocutionary frustration* highlights.

Bertrand's 'typology of silencing' can be illustrated allegorically with the three-monkey motif of the Japanese proverb 'see not, hear not, say not.' While the three wise monkeys in Japan have the meaning 'to wisely overlook bad things,' in its modified meaning in the West they stand for 'not wanting to acknowledge anything bad' and thus stand for a lack of civil courage or unquestioning loyalty.

Table 1: Silence Dilemma & Three Wise Monkeys

Type of silencing	Translation	Monkey...
Locutionary silencing	"Say not"	...covering its mouth.
Illocutionary frustration	"See not"	...covering its eyes.
Illocutionary disablement	"Hear not"	...covering its ears.

Source: Own creation.

Bertrand concludes that the inability of the subaltern to securitise gives way to a 'double' or 'colonial' move of silencing the subaltern by attempting to securitise on its behalf, which "easily end up silencing the very people one tries to give a voice to."[81] According to Bertrang, 'securitising for' can occur "by political action designed to remediate or take advantage of the 'silence-problem', by normative claims intending to critique the 'silence-problem', as well as by mere analysis aimed at locating and uncovering the 'silence-problem'."[82]

Bertrand criticizes the Copenhagen School that securitisation can only come into being through the successful completion of a speech act. Yet, she argues, even a well-meaning critique of the marginalizing effects of securitisation must invoke (in)security before a subaltern actor successfully completes the speech act, thereby erasing or marginalizing the subaltern's agency or voice. Bertrand argues that this aspect is structurally baked into securitisation's reliance on the speech act and does not emerge from historical contingency.[83] Bertrand's critique implies that securitisation falls short as an

---

79   Walter D. Mignolo and Catherine E. Walsh, eds., *On decoloniality: Concepts, analytics, and praxis*, On decoloniality (Durham, London: Duke University Press, 2018), p. 114.
80   Bertrand, "Can the subaltern securitize?," p. 289.
81   Bertrand, "Can the subaltern securitize?," p. 289.
82   Bertrand, "Can the subaltern securitize?," p. 288.
83   Bertrand, "Can the subaltern securitize?," pp. 291–92.

empowering transformative approach for subaltern actors. The suggestion that securitisation is thereby disqualified as a critical theory oversimplifies the issue.[84]

Table 2: Securitisation's Silence Dilemma resulting from....

Exclusion (failure to complete securitising speech acts)	Remedy against Superimposition (speaking security 'for' others)
Locutionary silencing	Active remediation of the silence problem
Illocutionary frustration	Normative critique of the silence problem
Illocutionary disablement	Analysis uncovering the silence problem

Source: Bertrand, "Can the subaltern securitize?," p.290.

According to Bertrand, it becomes impossible for a securitisation scholar to assume that a subaltern actor genuinely faces a security problem. This is particularly because, even if the subaltern actors should, in principle, be able to securitise their concerns, Bertrand argues that this assumption is unattainable within the specified epistemological framework. The consequence of this argument is that it sidesteps the potential scenario where the subaltern actor, despite not swaying the relevant audience, may have successfully persuaded the scholar. Furthermore, in her critique, Bertrand keeps speech act theory out of the proverbial line of fire: "the main reason behind securitization theory's 'silence-problem' lies in its specific epistemological choice to locate security within speech act theory."[85] Yet, Claudia Aradau righteously contents that it is not clear how this distinction is drawn between speech act and its particular deployment in securitisation theory.[86] Therefore, Aradau champions to prioritize the *perlocutionary act*, that is, context- and consequences-focused analysis of securitisation for it may "open up the possibility of taking into consideration the sedimentation of 'elaborate institutional structures of racism as well as sexism'."[87] The present study takes up this impulse, whilst Bertrand's taxonomy of 'securitising for' still captures the formalised guardian-ward-relationship of colonial and trusteeship regimes that is the focus of this work.

Securitisation & the Trusteeship Constellation

As indicated above, on the one hand, the subaltern subject position might be a hindering condition for a securitising actor in an uneven playing field simply because securitisation moves are discursive devices, which take place in a world that has been shaped for

---

84   Bertrand, "Can the subaltern securitize?," p. 291.
85   Bertrand, "Can the subaltern securitize?," p. 297.
86   Aradau, "From securitization theory to critical approaches to (in)security," p. 302.
87   Aradau, "From securitization theory to critical approaches to (in)security," p. 302.

centuries by colonial discourse. On the other hand, many of the issues in the theoretical debate on securitisation also revolve around who the audience is, what its function is and whether it is relevant.

Regarding these aspects, a securitisation analysis of the debates in the United Nations Trusteeship System promises to be relatively straightforward: The Trusteeship Council represented a specific and closed audience whose powers and terms of reference were clearly stipulated in the Charter and its *rules of procedure*. In the Trusteeship System, the people of the trusteeship territories had the *right to petition*, which was supposed to protect them against the abuses of the Administering Authorities. As such, petitions in their written and oral form represented complaints to a competent body for the redress of their grievances. In other words, for the most part, they represented securitising moves by their very premise. The roles of the relevant audience (state representatives) and the securitising agents (petitioners) were clearly distributed, and their debates meticulously recorded.

Yet, the Copenhagen School's *grammar of security* assumes in a sense a 'neutral audience.' Yet, the UN Trusteeship System represented a colonial constellation that contorted not only the context in which security speech acts are uttered but also the internal logic or structural constraints of the *grammar of security*. In the Copenhagen School, the default approach of a securitising actor is to address a relevant audience to draw its attention to an existential threat to a referent object. However, in the context of trusteeship, anti-colonial actors had to address the very members of the audience, which embodied the threat to their freedom, independence, etc. This corresponds to Vuori's observation that the audience may very well represent the very security predicament of the securitising actor.[88] Unlike Ketzmerick, who interprets the Trusteeship Council as an "uninvolved and supposedly rational third party,"[89] the current analysis holds that the UN Trusteeship System was a special colonial constellation in which the audience had a decisive influence on the securitisation process.

Moreover, as Adam Côté noted "securitization is less of a one-way, linear process in which the actor articulates a security reality to the audience, and more of a deliberation between actor and audience, consisting of multiple iterative, contextually contingent interactions between actor(s) and audience(s) regarding a single issue over time."[90] This holds especially true for the specific make-up of the United Nations Trusteeship System, where the two principal venues or 'audiences', that is the Trusteeship Council and the General Assembly's Fourth Committee, were also characterized by internal dependencies. For example, against their better judgment, some members of the Fourth Committee chose not to follow the securitising arguments of petitioners because they feared to be sanctioned by the Administering Authorities in the later run. Audiences, so argues Côté, must therefore be theorized as heterogeneous entities. Thus, it is not the securitising move by the securitising actor that drives the decision of the audience to (dis)agree to a securitising message, but rather the (de)securitising moves by members within the au-

---

88   Vuori, "Illocutionary Logic and Strands of Securitization," p. 81.
89   Ketzmerick, *Staat, Sicherheit und Gewalt in Kamerun*, p. 80.
90   Côté, "Agents without agency," p. 552.

dience itself, who may be driven by factors that might have nothing to do with the move of the securitising actor.

Furthermore, following the Copenhagen School, which assumes that, by building on *the grammar of security*'s linguistic framework and universal set of rules, each social sphere produces its own different 'security dialects,' the present study assumes in the context of the Trusteeship System a predominance of a 'colonial dialect,' whose adoption facilitates securitising moves rather than an 'anti-colonial dialect'. It is held, that to be heard vis-à-vis the dominance of liberal ideology, securitising actors must "use appropriate words and cogent frames of reference,"[91] or in other words: "to tune his/her language to the audience's experience'"[92] by adopting specific conceptual vocabulary concurrent with Western thought and language to rework securitising attempts. Jane Cowan's analysis of the *violent-language*-rule of the League's minority regime provides an insightful example.[93] In the aftermath of World War I, Cowan explores how League diplomats, committed to world peace, instituted a diplomatic code that prioritized politeness and indirect language, barring what they deemed as "violent language." Applied to the theoretical framework used here, the prohibition of "violent language" restricted the use of vocabulary typically used in securitising speech acts and prevented petitions directed against colonial grievances from reaching the public, as they had to be toned down to conform to prescribed language norms.

3.2 Paris School

Within Critical Security Studies, the so-called Paris School is more sociologically grounded than the Copenhagen School. The Paris School draws primarily from post-structuralist approaches, particularly from concepts of French sociologists such as Pierre Bourdieu and Michel Foucault. In contrast to the Copenhagen School, the Paris School does not emphasize extraordinary measures but, beyond the study of official speech acts, focusses on ordinary routines, bureaucracies of security,[94] and the power/knowledge processes that unfold within them.[95] Criticizing the Copenhagen School, Paris School scholars, such as Didier Bigo and Anastassia Tsoukala, maintain that the social and political consequences of security are not due to a single actor's speech act, but to a multitude of actors within a Bourdieu-inspired field of (in)security from completely different professional logics.[96] It is not the individual speech act that is of interest, but

---

91 Balzacq, "The Three Faces of Securitization," p. 192.
92 Ezeokafor and Kaunert, "Securitization outside of the West," p. 87.
93 Cowan, "Who's Afraid of Violent Language?"
94 Didier Bigo, "When Two Become One," in *International relations theory and the politics of European integration: Power, security, and community*, ed. Morten Kelstrup and Michael C. Williams (London: Routledge, 2000); Didier Bigo, "Security and Immigration," *Alternatives: Global, Local, Political* 27, Special Issue (2002): 73, https://doi.org/10.1177/03043754020270S105.
95 Aradau, "From securitization theory to critical approaches to (in)security," p. 302.
96 Pierre Bourdieu, *Distinction: A social critique of the judgement of taste* (London: Routledge & Kegan Paul, 1984); Pierre Bourdieu, *Language and symbolic power*, ed. John B. Thompson (Cambridge, MA: Harvard University Press, 1991); Didier Bigo and Anastassia Tsoukala, *Terror, insecurity and liberty*:

rather the complex social practice, which it represents. The result, taking up a concept by Deleuze, is an "(in)security assemblage,"[97] that is, a new ensemble of practices, applications, and technologies of security, which in turn give rise to a new space for action. Such a reading is conceptualized by Christopher Daase as "security culture."[98]

Consequently, Bigo holds from this perspective that "securitization results from power positions,"[99] including non-discursive practices. Thus, from the Paris School's perspective, securitisation can be discursive as well as non-discursive, intentional, and non-intentional, and performative. Since the Paris School does without an audience that grants extraordinary measures, its representatives speak rather of *in*securitisation.[100] Drawing from Foucault's governmentality, and especially his security *dispositif*, insecuritisation is not conceived as a state of exception or developed from a logic of the exceptional or the extraordinary, but as the normal state of a liberal society. Security practices are practices of normalization.[101] Thus, police practices, surveillance technologies and human rights discourses, in short, the whole contextual range of security routines are important to understand processes of *in*securitisation.

Due to the exclusion of the audience Copenhagen School scholars repudiated that "one cannot make the actors of securitization the fixed point of analysis."[102] Although at first glance the opposition between exceptionality and routine seems irreconcilable, there are fruitful overlaps between the Paris and Copenhagen School. For example, Balzacq's discussion on the importance of context has found its way into the Copenhagen School, as well as the Bourdieu-inspired terminology of symbolic, social, or cultural capital of the securitising actor.[103] Balzacq sees the performative dimension of security, understood as situated acts that mediate the habitus of the actor, as important for the process of securitisation.[104]

A core tenet of the Paris School is that security discourses and practices can diverge: Security practices in the form of routines or bureaucratic acts can create insecurity even if they are not publicly designated as such.[105] It is argued that when security professionals go about their *métier*, insecurity is inevitably created, just like the dictum 'When you are holding a hammer, everything looks like a nail.' Accordingly, security professionals constantly reproduce the insecurities they aspire to eliminate. Insecuritisation is seen

---

Illiberal practices of liberal regimes after 9/11, Routledge studies in liberty and security (London, New York: Routledge, 2008), p. 5.

97 George F. McHendry, "The politics and poetics of airport (in)security rhetoric: Materialism, affect, and the Transportation Security Administration" (Dissertation, Department of Communication, University of Utah, 2013), available from https://core.ac.uk/download/pdf/276265588.pdf.
98 Christopher Daase, "Sicherheitskultur," *Sicherheit und Frieden* 29, no. 2 (2011)
99 Bigo, "Security and Immigration," p. 74.
100 Côté, "Agents without agency," p. 549.
101 Conze, *Geschichte der Sicherheit*, p. 104.
102 Buzan, Wæver and Wilde, *Security*, p. 30.
103 Balzacq, "The Three Faces of Securitization," p. 191.
104 Balzacq, "The Three Faces of Securitization," pp. 187–90.
105 Thierry Balzacq, ed., *How Security Problems Emerge and Dissolve* (London: Routledge, 2011), p. 2; Karine Côté-Boucher, Federica Infantino, and Mark B. Salter, "Border Security as Practice: An Agenda for Research," *Security Dialogue* 45, no. 3 (2014), https://doi.org/10.1177/0967010614533243

as the "management of unease."[106] As a prime example, the Paris School draws on the insecuritisation of the migrant, who is made visible as the Other.[107] Drawing from Foucault, Bigo takes fault that the "form of governmentality of postmodern societies is not a panopticon in which global surveillance is placed upon the shoulders of everybody, but a form of ban-opticon in which the technologies of surveillance sort out who needs to be under surveillance and who is free of surveillance, because of his profile."[108]

For the Paris School, internal security agencies such as police, border guards or customs increasingly identify threats beyond state borders, not least through discourse on criminal networks (made up of migrants, asylum seekers, diaspora communities and, not least, Muslims with alleged links to terrorism, drug trafficking and transnational organised crime). Discussing responses of Western border control agencies, Didier Bigo holds that securitisation and liberalism are in fact the same process, whereby the humanitarian discourse "is itself a by-product of the securitization process."[109] The resulting convergence of the internal and external gives rise to "transversal threats" that make borders more fluid. Bigo uses the image of the Möbius strip for this purpose: "Inside and outside no longer have clear meanings for the professionals of threat management. A Möbius ribbon has replaced the traditional certainty of boundaries. It destabilizes the figures of threat as well as the borders of activities between the institutions."[110]

3.3 Research Perspective

Noting that, on the one hand, security must be thought of as a mode of communication, that facilitates issues to be placed on the agenda as security problems, and, on the other hand, as a non-discursive, performative practice of security professionals, the study applies a post-colonially informed reading of the Copenhagen and Paris School. In doing so, the study takes special note of Ruzicka's contention that securitisation is under-theorised because it suffers from a case-selection bias favouring successful securitisations, powerful actors, and facilitating contextual conditions.[111] However, as Ruzicka notes, it is equally important to think about failed securitisation, subaltern actors, and *hindering* contextual conditions.[112] To do justice to this contention, the analysis primarily turns to Bertrand's postcolonial reading of the Copenhagen School, that is, *locutionary*, *illocutionary*, and *perlocutionary silencing*, to render visible petitioners' securitisation efforts in the state-building process at play under the Trusteeship System. The three mechanisms will be illustrated by showing how:

---

106   Bigo, "Security and Immigration," p. 64.
107   Bigo, "Security and Immigration," p. 81.
108   Bigo, "Security and Immigration," p. 82.
109   Bigo, "Security and Immigration," p. 79.
110   Bigo, "Security and Immigration," p. 76.
111   Ruzicka, "Failed Securitization"
112   Ruzicka, "Failed Securitization," p. 373.

a) the Administering Authorities tried to limit the scope of acceptance and consideration of petitions via the constant adjustment of the rules of procedure and resorted to repressive measures in the trusteeship territories themselves (*locutionary silencing*),
b) the Administering Authorities were unwilling to consider the petitioners' securitisation moves / refused to implement General Assembly recommendations and presented their own counter-securitising views (*illocutionary frustration*), and
c) the discursive construction of the Administering Authorities and mandated peoples inscribed into the Trusteeship System disabled the petitioners' securitisation moves before United Nations venues (*illocutionary disablement*).

Equally, the Paris School finds its way into the analysis. Although for the Paris School, the trans-nationalisation of the security field began only in 1990 through the increasing interaction of different security professionals in the border region, it will be shown here that the European nation states and imperial states did cooperate in the field of colonial security. A particular focus will be placed on the security architecture and practices of the trusteeship administration, such as that of the Special Branch. With reference to the last, that is, aspects of colonial policing and the system of intelligence agencies that collected a wide range of information about the inhabitants, Foucauldian security policy posits that colonies like Togoland were essentially turned into panopticons. In the analysis, agency as well as the performative dimension, symbolic power, or social capital of security actors are important, as was contextual mobilisation. The empirical chapters show for example how colonial powers created contexts and structures that did not provide a level playing field for anti-colonial actors.

In conclusion, this study will utilize the Copenhagen School to analyse expressions of (anti-)colonial fears and threat constructions in the foreground – before the global audience, involving entities such as the Trusteeship Council or the UN General Assembly. Simultaneously, it will turn to the Paris School to contrast these foreground expressions with those articulated in the background, specifically within the colonial administration and ministries, occurring away from the public eye.

4. Methods

> "The nature of African states, and the opposition they encountered, has to be inferred from problematic and incomplete sources."[1]

This chapter focuses on the methodological considerations and reflects on the processes of data collection and analysis. It will show how archival research can enrich theoretical discussions within the study of International Relations and connect security studies with postcolonial theory by means of a historical perspective. Chapter 4.1 introduces the general constructivist perspective employed in this study, emphasising of socially constructed nature of (in)security and history, and its implications. This section also comments on the comparative perspective of this study regarding French and British Togoland. Chapter 4.2 will delve into the details of the archival field research, including reflections on analysing records *along* or *against* the archival grain. Furthermore, this section will provide an overview of the archives visited along with addressing the associated challenges. It concludes with a presentation of the research and evaluation procedure that was followed to operationalise the used securitisation framework.

4.1 Research Design

4.1.1 A Constructivist Study

This study takes a constructivist perspective. As an epistemological stance within the social sciences, constructivist approaches now form a broad field of research, yet, the minimal consensus is that the social world(s) around us (and thus all objects of research) are socially constructed through actions, shared ideas, expectations, and the production of

---

1 Skinner, *The Fruits of Freedom in British Togoland*, p. 211.

knowledge.[2] The implication for the present study is that both (in)security and history are equally perceived as socially constructed and thus as contingent. In the case of security, the study follows perspectives that consider security as a "derivative concept,"[3] meaning that the underlying understanding of security 'derives' from one's political attitudes and philosophical worldview. From a constructivist critical discourse point of view, the question does not arise as to whether these ideas correspond to 'reality'.

Constructivist approaches to knowledge production come with ontological and epistemological implications. At the core of constructivism are questions about what constitutes reality and the possibility and status of our knowledge about this reality. Constructivist approaches assert that (social) reality is contingent and socially constructed, experienced differently by those who observe, interpret, or assign meaning to it, including constructivist researchers themselves.[4] Constructivist approaches thus elude positivist notions that set out to pinpoint a 'true' state of any given research object to a stable 'reality.' These implications lead necessarily to the questions of actors' subjectivity,[5] and the relationship between agency and structure, which social constructivism assume to be mutually dependent.[6] These notions have found their way into constructivist approaches to security research.

> "We do not try to peek behind this to decide whether it is *really* a threat (which would reduce the entire securitization approach to a theory of perceptions and mis-perceptions). Security *is* a quality actors inject into issues by securitizing them, which means to stage them on the political arena in the specific way [...] and then to have them accepted by a sufficient audience to sanction extraordinary defensive moves."[7]

From this constructivist perspective, security is thus not to be seen as an object, but as a historically evolved negotiation between power, knowledge, and authority. The epistemological interest of the work therefore does not aim to identify and analyse security problems, but rather to pursue the question of how and under what conditions empirical objects become security problems in the first place. Constructivist works therefore focus on the contextual conditions in which a text or statement is produced and on language as a carrier of discourse.

The research question and its sub-questions in this study emerged from an assessment of the existing body of research, and the underpinning theoretical foundations but

---

2   Alexander Wendt, *Social theory of international politics*, Cambridge studies in international relations 67 (Cambridge: Cambridge University Press, 1999), p. 1; for a more specific appreciation of constructivist understandings in IR see the seminal work by Wendt, "Anarchy is what States make of it"
3   Peoples and Vaughan-Williams, *Critical Security Studies*, p. 22.
4   Teresa K. Beck and Tobias Werron, "Gewaltwettbewerbe," in *Ordnung und Wandel in der Weltpolitik: Konturen einer Soziologie der internationalen Beziehungen*, ed. Stephan Stetter, 1st ed., Leviathan Sonderband 28 (Baden-Baden: Nomos, 2013), p. 250.
5   Huysmans, "Agency and the politics of protection," p. 5.
6   Anthony Giddens, *The constitution of society: Outline of the theory of structuration* (Berkeley: University of California Press, 1984).
7   Emphasis in original. Buzan, Wæver and Wilde, *Security*.

especially from these ontological reflections. The inquiry extends beyond the construction of actors' social identities, delving into the examination of the practices and policies facilitated within the framework of these constructions. In this manner, it is elucidated how power dynamics play a constitutive role in shaping subjectivities.[8] Furthermore, the study explores how actors categorise and interpret events, organising these perspectives based on varied reactions and strategies. The research interest is to capture and understand the arguments and constructions of meaning of the individual actors around security. To investigate these inquiries, an abductive-oriented content analysis was employed, and the discourse-analytical question was posed: How does a security threat manifest? Causal and processual questions were intricately connected with the objective of scrutinising power dynamics and the evolution of subjectivity and agency.

Constructivist perspectives, as paraphrased from Neta Crawford, emphasize the historical and social construction of institutions and practices, providing context to the present by illustrating how we arrived at the current state. Yet, "constructivists have little to say about what needs to be done."[9] Epistemological-constructivist works align with post-structuralist theories, asserting that every theory is simultaneously a political-social practice, challenging the notion of objectivity in research. In this framework, all social processes, including scientific works, are understood as discursively negotiated. Scientific contributions are acknowledged as part of the construction and legitimation of social reality, highlighting that no research is neutral, as the research process itself is based on prior political decisions. Claudia Aradau and Jef Huysmans argue that methods in research are not merely for acquiring information but are also performative and integral to the world they engage with.[10]

4.1.2 A Qualitative & Comparative Study

Togoland was chosen as a case study because of its status as a UN trusteeship territory, which renders it historically distinct. As an internationally supervised UN trusteeship territory, Togoland stands out as a unique and significant case within the broader context of decolonisation. Consequently, it presents a distinctive and compelling situation for researchers to explore and analyse. Through the involvement of the UN, insight can be gained into the discourses and practices of a decolonisation and statebuilding process that took place in the global context of decolonisation struggles. Due to their accountability to the UN, the French and British Administering Authorities left archival trails of reports, verbatim records, transcripts, minutes, and publications. These materials serve as valuable resources for discerning how the administration was conceived and executed, as well as identifying perceived dangers throughout process. In the case of Togoland, the examination of security dynamics during decolonisation not only illuminates its impact

---

8   Doty, *Imperial encounters*, p. 4.
9   Crawford, *Argument and change in world politics*, p. 427.
10 Claudia Aradau et al., eds., *Critical security methods: New frameworks for analysis*, New international relations (London, New York: Routledge, 2015); Claudia Aradau and Jef Huysmans, "Critical Methods in International Relations: The Politics of Techniques, Devices and Acts," *European Journal of International Relations* 20, no. 3 (2014), https://doi.org/10.1177/1354066112474479.

on an anti-colonial movement but also facilitates a direct understanding of trusteeship territory administration. This insight reveals how the concept of colonially led decolonisation unfolded on a broader scale.

Since the decolonisation process of the two Togolese trusteeship territories was primarily about their reunification, a comparative qualitative study becomes imperative. However, due to disparities in archival records and blank spaces, a direct comparison is unfortunately only possible to a limited extent. Coincidentally, archival sources pertaining to the colonial security apparatus in the British trusteeship territory have endured and are accessible in the British National Archive. Conversely, in the French colonial archives, similar files are either restricted from release, no longer available, or only accessible to a restricted extent. Nevertheless, the focal point for all cases remains the discursive constructions of security, particularly the responses of the Administering Authorities to the reunification movement in Togoland. The archives reveal coordinated, joint, or congruent responses to the reunification movement for both the French and British trusteeship territories.

Moreover, within the Trusteeship System, hardly any other trusteeship area has generated so much attention and challenged the UN Trusteeship System. Its nearly 15-year trusteeship period results in a long period of investigation. A coding procedure was used for a qualitative content analysis.[11] Data were collected through method triangulation, that is, diverse sources were included, and different methods were used to generate the corresponding data.[12] The archival work had to be mediated between the methodological considerations from historical science and the political science requirements for dealing with data. The following gives an insight into the archival work, the data material, and the procedure for collecting and analysing the data.

4.2 Archival Research

Since the 'archival turn' archival work has gained prominence in International Relations.[13] However, although its history constitutes an entire subfield of the discipline, archival research methods, especially in Critical Security Studies, are still very much in their infancy. There is little methodological International Relations literature on working with archival records.[14] This circumstance forms the basis for much criticism

---

11 Philipp Mayring, *Qualitative content analysis: theoretical foundation, basic procedures and software solution* (Klagenfurt, 2014), http://nbn-resolving.de/urn:nbn:de:0168-ssoar-395173
12 Mayring, *Qualitative content analysis*, p. 8.
13 Davis E. Alexander, "An Archival Turn for International Relations," ISA Singapore; Shiera S. el-Malik and Isaac A. Kamola, eds., *Politics of the African anticolonial archive*, Kilombo: International Relations and Colonial Questions (Lanham: Rowman & Littlefield, 2017); Michael S. Moss and David Thomas, eds., *Archival silences: Missing, lost and, uncreated archives* (London, New York: Routledge, 2021).
14 The proverbial exception that proves the rule: Luis Lobo-Guerrero, "Archives," in *Research methods in critical security studies: An introduction*, ed. Mark B. Salter and Can E. Mutlu (London, NewYork: Routledge, 2013)

that with "its obsession of the present"[15] the study of International Relations can hardly take credit for "trying to transcend its imperial, colonial and racist roots."[16] Despite the increasing importance and reorientation of International Relations to history many International Relations scholars that work historically continue to rely on less theory-driven approaches from historical scholarship.

Coloniality of Archives

By stating that the colonial archive is "a force field that animates political energies and expertise, [which] inscribes the authority of the colonial state and the analytic energies mobilised to make its assertions,"[17] authors like Stoler caution historians about the coloniality of the archives. Research has shown how writing was crucial to the exercise of state power in colonial contexts. For example, Skinner argues that writing made colonialism possible: "It was a technology of control which categorised people, extracting them from a world of their own experience, locating them in the 'world on paper', and thereby enabling their appropriation as the subjects of bureaucratic regimes."[18] But this supposedly philosophical admonition has quite practical catches: archival material is subject to a historical conditionality and paths of transmission. Reflecting on her archival material, Skinner concludes that the administrative grid structures the way we write history, making some pasts easier to recover than others. In the archives, Africans mostly appear when they reacted to or obstructed the structures that colonial administrators tried to put in place.[19] Colonial archives thus have a lasting effect. The formations of various archives are complicit in the histories which have been written, that is, the stories that historians 'dig up' or 'extract' from archives depend largely on what archivists considered worth archiving. They distort the balance of what can be told about whom and how.

The fact that many archives of Western creation are either colonial archives or state archives, each emphasising the colonial or state perspective, should not go unconsidered as scholars of international relations increasingly reaches out to the "Global South." Historians studying international relations must also be aware that the history of diplomacy is always intertwined with the prevailing theoretical paradigm of the time. Both diplomatic history and international relations theory dawned with the rationalist assumptions of realism and empiricism, that is, scholarly historical and positivist assumptions about world order. Where diplomatic historians turn to the archive, scholars of International Relations turn to a theory-driven analysis.

Reading Against or Along the Grain?

By building a methodological bridge, this study draws on approaches to historical discourse analysis,[20] but its goal remains one of political science: archival documents were

---

15   Booth, *Theory of world security*, p. 100.
16   Sabaratnam, *Decolonising intervention*.
17   Ann Laura Stoler, *Along the archival grain: Epistemic anxieties and colonial common sense* (Princeton, NJ: Princeton University Press, 2009), p. 22.
18   Skinner, *The Fruits of Freedom in British Togoland*, p. 25.
19   Skinner, *The Fruits of Freedom in British Togoland*, p. 16.
20   Achim Landwehr, *Historische Diskursanalyse*, 2nd ed., Historische Einführungen 4 (Frankfurt/Main: Campus, 2009); Geert Castryck, Silke Strickrodt and Katja Werthmann, eds., *Sources and methods*

used as material for a theory-driven analysis of events in Togoland. Thus, this study is inspired by two approaches that at first blush seem to contradict each other: on the one hand, postcolonial approaches on reading archives *against the grain*, in particular Said's *contrapuntal reading*,[21] and, on the other hand, Ann Laura Stoler's approach to read *Along the Archival Grain*.[22]

Drawing attention to voids and marginalized voices within archival holdings, in particular postcolonial studies advocated for reading documents 'against the grain,' suggesting that the historical condition of archives led historians in a particular, that is, 'wrong' direction. Their drive was to write a history "from the bottom up" by focusing on human agency of the colonised in gestures of resistance or silence.

In the form of *contrapuntal reading*, Edward Said has conceptually developed this demand further.[23] Said – a lover of music – borrowed the musical term 'counterpoint,' that is, the combination of two or more melodic voices that are harmonically coordinated but rhythmically and melodically independent, as a metaphor to interpret colonial texts by considering the perspectives of both the colonizer and the colonized, the perspective of imperialism and the resistance to it.

On the other hand, Ann Stoler argues that it is also important to read *along the archival grain*, that is, to rethink established assumptions about the function and workings of concepts.[24] Stoler's intention is to shift the focus from the content of the archive to its form, that is, to "move away from treating archives as an extractive exercise to an ethnographic one."[25] According to Stoler, colonial records fashioned "grids of intelligibility" from "uncertain knowledge" and, thus, can be considered "artifices of a colonial state [...] in efficient operation."[26]

Stoler advocates not to examine what is unknown and unfamiliar, but precisely what is known and familiar, and, mutatis mutandis, "going right where we have already been."[27] Reading along the archival grain means reading along the colonial anxieties trying to create a sense of order where there was none (or at least no order they could recognise and were willing to endorse), and thereby allowing moments of confidence in the effectiveness and legitimacy of their own power. Stoler focuses on the preoccupations of the archivists and their concerns on what is and is not included in an archive.

On the one hand, the strategy to read archives 'against the grain' involved identifying prominent themes, concentrating on singularities that disrupted the apparent narrative, and subsequently delving into the nuanced connections between them. This approach is crucial for bringing forth the anti-colonial perspective, which often lacks representation in colonial archives. On the other hand, screening archival documents precisely in the sense of reading them 'along the grain' brought affects and colonial anxieties and thus

---

for African history and culture: Essays in honour of Adam Jones (Leipzig: Leipziger Universitätsverlag, 2016) Adam Jones

21 Chowdhry, "Edward Said and Contrapuntal Reading"
22 Stoler, *Along the archival grain*.
23 Chowdhry, "Edward Said and Contrapuntal Reading"
24 Stoler, *Along the archival grain*.
25 Stoler, *Along the archival grain*, p. 47.
26 Stoler, *Along the archival grain*, p. 2.
27 Stoler, *Along the archival grain*, p. 31.

security logics to light, which can be deciphered in exceptional cases with the Copenhagen approach on the one hand and in routine cases with the Paris approach on the other.

4.2.1 Archives Visited

The involvement of many international actors in Togoland's decolonisation process dispersed its main archival documentation across continents. Due to the geographical distribution of the relevant documents, the archives were selected based on preliminary work and directories of other researchers working on related topics, which helped to include archives that would otherwise have been overlooked.

Archival research was conducted between July 2018 and Mai 2019 in five main sites (New York, Aix-en-Provence, London, Lomé, and Accra) and several secondary sites. 16,361 document pages (including petitions, letters, telegrams, reports, minutes) were collected. Interviews during the archival visits complemented the document analysis to break down the coloniality of the archive with collaborative approaches.

New York

In New York, the holdings of the *United Nations Archives and Records Management Section* (UN ARMS) have provided insight into the workings of the Secretariat of the UN Trusteeship Department. Benefiting from the ever-increasing availability of digitised documents in recent years, such as the verbatim minutes of the Trusteeship Council meetings published in the UN's digital libraries, the countless and steadily digitised petitions from Togoland, stored offsite at Long Island, were similarly extensive.

Since, contrary to UN policy, Dag Hammarskjöld's papers were not transferred to the UN archives after his death in 1961, but were taken to his home country of Sweden, potentially important correspondence between the former UN Secretary-General and unification/independence leader and later President of Togo, Sylvanus Olympio, could not be viewed. However, records of Andrew Cordier, Hammarskjöld's assistant, could be consulted in the holdings of Colombia University, where Cordier later taught.

The holdings of the New York Public Library provide insight into how the reunification and independence movement cultivated support with non-state, international actors outside the UN, for example Roger Baldwin, director of the *International League for the Rights of Man* (ILRM).

The Ralph Bunche holdings in *Schomburg Center for Research in Black Culture* (SCRBC) in Harlem, were of particular interest: Bunche was not only Director of the UN Trusteeship Department. As he focussed his PhD thesis on a comparative study of the French colony of Dahomey and the Mandate Territory of French Togoland, he acquired sufficient academic authority to partake in the UNCIO negotiations at San Francisco as member of the US delegation, leaving an influential mark on the working of the future Trusteeship System.

France

In France, the bulk of archival documents was collected in the *Archives Nationales d'Outre-Mer* (ANOM) in Aix-en-Provence. In addition to the holdings under the rubric "Affaires politiques" the holdings on "Délégation du Cameroun et du Togo 1947–1959" (DPCT) should be highlighted: the 60 boxes, which largely cover the Togolese trusteeship territory, contain predominantly documents of the French administration of Cameroon and Togo between 1947 and 1959, compiled by the French administration or downstream by French archivists. This collection illustrates the exchange between the regional administration and the metropolis as well as the communication of individual services, such as the security service.

The *Archives Nationales de la France* (ANF) in Pierrefitte-sur-Seine, Paris, were a promising place to start research on intelligence and security services. Of note are especially the holdings of Jacques Foccart, known as the "Grey Eminence" and chief adviser to French presidents on African affairs as well as his subordinate, Claude Rostain, responsible for Togo. Yet, document-ordering-deadlines that needed to be met several weeks in advance and a several months-lasting security clearances to view these "highly sensitive" documents soon put a stop enterprise during the brief research trip.[28] In contrast to the British policy of archive opening, the French one is still very restrained.

The *Archives Diplomatique du Ministère des Affaires Étrangères* (MAE) in La Courneuve, Paris, were of particular interest as regards correspondence with the French UN delegation in New York, but also correspondence with other embassies in order to seek approval or rejection for resolutions to the French liking or dislike, respectively. Although the administration of Togoland was under the direct responsibility of the French Colonial Ministry, questions of the General Assembly and the Trusteeship Council as a UN body fell under the diplomatic purview of the Ministry of Foreign Affairs. After Sylvanus Olympio's electoral success in 1958 (although Togo was still under trusteeship), the autonomy of the territory had progressed to the point where the French Ministry of Foreign Affairs, rather than the Overseas Ministry, took over Franco-Togolese relations. Most archival documents of the final but important transition phase from autonomy to independence can therefore be found in the diplomatic rather than colonial archives.

Much larger holdings, especially on confidential diplomatic correspondence with French embassies across West Africa, are stored in the *Archives Diplomatiques* in Nantes, especially regarding the weekly political and intelligence reports of the French Consul General in Accra, Charles Renner, who informed Metropolitan France about events concerning the Togolese unification movement on the British side of the Togoland border. However, due to extended renovations and construction work, the archive was closed during my research trip to France and subsequent trips were thwarted by the Corona pandemic – that is the misfortune of research projects planned far in advance.

Togo

The fragmentary holdings in the *Archives Nationales du Togo* (ANT) might disillusion researchers a little. The existing holdings on the French administration consist of a post-independence compilation of the leftover documentation of the individual *administrations de cercles*. Holdings from higher administrative levels are only scattered

---

28   See Jean-Pierre Bat, Olivier Forcade and Sylvain Mary, *Jacques Foccart: Archives ouvertes (1958–1974) la politique, l'Afrique et le monde,* Mondes contemporains (Paris: Presses de l'Université Paris-Sorbonne, 2017).

therewithin. It seems that unlike the British administration, the French administration was much more thorough in clearing incriminating records. Most of the documents, especially those concerning political or security affairs with the potential to compromise the French administration, went to metropolitan France, were burnt on-site, or destroyed by termites due to lack of protection. Finding aids, created in the mid-1980s and already quite worn out, were only sporadically updated by hand and have thus, over time, virtually become archive material themselves. To complete the inventory to some extent, there are also private family archives and oral sources, which are not easily accessible given the reluctance of some to open their archives to researchers on this or that subject.

The collection of the *Bibliothèque Nationale du Togo* next door is also meagre, but there is early secondary literature on the history of Togo by some French and Togolese authors, which was difficult to find even in France.

Britain

Regarding archival research on security matters, *The National Archive* (TNA) turned out to be a goldmine. Fortunately, in 2011, the British government lifted an embargo on colonial security papers. This was the result of a lawsuit filed by a group of Kenyans who accused British officials of deliberately removing records documenting extreme abuses and crimes committed by the colonial state during the Mau-Mau crisis in the 1950s. The ensuing investigation led the Foreign Office to acknowledge the existence of such records and to begin a lengthy process of reviewing and releasing them to the public holdings of the TNA. Known as the "Hanslope Disclosure", this release includes some 8,800 files from the late colonial period.[29] Although some of these papers are still withheld or censored for reasons of state security, they provide a previously inconceivable overview of security and intelligence work throughout the British Empire, including everything from intelligence summaries produced by local Special Branch officers to debates these reports sparked among local police and city officials.

Due to a lucky coincidence, some of the reports of the Gold Coast's *Local Intelligence Committee* (LIC) survived, though in an incomplete form. These reports were supposed to be burnt by the local Special Branch officer in the first week of each quarter while a return slip had to be returned to the *Central Security Committee* (CenSeC). Yet some of the return slips still bore their copies. The CenSeC produced its own material: the Political Intelligence Summaries. These were also marked "secret" and supposed to disappear. However, some, but by no means all, of their contents can be seen in the CO 537 series, where the edited versions are variously referred to as *Political Intelligence Summaries, Reports or Notes*. While the CO 537 series mainly comprises the "products" of the security services, the FCO 141 series brings to light how the British administration organised the security services. The series contains interesting material on Anglo-French cooperation in security and intelligence matters, how the Special Branch should operate in the future and how African staff should be involved.

---

29 Anthony Carry, "Cary report on release of the colonial administration files" (Foreign & Commonwealth Office, 2011), available from https://www.gov.uk/government/publications/cary-report-on-release-of-the-colonial-administration-files.

Ghana

The Ghanaian National Archives, called *Public Records and Archives Administration Department* (PRAAD), has a head office in Accra and a branch archive in Ho, capital of the former Trusteeship Territory of Togoland under British administration. While in Accra some documents of general nature were of interest for this study, the Branch Office in Ho was of acute importance. The holdings in Ho include some documents on the security architecture shortly after Ghana's independence and show how the transition was supposed to happen in relation to security services.

As Kate Skinner noted already in 2010,[30] the Ho archive is still awaiting improvements in storage and cataloguing. Moreover, it can be assumed that a not so insignificant part of the archive was deliberately destroyed after the 1966 coup that overthrew Nkrumah. In addition, an accident shortly before my arrival made research difficult. A large part of the holdings is stored in cellars, and shortly before my arrival, a particularly strong storm caused the storeroom to be flooded and many files and folders to be affected. Once again, I would like to thank the archivist, Augustine Julius Gede, who made documents available to me that have not yet been catalogued in the directory.

4.2.2 Challenge of Access & Supplementary Sources

Archives in France are slow to open due to French archival law, as files are still subject to a special clearance and security review procedure due to the 60-year retention period for documents concerning the private lives of individuals or the security of the state and national defence. For example, it was not possible to gain full access to Jacques Foccart's documents, which could have provided essential information on the strategic bearings of French colonial or post-colonial foreign policy. The staff member of the French National Archive, who had the appropriate security clearance, described Jacques Foccart's collections as "very sensitive" holdings. Thus, an exemption for consultation had to be applied for at the French Ministry of Culture, which they granted to me only partially after a 10-month waiting period. For historians of security, such procedures have a foreboding aftertaste. Only recently, the descendants of Sylvanus Olympio renewed their efforts to gain access to the French archives dealing with the assassination of Sylvanus Olympio on 13 January 1963.[31] In 2021, the Togolese bi-weekly newspaper *L'Alternative* ran the headline that France had sent French archival documents on the assassination to the family's lawyers.[32]

Another challenge was the selection of the documents, as the *Archive Nationale d'Outre Mer* (ANOM) has restrictive security regulations: Only 6 boxes may be ordered per day, regardless of the number or content of the documents they contain. Moreover, the explanation that, for security reasons, there is no Wi-Fi in the reading room, of all places, is perplexing in these times of advancing digitisation. Direct transfer of the collected docu-

---

30   Skinner, "Local Historians and Strangers with Big Eyes," p. 141.
31   Fanny Pigeaud, "La Famille Du Président Du Togo Tué En 1963 Réclame L'accès Aux Archives Françaises," *Mediapart*, 21 June 2021
32   *L'Alternative*, "La France Transmet Des Archives Aux Avocats De La Famille," 15 October 2021.

ments and storage in a digital archive in the cloud or server-supported optical character recognition are therefore not possible.

In addition, one challenge is the geographical span of the archive locations: the archival material on the French administration in Togoland is partly in the *Archive National d'Outre-Mer* (ANOM), partly in the *Archive Nationale* in Pierfitte-sur-Seine, Paris, or in the *Archive diplomatique* in Nantes, all several hundred kilometres away from each other. However, the archival sources on Togoland extend not only to the mandate powers of the two trusteeship territories, but also to the UN and to actors scattered around the world. For example, contrary to UN regulations, part of the correspondence between Sylvanus Olympio, former leader of the reunification movement and later President of Togo, and the then UN Secretary-General Dag Hammarskjöld, after the latter's death in 1961, was transferred to archives in Stockholm rather than to the UN archives in New York. Another example: Since Sylvanus Olympio was assassinated on the grounds of the American Embassy in Lomé in 1963, the documents on the still unclear events of that night, which are important for security policy research, are in the holdings of the US State Department in the United States National Archives in Maryland. Furthermore, due to Olympio's untimely death and thus prematurely ended role in the post-colonial order of the African continent, he was less received in documentary, cinematic or literary terms than some of his contemporaries, despite his prominent role in the reunification movement, in the UN negotiations, and the decolonisation process of Togo in general.

All these limitations, challenges, and the hurdles demand time, money, travel, and academic career privileges that structurally exclude a considerable proportion of historians from the countries concerned. Despite the pretence to do justice to postcolonial aspirations, this work would have been difficult to write without the privileged access to the field, archives, and academic support structures.

The underfunding of archives in Togo and Ghana poses problems for domestic and external researchers of colonial history. Since it is not only domestic archival material there that deals with interrelated history that Europe would rather forget, not only the local authorities should be called to task, but also the international donors. For example, the archival holdings in Ho were stored in a basement. A heavy downpour a few days before my arrival flooded the archives and soaked many boxes. The archivist on-site, Augustine Julius Gede, did the utmost while at the same time taking care of my requests. Personal contacts on site were immensely helpful when it came to finding basic documents that were not (yet) recorded in the electronic databases.

Regardless of challenges access and the hurdles, much material is destroyed anyway and lost to historical research forever. Efforts were made to think about this blank space and reflect it in the research question. To fill these gaps identified early on, interviews were to be conducted with former activists. This proved difficult, as many activists have since died due to the historical distance or were too young to be actively involved in the Togoland unification movement. What remained were contacts at universities and interviews with Togolese historians. Memoirs, autobiographical, or historical accounts for Togoland and the decolonisation period were also used. Inspiring were especially accounts of Emanuel Kodjo Bruce,[33] a tutelary of the German colonial administration, who accompanied the independence process, or the Ghanaian academic and politician, Obed Asamoah, who was born in Likpe, the traditional area of the Volta Region, and thus not impartial regarding the Togoland reunification question.[34]

Ultimately, however, non-recorded voices will always represent archival voids. To address this issue, radio, and film recordings as well as oral history conversations were collected. To get an impression of the context where the supposed security-related speech acts occurred and a sense of the narratives during the trusteeship period, photographic material and film recordings were used, though admittedly, these were almost exclusively recordings in which the white gaze operated behind the camera (or the microphone). These media gave a sense of the atmosphere in the UN negotiations and the rallies in the territories, which clarified the analytical context. Although they were not used systematically as a theory, these materials were helpful in the research process as they functioned as a sounding board to better understand processes of securitisation, and to locate rumours and narratives that emerged in the material studied. Furthermore, the photos presented throughout this study served as a basis of conversation for some of the interlocutors.

Oral History

Skinner holds that "oral history was critical to the de-centring of 'western' political-scientific theories and the re-centring of the ideas and experiences of African protagonists in political mobilizations and events."[35] Thus, many historians of contemporary Africa find that their methodological inclination towards oral tradition is challenged by the passage of time.[36] What is not written down now is subject to the vagaries of oral tradition or, in the worst case, lost forever and thus subject to speculation. Many of the contemporary witnesses to the decolonisation of Togoland are either deceased or were so young at the time that active key participation in the events was hardly possible. This is particularly tragic for historians working on their case as it makes the transition from contemporary history to archival history.

The history professor and former president of the University of Lomé, Théodore Nicoué Lodjou Gayibor, systematically takes up the main themes of the oral sources debate.[37] In May 2011, Gayibor invited historians, anthropologists, and archaeologists to meet in Agbodrafo, Togo, to take stock of the contribution of oral sources to the historiography of Africa and to examine the prospects for research. The resulting volume included several Togo-related chapters, which offer perspectives for methodology and

---

33 Emanuel G. K. Bruce, "Vom Kolonialen Zum Unabhängigen Afrika," (unpublished manuscript, 2007), PDF; Asamoah, *The political history of Ghana (1950–2013)*.
34 Asamoah, *The political history of Ghana (1950–2013)*.
35 Skinner, "West Africa's First Coup," p. 378.
36 Erin Jessee, "The Limits of Oral History," *The Oral History Review* 38, no. 2 (2011), available from https://www.jstor.org/stable/41440904.
37 Nicoué Lodjou Gayibor, *Sources orales et histoire africaine: Approches méthodologiques*, with the assistance of Moustapha Gomgnimbou, and Komla Etou (Paris: Harmattan, 2011).

analysis using oral sources. These highlight the pitfalls that await the historian in this field, including the disappearance of certain categories of informants.[38]

But, as Erin Jessee holds, even these approaches are not without controversy.[39] Oral history is valued for its humanising potential and its ability to 'democratise' history by making visible the narratives of people and communities that are normally missing from archives, thus bringing them into conversation with the narratives of the political and intellectual elites who normally write and disseminate history. However, considering her highly politicized research environment, Rwanda and Bosnia-Herzegovina, Jesse questions the idea that oral history allegedly promotes the democratization of history: "By uncritically disseminating the narratives of complex political actors who seek to delegitimize their governments or justify their involvement in mass atrocities, for example, oral historians risk inadvertently becoming part of the machinery of propaganda by promoting memories and myths that could be used to promote further bloodshed between communities."[40] The attempt to contextualize these narratives historically or politically compromises the very goal of allowing people to tell their stories on their own terms and giving them a voice not normally found in history or the archive. In other words, it might silence them. This is precisely what oral historians seek to avoid, for it undermines efforts to share and democratize the authority of historiography.

Interviews were only possible to a limited extent. During the research stays in Togo, Ghana, Paris, and New York, interviews were conducted with only a few contemporary witnesses that are still alive, but these were of great benefit. The interviewees exchanged views on current relations between Togo and France or Ghana and Great Britain. During the conversations, it became evident how contentious the role of the trustee powers was in the decolonisation process and the unsuccessful reunification attempt. When asked about perceptions and ideas of security, reference was immediately made to the lack of fulfilment of state tasks in the social and societal sphere by the current regime under Faure Gnassingbé or the government under Akufo-Addo. However, against the backdrop of violent unrest in Togo in 2017 and 2018, and the crackdown in Ghana in 2019 to 2021, one should be wary of relegating individuals and their readings to the accuracy of historical events in a study. Kwame Kudzordzi and Kosi Kedem may have been contemporary witnesses to the fate of British Togoland, but their interpretation is regarded as rather peculiar, even among Ghanaian historians.[41] Moreover, in the view of political actors seeking to delegitimize their governments, such as Charles Kwame Kudzordzi, for example, oral historiography is not immune from inadvertently becoming part of propaganda that seeks to promote memories and myths that could lead to, rather than prevent, an escalation of conflict.[42] Thus, it is important to distinguish between oral history, that is, orally transmitted cultural history and personal accounts of historical events. Undertak-

---

38   Nicoué L. Gayibor, Dominique Juhé-Beaulaton and Moustapha Gomgnimbou, eds., *L'écriture de l'histoire en Afrique: L'oralité toujours en question*, Hommes et sociétés (Paris: Karthala, 2013).
39   Jessee, "The Limits of Oral History"
40   Jessee, "The Limits of Oral History," pp. 299–300.
41   Most notably Amenumey, "The brouhaha over Togoland Plebiscite. The historical fact."
42   Jessee, "The Limits of Oral History," 300–301.

ing this study based primarily on documentary sources available in public repositories, which I am responsible for interpreting, seemed more sensible to me.[43]

Because of the present study's focus on archival documents, it is inherently subject to a bias,[44] which considering alternative oral histories suffers from what Edward H. Carr called "fetishism of documents."[45] Most of the actors who speak from the archives are colonial administrators, whose notions of threat and security are prominently foregrounded by the sources. Archive-based studies cannot avoid relying almost exclusively on the observations of European imperialists and their activities. In any case, the relevant archival materials for this study are located within Europe and North America and only to a lesser extent in West Africa. Limited to the same archival materials, few have attempted to emphasize the African experience during this historical episode, for example, through the inclusion of handed down oral histories.

4.2.3 Research Procedure & Evaluation

The research procedure was similar in each archive: to be successful in the search, it was essential to understand the 'logic of classification' according to which the archive and its catalogue were constituted. Often overlooked, the archival structures and accompanying comments provide information about colonial or security consideration for the provenance of the documents. For example, the accompanying commentary of the British *National Archives* candidly writes:

> "The general rule, as set out in a Colonial Office guidance telegram of 3 May 1961 on the 'disposal of classified records and accountable documents', was that successor Governments should not be given papers which, might embarrass HMG or other governments; might embarrass members of the police, military forces, public servants or others e.g. police informers; might compromise sources of intelligence information; or might be used unethically by Ministers in the successor government. [...] There would be little object in handing over documents which would patently be of no value to the successor government."[46]

Many documents were destroyed on this basis. In the case of the Ghanaian archives (PRAAD), the logic mimics the bureaucratic organization of the British colonial state. Documents from the Admiralty are kept under the entry "ADM" and are classified thereafter by topic and year. Although the archival documents were created in the same

---

43   Compare these reflections with Skinner, "West Africa's First Coup," p. 379.
44   Danso and Aning, "African experiences and alternativity in International Relations theorizing about security," pp. 78–79.
45   Edward H. Carr, *What is history? The George Macaulay Trevelyan lectures delivered in the University of Cambridge, January– March 1961*, 2nd ed., ed. R. W. Davies, Penguin history (London: Penguin Books, 1990), p. 16.
46   TNA, "Foreign and Commonwealth Office and Predecessors: Records of Former Colonial Administrations: Migrated Archives," accessed 03 April 2023, available from https://discovery.nationalarchives.gov.uk/details/r/C12269323.

period, the British National Archives (TNA) arrange the documents according to ministerial jurisdiction: "CO" for Colonial Office, "FO" for Foreign Office, "FCO" for Foreign/Commonwealth Office. This is significant because as a trusteeship territory Togoland fell under the jurisdiction of both the Colonial Office and, in terms of the United Nations, was assigned to the Foreign Office. The archival holdings of the Togolese National Archives (TNA) are not arranged thematically but according to the places of origin, that is, the administrative regions: the *cercles*. Therefore, a new strategy to read through the archive structures had to be adopted repeatedly to assign individual documents to a series and thereby reconstruct entire exchanges.

After reviewing the respective archive structure, documents relevant to the research project were requested. Depending on the importance and significance for the research question, the document pages were photographed, underwent optical character recognition, and then were transferred to a personal digital archive according to their position in the archival structure. Notes on the research work were made to record daily impressions and questions that guided the further research process.

After the material was collected, the evaluation process began. The methodology is based on the procedure of qualitative data analysis according to Mayring.[47] However, the evaluation process was not inductive, but abductively designed, that is, the formation and refinement of theoretical assumptions was always compared with the collected material and modified in order to draw conclusions about regularities.[48] The study uses content-analytical methods, but explicitly analyses the collected data as part of a colonial discourse.[49]

Based on the overarching research question, the evaluation was guided by sub-questions such as how was (in)security communicated and what experiences have been revealed in the process? Which threat constructions were mobilised (terms and categories)? What shifts in security communication seem interesting? How is threat interpreted and to which audience is it communicated? Which security mode is established and what function do individual security speech acts fulfil?

The digitized archival documents were screened using Citavi computer software. During an explorative screening, initial categories were formed according to epistemological interest and text passages were indexed accordingly. Subsequently, the items of knowledge belonging to a keyword were subjected to a second, more in-depth sequence analysis for individual arguments, to refine indexing on the one hand and to establish cross-material references on the other, for example, to reconnect documents that were separated due to the way the archive was set up with response letters in other holdings. In addition, following the pragmatic reading of the contextual strand of securitisation,[50] the material was examined for security terminology in a theory-based manner by identifying text excerpts in which certain terms occur together, for example, 'Ewe' or

---

47 Mayring, *Qualitative content analysis*.
48 Udo Kelle and Susann Kluge, *Vom Einzelfall zum Typus: Fallvergleich und Fallkontrastierung in der qualitativen Sozialforschung*, 2nd ed., Qualitative Sozialforschung 15 (Wiesbaden: Verlag für Sozialwissenschaften, 2010), pp. 21–27.
49 Landwehr, *Historische Diskursanalyse*.
50 Balzacq, "The Three Faces of Securitization," p. 172.

'Togoland unification' and 'threat' or 'danger'. These securitisation text excerpts were also subjected to the procedure presented above and evaluated in terms of power relations, positionalities, narratives, the political background of the debates, and ideas about actors' political strategies.

5. Historical Background: From Slave Coast to Mandate Territory

> "I cannot forget that the natives are not represented amongst us, and that the decisions of the Conference will, nevertheless, have an extreme importance for them."[1]

In 1884, with the Scramble for Africa, most of the Ewe people fell under the German protectorate of Togoland. Shortly after the outbreak of World War I, French-led troops occupied the eastern part and British-led troops the western part of the German protectorate. At the Paris Peace Conference, German Togoland was divided among the victorious powers; the eastern two thirds became a League of Nations mandate territory under French administration and the remaining third of (Western) Togoland became a mandate territory under British administration. Eventually, France wanted to keep French Togoland in the French Union and Britain wanted to keep British Togoland within the Commonwealth by integrating it into the Gold Coast. However, the new colonial border demarcation cut through the traditional settlement area of the Ewe people, which found itself split among three territories: the British Gold Coast Colony, British Togoland, and French Togoland.

After World War II, this division led to the formation of a unification movement, which campaigned first for the unification of the Ewe and later for the unification of both Togolands before the UN Trusteeship Council and General Assembly – a right which hardly any other dependent people had dreamed of having recourse to. While France and Britain saw their prestige at stake, the movement was perceived as a threat within the colonial administration and attempts were made to hamstring through various means. At the UN, acting as the Administering Authorities of the two territories, they presented the reunification thesis as a minority demand, unfeasible and particularly as a threat that could set a potential precedent for the balkanisation of the African continent. After years of tough negotiations at the UN between the Anglo-French and anti-colonial positions, political campaigns and colonial repression in the Togolese trust territories, an

---

1   TNA (London), FO 341/1, *Protocols and the General Act of the West African Conference*, Parliamentary Papers 1885 [LV mf. 91.435], Protocol No. 1, 15 November 1884, p. 11.

UN-supervised referendum in 1956 finally led to the incorporation of British (Western) Togoland into the neighbouring Gold Coast to form the nation state of Ghana. The unification leadership criticized this result, especially since it degraded the Ewe to an ethnic minority within Akan-dominated Ghana and further removed them from the Ewes in French Togoland.

5.1 Precolonial Era & Introduction of European Rule

5.1.1 From 'Gold Coast' to 'Slave Coast'

In 1471, the Portuguese were the first Europeans to reach the coast of West Africa, where they encountered several African kingdoms, some of which controlled territories with significant gold deposits, which is why the Portuguese navigators named the coastal strip "Gold Coast," where they built their first fort called "El Mina" (the mine) in 1482. Eastwards along the coast of the Gulf of Guinea,[2] only a few rivers manage to break through the sandbank that has been thrown up by the strong surf over centuries. One of these main rivers, 250km east of Elmina, was called by the Portuguese "Volta" (leaping water) because of its striking rapids.[3] Lagoon systems formed along the coast where the rivers did not break through the sandbanks. Because of these Lagoon systems the Portuguese would call one of their settlements 600km east simply "Lagos" (lake/lagoon). The Ewe, too, which would later settle between the delta of the Volta and the Mono, would name one of their settlements on the northern shore of one of these lagoons simply "Togo" ("behind the water"). Under German colonial rule this village became the namesake of Togoland.

Despite the ever-advancing conquest of the Americas and the beginning slave trade dominated by Portugal in the early 15th century, African populations were at first able to limit European domination to the coastal forts and the area they were able to secure within range of their cannons.[4] Since the number and the power of the coastal forts remained limited, the competing European powers depended for four centuries on African regents whose role in the incipient triangular Atlantic trade was that of slave procurers for the plantations and mines in the Americas. The slave trade along the coast was so important that from the 17th century onwards, Europeans marked the once Portuguese-coined "Gold Coast" on their maps as the "Slave Coast."[5]

---

2   Theories about the origin of the name "Guinea" assume either a corruption of "Ghana," the African kingdom the Portuguese heard about in the Maghreb, or "aguinaou," the Tamazight word used to refer to Black people south of the Sahara.
3   Sebald, *Die deutsche Kolonie Togo 1884–1914*, 11.
4   In any case, this limited exercise of power was primarily directed against European competitors: Even today, the cannons on the fortifications of Elmina point out to the ocean. Consequently, the ships of the other European powers, such as the Dutch, Prussians, Danish, Swedish, British, and French, sailed past Elmina at some distance and built their own forts on the Gold Coast. Even the Hohenzollerns, trying to tap into the transatlantic slave trade, maintained fort "Großfriedrichsburg" near today's Princes Town between 1683 and 1717.
5   Sebald, *Die deutsche Kolonie Togo 1884–1914*, p. 13.

5.1.2 Ewe Heterogeneity

Both older and current literature emphasize the historical heterogeneity of the Ewe – the trusteeship powers argued all the way to the point that the Ewe-speaking population cannot be considered as a distinct people at all. According to the traditional history of the Ewe people, following their migration from the Niger Valley, they settled in Notsé. In the 17th century, Ewe[6] and Ané settled in the coastal region between the Volta and the mouth of the Mono river. Fleeing from Asante slave hunting campaigns on Elmina, the Ané are commonly called "Mina." European cartographers and missionaries in the pre-colonial era used the term 'Mina Republics' to denote the decentralized polities along the Aného coast and its hinterland, though, the entities were neither always Mina nor politically republican.[7] Though ethnically distinct from the Ewe, they eventually adopted the Ouatchi-Ewe dialect. Although described as a single language group, the variation in Ewe dialects signifies that mutual intelligibility proved to be exceedingly difficult at times.

According to a myth later popularised by German missionaries,[8] the Ewe migrated from Notsé to the south around 1720 due to the excesses and insistence of King Agokoli III (1670–1720) to build earthen walls around the royal capital of Notsé. Allegedly, the painful memories of Agokoli's brutal and autocratic rule contributed to the Ewe's later aversion to centralised monarchical rule and tendency toward political fragmentation.[9] Although the accuracy of the myth is widely disputed,[10] the fact remains that at the beginning of the 20th century the Ewe were not a politically unified people but remained instead a series of some 120 clans ("dou" or "states"), each governed by a chief or a paramount chief.[11] This is where the securitisation of Ewe cultural history diverges from Jutila's assumptions about nation-building projects: instead of putting a securitised origin story in the service of achieving national cohesion, the effect of the securitising Notsé myth led to the opposite.

The political fragmentation is substantiated by instances of Ewe states fighting one another in concert with non-Ewe allies in 1750, 1767, 1776 and 1784.[12] Thus, while the Notsé myth is able to explain that the political fragmentation of the Ewe was due to fear of the *internal* threat posed by a dominant central state, such as Agokoli's rule, it also explains the Ewe states' vulnerability to *external* threats, such as slave raids by larger neighbouring and more centralized kingdoms like Asante to the west.

---

6 Around 1720, Ewe founded the village "Alome," which means "in the Alo bushes" and later became Lomé.
7 Samuel Decalo, *Historical dictionary of Togo*, 3rd ed., African historical dictionaries 9 (London: Scarecrow Press, 1996), p. 212.
8 Skinner, *The Fruits of Freedom in British Togoland*, p. 38; Greene, "Notsie Narratives"; Nugent, *Smugglers, secessionists & loyal citizens on the Ghana-Togo frontier*, p. 161; Keese, *Ethnicity and the Colonial State*, p. 233.
9 The Notsé dispersal is a major annual Ewe celebration commemorated in the *Hogbetsotso* ("Hogbechocho") festival.
10 Keese, *Ethnicity and the Colonial State*, p. 223.
11 Lawrance, *Locality, Mobility, and "Nation"*, p. 27.
12 Amenumey, *The Ewe Unification Movement*, p. 3.

Map 4: Ewe Settlements

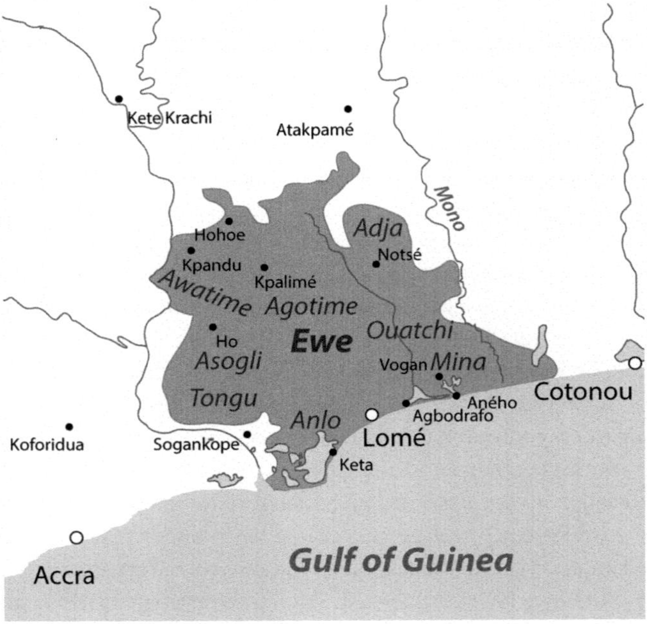

Source: Own creation.

In the 19th century, the demand in slaves led in part to an alliance between the Asante and the chiefdom of the Anlo-Ewe for slave raiding campaigns east of the Volta against the Krepi-Ewe,[13] who in turn fought alongside the Buems and Guans.[14] As Jutila also argued, that history plays a role in the securitisation of the other,[15] Skinner notes that the Togolese Ewe unificationists pressed history and past experiences of invasions and raids by neighbouring Ewe groups in their service.[16] For example, the Anlo, a faction of the Ewe who would later fall within the boundaries of the British Gold Coast colony, were opposed by many Ewe from Togoland not only because of their higher levels of education and elevated status. The association of the Anlos' past with the slave trade and the memory of their role in smuggling Ashanti armies into the Ewe hinterland in the 19th century were securitised in a way that reinforced a distinctly Togolese Ewe identity. In absence of a unifying precolonial Ewe identity, Keese notes that "[i]n all the warring after 1860s Ewe solidarity didn't play a role,"[17] which bears witness to the political fragmentation of the Ewe.[18] Skinner, Nugent and Keese stress the absence of any ethnic nationalism amongst

---

13 The Ewe settlements near the coast joined together to form an Ewe state, which became known as Anlo. Europeans remained in the dark about the nature of the Ewe-speaking interior, which they referred to as the "Krepe." See Skinner, *The Fruits of Freedom in British Togoland*, 5–7.
14 Keese, *Ethnicity and the Colonial State*, pp. 235–36.
15 Jutila, "Securitization, history, and identity"
16 Skinner, *The Fruits of Freedom in British Togoland*, p. 26.
17 Keese, *Ethnicity and the Colonial State*, p. 239.
18 Amenumey, *The Ewe Unification Movement*, p. 3.

the Ewe while the label "Ewe" in itself has to be regarded rather as a colonial invention.[19] According to Brown, the political agitation for and emergence of an Ewe identity is phenomenon of the late 19th century that was rather due to "the adjustment of boundaries in the interest of sub-ethnic collectivities."[20]

5.1.3 The Emergence of 'Eweness'

In fact, Enlightenment ideas such as that of the "Ewe-nation," were brought in from outside by a yet-to-be-formed Ewe-elite that was no longer entirely autochthonous in nature. The background for this development was the industrialisation of Britain, the number one maritime power, which changed the structure of Atlantic trade in West Africa.

Britain's need for new liberal type of 19th century Atlantic trade no longer required slave labour and the traditional coastal forts. The British banned the transatlantic slave trade in 1807, yet, since slavery had not yet been banned in the southern United States before 1863, there was still an extensive slave trade to North America, but also to cash crop producing states such as Cuba or Brazil.[21] British warships patrolled West African ports, such as Porto Seguro (today Agbodrafo). Testimony to the once Portuguese influence in the slave trade still bears on the naming of Porto Seguro ("safe haven"), which did not refer to the ability to dock safely at the harbour (the surf was just as dangerous as anywhere else on the coastal strip), but "safe haven" referred to the safety from the pursuit from British warships for illegal slave trade. British naval predominance slowly changed the balance of power on the coast,[22] monopolizing Britain's presence after 350 years of competition between various European powers. While British warships were spoiling business for Portuguese slave traders, Napoleon's campaign in Europe forced the Portuguese royal family to flee to Brazil.

The signs of the Portuguese empire's decline significantly set the stage for Brazil's independence in 1822 and several subsequent upheavals that were to become important for a forming Ewe elite. At the beginning of the 19th century, there were several slave revolts in Bahia, Brazil, to which the Brazilian state responded with violent repression and restrictions: free blacks were denied owning property and were subjected to strict taxation. When in the mid-19th century, the US-sponsored establishment of the Republic of Liberia (1847) gave rise to the repatriation wave of former slaves to West Africa, the 17-year-old Francisco Olympio da Silva, a mestizo of mixed Portuguese, indigenous and African descent, went along and migrated from Bahia, Brazil, to Keta, east of the Volta Delta in search of economic opportunities. Francisco Olympio dropped the "da Silva" part of his name, under which he had been a slave in Brazil, worked for a decade in the slave trade in various places along the coast east of Volta until he settled and founded the Olympio

---

19 Paul Nugent, "Putting the History Back into Ethnicity," *Comparative Studies in Society and History* 50, no. 4 (2008), available from https://www.jstor.org/stable/27563713; Skinner, *The Fruits of Freedom in British Togoland*, p. 12; Keese, *Ethnicity and the Colonial State*, p. 233.
20 Brown, "Borderline Politics in Ghana," p. 579.
21 Sebald, *Die deutsche Kolonie Togo 1884 – 1914*, p. 15.
22 The British administration of the Gold Coast Colony (now Ghana) was able to buy out the Danish coastal forts in 1850 and the Dutch coastal forts in 1870.

family in Porto Seguro, where there was already an emerging urban society, a bustling Brazilian community, and a Catholic chapel.[23]

In the 1850s, German missionaries of the Bremen-based "Norddeutsche Missionsgesellschaft", known as "Brema" for short, established their first stations in the coastal area of Keta and a few years later also in its hinterland.[24] Though missionary societies were not part of the approaching state colonialism (which at times they opposed in fact),[25] they certainly trailblazed it.[26] In their self-understanding and missionary vocation far from the life in Germany, the missionaries saw themselves as "saviours," rescuing the African population from the purgatory of the afterlife – a self-empowerment that was not far from the vocation of the *mission civilisatrice*. From the first missionary foundations of the Bremen Missionary Society in the early 1850s until the end of the German colonial period, only about 100 priests undertook missionary work, which according to Skinner was painfully slow. In the first decade of their evangelistic efforts, only fourteen conversions of 'free Africans' were recorded. This record led to about a hundred slave children being bought, 'freed' and converted between 1857 and 1868. The efforts were set back even further as the Bremen and the Basel mission station in the Volta basin were destroyed in 1869 by slave-hunting campaigns from the Asante in the Ewe settlement area.[27] And yet, these missionary ventures were the reason that most Ewe later found themselves in the Ewe Presbyterian Church. Even today over half of the southern Togolese elite are still Protestant, while the majority of Christians in French West Africa, and especially the Afro-Brazilian elite in the present-day Togo are Catholic.[28]

Due to their knowledge of several European languages, the new generations of "Brazilians," who were born and raised on the coastline, soon assumed the role of agents for the various European wholesalers from England, France, Portugal, and Germany, who settled on the coast founding outposts of their trading companies. The first German company, Friedrich M. Vietor & Söhne; established itself in 1874 in Be Beach (later Lomé), having already operated the trading business of the North German Mission Bremen in Keta in the Gold Coast Colony since 1857, whilst the trading house Wölber & Brohm was active in "Little-Popo" (later Aného).

For the operation of the European trading posts, the coastal chiefs and family clans, who considered the shore their legitimate domain, demanded both land taxes and export duties. Fuelled by the political fragmentation of the Ewe, rival chiefs often sought support from equally rival European powers. The 50-kilometer-long coastal strip east of the Gold Coast Colony boundary, was not yet officially occupied by any colonial power. Yet,

---

23   Alcione M. Amos, "Afro-Brazilians in Togo," *Cahiers d'études africaines* 41, no. 162 (2001): 293–95, htt ps://doi.org/10.4000/etudesafricaines.88.
24   Skinner, *The Fruits of Freedom in British Togoland*, p. 38.
25   Habermas (2016) highlights moments when the Bremen or Steyer Mission joined forces with the Togolese petitioners and denounced the ruling practices of the German colonial administrations in the Reichstag.
26   Rainer Alsheimer, *Zwischen Sklaverei und christlicher Ethnogenese: Die vorkoloniale Missionierung der Ewe in Westafrika (1847 – ca. 1890)* (Münster: Waxmann, 2007), http://www.waxmann.com/kat/in halt/1764.pdf
27   Skinner, *The Fruits of Freedom in British Togoland*, p. 43.
28   Decalo, *Historical dictionary of Togo*, p. 74.

British merchants clearly dominated in the growing presence of Europeans traders and missionaries.[29] By virtue of their own business interests, African intermediaries such as the "Brazilian" elites were trailblazers of British colonial expansion.

Francisco Olympio, who himself had grown up speaking Portuguese, initially had his two sons Epiphanio and Octaviano learn Portuguese from a Catholic priest. However, as almost all Europeans involved in the Atlantic trade used the English language, coins, weights, measures and legal norms,[30] Francisco Olympio sent his two sons to London to receive higher-level education in accounting and business. Upon their return, Epiphanio worked in the British trading house Miller Brothers in Agoué (present-day Benin). In 1902, Epiphanio had a son with a Mamprusi slave (an ethnic group from the north of contemporary Togo), who was sold to the Olympio family: the later Ewe nationalism leader, independence fighter, and first president of Togo, Sylvanus Olympio, was thus not himself from an Ewe lineage. Meanwhile, Epiphanio's brother, Octaviano, worked for the British trading house A. and F. Swanzy, where he secured commercial property for coconut plantations in the northwest of Lomé.

While the Afro-Brazilian community on the coastline was expanding, Octaviano became by far the richest and most influential indigenous citizen of Lomé. For six decades and under three colonial powers, he was one of the most respected members of Lomé's commercial and political elite.[31]

5.2 The 'Schutzgebiet Togoland'

With 1870/71 defeat of France, which was the leading colonial power alongside Great Britain, the German Empire emerged as the new great power in Western Europe, almost inevitably turning its attention to colonial policy. Although Otto von Bismarck had little to no sympathy for the colonial ambitions of large sections of the German population, the statement written in 1897 by the then German Foreign Minister, Bernhard von Bülow, "We don't want to outshine anyone, but we also demand our place in the sun"[32] soon became the new political slogan.

However, it was rather by chance that Togoland came under German control: In 1881, the French and British had received petitions from rival kings, each asking the other power for 'protection.' If it was not for consideration of other domestic power relations, either power could have occupied this territory permanently as a protectorate even before the Germans appeared.[33] Yet, in the run-up to the Berlin Congo Conference, which ultimately decided the colonial division of the African continent, the German Consul-General, Gustav Nachtigal, was traveling by sea to secure claims to Cameroon. Previously, Bremen- and Hamburg-based trading houses indicated their business interests on the

---

29   Sebald, *Die deutsche Kolonie Togo 1884 – 1914*, p. 15.
30   Sebald, *Die deutsche Kolonie Togo 1884 – 1914*, p. 16.
31   Amos, "Afro-Brazilians in Togo," p. 296.
32   James Holmes, "Mahan, a "Place in the Sun," and Germany's Quest for Sea Power," *Comparative Strategy* 23, no. 1 (2004), https://doi.org/10.1080/01495930490274490.
33   Sebald, *Die deutsche Kolonie Togo 1884 – 1914*, p. 18.

'Togo coast' and demanded political and military backing by the Empire. During an unscheduled stopover, Nachtigal intervened in a local conflict between German and British trade representatives, which led to the signing of a protection agreement with the Ewe-chief Mlapas on 5 July 1884.[34] The document was decisive for German territorial claims at the Berlin Congo Conference, thus establishing the protectorate of Togoland.

The Berlin Congo Conference, which at Reichschancellor Bismarck's invitation brought together 15 powers, ultimately cemented Germany's colonial-territorial claims to Togoland. Born out of the conference, the Berlin General Act echoed Edmund Burke's idea of humanitarian colonial trusteeship whilst the 'level of civilization,' which was still embedded in the concept of 'trust,' remained untouched. Edward Malet, the British ambassador to the Berlin Conference conveyed this conviction by saying: "I cannot forget that the natives are not represented amongst us, and that the decisions of the Conference will, nevertheless, have an extreme importance for them."[35]

Certainly, colonial trusteeship was only a pretext. The conference was primarily an attempt to contain an escalation of imperial tensions between European states and secure primarily private-sector access to the African continent before the onset of state-directed colonization. This was expressed through the *open-door* principle, which stipulated that the markets of the colonies were to be open to European traders and that no European power could impose preferential tariffs within its domains. This was a policy that was presented as beneficial to the economies of the metropolitan states and, in the spirit of the *civilising mission*, to the colonies as well.

Humanitarian aspects, such as the prohibition of the slave trade, were marginal, especially since the British Empire had already banned the slave trade in 1807 and abolished slavery in 1833. Yet the securitising narrative of a more regulated colonialism that had a civilizing effect by eliminating alcoholism or slavery provided legitimacy to the colonial project. It was only through the addition of trusteeship principles that a securitisation of the civilising mission and thus the legitimisation of the colonial enterprise, that is, the 'Scramble for Africa,' became possible. This colonial-securitising logic is evident in linguistic paraphrases such as 'protectorates' and self-empowerment through trusteeship responsibilities such as the abolition of the still rampant slavery – an irony, given that the European powers themselves were responsible for the emergence of the transatlantic slave trade. That this was only a hypocritical securitisation for purposes of legitimisation becomes clear when considering that the use of forced labour – as a more humane alternative to slavery – was presented as a necessary evil (exceptional measure) to civilise (or 'salvage') the 'less civilised people' (referent object). The need for trusteeship and the

---

34   While "occupation" was de jure only possible for territories that were unilaterally declared "terra nullius," "protectorate" presupposed an already sovereign state that voluntarily placed itself under the protection of another through a treaty. De facto, however, it was an occupation and the official designation of the German colonies as "protectorates" by no means clearly reflected the legal relationship. Rather, the choice of words "protectorate" and "pacification operations" was a linguistic de-securitisation of colonial violence. Hiding behind terms like "sovereignty" and "statehood" perpetuates the colonial logic of their emergence. Stefanie Michels, "Koloniale Beutekunst," *Forum Recht*, no. 3 (2011): 79

35   TNA (London), FO 341/1, *Protocols and the General Act of the West African Conference*, Parliamentary Papers 1885 [LV mf. 91.435], Protocol No. 1, 15 November 1884, p. 11.

civilizing mission were formulated in the *grammar of security*. Not surprisingly, during the Scramble for Africa, 'protection treaties' secured territories as "protectorates," whilst the German 'Schutztruppe' subjugated the "Schutzgebiet Togoland."[36] 'Pacification campaigns' were a linguistic form of de-securitisation of colonial violence. These terms "obscured responsibilities that would come with sovereignty from one state over another."[37]

5.2.1 Drawing Borders & Conquest of the Hinterland

The first years of German rule were mainly confined to the coastal region.[38] Bracketed between the British-controlled coastal strips to the west and French-controlled coastal strips to the east, the German colonial officials found themselves in a race with France and Britain to negotiate the course of the hinterland border northwards. This European race to penetrate the West African hinterland, that is, to draw the border in a north-south direction, perpendicular to the coast, cut for the most part through the population belts which tended to run parallel to the coast, that is, in an east-west direction.

Photo 1: Schutztruppe in German Togoland

Source: Bildarchiv der Deutschen Kolonialgesellschaft, Universitätsbibliothek Frankfurt am Main, N° 037–0601-35 (no date).

---

36   Wilde, *International territorial administration*, p. 300.
37   Wilde, *International territorial administration*, p. 300.
38   The German colonial central administration of Togo was initially located in Aného and only later in Lomé.

It was not until a decade after the signing of the protection treaty that the German colonial rulers extended their sphere of influence also factually northwards with a series of 'pacification', that is, punitive campaigns. In order to quickly enforce the colonial order, Bismarck ordered the establishment of a *Polizeitruppe* for Togoland just one year after the signing of the treaty of protection. The *Polizeitruppe* consisted mainly of African mercenaries from neighbouring territories and to some extend of 'ransomed' slaves who had to work off their purchase price at which the Germans acquired them. Since the '*Schutzgebiet*' did not have its own protection force, the police force was also used for military tasks and securing the territory against colonial competitors. An expeditionary company, the so-called '*Schutztruppe*,' was stationed in Lomé to be used in the event of uprisings.

Map 5: German Togoland (1885–1915)

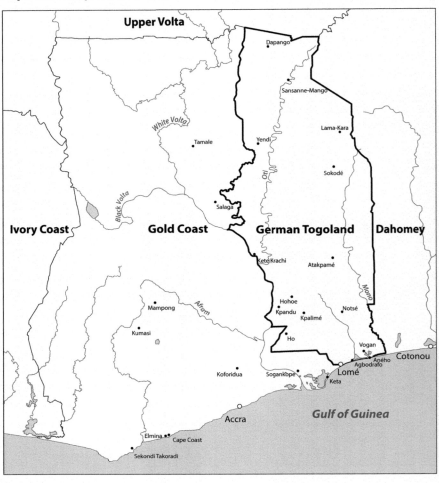

Source: Own creation.

Acting under the maxim of exercising control through the maximum threat of violence, the Germans concealed their numerical inferiority through a policy of selective terror. Enabling them to establish a monopoly of power, massacres and burning villages were considered the best means of achieving maximum intimidation with minimum use of resources.[39] Between 1894 and 1900 alone, the *Schutztruppe* was deployed on 35 campaigns and 50 smaller skirmishes. Uprisings, mainly local in nature, such as the Tové-revolt in March 1895, were soon put down. In 1896, Governor Otto Gleim used a trifle to justify an assault of the Togo-Village.[40] In 1896, the Germans defeated a 7000 men strong army of the Dagomba and soon destroyed their capital Yendi. This was followed by a punitive campaign against the Bassari. In 1897 an attack by the Konkomba defeated 23 mercenaries of the *Schutztruppe*. Commander von Massow responded with a punitive campaign, destroying 50 villages. Three other punitive campaigns were conducted against the Kabré. However, unlike in German East Africa and South-West Africa, no major anti-colonial uprisings took place.

5.2.2 Exploitation & Modernization

The German maxim was that colonies must be profitable. Yet, the colonial project was supposed to be economically affordable. The colonial administration imposed heavy taxation, which drove Africans into production for export. Those who could not raise enough money or goods had to pay 'muscle tax.' Since the German Empire, established under the trusteeship principles of the Berlin Conference, that slavery was no longer acceptable for 'civilisation' at the end of the 19th century, German colonial officials resorted to forced labour to realize these modernisation projects. In accordance with colonial logic, this form of exploitation also fulfilled the function of 'educating Africans for labour'. The Germans used force against those who did not comply. Togoland was soon known as the land of the 25 lashes, famous for the saying 'And one for Kaiser!' for the final additional lash. One of Lomé's neighbourhoods was dubbed 'Moabit,' after the famous prison in Berlin's district of the same name. Sebald notes that "Twelve prisons but only four schools were built by the German Administration. In Western Togo, which today is part of Ghana, the Germans built not even one school but four prisons."[41]

The Germans were primarily interested in colonially exploiting coveted agricultural goods such as peanuts, cocoa, copra, and coffee – but in particular: cotton.[42] Large cotton plantations were established along the coast and the German administration even arranged for an expedition of Afro-American cotton experts from the south of the United

---

39   Trotha, *Koloniale Herrschaft*, 42.
40   The Togo village was located on the northern shore of the coastal lagoon, Lake Togo, and could be reached by pirogues today as it was then. The name "Togo," which loosely translated means "behind the waters" in Ewe, was later to give its name to the entire area.
41   Sebald as cited in Kofi Amenyo, "Deutschland Uber Alles – What If Germany Had Not Lost Its Colonies in Africa?," GhanaWeb, 06 March 2017; Michael Weisfeld, writer, *Sonntagsspaziergang*, "Togo," aired November 17, 2013, on Deutschlandfunk, available from https://www.deutschlandfunk.de/togo-wie-der-niederrhein-mit-palmen-100.html.
42   Sebald, *Die deutsche Kolonie Togo 1884 – 1914*, pp. 93–98.

States.⁴³ To ensure that the goods could be transported quickly to the coast, in the early 1900s, the German colonial administration initiated large economic and infrastructural development projects. Africans were forced to build roads, bridges, and several railway lines named after their purpose: In 1904 a 350-meter-long iron pier with railway tracks was built in Lomé connecting the "Coconut Railway" (Lomé-Aného) and "Cocoa Railway" (Lomé-Kpalimé), which opened in 1905 and 1907 respectively, while in 1913, the 167km-long "Cotton Railway" (Lomé-Atakpamé) was opened. In 1907, a telegraph link from Lomé to Atakpamé went into operation. Hospitals in Lomé and Kpalimé were opened. One of the most outstanding and yet short-lived construction projects was the transcontinental radio station in Kamina, which, due to its size, was able to establish a connection to Nauen near Berlin, 5,000 km away, and which, due to its location, was important as a telecommunication point for the German Empire's overseas communications with its colonial territories of German Kamerun and German Southwest Africa.

Soon the myth of the "Musterkolonie" (model colony) developed, since it was the only colony that allegedly had a balanced budget.⁴⁴ German Togoland remained a minimal state and neither became a full-scale plantation nor a settler colony. During the entire German colonial period, the number of Europeans never rose above 500. It remained a modest trading colony whose foreign trade in the colonial economic peak of the "protectorate" reached just 0.1% of the value of the total foreign trade of the German Reich.⁴⁵

As to the societal effects of the German modernization campaign, Keese holds that there is no proof for a strong feeling of Ewe unity under the coming German rule.⁴⁶ Amenumey and Lawrance hold that "German rule had exceptional importance for the consolidation of Ewe identity,"⁴⁷ especially the missionary efforts, laying the basis for the resistance during the French and British mandate and trusteeship period: the Bremen Missionary Society, united the majority of the native society in a Protestant church. German missionaries established schools and conducted ethnological research on the Ewe language and culture. Diedrich Westermann, a pastor of the Bremen Missionary Society, standardized grammar, introducing the first Ewe language script and Ewe-Bible.⁴⁸ It was precisely under missionary efforts such as by Jakob Spieth that the Ewe were intensively exposed to German Protestant ideals of the *Volk*.⁴⁹

43　Andrew Zimmerman, *Alabama in Africa: Booker T. Washington, the German empire, and the globalization of the new South*, America in the world (Princeton, N.J.: Princeton University Press, 2010), http://site.ebrary.com/lib/alltitles/docDetail.action?docID=10640072; Habermas, *Skandal in Togo*.

44　Already in 1969 Amenumey pointed out that the "model colony" was nothing more than colonial propaganda; D. E. K. Amenumey, "The Pre-1947 Background to the Ewe Unification Question," *Transactions of the Historical Society of Ghana* 10 (1969), available from https://www.jstor.org/stable/41406350.

45　Trotha, *Koloniale Herrschaft*, p. viii.

46　Keese, *Ethnicity and the Colonial State*, p. 246.

47　Lawrance, *Locality, Mobility, and "Nation"*, p. 123; Amenumey, *The Ewe Unification Movement*.

48　It should be noted that the Anlo dialect was used to standardize the Ewe language and Bible, that is, an Ewe dialect spoken in the British Gold Coast outside of German Togoland.

49　Andreas Jakob Spieth, *Die Ewe-Stämme: Material zur Kunde des Ewe-Volkes in Deutsch-Togo* (Berlin: Reimer, 1906), https://archive.org/stream/dieewestmmematoospie#page/n9/mode/2up; Skinner, *The Fruits of Freedom in British Togoland*, p. 21.

5.2.3 Petitions as Anticolonial Resistance

Sebald was one of the first to document how, at the beginning of the 20th century, a protest movement was formed that did not want to wait for reforms from above, but rather, by relying on its own efforts, strove for change.[50] Since, under the conditions at the beginning of the 20th century, the success of violent anti-colonial resistance was just as impossible as the open refusal of a colonial order, in the last decade of German colonial rule in Togo petitions were the means of choice.

Starting in August 1902, by employing the services of Octaviano Olympio, who was by far the most influential Afro-Brazilian in Togo, the chief of Atakpamé, Kukowina, complained in a petition to Governor of German Togoland, Woldemar Horn, about the District Officer of Atakpamé, Geo A. Schmidt, who arrested the minor, Adjaro Nyakua, for unlawful rubber harvesting and, in the exuberance of his power, abused her.[51] Kukowina, whose complaint was not against colonial rule per se but merely against an excess of repressive measures, was referred back by Horn to the District Officer Geo A Schmidt. Yet, since Kukowina did not withdraw his complaint, Schmidt ordered to put Kukowina in prison, where he was subjected to such ill-treatment that he died upon his release in January 1903.

When Schmidt also took action against students of the Catholic Steyl Mission in Atakpamé, the mission made itself the advocate of complaints for Africans. The administration and missionaries turned to the higher authorities in Germany, by sending petitions and letters, including to the Reichstag, to (de)securitise the state of affairs in the German protectorate. However, in the sense of the *illocutionary disablements*, Habermas characterizes the treatment these petitions received as "eloquent silence," because stereotypical rather than realistic images of Africa and Europe were mobilized, thereby concealing more than bringing to the fore.[52] Habermas notes that the "very act of writing a petition must have seemed *threatening*, since the choice of the petition as a medium for expressing dissatisfaction presupposed a considerable political will and initiative on the part of the local population (or at least its elite)."[53] Habermas argues that petitioning meant using a medium of the colonial power (including writing and a European language) to gain access to a political space and to initiate a process of negotiation on one's own behalf, including a sense of entitlement to be heard as a political and social subject with legitimate concerns, which might not have had the same rights as a European, but was by no means without rights.[54] The potency of a presentation of grievances classified as a petition lies in its official nature. So, even if petitions were not granted, they may have been successful through sheer visibility. In short: petitioning

---

50   Thea Buttner, ed., "Leadership and National Liberation Movement in Africa," special issue, *Asia, Africa, Latin America*, no. 7 (1980)
51   Habermas, *Skandal in Togo*.
52   Habermas, *Skandal in Togo*, p. 130.
53   Author's translation, emphasis added, Habermas, *Skandal in Togo*, p. 131.
54   Habermas, *Skandal in Togo*, pp. 132–35; Bright C. Alozie, "Female Voices on Ink," *The Journal of the Middle East and Africa* 10, no. 4 (2019), https://doi.org/10.1080/21520844.2019.1684719.

expressed potential for anticolonial agency, though, petitions were part of a process by which colonial subjects sought to reform rather than to overthrow the state.[55]

The consequences were disillusioning Schmidt was transferred to German Cameroon, and the chief representative of the Steyl Mission and two critical priests as well had to German Togoland and were replaced by missionaries who subordinated themselves willingly. Octaviano Olympio concluded that no excessive hopes should be placed in the missionary societies and that the Africans should therefore formulate anti-colonial goals themselves. Starting in 1907, Octaviano Olympio, lead the indigenous leadership of Lomé, sent regularly petitions to the German governor Count Julius von Zech, demanding, among other things, equal treatment of natives under the law, the abolition of unwarranted arrests, chains and flogging, a better prison regime, the inclusion of indigenous representatives in government council meetings, tax reductions and permission to trade freely.[56] The colonial administration reacted with suspicion to every criticism and proposal for change, simply because it came 'from below,' because it was put forward by the African side. Generally, the administration considered these petitions as a fundamental attack on its claim to rule and reacted accordingly. Governor von Zech and subsequent governors reacted repressively to such petitions, with corporal punishment or fines. Occasionally authors of such petitions, including Octaviano Olympio, were arrested. In addition to petitions, newspapers were also put to the service of written protest. Although Africans were not allowed to publish their own newspaper in Togo, in the British Gold Coast colony, where the colonial administration relied on the much more liberal indirect rule, the African newspaper The Gold Coast Leader appeared weekly from 1902. There were no separate articles on Togo until 1911, but from 1913 on, in each issue one or two articles, mostly from anonymous contributors, dealt exclusively with German Togoland.[57]

Sebald noted that Octaviano Olympio seemed to accept the legend of the model colony in his petition and never mentioned German colonialists by name.[58] From a securitisation-strategic perspective, it is quite possible that Octaviano did not accept the legend of the model colony, because, after all, the Germans discriminated against the Olympio family to the utmost, but Octaviano knew how to use the legend of the model colony skilfully in his securitisation, because in Germany there would have been nothing more to fear if the legend of the 'model colony' burst like a soap bubble. Sebald himself noted that only the beginning of the World War I in August 1914 prevented the petitions from being discussed in the Reichstag. If the war had broken out only a few months later, the 'model colony' of Togo might have served as a very different role model for the other German colonies in the Reichstag, namely as a model for anti-colonial protest.[59] Not naming certain colonialists could also have been a strategic means of

---

55   Streets-Salter and Getz, *Empires and colonies in the modern world*, p. 413.
56   Amos, "Afro-Brazilians in Togo"; Habermas, *Skandal in Togo*.
57   Sebald, *Togo 1884–1914. Eine Geschichte der deutschen „Musterkolonie" auf der Grundlage amtlicher Quellen*, p. 171.
58   Sebald, *Togo 1884–1914. Eine Geschichte der deutschen „Musterkolonie" auf der Grundlage amtlicher Quellen*, p. 184.
59   Sebald, *Togo 1884–1914. Eine Geschichte der deutschen „Musterkolonie" auf der Grundlage amtlicher Quellen*, pp. 171–72.

securitisation, so as not to incur the wrath of a few specific people, but nevertheless to securitise the colonial situation with sufficient vagueness. Regarding Togolese identity, Sebald postulates with reference to Olympio's petition that "It was not until 25 years after the German takeover that African sources prove that, for example, the spokesmen of the anti-colonial protest used the term Togo. People began to think and act in terms of the new entity 'Togo' and to transform the term originally imposed by force by the colonial power into 'our Togo,' to 'Africanise' or 'nationalise' it."[60] Confronted with this constant and everyday threat, this inevitably led to communalisation among the local population.

The brute methods of the German administrators led to many inhabitants emigrating westwards to the British Gold Coast, where economic opportunities, especially in cocoa and mining, were more promising. At the Gold Coast, such a poll tax existed only from 1852 to 1861, but due to misappropriation of funds, the tax was repealed, and the imposition of poll taxes was completely abandoned because the colonial government relied on import and export duties on cocoa, which were cheaper to collect and much more profitable. The notion that British administration meant leniency and better opportunities for African advancement took root in the period of German rule.[61] Besides, Pidgeon-English, also spoken by the German colonial officials, was already the lingua franca on the West African coast. Africans who spoke English could simply make more of their lives if they went to the Gold Coast, where they could acquire citizenship rights.[62]

To regulate this migration and the flow of goods, strict restrictions were imposed between the two colonies and trade across the Anglo-German border on the Volta River was virtually halted between 1904 and 1914, until the outbreak of World War I.[63] Since it was expected that the looming World War I will be fought on the battlefields of Europe, no military had been stationed in Togoland. There was only the *Polizei-* or *Schutztruppe* consisting of a dozen German officers and about 500 local policemen. Indeed, the French and British allies achieved one of their very first victories in the Great on Togolese soil, only after three weeks (6–26 August 1915) with the surrender of German troops to British and French forces. While the British occupied the western parts of the protectorate, including Lomé, the French occupied large parts of the north and east (see Map 5).

5.3 Togoland under Mandate

5.3.1 Creation of the Mandates System

Bain notes that during the Paris Peace Conference, "[s]o long as the war remained primarily a European affair, colonial questions attracted little attention." Unsurprisingly for most of the press, the war took place primarily in Europe and the negotiations were thus seen as a European affair. Yet from the beginning, the mandate question was one of the most important and controversial items on the agenda of the Paris Peace Conference.

---

60   Sebald, *Die deutsche Kolonie Togo 1884–1914*, p. 165.
61   Welch, *Dream of Unity*, p. 53.
62   Sebald, *Die deutsche Kolonie Togo 1884–1914*, p. 158.
63   Brown, "Borderline Politics in Ghana," p. 578.

Ultimately the reasons for the establishment of the Mandates System are manifold, yet, it has been argued that political leadership, particularly in the USA, France, and Britain, was broadly committed to the development of international law in response to the crisis of World War I itself.[64] However, it is noteworthy that the victorious powers agreed on the outlines of the Mandates System within only three days (27–30 January 1919), indicating that, contrary to this historiography of international relations, the Mandates System was a rather spontaneous conclusion than an inevitable evolution of international law.

From the beginning, it was clear that France and Britain were averse to the idea to return the fourteen formerly German and Ottoman enemy territories conquered during the war, especially the former German colonies in Africa. France favoured the simple annexation of these territories. In fact, when in 1919, boundary commissioners were directed to avoid separating villages from their agricultural lands,[65] Hugh Clifford, Governor of the British Gold Coast, reported just a month prior to the Paris Peace Conference to the Secretary for the Colonies, Viscount Alfred Milner, that the French authorities pressured Togolese chiefs to sign testimonials in favour of French administration. The subsequent appeals made to the British led Clifford to the conclusion: "There can, I fear, be very little doubt that […] French rule in West Africa is in even worse odour among the natives than was that of the Germans before August 1914."[66] But in view of the approaching Paris Peace Conference the British Foreign Office warned Clifford not to fuel further discontent among the Togolese chiefs, as it might lead to a diplomatic incident with the French.

US President Woodrow Wilson, on the other hand, was aware that the League, as the new international peace organization, would become "a laughingstock if the annexation of enemy territory by the victorious powers were not invested with some 'quality of trusteeship'."[67] Therefore, he proposed to include in the Covenant specific references to self-determination and direct administration by the League.

A-, B-, and C-Mandates

Thus, during the negotiations in Paris, the dividing line of what to do with these territories lay between the demand for simple annexation, on the one side, and some mode of international rule, on the other.[68] The British defused the idea of direct international rule by advocating for indirect administration. As Pedersen pointed out, the British found Wilson's idea easy to accommodate because they fitted equally well with the British imperial practice of indirect rule.[69] Using the expression of a "sacred trust" once coined by Edmund Burke, the British delegation proposed an administration "on trust," that is, by

---

64   Chowdhuri, *International Mandates and Trusteeship Systems*, p. 3.
65   Coleman, *Togoland*, pp. 7–8.
66   As cited in Pedersen, *The guardians*, p. 79.
67   Tom Parker, *The Ultimate Intervention: Revitalising the UN Trusteeship Council for the 21st Century* (Sandvika, 2003), accessed 29 July 2019, available from www.bi.edu/globalassets/forskning/centre-for-european-and-asian-studies/pdf/03-03the_ultimate_intervention.pdf, p. 7.
68   Tom Parker, *The Ultimate Intervention: Revitalising the UN Trusteeship Council for the 21st Century* (Sandvika, 2003), accessed 29 July 2019, available from www.bi.edu/globalassets/forskning/centre-for-european-and-asian-studies/pdf/03-03the_ultimate_intervention.pdf, p. 7.
69   Pedersen, *The guardians*, p. 25.

the victorious states under international supervision.[70] The other powers, , were at first completely averse to the British compromise. Especially the French felt they should be compensated for the high price paid on the battlefields in Europe.

The proposal that eventually swayed the opposing powers was to create not a one-tier but a multi-tier system of A-, B- and C-mandates: A-mandates applied mainly to the ex-Turkish territories, which were considered almost "able to stand by themselves." B-mandates applied for African territories that were to be administered by a mandate power. C-mandates encompassed territories adjacent to territories of mandate powers and were created at the instigation of Australia and South Africa, which administered these as an extension of their own territory.

This classification ultimately reflected only the positions of the negotiators, but the Covenant's Article 22 legitimized the comprise by stating that "character of the mandate must differ according to the stage of the development of the people." It was Jan Smuts, co-author of the League of Nations Covenant, who based the Mandates System on the paternalistic foundation, which Cecil Rhodes once described as "the right relationship between whites and blacks in this country was the relationship between guardian and ward. This is the basis of the trusteeship."[71] Thus, in principle, the Mandates System reiterated the "sacred trust" spirit, which had been already established in the Berlin General Act.[72]

Yet, above all the proposed Mandate System yielded a decisively practical advantage for the French: the fact that the former German colonies, such as Togoland, were transformed into mandated territories under (limited) international supervision and did not *de jure* go to France and Britain as "spoils of war" meant that Germany could not count the loss of the territories as reparations already made.[73] Robert Lansing, a contemporary witness, noted:

> "Thus, under the mandatory system Germany lost her territorial assets, which might have greatly reduced her financial debt to the Allies, while the latter [France and Britain] obtained the German colonial possessions without the loss of any of their claims for indemnity. In actual operation the apparent altruism of the mandatory system worked in favour of the selfish and material interests of the Powers which accepted the mandates."[74]

The Mandates System functioned, thus, in part to retroactively legalize the redistribution of ex-German and ex-Turkish dependencies agreed upon in secret treaties during World War I.[75] Pedersen holds that "Out of this potent brew of liberal internationalism, imperial humanitarianism, and sheer territorial acquisitiveness the British proposals for the

---

70   The British Labour Party was against annexation.
71   Jan Christiaan Smuts, *The basis of trusteeship in African native policy*, New Africa pamphlet 2 (Johannesburg: R. L. Esson, 1942), p. 7. Pedersen's "The Guardians" is titled after this expression.
72   Bain, *Between anarchy and society*, p. 79.
73   Robert Lansing, *The Peace Negotiations: A Personal Narrative* (Boston, New York: The University Press Cambridge, 1921), pp. 156–57.
74   Lansing, *The Peace Negotiations*, pp. 156–57.
75   Thullen, *Problems of the Trusteeship System*, p. 11.

mandates system emerged."[76] Lansing noted that "[t]he principal European Powers appeared to be willing and even eager to become mandatories over territories possessing natural resources which could be profitably developed and showed an unwillingness to accept mandates for territories which, barren of mineral or agricultural wealth, would be continuing liabilities rather than assets."[77]

Given the fact that only Article 22, placed relatively at the end of the Covenant, dealt with the establishment of the Mandates System, colonial issues seemed to play a rather subordinate role in the overall composition of the Treaty of Versailles.[78] Nevertheless, Article 22 is one of the most extensive articles of the Covenant, which on the one hand indicates the importance given to the mandate question in the debates, but on the other hand also showcases the difficulties in circumscribing linguistically the sensitivity of the issue in the negotiations. The rhetoric of security legalized the principle of trusteeship and the *mission civilisatrice* in Article 22 of the Covenant of the League of Nations:

> "To those colonies and territories which as a consequence of the late war have ceased to be under the sovereignty of the States which formerly governed them and which are *inhabited by peoples not yet able to stand by themselves* under *the strenuous conditions of the modern world*, there should be applied the principle that the well-being and development of such peoples form *a sacred trust of civilisation* and that securities for the performance of this trust should be embodied in this Covenant."[79]

Here, too, the humanity-hierarchizing *mission civilisatrice* was the underling heuristic to securitising and thus legitimizing the transfer of territories under the 'guardianship' of mandate powers. Representing a precedent in the young history of intergovernmental organisations, the acceptance of the mandates as "a sacred trust of civilization" (extraordinary measure) was circumscribed to protect "peoples not yet able to stand by themselves" (referent object) from the "strenuous conditions of the modern world" (existential threat).

Another key concept expressed in the Covenant's section of the C-Mandates was the 'open door' policy. It was enshrined in the Berlin General Act, the League of Nations Treaty and later in the UN Charter articles on the Trusteeship and the Non-Self-Governing Territories. The markets of the mandated territories were to be open to traders from all European powers. This 'open door' policy was a key feature of the 'dual mandates' of the architect of British colonial policy and later member of the Permanent Mandates Commission, Sir Frederick Lugard,[80] who put it this way:

> "Let it be admitted at the outset that European brains, capital, and energy have not been, and never will be, expended in developing the resources of Africa from motives

---

76 Pedersen, *The guardians*, p. 27.
77 Lansing, *The Peace Negotiations*, p. 158.
78 Bain, *Between anarchy and society*, p. 80.
79 *League of Nations*
80 Lugard (1858–1945) was Governor-General of Nigeria (1912–19) and the British member of Permanent Mandates Commission (1923–36).

of pure philanthropy; that Europe is in Africa for the mutual benefit of her own industrial classes, and of the native races in their progress to a higher plane; that the benefit can be made reciprocal, and that it is the aim and desire of civilised administration to fulfil this dual mandate."[81]

On the other hand, imperial rivalries were to be defused by the open-door policy, which thus functioned as a security warrant. In other words, the joint exploitation of colonial possessions was codified in the Covenant to create mutual securities between the major European powers.

Similar security motives found their way into the section for the B-mandates. The League of Nations' strategy for preventing future wars lay in prohibiting the construction of fortifications or military and naval bases, as well as the military training of locals for purposes other than policing and defending mandated territories. After all, the Versailles Treaty and the mandate system were negotiated at the Paris *Peace* Conference. Brokering peace and *not* security was the top priority.

While South West and Central Africa are explicitly mentioned in the Covenant, Togoland and Cameroon were also put in the B-mandates because their peoples were regarded "as unable to express a rational choice as to the mandatory power to be selected."[82] Though at first, France did not want to accept the mandate system at all, especially the so-called A-mandates,[83] ultimately Clemenceau realised that the acceptance of the Mandate System, which largely corresponded to the norms and principles of British imperial ideals, mitigated Anglo-French antagonisms.[84] Nevertheless, the price for France's approval of the Mandates System was an exception to the general formula of non-militarisation envisaged for the "B" mandates: the French secured the right to raise indigenous troops in Togoland and Cameroon to defend the homeland in the event of a general war.[85] Furthermore, the C-mandates contained a clause that allowed the mandated power to administer the territory "as an integral part of its territory." France insisted on the introduction of a similar clause in the mandate agreements of Togoland and Cameroon. This clause was to reappear in the later trusteeship agreements and to cause some stir during the UN's founding conferences in San Francisco and London.

Redrawing Borders of Togoland: The Simon-Milner Agreement
When the main negotiators left Paris, some the sub-negotiators, who were tasked with settling all the remaining issues, seemed to want to throw some concepts out the window.[86] On 7 May 1919, the British Secretary of State for the Colonies, Viscount Alfred Milner, met bilaterally with his counterpart, the French Colonial Minister Henri Simon, to negotiate the final boundary between French-occupied and British-occupied Togoland.

---

81 Frederick Dealtry Lugard, *The Dual Mandate in British Tropical Africa*, 3rd ed. (Blackwood, 1926), p. 617.
82 As cited in R. B. Bening, "The Ghana-Togo Boundary, 1914–1982," *Africa-Spectrum* 18, no. 2 (1983): 193
83 Pedersen, *The guardians*, pp. 33–34.
84 Pedersen, *The guardians*, p. 12.
85 Chowdhuri, *International Mandates and Trusteeship Systems*, p. 60.
86 Pedersen, *The guardians*, p. 31.

After the two-week long Togoland campaign (the first victorious battle of the allied powers in World War I), the British still occupied Lomé, its port, and large parts of the German railway network, which France was keen on. Milner eventually consented to Simon's request that, due to the narrowness of Dahomey, its limited coastline and lack of ports, Lomé and the coastal area be exchanged for territorial gains in the north, which eventually united the Mamprusi and Dagomba under British rule.[87]

Map 6: Simon-Milner Boundary Accords (1920)

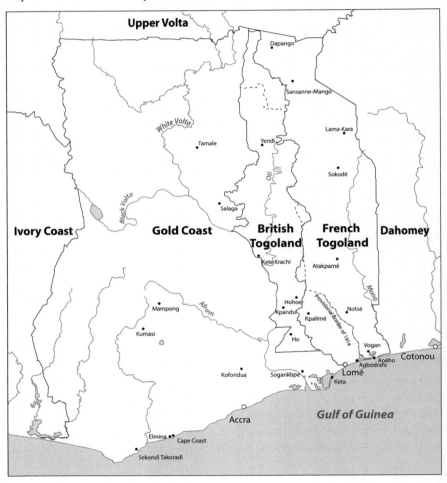

Source: Own creation.

Simon and Milner agreed that the "small strips" of Togoland should simply be incorporated into neighbouring French Dahomey and the British Gold Coast "without any

---

87   TCOR, "2nd Session" (1947), p. 321.

question of mandate."[88] Especially Simon championed the "pure and simple" annexation of Togoland to ensure the effective protection and development of the natives "towards a higher plane of civilization," maintaining that the "work of civilization, could only be carried out under the auspices of the sovereignty of a country," that is, French sovereignty.[89] But pressured by large sections of the British public, especially the Labour Party and the American delegation, the British Prime Minister, Lloyd George, had to put a spoke in the wheel of Simon's and Milner's colonial ambitions and maintained that West Africa could not be excused from the new mandate regime. Pedersen maintains that "[h]ad Milner and Simon been left to their own devices, they might have made short work of the mandates system altogether."[90] Thus, on 10 July 1919, with the signing of the Milner-Simon agreement, the eastern two-thirds of Togoland came under French control and the remaining western third came under British control.

The new colonial demarcation cur across the homeland of the Ewes,[91] who were was subsequently divided between the British Gold Coast, British-mandated Togoland, and French-mandated Togoland. A look at the population distribution of the Ewe at the time shows how Milner and Simon caused the future headaches of the two mandate powers:

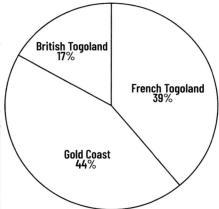

Map 7: Border Demarcation across Eweland (1920–1956)

Source: Own creation.

Figure 1: Distribution of the Ewe-speaking population (1947)

Source: Own creation. Based on TCOR "7th Session: Reports of the United Nations Visiting Mission to Trust Territories in West Africa" Supplement No.2 (T/793) (1951), p. 72.

---

88 Milner as cited in Pedersen, *The guardians*, p. 31.
89 Chowdhuri, *International Mandates and Trusteeship Systems*, pp. 46–47.
90 Pedersen, *The guardians*, p. 31.
91 Bening, "The Ghana-Togo boundary, 1914–1982"

Since the coastal areas were more densely populated, more than half of the Ewe-speaking population was under British influence, reinforcing the already strong 'British pull factor' on the Ewe. At the same time, more than half of the Ewe lived in a mandated area, that is, under international supervision, which was to provide the Ewe representatives with the argument before the international organisations that they should have a decisive say in their future fate as a unified people. If most of the Ewe had ended up outside the mandated area, then the international organisations would have placed the Ewe issue outside their jurisdiction.[92]

Proto-Nationalist Ewe-Petitions to the League

The division gave rise to several petitions by the *Committee on behalf of Togoland Natives*, which was made up by several English- and German-speaking Ewe chiefs and merchants and led by none other than Octaviano Olympio, Lomé's wealthiest merchant.

Olympio's plea first came to the attention of Alfred Milner on 10 September 1919, that is, only two months after the publication of the accord negotiated between Milner and Simon.[93] The letter, penned by Olympio, stated that the mere possibility of Togoland being transferred to another power "had filled them with great apprehension" and that they wished to be under British administration for "tribal, territorial, educational, and economic reasons." The dispatch further stated that "the absorption of Togoland in France's Colonial Possessions will sever members of the Ewe-speaking tribe in Togoland from those in the South-Eastern portion of the Gold Coast Colony and seriously interfere with their economic progress,"[94] and concluded: "The feelings of his Lordship's petitioners will be more clearly understood when they are considered side by side with those of the inhabitants of Alsace and Lorraine at the time of their annexation to Germany in 1871."[95] Olympio requested furthermore that the petition be placed before the League of Nations for due consideration.

It is difficult to say to what extent Olympio's petition was motivated by an authentic sentiment of Ewe-ness,[96] or whether he was using the division of the Ewe for a rather self-serving end. For sure, Olympio, as an already-Anglophile member of Lomé's commercial elite would have greatly benefited if his favoured protective power, Britain, would have remained in control over Lomé. Whatever the reason, it is not difficult to see that Olympio securitised the division of the Ewe by comparing it to Alsace and Lorraine – a fresh reminder of the recent horrors of World War I, as it was one of the very points of

---

92 There are only estimates of the size and proportion of the Ewe in the total population. The report of the first United Nations visiting mission to the trusteeship territories in West Africa puts the number of Ewe in 1947 at 800,000, of whom about 330,000 lived in the Volta Triangle of the Gold Coast, about 126,000 in British Togoland and about 290,000 in French Togoland. In British Togoland, the Ewe made up between one third and one half of the total population, in French Togoland more than one third.

93 United Nations (UN) (Geneva), R20/1/4900/3099, *Letter protesting against the present division of Togoland*, 1920, petition by Olympio to Milner, 16 September 1920 [p. 2]

94 As cited in Welch, *Dream of Unity*, p. 57.

95 As cited in TCOR, "2nd Session" (1947), p. 322.

96 Keese, *Ethnicity and the Colonial State*, p. 248.

contention that brought the archenemies, France and Germany, to the trenches of the Great War.

Although at the Paris Peace Conference, George Lloyd, Woodrow Wilson, and Jan Smuts had made proposals on the right of mandated peoples to petition,[97] it was Henri Simon who argued that if a right to petition would be granted to individual inhabitants of mandated territories "all administration would be impossible."[98] Thus, Milner, who had personally negotiated the partition of German Togoland, simply rejected Olympio's petition. Thus, Olympio sent his complains protesting the introduction of French rule in Togoland to promising anti-colonial advocates, the most prominent of which was US President Harding. Olympio stated:

> "Togoland handed to a Government other than British is a ruin to Togoland because of its connection with the Gold Coast. [...] Please allow us to say that the French method of administration as we see it is worse than that of the Germans... During the German regime there were some methods of administration which we disliked and protested against; now they are being recalled into the colony, such a as the poll-tax, market-tax, forced labour, oppression, etc."[99]

Furthermore, Olympio made use of his contacts from his time in Liverpool, sending cables to representatives in Liverpool's Chamber of Commerce, the Liverpool-based *Association of West African Merchants*, and to correspondents of the *Daily Telegraph*, whereby his petitions made their way into English newspapers and thus, by January 1921, came to the attention of the League's Council.[100]

Togobund

Not a year had passed since the Simon-Milner-Accord when in 1920 African pupils, employees, and ex-clerks of the former German Togoland, who were now unemployed due to the changed language skills required on both sides of the new border, founded the *Bund der deutschen Togoländer* (Togobund). The Togobund was largely led by Ewe-exiles from French Togoland living in Accra. Notable members were Emmanuel Bruce and Gerald Otto Awuma. It is difficult to estimate how large the audience of the Togobund was, but it may have gone beyond a few nostalgic ex-clerks as Germanophilia was widespread among the common people and the advanced elite.

---

97   Momirov, "The Individual Right to Petition in Internationalized Territories," p. 217.
98   As cited in Pedersen, *The guardians*, p. 78.
99   Raymond Leslie Buell, *The Native Problem in Africa* 2 (New York: Macmillan, 1928), p. 362.
100 United Nations (UN) (Geneva), R20/1/4900/3099, *Letter protesting against the present division of Togoland*; See also Pedersen's analysis Pedersen, *The guardians*, p. 79.

Photo 2: Meeting of the Togobund, Accra (26 July 1931)[101]

Source: Bildarchiv der deutschen Kolonialgesellschaft, Universitätsbibliothek Frankfurt am Main, N° 041-0235-52.

The Togobund took a strong interest in ameliorating the impoverished lives of peasant communities, claimed support throughout partitioned Eweland. With the establishment of German colonial rule, almost all the Ewe chiefdoms had been united under one rule for the first time in their history, while now since World War I they saw themselves separated again. The German period had left behind the memory of a region that was less artificially fragmented than it had been after 1919, and the memory fed resentment. This promoted nationalist efforts for unity, especially among parts of the Ewe elite, as they also manifested themselves in the German Togobund. The Togobund's own designation "Bund deutscher *Togoländer*" was the first self-reference expressing a "Togolese" identity, although its membership and activities drew mainly from the Ewe population.

Lawrance holds that "the amorphous idea of Togolese unity was superimposed on a more tangible concept of Ewe unity, [...] Bundism was an evolving and changing Ewe expression of Togolese nationalism, [...] its failure provides an important explanation for the failure of the post-war Ewe Reunification Movement."[102]

Petitions to the League

Octaviano Olympio also petitioned directly to the newly created League of Nations.[103] Since its Permanent Mandates Commission (PMC), responsible for the supervision of the mandate administrations, has not yet been convened, its designated director, William

---

101 Translation: "Our faithful Togo people in exile."
102 Lawrance, *Locality, Mobility, and "Nation"*, p. 122.
103 Amenumey, *The Ewe Unification Movement*, pp. 22–26.

Rappard, saw no other alternative than to forward selected protests (among them Olympio's petition) to individuals of the Commission and state representatives of the League's Council. As Momirov posits: "Understandably, such practice of in fact un-institutionalized blaming and shaming of certain mandatory powers was not welcomed with fanfare."[104] Even before the first meeting of the PMC in October 1921, the Council had already received 71 petitions (most of them from the A-mandates, such as Palestine and Syria)[105] and a petition from Palestine, received in July 1921 represented the last straw for the British. The new minister of colonies, Winston Churchill, stated that it was "obviously unsuitable that petitions of this nature which are generally *ex parte* statements directed either against His Majesty's Government or against the local Government, should be circulated in this way."[106]

As such, the matter of petitions and their circulation was raised at the very first meeting of the PMC in October 1921, but the commission refused to formalize the growing petition practice. Fearful of the power und publicity, which the petitions might confer on colonial subjects, the British drafted procedural rules for the petition process,[107] that were modelled on the minority regime of the League of Nations and distinguished remedially between "receivable" and "non-receivable" petitions.[108]

Receivable petitions could not

- stem from an anonymous source,
- cover ground already gone over by another petition,
- be composed in a 'violent language,'[109] and
- call the terms of the mandate itself into question.[110]

While the rule not to question the Mandates System quite literally ruled out its securitisation in the first place, the rule on 'violent language' represented *locutionary silencing* in a particular aspect. The requirement that petitions not be written in "violent language" did not refer to the use of swear words, but to descriptive terms such as 'terror, atrocities, or bloodshed.'[111]

While 'receivable' petitions had to be submitted through the mandate power, oral hearings were ruled out entirely. The issue of oral hearings was discussed at the 3rd, 8th, and 9th Sessions of the PMC, which rarely was able to make an informed decision on a

---

104 Momirov, "The Individual Right to Petition in Internationalized Territories," p. 217.
105 van Ginneken, "Volkenbondsvoogdij," 205, footnote 9.
106 TNA (London), FO 371/7051, *League of Nations*, 1921, "Churchill to the Premiers of Australia, New Zealand and South Africa", 14 July 1921, p. 109–110.
107 Submission to the League of Nations of Petitions from Inhabitants of Mandated Territories; Memorandum by the British Representative of Procedure to be Adopted.
108 League of Nations, *The Mandate system: origin, principles, application*, Series of League of Nations Publications (Geneva), p. 41.
109 For the origine within the League's minority regime see Cowan, "Who's Afraid of Violent Language?"
110 The proposal presented through a report to the Council was adopted in January 1923; see League of Nations, *Official Journal* (1923) League of Nations Official Journal 4, no. 3, 298–300, 1427.
111 Cowan, "Who's Afraid of Violent Language?," p. 283.

petition as it was not empowered to hear the petitioner in person. As was to be expected, all mandate powers rejected this proposal because it would render the petition procedure comparable to court proceedings, which were regarded "inconsistent with the very nature of the mandatory system."[112] As Balakrishnan Rajagopal rightfully noted: "The net result of this policy was that the PMC adopted or was made to adopt by the council an *attitude of containment* towards the petitions, wherein the most serious allegations were either *put off by bureaucratic techniques.*"[113]

Petitions that were considered receivable were referred to a member of the PMC who functioned as a "rapporteur." After discussing the petition in closed session with an accredited representative of the respective mandate power, the rapporteur formulated his/her own conclusions for submission to the Council.[114] After discussing petitions received, the PMC could decide which petition (if any) should be circulated to the Council. The minutes of the meeting at which the petitions were discussed had to be attached. The Council, dominated by the four permanent members, Britain, France, Italy, and Japan had the power decide if there are reasons for circulating any of these petitions to other members of the League, which they usually did not find.[115]

Most petitions that *reached* the League, about 87% (2,642), were considered 'receivable'. However, this seemingly positive statistic was overshadowed by the fact that petitions had to be submitted via the mandate power itself. But many potential petitioners were discouraged from submitting their petitions directly to the mandate powers for fear of consequences. Furthermore, as Pedersen notes, it is impossible to estimate how many petitions were sorted out.[116] In the 25 years of the formal existence of the Mandates System, only one petition was received from British Togoland, 71 from French Togoland and 3 from both territories. Regardless, most of the petitions that were considered 'receivable' never got far because the PMC had little external information and was unable to conduct independent investigations with which to challenge the mostly negative response of the mandate powers.[117]

An instructive example of petitions against the abuses of rule in French Togoland is the case of the Adjigo family. Like most influential families on the Togo coast, the Adjigo family was an Anglophone merchant family that had riveled with the Lawson family over the stoolship of the Togolese town of Aného, the early capital of German Togoland. Before the war, the German colonial administration had decided to use the Lawson family for its own purposes and deported the Adjigo family to Atakpamé up north. When, after the war, the French Mandate was established, the Adjigos hoped to be rehabilitated. However, France's first governor, Auguste Bonnecarrère, did not rehabilitate the

---

112 League of Nations, *The Mandate system*, p. 41.
113 Emphasis added; Balakrishnan Rajagopal, *International law from below: Development, social movements, and Third World resistance* (Cambridge, U.K, New York: Cambridge University Press, 2003), https://search.ebscohost.com/login.aspx?direct=true&scope=site&db=nlebk&db=nlabk&AN=120466, p. 69.
114 Chowdhuri, *International Mandates and Trusteeship Systems*, p. 206.
115 League of Nations, *Official Journal* (1923) *League of Nations Official Journal* 4, no. 3, p. 300.
116 Pedersen, *The guardians*, pp. 86–87.
117 Hall, *Mandates, Dependencies and Trusteeship*, p. 202.

Adjigo family, but sent their leaders to "obligatory residence" in northern Togoland. After the Adjigos' own appeals to return from exile failed, the Gold Coast lawyer, Joseph Ephraim Casely Hayford, took on their case and sent three successive petitions to the PMC on their behalf. As a lawyer, Casely Hayford addressed the PMC as the "final Court of appeal."[118] The largest petition he sent amounted to over one hundred pages, including at least thirty appendices. Yet, the PMC rejected Casely Hayford's petitions. More to the point, the PMC's French member, Pierre Orts, claimed that representation of a single family by a foreign lawyer was "an abuse of the right of petition," adding that Casely Hayford had falsely claimed that the French administration had not forwarded one of his petitions to the PMC. The PMC's refusal to accept Casely Hayford's petition was particularly absurd because Paris itself later called French Togoland's Governor Bonnecarrère to order and nearly removed him (albeit for reasons other than the petition). Finally, the Adjigo family returned from exile.

Anique van Ginneken compiled a comprehensive set of statistics on petitions that reached the PMC.[119] She establishes that until the League's dissolution in 1945, the PMC received in total 3,044 petitions among which it considered 13% (402) as 'not receivable': 4 were anonym (rule a), 183 raised issues that were already dealt with by the PMC (rule b), 19 contained 'violent language' (rule c), and 49 were protesting the Mandates System (rule d). For the remainder, the PMC considered them either not within its competence (67), too general (41), vague (24), or trivial (12).[120] These petitions underwent classic *locutionary silencing* because they were either not forwarded to the League or classified as 'not-receivable'.

In quantitative terms 80% of petitions were either rejected (1,638) or no decision was found (841), whilst of all petitions only 14% (416) were partially and 5% (149) were fully 'considered'. 'Considered', however, did not automatically mean that a petition was acted upon according to its demands, but merely that the PMC made a recommendation to the respective mandate power. In fact, the League pronounced 15 reprimands against France and one against Britain for not acting on the petitions that emanated from Togoland.

As Pedersen notes, most petitions 'failed' because they clashed with the mandate powers' conception of the system, that is, not to challenge the basic premises of the system itself. After all, territories were placed under mandate because their inhabitants were "not yet able to stand by themselves."[121] Though, almost three-quarters of all petitions were essentially political in nature,[122] remarks such as that petitioners from mandated territories 'do not understand the terms of the mandate system' usually disqualified criticism towards the mandate powers because the petitioners' alleged backwardness rendered them incapable of recognising their need for foreign rule. In fact, the very proposal that established the rules of procedure of the PMC stated that "peoples of a less-advanced civilisation are always ready to address, to any authority, complaints

---

118 Lawrance, *Locality, Mobility, and "Nation"*, p. 55.
119 The research results regarding the numbers, origin, nature and effect of the mandate petitions are those of van Ginneken, "Volkenbondsvoogdij," pp. 211–18.
120 The reason for the three remaining petitions is not known.
121 *League of Nations*
122 van Ginneken, "Volkenbondsvoogdij," p. 214.

about the most insignificant matters for reasons which have little, if any, foundation"[123] Thus, the PMC's civilizational attitude, which was formalized in the Covenant's mandate article, indicated *illocutionary disablement*, while the overwhelming majority of petitions underwent *illocutionary frustration* because they were either rejected or no decision was found because the PMC was incapable to challenge the negative response of Mandate Powers.

5.3.2 French & British Togoland under Mandate

The period of French mandated Togoland can roughly be divided into two phases: The first phase (1922–1930) was characterised by the new role of the chiefs in conjunction with a relatively prosperous economic climate.

French Mandate Organisation

Akin to the other French possessions in West Africa, the mandate administration was highly centralized: at the top of the administration was the Governor, the *Commissaire de la République*, who reported directly to the Ministry of the Colonies in Paris at Rue Oudinot and not to the AOF Governor-General in Dakar. The highest colonial officials at the regional level were the 7 *Commandant de Cercle* (district commissioners) to whom the total of 11 *Chefs de Subdivision* were subordinate. The French established a rigid hierarchical system of Chiefs (*chefs du village*) and superordinate Paramount Chiefs (*chefs du canton*), each of whom had a set of responsibilities in a descending hierarchy of power. Chiefs had the task of transmitting and supervising the execution of directives and orders from the district commissioner, controlling the activities of their subordinate chiefs, whose most important functions were the census and the collection of the poll tax.[124]

African participation in government was limited to the so-called *Conseils de Notables*. Each composed of up to 30 elected rural or urban chiefs, the councils had only an advisory function in the areas of taxation, public works, and the local budget. This experiment with elected offices displaced the former role of urban tribal chiefs and village heads in administration.[125] Needless to say, the influential Octaviano Olympio was the president of the *Conseil des Notables* in Lomé. Nonetheless, these *Conseils de Notables* had little influence on the decisions of the district commissioners.

The French colonial doctrines, which were also applied to the mandate territories, were politically underpinned by a sense of cultural mission of the *civilisation française*. Based on the unquestioned superiority of French culture and its suitability for all populations, a basic tenet of French colonial policy in Africa was the slow cultural *assimilation* of the colonial population. Those colonial subjects who had acquired the characteristics of French civilization, that is, French language, dress, customs, education, religion, were accorded the status of *assimilé* or *evolué*. With this status came the right to vote, jurisdiction under French civil and criminal law (instead of customary law), and exemption from the *indigénat* code. Introduced in 1924, the *indigénat* code replaced constitutional rights

---

123 League of Nations, *Official Journal* (1923) *League of Nations Official Journal* 4, no. 3.
124 Lawrance, *Locality, Mobility, and "Nation"*, p. 47.
125 Lawrance, *Locality, Mobility, and "Nation"*, p. 19.

of indigenous people (*indigènes*) and applied them exclusively to Europeans and *assimilés* (citoyens). Ironically, the League of Nations itself was a factor in this development, for in order to prevent a "creeping annexation" of mandate territories, in 1923 the League of Nations disallowed the mandate powers to grant citizenship to mandate residents – only "naturalisation" was allowed.[126] The de facto restriction of civil and political liberties allowed the French administrators for example to impose forced labour or to sentence the natives according to customary law (instead of French civil and criminal law). The gross abuses and often arbitrary application of the *indigénat* code was one of the greatest sources of emerging anti-French sentiment within French Togoland.[127]

Active until the late 1940s, the Togobund sent a stream of petitions to the PMC from 1925 on, documenting what it described as human rights violations such as arbitrary arrest and called on the League of Nations to persuade France to leave and reunify Togoland under German control.[128] The Togobund's strategy was aimed at discrediting the French regime and showing its unfitness to rule. This mythologisation of the German rule (which is still widespread today) did not arise on its own merits but can rather be understood as a means of criticising the French regime. The French feared the ambitions of the Togobund since their goal was to take the French possessions away. The French in return did their best to deny the Togobund access to the international press and to send representatives to the PMC. Eventually, the PMC did not address the demands of the petitions, holding the restitution of the territory to Germany to be incompatible with the provisions of the Mandates System.[129]

As a counterweight to the Togobund, which put itself at the service of the colonial claims of Hitler's Third Reich, the French Governor Montagne founded on 5 September 1936 a *Cercle des Amitiés Françaises* whose vice-presidency was assumed by one of the most respected merchants of Lomé: Sylvanus Olympio. Dormant at the beginning, the *Cercle des Amitiés Française* led to the foundation of the *Comité du l'Unité Togolaise du Nord et du Sud* by decree in 1941.

Security under Mandate

Between 1920 and 1946, many developments took place in the field of colonial forces of order, which were a Foucauldian-like "institution of permanent reform."[130] The security architecture of the French Empire was organised along colonial rather than populace-protection lines. Thus, the directors of the General Security AOFs were not chosen from among senior officers of the municipal police but from among the colonial administrators, as the colonial ministry preferred 'specialists in the colonial field' rather than in policing techniques in this position. Due to the mandate status, things in Togoland were

---

126 Gouvernement Français, "Rapport Annuel: 1955" T/1300 (1957)
127 Gregory Mann, "What Was the Indigénat?," *Journal of African History* 50, no. 3 (2009), https://doi.org/10.1017/S0021853709990090.
128 SDN, R 37 FMT (12226) N°32095: "Wir Togoleute hatten uns s[einer] Zeit *freiwillig* unter deutschen Schutz gestellt, während wir unter die französische Herrschaft *gezwungen* wurden" (emphasis in original). Lawrance, *Locality, Mobility, and "Nation"*, p. 224.
129 PMC, 15th Session. C.305 M.105 VI. p. 10.
130 Glasman, *Les corps habillés au Togo*, p. 189.

forced to take a different direction. The *tirailleurs sénégalais*, responsible for the territorial defence of French West Africa, had been deployed in Togoland since the campaign of World War I. However, Togoland's mandate status prohibited the conscription of military forces except for police purposes. Since the PMC insisted on the withdrawal of the *tirailleurs sénégalais*, France therefore created in 1924 from the territory's own budget a police force, the so-called *garde indigène*, which consisted mainly of mercenaries trained and led by French officers. The French administration then separated from the *garde indigène* a so-called *companie de milice*, which it stationed in various parts of the territory from 1927 onwards. The *companie de milice* could be reinforced by reservists at any time. It was subordinate to the West African General Command. The *companie de milice* thus became a kind of substitute army and elite force of the *garde indigène*. Moreover, it offered an advantage over regular armed forces, as the militias' costs were much lower than the military costs under German rule and even lower than British military expenditure in Tanganyika.[131]

Based on the French annual reports to the PMC, Glasman calculated that in 1929 French Togoland comprised a staff of 1.608, of which 1.383 were natives.[132] The *garde indigène* and *companie de milice* (534) thus made up roughly a third of the administration's entire personnel. If the hygiene guards and border guards are added, forces of order made up as much as 43.2% of the colonial state's indigenous personnel. Considering the extent of the territory and a population of about 750,000, however, there was on average only one state servant for every 500 inhabitants. Thus, the French administration constituted a weak state whose proportion of law enforcement officers was, however, disproportionately high. Until the 1933, the *garde indigène* and *companie de milice* formed the almost sole forces of law enforcement.[133]

The 1933 Riots & Service de Police et de Sûreté

Between 1914 and 1920, that is, the interim period from the surrender of the German troops to the time when the British-occupied areas around Lomé were ceded to the French, the local population welcomed the British waiving most of the taxes that the Germans had introduced.[134]

Yet, in the wake of the global stock market crash of 1929 and to raise funds during the worldwide economic downturn, the French administration announced in 1933 that it would reintroduce a dozen taxes that had already existed under German rule. Led by Lomé's market women, local district and cantonal chiefs submitted petitions to the Lomé police headquarters on 22 January 1933 demanding the withdrawal of the new taxes, especially those on market stalls. The French administration responded to the petitions by arresting two of the leaders. That same afternoon, a crowd of 3,000 people marched through the streets, calling for a general strike and the release of their leaders. Although the arrested were released that same evening, the crowd still did not disperse the next day

---

131   Wright, *Mandates under the League of Nations*, p. 564.
132   Glasman, *Les corps habillés au Togo*, p. 195.
133   Glasman, *Les corps habillés au Togo*, p. 223.
134   Nugent, *Smugglers, secessionists & loyal citizens on the Ghana-Togo frontier*, p. 149.

and vandalized several buildings (including the house of Jonathan Savi de Tové, secretary of Lomé's *Conseil de Notables*, who was considered a lackey of the French administration).

As tensions increased, some 170 *tirailleurs* were brought in from the Ivory Coast. On 3 February, a skirmisher, Moussia Diarra, killed twelve Togolese and wounded three for no apparent reason: the governor invoked a "a stroke of madness." In the counter-repression, many villagers were killed, and women raped. In the subsequent trials of the revolt, fourteen Togolese were sentenced to death, entire villages and neighbourhoods were collectively fined thousands of francs and sentenced to several thousand days of forced labour. Some were jailed for up to five years for minor offenses such as unauthorized travel.[135]

To prevent such revolts in the future the French administration created in less than a month after the revolt the *Service de Police et de Sûreté*. The French Governor, Robert de Guise, pressured officials to keep in closer contact with village authorities and to report any activity they considered subversive or likely to endanger order and security to the administering authority.

The *Service de Police et de Sûreté*, which represented a new, that is, civil police service, whose urban commissariats now formed the central authority for maintaining order, marked a break with the *garde indigène* and its mere military presence in the streets. In the face of a civilian and otherwise peaceful population, the use of machine gun fire no longer seemed appropriate, especially in a territory particularly observed by the international press, the League of Nations and competing major powers.[136] Control of the streets was, thus, handed over to the municipal police station, which now represented the central site of colonial order and political control of the territory.

The creation of the *Service* entailed the bureaucratisation and emergence of a remote policing, which increasingly made use of surveillance techniques.[137] Henceforth, written reports formed the primary relationship between the police and the population. Not military experience was required any more, but scholarly experience. The commissariats issued numerous documents (certificates of good conduct, certificates of residence, loss certificates, et cetera). They documented their daily work. A good commissioner was one who writes good protocols. Anthropometry, that is, measuring people (length of feet, legs, etc.) to establish identities. In 1941, a special archival section of the police was founded[138] and by 1947, that is, from the transition from the mandate to the trusteeship era, the police authorities had created an archive of 11,338 fingerprint samples.[139] Although *la force d'ordre* in Togo was not as militarized as in the rest of French West Africa, the creation of the *Services de Sûreté* represented a reform of the previous law enforcers. Whereas previously the tasks of the *force d'ordre* had been those of colonial administration, tax collection, supervision of forced labour, et cetera, now it was a matter of preventing plots against the colonial powers, controlling the borders and directing

---

135 Decalo, *Historical dictionary of Togo*, pp. 196–97.
136 Glasman, *Les corps habillés au Togo*, p. 205.
137 Glasman, *Les corps habillés au Togo*, pp. 198–207.
138 Arrête 759, 27 December 1941.
139 Gouvernement Français, "Rapport Annuel: Togo placé sous la Tutelle de la France" T/221 (1948), p. 36.

the flow of population. However, this new urban police force was less concerned with fighting crime than with maintaining colonial power by criminalising political opponents. The bureaucratisation of the police was not synonymous with its pacification, but perfectly compatible with an exacerbation of police violence.

To summarise, then, there was a Foucauldian tendency towards the panopticon in France's colonial security system. While initially it was repression and brute force that held the colonial empire together, after 1933 Togo's *Service de Sûreté* was a knowledge institution that played an essential role in the construction of the threat in the preparation of threat assessments. The reactive-repressive police force was joined by a pre-emptive police force.

British Mandated Togoland

In contrast to French Togoland, the British were not willing to establish a separate administration and legislature, so that an administrative union was set in place between British-mandated Togoland and the neighbouring colony of Gold Coast. Thus, at the top of the mandate administration stood the governor of the neighbouring colony of the Gold Coast, who was based in Accra, while the *district commissioners* at the lower level of the colonial chain of command represented the local "barons." The Northern Section was administered as an integral part of the Northern territories of the Gold Coast and a Southern Section administered as an integral part of the Southern third of the Gold Coast (itself referred to as Gold Coast Colony).[140] Some divisions, whether Native States or administrative districts, thus extended across the borders between the Gold Coast and British Togoland.

In contrast to the French policy of centralised assimilation, British colonial policy was imbued with what Lugard called *indirect rule*, which consisted of a gradual devolution of authority into the hands of indigenous *Native Authorities* (that is, political groupings at the local level based on traditional elites and alignments) first as units of local administration and later as units of local government. The amalgamation of the divisions into *states* and *Native Authorities* under one paramount ruler has been a continuous process since the British Government assumed the mandate at the end of World War I. At the end of the mandate, four such states existed in southern section of British Togoland. Native Authorities had limited administrative, legislative, and executive powers, encompassing orders to natives subject to its authority and make rules providing for public order and police. *States* and *Divisions* had the power to enquire into all disputes of constitutional or political nature. The British refrained from forming larger states on the scale of the French cantons so as not to provoke chieftaincy disputes.[141]

While due to the French policy of *assimilation*, that is, *direct rule*, nationalist movements and self-government in Togoland were seen as a challenge and to some degree even a threat to the colonial system and suppressed accordingly, similar groups in British Togoland were not only legitimate and enjoyed greater freedoms, but also fulfilled a functional role: Native Authorities were created ostensibly to look after their own local affairs,

---

140 Whereas the "Colony of the Gold Coast" refers to the entire colony, "Gold Coast Colony" referred to the southernmost of its four jurisdictions besides Ashanti, the Northern Territories and British Togoland.
141 Skinner, *The Fruits of Freedom in British Togoland*, p. 15.

but hedged about with the overriding authority of the Administrative Officers and the veto of the Governor, so that in effect they were only instruments for carrying out the orders of the European administrators, who reserved certain judicial functions.

Especially during the war years, but also before, migration from the French to the British Mandate territory was not atypical, as conditions in British Togoland were apparently better: No forced labour or indigénat, lower taxes, more liberal trading policies, better conditions for African advance.[142] It was easier to get an education in British Togoland, this implanted a favourable attitude towards British rule.[143]

World War II

When France and Vichy concluded an armistice in 1940, British-French tensions during World War II led to the complete closure of the border between British and French Togoland, which was only reopened with many restrictions, in June 1943, when French West Africa re-entered the war. The Allied blockade left Vichy-French Togoland struggling to cope in complete self-sufficiency at a time when hardships for the war effort were already mounting. Deprivations included poverty and hunger due to increased forced labour, taxation in money and kind, restrictions on freedom of movement, transport and trade, and requisition of goods and services. Nugent noted that shortages of commodities prompted the French regime to facilitate smuggling, and that life in British Togoland was far bleaker than in French Togoland because of the high market demand in Lomé and elsewhere.[144]

In November 1942, before the invasion of North Africa by Anglo-American troops and the eventual break with the Vichy regime, the French administration in Lomé decided to detain representatives of foreign trading houses and Togolese who were known to be pro-British. Many fled over the border to British Togoland. Because Sylvanus Olympio was a representative of the United Africa Company, a Unilever subsidiary, and a former graduate of the LSE who regularly listened to the BBC radio, the Vichy-controlled administration interned him along with six of his colleagues for a fortnight in Djougou, north of Dahomey in November 1942. They were suspected of having links to the British and Gaullists. However, ironically, it was his internment that made Olympio a potential contact for the Gaullists in Algiers, who were gradually gaining influence in the French African colonies. Certainly, this was an experience that shaped resentment towards French administrative policy. Ironically, it was Nicholas Grunitzky, Olympio's later rival, who was a Gaullist underground member during World War II in Vichy-controlled Togoland.[145]

When representatives of Free France met with senior colonial officials from the African colonies at the Brazzaville Conference in early 1944 to involve the African colonies more fully in the struggle for the liberation of France, they recognised, in return for their support, the need for political, social and economic reforms in the French-controlled part of Africa and promised a fundamental reorganisation of relations between

---

142 Welch, *Dream of Unity*, p. 60.
143 Welch, *Dream of Unity*, p. 51.
144 Nugent, *Smugglers, secessionists & loyal citizens on the Ghana-Togo frontier*, p. 163.
145 Decalo, *Historical dictionary of Togo*, p. 154.

metropolitan France and its colonies. The administrators present recommended the abolition of the worst features of the old system, such as the indigénat, forced labour and compulsory tributes, while recommending the establishment of local territorial assemblies and representation of the territories in Paris. But they had reiterated an old principle of French colonial policy: namely that France's aims in its civilizing work in the colonies excluded any idea of self-government and any possibility of development outside the French empire. The formation of independent governments could not be contemplated. The reorganisation decided upon at the Brazzaville Conference merely provided for the transformation of colonial relations into a newly born *French Union*.

Contemporaries[146] and literature,[147] undoubtedly identify World War II as an awakening of political consciousness in Togoland. Nugent highlights the permeability of border in interwar years.[148] The hardships of the World War II, translated into the rise of Ewe nationalism.[149] When the Vichy regime imposed increasing economic burdens on the population of French Togoland for the war effort, again in 1943 a petition to the Secretary of State for the Colonies, Oliver Stanley, and several newspaper articles in 1944 called for the unification of all Ewes under British administration.[150] Similarly, on 24 August 1944, the Asogli State Council addressed a memorandum to Sir Alan Burns, Governor of the Gold Coast, stating that the restoration of Ewe unity was as important to them as the self-government promised by the British government, since the Atlantic Charter and other wartime conferences.

Likewise, former members of the Togobund hoped that under Hitler the Germans would return to reunite Togoland and the members of the Federation would regain their former jobs and status. In 1943, when Oliver Stanley's visit a group of teachers in southern British Togoland, many of them educated by the Bremen Missionary Society, such as Francis Yao Asare, Kofi Dumoga and Gerald Otto Awuma, revived the idea of a united Togoland by founding the *Togoland Union*.[151] It is important to note that as its primary goal the Togoland Union did not seek the unification of Eweland. Though many of its members were Ewe, especially for the Akpini and Atando area, also many members were Buems. Its members were resentful of the fact that many of the more important posts in the education system of the Southern Section of Togoland were held by Ewes from the Gold Coast Colony (which is hardly to be wondered since there have been schools in the Gold Coast Peki and Keta areas for over 100 years). Although the Togoland Union signed a joint resolution in the autumn of 1948 supporting the unification of the whole of Eweland, it soon became an opponent of the Ewe unification movement, opposing all efforts that

---

146 Sylvanus Olympio, MAE (La Courneuve), 77QO-13, *Élections de 1958, travaux du Conseil de Tutelle*, Note sur M. Sylvanus Olympio, Mai 1958. Pedro Olympio TCOR, "6th Session" (1950), p. 156.

147 Welch, *Dream of Unity*, p. 41; John Kent, "The Ewe Question," in *The Internationalization of Colonialism*, ed. John Kent (Oxford University Press, 1992), p. 217; Lawrance, *Locality, Mobility, and "Nation"*, pp. 135–55.

148 Nugent, *Smugglers, secessionists & loyal citizens on the Ghana-Togo frontier*.

149 Amenumey, *The Ewe Unification Movement*, pp. 37–38.

150 ANOM (Aix-en-Provence), 1AFFPOL/3284/3, *Affaire Ewe*, Bulletin de Renseignement, N/175-932 S. D., p. 2

151 PRAAD (Accra), ADM 39/1/651, *Togoland Union and Togoland Association for the United Nation Association Statement subject and reasons etc*, Application for Registration of the Togo Union

would lead to the abandonment of the territorial identity of former German Togoland that would result from the integration of the Ewe territories into the Gold Coast.

6. The Securitisation of Ewe & Togoland Unification before the United Nations

> "The Ewe problem was the most critical that had yet emerged from the operation of the International Trusteeship system. The finding of an adequate solution must be regarded as a test of the Trusteeship System itself [...] a test of local administrative policies and also a test of the whole concept of colonialism. It raised the validity of the concepts of the British Commonwealth of Nations and of the French Union."[1]

6.1 Bringing Togoland under United Nations Trusteeship

During World War II, to mobilize global support for the Allied war endeavour, British Prime Minister Winston Churchill and US President Franklin D. Roosevelt publicly affirmed their commitment to the right of all peoples to self-government. This joint declaration, known as the Atlantic Charter, was made in August 1941. Churchill later tried to limit this promise to peoples living under Nazi occupation, but expectations had already been raised in the colonies since the Atlantic Charter was issued by various nations in January 1942 and later confirmed by the United Nations.[2] The US position, on the other hand, was initially to insist on a broad application of the Atlantic Charter's promise of self-determination and independence. In mid-July 1942, Roosevelt and his Secretary of State, Cordell Hull, set up a committee in the State Department whose working paper later served as the basis for the United Nations' institutional design, which also laid out the contours for the eventual establishment of a Trusteeship System.

---

1   Intervention by Philippine Representative Diosdado Macapagal, GAOR, "6th Session: 4th Committee" (1951), p. 189.
2   Tom Parker, *The Ultimate Intervention: Revitalising the UN Trusteeship Council for the 21st Century* (Sandvika, 2003), accessed 29 July 2019, available from www.bi.edu/globalassets/forskning/centre-for-european-and-asian-studies/pdf/03-03the_ultimate_intervention.pdf, p. 9.

At the so-called "Big Three Conferences" in Cairo and Tehran in late 1943, Roosevelt proposed to Churchill and Stalin that all dependent French territories, by then Vichy-controlled, be placed under international trusteeship. The plans included a powerful Trusteeship Commission, which would have been authorised to recommend and revise "charter terms, designate or replace administering authorities, and terminate trust status."[3] Roosevelt's suggestion was vehemently opposed by Churchill who regarded an all-powerful Trusteeship Commission as an implicit threat to the British Empire.[4] Furthermore, the US Military preferred to keep the question of trusteeship open until the US government had defined its final disposition of the Pacific Islands, which it conquered from Japan.

Over the following year, as a concession to the British but also the US military, the State Department retreated from its proposition and instead advocated for 'self-government' rather than independence and limited UN powers.[5] Nevertheless, dissatisfied with the revised proposals, the US military insisted that the question of trusteeship be dropped from the forthcoming Dumbarton Oaks Conversations that were taking place between August and October 1944. Much to the regret of Secretary of State, Cordell Hull, who considered American security interests fully protected trough the proposed Trusteeship System, it was agreed to omit Section IX from the "Tentative Proposals."[6] With the exception of the forthcoming strategic trusteeship provisions, the US State Department's plans laid out a decidedly vague blueprint for deliberations on the new Trusteeship System that appeased conflicting preferences of the US State Department, the US military and the interests of the colonial powers, especially the British. Principles of trusteeship would be applied to the administration of all colonies, but only territories voluntarily placed by the colonial powers under the Trusteeship System would fall under UN supervision.

Although the colonial question was an issue during the war, especially considering the burgeoning decolonisation movements, due to US-American security interests the Dumbarton Oaks proposals thus did not have much influence during the forthcoming negotiations in San Francisco and London.[7] Yet, one crucial proposal made at Dumbarton Oaks lingered its way into the later negotiations: As was done under the Mandates System, instead of the new international organisation, the Administering Authorities should prepare the terms of each trusteeship agreement and submit them to the organization for approval before placing a territory under trusteeship. This formula was proposed by the US government as a concession to the British in order to give them a free hand in determining the conditions by which they would place any of territory under trusteeship and so would circumvent direct UN administration or supervision by a powerful Trusteeship Commission.[8] Thus, the fact that contemporary peacebuilding

---

3   Thullen, *Problems of the Trusteeship System*, p. 33.
4   Tom Parker, *The Ultimate Intervention: Revitalising the UN Trusteeship Council for the 21st Century* (Sandvika, 2003), accessed 29 July 2019, available from www.bi.edu/globalassets/forskning/centre-for-european-and-asian-studies/pdf/03-03the_ultimate_intervention.pdf, p. 9.
5   Thullen, *Problems of the Trusteeship System*, p. 33.
6   Thullen, *Problems of the Trusteeship System*, pp. 33–34.
7   Falcón, *Power interrupted*, p. 42; TCOR, "1st Session" (1947), p. 2; Welch, *Dream of Unity*, p. 29.
8   Thullen, *Problems of the Trusteeship System*, p. 35.

missions comprise 'mandate agreements' derives from the tradition of mandate agreements once agreed upon during the Paris Peace Conference, and after World War II, at the Dumbarton Oaks Conference.

The first concrete proposal for international supervision was officially discussed in February 1945 at the Yalta Conference and already containing the demand of the US Military to classify future trusteeship territories either as *strategic* or *non-strategic*. While *non-strategic* territories would be overseen by the Trusteeship Council, *strategic* territories would be overseen by the future Security Council, where the US could protect its interests by exercising its right of veto.[9] John Foster Dulles, who participated in the Dumbarton Oaks and Yalta conferences, commented that these proposals "had the defects which usually occur when a few big powers get together to decide how to run the world [and]conclude that the best of all possible worlds is a world which they will run."[10] Thus, in the aftermath of World War II, the institutional design of the Trusteeship System emerged, driven not only by the perennial concern for power preservation but also by considerations of national and international security, as evident in the substantial involvement of actors such as the US Military.

6.1.1 Establishment of the United Nations Trusteeship System

It was planned that the relevant articles for the Trusteeship System in the United Nations Charter would be drawn up at the *United Nations Conference on International Organization* (UNCIO) in San Francisco. Since the Big Five failed to reach agreement at the UNCIO in San Francisco in April-June 1945, a subcommittee of the *Preparatory Commission* was appointed to continue negotiations in London. It took about eighteen months of debate and compromise before the Trusteeship System was born. As Sylvanna Falcón has shown, the negotiations of the Trusteeship System were marked by most blatant paternalism and racism. For example, the British negotiator, Robert Gascony-Cecil, regarded that:

> "Many of these areas are small, poor and defenseless and could not stand on their own feet. Many of them are extremely backward. Many need help building roads and communications, building modern health systems, introducing scientific methods to agriculture, and promoting the spread of education that is fundamental to all progress. Take your helping hand away, and such areas would quickly fall back into barbarism. What we can give them is freedom and free institutions. We can gradually train them to lead their own affairs, so that if independence eventually comes, they will be ready."[11]

Thus, even after the horrors of World War II, which the 'civilized world' brought upon itself and other world regions, non-Western peoples were described with the tropes of

---

9   Thullen, *Problems of the Trusteeship System*, p. 34.
10 Falcón, *Power interrupted*, pp. 32–33.
11 Department of State, *The United Nations Conference on International Organization: San Francisco, California, April 25 to June 26*, Conference Series 83 (Washington: U.S. Government Printing Office, 1946), p. 694.

being 'uncivilized,' 'wild,' 'backward' and 'primitive.' As had happened during the drafting of the now-to-be-replaced League of Nations Covenant, this paternal spirit found its way into the euphemistic wording of the Charter describing colonial territories 'non-self-governing' and their peoples as 'not yet fully self-governing.'[12] These negative formulations formed the phraseology of the trusteeship principle, suggesting that 'governmental authority' was understood as something that endows self-government only altruistically.

Since World War II represented a turning point in history, both in terms of the maintenance of international peace and security as well as in terms of its relationship to principles of trusteeship, security considerations also found their way into the trusteeship chapters of the Charter:

> "Members of the United Nations which have or assume responsibilities for the administration of territories whose peoples have nor yet attained a full measure of self-government recognize the principle that the interests of the inhabitants of these territories are paramount, and accept as a sacred trust the obligation to promote to the utmost, within the *system of international peace and security* established by the present Charter, the well-being of the inhabitants of these territories."[13]

Thus, the architects of the Charter identified the primary objective of the Trusteeship System to be the furthering of international peace and security. Unquestionably, the experience of World War II marked a shift from idealistic strands of International Relations to the dominance of realist thought. The common assessment was that while the League of Nations was still based on an idealistically inspired idea of peace, World War II turned this view upside down: no longer *peace* (which called for disarmament and cooperation) but *security* was regarded the paradigm of the hour and hence, the core function of the United Nations as embodied by the Security Council.

Thus, as a lesson from the failed *passive* peacekeeping measures of the League, such as the demilitarization of mandate areas, the Charter stipulated that each dependent territory should play an *active* role in the maintenance of international peace and security. As demanded by the US Military, trusteeship territories could be completely or partially declared as *strategic areas*, whose supervision would fall under the authority of the UN Security Council.[14] However, the Security Council was ultimately never to assume oversight over a *strategic* area since in 1949, during its first meeting on the strategic Trust Territory of the Pacific Islands (TTPI), the US proposed that regular oversight functions should be transferred to the Trusteeship Council.[15] Although the United States granted oversight rights to the Trusteeship Council, by designating the TTPI as a 'strategic area' in its 1947

---

12   Charter, United Nations (UN) (1945)
13   Emphasis added, *id.*, Chapter XI: Declaration Regarding Non-Self-Governing Territories, Article 73.
14   The background to this concept were security motives of the United States. In the event of international attempts to interfere in the management of its strategic areas in the Pacific, the United States would have been able to use her veto right in the Security Council.
15   Security Council Resolution 70, *Trusteeship of Strategic Areas*, S/RES/70(1949) (7 March 1949), available from https://documents-dds-ny.un.org/doc/RESOLUTION/GEN/NR0/055/07/PDF/NR005507.pdf?OpenElement.

Trusteeship Agreement, the US retained the ace up its sleeve that it could deny access to the oversight bodies at any time.

Nonetheless, in contrast to the Mandates System, the introduction of *strategic areas* implied not only a right but, in a sense, also a duty under the Trusteeship System to maintain armed forces and bases in trusteeship territories. The apparent insight was that security was not guaranteed by the absence of militarization, but rather by its expansion. This also meant a complete reversal of the function that mandated territories played in the global security architecture: Whereas before World War II the colonial narrative asserted that dependent peoples needed to be protected by colonial powers, after World War II they were meant to be instruments of global security. This about-face, however, was equally colonial, for behind the idea of 'developmental decolonisation' lay a rather self-righteous interest on the part of Western states regarding their national security.

Furthermore, whilst the Mandates System operated on a rigid classification of "A," "B" and "C" mandates "according to the stage of the development of the people," the Trusteeship System operated on a flexible division of territories into *strategic* and *non-strategic areas*, that is, Administering Authorities could freely decide under which circumstance a territory, partially or wholly, could be designated as a *strategic* area. Hence, the distinction between *strategic* and *non-strategic* trusteeship territories was not determined so much by geography or 'stage of development' but was functionally determined by security considerations.

Figure 2: Structure of the Trusteeship System

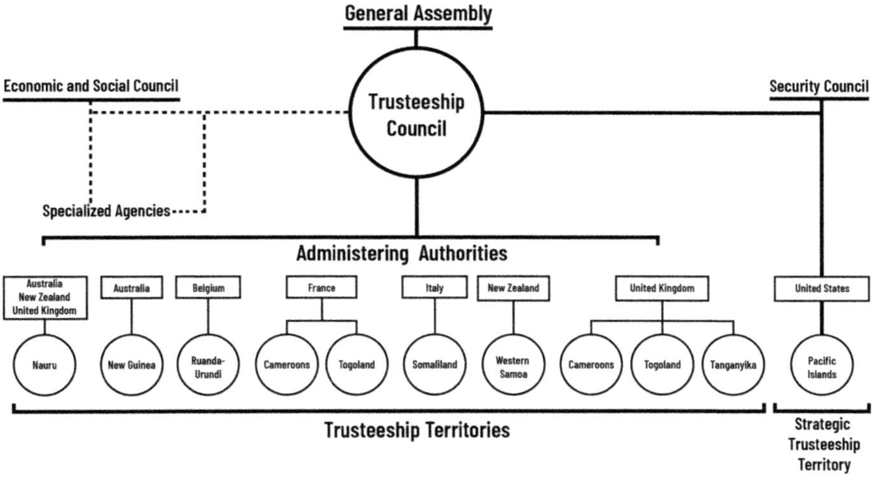

Source: UN Yearbook 1950, p. 104.

With regard to security issues, however, there were not only breaks with the Mandate System. While during the League of Nations period the principle of the 'dual mandate,' that is, the 'reciprocal benefit' of the mandated territories lay in their economic utility, under the Trusteeship System the benefit of 'dual mandate' seemed to have been replaced in the function of ensuring international security.

In sum, security interests of the Allied Powers overshadowed the interests of the inhabitants of trusteeship territories. Black American scholars such as Rayford Logan, who was the former mentor of the Trusteeship Division's Director-General, Ralph Bunche, found the submissiveness to the administering powers' security interests particularly worrying.[16] Now that "Every nation was talking in terms of its own security," one contemporary called the prevailing paradigm of Trusteeship System "security imperialism."[17] On the other hand, Bain argues:

> "it is a mistake of considerable proportion to suggest that the Trusteeship System, and the Charter in general, subordinates the well-being of dependent peoples to a narrow argument of security. [...] The Trusteeship System should not be viewed as expressing a narrow set of interests related exclusively to either security or welfare; nor should it be viewed as an isolated arrangement that is separate from the principles and purposes expressed elsewhere in the Charter, the most important of which relate to the problem of war and the conditions of peace."[18]

Besides the maintenance of international peace and security, the authors of the Charter spelled out more clearly the specific objectives of the Trusteeship System: to promote the political, economic, social, and educational advancement of the inhabitants, and to promote the progressive development towards self-government or independence. On the one hand, this was a departure from the Covenant's vague formulation to tutelage "peoples not yet able to stand by themselves" towards a clear commitment to political independence. On the other hand, this shifted the emphasis from mere "just treatment" of dependent peoples and prohibition of abuses under the Mandates System to positive aspects of constructive development, which was coined as a sort of 'developmental decolonisation.' In sum: "The architects of the United Nations trusteeship system believed that the welfare of dependent peoples could not be separated from the furtherance of international peace and security."[19]

6.1.2 The Instruments of International Supervision

The Trusteeship System introduced several innovations designed to increase oversight over and the accountability of the Administering Authorities. It is largely due to the American delegate Ralph Bunche, later Director-General of the UN Trusteeship Division, "that the International Trusteeship System is no mere prolongation of the mandates system under the League of Nations."[20] For his Ph. D. dissertation, which

---

16   Pedersen, *The guardians*, p. 401.
17   Falcón, *Power interrupted*, p. 55.
18   Bain, *Between anarchy and society*, pp. 125–26.
19   Bain, *Between anarchy and society*, p. 25.
20   TCOR, "1st Session" (1947), p. 4.

was entitled *French Administration in Togoland and Dahomey*,[21] Bunche carried out field research in West Africa, comparing the League of Nations mandate territory of French Togoland with the adjacent French colony of Dahomey (today: Benin). Although he noted that, because of the Mandates System, Togoland fared a little better than Dahomey, he concluded:

> "There is a grave need for some more effective method whereby the Mandates Commission can be made aware of the actual condition of the mandated territories and any abuse of administration which may occur. The natives are inadequately organized to effectively employ the *right of petition* to the Commission through the administration. It would be helpful if the natives were given the right to direct appeal to the League of Nations against any failure of the mandatory to keep its trust."[22]

As a member of the US delegation to the Preparatory Commission that negotiated the content of the Charter in San Francisco and London, Bunche himself had the opportunity to remedy the matter by introducing the triad of annual reports, visiting missions, and petitions. In a manner of speaking, annual reports would represent the official voice of the Administering Authorities, Visiting Missions would represent the eyes and ears of the United Nations, and petitions would represent the collective voice of the inhabitants.[23]

Yet, among the three instruments, it was really the *right to petition* that was considered the new "backbone of the system of international supervision."[24] For the first time in international law, the UN Charter established the *right to petition*, giving those governed under the Trusteeship System a voice in the new international organisation and the possibility to draw attention to abuses of Administering Authorities. The Charter formally established the right to petition, stating that the...

> "[...] General Assembly and, under its authority, the Trusteeship Council, in carrying out their functions, may [...] accept petitions and examine them in consultation with the administering authority."[25]

The peculiar wording of the article, stating that the United Nations had the right to receive petitions, rather than the inhabitants of the trusteeship territories having the entitlement to have their petitions considered, was likely instigated by the colonial powers. As the Council's first President, Francis B. Sayre, noted during the Council's 1st Session "it is for the Trusteeship Council to decide whether it shall consider a petition, and not for the petitioner so to decide."[26] The extent to which one can speak of a "right to petition" on

---

21   SCRBC (New York). Ralph J. Bunche, b. 12 f. 5, *Doctoral Thesis "French Administration in Togoland and Dahomey"*
22   Emphasis added, SCRBC (New York)Bunche, b. 12 f. 5, *Doctoral Thesis "French Administration in Togoland and Dahomey"*, p. 518.
23   Smith, "The formation and functioning of the Trusteeship Council procedure for examining petitions," pp. 79–80.
24   TCOR, "1st Session" (1947), p. 4.
25   *Charter*, Article 87.
26   TCOR, "2nd Session" (1947), p. 35.

the part of the petitioner is questionable in this context. In addition, the authors of the Charter thereby excluded an independent examination of the petitions without the participation of the Administering Authorities. The Administering Authorities would limit the *right to petition* by introducing ever more restrictive *rules of procedure*.

But also outside the Trusteeship System, the *right of petition* did not get off to an easy start: in January 1947, even before the first session of the Trusteeship Council, the two superpowers, the US and USSR, expressed at a meeting of the Commission on Human Rights that the UN should have neither the mandate nor the capacity to receive individual complaints about alleged human rights violations.[27] The USSR argued that any petition mechanism would be a direct violation of Article 2(7) of the UN Charter (concerning national sovereignty). That this was by no means a matter of principle for the USSR was shown by the quite different attitude it adopted regarding the Trusteeship System, where petitions could be directed primarily against Western powers.

Regardless, neither the Charter nor the Preparatory Commission set up an exact procedure for examining petitions. The Executive Committee's proposal of the Preparatory Commission of the United Nations was based on the League's previous procedure.[28] During the negotiations the Chinese delegate expounded "if on the one hand the natives of the Trust Territories were recognized as yet incapable of exercising sovereignty, it seemed only logical on the other hand not to maintain too exacting standards for the excellence of petitions."[29] Although the Chinese delegate advocated a liberal petition policy, the trusteeship principle underlying his argument indicated an *illocutionary disabling frame*, that is, silencing dependent peoples in their attempt to speak from a subaltern position.

Limits of Accountability

The United Nations Trusteeship System depended on the deliberate cooperation of the Administering Authorities. While according to Article 25 of the UN Charter resolutions by the Security Council are binding for all UN member states, there is no such provision for the resolutions of the Trusteeship Council. Its resolutions have, so to speak, only the character of recommendations. As such, these instruments of international supervision could only be applied to the extent permitted by the Administering Authorities. The Trusteeship Council was merely empowered to *review* annual reports, *consider* petitions, or *draw attention* to the recommendations of Visiting Missions. The colonial powers deliberately negotiated these limitations in San Francisco and London in the hoped to forestall any interference into the administration of their trusteeship territories. It was neither in the power of the Council nor of the General Assembly to coerce Administering Authorities to take certain action. If a member state felt that an Administering Authority was

---

27 Marc Limon, *Reform of the UN Human Rights Petitions System: An assessment of the UN human rights communications procedures and proposals for a single integrated system* (2018), p. 9.
28 United Nations, "Report to the Preparatory Commission of the United Nations" PC/EX/113/Rev.1 (1945), available from https://digitallibrary.un.org/record/703121, p. 61.
29 UN ARMS (New York), S-0504-0004-0001-00001, *Committee on Rules of Procedure (1–11th Meeting (Conference Papers Nos. 1–10)*, Conference Room Paper No. 6, p. 27

not acting in the spirit of the Charter, it could bring its contention merely to the attention of the General Assembly and, consequently, world opinion. However, world opinion rarely influenced the decision-making process of the Administering Authorities. Respecting the sovereignty of its member states and without any real means of sanctions, the United Nations could do little to prevent the Administering Authorities from treating their trusteeship territories as they pleased.

Thus, already during the negotiation of the Charter, the Administering Authorities were successful in eroding the relevance of the Trusteeship Council, which was ultimately not empowered to take extraordinary decisions. Aware that the Trusteeship System was based on voluntarism, representatives of other member states had to accept this fact. The Administering Authorities would not have allowed United Nations supervision without power to limit it. Without means of sanction, United Nations supervision was limited to observation. Rather than being a prototype of international state-building, trusteeship represented international observation of colonial state-building.

The establishment of *rules of procedure* remained in limbo, so that the negotiators simply delegated in Article 90 of the Charter the responsibility for adopting *rules of procedure* to the Trusteeship Council itself. Once again, this was most likely pressed at the instigation of the future Administering Authorities, as the power to set the *rules of procedure* would empower them to determine how the 'new system of international supervision' would be run.

Beyond the responsibilities of the Trusteeship System, the Fourth Committee of the General Assembly, responsible for decolonisation-related matters, also monitors compliance with the Charter's *Declaration concerning Non-Self-Governing Territories* in which all member states administering Non-Self-Governing Territories (NSGTs), that is, colonies, accepted to grant self-government or independence to its inhabitants. Colonial powers committed themselves to submit regularly annual reports on the social, educational, and economic conditions. These reports were reviewed by the General Assembly in its Fourth Committee. The UN had no authority to make periodic visits or accept petitions from NSGTs. These two functions were the unique features of the Trusteeship System. As such, the Trusteeship System was considered as a window through which the world could see that the interests of dependent people would not be harmed.

Trusteeship Agreements

As negotiated at the Dumbarton Oaks Conference, the Trusteeship Council could only begin its work after Trusteeship Agreements had been concluded between the General Assembly and the "states directly concerned."[30] Yet, neither the Charter nor the Preparatory Commission specified 'states directly concerned.' The demand for a definition led to months of delay. Deciding unilaterally for themselves the 'states directly concerned,' the United Kingdom, Belgium, Australia, New Zealand, and France, drew up eight draft Trusteeship Agreements without consultation of the indigenous inhabitants of the ter-

---

30 *Charter*, Article 85.

ritories.³¹ The United States and the South African Union did not.³² The subsequent negotiation of the draft Agreements in the Fourth Committee was a long, and challenging task, aggravated by a conflict of ideas and interests. Many anti-colonial nations considered the Charter's Trusteeship chapters already "a dead letter."³³

Indeed, the agreements for French and British Togoland followed the wording of the previous Mandate Agreements. Featured prominently at the beginning of both agreements, the mandate powers were in the first place responsible for the security of the territories: "The Administering Authority shall be responsible (a) for the peace, order, good government, and defense of the Territory and (b) for ensuring that it shall play its part in the maintenance of international peace and security."³⁴ Since neither area was attacked or strategically used during World War II, these prominently placed security provisions of the article, like Article 22 of the Covenant, functioned as a discursive authorization and justification of the quasi-colonial administration. In addition, the mandate powers secured provisions that allowed them to establish military bases and use volunteer forces in the trusteeship territories.

For all intents and purposes, the agreements contained progressive and democratic features, such as limitations on the exploration and tapping of territories' natural resources. Overall, the Trusteeship Agreements for French Togoland guaranteed "freedom of speech, of press, of assembly and of petition[!]," however, the agreement clearly expressed the possibility of restricting these fundamental rights "subject only to the requirements of public order."³⁵ The Trusteeship Agreement for British Togoland included a similar clause as basic freedoms "shall not, however, affect, the right and duty of the Administering Authority to exercise such control as it may consider necessary for the maintenance of peace, order and good government."³⁶

Between the agreements for British and French Togoland, there were small but notable differences. Both agreements provided administrative unions with their adjacent colonies. Hence, the British Agreement considered British Togoland as an "integral part of *his* territory,"³⁷ that is, using the possessive pronoun ("his"), Britain understood British Togoland as part of the Gold Coast, whilst the French wording considered French Togoland "in accordance with French law as an integral part of *French* territory" suggesting that France already considered the territory legally as a part of herself.³⁸

These agreements received sharp criticism from the Soviet Union, on the grounds that the provisions for administrative unions were "equivalent to the annexation of the

---

31   They concerned Tanganyika, British Togoland, British Cameroon, Rwanda-Urundi, French Togoland, French Cameroon, New Guinea, and Western Samoa.
32   The US State Department and US military did not yet agree on the strategic value of the former Japanese islands. The US' veto power in the Security Council safeguarded them from external intervention. The U.S. military, however, feared that the USSR's veto power might affect the administration of these "strategic areas" in the same way.
33   TCOR, "1st Session" (1947), p. 2.
34   TCOR, "Trusteeship Agreements" T/8 (1947)
35   TCOR, "Trusteeship Agreements" (1947), Agreement for French Togoland, Art 10.
36   TCOR, "Trusteeship Agreements" (1947), Agreement for British Togoland, Art. 5.
37   TCOR, "Trusteeship Agreements" (1947), Agreement for British Togoland, Art. 5.
38   SCRBC (New York). Ralph J. Bunche, b. 45 f. 16, *Proposed Agreement: French Togoland*, [1947]

Trusteeship Territories by the mandatory Powers."[39] During the subcommittee's negotiations, the Soviet Union proposed to delete the phrase 'as an integral part of his/French territory' from the trusteeship agreements. The subcommittee rejected the deletion,[40] but the Fourth Committee as a whole approved the deletion.[41] The Administering Authorities rejected the Soviet amendment and refused to cooperate if they were forced to agree to amendments that were unacceptable to them. In consequence, the General Assembly approved the Trusteeship Agreements as they were written by the Administering Authorities, including the 'integral part' provision.[42]

Ultimately, the Trusteeship Agreements were a matter of compromise on the part of anti-colonial states, who considered a poor Trusteeship System better than none. The debates on the Trusteeship Agreements reveal much dissatisfaction, but the primary desire of the General Assembly was to get the Trusteeship Council on the way. Therefore, Trusteeship Agreements were adopted, which were to the liking of the Administering Authorities. Thus, within a few weeks, the Fourth Committee negotiated eight separate agreements. In the end, only Liberia and states of the eastern bloc voted against the agreements. The Soviet Union subsequently boycotted the 1st Session of the Trusteeship Council, arguing that the Trusteeship Agreements were not in conformity with the Charter and that equal membership in the Council made it impossible to take constructive resolutions.

Trusteeship as a Communicative Space

In contrast to the League's Permanent Mandates Commission, which solely comprised *individuals* with 'expertise' in colonial matters,[43] the Trusteeship Council comprised *state representatives*. While all Administering Authorities and members of the Security Council were permanently represented, several non-Administering states were elected for three-year terms, so that the number of Administering and non-Administering Authorities remained equal. Unlike the General Assembly or the Security Council, the Trusteeship Council had only two official working languages: English and French – a communicative aspect that impressively illuminated the symbolic supremacy of the colonial powers. Administering Authorities, such as Belgium, France, and Britain, were mostly represented by veteran colonial governors.[44] Indeed, by addressing themselves mutually as 'gover-

---

39   GAOR, "1st Session: 62nd Plenary Meeting" A/PV.62 (1946), p. 1277.
40   GAOR, "1st Session (2nd Part): 4th Committee" (1946), p. 123.
41   GAOR, "1st Session (2nd Part): 4th Committee" (1946), p. 141.
42   GAOR, "11th Session: Plenary," p. 1286.
43   Mandate powers almost exclusively appointed former colonial governors to the Permanent Mandates Commission.
44   During the first decade of the Trusteeship Council, for example, the Belgian permanent representative was Pierre Ryckmans (Governor-General of Belgian Congo, 1934–1946). French permanent representatives were Henri Laurenti (promoted to 'Governor of the Colonies' in 1942 and in charge of the organisation of the Brazzaville Conference), Léon Pignon (High Commissioner in Indochina, 1948–1950), Robert Bargues (High Commissioner in Madagascar, 1950–1954), and Jacques Kosciusko-Morizet (cabinet director of Félix Houphouët-Boigny in Côte d'Ivoire, 1956–1957). The British permanent representative was Sir Alan Burns (Governor of Belize, Nigeria, and the Gold Coast, including British Togoland, 1934–1947). Burns was strongly influenced by Sir Frederick (later Lord) Lugard, for whom the former was private secretary during the latter's gov-

nor', the composition evidenced the continued colonial spirit of the Trusteeship Council rather than a spirit of growing international governance.[45] Alan Burns, who was Governor of the Gold Coast and British Togoland shortly before his appointment as British representative to the Trusteeship Council, readily displayed his 'professional expertise' to the representatives of non-Administering Authorities:

> "As one who had had many years' experience in various parts of the world in the extremely complex task of bringing rapidly forward those peoples who had, through accidents of history and geography, remained over-long in a backward state, he would emphasize that even the best will in the world and the best policies in the world could not always overcome as quickly as might be desired every obstacle and every difficulty."[46]

Furthermore, while petitioners could seek to be heard at oral hearings, they usually did not have the right to speak at the subsequent general discussion unless a state representative called on the petitioners to do so. The right to appeal to statements of the Administering Authorities for example was a prerogative of state representatives.

The composition of the Trusteeship Council was an essential feature, which polarised its deliberations usually along two camps: Administering Authorities and anti- non-Administering Authorities were holding the balance, whereas the United States occasionally sided with one or the other. The balance meant that any rebukes from the Council were defeated by the need for compromise. Thus, although evenly distributed, the Trusteeship Council gave an advantage to the Administering Authorities. Therefore, Groom holds that the Trusteeship Council "was essentially a lowly and docile body since it was dominated by the veto-holding powers and the administering powers. The great debates on colonialism took place elsewhere, chiefly in the General Assembly and in its [Fourth] committee."[47]

The parity of membership was seen as a constitutional protection against an encroachment by the General Assembly. Since the membership of the General Assembly was correspondingly wider than that of the Trusteeship Council, hence, comprising more anti-colonial states, its Fourth Committee tended to press for more rapid implementation of self-government or independence than the Trusteeship Council. Although according to article 85 of the UN Charter, the Trusteeship Council operated under the authority of the General Assembly, during the negotiations in London the colonial powers managed to obtain a safeguard against its interference, namely the requirement of a two-thirds majority for all decisions affecting trusteeship.[48] This requirement forced moderation in the drafting of resolutions and before voting often led to the deletion of radical passages.

---

ernorship of Nigeria. Lugard was *the* ideological promoter of British colonialism and a member of the Permanent Mandates Commission of the League of Nations (1923–1936).
45   See for example at TCOR, "2nd Session" (1947), pp. 350–51.
46   GAOR, "7th Session: 4th Committee" (1952), p. 201.
47   Groom, "The Trusteeship Council," p. 161.
48   *Charter*, Art. 18.

As a last resort, the Administering Authority could simply ignore General Assembly resolutions that ran counter to its own judgement and wishes. Yet usually, the Trusteeship Council sought to avert such a crisis by forcing a compromise. There was a limit to how far the administrations were willing to go, and this was recognised by the anti-colonial powers.

6.2 The All-Ewe-Conference & First Petitions under Trusteeship

6.2.1 Formation of the 'Ewe Parties'

Before World War II, the governor of French-mandated Togoland, Michel Montagne, had decreed the creation of the *Comité du l'Unité Togolaise du Nord et du Sud*, as a counterweight to the Nazi loyalists of the *Bund der deutschen Togoländer*. After World War II, during negotiations on the UN Charter in San Francisco, this *Comité* was transformed into a political party, the *Comité du l'Unité Togolaise* (CUT). Under the presidency of the wealthy 'Brazilian' merchant, Augustino de Souza, the CUT campaigned for the 1946 elections of the representative assembly, the *Assemblée Réprésentative du Togo* (ART), which consisted of two electoral colleges. The first college was composed of 6 citizens of metropolitan France over-representing the French community of only 1,500 voters, while the rest of French Togoland's native male population elected the 24 African representatives of the second college. In the election, the CUT won 14 seats, the pro-French *Parti Togolais du Progrès* (PTP) one seat and the remaining 9 seats went to independent candidates. Sylvanus Olympio was elected President of the Assembly and Jonathan Savi de Tové was elected as the Togolese member for the Council of the French Union.

Whereas before the war, the name, "*Comité du l'Unité Togolaise*", stood programmatically for the cohesion of French Togoland in opposition to the threat posed by the Germanophile elements of the Togobund, it now stood programmatically for the (re)unifying tendencies of an Ewe elite around Sylvanus Olympio, Augustino de Souza, and Jonathon Savi de Tové. For the already Anglophile Olympio, the memory of his internment by the French authorities in 1942 must still have been fresh in his mind and led to an unequal preference to unify the Ewe under British administration.

In British Togoland, Daniel Ahmling Chapman, another key figure in the early development of the Ewe unification movement, undertook similar efforts. Chapman was an Anlo-Ewe, born in Keta in 1909, that is, a Gold Coast Ewe, but received an early German education at the Bremen Missionary Society in Lomé, which probably resulted in his friendly relationship with the Germanophile ex-Togobundarian Kofi Dumoga.[49] Much like the other Ewe elites, Chapman was sent to study at anglophone institutions such as Oxford and Columbia University. Upon his return he worked himself up to become a Geography professor at Achimota College in Accra.

In January 1945, Chapman hosted a cocktail party at his home, where many prominent Ewe raised the possibility of assisting the Ewe in French Togoland that suffered

---

49 ANOM (Aix-en-Provence), 1AFFPOL/3297/1, *Affaires politiques*, Discours de D.A. Chapman devant la conférence Pan – Ewe, 3

privations due to the war efforts. In fact, by December 1945 the French administration already grew concerned about the substantial exodus of the population from French Togoland to British Togoland.[50] Chapman decided to start publishing an Ewe information leaflet, the *Ewe Newsletter*, the first issue of which appeared in May 1945, in English.[51] Chapman wrote about the history of the Ewe, about the privations in French Togoland, about the need to overcome divisions in Ewe society, to unite the Ewe under British administration, and about the importance of the new institutions of the United Nations. The Ewe Newsletter addressed the English-speaking Ewe population and was an important vehicle for disseminating information about the discussions taking place in San Francisco and London at the time on the new provisions of the UN Trusteeship System. Although mostly writing in a mild, teacherly tone, Chapman used more drastic, that is, securitising language in his criticism of the administration of French Togoland:

> "The people of French Eweland want personal security; the right to work at a reasonable way instead of forced labour under the whip without renumeration; the right to have an effective voice in the election of their own chiefs; above all, they want union with their kinsmen on the British side of the frontier."[52]

In fact, on New Year's Eve, 1945, Chapman signed a petition together with 25 influential Ewe-personalities from the Anlo and Peki areas, among them the ex-Bundarians Kofi Dumoga and Gerald Otto Awuma to the Secretary of States for the Colonies, George H. Hall, pleading for the unification of the Ewes.[53] Furthermore, Chapman endeavoured to create *the Ewe Unionist Association*, a political movement for all Ewes.[54] The numerous Ewe associations in the Gold Coast, such as the Ewe Central Committee, the Ewe Labour Committee, the Ewe Benefit Association, the Ewe-Speaking Catholic Union, the Ewe-Speaking Society, the Ewe Charity Union and the Ewe Central Fund, the Togoland Union, and the Trans-Volta Ewe Union unreservedly joined the call for unification.[55] The crowning result was a mammoth meeting with a few thousand participants, in Accra on 9 June 1946, at which the *All-Ewe Conference* (AEC) was established. Under the auspices of Chapman, the AEC adopted an "Ewe Convention," which would reject any trusteeship measure, which did not involve the establishment of a single administration for a 'unified Eweland.'

In August 1946, the AEC sent petitions to the UN, pointing out that no one had consulted the Ewe on the drafts of the Trusteeship Agreement and that Ewe representatives should have a say in the Trusteeship Council. These claims were discussed at an Anglo-French meeting in September 1946. Follow-up minutes show, that the British were torn

---

50 ANT (Lomé), 2APA Aného/71Add, *Affaires Politiques*, Exodes des populations du Togo français vers la Gold-Coast et le Togo britannique, N° 35e, 3 December 1945.
51 A major collection of these Newsletters can be found at PRAAD (Accra), ADM 39/1/339, *Unification of Ewe speaking Peoples*.
52 PRAAD (Accra), ADM 39/1/339, *Unification of Ewe speaking Peoples*, Ewe Newsletter no. 6.
53 PRAAD (Accra), ADM 39/1/339, *Unification of Ewe speaking Peoples*, A Resolution on Eweland.
54 PRAAD (Accra), RG 17/1/224, *Daniel Chapman*, Note sur D. Chapman
55 Lawrance, *Locality, Mobility, and "Nation"*, p. 156.

between seriously considering the Ewe claims and not spoiling Anglo-French relations in colonial matters:

> "Admittedly the U.K. might be able to say that these petitions are technically out of court because they were written before the territories came under trusteeship, but it is doubtful whether this legal quibble would now do us any good and in any case the Ewes (or Dr. Chapman himself) could very quickly write a new petition."[56]

On 7 October 1946, Stephen Tonato Agbeko, President of the AEC, sent another telegram regretting that the French draft agreement for Togoland had not been communicated to the people of the territories and that the AEC opposed the British drafts, which ignored Ewe aspirations for a unified administration. However, as the Trusteeship System was not yet in place, the General Assembly did not consider itself the relevant audience and disregarded the telegram, adopting the draft agreements accordingly – simple *illocutionary silencing*.

Almost simultaneously with the General Assembly adopting the Trusteeship Agreements for French and British Togoland, Chapman was to leave the Gold Coast to accept a position as an area specialist at the *United Nations Secretary Department of Trusteeship and Information from Non-Self-Governing Territories*, where he worked until his return in 1954. It may be no coincident that Chapman worked at the UN when the first Ewe petitions arrived, and the British were already concerned that Chapman, in the role of an international civil servant, might be part of a future UN Visiting Mission to the Ewe areas.[57] In May 1947, Chapman wrote to Gerald O. Awuma, the ex-Bundarian and co-founder of the Togoland Union, to establish a United Nations Association in British Togoland, provided him with pamphlets, reports, illustrations, etc. on the work of the United Nations. Chapman thought that "this is the best, quickest and least expensive way of getting the information across to our people."[58]

The *Togoland United Nations Association* (TUNA) was short-lived. Yet, a particularly diligent young member of TUNA, the teacher Senyo Gatror Antor, published the Togoland United Nations Association newsletter from 1947 onwards, which, thanks to the information material provided by Chapman, kept the people of the trusteeship territory informed of what was happening at the United Nations.[59] Antor, who was himself a Guan and not an Ewe, was to break with Awuma in 1950 and become the leading figure in the unification movement on the British side of the Togoland border. One of the reasons for his desire to reunify Togoland lied in his simultaneous position as Secretary of the *Togoland Farmers Association*, which advocated for independence from the Gold Coast Cocoa

---

56 TNA (London), CO 537/2037, *Problem of the Ewe people in British and French Togoland*, 1947, K.E. Robinson, no title.
57 TNA (London), CO 537/2037, *Problem of the Ewe people in British and French Togoland*, K.E. Robinson, no title.
58 UN ARMS (New York), S-1554-0000-0003, *Africa – Cameroon and Togoland -Visiting Mission*, 1949, The United Nations and the People of Western Togoland, by Gerald O. Awuma, p. 7.
59 UN ARMS (New York), S-1554-0000-0003, *Africa – Cameroon and Togoland -Visiting Mission*, The Togoland U.N.A. Newsletter, Vol. 1., No. 3, September 1947.

Marketing Board, so that cocoa from British Togoland could be marketed independently and the revenue would not go to projects in the Gold Coast.

Chapman's trajectory in the further development of the unification campaign is more than ironic when gauged from a security-focused point of view: though his role was somewhat foundational for the post-war Ewe unification movement, upon his return to the Gold Coast he decamped from the AEC to Nkrumah's *Convention People's Party* (CPP), which advocated for the integration of British Togoland into the Gold Coast. After Ghana's independence, Chapman himself would assume the Chairmanship of Ghana's highest intelligence body, the Local Intelligence Committee (LIC), gathering intelligence for example on the Togoland Congress while his brother, Charles H. Chapman, would become Regional Commissioner in Trans-Volta-Togoland (TVT) and enforce the Avoidance of Discrimination Act and the Preventive Detention Act to quell Ewe and Western Togoland unrest.[60]

6.2.2 Establishment of the Petition Procedure

Before the start of the Trusteeship Council's 1st Session (1946), the unpleasant petitions from the AEC were again subject of an Anglo-French inter-ministerial meeting at Whitehall in March 1947. There, the possibility of the British offering Gambia or British Cameroon in exchange for the French parts of Togoland was discussed, but this was rejected on the grounds that it would be heavily criticised by the United Nations and would not appeal to the populations concerned.[61] In any case, the prestige of the colonial powers would be tarnished if they allowed themselves to be driven by the aspirations of a 'minor' nationalist movement and it was feared that giving in on this point would set a precedent for other nationalist movements, which could lead to the 'balkanisation' of the African continent.

At the end of the month, the Trusteeship Council was ready to start its work in New York. In admonitory words, UN Secretary-General Trygve Lie recapped during the inauguration of the Trusteeship Council that the debates in San Francisco and London...

> "... may have raised the question in people's minds whether the interests of the nations or the interests of the inhabitants of the prospective Trust Territories were the paramount consideration. The Administering Authorities may have wondered on occasion whether they or the Trust Territories most needed United Nations protection."[62]

It was a sharp reminder that the Soviet Union boycotted the 1st Session of the Trusteeship Council. That's why, during the 1st Session, the non-administering Council members

---

60 The Prevention of Discrimination Act (1957) had a progressive veneer in name, but ultimately banned all parties based on ethnic, regional, or religious grounds. Parties like the Togoland Congress or the Ewe Associations became illegal groups practically overnight. The Preventive Detention Act (1958) gave the Ghanaian government the power to detain an individual for up to five years without the right of appeal.

61 TNA (London), FO 371/67718, *Problem of the unification of the EWE ethnic group in Togoland (under British and French trusteeship)*, 1947, Minutes "The Ewe Problem", William Blanch, 21 March 1947.

62 TCOR, "1st Session" (1947), p. 1.

were outnumbered by 4:5.[63] This allowed the colonial powers, whose primary concern was preserving their prerogatives by limiting the *rules of procedure* for the examination of petitions to the minimum requirements of the Charter. The history of the Trusteeship System could have been much different had the Soviet Union simply assumed its membership during the Trusteeship Council's first session and used its voting power with respect to the *rules of procedure*. The Council spent much more time and drafted more rules of procedure for petitions than for annual reports and Visiting Missions combined. Most of the rules of procedure were proposed on the initiative of the Administering Authorities, while the non-Administering Authorities mitigated excessive restrictions.[64]

Already in the 1st Session (1947), disagreements on the petition procedure arose between the representatives of the colonial powers and non-Administering powers. With the AEC petitions in mind and concerned with a potential compromise of their positions, the French and British representative insisted that, if petitions could not already be "solved on the spot,"[65] they should – like the provisions of the Mandates System – be submitted exclusively through Administering Authorities. The Iraqi Council representative, Awni Khalidy, strongly objected:

> "If you want to accuse Mr. X, you do not submit the accusation to Mr. X. That is to say, petitions are mostly, if not always, some sort of accusation, and if the inhabitants are to present accusations against the Administering Authorities to the Administering Authorities, then why have the Trusteeship Council at all? In fact, when it comes to that, why have the United Nations?"[66]

For the Administering Authorities, security was a pivotal aspect during the petition debate: The representative of New Zealand, Carl Berendsen, defused Khalidy's objection via the argument of security: "There is great validity in that point of view. But may I suggest that Mr. X in this case is a very peculiar and particular Mr. X? Mr. X is the Authority responsible for the peace and the order and the good government of the Territory."[67] Similarly, the Australian representative, Norman Makin, raised security considerations to express his concern about the publicity that would result if petitions were circulated immediately in the Trusteeship Council or the Secretariat, or if public access to the petition register were established.[68] The Mexican delegate, Luis Padilla Nervo, countered:

> "I do not think the fact that the members of the Council knew of petitions would present any danger to the Administering Authority. We already know of some petitions that have been addressed to us. We know also that in the Security Council complaints of one State against another have been sent in and have been circulated

---

63 As the United States did not yet bring any territories under the Trusteeship System, administering members were Australia, New Zealand, Belgium, the United Kingdom, and France. Non-administering members were Iraq, Mexico, China, the United States, and the Soviet Union.
64 TCOR, "1st Session" (1947), 83, 87–89, 139, 145.
65 TCOR, "1st Session" (1947), p. 83.
66 TCOR, "1st Session" (1947), p. 90.
67 TCOR, "1st Session" (1947), p. 116.
68 TCOR, "1st Session" (1947), p. 94, pp. 174–175.

among the members long before the defendant State could have had an opportunity to answer or to send its comments. And those are matters relating to the maintenance of peace and security."[69]

Finally, the Council's President, the American representative Francis B. Sayre, put his foot down: "We must not delude ourselves into thinking that surrounding with restrictions the formalities of sending the petition through the Administering Authority will give adequate security to that Authority so far as concerns publicity and the danger of prejudicing the public because it has not heard the other side."[70]

The Administering Authorities believed their position would be compromised if the petitions were forwarded to Council members before the official comments from the trusteeship territories were available. The most extreme position on this issue was taken by the chairman of the French delegation, Roger Garreau, who believed that no petition should be submitted before the Administering Authority's views had also been communicated to the Council members. In any case, he insisted that a special representative of the Administering Authority be present when the Council discusses a petition so that always "both sides of the problem"[71] should be presented at the same time, that is, a colonial officer in persona on one side and the paper petition on the other.

Finally, it was agreed that petitions had to be submitted at least two months before the date of the next following regular session, to allow the Administering Authorities enough time for an official response to a petition. It was resolved that petitions could be sent to the UN in three ways: via the Administering Authority, the Secretary-General, or a UN Visiting Mission. The Belgian representative, Pierre Ryckmans, insisted that the UN Secretariat "should never take the initiative of adding any comment whatsoever, which in any case might be misinterpreted. The rules of procedure should not even mention the possibility."[72]

The French delegation proposed an *ad hoc* Committee, almost identical to the Mandates System, which would have been empowered to discriminate between admissible and non-admissible petitions.[73] The proposal provoked concern from non-Administering Authorities about public criticism if petitions, especially anonymous ones, would be excluded from examination.[74] Ultimately, the Council agreed on the *ad hoc* Committee, which, however, had no power to "throw out" petitions,[75] except if local courts were com-

---

69   TCOR, "1st Session" (1947), p. 96.
70   TCOR, "1st Session" (1947), p. 98.
71   TCOR, "1st Session" (1947), p. 123.
72   TCOR, "1st Session" (1947), p. 126.
73   T/15, *Amendment proposed concerning chapter XIV of the draft provisional rules of procedure of the Trusteeship Council / Delegation of France* (31 March 1947) available from digitallibrary.un.org/record/675417.
74   TCOR, "1st Session" (1947), pp. 133–43.
75   TCOR, "1st Session" (1947), p. 141.

petent to deal with the issue raised in them.⁷⁶ The *ad hoc* Committee was supposed to pre-examine petitions regarding their admissibility and possible order of consideration, but any appraisal of the substance was strictly prohibited – this was solely the prerogative of the Administering Authorities, through their comments, and the Council during its debates. Oral hearings of petitioners would only be granted in support of previously submitted written petitions.

In sum, the Council decided upon a procedure like under the Permanent Mandates Commission: the appointment of an *ad hoc* Committee to examine petitions, followed by a general discussion of the petitions by the Council itself including the questioning of a special representative, whereafter the *ad hoc* Committee formulated a resolution based upon the Council's discussion.

First Written Petitions

Since the Trusteeship System's establishment, Ewe petitioners addressed the Council. Even before the start of the Council's 2nd Session (1947), the Secretariat had received seven petitions by the AEC requesting the unification of the Ewe people.

When the French were informed about these petitions, at first they considered them a ploy by the British to appropriate all of Togoland rather than a genuine anti-colonial challenge.⁷⁷ Thus, another inter-ministerial Anglo-French meeting was convened at Rue Oudinot in May 1947 to coordinate official observations on the Ewe petitions before the Council's 2nd Session (1947).⁷⁸ The French and British ministerial representatives agreed that a joint Anglo-French memorandum should be submitted to the Trusteeship Council. The memorandum virtually securitised the demand voiced in the Ewe petitions as a danger of 'balkanizing' the African continent. Accordingly, the memorandum stated that "the proper policy in West Africa is not to create a large number of small, isolated units. […] It would seem to be a mistaken policy if the powers responsible for West Africa […] should embark upon a policy which would result in dividing the Continent into a mosaic of rival countries."⁷⁹ Furthermore, it was stated that in the long run, a political entity consisting only of the Ewe would be too small and would not have the economic and other foundations necessary for an independent state.⁸⁰ The memorandum furthermore attempted to depoliticize the demand of the petitions by presenting the Ewes' claim as a demand

---

76   The Administrating Authorities were concerned to convert the Council into a court of appeal. The concern seemed justified as in 1955 the issue was raised before the Fourth Committee question whether petitioners could be represented by lawyers (United Nations, "Art. 85," in United Nations (UN) *Repertory of Practice of United Nations Organs*, Vol. Vol. II.
77   ANOM (Aix-en-Provence), 1AFFPOL/3297/1, *Affaires politiques*, Confidential Letter to Minister of Overseas France, N° 49, APA, 2 May 1947, p. 9; also see Michel, "The Independence of Togo," p. 298; Ansprenger, *Politik im Schwarzen Afrika*, p. 210; Amenumey, *The Ewe Unification Movement*, p. 49.
78   ANOM (Aix-en-Provence), 1AFFPOL/3284/1, *Affaire Ewe*, Réunion Franco-Britannique au sujet du problème Éwe.
79   TCOR, "Memorandum on the Petition of the All Ewe Conference to the United Nations" T/58 (1947), p. 12.
80   ANOM (Aix-en-Provence), 1AFFPOL/3284/1, *Affaire Ewe*, Aecret Letter to Laurentie, 25 July 1947.

that merely appealed to the economic hardships caused by the frontier, rather than considering the petitions as a political movement with nationalist ambitions. Therefore, the memorandum proposed to conduct a study on the possible creation of a conventional zone, which would function as a single customs regime, and to create a Consultative Commission where elected African representatives could advise the administration to mitigate cultural and economic hardships which the border causes. However, a general debate on the course of the border as such was ruled out.

The Commission's name *Consultative Commission on Togoland Affairs* said it all: "Consultative" meant that the Commission had no say, and "on Togoland affairs" had been agreed upon at the instigation of the French because they were very anxious that the Commission should indeed be a Togoland and not a purely Ewe affair.[81] The Consultative Commission had to deal not only with the border running through Ewe territory, but with the whole of Togoland. This was advantageous for the Administrative Authorities, as they could point out the difficulty of making arrangements for the entire border.[82]

The minutes of the inter-ministerial meeting of May 1947 show that the French in particular hoped to silence the Ewe petitions by questioning their admissibility.[83] During the meeting the French and British representatives agreed that the submission of the memorandum should be as late as Article 86 of the Council's rules of procedure allow in order to keep the window of opportunity for the Trusteeship Council and room for manoeuvre for the petitioners as small as possible[84] – a strategy that was to shape the next decade of petition examinations. During the Trusteeship Council's examination of the petitions Thomas Mead and Henri Laurentie were selected to act as special representatives of Britain and France respectively.

The Administering Authorities pursued a dual strategy: on the one hand, by employing the Balkanization argument, they sought to securitize the Ewe demands. On the other hand, they attempted to depoliticize these demands by framing the call for Ewe unification as an economic issue rather than a political one.

First Oral Hearing

One of the seven Ewe petitions was a request for an oral hearing by Sylvanus Olympio. In retrospect, the Ghanian diplomat, Alex Quaison-Sackey, noted that none of the Council members had expected such an early request for an oral hearing. The American Council president, Francis B. Sayre, was apprehensive: "hearing of oral petitions is a matter of favour and not of right [...] it is for the Trusteeship Council to decide whether it shall consider a petition, and not for the petitioner."[85] Yet, following the expression of concern

---

81 PRAAD (Accra), ADM 39/1/676, *Standing Consultative Commission for Togoland*, Anglo-French Consultative Commission for Togoland, L.H. Gorsuch, 2 December 1948, p. 2.
82 PRAAD (Accra), ADM 39/1/677, *Agenda notes and minutes of the Standing Consultative Commission for Togoland*
83 ANOM (Aix-en-Provence), 1AFFPOL/3284/2, *Affaire Ewe*, Projet de mémorandum sur la pétition de la "All Ewe Conference" aux Nations Unies.
84 ANOM (Aix-en-Provence), 1AFFPOL/3284/1, *Affaire Ewe*, Annex II, Joint Memorandum: Concerning the attitude to be adopted on the Ewe question at the Trusteeship Council by the French and British Delegations, p. 1.
85 TCOR, "2nd Session" (1947), p. 34.

from anti-colonial Council members,[86] the request was ultimately granted. An anonymous observer recalled the prejudice and suspense of the eagerly awaited first oral hearing before the UN:

> "we had heard that there was a petitioner coming from Africa and didn't know quite what to expect. None of the delegates knew much about Africa, and I sincerely believe many of them expected someone to come rushing into the Council in a leopard skin and accompanied by a rumble of drums."[87]

Yet, addressing the Council in impeccable English and French, it was rather Olympio's westernized demeanour that caused a sensation. Olympio brought the necessary Bordieuan habitus into the play: Olympio belonged to the Afro-Brazilian merchant elite of Togoland. After completing a business degree at the London School of Economics in the mid-1920s, he worked as a representative of the United Africa Company – a branch of Unilever's West Africa operations. In the late 1930s, he was appointed director-general for West Africa and almost simultaneously became vice-president of French Togoland's first political party, the *Comité de l'Unité Togolaise* (CUT). Without question, Olympio provided the Western habitus and cultural capital needed to voice the demand of Ewe unification in such a colonial forum as the UN Trusteeship Council.

Meticulously listing previous petitions sent to the League of Nations and British Government (some of which had been written by his uncle Octaviano), Olympio did not appeal for straightforward independence, but merely for the unification of "his people," the Ewe, under a single and preferably British administration. He pointed out that for no apparent reason the French administration had banned a meeting between the Ewes living in the French zone and those living in the British zone just before the Council's current session.[88] Furthermore he criticised the Anglo-French memorandum's proposal to establish a Consultative Commission for Togoland because its terms of reference were limited to economic and cultural matters, the manner in which the two representatives of the inhabitants were to be chosen was not defined and the proposed permanent secretariat, which was to co-ordinate the efforts of the two Administrations, would be composed solely of men nominated by France and Britain, without any reference whatsoever to the wishes of the Ewe people.[89]

Yet, even despite his eloquent appearance, during the questioning Olympio faced the racist stereotypes. For example, the representative New Zealand asked:

> "This is not the first occasion upon which the matter of consultation with Africans has been brought before the United Nations. We actually had such a consultation in connexion with the inhabitants of South-West Africa, and the General Assembly saw fit to decide, rightly or wrongly, that the inhabitants of South-West Africa were so back-

---

86   TCOR, "2nd Session" (1947), p. 33.
87   Alex Quaison-Sackey, *Africa unbound: Reflections of an African statesman* (New York: Praeger, 1963), pp. 129–30.
88   TCOR, "2nd Session" (1947), p. 348.
89   TCOR, "2nd Session" (1947), pp. 327–28.

ward that they really were not able to express their views as to what should happen to them. Is there any such risk with regard to the Ewe people?"⁹⁰

This comment stands out as one of the few unequivocal illustrations that highlight compellingly silencing by *illocutionary disablement*. This instance is particularly noteworthy as it directly addresses the notion of the ability to express oneself.

Photo 3: Sylvanus Olympio & Ralph Bunche, Lake Success (8 December 1947)

Source: UN Photo.

But it played into Olympio's favour that he could keep his composure, putting France on the spot, especially since the joint administration of Nauru by Australia, New Zealand and Great Britain did not rule out a possible joint administration of Eweland. The Anglo-French attempt to depoliticise the Ewe movement by portraying it as a movement for economic grievances backfired. In fact, the French Special Representative, Henri Laurentie, was now virtually forced to argue that the proposed Consultative Commission was 'political enough' and represented "really a political commission, for no commission which was not political could hold such power."⁹¹ Furthermore he downplayed the importance,

---

90 TCOR, "2ⁿᵈ Session" (1947), pp. 348–49.
91 TCOR, "2ⁿᵈ Session" (1947), p. 358.

which Olympio attached to petitions that had been send previously to the League's Permanent Mandates Commission:

> "The fact that there was a series of written statements – though there were not really many of them – does not imply that partition had given rise to any difficulty whatsoever. In principle, it was perhaps a matter for regret that tribal unity had not been preserved in the delimitation of the frontier. In the territory itself, however, no open crisis was created by this frontier separating the two parts of the tribe."[92]

Laurentie underlined the Anglo-French position before the Trusteeship Council by echoing the securitising argument of a dangerous balkanization, arguing that…

> "…if we were to allow ourselves to be carried away by the [Ewe] movement, […] Africa would return to that condition of disintegration in which it was found by the European colonizers when they penetrated into the continent. Thus, we would be promoting a spirit of rivalry and of disunity which would certainly be contrary to the general interest of Africa. […] Togoland is not alone in being divided between the United Kingdom and France; the whole of West Africa is divided between those two Powers. […] To unify Togoland as if Togoland were not part of West Africa would be to upset the equilibrium of the whole of that part of the continent, to ignore one of the facts of the present political situation in Africa. This partitioning of the territories between British and French Administrations is, I repeat, an important factor, one of the most important factors, to be taken into consideration in an examination of the state of present-day West Africa. […] If we are in a transitional period, we should take transitional measures; measures which might create precedents and might unduly prejudice the future seem to me to be rather dangerous for the welfare of all sections of the population." [93]

The British special representative, Thomas Mead, furthermore, argued that the Ewe cannot even be considered a single nation because they are too fragmented. He concluded that some sub-grouping, such as the Mina or the Awatime, although speaking an Ewe-dialect, cannot be considered Ewe because they do not share the Notsé myth.[94] With regard to the prohibition of the meeting between Ewe from French and British Togoland, Laurentie replied that…

> "…the French Authorities considered that on the very eve of the Trusteeship Council's consideration of this matter it was quite useless, and probably improper, to hold a large conference which would have added only *useless noise* to a situation that had been perfectly well defined by previous Conferences […] Indeed, it was even out of respect, so to speak, for the Trusteeship Council that the French Government thought it inopportune for a manifestation of this kind to take place on the eve of the debate on these questions by our Council."[95]

---

92 TCOR, "2nd Session" (1947), p. 353.
93 TCOR, "2nd Session" (1947), pp. 355–57.
94 TCOR, "2nd Session" (1947), pp. 361–63.
95 Emphasis added, TCOR, "2nd Session" (1947), p. 380.

By seeking to pre-empt *illocutionary disablement* through the prevention of 'useless noise,' Laurentie ironically ended up silencing the Ewe conference through *illocutionary frustration*. That was a highly adventurous line of argumentation, which did not go unnoticed: The American representative, Francis B. Sayre, expressed concern about the banning of the meeting, whereupon Laurentie assured him that freedom of assembly not only existed but was even guaranteed in the French constitution (unless, apparently, it constitutes 'useless noise'). Yet again he repeated that "the French Authorities thought it inadvisable to allow discussion in the public square of what was about to become the business of the Council."[96] Finally, the Council recommended that the proposed Anglo-French Consultative Commission be set up as soon as possible on the terms proposed in the Anglo-French Memorandum, so that the Visiting Mission scheduled for 1949 could examine the Commission's work. Although Olympio's petition was factually rejected, the Council's president, Francis B. Sayre, judged Olympio to have "set a record-breaking international precedent" and a "'live example of implementing' the goals of independence as set out in the UN Charter."[97]

Olympio's return and the Consultative Commission on Togoland Affairs

After the media spectacle in New York, Olympio was celebrated on his return to Lomé, where he gave a lively account of his hearing before the Trusteeship Council to some 5000 CUT and AEC supporters.

Photo 4: Olympio addressing a crowd at Hotel Tonyeviadji, Lomé (4 January 1948)[98]

Source: ANOM (Aix-en-Provence), 1AFFPOL/3297/1, Affaires politiques.

---

96 TCOR, "2nd Session" (1947), p. 384.
97 "The Trust Territory of Togoland: An International Precedent," *The International Law Quarterly* 2, no. 2 (1948): 257; Editorial Notes, available from www.jstor.org/stable/763176.
98 ANOM (Aix-en-Provence), 1AFFPOL/3297/1, *Affaires politiques*

Photo 5: CUT Meeting after Olympio's return, Lomé (4 January 1948)[99]

Source: ANOM (Aix-en-Provence), 1AFFPOL/3297/1, *Affaires politiques*.

Photo 6a & 6b: AEC Meeting after Olympio's return, Ho (11 January 1948)

Source: ANOM (Aix-en-Provence), 1AFFPOL/3297/1, Affaires politiques, "Retour S. Olympio de New York à Ho. Conference." 11 January 1948. Photo by Alex A. Acolatsé.

The French, who intended to integrate Togoland into the French Union eventually, felt reaffirmed that Olympio and the unification-demanding petitions were a ploy by the British to appropriate all of Togoland. Especially the French Governor, Jean Noutary, was firmly convinced that the whole Ewe affair was a British ruse, and that Sylvanus Olympio was an Anglo-American agent.[100]

---

99 At centre: Augustino de Souza (left) and Sylvanus Olympio (right).
100 ANOM (Aix-en-Provence), 1AFFPOL/3297/1, *Affaires politiques*, Comité Unité Togolaise, N° 49 /APA, 2 May 1947.

As for the situation in New York, there was little concern, by March 1948, the deputy chief to the French delegation, Henri Laurentie, concluded (with a little exaggeration) that the Trusteeship Council has "established itself once for all in the most authentic colonialism."[101] However, the perspective on how to deal with it on-site appeared quite different:

> "The tactic, therefore, is to limit ourselves, for the time being, to the maneuver that is perfectly expressed by the sending of the petition requesting unification. [...] It is up to us to make this maneuver fail [yet] a success before the Trusteeship Council will not solve the issue at the local level."[102]

The French clearly tried to silence the movement and repress it locally. Accordingly, the French administration began to ostracize the unification movement, especially Olympio's party, the CUT. The French planned to replace the *Conseils de Notables*, established in 1922, with the *Conseils de Circonscription* (District Councils). As purely advisory bodies, they had no executive power, but especially in the rural areas, the French administration saw them as a way of giving small peasant producers a voice vis-à-vis the southern Ewe chiefs and merchant houses, likely breaking the hold of the CUT.[103]

Through secret funds, the government also provided financial support to the newly formed pro-French *Parti Togolais du Progrès* (PTP),[104] which under the leadership of Nicholas Grunitzky also petitioned the Trusteeship Council. At the 3rd Session (1948), the French delegation tried to stress the importance of the PTP petition, albeit with moderate success,[105] since the French representatives themselves had insisted that consideration of all present and future Ewe petitions to be postponed until the report of the 1949 Visiting Mission to West Africa would shed new light on the matter.[106]

The French administration surveilled Olympio and the CUT via the *Service de Sûreté*,[107] which had already been introduced after the Lomé riots of 1933. Its informants, the so-called "fils invisible," infiltrated a meeting held on 5 April 1948 at the de Souza estate. Since the CUT dominated the *Assemblée Représentative du Togo* (ART) since 1947, it had unsurprisingly elected Olympio as the African representative to the Consultative Commission on Togoland Affairs. The *Service de Sûreté* reported that after the AEC planned to adopt a resolution calling for the abolition on the border between British and French Togoland during another mammoth meeting at Kpalimé on 16 May 1948, that is, ten

---

101 ANF (Pierrefitte-sur-Seine), 72AJ/537, *Henri Laurentie*, Laurentie to Labonne, 13 March 1948.
102 ANOM (Aix-en-Provence), 1AFFPOL/3297/1, *Affaires politiques*, Note pour le Ministre, 19 September 1947, p. 1, translation.
103 ANOM (Aix-en-Provence), 1AFFPOL/3297/1, *Affaires politiques*, Note pour le Ministre, 19 September 1947, p. 3.
104 Alexander Keese, "Rigged Elections?," in *The French Colonial Mind: Mental Maps of Empire and Colonial Encounters*, ed. Martin Thomas, 2 vols., France Overseas: Studies in Empire and Decolonization Series 1 (Lincoln: University of Nebraska Press, 2011), p. 335.
105 TCOR, "3rd Session" (1948), p. 226.
106 TCOR, "3rd Session" (1948), pp. 130–31.
107 ANOM (Aix-en-Provence), 1AFFPOL/3297/1, *Affaires politiques*, Service de la Sûreté N° 36: Réunion du CUT

days before the first meeting of the Consultative Commission. Cédile informed his counterpart, the British Governor, Charles Arden-Clarke, that…

> "[…] As far as I can see, there are no reasons at the moment which would cause me to forbid the holding of this Congress which does not seem, so far as my present information goes, likely to lead to a breach of the peace. Nevertheless, I propose to take, in due course, all steps necessary for keeping it under surveillance, and I am at once issuing orders for the maximum of information."[108]

Thus, although the AEC resolution was not welcomed by the two Governors, they were not surprised when at the 1st Meeting of the Consultative Commission in May 1948 Olympio and the other African representatives presented their resolution.[109] At the 2nd meeting of the Commission in December 1948, the question arose whether the work of the Commission related only to Eweland or to the two Togolands. Of course, the British and the French insisted that the Commission should deal with all of Togoland as a whole. At the 4th meeting of the Commission in October 1949, Olympio called for a review of the area covered by the Commission, demanded that more African members be part of the Commission and that the mandate for the African representatives from British Togoland should last longer.[110] Olympio threatened to boycott the Consultative Commission and since the arrival of the UN Visiting Mission was near the British were trying to convince the French to extend the terms of reference of the Consultative Commission so that the unificationist representatives would not boycott the Commission altogether.[111]

Cédile's decision to share information on the unificationists marked the slowly occurring turning point in the Anglo-French cooperation in intelligence and security policy in colonial Africa, which was virtually non-existent up to this point in time. Although France and Britain were allies in World War II, French Togoland was controlled by the Vichy regime, virtually freezing Anglo-French security cooperation across the Togoland border.[112]

Two factors were to unfreeze Anglo-French cooperation in colonial security and intelligence matters: First, the Ewe unification movement was a trans-territorial problem and the French as well as the British relied on mutual intelligence to know what was happening on the other side of the border. The second factor was the general strike and rumours of approaching protests in the Ivory Coast, which began shortly after the Accra Riots of 1948. Both colonial powers saw these events as a threat to the colonial order, resulting from a lack of political intelligence. Although France and Britain reacted differently to

---

108 PRAAD (Ho), VRG/AD/250, *Standing Consultative Commission for Togoland*, 1948, Governor Cédile to Governor Arden-Clarke No. 82/Cab [Translation], 12 April 1948.
109 PRAAD (Ho), VRG/AD/250, *Standing Consultative Commission for Togoland*, Minutes of the 1st Session of the Standing Consultative Commission for Togoland, p. 2.
110 PRAAD (Accra), ADM 39/1/677, *Agenda notes and minutes of the Standing Consultative Commission for Togoland*, Standing Consultative Commission, 4th Session. Supplementary agenda [71].
111 PRAAD (Ho), VRG/AD/1027, *Standing Consultative Commission for Togoland*
112 Only after France deposed the Vichy regime, there was a French Security Liaison Officer in Accra with whom there was constant exchange.

their respective troubles, they agreed (albeit somewhat half-heartedly) to cooperate on security issues.

6.3 Security Matters: Trouble in Accra & Abidjan (1948–1951)

6.3.1 The Accra Riots & the Special Branch

During World War II, thousands of troops from across Africa fought for the British Empire. The British's Gold Coast Regiment was sent via India to Burma to fight the Japanese. Many African servicemen were affected by the experience of the war and during their time in India particularly by the exposure to Gandhi's leading voice in the struggle for independence from the British. For the part they played in the War, the African servicemen were promised pensions and jobs, yet upon their return, they faced the deteriorating social and economic situation after World War II, which led to an increased social discontent. The Swollen Shoot Virus certainly exacerbated the general economic situation, which affected particularly cocoa farmers in Southern Togoland, where cocoa was the main source of the entire territory's revenue.

In January 1948, boycotts of imported European goods were coordinated in protest of exorbitant pricing and the control of trade cartels such as the all-powerful Cocoa Marketing Board holding the cocoa price down.[113] On 28 February 1948, the veterans of the Gold Coast Regiment organized a protest march in coordination with the colonial authorities. The ex-servicemen intended to present a petition to Governor Gerald Creasy as a reminder to keep the promises, which were made during the war.[114] Yet, the approved procession diverted from its prescribed route and headed for the governor's seat at Christiansborg Castle, where the police stopped it. While the local police officers refused to open fire on the crowd of 2,000 people, the commanding Superintendent of Police, Colin Imray, panicked as he was facing…

> "[…] a vast milling crowd of very excited shouting men, filling the road and even now starting to envelop our flanks. Two thoughts dominated: 'They must not pass' and 'Minimum force'. Many were in fact waving sticks, cudgels, and anything else that came to hand […] baton charges were clearly out of the question. Again, I shouted, but this time it was 'Disperse or I fire'. More and more stones and yells of derision. Desperately I tore the rifle and bandolier from the nearest man, stuffed six rounds into the magazine, levelled on the man with the horn – now very close – and fired. He went down in a heap."[115]

---

113   Alence Rod discusses the emergence of cocoa marketing boards in the Gold Coast in the context of tensions between the interests of the colonial state and the peasant population. Rod Alence, "Colonial Government, Social Conflict and State Involvement in Africa's Open Economies," *The Journal of African History* 42, no. 3 (2001)

114   His/Her Majesty's Stationery Office, "Report of the Commission of Enquiry into Disturbances in the Gold Coast," Colonial Reports 231, pp. 96–97.

115   Colin Imray, *Policeman in Africa* (Lewes: Book Guild, 1997), pp. 124–26.

Three protesters, who were in fact ex-servicemen, were killed at the crossroads.[116] Witnessing the excessive and unjustified violence against the unarmed men, the protesters took their anger to the streets, attacked European businesses and property in Accra as well as in other cities. On 1 March, two days after the fatal shooting, Governor Creasy, passed the Riot Act declaring a state of emergency. It took the Gold Coast security forces five days to get the riots back under control. British and French reports speak of around 14 people being killed and around 140 wounded in the following days.[117]

The British set up a commission of inquiry to investigate the disturbances and find viable solutions to prevent such events in the future. Chaired by Andrew Aiken Watson, the commission's report states prophetically: "The riots cannot be regarded as isolated incidents which developed because of the shooting at the Christiansborg crossroads. They have a history, and they have a sequel."[118] The Accra riots were considered not as a singular event but symptomatic of a much bigger problem: the post-war years showed that anticolonial discontent grew across the British Empire and that the colonial administrations were notoriously incapable of predicting and containing the frequent disturbances. Similarly, Michael Ensor, then Permanent Secretary in the Gold Coast's Ministry of Defence & External Affairs, held that the shootings and the riots of 1948 demonstrated violently "the Gold Coast Government's failure to appreciate the seriousness of the several strands of post-war discontent and the unpreparedness of almost everyone in authority for a serious outbreak of violence."[119] The Colonial Secretary and Deputy Governor, Reginald Saloway, held that "the forces of law and order were utterly inadequate."[120] As an immediate remedy, Governor Creasy was replaced by Charles Arden-Clarke, yet for a long term strategy the 'Watson-Commission' recommended a two-pronged approach.

On the one hand, while completely exonerating Superintended Imray for the shooting at the Christiansborg crossroad, the Watson-Commission concluded that the government was clashing with the realities of the time. The 1946 'Burns-Constitution,'[121] named after the then-Governor Alan Burns, who by that date was sitting as the British Permanent Representative in the Trusteeship Council, was regarded as "outmoded by birth."[122] The Watson-report recommended a new constitution to strengthen the participation of local representatives and the Africanisation of government. To make suggestions on this new constitution, the colonial administration set up an all-African

---

116   Ex-Private Odartey Lamptey, ex-Corporal Patrick Attipoe and ex-Sergeant Cornelius Francis Adjetey.
117   ANOM (Aix-en-Provence), 1AFFPOL/2115/1, *Dossiers généraux A.F.P., Des Incidents dans la colonie britannique de la Côte de l'Or* (without number), no date.
118   His/Her Majesty's Stationery Office, "Report of the Commission of Enquiry into Disturbances in the Gold Coast," p. 89.
119   Imray, *Policeman in Africa*, p. 49.
120   As quoted in Rathbone, "Police intelligence in Ghana in the late 1940s and 1950s," p. 107.
121   Named after Alan Burns, Governor of the Gold Coast between June 1942, and August 1948. His governorship is undoubtedly partly responsible for the occurrence of the social unrest six months later. By the time of the Accra riots, Burns functioned as the British permanent representative in the UN Trusteeship Council.
122   His/Her Majesty's Stationery Office, "Report of the Commission of Enquiry into Disturbances in the Gold Coast," p. 24.

Committee, presided by Justice H. Coussey. On the other hand, the Watson-Commission also recommended that "early steps be taken to reorganise and strengthen the Intelligence Branch of the Police Force"[123] – the so-called Special Branch.

Origin of the Special Branch

The Special Branch was originally created in March 1883, when it was formed as unit of London's Metropolitan Police to acquire intelligence on the Irish Brotherhood, which was responsible for a series of dynamite bombings throughout England in the 1880s.1005F[124] Special Branch members were Metropolitan police officers that have gone through the usual police work of directing traffic and taking down numbers. While so engaged in their early years, they were hand-picked for the Special Branch because of their special knowledge of languages, foreign countries, commerce, industry, the arts, or sciences. During World War I, the nucleus of the Special Branch consisted of Army officers of field rank, carefully selected from the Intelligence Corps. The principal task of the Special Branch was to acquire political intelligence to ensure the security of the state. After World War II, England and Wales alone had no less than 126 separate police forces independent of each other, most of which had their own Special Branches. The main function of creating the British Security Services (MI5)[125] was to collate and coordinate all the reports from the Special Branches throughout Britain.[126] Thus, when the British Empire spread across Africa, so did the Special Branch. Yet, it is noteworthy that this happened under the aegis of the British *domestic* intelligence service MI5 and not the British *foreign* intelligence service MI6. Thus, it can be deduced that, in good colonial fashion, developments in the overseas colonial possessions were viewed as an internal rather than an external security problem. The distribution of tasks among the security agencies was indicative regarding the UK's understanding of 'home affairs'.

Before the Accra riots, police forces played only a minor role in the politics of the Gold Coast and British Togoland.[127] Certainly, since its advent colonial police was frequently used to violently secure territory, impose colonial rule and 'pacify' local disturbances. At times, colonial police certainly resembled rather more than less colonial para-military forces.[128] In fact, during World War I, Gold Coast police forces were conscripted as an arm to the British military, which was deployed in the Togoland campaign.[129] Yet, once the League of Nations approved the British mandate over Togoland, thereby enforcing its non-militarization imperative, urban police were spending more time on 'non-political' tasks such as petty crime, monitoring of licensing or traffic regulation. Until the Accra

---

123 His/Her Majesty's Stationery Office, "Report of the Commission of Enquiry into Disturbances in the Gold Coast," p. 15.
124 TNA (London), FCO 141/4990, *Gold Coast: Security Liaison Officer, West Africa*
125 Fifth Section of Military Intelligence, also known as "Security Service."
126 TNA (London), FCO 141/4992, *Gold Coast: Special Branch; security and training*, Draft Paper, Post-Independence Intelligence Organisation (without number), 16 January 1957.
127 Rathbone, "Police intelligence in Ghana in the late 1940s and 1950s," p. 107.
128 Brogden, "The emergence of the police," p. 13.
129 F. J. Moberly, *Military operations: Togoland and the Cameroons, 1914–1916* (London: H.M.S.O., 1931), p. 32.

riots of 1948, little attention had been paid to a policy, which would standardise the organisation of police and its role within the colonial state.[130] In fact, there was only a single Special Branch Officer operating in the entire Gold Coast.[131] The Accra riots of 1948 would change this fundamentally.

While it is acknowledged that the riots led to widely visible constitutional developments, put forward by the Coussey Committee, the riots also led to less visible developments in the colonial security structures, even well beyond the Gold Coast. Following the Watson-report, the British government despatched high ranking security and intelligence officers for audit tours in the territory: In 1948, Alexander E. Kellar, head of MI5's E-Branch;[132] in 1949, William Johnson, first Colonial Police Advisor;[133] in 1950, Arthur Young, Commissioner of Police of the City of London; and in 1954, Derek Franklin Deputy, Inspector General of the Colonial Police (Special Branch Kenya) as well as Alex M. MacDonald, MI5's first Security Intelligence Advisor.

Yet, with the Accra riots as the trigger, the empire-wide colonial security reforms were first implemented in the Gold Coast and, in extenso, in British Togoland. Police staff was increased, and tear-gas was stocked,[134] which "would have deprived the nationalists of the martyrs at the Christiansborg crossroads."[135] The police force doubled in size between 1947 and 1952 in the Gold Coast and British Togoland. In British Togoland alone, police forces quadrupled, and spending doubled between 1948 and 1955.[136]

And yet it should be noted that British Togoland by no means became a police state but rather remained a minimal state, since the police force, not even 100 men strong, was supposed to watch over an area that roughly corresponded to the size of Slovenia. Although British Togoland accounted for about 16% of the total territory administered by Accra, in 1956 it accounted for only about 3% of all stationed police forces, as they were posted mainly in the populous coastal areas. Togoland was just a sideshow.

---

130 Only during WWII did MI5 maintain a Security Liaison Officer for the whole of West Africa to: Colonel M.H. Haigh-Wood 08/1941-1944; Colonel P.E.L. Russel 04/1944-194[8]; Colonel Stephens (transferred to Middle East mid 1951; P. Kirby-Green (coming from Singapore until about mid-1954). The post of the SLO West Africa was then abolished and there was only the SLO in Nigeria and Gold Coast.
131 TNA (London), FCO 141/4992, *Gold Coast: Special Branch; security and training*, Special Branch Instruction No. 1, March 1948.
132 Since 1941, the E-Branch was responsible for 'alien control'.
133 See Georgina Sinclair, *At the end of the line: Colonial policing and the imperial endgame, 1945–80*, Studies in imperialism (Manchester: Manchester University Press, 2010), p. 56.
134 TNA (London), FCO 141/4999, *Gold Coast: security and political intelligence; policy*, p. 7.
135 Richard Rathbone, "The Government of the Gold Coast After the Second World War," *African Affairs* 67, no. 268 (1968): 215, available from https://www.jstor.org/stable/719904.
136 Calculations based on Annual Reports (1948–1955). The reports were written in such a way that it was difficult to discern these changes at first glance.

Figure 3: Police Force in British Togoland (1947–1955)

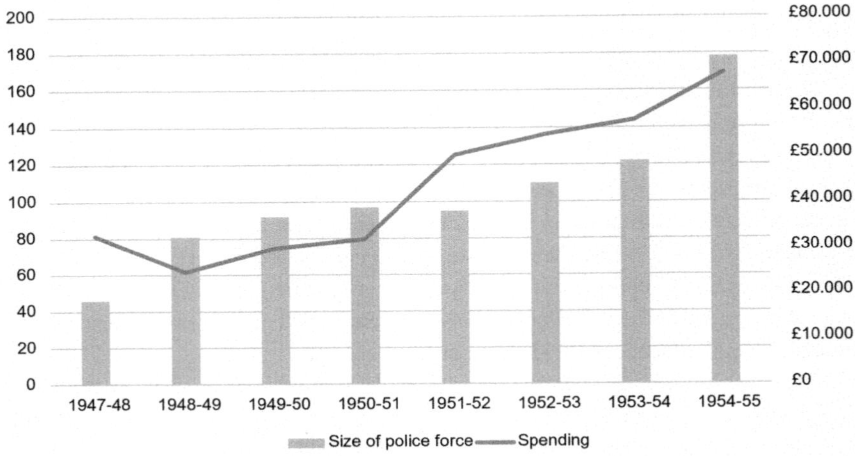

[Bar and line chart showing Size of police force (bars) and Spending (line) across years 1947-48 through 1954-55. Police force size grows from ~45 to ~180; spending grows from ~£30,000 to ~£70,000.]

Source: Own creation. Calculations based on Annual Reports (1948–1955).

Tasks of Special Branch

Before the Accra riots, the Special Branch was virtually inexistent in the Gold Coast. The sole Special Branch officer was part of the Criminal Investigation Department (CID) covering the whole territory.[137] Therefore the Gold Coast's Commissioner of Police, Richard Ballantine, wrote just a month after the Accra riots to the Colonial Secretary, Reginald Saloway:

> "the emergence of organised subversion inside the Colony and the probability of its stimulation by outside agencies raises a clear and immediate need for widening the scope and activities of the Special Branch. [...] this Force can only hope to meet its future responsibilities to Government, in the directions indicated, if a systematic and long-term penetration of all organisations and persons potentially dangerous to Government is commenced now, and accorded a high degree of operational priority."[138]

To ensure a continuing review of internal security measures, Alexander Kellar, head of the MI5's E-Branch, recommended just one month after the riots the creation of a *Central Security Committee* (CenSeC) – a weekly meeting of the Governor, the Senior Colonial Secretary (Ministry of Defence), the Chief of the Gold Coast Regiment, and the Commissioner of Police.[139] By 1 April 1948, the Special Branch of the Criminal Investigation Department operated under a revised organisation and procedure. Six Special Branch officers were immediately employed to provide the CenSeC with political intelligence.

---

137 TNA (London), FCO 141/4992, *Gold Coast: Special Branch; security and training*, Special Branch Instruction. No. 1. Reorganisation. (without number), March 1948, p. 1.

138 TNA (London), FCO 141/4992, *Gold Coast: Special Branch; security and training* Commissioner of Police to Colonial Secretary (S.F. 770 Secret), 9 April 1948.

139 Rathbone, "Police intelligence in Ghana in the late 1940s and 1950s," p. 110.

Their targets were comprehensive but primarily comprised subversive indigenous societies, labour organisations, and communist activities.[140]

The main source for information of the Special Branch were paid secret informers[141] or officers screening mail at the Post & Telegram Department.[142] Security reports were written by Special Branch and Police officers but also from officers working in the Ministry of Labour. District Officer evaluated the collected intelligence and forwarded it for submission to CenSeC.[143] The emergence of this new mode of obtaining information undoubtedly undermined the once virtually untouchable power of the chief commissioners, the "barons" of the Gold Coast.[144] Now reports and records played an essential role and had high operational aspect reflecting "the Intelligence 'Order of Battle' now planned by S.B."[145] Yet, the Special Branch's terms of reference, set out by Young in his report, clearly restricted its powers:

> "The purpose of the Special Branch is confined to the provision of intelligence regarding those who seek to injure or destroy the Government, or the Constitution, or the country by unconstitutional or subversive means. The Special Branch gives warning by reporting such facts, but any subsequent action which the authorities may take as part of their responsibility to protect the country from harm is in no way a function of the Branch."[146]

The Special Branch was, thus, a pure intelligence service without executive powers, that is, lacking the plenary powers, the Special Branch officers were merely allowed to 'smell out and report,' yet, not allowed to make arrests themselves for example. Thus, the Special Branch was at the same time part of and separate from the police.

Spying on Political Parties

The reorganisation of the Special Branch was a response to newly perceived menaces to colonial domination. It is ultimately the plague (if not the fate) of historical security and intelligence research that empirical material is scarce. Only a handful of these reports still exist as each of the reports, displaying incriminating intelligence practices, was supposed to be destroyed in the first week of each quarter.[147] The documents that still can be found in *The National Archives* (TNA) were supposed to disappear in Accra and allow only a slight glimpse into the whole picture. The collected material remains rather suggestive. The Special Branch Summary Reports from July 1951 until December 1952,[148] which were probably all penned by L. Chapman, Head of the Gold Coast Police in charge of Special

---

140 TNA (London), FCO 141/4992, *Gold Coast: Special Branch; security and training*, Special Branch Instruction. No. 1. Reorganisation. (without number), March 1948. p. 1.
141 TNA (London), FCO 141/5001, *Gold Coast: security and political intelligence; policy*, 1957
142 TNA (London), FCO 141/4992, *Gold Coast: Special Branch; security and training*
143 TNA (London), FCO 141/4999, *Gold Coast: security and political intelligence; policy*, T.I.K. Lloyd to Charles Arden-Clarke, *Securtiy and Political Intelligence* (without number), 29 April 1953, pp. 2–3.
144 Rathbone, "Police intelligence in Ghana in the late 1940s and 1950s," p. 125.
145 TNA (London), FCO 141/4992, *Gold Coast: Special Branch; security and training*
146 TNA (London), FCO 141/5001, *Gold Coast: security and political intelligence; policy*
147 TNA (London), FCO 141/4992, *Gold Coast: Special Branch; security and training*, p. 62.
148 TNA (London), FCO 141/4997, *Gold Coast: Special Branch Summaries*

Branch, deal for the most part with the activities of *Convention Peoples Party* (CPP) founded by Kwame Nkrumah,[149] who had decamped from the *United Gold Coast Convention* (UGCC) in June 1949 and openly displayed sympathies for communism when sought "Self-Government NOW" by means of a non-violent *Positive Action* campaign.[150] In early 1950 with growing popular support that led to widespread strikes and violent unrest, Nkrumah was promptly arrested and jailed for sedition.

Another focus of the Special Branch lay on the various trade and labour unions in the Gold Coast, which since the Accra riots were regarded as the primary incubator for communist or anti-colonial disturbances. Thus, in August 1948, the Germanophile *Togoland Union*, also came under the scrutiny of the Special Branch since it applied for registration as a trade union.[151] Many of its members were members of the *Bund der deutschen Togoländer*. Although it championed the reunification of British and French Togoland in its German borders, in autumn of 1948, the Togoland Union was still able to sign a joint resolution with the All-Ewe Conference, supporting the unification of all Ewelands. Yet, when in August 1949 (only three months before the arrival of the UN Visiting Mission) the British administration inaugurated the Southern Togoland Council in an effort to unite the Ewe of the Volta Triangle with those of southern British Togoland into a single administrative district, the Togoland Union was determined to resist the political influence of the Gold Coast Ewes and their efforts to integrate British Togoland into the Gold Coast.[152] The Togoland Union was aggravated that it was not represented in the Coussey Commission on Constitutional Reform, which recommend the establishment of the Southern Togoland Council. The Union's leadership feared that this Council would become a legislative body and protested the election of a representative of the Southern Togoland Council as a member of the Gold Coasts Legislative Council, since this would further manifest Togoland's integration into the Gold Coast.[153]

Within the Togoland Union Ex-Bundarians in particular took a liking to drastic words. Thus, already in June 1949, Gerald O. Awuma, co-founder of the *Bund der deutschen Togoländer* wrote to the British Secretary of State for the Colonies:

---

149 TNA (London), FCO 141/4997, *Gold Coast: Special Branch Summaries*. The summary reports (all written by the Gold Coast's Chief Commissioner of Police, L. Chapman) comprised about 10 pages per monthly summary.

150 "Positive Action" was a campaign of political protests and strikes launched by Kwame Nkruma in the run-up to the Accra riots of 1948. Launched to fight imperialism through non-violence and popular awareness, the campaign ended with the election of Nkrumah in 1951, which initiated the transformation from a British colony to an independent nation, ending the decolonisation process.

151 PRAAD (Accra), ADM 39/1/651, *Togoland Union and Togoland Association for the United Nation Association Statement subject and reasons etc*, Application for Registration of the Togo Union, 9 August 1948.

152 PRAAD (Accra), ADM 39/1/105, *United Nations Organisation Visiting Mission – Petitions*, Resolution of the Togoland Union on Behalf of the Natural Rulers and the People of Togoland under United Kingdom Trusteeship, [14 August 1949].

153 PRAAD (Accra), ADM 39/1/651, *Togoland Union and Togoland Association for the United Nation Association Statement subject and reasons etc*, Reform in Togoland Constitution.

"It appears that a rule of terror still exists in Western Togoland, and that freedom of speech is still unknown. [...] all the key position in the Government, the Schools, Commerce, and even the Native Administration, are filled with adventueres [sic] from Gold Coast Eweland. [...] Should the inborn Togolander then be judged unreasonable when he rightly concludes that the Gold Coast Government, conspired to support the Gold Coast Ewes in their intrigues and trickery to set up a Totalitarian Tyranny in Togoland and dominate, supplant and oppress the Togolander in his own home?"[154]

Security Liaison Officer

To ensure a continuing review of internal security measures, Alexander Kellar, head of the MI5's E-Branch, recommended the permanent posting of an MI5 *Security Liaison Officer* (SLO) to assist local police in intelligence services.[155]

During World War II, MI5 had sought to install basic intelligence and security programs in West Africa. They had originally been motivated by indications in 1939 that German agents were gathering information on Allied shipping in the South Atlantic to disrupt wartime aid from America. Although these indications were in hindsight unfounded, MI5 responded by posting SLOs at the headquarters of the West Africa Command in Accra.[156] SLOs were thus the most important representative of MI5 in British West Africa, whose principal task was to advise local authorities on how to prevent subversion and protect sensitive information from foreign agents.[157] As part of the '*normal* Commonwealth defence apparatus,' SLOs were local agents of a network for the empire-wide provision and exchange of defence information. The network of SLOs around the world was intended to enable the acquisition of security-related information for individual territories. For example, if a person classified as dangerous intended to visit a British colony, relevant information was forwarded from the local SLO to London or to SLOs in corresponding territories.[158] Instead of acting on its own, the SLO primarily maintained contact with security and intelligence agents. The SLO was not supposed to initiate agent operations or use informants unless asked to do so and had the permission of the police commissioner. Nevertheless, the SLO's identity was often kept secret because, since as a node of the security and intelligence links, the SLO was usually in the possession of sensitive security information and therefore had to be shielded from being the target of foreign intelligence gathering.

Since no procedure to collate intelligence existed for the British colonies before the Accra riots, the appointment of the first official Colonial Police Advisor, William Johnson in November 1948 would mark the beginning of the Colonial Office's attempts to unify and reform the 43 separate police forces of the Colonial Police Service. In 1949 alone, Johnson visited Cyprus, Gambia, Sierra Leone, the Gold Coast, Nigeria, Hong Kong, Singa-

---

154 PRAAD (Ho), D/DA/376, *Togo Union*, 1951, Gerald O. Awuma to Colonial Secretary, 7 June 1949.
155 During World War II the Security Liaison Officer at the West Africa Command was the principal MI5 Representative in West Africa TNA (London), FCO 141/4990, *Gold Coast: Security Liaison Officer, West Africa*.
156 Colonel M.H. Haigh-Wood from 1941 until 1944 and Colonel P.E.L. Russel from 1944 until 1948[?].
157 TNA (London), FCO 141/4990, *Gold Coast: Security Liaison Officer, West Africa*.
158 TNA (London), FCO 141/4992, *Gold Coast: Special Branch; security and training*, Post-Independence Intelligence Organisation, p. 10.

pore, Malaya, north Borneo, Brunei, and Sarawak. "Suddenly," Georgina Sinclair noted, "the Colonial Office was preoccupied with global security."[159]

6.3.2 The Abidjan Troubles & the Service de Sûreté

But the French also had their own problems to contend with. Ever since Felix Houphouët-Boigny and the *Rassemblement Democratique Africain* (RDA), instigated a general strike in 1948, the French considered the Ivory Coast as a "hotbed of communism."[160] The French feared that the RDA would spread Communism to other African colonies and, thus, began liaising with the British over the RDA. The British received most of the intelligence through the General Consul of France in Accra, Charles Renner, who operated a network of informants in the Gold Coast, yet whose information was mostly based on rumours. His information was therefore usually always treated with caution by the British. For example, an informant of the French Overseas Ministry leaked information to the British that Sylvanus Olympio, although not a Communist himself, was in close touch with the RDA.[161] However, Governor Cédile, in a private conversation with Security Liaison Officer Robin Stephens, was "emphatic that there was no communist or fellow-traveller tie-up with the Ewe Movement."[162]

Especially the French wanted to intensify the exchanges on security and intelligence matters. In July 1949, the Assistant Cabinet Chef of the High Commissioner in French West Africa in Dakar, M. Lefevre, responsible for political and security intelligence for French West Africa, visited Accra for exchanges in colonial security affairs. Although Lefevre informed the Gold Coast authorities that the Ivory Coast's new Governor, Laurent Péchoux, was successful in its hard-handed crackdown of the RDA, he agreed to exchange reports regarding the activities in the Ivory Coast of interesting Gold Coast political figures and vice versa. According to the British records, Lefevre was "very anxious to collaborate closely with British authorities in intelligence matters,"[163] so that he returned once more to Accra in May 1950.

In British Togoland, guided by the policy of *indirect rule*, nationalist tendencies were legitimate and therefore enjoyed greater freedom. The British were more afraid of communist personalities like Kwame Nkrumah. Thus, the British were interested in obtaining information regarding communist activities in French West Africa,[164] which were "a

---

159   Sinclair, *At the end of the line*, p. 56.
160   TNA (London), FCO 141/5026, *Gold Coast: Anglo-French cooperation on security matters in West Africa*, Secret Letter Pol.F.16/1/1, S.L.O. R. Stephens to Colonial Secretariat, 13 April 1949.
161   TNA (London), FCO 141/5026, *Gold Coast: Anglo-French cooperation on security matters in West Africa*
      TNA (London), FCO 141/5026, *Gold Coast: Anglo-French cooperation on security matters in West Africa*, Summary of a Discussion About Political Development in French West Africa.
162   TNA (London), FCO 141/5026, *Gold Coast: Anglo-French cooperation on security matters in West Africa*, Secret Letter, G.W. Thom to R. Scott, 5 February 1949.
163   TNA (London), FCO 141/5027, *Gold Coast: Anglo-French cooperation on security matters in West Africa*, personal note, 17 March 1950.
164   TNA (London), FCO 141/5026, *Gold Coast: Anglo-French cooperation on security matters in West Africa*, Saving Telegram No. 2047, Arden-Clarke to Secretary of State for the Colonies, 3 November 1949.

beam of light in the eye of the S.B."[165] For example, when George Sinclair, a Senior Assistant Colonial Secretary, wanted to enquire about French information on the apparently workers' strike-related events in Abidjan,[166] he called the SLO for West Africa, Colonel Robin Stephens. The latter, in turn, was very displeased with this unorthodox approach, explaining he reported directly to the Governor and would not work with "underlings." Sinclair speculated that Stephens was just acting angrily because he had no information about Abidjan, since he had to focus all his attention on Nigeria. Sinclair later wrote that Stephen's "failure to let us know immediately of the recent troubles in Abidjan is typical of the lack of useful Service that he has so far rendered to this Government."[167] Because of this disagreement, CenSeC decided in October 1949 that the Gold Coast needed its own SLO and on a transitional basis appointed Sinclair as the first Gold Coast SLO from 1949, whose duties included personal visits to all stations in the Gold Coast, assistance in the preparation of security schemes and the collation of information, and submission of reports on all security matters.[168] Sinclair, who later obtained the information about the Ivory Coast from Superintendent of Police, L. Chapman, was aware that the latter could not spare another officer to inquire on the Ivory Coast because the Special Branch was too busy keeping an eye on the CPP. Sinclair therefore proposed an Anglo-French security exchange.[169] As Senior Assistant Colonial Secretary, Sinclair's forays into Anglo-French security cooperation were to be of later use, since in 1952, in his capacity as Chief Regional Commissioner of the Trans-Volta-Togoland Region, his information was instrumental in coordinating French responses regarding the Togoland unification movement.

In contrast, the French, guided by the policy of assimilation, perceived nationalist movements primarily as a challenge to their direct rule and were, thus, interested in obtaining intelligence on nationalist movements in British territories, such as the All-Ewe-Conference. Yet, in fact, there was no security or intelligence report exchange between French and British Togoland officials – one of the reasons why pleadings for more Anglo-French cooperation in colonial security matters was not always condoned. For example, the Commissioner of Police, L. Chapman, demanded that a more considerable effort be made to work more closely with French officials, emphasizing personal contact. Yet, Michael Ensor, Permanent Secretary at the Gold Coast's Ministry of Defence, already felt a degree of unease regarding the informants of French Consul General in Accra, Charles Renner: "There are it seems to me already far too many French officials and semi officials who drift about in the Gold Coast. [...] They [the French] have rarely seem to pass on information to the French Consulate or ask the Consulate for information."[170] Likewise, whilst the French suggested that a representative of the Sûreté's *Service de Documentation*

---

165 TNA (London), FCO 141/5027, *Gold Coast: Anglo-French cooperation on security matters in West Africa*, handwritten note, Ensor, 31 November 1950.
166 TNA (London), FCO 141/5026, *Gold Coast: Anglo-French cooperation on security matters in West Africa*, Liaising with French African Police, 11 April 1949.
167 TNA (London), FCO 141/5028, *Gold Coast: security reports from the French*, Anglo-French Intelligence and R.D.A. troubles in Abidjan, handwritten note, 3 February 1950, para. 3–4.
168 TNA (London), FCO 141/4990, *Gold Coast: Security Liaison Officer, West Africa*, p. 14.
169 TNA (London), FCO 141/5028, *Gold Coast: security reports from the French*
170 TNA (London), FCO 141/5027, *Gold Coast: Anglo-French cooperation on security matters in West Africa*, handwritten note, Ensor, 31 November 1950.

et de Contre-Espionage (SDECE), an equivalent to MI6, should be stationed in Accra, the British Secretariat of State for the Colonies found:

> "the question of security generally in France, and therefore in French Colonial territories, gives cause for anxiety [...] An S.D.E.C.E. representative in Accra would have special opportunities for obtaining information and would necessarily be free to tour without restriction in West Africa, and his reports might reach the wrong quarters both in France and Africa. [...] any proposal for posting of a representative of M.I.6. in one of the French territories would be unlikely to be acceptable to the French authorities, and this may be thought to be a further argument against agreeing to a corresponding appointment in British territory."[171]

Therefore, Anglo-French exchanges on security and intelligence matters were, thus, put on hold until the reorganization of the Gold Coast's intelligence services in 1951.

6.4 Securitising Petitions I: Trusteeship Council (1949–1951)

6.4.1 New Restrictions for Petitions & Visiting Missions (1949)

Following Olympio's presentation during the 2nd Session of the Trusteeship Council, the Administering Authorities postponed the consideration of all petitions until after the Visiting Mission. Consequently, there was no progress regarding petitions. Then, between 3 and 5 January 1949, representatives of France, Belgium, and the United Kingdom, that is, three of the five administering powers met at the Colonial Office to coordinate joint tactics for the Trusteeship Council's upcoming 4th Session. It was agreed that a revision of the favourable rules of procedure, which had been secured because of the Soviet Union's absence during the 1st Session (1946), had to be resisted under any circumstances.[172] It was agreed that Soviet criticism regarding inadequate health, education, and other social services in the Trusteeship Territories should not, as a rule, be answered by counterattacks on practices in the Soviet Union and its satellite countries – only in the case of criticism regarding economic exploitation and human rights should the representatives of the Administering Authorities make use of material to silence criticism by counterattacking such practices in the Soviet Union.[173]

Yet, in any case, it was recognized that the other non-Administering Authorities were a more difficult problem than the Soviet representative. It is noteworthy how in the emerging schism of the Trusteeship Council, the Administrative Authorities, in good

---

171 TNA (London), FCO 141/5027, *Gold Coast: Anglo-French cooperation on security matters in West Africa*, Saving Telegram No. 14, Secretary of State for the Colonies, 31 November 1950.

172 ANOM (Aix-en-Provence), 1AFFPOL/3316/3, *Affaire Ewe*, Note of Provisional Conclusions reached at Anglo-French-Belgian discussions held at the Colonial Office in London 3rd to 5th January, p. 6.

173 ANOM (Aix-en-Provence), 1AFFPOL/3316/3, *Affaire Ewe*, Copy N° 14, Confidential resumé of a general discussion between representatives of Belgium, France, and the United Kingdom on future policy towards the Trusteeship Council, p. 1.

old colonial fashion, imagined themselves as impartial experts to vindicate the criticism of the trusteeship constellation:

> "the Trusteeship Council might find itself faced with an apparently unbridgeable cleavage between administering and Non-Administering Authorities. The Administering Authorities, however, from the majority of the permanent members, and they alone are in a position of gradually to establish a tradition of impartial and at least non-political, if not informed, approach to the questions before the Council. If they adhere constantly to this line, there is at least a reasonable change that such a tradition, which alone can make the Council a workable body, may eventually prevail."[174]

It was agreed that the arrangements for the Visiting Mission to Togoland should be debated as late as possible and that the subject of petitions should be kept as low as possible on the agenda.[175]

However, at the beginning of the Council's 4th Session (1949), the Council was informed that the Secretariat had received two petitions marked "Private" and "Confidential." In one of them the petitioner had specifically requested that the subject of his petition should not be made known to the Administering Authority. The Secretariat requested guidelines from the Council, since there was no provision in the rules of procedure for such cases.[176] In the ensuing debate, the divide between the positions of the Administering and non-Administering Authorities became apparent once again: The French representative, Roger Garreau, recalled that when the rules of procedure were being drafted, he had warned the Council of the results of making the petitions system too wide in scope: "If the *right of petition were abused*, the Secretariat and the Trusteeship Council might often be placed in a difficult position."[177] All Administering Authorities rallied behind the proposal made by the Belgian representative, Ryckmans, that…

> "[…] When the petitioner asks specifically that the subject-matter of his petition should not be brought to the notice of the local authority, […] the petitioner should be informed that all petitions received by the Secretary-General will, as soon as they, are transmitted to the Trusteeship Council, necessarily be known by the Local and Administering Authorities. The petitioner should be asked whether, in those circumstances, he wishes his petition to be transmitted to the Trusteeship Council."[178]

Again, Garreau maintained that only signed petitions should be considered as written in good faith and therefore underlined:

---

174 ANOM (Aix-en-Provence), 1AFFPOL/3316/3, *Affaire Ewe*, Copy No. 14, Confidential resumé of a general discussion between representatives of Belgium, France and the United Kingdom on future policy towards the Trusteeship Council, p. 2.
175 ANOM (Aix-en-Provence), 1AFFPOL/3316/3, *Affaire Ewe*, Note of Provisional Conclusions reached at Anglo-French-Belgian discussions held at the Colonial Office in London 3rd to 5th January, p. 2.
176 TCOR, "4th Session" (1949), p. 29.
177 Emphasis added, TCOR, "4th Session" (1949), p. 30.
178 TCOR, "4th Session" (1949), p. 65.

"The author of a petition should always assume responsibility for his statements. There was no Trust Territory in which any person had a valid reason for remaining anonymous, or needed to fear reprisals from the Administering Authorities. [Even] If such a case should arise, the Secretariat could not take a decision; that was a matter for the Council."[179]

Similarly, the British representative, Burns, echoed: "No anonymous document should be received as a petition by the Trusteeship Council. There was no reason why any petitioner in a Trust Territory should fear reprisals."[180] Only the Iraqi representative, Abdullah Bakr, expressed concern that a petitioner should have the right to have his or her name kept secret if he or she so desired. Yet, with so little resistance, the proposal was thus adopted by eight to four votes.[181]

However, the proposal only covered petitions where the author was known but wished his or her identity to remain confidential. Although the Secretariat had not received any anonymous petitions so far, the Administering Authorities immediately made the initiative that anonymous petitions should not be treated as petitions at all. The Belgian representative, Ryckmans, urged to speak of "anonymous *communications*" because in his opinion "there was no such thing as an anonymous petition."[182] Also, the American representative, Sayre, doubted that anonymous petitions could be regarded as petitions at all since "they lacked the weight of a signed document and were therefore 'inconsequential'."[183] Once, again, a proposal was made by Ryckmans that no anonymous communications should be published as unrestricted documents. He maintained that that his proposal was designed only to restrict the publicity given to anonymous petitions but in no way prejudged the further treatment they should receive.[184] Garreau felt that Ryckmans' proposal did not go far enough, probably because the proposed restrictions still gave too much authority to the UN Secretariat on how to deal with potentially compromising petitions. He championed that anonymous communications as well as confidential petitions should not be considered first by the Secretariat but by the *Ad Hoc* Committee, which should have the right to accept or reject them. In the end, it was agreed that "anonymous communications sent as petitions should not be circulated as unrestricted documents unless the Council decides otherwise."[185]

The rule concerning anonymous petitions forced authors of written petitions into Hansen's *silence dilemma* of securitisation because the disclosure of their identity might have provoked reprisals of the Administering Authorities or observation by their secret police. This amendment to the rules of procedure was only the beginning of the Administering Authorities' campaign against anonymous petitions. Petitions, whether anonymous or confidential, could now no longer securitise the administration without running into the silence dilemma.

---

179   TCOR, "4th Session" (1949), p. 67.
180   TCOR, "4th Session" (1949), p. 67.
181   TCOR, "4th Session" (1949), p. 69.
182   TCOR, "4th Session" (1949), p. 71.
183   TCOR, "4th Session" (1949), p. 67.
184   TCOR, "4th Session" (1949), pp. 70–71.
185   TCOR, "4th Session" (1949), p. 71.

When in the course of the session, the Council dealt with the examination of the 1947 annual reports for Togoland, the French and British delegations presented the Trusteeship Council with a joint interim report, describing the work of the Consultative Commission and the measures implemented by both administrations in the Togolands.[186] The conclusions of the report pointed to the need to reorganise the economic relations between the colonial territories in West Africa as a whole and to establish a commission to study the economic problems of West Africa. The idea of a formal commission to investigate general economic relations in colonial West Africa found both supporters and opponents in the Colonial Office, but by July 1949 the French Overseas Ministry was to express its opposition. The French preferred to limit cooperation to a joint mission investigating the problem of Togoland and the Conventional Zone, but to leave aside the broader question of economic relations.[187]

At the beginning of the 5th Session (1949), the question arose on how to deal with petitions submitted to UN Visiting Missions since the number of petitions considered by the Council increased somewhat, mainly due to petitions received by the 1948 UN Visiting Mission to the trusteeship territories in East Africa, that is, Ruanda-Urundi and Tanganyika. The procedure of the *ad hoc* Committees revealed its first problems due to the lengthy discussion in the Council and, in addition, the Administering Authorities repeatedly asked for further postponements in the submission of their written statements. Thus, in view of the forthcoming 1949 Visiting Mission to the trusteeship territories of Togoland and Cameroon, the Soviet delegate, Aleksander Soldatov, sought to broaden the terms of reference for the Visiting Missions by allowing them to investigate petitions on the spot. Expectedly, the Administering Authorities rebutted this initiative, arguing that only the Council was vested with the sufficient authority to decide upon petitions, not the Visiting Missions. Thus, the Soviet amendments to the rules of procedure were defeated,[188] and the French insisted successfully that consideration of all present and future Ewe petitions be postponed until the Council had begun consideration of the report of the Visiting Mission during the next session.[189]

Documents of the British administration in the Gold Coast reveal that the French were "most anxious that the Visiting Mission to West Africa should go to the Cameroons before the Togolands. [...] if the Mission starts by becoming preoccupied with the Ewes it will think of little else during its time in West Africa and everything else it sees will be coloured by the aspirations of the Ewes."[190] As concluded during the Council's debates, the French and British authorities, thus, gave instructions to the local authorities that Visiting Missions merely had power to "accept" petitions, yet, not to "investigate" them.[191]

---

186   TCOR, "4th Session" (1949), p. 288. T/255, *Examination of annual reports: Togoland under British administration, 1947, Togoland under French Administration, 1947: statements by the delegations of France of the United Kingdom*.
187   Kent, "The Ewe Question," p. 236.
188   TCOR, "5th Session" (1949), p. 28.
189   TCOR, "5th Session" (1949), p. 54.
190   PRAAD (Ho), VRG/AD/1185, *Trusteeship Council 6th Session June 1950*, Secret Letter [25165/2/49], L.H. Gorsuch to Robert Scott, 14 July 1949.
191   PRAAD (Ho), VRG/AD/1185, *Trusteeship Council 6th Session June 1950*, Telegram No. 530, Governor of Gold Coast to Secretary of the Colonies, 25 June 1949, p. 2.

In addition, during the Council's debate, the French and British delegation also suggested a change in the rules of procedure that would have resulted in the report of the Visiting Mission being sent directly to the Council's member delegations and not being distributed as an official trusteeship document until after the Administering Authorities had attached their comments on the report to the report itself.[192] This proposal was met with astonishment by the non-Administering Authorities. The Philippines' delegate, José Inglés, saw the proposal as exacerbating the already unequal distribution of voices in the Trusteeship System:

> "[…] if it could be supposed that the report of a visiting mission might be unjustly unfavourable to the Administering Authority, it might equally be supposed that such a report might lack impartiality about the population of the Territory visited. If, therefore, it was desired to grant the Administering Authority concerned the right to reply to the comments of the visiting mission, the same right should be granted to the population of the Territory visited. The Administering Authorities were represented on the Council; they had the right to have a special representative present and taking part in the Council's discussion of the visiting mission's reports; experts of the Power administering the Territory customarily accompanied the visiting mission to that Territory, and that Power was able to submit to the Council its comments on the visiting mission's report. The peoples of the Territory visited, on the other hand, had only the right to address petitions to the Council if the visiting mission's report lacked impartiality towards them. How could they exercise that right if they were unable to take cognizance of the contents of that report? The Council should have before it the comments of both the Administering Authority concerned and of the peoples of the Territory visited before it drew its own conclusions and made its own recommendations on the visiting mission's report."[193]

The Soviet delegate seconded this view, stating that…

> "The proposal before the Council would have the effect of still further restricting the means by which the populations of the Trust Territories could inform the Council of the real conditions in those Territories. A certain tendency was discernible to bring the work of the visiting missions under the control, or even the censorship, of the Administering Authority of the Territories they visited."[194]

The British delegate, Alan Burns, regretted to note that all the statements made by the delegation of the Philippines and the USSR…

> "[…] clearly betrayed suspicion of the Administering Authorities and of any proposals put forward by them. It was most unfortunate that the Council should be divided into Administering Powers and non-administering Powers; […] as long as the latter per-

---

192   TCOR, "5th Session" (1949), p. 12.
193   TCOR, "5th Session" (1949), pp. 313–14.
194   TCOR, "5th Session" (1949), p. 314.

sisted in the attitude they had thought fit to adopt, the Council could not function as it should, and the blame would not rest with the Administering Authorities."[195]

Due to the irreconcilable positions, it was decided to postpone a decision in this regard until the next meeting. This heated exchange illustrated that while anti-colonial Council members repeatedly pushed for petitions to be dealt in a timely and effective manner, the colonial powers tried to drag out the review process. The frustration of the anti-colonial Council members was best captured by the Soviet delegate, Aleksander Soldatov:

> "Petitions were very important documents; their examination was one of the Council's principal functions. The examination had been postponed from the fourth to the fifth session; it might well be deferred from the fifth to the sixth or even longer. The Council should not treat petitions in such an off-hand fashion but should act upon them immediately."[196]

Given the Cold War dynamics, the Soviet stance was transparent. Just a few years earlier, the Soviet Union had positioned itself against the right of individuals to petition the UN. However, if petitions could be directed against the Western trusteeship powers, the Soviet Union strongly supported this instrument and once-colonised states pushed to facilitate the petition process.

Thus, when during the General Assembly's 4th Session (1949), its Fourth Committee, responsible for trusteeship- and decolonisation-related matters, was informed about the influx of petitions, it resolved on basis of an Egyptian-sponsored resolution that the Council shall facilitate and expedite its examination procedure ensuring that the findings of Visiting Missions should be promptly and effectively acted upon.[197]

The 1st Visiting Mission (1949)

During the Council's 6th Session (1949), the chairperson of the 1949 UN Visiting Mission to the Cameroons and Togolands, Awni Khalidy, released the Mission's report to the Council. The Mission concluded that the existing frontier between British and French Togoland was a hardship for the people and confirmed that much of the Ewe people seemed to favour the formation of a unified Eweland comprising, the southern section of the two Togolands and two neighbouring districts of the Gold Coast. Merely eliminating the economic disadvantages resulting from the border would not meet the Ewe unification movement's objectives.[198] The mission noted that "If unification is not satis-

---

195   TCOR, "5th Session" (1949), p. 317.
196   TCOR, "5th Session" (1949), p. 265.
197   General Assembly Resolution 321, *International Trusteeship System: petitions and visiting missions*, A/RES/321(IV) (15 November 1949), available from undocs.org/en/A/RES/321(IV).
198   TCOR, "6th Session: Special Report of the first Visiting Mission to the Trust Territories of Togoland under British Administration and under French Administration on the Ewe Problem" T/463 (1950), available from digitallibrary.un.org/record/794632, p. 35.

fied to some appreciable degree, the *danger* of an intensified local nationalism [...] seems unavoidable."[199]

Such distinct assessments on the part of the Visiting Mission were a result of meetings with the unification movement, during which the unification of the Ewes was securitised. For example, photographs taken by the Visiting Mission clearly show that the UN was approached as an audience to save the Ewes from "cruel frontiers" by reunifying Eweland (see Photo 7).

Photo 7: Ewe Unificationist awaiting the Visiting Mission, Lomé (December 1949)

Source: UN Photo.

Yet, the mission also reported that another very large section of public opinion, spearheaded primarily by the *Togoland Union*, considered that "self-government or independence, [...] must take the form of a Togo State with frontiers more or less corresponding to those of the former German Togoland."[200] In northern part of French Togoland, the majority of the population was indifferent about the Ewe cause while

---

199 Emphasis added, TCOR, "6th Session: Special Report of the first Visiting Mission to the Trust Territories of Togoland under British Administration and under French Administration on the Ewe Problem" (1950), p. 34.

200 TCOR, "6th Session: Special Report of the first Visiting Mission to the Trust Territories of Togoland under British Administration and under French Administration on the Ewe Problem" (1950), p. 35.

"many chiefs and notables, while expressing themselves in favour of the idea of a reunited Togoland, [...] are opposed to any change of trusteeship authority [...], and have also voiced their fear of possible Ewe domination in the event of immediate unification."[201] In the northern part of British Togoland "public opinion, as expressed in the statements of the tribal chiefs, appears to be hostile to the reconstitution of Togoland within its pre-1914 boundaries,"[202] thus, reflecting to some degree the position of the Administering Authorities, that more difficulties would be created than solved by reuniting the two Togolands, which would separate other groups, such as the Dagomba.

The Mission proposed solutions, echoing the ambiguousness of the Anglo-French interim report, as they were so vaguely formulated that they opened the door to a wide range of interpretations:

"(a) a *political* solution within the framework of the two existing Togolands;
(b) an *economic* solution within the framework of the two existing Togolands; or
(c) a *general* solution to be sought within a wider political and economic framework including the two Togolands."[203]

Yet, like a securitising drumbeat, the final sentence of the report reads "the Mission feels that it is its duty to point out that the problem has attained the force and dimensions of a nationalistic movement and that a solution should be sought with urgency in the interest of peace and stability in that part of the world."[204]

The Administering Authorities on the other hand noted in their joint observations attached to the report that "the Ewe [...] are far from being agreed themselves upon a political and administrative solution [...] also between different representatives of the Ewe themselves."[205]

Apart from its report, the Visiting Mission flooded the Council with petitions to such an extent that in retrospect the British Council representative, Alan Burns, noted disparagingly that petition writing had become "a national sport in tropical Africa."[206] The mission had received a total of 255 petitions, almost a quarter of which related exclusively to the Ewe question.[207] Overall, the petitions included demands for greater economic development, better treatment by the colonial powers, more political freedom and the

---

201 TCOR, "7th Session: Reports of the United Nations Visiting Mission to Trust Territories in West Africa" Supplement No.2 (T/793) (1951), p. 82.
202 TCOR, "6th Session: Special Report of the first Visiting Mission to the Trust Territories of Togoland under British Administration and under French Administration on the Ewe Problem" (1950), p. 36.
203 TCOR, "6th Session: Special Report of the first Visiting Mission to the Trust Territories of Togoland under British Administration and under French Administration on the Ewe Problem" (1950), p. 37.
204 TCOR, "6th Session: Special Report of the first Visiting Mission to the Trust Territories of Togoland under British Administration and under French Administration on the Ewe Problem" (1950), p. 38.
205 TCOR, "7th Session: Reports of the United Nations Visiting Mission to Trust Territories in West Africa" (1951), p. 83.
206 Burns, *In defence of colonies*, p. 119.
207 TCOR, "6th Session: Special Report of the first Visiting Mission to the Trust Territories of Togoland under British Administration and under French Administration on the Ewe Problem" (1950), p. 39. A broad selection of these can be found at UN ARMS (New York), S-1554-0000-0004, *Africa – Togoland – Visiting Mission – Petitions and Communications*, 1949.

revision of local laws. A significant number of petitions considered the main cause of their problems to be the border, which separated communities from their fields and imposed tariffs on them: 39 petitions requested Ewe unification and 30 petitions requested the unification of British and French Togoland.[208] A large number of the petitions emphasized the "artificiality" of the border and echoed the AEC's proposal for a referendum. Criticism, especially that of a few anonymous petitions, was directed particularly against the French administration and its election methods for the half-heartedly established Anglo-French Consultative Commission, which was supposed to remedy all these problems.

At the very beginning of its 6th Session (1950), even before the discussion of the report began, the Council decided to establish a sub-Committee to find a solution to the volume of petitions by revising the Council's rules of procedure.[209] Eventually the sub-committee[210] recommended that the *ad hoc* Committees should classify all petitions into three categories:

a) petitions, which specifically called for an intervention by the Council,
b) all others,
c) except those, which were manifestly inconsequential, such as notes of appreciation.[211]

In practice, this meant that the sub-Committee did not consider expanding the *ad hoc* Committees' review process or making it more efficient, but simply recommended to limit the number of communications that would be classified and still considered as petitions under the Council's lengthy examination process. The ulterior motive behind this proposed classification scheme became clear when Ryckmans' stated that "a petition of a general character was not a true petition, which, by definition, must seek redress for a personal or collective grievance."[212] Ryckmans' comment foreshadowed the silencing of petitions in the coming years, in which petitions of general character, such as the ones demanding Ewe or Togoland unification, were grouped together and treated as a single petition. In other words: they were swept under the carpet.

Yet, the sub-Committee also recommended to undo the Council's previous decision that anonymous petitions may only be circulated after the Council's approval, allowing

---

208 Welch, *Dream of Unity*, p. 92.
209 TCOR, "6th Session" (1950), p. 4.
210 Composed of representatives of Argentina, Australia, Belgium, Iraq, Philippines, and the United Kingdom.
211 TCOR 6th Session, Annexes (T/6S/Annex (Vol.I)), *Item 10 of the Agenda: Revision of the Procedures of the Council*, T/L.8 and T/L.13, 92, available at digitallibrary.un.org/record/1626202. However, this was also in the eye of the beholder. As early as 1947, the Secretary-General classified a petition as "manifestly inconsequential" which called for the reunification of French and British Cameroon. The reason for this classification could have been that it was only a postcard and the sender lived in the USA. See *Petitions Received by the Secretary-General*, T/180 (14 June 1948), available from https://digitallibrary.un.org/record/3848545.
212 TCOR, "6th Session" (1950), pp. 267–68.

the *Ad Hoc* Committee to recommend that anonymous petitions be circulated without restriction.[213] As a response to this proposal, the colonial powers proposed that anonymous 'communications' should not be considered petitions and only signed communications requesting redress for specific grievances should be classified as petitions at all.[214] The anti-colonial members of the Council considered this proposal a rigorous curtailment of the right to petition.[215] The representative from the Philippines, José Inglés, protested that "Administering Authorities were sufficiently protected against slanderous communications […] to the effect that anonymous petitions should first be circulated to members of the Council only," adding the concern that "Law enforcement and detection agencies had been known to act on anonymous communications."[216] The British representative, Alan Burns, replied to this accusation:

> "it was the duty of the Trusteeship Council to assist the Administering Authority in its task of leading the people living under the trusteeship system towards self-government, by promoting their general development. Nothing could be more detrimental to their moral development than to encourage them to submit anonymous petitions, a cowardly practice which the Council should in no way condone."[217]

The French representative, Henri Laurentie, also argued his opposition to anonymous petitions with reference to the superior European moral code:

> "the Trusteeship Council had never judged those practices by the moral code of the so-called backward peoples but had invariably done so on the basis of the European moral code […] He saw no reason why the Council should depart from that policy in dealing with anonymous petitions which, since the existence of free speech in the Trust Territories had not been questioned, must be motivated by some other reason of a questionable moral nature. In addition, from his experience in Africa he was convinced that anonymous petitioners were aware of the impropriety of their action."[218]

In suppressing anonymous petitions, Laurentie sought to influence Council members by insisting on evaluating them according to European norms, thereby dismissing these petitions as morally questionable. This illustrates *illocutionary disablement*, wherein power dynamics, including colonial influences, distort securitising speech acts to the extent of incomprehensibility, effectively silencing them through epistemic violence.

Awni Khalidy and José Inglés expressed concern that the *rules of procedure* were being instrumentalized to eliminate anonymous petitions even though there were not even many of them.[219] It did not seem that the issue could be resolved. The Administering Au-

---

213 TCOR, "6th Session" (1950), p. 185.
214 UN ARMS (New York), S-0504-0004-0001-00003, *Committee on Rules of Procedure (1–11th Meeting (Conference Papers Nos. 1–10)*, Conference Room Paper N° 12, Final Report to the Trusteeship Council, p. 3
215 TCOR, "6th Session" (1950), p. 269.
216 TCOR, "6th Session" (1950), pp. 265–66.
217 TCOR, "6th Session" (1950), p. 266.
218 TCOR, "6th Session" (1950), pp. 268–69.
219 TCOR, "6th Session" (1950), p. 269.

thorities seemed eager to set a small-scale example when the Council rejected the consideration of an anonymous petition from Rwanda-Urundi by a narrow majority of 7 to 4 explicitly on the basis of its anonymity.[220]

When the discussion resumed on the volume of petitions received by the 1949 Visiting Mission to West Africa, it revolved, on the one hand, around the question of how the petitions received so far can be processed most effectively and, on the other hand, whether it is at all possible for the Council to consider all those petitions in its debates during current session, since the Mission had received 255 petitions, rounding up to some 2000 pages.[221]

The Iraqi representative, Jamili, complained about the rule previously adopted by the Council that Visiting Missions themselves could not consider petitions. He pointed out that this called into question the validity and value of any Visiting Mission. Conversely, by lifting the restriction, the Visiting Missions could ease the burden on the *Ad Hoc* committee, which until then had to assess petitions on its own.[222] Based on this, the American representative, Francis B. Sayre, suggested an *ad hoc* Committee to submit a further report on procedure for dealing with the petitions presented to the Visiting Mission to West Africa.[223]

Yet, the Belgian and British representative, Ryckmans and Burns rejected, this suggestion and repeated their proposal to identify petitions of general character so that "the Council could accordingly dispose of them quickly, and so be free to deal properly with the remaining petitions sooner than was at present thought possible."[224] The French representative, Garreau, pointed out that a large number of such 'general petitions' referred to "matters such as the unification of the two Togolands, which were not within the purview of the Council."[225] He warned the Council that there was grave danger of it exceeding its competence. As was already indicated by the 1947 proposal for the petition examination procedure, the French delegation wanted to return to the protective provisions, which were in place for the examination procedure of the Mandate System. By calling into question the Council's competence, Garreau was paving the ground for the petitioners' forthcoming *illocutionary frustration*.

The French delegation concluded that the Council would not be able to complete its agenda by the scheduled end of the session and requested that consideration of the annual reports on the two Togolands be postponed until the Council's 7th Session (1950). The representatives of Britain and France agreed that by then, they would present a plan to the Council to resolve the Ewe problem. The Belgian representative, Ryckmans, additionally urged that the consideration of the annual reports on the two Togolands, the reports of the Visiting Mission and the "relevant general petitions be grouped together under one

---

220 TCOR, "6th Session" (1950), p. 271.
221 TCOR, "6th Session" (1950), p. 298.
222 TCOR, "6th Session" (1950), p. 298.
223 TCOR, "6th Session" (1950), p. 298.
224 TCOR, "6th Session" (1950), p. 300.
225 TCOR, "6th Session" (1950), p. 315.

agenda item so that the Council could consider the situation in the two territories and report to the General Assembly on the question as a whole."²²⁶

Thus, the concern, which the Soviet delegate, Aleksander Soldatov, had expressed at the previous session proved to be fully accurate. Consideration of all petitions received by the UN since Olympio's oral hearing in December 1947 had been deferred until the second half of 1950. Some petitions, whose authors had been waiting for a response for more than two years, were not even considered yet by the Council.

Oral Hearing

Yet, toward the end of the session, a three-member delegation from the AEC, comprising Ephraim Amu, Albert Simpson, and Sylvanus Olympio, made its way to Geneva, where they were heard by the Council on 20 March 1950.

Photo 8: Amu, Simpson & Olympio at Palais de Nations, Geneva (20 March 1950)

Source: UN Photo.

Olympio pointed out that the report of the Visiting Mission had recognized the inadequacy of a purely economic, social, and educational approach, arguing that the Standing Consultative Commission (SCC) had had its day and needed to be replaced by a body with broad powers to deal with all aspects of the Ewe question. Olympio repeated that the AEC did not call for the creation of a fully independent Ewe state but argued that once the Ewe territories had been unified under a single administration, the Ewe could one day occupy a proper place in a system of federated states that could be developed for West Africa as a whole.²²⁷

The subsequent questioning was the first time that Olympio expressed his frustration by securitising the passivity of the Administering Authorities before the Council – a

---

226 TCOR, "6ᵗʰ Session" (1950), p. 413.
227 TCOR, "6ᵗʰ Session" (1950), p. 499. Olympio's foresight regarding what was to become ECOWAS was as prophetic as it was a thorn in the side of the French and British, who had their own associations of states in mind rather than African ones.

foretaste of the securitisation moves that were yet to follow in the coming years. Olympio expounded that "the whole problem had so many aspects that if it was not solved the difficulties would become so complicated that they might get out of hand."[228] Olympio's securitising insinuation was picked up by the Iraqi representative, Awni Khalidy, who asked what Olympio meant by the words "getting out of hand?" Olympio assured that the AEC was "composed of responsible people who desired an orderly solution of the problem in co-operation with the Administering Authorities, but if there was much further delay in solving the problem, it might pass into the hands of people who preferred different methods of dealing with it. The situation might then become *dangerous*."[229] Khalidy asked whether, in the event of the Ewe people not receiving satisfaction, the movement was likely "to follow the same dangerous course as was usually followed by nationalist movements which were thwarted."[230] Olympio said the Accra riots of 1948 and the recent developments in the Gold Coast were an example of what he had in mind. Khalidy felt incapable to compare the Ewe movement with the Accra riots, since the Council was not in possession of precise information on happenings there.

In fact, the British effectively attempted to present their administration as being firmly in control of the situation, guaranteeing law and order. The annual report for Togoland under British administration bagatellised the 1948 territory-wide riots as a "minor disturbance [...] arising from a variety of causes."[231] And maintained the "population receives little social benefits other than peace and security."[232] The annual report's passage covering the disturbances did not mention any killings, played down the riots and in turn blamed the rioters for looting European businesses:

> "Associated with these disturbances was a *small* dissatisfied band of ex-Servicemen comprising a *very small* portion of the total number of men demobilised, and allied to certain disorderly elements in the population. [...] Representatives of the ex-Servicemen demanded from the stores to be supplied free of charge with small supplies of petrol and other commodities and in most cases obtained what they wanted. [...] The men involved in this incident were arrested [...] Police was reinforced [...] and order was restored without difficulty."[233]

However, a discussion in the Trusteeship Council about the implications for the British trusteeship administration never came about. Just before Olympio's hearing, the Council had decided to postpone the debate on the annual report. The British intention may have been to avoid uncomfortable debates in the run-up to the AEC hearing.

---

228 TCOR, "6th Session" (1950), p. 501.
229 Emphasis added, TCOR, "6th Session" (1950), p. 501.
230 TCOR, "6th Session" (1950), p. 501.
231 HMG, "Togoland under United Kingdom Administration: Report for the Year 1948," Colonial Reports 243 (1949), p. 54.
232 HMG, "Togoland under United Kingdom Administration: Report for the Year 1947," Colonial Reports 225 (1948), p. 93.
233 Emphasis added, HMG, "Togoland under United Kingdom Administration: Report for the Year 1948" (1949), p. 54.

Nonetheless, Olympio's insinuation resonated with the non-Administering Council members. As ex-Chairman of the Visiting Mission to West Africa, the Iraqi representative, Awni Khalidy, stated that "the Mission had considered that the Ewe unification movement was being conducted in a very orderly manner. But it was a nationalist movement, with dangerous elements like all nationalist movements; it should not be thwarted and so encouraged to develop along violent lines."[234]

Olympio's plea was supported by the representatives of the non-Administering Authorities, such as the Philippines, China, the Soviet Union, and Iraq. As such, the representative of the Philippines introduced a draft resolution, which supported Olympio's expositions by calling on the French and British authorities to develop and to include a *political* solution to the Ewe problem in the memorandum they would submit to the Council at its 7th Session. Yet, in view of the already-taken decision to postpone the discussion of all petitions from Togoland until the 7th Session, this motion was not voted on and the debate was adjourned.

6.4.2 The Anglo-French "Master Stroke" (1950)

At the 7th Session (1950), the French and British delegation presented their Joint Memorandum, which recommended to replace the Standing Consultative Commission (SCC) with an Enlarged Consultative Commission (ECC). Nugent considered this move a "master stroke."[235] Originally, the instruction to establish the SCC, which the Trusteeship Council gave to the Administering Authorities in 1947, was primarily a response to the Ewe petitions of 1946 and 1947, calling for the unification of their territories. But the French and British established a Joint Anglo-French Consultative Commission on *Togoland* Affairs, thereby emphasizing that they were committed to taking a broader view, as they were obliged to the entire population of both territories. Yet, as mentioned before, already at the SCC's 2nd meeting in December 1948, frustration was caused amidst the African representatives whether the work of the SCC related only to Eweland or to the two Togolands.

As the memorandum outlined, by increasing the number of the Commission's elected representatives to 45 and weighting the seats according to population, with 28 seats going to French Togoland and 17 to British Togoland, the Administering Authorities were able to give the appearance of treating the two Togolands seriously as one, while at the same time drown out the voices of the unificationists. With this new arrangement, there were also representatives from the northern regions of both territories who were aloof to the Ewe cause. With French Togoland accounting for almost two-thirds of the seats, it was easy for the French to marginalize the demand of the Ewe, who would find themselves in the minority in the Commission.

Following the decision to discuss the Visiting Mission's report at its 7th Session, the Council heard for the first time several representatives from other political organizations from Togoland. In addition to Sylvanus Olympio, who again represented the AEC, Fran-

---

234 TCOR, "6th Session" (1950), p. 501.
235 Nugent, *Smugglers, secessionists & loyal citizens on the Ghana-Togo frontier*, p. 177.

cis Y. Asare and Senyo G. Antor appeared for the for the *Togoland Union*, the *Natural Rulers of Western Togoland*, and the *Togoland Farmers Association*.

Photo 9: Asare, Antor & Olympio before Hearing, Lake Success (11 July 1950)[236]

Source: UN Photo.

Pedro Olympio, ironically a cousin of Sylvanus Olympio, represented the pro-French PTP, and Derman Ayeva appeared for both the PTP and the pro-French *Union des Chefs et des Populations du Nord* (UCPN).

Sylvanus Olympio recalled the first Ewe petitions of 1946 and tried to discount the opposition to Ewe unification voiced in some parts of Togoland. Whilst he agreed with the mission report that the movement was met with indifference in the north, he expressed that their legitimate preference not to unite with the people in the south should not prevent the Ewe from realizing their unification. He announced that the AEC would boycott the announced EEC since he was convinced that "that body's terms of reference would not permit it to study the question of the unification of the Ewe people as it ought to be studied."[237] Olympio noted that while the mission report mentioned the opposition of the Togoland Union and PTP to the unification of the Ewe, there were no serious disagreements between the AEC and the Togoland Union. The difference lay with the PTP, which "consisted mostly of employees of the French administration who feared that unification would involve a reorganization of that administration and hence cause them to lose their posts."[238]

---

236 From left to right: Francis Y. Asare, Senyo G. Antor, and Sylvanus Olympio.
237 TCOR, "7th Session" (1950), p. 148.
238 TCOR, "7th Session" (1950), p. 148.

*Photo 10: Ayeva & Olympio before Council Hearing, Lake Success (11 July 1950)*²³⁹

Source: UN Photo.

In an approach that was unusual for oral hearings, the French representative, Garreau, interposed the question "whether Mr. Olympio realized the limitations of the Council's competence in the examination of petitions. The conclusions of [his] statement suggested that Mr. Olympio did not realize those limitations. [...] Mr. Olympio was quite wrong in thinking that the Trusteeship Council was competent to deal with certain questions which were actually beyond the scope of its competence."²⁴⁰ While the question caused bafflement among non-Administering Council members, the Belgian representative, Ryckmans, was backing Garreau, stating that "Mr. Olympio had been invited by the Council to express the point of view of the All-Ewe Conference and not to construe the terms of the Charter."²⁴¹ When thereafter Garreau then followed up with the question whether Olympio "had been in direct contact with certain officials in the Secretariat of the United Nations and, if so, who those officials were,"²⁴² even Ralph Bunche had voiced his puzzlement that there was actually another matter at hand. Garreau prepared the ground for unificationists' *illocutionary frustration*, yet the floor was given to the representatives of the Togoland Union.

---

239   Derman Ayeva (left) and Pedro Olympio (right).
240   TCOR, "7ᵗʰ Session" (1950), p. 149.
241   TCOR, "7ᵗʰ Session" (1950), p. 149.
242   TCOR, "7ᵗʰ Session" (1950), pp. 149–50.

Antor and Asare demanded the immediate unification of the two Togolands under a single administration. They were not opposed to Ewe unification, yet, declared that Ewe unification alone would lead to the disintegration of both territories. They protested the creation of the Southern Togoland Council and the administrative union with the Gold Coast, proposing that the Council should initiate a program of development which would enable Togoland to attain self-government within five years. Antor claimed that the proposed Consultative Commission was instrumental in maintaining the barrier and that the French and British claim about the disunity of the Ewe "was but a mere excuse intended to confuse world opinion and to prevent the United Nations from seeing the problem in its true light and from taking a decision consistent with the principles of the Trusteeship Agreement and the Charter."[243]

Antor complained about the lack of accountability of the Administering Authorities since the report of the Visiting Mission asserted that the recommendations and resolutions of the Trusteeship Council and of the General Assembly were not binding upon the Administering Authority, which was free to accept or reject them. It would therefore appear, he argued, that "the Administering Authority could do as it pleased regardless of the wishes and interests of the inhabitants."[244]

It is worth highlighting how Antor and Asare distinguished themselves from the other petitioners in their language. Neither Antor nor Asare spoke of 'British Togoland' but instead spoke consistently of 'Western Togoland' whilst highlighting the alleged harmony when Western and Eastern Togoland were under a single, that is, German administration. Although they did not (yet) follow a straightforward grammar of security, for example by specifying an existential threat, they nevertheless used a vocabulary and rhetorical figures of (in)security: Asare securitised "the barrier between people of the same ethnic group, [as] it had *destroyed* the community of interests and the harmony which they had learned to enjoy during the long period when they had lived together under one government."[245] Furthermore he declared that "The Trusteeship Council had a human problem to solve. It must repair a great wrong and *free the peoples of Togoland from serfdom.*"[246] Antor's rhetoric was even more drastic. In his opening statement he paid tribute "to the Trusteeship Council's efforts to promote world peace," highlighting that "he had not made the journey from far away Africa to North America to ask for guns or tanks [...] but merely to request that the peoples of Togoland should be allowed to live in peace and harmony in their own territory."[247]

Pedro Olympio and Derman Ayeva, on the other hand, opposed both Ewe and Togoland unification. They argued that any change of administration would only delay the move toward self-government. They argued that not the border, but unification was an artificial idea suggested by an elitist group of Ewe, especially from the Gold Coast, and if it came about, it would separate the Ewe people from the other peoples of the north with whom they had formed a common administration for two generations. They also

---

243   TCOR, "7th Session" (1950), p. 151.
244   TCOR, "7th Session" (1950), p. 152.
245   Emphasis added, TCOR, "7th Session" (1950), p. 150.
246   Emphasis added, TCOR, "7th Session" (1950), p. 151.
247   TCOR, "7th Session" (1950), p. 151.

repeated the French and British securitising argument of a balkanizing domino effect, that is, if Ewe unification would be granted other ethnic groups would also begin to demand unification under an administration of their choosing, thus balkanizing Togoland into impossibly small units.[248]

Pedro Olympio's plea served as a smokescreen for the Administering Authorities. His testimony demonstrated for the Belgian representative, Ryckmans, that "a change in administration would be *virtually catastrophic*,"[249] and for the French representative, Garreau, that the Council could not accept that Sylvanus Olympio was speaking on behalf of all Ewes. The latter, obviously frustrated, repeated his demand that the UN could have easily supervised a referendum on the Ewe issue.[250]

The representative of the Philippines, José Inglés, who had distinguished himself as a champion of the right of petition, noted Olympio's frustration and asked him point-blank before the Council whether the Ewe still considered petitions to the United Nations to be at all useful and effective.[251] Inglés seemed convinced that even though the Administering Authorities recognized the justice of the Ewe cause, they did not wish to see unification achieved.[252] Olympio repeated his statement of the previous year that frustration of the Ewe movement could lead to disturbances comparable to the Accra riots. Garreau used this insinuation as an opportunity to suggest that Olympio has sympathies with the communist rioters and should be careful not to incite young people to violence: "The question which the Council was endeavouring to settle was of great importance. It could not be solved by childish methods."[253] The British special representative, however, felt compelled to admit that there had been disturbances in the Gold Coast only to relativize that in the British trusteeship territory itself there had been only a slight outbreak, which had been "caused by infiltrating agitators." However, in order not to get caught up in the debate, he quickly added that the "Ewes would never permit disturbances in their midst."[254] Yet, the British delegate, John Fletcher-Cooke, used Olympio's repeated warnings of possible violence against him:

> "The work of the Trusteeship Council did not involve it in those questions of violence and aggression with which other organs of the United Nations had to deal and it was therefore strange that anyone in the Council should allude to possible resort to violence. Threats of violence, however discreet they might be; could have no part in the deliberations of the Council. Any suggestion to the contrary would betray the very principles on which Chapters XII and XIII of the United Nations Charter were based."[255]

Olympio's securitising moves were rebuffed. Yet, the Administering Authorities, securitised that "if the Council allowed the Ewes alone to decide the question of unification, it

---

248 TCOR, "7th Session" (1950), pp. 152–54.
249 Emphasis added, TCOR, "7th Session" (1950), p. 154.
250 TCOR, "7th Session" (1950), pp. 164–65.
251 TCOR, "7th Session" (1950), pp. 173–74.
252 TCOR, "7th Session" (1950), p. 177.
253 TCOR, "7th Session" (1950), p. 175.
254 TCOR, "7th Session" (1950), p. 177.
255 TCOR, "7th Session" (1950), p. 204.

would implicitly decide the question of the right to secede, and it would thus establish a precedent of incalculable importance, since there were numerous other territories, now independent, whose original frontiers had been arbitrarily drawn."[256] While the unificationist petitioners securitised non-reunification as a danger, the British and French securitised the opposite. The audience for this spectacle of securitising arguments were the other supposedly impartial Council members. But as permanent members of the Council, the British and French had the longer leverage.

The Philippines,' Chinese, and Iraqi representatives were captured by the securitisation of the unification argument and unreservedly defended the Ewe cause, stating that the AEC's claim to represent the Ewe aspirations was indisputable. The Iraqi representative, Khalidy, found that…

> "[…] anyone reading the [Visiting Mission's] report must realize the necessity, not only of finding within the shortest possible time a solution […] in the interests of peace and security in that part of the world. […] The Ewe movement […] presented their case peacefully and with dignity. However, there were circumstances in which the dividing line between peace and violence and between justice and injustice tended to disappear on the slightest provocation. That state of affairs must not be allowed to develop in Togoland."[257]

The non-Administering Authorities criticized the joint Anglo-French position as tending to increase disagreement among the Ewes and delay the realization of their just aspirations. They considered the establishment of the EEC superfluous, since all the necessary information was available to the Council.[258] Yet, Garreau, on the other hand, repeated that "questions involving boundary changes clearly did not come within the jurisdiction of the Trusteeship Council or the United Nations. Future questions of competence could, under the Charter, be considered only by the International Court of Justice."[259]

The American and Argentinian representatives tended toward the presentation of the British and French and supported the idea of the EEC. They submitted a draft resolution,[260] welcoming the new Franco-British proposals and recommending that the Administering Authorities take steps to preserve the common characteristics and traditions of the Ewe people in both areas until a final solution can be found.

The Chinese, Iraqi, and Philippines' representatives jointly submitted an amendment,[261] urging the AEC to consult with the Ewe people and other residents of the Ewe-inhabited areas and recommend that the Administering Authorities unify the Ewe in both areas. Yet, since Argentina was the only non-Administering Authority to side with the colonial powers, and the Soviet Union was absent throughout the Council's 7th Session, predictably the amendment was rejected, and the original US-Argentine draft

---

256 TCOR, "7th Session" (1950), p. 205.
257 TCOR, "7th Session" (1950), p. 221.
258 TCOR, "7th Session" (1950), pp. 221–23.
259 TCOR, "7th Session" (1950), p. 235.
260 T/L.100 available at TCOR 7th Session, Annexes, (T/7S/Annex Vol. II), *Agenda Item 5*, p. 10.
261 T/L.102, available at TCOR 7th Session, Annexes, (T/7S/Annex Vol. II), *Agenda Item 5*, p. 39.

resolution was adopted.²⁶² The Administering Authority were finally asked to report to the Council at the next meeting on steps taken to implement the plan for the EEC.

Thus, at the Council's 7th Session (1950), in three resolutions alone, more than 200 petitions were "settled" by simply referring the petitioners to the positions set forth in the annual reports of the Administering Authorities, which were virtually mandated by themselves to take such action as it deemed appropriate.²⁶³ The Dominican representative, Enrique de Marchena would later comment, that the procedure gave the impression that "the vast majority of petitions were dealt with according to a fixed routine, that mere 'rubber stamp' decisions were taken."²⁶⁴

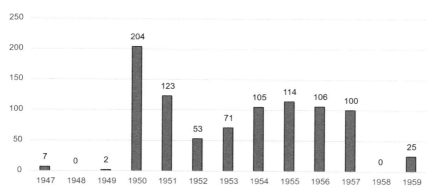

Figure 4: Written Petitions from Togoland handled by the Council (1947–1959)

Source: Own creation. Calculation based on Repertory of Practice of United Nations Organs Art. 87 (1947–1959).

The *Repertory of Practice* is the most comprehensive statistical source available on the petitions of the Trusteeship System. Yet, the abovementioned debate demonstrates, that the informative quality of the Repertory should be treated with caution. On the one hand, the repertory only shows how many petitions the Council dealt with, not how many it

---

262 TCOR, "7ᵗʰ Session" (1950), p. 239.
263 Resolution 250 concerning the "Ewe Question" dealt with 140 petitions, while Resolution 272 and 281 concerning British and French Togoland respectively dealt with 68 petitions. Trusteeship Council Resolution 250, Petitions concerning the Ewe question, frontier difficulties and the unification of the Trust Territories of Togoland under British administration and Togoland under French administration, T/RES/250(VII) (14 July 1950), available from https://digitallibrary.un.org/record/216247; Trusteeship Council Resolution 272, Question of a general nature as raised in certain petitions concerning Togoland under British administration, T/RES/272(VII) (17 July 1950), available from https://digitallibrary.un.org/record/216319; Trusteeship Council Resolution 281, Questions of a general nature as raised in certain petitions concerning Togoland under French administration, T/RES/281(VII) (17 July 1950); some petitions were covered by more than one resolution, see GAOR, "6ᵗʰ Session: 4ᵗʰ Committee" (1951), p. 169.
264 GAOR, "8ᵗʰ Session: 4ᵗʰ Committee" (1953), p. 437.

had before it. On the other hand, it is also not clear from the Repertory how many communications that were intended as petitions were not classified as such by the Council. This inadequacy is evident from the debate on anonymous petitions and petitions that raised questions of 'general nature.' Furthermore, the example of the unification petitions shows that it is also not apparent from the Repertory how the subject matter of petitions was considered. In other words, the statistics in the repertory evoke the impression that the petition examination procedure was a successful enterprise. This impression does not stand up to a qualitative examination.

Decision to Boycott (1950)

When the Administering Authorities announced the election to the Enlarged Consultative Commission (ECC), the unificationists, particularly the AEC and the CUT, opposed the two-stage election procedure that the French administration introduced. During the first stage, village chiefs, which were previously appointed by the French administration itself, elected so-called *grand electeurs*, who in a second stage elected the eventual representatives to the ECC. Through this system of indirect elections, the French wanted to ensure that the pro-French candidates of the UCPN and the PTP were elected. The first stage of the elections for the ECC took place on 10 October 1950. Yet, at the second stage on 20 October 1950 the CUT decided to boycott the election for the ECC. Expectedly, the opponents of the unificationists won twenty-seven of the 30 seats allocated to French Togoland.[265] De Souza, the President of the CUT, and Olympio petitioned the UN complaining about the electoral process by means of chiefs that were appointed by the French administration in the first place. They raised serious allegations of pressure and excessive influence from administrative officers, arbitrary arrests, and persecutions during the electoral period.

While the AEC and the CUT decided to boycott the elections entirely, the question of whether to boycott the EEC led to a split in the Togoland Union: on one side were the founding members, the ex-Bundarians Awuma, Dumoga, and Asare, willing to cooperate with the Administering Authorities. On the other side were those around the newcomer Senyo G. Antor, who supported the total boycott of the ECC.

The Togoland Union participated in the British Togoland election between 14 August and 9 September, sending the ex-Togobundarian Kofi Dumoga to the ECC. Less than a week before the EEC's first meeting, on 2 November 1950, Antor organized a meeting of prominent members of state, local government, political parties, and peasant organizations in Borada, Buem State. Informants of the Special Branch were also present.[266] This meeting reflected the waning influence of ex-Bundarians in the Togoland Union, and the incipient formation of Antor's *Togoland Congress* six months later. The meeting resolved the demand that the ECC should be postponed "until the protests and petitions already

---

265 Amenumey, *The Ewe Unification Movement*, p. 96.
266 TNA (London), FCO 141/5004, *Gold Coast: the Ewe and Togoland unification problem*, Superindendent to Gold Coast Police Commissioner, 9 November 1950.

made be fairly considered and replies received by the various petitioners in the joint territories."²⁶⁷ But all the same the EEC held its first session in November 1950.

Photo 11: Enlarged Consultative Commission (7 November 1950)²⁶⁸

Source: ANOM (Aix-en-Provence), 1AFFPOL/3297/1, *Affaires politiques*.

Representing the minority opinion for reunification, Kofi Dumoga criticized the other representatives for being more concerned about their "personal security" and, in extension, "the security of Britain and France" than about the future of Togoland as envisioned in the Trusteeship Agreement and the UN Charter. While he viewed the Togoland Union and a unified Togoland state as a peaceful objective, he securitised that "the members of the Commission did not want the situation in Korea to be repeated here."²⁶⁹ Criticisms such as the Anglo-French language barrier between the two territories could be refuted by peaceful examples such as Quebec. But for all that, Dumoga's voice drowned in the preponderance of the anti-unification representatives and upon his return his own party forced him to resign as Secretary-General,²⁷⁰ thus clearing the way for Antor to take over the Togoland Union.

It was not until a month after the first session of the EEC that the methods for electing its members were brought up during the General Assembly's 5th Session (1950). In the Fourth Committee, several anti-colonial states, especially the representative of the

---

267 PRAAD (Accra), ADM 39/1/676, *Standing Consultative Commission for Togoland*, Commentary on Mr. Antor's statement to the Trusteeship Council, p. 3.
268 First Meeting of the Enlarged Consultative Commission. In the middle: Charles Arden-Clarke (to his left Mr Dickson and Pédro Olympio) and Governor Yves Digo (to his right Mr. Guillou, Secretary General, and Charles Renner, Consul General of France in Accra.
269 PRAAD (Accra), ADM 39/1/677, *Agenda notes and minutes of the Standing Consultative Commission for Togoland*, Minutes of the 1st Session of the Enlarged Standing Consultative Commission for Togoland, p. 7.
270 PRAAD (Accra), ADM 39/1/94, *Administration of Southern Togoland*, Michael Batse to UN Secretary-General, Togoland Affairs, 11 May 1951, p. 3.

Philippines, confronted France with the petitions by Olympio and de Souza accusing the French authorities of organizing the elections in such a way as to favour the part of the population that was against the unification of the Ewes.

At the same time, several other anti-colonial members of the Fourth Committee complained particularly about the hostility, which the Administering Authorities have adopted toward anonymous petitions.[271] The Yugoslav representative, Sudjan Prica, criticized the Trusteeship Council for having "too often replied in the vaguest terms to interesting and useful petitions."[272] The representative from the Philippines, Diosdado Macapagal, noted that the Council "tended to discourage appeals to the United Nations against any act or policy of the Administering Authorities and thus to render illusory the right of petition."[273] Furthermore, Macapagal noted that it was also difficult to reconcile the fact that arrests were taking place on the eve of elections with the pledge given by the Administering Authority during the Council's previous session.[274] The delegates of India, Indonesia, Iraq, the Philippines, and Yugoslavia submitted a joint draft resolution urging the General Assembly to persuade the Trusteeship Council and the Administering Authorities that it was not only important to find an appropriate solution as soon as possible, but also to conduct the elections to the ECC in a democratic manner.[275] In particular, the joint resolution called on France, to investigate the practices objected to in the petitions and to report on them at the next meeting of the Trusteeship Council. In addition, the General Assembly requested the Trusteeship Council to report separately to the General Assembly on all steps taken in connection with the Ewe issue.[276]

Furthermore, the Fourth Committee called on the Council to transform the *ad hoc* Committees on petitions into a *Standing* Committee on petitions, which would be empowered to examine petitions between Council sessions, requiring colonial powers without delay to provide comments and information on measures taken.[277] The reaction by General Assembly towards the new procedure was prelude to the decade-long exchange of blows between the Assembly's Fourth Committee and the Trusteeship Council.

6.4.3 From Ewe to Togoland Unification (1951)

The boycott of the ECC was an expression of frustration with the Trusteeship Council's passivity toward the demands of the unification movement. Thus, on 7 January 1951, the AEC, the CUT, and the Togoland Union held a joint meeting in Agomé, near Kpalimé, and adopted a resolution that was course-changing in several respects.

---

271 GAOR, "5th Session: 4th Committee" (1950), pp. 15–20.
272 GAOR, "5th Session: 4th Committee" (1950), p. 15.
273 GAOR, "5th Session: 4th Committee" (1950), p. 20.
274 GAOR, "5th Session: 4th Committee" (1950), p. 21.
275 A/C.4/L.82/Rev.1, available at GAOR 5th Session, Annexes, (T/5/Annexes Vol. I), *Agenda Item 13*, pp. 21–22.
276 GAOR, "5th Session: 4th Committee" (1950), p. 126.
277 GAOR, "5th Session: 4th Committee" (1950), p. 176. General Assembly Resolution 435, *Examination of petitions*, A/RES/435(V) (December 2, 1950), available from undocs.org/en/A/RES/435(V).

First, the joint resolution included the clear demand for independence. Previously, the AEC had called only for the reunification of all Ewe under a single colonial power – not for straightforward independence.

Second, the AEC had accepted the fact that the UN did not have the authority to decide on the Ewe populated areas of the Gold Coast – a matter, which the AEC had previously consistently denied in petitions and oral hearings as a technicality. However, confronted with the Administering Authorities' apparent unwillingness to bring about Ewe unification, Olympio now argued that unification of the Ewe majority could only be achieved through Togoland reunification and independence. Thus, overall Olympio championed a new program that aligned the AEC's and CUT's position more closely with that of the Togoland Union by calling for the independence of a reunified Togoland within five years under UN auspices. The drive to prioritise the unification of Togoland over the unification of the Ewes divided many Ewe unificationists and led to many notable members such as Francis Asare, Komla Gbedemah and Daniel Chapman (after all the founder of the AEC), turning their backs on the AEC and joining Kwame Nkrumah's Convention Peoples Party, which would win the General Elections in the Gold Coast in the following month.

Third, it did not escape the movement's attention that in recent months it had been supported by non-Western members on the Trusteeship Council and that the majorities in the General Assembly had already resulted in several resolutions in its favour. Thus, the movement sought to by-pass the Trusteeship Council, dominated by the colonial powers, to appear before the Fourth Committee of the General Assembly, where most of the delegates was favourably disposed to the anti-colonial cause of the unification argument. The securitizing actors were looking for an audience that was easier to attract.

Fourth, because the unificationist had been particularly successful in the past with their securitising language, especially regarding delegates from the Global South, the language of written and oral petitions became more drastic. This change in language is also evident in the adopted resolution, which resolved that...

> "[…] in carrying out the unification the wishes of that part of the section of the Ewe peoples which inhabit the South Eastern part of the Gold Coast Colony which the Trusteeship Council accepts is outside the competence of the Trusteeship Council be seriously considered by United Nations in the interest of the *peaceful development of the Trust Territory and the maintenance of world peace and security for which the United Nations stands.*"[278]

Thus, the unificationists adapted their language by addressing the UN in the spirit for which it was created after World War II in the first place: as *the* international organization to prevent armed conflict. Thus, the Togoland Union, which was taken over by Antor, addressed a cablegram not to the UN Trusteeship Council but the UN Security Council, requesting the withdrawal and replacement of the current Trusteeship Agreement.[279]

---

[278] Emphasis added, PRAAD (Accra), ADM 39/1/676, *Standing Consultative Commission for Togoland*, Resolution adopted on 7th January 1951, p. 1.

[279] PRAAD (Ho), D/DA/376, *Togo Union*, Cablegram [59]. Togoland did not fall under the jurisdiction of the Security Council and was, therefore, dismissed.

Several other written petitions and short cablegrams heavily securitised Togoland unification: "Farmers indignant [regarding] delay Togo Unification. Approval vitally necessary to safeguard peace in territory."[280]

After Antor's successful takeover of Togoland Union, its new General-Secretary, Michael Batse, wrote:

> "The patience of the people in the Trust Territory is now exhausted and it is feared these peace-loving people of the territories may soon lose their hithertoo [sic] levelheadedness and the matter may get out of control unless the two territories are unified in the very near future. It is hoped that for the maintenance of the principles of the Charter, the United Nations will be more prepared to appoint peaceful commissions now to *implement immediate unification than to send Military Missions at a later date*. The people of the territories are wide aware of the activities of the Administering Authorities to frustrate their demand for unification. In the interest of peace and good order therefore, it is respectfully requested that the General Assembly set up a suitable machinery for the immediate unification of the two territories."[281]

Nevertheless, during the Trusteeship Council's 8th Session (1951), the Administering Authorities continued their course to frustrate the unificationist petitions. Although the report of the French *Procureur Général*, Paulin Baptiste, expectedly attested that the electoral system implemented in French Togoland was the only one which, "in view of the tribal state of development of the people of Togoland, enabled the population to express its views,"[282] the Council noted that the EEC had failed due to the boycott of the unificationist parties. The Council took note of the petitioners' grievances but followed the French account of the situation, urging the unificationists to co-operate with the Administering Authorities to find a solution to the problem.[283]

Moreover, since the Council resolved at its 7th Session (1950) to defer consideration of the 1949 Annual Reports on Togoland and the 1949 Visiting Mission report, it had decided at its 3rd Special Session (November 1950) not to consider the reports at the next possible session, that is, the Council's 8th Session (1951), but only six months later at the 9th Session (1951).[284] It was only at the beginning of the 8th Session that the Non-Administering Authorities took note of the ulterior motive behind this move, that is, in this way the Administering Authorities intended to postpone also the discussion of all petitions, which, as they put it, were raising questions of general character. Again, France, Britain, and Belgium argued that those petitions be best considered during the debate of the Annual Reports and the Visiting Mission.[285] And thus, with only a narrow majority the Council

---

280 PRAAD (Accra), ADM 39/1/94, *Administration of Southern Togoland*, Cablegram, 21 June 1951, Thomas Egbadzo to UNations.
281 Emphasis added, PRAAD (Accra), ADM 39/1/94, *Administration of Southern Togoland*, handwritten letter "Togoland Affairs", Michael Batse to Secretary-General, 11 May 1951, p. 3 [110].
282 TCOR 8th Session, Annex (T/8S/Annex), *Agenda Item 17*, p. 19.
283 TCOR, "8th Session" (1951), p. 197. Trusteeship Council Resolution 306, *The Ewe problem*, T/RES/306(VIII) (9 March 1951), available from digitallibrary.un.org/record/216359.
284 TCOR, "3rd Special Session" (1951), p. 7.
285 TCOR, "8th Session" (1951), p. 225.

decided to postpone all "those petitions from trust territories in Africa which are regularly before the Council."[286] Since 7 of the 11 UN Trusteeship Territories were in Africa, this affected virtually all petitions. However, petitions from Togoland were particularly affected, because of the total of 317 petitions brought before the Council at this session, 123 petitions, that is, more than one third originated from Togoland alone.[287] Many of them were anticipated to remain unexamined for two years following their dispatch.

Yet, two days after the postponement, on 15 March 1951, Antor appeared before the Council as a representative of the yet-to-be-officially-constituted Togoland Congress and presented the main lines that the unification movement had adopted at the Kpalimé Conference in January 1951. Antor laid down the demand that no part of Togoland should be integrated into a neighbouring territory as long as Togoland was not unified, and its people could thus decide for themselves on a possible union or federation with the Gold Coast. He repeated the call, which Olympio had made as early as 1947, for a plebiscite to determine the wishes of the people and wished the UN to set the transition period to independence at a maximum of five years.[288]

After Antor's hearing, the Soviet representative, Aleksander Soldatov, wished to reverse the earlier decision to postpone consideration of the petitions until the next session in order to take a decision immediately after the hearing. Yet, the Administering Authorities rebuffed the motion considering it "grossly unfair"[289] to other opinions held in the territory if the Council reaches a decision immediately after hearing from only one side.[290] Conversely, the Council resolved to postpone also consideration of the Assembly resolution that demanded to turn the *Ad Hoc* Committee procedure for examining petitions into a Standing Committee for examining petitions.[291]

Following the Council's 8th Session (1951), the French and British Colonial Ministers Pierre Pflimlin and Oliver Lyttelton, agreed during an intermenstrual meeting at the end of March 1951 to maintain the status quo in the territories.[292]

Founding of the Togoland Congress (1951)

The unification parties decided to ignore the Council's resolution urging them to attend the second meeting of the ECC, which was scheduled for 15 May 1951. As a result, the ECC proved to be a failure. The continued boycott of the ECC prompted Awuma, who had been expelled by the Togoland Union, to write a hateful letter to Antor in June 1951, expressing that although they were pursuing the same goals, they differed in their means: „we condemn without reserve and shall ever resist ruthlessly any Fascist attempt to achieve this

---

286 Trusteeship Council Resolution 341, *Deferment of the consideration of certain petitions*, T/RES/341(VIII) (March 13, 1951), available from https://digitallibrary.un.org/record/216428.
287 Calculation based on United Nations, "Art. 87," in *Repertory of Practice of United Nations Organs*, 1945–1954, Vol. VI, 425–399, available from legal.un.org/repertory/art87/english/rep_orig_vol4_art87.pdf, p. 390.
288 TCOR, "8th Session" (1951), pp. 241–49.
289 TCOR, "8th Session" (1951), p. 249.
290 TCOR, "8th Session" (1951), p. 264.
291 TCOR, "8th Session" (1951), pp. 264–65.
292 ANOM (Aix-en-Provence), 1AFFPOL/3341/2, *Entretiens franco-britanniques sur le Togo-Cameroun*, without title [compte-rendue], 7 February 1953, p. 1.

end through gangster methods by your Boycott Party."[293] Awuma's fascism-insinuations were not far-fetched, since, when under the leadership of Antor, the Togoland Congress was officially constituted on 7–8 July 1951, the Special Branch reported that the Togoland Congress' Working Committee had adopted the swastika as its flag and emblem a month later.[294] Although Awuma was an ex-member of the *Bund der deutschen Togoländer*, he was likewise an objector of Naziism. As early as 1 August 1951, Awuma wrote to the Gold Coast Ministry of Defence and External Affairs and to the Senior District Commissioner in Ho, asking that members of the Togoland Congress be warned not to let the Swastika fly anywhere in Togoland.[295] The adoption of the Swastika by the Congress sparked controversy,[296] but it passed soon as even the Commissioner in Ho acknowledged that the Togoland Congress has shown merely a lack of foresight and disregarded the Swastika-flag-incident as irrelevant.[297] The incident nevertheless shows that Antor and his followers were prone to naive Germanophilia – no wonder, since they wanted Togoland to be reinstated within its former 'German borders.'

However, it was not the former founders of the Togoland Union who were to lead to the most challenging antagonism of the Togoland Congress, but the political developments in the Gold Coast that led to the formation of a new anti-colonial party: the *Convention Peoples Party* (CPP), led by Kwame Nkrumah.

Harnessing Nkrumah for Togoland Annexation (1951)

The 1948 Accra riots forced the British government to make gradual constitutional concessions. When the all-African Commission under the chair of Justice H. Coussey completed its work, a new constitution was adopted on 29 December 1950, which fundamentally changed the entire structure of local government. The new constitution provided that the Gold Coast government's cabinet would be composed of a large majority of eight African ministers and created an 84-member legislative assembly, of which just under half (38) were to be popularly elected and 37 would represent the territorial councils.

Yet, six members (all white) were appointed by the governor to represent commercial interests and three were the *ex-officio* ministers: the Financial Secretary, the Attorney General and the Chief Secretary, who was in charge of Defence and External Affairs. Thus, despite the majority of African ministers, core executive power remained in the hands of the British colonial administration, and the legislature was tailored to be subject to control by traditionalist interests. The merging of Defence and External Affairs is noteworthy since any official diplomatic interaction, whether with France, French Togoland or

---

293   PRAAD (Accra), ADM 39/1/676, *Standing Consultative Commission for Togoland*, Otto Awuma to Senyo Antor, 5 June 1951, p. 3.
294   TNA (London), FCO 141/4997, *Gold Coast: Special Branch Summaries*, Special Branch Summary No. 30, July 1951, p. 15.
295   PRAAD (Accra), ADM 39/1/94, *Administration of Southern Togoland*, Letter BA.93/191, September 1951; Without Title, Senior District Commissioner, 6 September 1951.
296   PRAAD (Accra), ADM 39/1/94, *Administration of Southern Togoland*, Ianthe Lee, "The Significance of the Swastika to the Joint Togoland Congress," 12 September 1951.
297   PRAAD (Accra), ADM 39/1/94, *Administration of Southern Togoland*, Chief Commissioner: "Flying of the Swastika Flag", 4 October 1951.

regarding the Trusteeship Council, was thereby always underpinned by security considerations. The ex-officio Minister of Defence, Reginald Saloway, would become as much a scapegoat for the Togoland Congress as Governor Arden-Clarke.[298]

Although the new constitution represented enormous progress, it fell far short of the CPP's demand for complete self-government. When elections to the Legislative Assembly created by the new constitution were held on 8 February 1951, the CPP's leader, Kwame Nkrumah, was still imprisoned. However, this only strengthened his reputation as a leader and hero of the anti-colonial cause, lending him the status of a martyr. The CPP won an impressive victory with a two-thirds majority of the seats, including one for the still-imprisoned Nkrumah. The governor, Charles Arden-Clarke, released Nkrumah and allowed him to form a government as head of affairs, a position similar to that of prime minister.

Shortly after his electoral victory, Nkrumah travelled to London in June 1951. A British cabinet paper records that during Nkrumah's visit, he had a private meeting with Thomas Cooke, the parliamentary Under-Secretary of State for the Colonies, who involved Nkrumah in the British plans to integrate British Togoland into the Gold Coast.[299] The British needed Nkrumah for the plan because they could afford to be seen as the main actors.[300]

The priority that the Togoland question had for the British was further expressed in the fact that in the same month the British carted Nkrumah to New York. There, he discussed the Ewe question with Ralph Bunche, Director of the UN Trusteeship Division and Daniel Chapman, UN Senior Area Specialist on African Affairs. Chapman, who was after all, the founder of the Ewe Newsletter and the AEC, as well as other prominent members of the AEC, such as Komla Gbedemah, henceforth advocated for Nkrumah's and the CPP's push for the "integration" of British Togoland into the Gold Coast as a first step toward Ewe liberation.

A Special Branch report recounts how just one month later, on 4 August 1951, at a CPP party convention held in Ho (that is, the capital of British Togoland) Nkrumah "sought to bring great weight to his promises of the benefits that would accrue to the Togoland peoples when their territory was "annexed'."[301] Approximately half a year later, on 5 February 1952, Nkrumah declared his intention to "liberate" French Togoland once the Gold Coast was independent along with British Togoland.[302]

Thus, slowly a line of conflict formed between the CPP, which demanded the *integration* of British Togoland into the Gold Coast, and the Togoland Congress, which wanted *unification* of British and French Togoland in their former borders under German rule.[303]

---

298 See comment by J.K.A. Quashi (Togoland Congress) in TNA (London), FCO 141/4997, *Gold Coast: Special Branch Summaries*, Special Branch Summary No. 30, July 1951, p. 10.
299 Kudzordzi (private) (Ho), *Kudzordzi Archives*, Memorandum by the Secretary of State for the Colonies [C.(54) 169], Cabinet Meeting 19th May 1954, p. 2
300 Kent, "The Ewe Question 1945–56," p. 197.
301 TNA (London), FCO 141/4997, *Gold Coast: Special Branch Summaries*, Special Brunch Summary No. 30, July 1952.
302 Luchaire, *Du Togo français sous tutelle à la République autonome du Togo*, p. 79.
303 Nugent, *Smugglers, secessionists & loyal citizens on the Ghana-Togo frontier*, pp. 183–97; Skinner, *The Fruits of Freedom in British Togoland*, pp. 149–54.

Local Intelligence Committee (1951)

In British Togoland, a new era dawned in 1951 in terms of the attitudes of the security services, albeit not equally repressive. Yet, security and intelligence operations intensified: After Arthur Young ended his two-month tour in 1950, his 1951-report followed the recommendation of his predecessor, William Johnson, to unify and overhaul the Gold Coast's police force. Young concluded that, with merely ten European Special Branch officers, the British administration had only extremely limited sources of intelligence and recommended the broadening and Africanization of the Special Branch in the territory.[304] Furthermore, in September 1951, Security Liaison Officer, Philip Kirby Green, requested a general authority from the Minister of Defence, Reginald Saloway, to exchange information with French officers equivalent to the British Security Liaison Officers.

With the broadening of security intelligence measures, especially those of the Special Branch, CenSeC decided in October 1951 on the creation of a *Local Intelligence Committee* (LIC), tasked with the "purpose of collating and assessing all intelligence which had a bearing on the security of the country."[305] While CenSeC was staffed exclusively with administration members responsible for *external* security, with the exception of the Police Commissioner, LIC comprised mainly members concerned with *internal security*, namely the Governor, the Permanent Secretary of the Ministry of the Interior, the Head of Special Branch, the Security Liaison Officer, and military intelligence officers of Gold Coast Forces. LIC and CenSeC autonomously generated their intelligence and security reports, each focusing on their respective areas of concern.

It should be noted that after Nkrumah's election victory that the British intelligence apparatus lost one of its most important surveillance targets and sources of insecuritisation. Thus, it should come as no surprise that the formation of the LIC corresponded to a reorganization of the intelligence apparatus that followed only after Nkrumah's inclusion into British annexation plans.

Maintaining 'Public Order' in French Togoland

In French Togoland the unification parties were increasingly losing ground by 1951, since the French administration made it cumbersome for unificationist parties to hold regular rallies. The CUT continuously complained about collusion between the PTP and the police. For example, after the CUT applied to the relevant authority for a permit to hold a meeting and indicated the time and place of the meeting, the PTP scheduled a meeting at or near the same place and time. Both meetings were therefore prohibited to avoid a clash between the rival parties and a threat to public order. Amenumey provides an overview of the range of tactics used by the French administration to use trifles, such as missing bicycle licenses or incomplete first aid boxes to hinder attendance to rallies.[306] The

---

304 TNA (London), FCO 141/4999, *Gold Coast: security and political intelligence; policy*, Minutes of the Twentieth Meeting of the Central Security Committee, 7.
305 TNA (London), FCO 141/5000, *Gold Coast: security and political intelligence; policy*
306 D. E. K. Amenumey, "The General Elections in the 'Autonomous Republic of Togo', April 1958," *Transactions of the Historical Society of Ghana* 16, no. 1 (1975): 50–51, available from http://www.jstor.org/stable/41406580.

obstructions were significant because public rallies were often the only means of communicating with the masses, many of whom were still illiterate, including some of the traditional representatives of the people: the chiefs. Thus, after the PTP failed to oust the CUT, the French administration turned to the northern chiefs, who according to government propaganda would lose out in the event of an Ewe Union, and thus in 1951 helped founding the *Union des Chefs et des Populations du Nord* (UCPN).

The fact that the police were recruited almost exclusively from the north, which according to French propaganda would lose out on unification of the Ewe, increased the enthusiasm with which they conducted the orders of their officers. Many younger people, especially Kabré from the North, who had little to no education were attracted by the career opportunities offered by the police but also the military during the colonial period. Yet, though France was allowed to maintain military bases in its trusteeship territory, it was prohibited to actively recruit within Togo. With the knowledge of the French, many North-Togolanders simply crossed the border into Dahomey and (usually) posed as Dahomeans at the recruitment centre in Djougou, where Olympio was imprisoned during World War II.[307] Trained as riflemen, some were later recruited as the so-called *gardes-cercles*, a civilian local police force under the authority of the local chiefs and de facto of the *commandant de cercle*.

Finally, in the elections of the Togolese deputy to the French National Assembly on 17 June 1951, Martin Aku (CUT) lost to Nicolas Grunitzky (PTP), reversing the November 1949 election, in which Aku defeated Grunitzky. The frustration over the obstruction of rallies and the electoral defeat led to a brawl between members of the CUT and the PTP during a public meeting organized by the CUT on 3 July 1951. French law of 30 June 1881 and the Trusteeship Agreement provided that freedom of assembly was subject to the condition that the police had the right to prohibit demonstrations or meetings that might disturb the peace or public order.[308]

In the name of public order, the French Governor, Yves Digo, systematically exploited this provision to prohibit public gatherings planned by the CUT as he issued two days later, on 5 July, a decree banning all public meetings in the southern districts of Kpalimé and Lomé (strongholds of the CUT) for the month of July. On the very same day, the French administration's police forces stormed a private CUT meeting at Augustino de Souza's estate, claiming that the crowd in front of the estate was blocking the road. As a result, several people were injured on the part of both the participants and the forces of order. Governor Digo was forced to justify the heavy-handed intervention before the French Overseas Ministry, which feared that Governor Digo's course could lead to reprimands from the Trusteeship Council:

> "As far as the police force was concerned, I had no other way to maintain order and calm in the Lomé region without brutality. By acting otherwise, I would have found

---

307 Decalo, *Historical dictionary of Togo*, p. 48.
308 TCOR, p. 303.

myself one day constrained to extreme means in front of people who would have been given widely at the same time the council of violence." [309]

The ban on meetings in July naturally had a particular aftertaste ahead of the August elections to the newly created *Conseils de Circonscription*, which advised the French administration on certain matters, much as the *Conseils de Notables* had done before World War II. These were largely inactive until Governor Digo re-established the *Conseils de Circonscription* in July 1951 with slightly wider powers as way to counterbalance the southern elites und pro-unificationists. Of the six *Conseils de Circonscription* in the south, the CUT took control of two in the south (including Lomé) and provided half of the twelve members in the *Conseil de Circonscription* in Kpalimé. The UCPN, on the other hand, took control of all six Conseils de Circonscription in the north. In French Togoland as a whole, the CUT won only 22 seats, compared with 48 for the PTP and 82 for the UCPN.[310]

Joint Council for Togoland Affairs (1951)

At the Trusteeship Council's 9th Session (1951),[311] the French and British delegations presented yet another joint memorandum in which they announced to dissolve the EEC to establish a *Joint Council for Togoland Affairs*.[312] It was now the third joint Anglo-French memorandum proposing this kind of joint consultative body. The memorandum dismissed the solutions proposed so far by the unificationists as unworkable, claiming that neither Ewe nor Togoland unification met the wishes of more than a minority of the population. Despite the boycott of the unificationists, the Administering Authorities claimed that the ECC had shown that none of the border changes proposed so far would meet the general approval of the population. Yet, the proposal by the unificationists to conduct a plebiscite to elicit this assertion was rejected by the Administering Authorities on the ground that the matter of Togoland unification would be too complex for the conduct of a plebiscite, which would overwhelm the electorate. Furthermore, they argued that in the event of a plebiscite it would then be unjustifiable to deprive the non-Ewe sections of the population the right to express its views.[313] In other words: in colonial fashion, it was argued that, on the one hand, the Ewe could not be granted a democratic voice because the danger of democratic participation by other ethnic groups endangered the continuation of the colonial order, and that, on the other hand, the population was overwhelmed in articulating its own interests. The racist assertion unveiled *illocutionary disablement*, specifically, the silencing of the unification movement, as the colonial mindset proved resistant to engaging with the unificationists' ability to express their views.

The Soviet representative, Aleksander Soldatov, was overly critical of the memorandum, charging that French Togoland's membership in the French Union violated the

---

309 ANOM (Aix-en-Provence), 1AFFPOL/3283/4, *Affaire Ewe*, Secret Letter N° 428, Govenor Digo, 13 July 1951.
310 Gouvernement Français, "Rapport Annuel: Togo placé sous la Tutelle de la France" T/994 (Année 1951, 1952), p. 197.
311 TCOR, "9th Session" (1951), pp. 264–65.
312 T/931 available at TCOR 9th Session, Annex (T/9S/Annexes), *Agenda item 12: The Ewe problem*.
313 T/931, pp. 6–7.

Trusteeship Agreement.³¹⁴ The proposed *Joint Council for Togoland Affairs* would be virtually as ineffectual as the ECC. The French representative, Pignon, dismissed this as the "usual criticisms" of the representative of the USSR and did not even try to refute them.³¹⁵ The French and British representatives tried to convince the Council that the problem had a different character than the unificationists intended to portray. The problem had arisen from rigid boundaries during World War II, but since then the improved conditions, including the constitutional development in the Gold Coast, and the political awakening of the population had shaken the widespread belief that improvements could be achieved only through unification.³¹⁶

In the meeting that followed, Antor was granted an oral hearing, in which he accused the Administering Authorities of engaging "in a conspiracy to discredit the unification movement."³¹⁷ Furthermore, he maintained that their annual reports gave no accurate picture of the situation in the territory. He did not restrain himself in his securitising choice of words, expounding that while "the British used persuasion, intrigue and occasionally intimidation to achieve their plan of annexation, the French had established a *reign of terror.*"³¹⁸ With these drastic words, Antor referred to the obstruction of the campaign of the unificationists for the June 1951 election of the Togolese deputy to the French National Assembly and the subsequent storming of the de Souza estate, as well as the meeting ban for July, ahead of the elections of the *Conseils de Circonscription*. For instance, Antor referred to several petitions explaining how the French administration blocked transportation facilities for pro-unificationist rallies and maintained that "the unification of Togoland was of minor importance in comparison to the international solidarity and security between France and Britain [... which] must be achieved at the expense of the demand of the peoples of Togoland."³¹⁹ Following this exposition, Pedro Olympio (PTP) strongly opposed unification unless it were to take place under French aegis. He accused the unificationists of using false reports and intimidation to reach their goal.³²⁰

Despite the apparent schism in the Trusteeship Council, all Council members agreed that regarding the accounts they had just heard, a continuation of the ECC did not make sense. The USSR and Iraq, however, opposed the Franco-British proposal to create yet another institution that would not differ significantly from the existing ECC. The Iraqi Council member pointed out that "after several years of discussion and study, the Ewe question was still as far as ever from an effective solution and was threatening to lead to violence."³²¹ The French representative, Pignon, rejected the allegations as mere exaggerations, yet admitted that the French authorities had forbidden meetings under the law of

---

314 TCOR, "9ᵗʰ Session" (1951), pp. 289–90.
315 TCOR, "9ᵗʰ Session" (1951), p. 291.
316 TCOR, "9ᵗʰ Session" (1951), p. 296.
317 TCOR, "9ᵗʰ Session" (1951), p. 297.
318 TCOR, "9ᵗʰ Session" (1951), p. 299.
319 T/PV.380 as quoted in George Arthur Padmore, *The Gold Coast revolution: The struggle of an African people from slavery to freedom* (London: Dennis Dobson Ltd, 1953), p. 154; corresponds to; TCOR, "9ᵗʰ Session" (1951), p. 299.
320 TCOR, "9ᵗʰ Session" (1951), p. 300.
321 TCOR, "9ᵗʰ Session" (1951), p. 303.

30 June 1881 that allowed the administration to prohibit meetings likely to disturb public order.

Without being able to get to the bottom of the repression allegations for the time being, the Council contented itself with the submission of draft amendments by the representatives of the United States, Thailand, and the Dominican Republic, aimed at broadening the scope of the proposed *Joint Council for Togoland Affairs*, authorizing it to deal specifically with matters relating to the Ewe problem. This proposed amendment was adopted as it satisfied the members who had opposed the Franco-British proposal.[322]

The *Joint Council* was, of course, only a temporary device for the two Administering Authorities to keep the United Nations and the unification movement quiet for the time being. The French and British could not afford for the *Joint Council* to become a truly effective body, because it would rival the existing representative bodies and could be seen as the nucleus of a unified Togolese parliament. In the words of the Colonial Office's Deputy Under-Secretary of State, William Lethbridge Gorell Barnes, the French and British found themselves on a tightrope walk to "breathe sufficient life into the Joint Council to make it live for the Fourth Committee, while ensuring that it does not become a Frankenstein."[323] Gorell Barnes found: "We must preserve to ourselves the ability to frustrate the unificationists both locally and in New York if they show signs of seeking to sabotage the Joint Council."[324]

Later during the session, the Trusteeship Council eventually considered the Assembly resolution that urged the Trusteeship Council to expedite its petition examination procedure. Since Thailand sided with the Administering Authorities, the Council merely resolved with seven votes to five abstentions to slightly change the wording of its rules of procedure: instead of "asking," the rules of procedure now "required" colonial powers "when possible" to transmit observations on petitions in a timely manner. Information on measures had to be provided merely "where the Council had indicated it to be necessary."[325] Since the colonial powers ignored the Assembly's call to establish a Standing Committee, the anti-colonial Council members did not consider the changes in line with the General Assembly resolution.[326]

---

322 TCOR, "9th Session" (1951), p. 304. Trusteeship Council Resolution 345, *The Ewe Problem*, T/RES/345(IX) (24 July 1951), available from digitallibrary.un.org/record/216583.

323 TNA (London), CO 554/668, *Togoland under UN Trusteeship: future policy*, Secret Letter No. 31614/23, from Gorell Barnes to Arden-Clarke, 13 March 1952, p. 4–5.

324 TNA (London), CO 554/668, *Togoland under UN Trusteeship: future policy*, Secret Letter No. 31614/23, from Gorell Barnes to Arden-Clarke, 13 March 1952, p. 7.

325 Trusteeship Council Resolution 347, *Examination of petitions*, T/RES/347(IX) (30 July 1951), available from digitallibrary.un.org/record/216433.

326 TCOR, "9th Session" (1951), p. 323.

6.5 Securitising Petitions II: The General Assembly (1951-1955)

According to Ginette Kponton the months following the Council's 9th Session (1951) heralded a new era of repression in French Togoland,[327] evidenced by a series of incidents:

- 10 August 1951, Agbétiko: one dead
- 23 August 1951, Vogan: eight dead and several injured
- 27 October 1951, Mango: 63 arrested

Paraphrasing Pierre Alexandre, an agent of the French administration, Amenumey concurs that under the direction of the French Governor, Yves Digo, the French administration went "into an open war against the CUT, with the result that the latter lost its most fervent supporters."[328] Furthermore, in 1950 the French Overseas Ministry had already pressured the United Africa Company to transfer Sylvanus Olympio, the company's general manager, from Togoland to Paris to keep his activities on a short leash. But when Olympio showed defiantly continuing effort to unify the Ewe, Louis Jacquinot, Minister of Overseas Affairs, demanded his transfer to London in 1951, hoping to "put on him the label of Anglophile and damn him."[329] The effort backfired: Olympio resigned from the Paris office of the United Africa Company in December 1951 to devote himself entirely to the unification movement.

The electoral defeats preceding the Council's 9th Session (1951) and the upcoming elections for the *Conseil de Circonscription* heated up the tempers: On 10 August 1951, in Agbétiko, a large village in the southeast, a scuffle between members of the CUT and PTP over the enthronement of a pro-French chief resulted in a death among the affiliates of the new chief.[330] Yet, the most serious incident, would occur two weeks later, when on 23 August 1951, a conflict between members and opponents of the CUT over the leadership of the Vogan chiefdom degenerated into an attack on the local administrative post, whereupon the guard returned fire, killing eight people.[331] Governor Digo took advantage of the incident to crack down on the unificationists, indicting fifty-one people (five of them in absentia). The trial against them took place in January 1954 and ended with harsh punishments in the form of forced labour and imprisonment. The guard who fired the lethal shots on the other hand was acquitted.

The incident was the dominant theme at a joint conference of the AEC and the Togoland Congress in Accra on 2 September 1951, at which about 150 people were present.

---

327   Kponton, Ginette A. "Réactions Populaires Au Pouvoir Colonial: Agbetiko, Vogan Et Mango (1951)." In Gayibor, *Les Togolais Face À La Colonisation*, 173-93.
328   Amenumey, "The General Elections in the 'Autonomous Republic of Togo', April 1958," p. 50; Pierre Alexandre, pseud. Praetor Africanus, "Vers Une Federation Franco-Africaine," *L'Afrique et l'asie* 11, no. 36 (1956): 18–19
329   As quoted in David Fieldhouse, "British Merchants and French Decolonization," in *L'Afrique noire française: l'heures des Indépendences*, ed. Charles R. Ageron and Marc Michel (Paris: CNRS Éditions, 1992), pp. 491–92.
330   ANOM (Aix-en-Provence), 1AFFPOL/3283/4, *Affaire Ewe*, Secret Letter, Observations relatives aux pétition, 1.
331   Kponton, "Réactions populaires au pouvoir colonial: Agbetiko, Vogan et Mango (1951)," pp. 180–90.

Delegates such as Raphael Armattoe expressed reservations about the practice of petition writing: "Independence for Togoland would never be achieved by petitions unless they were backed by active demonstrations."[332] Yet, no fewer than 19 petitions were to reach the Trusteeship Council in response to the incidents in Vogan, such as the petition by the CUT's president, Augustino de Souza, who used the incident at his estate and in Vogan to securitise Ewe unification:

> "[...] now that there has been blood shed, we implore you, in the name of all anxious Togolanders and Ewes, to hasten to intervene so that the next session of the United Nations General Assembly may deal with the question of the unification of the Ewes in the light of the general insecurity which must of necessity result from the attitude of the French Government."[333]

The Togoland Congress also securitised the immediate removal of Governor Digo and the establishment of an interim government before independence, accusing the police of French Togoland of an "indiscriminate massacre [of] peaceful civilians."[334] Digo himself reasoned to consider these petitions inadmissible, since according to the Trusteeship Council's *rules of procedure* all petitions whose subject matter could be dealt with by local courts could be considered as not admissible.[335] Rue Oudinot followed this line of reasoning, yet, nonetheless, the French administration feared a different situation regarding the Fourth Committee of the General Assembly, where the incident might be raised at the upcoming session. In any case, the intention of the French administration was to ensure that no documents of the impending trial would be leaked before the proceedings were initiated, so that only the French delegation itself could use the documents from the administration as a basis for discussion before the Fourth Committee.[336]

The Vogan incident was certainly also a determining motive a month later for the formation of the *Mouvement de la Jeunesse Togolaise*, or *Juvento* for short. Led by Anani Santos, Messan Aithson, and its Secretary-General Firmin Abalo, Juvento was the more radical youth wing of the CUT, distinguished from it by its more resolute anti-French stance, its pro-Nkrumah pan-Africanist views, and more inflexible attitude toward the Ewe movement.

---

332 TNA (London), FCO 141/4997, *Gold Coast: Special Branch Summaries*, Special Branch Summary, September 1951.

333 UN ARMS, T/Pet.7/287, *Petition*, 26 September 1951, p. 3.

334 ANOM (Aix-en-Provence), 1AFFPOL/3283/4, *Affaire Ewe*, cablegram to United Nations, 25 August 1951

335 ANOM (Aix-en-Provence), 1AFFPOL/3283/4, *Affaire Ewe*, Secret Letter N° 770, from French Commissioner to Minister of Overseas France, 29 October 1951, 1

336 ANOM (Aix-en-Provence), 1AFFPOL/3283/4, *Affaire Ewe*, Secret Letter of Minister of Overseas France to French Commissioner, Incident of Vogan [without date].

6.5.1 After Vogan: Double Standard for Examining Petitions (1951)

Throughout the period of trusteeship, oral hearings were used almost exclusively by African petitioners,[337] particularly petitioners from Togoland. In fact, until 1950, the Ewe and Togoland unification movement was the only group that appeared in oral hearings before the Trusteeship Council[338] and the first group that appeared before the Fourth Committee in 1951.

Thus, for the first time, during the General Assembly's 6th Session (1951), the leadership of the unification movement, namely Sylvanus Olympio, Senyo G. Antor, and Martin Aku, requested oral hearings before the Assembly's Fourth Committee. The Belgian representative, Ryckmans, sought to have the Trusteeship Council rather than the Fourth Committee hear the petitioners, but after an objection from anti-colonial delegations, the requests for the first oral hearing before the Fourth Committee were unanimously granted.[339]

Meanwhile, the British and the French delegations finally submitted a joint memorandum on the establishment of the *Joint Council for Togolese Affairs*, which set out its composition, method of election, procedure, and mandate. The *Joint Council* was to have 21 members: 15 for French Togoland and 6 for British Togoland. Again, its terms of reference were limited to "discuss and advise the Administering Authorities"[340] on the amelioration of conditions caused by the existence of the frontier. However, the *Joint Council* was specifically prohibited from altering its own terms of reference.

When Olympio, Aku, and Antor appeared before the Fourth Committee, they made it clear that the proposal would not provide anything essentially different from the previous *(Enlarged) Consultative Commission* and they went over to exploit the Vogan incident: Olympio expounded to the members of the Fourth Committee that "almost every conceivable weapon had been used against the Ewe people [...] to crush the unification movement."[341] He accused the French government of arbitrary arrest of unificationists and rigging of representative elections. Now the "Committee had before it details of the most recent and most serious provocations [...] leading to the tragic death of a number of people – all in continuation of the campaign against the Ewe people."[342]

Antor maintained that he lived "in a country where maintenance of law and order had been made an excuse for the suppression of human rights and fundamental freedoms and for the use of armed force against a law-abiding population."[343] He reasoned that the French administration's attitude originated from the threat that "the loss of Togoland would lead sooner or later to the disintegration of the whole French Union."[344] Antor also made his opinion on the Council's petition procedure clear:

---

337 Chowdhuri, *International Mandates and Trusteeship Systems*, p. 155.
338 Amenumey, *The Ewe Unification Movement*, p. 189.
339 GAOR, "6th Session: 4th Committee" (1951), 8–9.
340 GAOR, "6th Session: 4th Committee" (1951), p. 159. See A/C.4/198 available at GAOR 6th Session, Annex (A/6/Annexes), *Agenda item 12: Report of the Trusteeship Council*, pp. 14–15.
341 GAOR, "6th Session: 4th Committee" (1951), p. 162.
342 GAOR, "6th Session: 4th Committee" (1951), p. 162.
343 GAOR, "6th Session: 4th Committee" (1951), p. 163.
344 GAOR, "6th Session: 4th Committee" (1951), p. 163.

"For many years, the people of Togoland had sent petitions, resolutions and cablegrams to the United Nations. [...]. The petitions, however, had merely been referred to the Trusteeship Council, and the Council's resolutions on them had frequently concluded with the phrase 'draws the attention of the petitioners to the recommendations adopted by the Trusteeship Council in connexion with its examination of the annual report on the administration of the Territory' or 'draws attention of the petitioners to the observations of the Administering Authority.' Such meaningless resolutions had impaired the prestige of the United Nations among the peoples of the Trust Territories, who had seen *the Administering Authorities gain a stranglehold on the Trusteeship Council* during the past few years. That was why they had decided to bring their case before the General Assembly."[345]

Martin Aku's opening statement is a textbook example of securitisation:

"Events since the Second World War had shown the peoples of Togoland that their aspirations to freedom, progress, well-being, democracy, peace and security could only be achieved through the abolition of the colonial system. [...] The first task of the United Nations was the maintenance of peace and security, and it should be able to remove the burden which weighed on the countries dominated by the Powers of the so-called free world. So far no dependent people had been able to acquire self-government by peaceful means within the framework of French imperialism. The people of Togoland were the first African people to express their aspirations to political emancipation before the United Nations and they were conscious of their responsibility as the spokesmen of all Africa. The objectives of their movement for national liberation were essentially peaceful and consistent with the principles of the Charter. The Fourth Committee should bear in mind the fact that to find a just and pacific solution of the urgent problems which existed in Togoland would open the way to a pacific settlement of the whole colonial problem."[346]

Unambiguously, Aku's presentation ended by addressing the General Assembly as the relevant audience: "the French local Administration had declared war on the *Unité togolaise*. Hence the people of the Territory appealed to the United Nations in the hope that at last their aspirations might be fulfilled."[347]

These statements had an impact – at least on anti-colonial states, which made up the majority of the Fourth Committee. The Yugoslav representative, Ivo Vejvoda, noted that the Council had merely paid lip service to the Ewe petitions, as it "had merely drawn up seven stock decisions for dealing with petitions,"[348] and purposefully delayed the establishment of a Standing Committee on petitions. The Philippines' representative, Diosdado Macapagal, said that "the Ewe problem was the most critical that had yet emerged from the operation of the International Trusteeship System. The finding of an adequate solution must be regarded as a test of the Trusteeship System itself [...] and also a test

---

345 Emphasis added, GAOR, "6th Session: 4th Committee" (1951), p. 180.
346 GAOR, "6th Session: 4th Committee" (1951), pp. 164–65.
347 GAOR, "6th Session: 4th Committee" (1951), p. 165.
348 GAOR, "6th Session: 4th Committee" (1951), pp. 169–70.

of the whole concept of colonialism. It raised the validity of the concepts of the British Commonwealth of Nations and of the French Union."[349]

For the ease of the Administering Authorities, briefly afterwards, the Fourth Committee heard Robert Ajavon (PTP), Nicholas Grunitzky (PTP) and Mama Fousseni (UCPN), all of whom rejected unification and preferred the status quo.[350] Remarkably, before the general discussion began, Sylvanus Olympio wished to bring the silence dilemma of his movement to the attention of the Fourth Committee: "The Ewe people had had troubles before they appealed to the United Nations, but they had been free to organize and to fight for justice. Now they had lost those freedoms; since their case had come into the international limelight every effort was being exerted to suppress them."[351]

During the general discussion, a number of delegations, mainly Western powers, supported the Anglo-French memorandum concerning the *Joint Council for Togoland Affairs*, whilst representatives of nine anti-colonial states, however, jointly submitted an amendment which gave more teeth to the draft resolution,[352] recommending that the French and British authorities ought to extend the powers of the Joint Council to deal with *all* aspects of the Ewe and Togoland problem and devise a procedure for the election of representatives satisfactory to all parties. Furthermore, the amendment provided that the Trusteeship Council should allow sufficient time for the next UN Visiting Mission to undertake a thorough study of the *Joint Council* and the unification problem. The Mission then had to submit a detailed report to the Trusteeship Council as well as to the General Assembly with specific recommendations that should take full account of the real wishes of the people concerned. As amended, the draft resolution was adopted.[353]

Thullen notes that while the overall reaction to the petitioners' statements was in favour of reunification, the General Assembly did not take a definitive position. In particular, the Indian delegation, which had previously been a resolute supporter of reunification, showed itself to be moving away from this position, as reunification was delaying the rapid independence of the Gold Coast.[354]

General versus Specific Petitions

The debate on the Ewe and Togoland unification problem was immediately followed by a debate on the right to petition. Anti-colonial state representatives, especially from the Global South, increasingly saw the Administering Authorities' maintenance of the status quo as an unbearable problem. While the Trusteeship Council's *ad hoc* Committees could not satisfactorily deal with the increased number of petitions, these representatives noted that the Council had merely drawn up non-committed resolutions.[355] The

---

349   GAOR, "6th Session: 4th Committee" (1951), p. 189.
350   GAOR, "6th Session: 4th Committee" (1951), pp. 209–14.
351   GAOR, "6th Session: 4th Committee" (1951), p. 217.
352   Brazil, Ecuador, Egypt, India, Indonesia, Iraq, Pakistan, Philippines, and Uruguay. A/C.4/L.168
353   GAOR, "6th Session: 4th Committee" (1951), p. 221. General Assembly Resolution 555 (VI), *The Ewe and Togoland unification problem*, A/RES/555(IV) (18 January 1952), available from https://documents-dds-ny.un.org/doc/RESOLUTION/GEN/NR0/068/10/PDF/NR006810.pdf?OpenElement.
354   Thullen, *Problems of the Trusteeship System*, p. 140.
355   GAOR, "6th Session: 4th Committee" (1951), p. 223.

anti-colonial state representatives grew aware that the bureaucratic overload of the *ad hoc* petition examination procedure was a feature for the colonial powers, not a bug. Once again, anti-colonial states drafted a resolution calling upon the Trusteeship Council to act without delay to constitute a Standing Committee on Petitions that should be enabled to meet whenever necessary during and between Council sessions.

The colonial powers attacked the draft resolution, arguing that the number of petitions was exceptionally high only because of the enormous number of petitions on the Ewe question and that it would be unwise to introduce a special procedure until the number of petitions returned to normal. The French delegation in particular was concerned about the draft's provision that the Standing Committee could seek information from sources other than those supplied by the colonial powers themselves.[356] The Belgian representative, Ryckmans, defended the Council's prerogatives: "The Assembly was not in a position to give directives to the Council with regard to its rules of procedure, for, under the Charter, the Council was master of its own procedure."[357] Yet, since anti-colonial states were in the majority in the Fourth Committee and only the colonial powers were opposed, the resolution was adopted anyhow.[358]

Thus, despite the opposition from the Belgian representative, at its 10th Session (1952), the Council finally inaugurated a procedure for a six-member Standing Committee.[359] However, Standing Committee was not established in the spirit of the General Assembly resolution because it was not authorized to meet between Council sessions. Similarly, the Assembly had requested colonial powers to provide specific information on the measures taken. Yet, the Council included the following convoluted and negatively worded provision in its rules of procedure:

> "The Standing Committee on Petitions shall submit recommendations to the Trusteeship Council specifying petitions in respect of which special information on the action taken on the recommendations of the Trusteeship Council by the Administering Authority concerned is not required."[360]

Furthermore, the Standing Committee was tasked to distinguish which of the communications it received were to be treated as *specific* petitions, which as *general* petitions, and which as petitions at all.[361] *Specific* petitions comprised only complaints and grievances which explicitly sought action by the Trusteeship Council. Such communications were

---

356 GAOR, "6th Session: 4th Committee" (1951), p. 227.
357 GAOR, "6th Session: 4th Committee" (1951), p. 255.
358 General Assembly Resolution 552, *Examination of petitions*, A/RES/552(VI) (January 18, 1952), available from undocs.org/en/A/RES/552(VI).
359 Three members of Administering Authorities and three members of Non-Administering Authorities. Trusteeship Council Resolution 467, *General procedure of the Trusteeship Council*, T/RES/467(XI) (July 22, 1952), available from https://digitallibrary.un.org/record/216684.
360 Rules of procedure of the Trusteeship Council (as amended up to and during its 17th session), T/1/Rev.4 (June 5, 1956), p. 16, available from https://digitallibrary.un.org/record/678772.
361 Rules of Procedure of the Trusteeship Council (as amended up to and during its 11th session), T/1/Rev.3 (1952), Rule 90, p. 15, available from https://digitallibrary.un.org/record/675438.

duly processed: after screening these petitions and examining comments by the colonial powers, the Standing Committee was authorized to invite representatives, submit a summary report with background information and recommendations. Each specific petition was dealt with by the Council in lengthy debates individually and independently of the overall oversight of the respective trusteeship territory. This procedure consequently slowed down the work of the Committee and the time available for dealing with other petitions. Classifying the petitions as specific, as if they had nothing to do with the general problems in the territories, was at best misleading to the petitioners, as the specific problems in the petitions resulted from the general conditions in the trusteeship territories. Furthermore, often discussions of specific petitions were postponed to a future Council session rather than the next possible one. The consideration of as many as 85 petitions, received by the 1952 Visiting Mission, were postponed until 1954.

Regarding *general* petitions, as well as anonymous petitions or petitions on subjects on which the Council had already adopted resolutions, no examination procedure was laid down in the rules.[362] In this way, the colonial powers virtually managed to revive, through the back door, the former rules of the Mandates System that stipulated to not process petitions that either originated from an anonymous source, referred to an issue already covered by another petition or questioned the terms of the mandate itself. Virtually all petitions requesting either Ewe or Togoland unification were therefore not processed. Hundreds and at times thousands of individual petitions that raised general questions were grouped together and subsequently treated as a single petition.[363] Usually, the Standing Committee recommended that general petitions be deferred, and the issues raised in them not be placed on the agenda until the Council considered an annual report, which represented the colonial power's voice on the administration of a trusteeship territory.

Moreover, there were regularly considerable delays between the submission and examination of written petitions. With only six members, the Standing Committee was understaffed and found it impossible to deal with the large volume of petitions efficiently and thoroughly as the colonial powers deliberately submitted written observations extremely late. At the 13th Session (1954), even though the Standing Committee met daily, it was unable to report to the Council on ten petitions on which the colonial powers had already provided their observations. This was only resolved in 1954, when the procedure was changed so that the Standing Committee could finally meet as often as necessary between sessions – four years after the Fourth Committee first urged the Council to do so! But still, the number of postponed petitions rose: 56 general petitions concerning the Togoland unification question and 287 specific petitions were postponed from the Council's 16th Session (1955) to its 17th Session (1956).[364] Often two to three years had passed before petitioners had received the Council's decisions. Through this procedural system the Administering Authorities managed to silence written petitions.

---

362 United Nations (UN), "Art. 87," p. 343.
363 Lohrmann, *Voices from Tanganyika*, p. 29.
364 United Nations, "UN Yearbook 1955" (1955), pp. 296–97.

Figure 5: Written Petitions on the Trusteeship Council's Agenda (1954–1957)

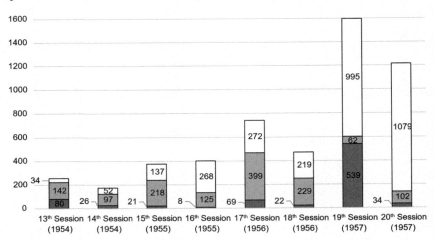

Source: Own creation. Calculation based on *Report of the Committee on Procedures regarding Petitions*, T/L.777 (June 10, 1957), 4.

The Soviet representative, Aleksander Soldatov, protested that "the Trusteeship Council itself must receive and examine petitions in order to protect the indigenous inhabitants against the abuses of the agents of the Administering Authorities."[365] The representative of the USSR reiterated at the 11th Session of the Council (1952) that this new classification would set aside all general petitions.[366] The anti-colonial members of the Standing Committee also pointed out that just because the Council had already addressed petitions raising general questions, did not mean that they do not raise new issues.[367] Thus, the new classification system resulted in many petitions being addressed in Council resolutions without their subject matter being considered.

While in the foreground general petitions were given secondary treatment in the Trusteeship Council, behind closed doors the French and British, who had by then moved to full cooperation in Trusteeship matters,[368] agreed to discuss with priority every general petition in their bilateral meetings between colonial ministries.[369] The Administering Authorities effectively defused the threat, which written petitions posed to their reputation. Written petitions thus virtually went nowhere.

---

365 TCOR, "10th Session" (1952), p. 87.
366 TCOR, "11th Session" (1952), p. 2.
367 Report of the Standing Committee on Petitions, *Procedure for the Examination of Petitions*, T/L.465(XIV), (1954), p. 2.
368 Kent, "The Ewe Question 1945–56," p. 196.
369 ANOM (Aix-en-Provence), 1AFFPOL/3341/2, *Entretiens franco-britanniques sur le Togo-Cameroun*, III.-Nations Unies, p. 2.

Figure 6: Trusteeship Council Resolutions on Petitions (1952–1956)

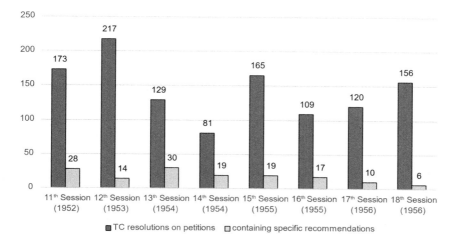

Source: Own creation. Based on Smith 1957, p. 73.

For the unificationists it became clear that from then on only oral petitions before the General Assembly could still exert some degree of influence. Yet, the British administration already had deliberated which petitioners from the Gold Coast and British Togoland could be brought before the Fourth Committee as an "antidote to Antor."[370] They had Komla Gbedemah in mind. Gbedemah was an Anlo-Ewe from the Gold Coast and a former member of the AEC. Yet, since the Olympio-faction of the AEC espoused Togoland unification, which would unify the Ewes of French and British Togoland but leave out the Ewes of the Gold Coast, Gbedemah decamped to Nkrumah and the CPP in the hope of unifying the Ewes of British Togoland and the Gold Coast.

6.5.2 Political Development under Security Surveillance (1952)

In December 1951, the *Assemblée Représentative du Togo* (ART) was re-elected. However, partly due to the criticism levelled by the unification parties at the General Assembly, the French administration was forced to abolish the dual college system for the ART. Thus, only three months after the ART election, in March 1952, the administration held elections for the newly constituted *Assemblée territorial du Togo* (ATT). Thus, apart from Senegal, French Togoland became the only sub-Saharan territory under French rule without electoral discrimination. However, as with the composition of the ECC before, the expansion of the electorate was not an altruistic act by the French government. Rather, the expansion of the electorate, coupled with active French support for the UCPN and the PTP, was well timed to break the previous supremacy of the CUT and Juvento.

---

370 TNA (London), CO 554/668, *Togoland under UN Trusteeship: future policy*, The Togoland Unification Issue before the United Nations, 1952, p. 2.

Table 3: Results Togolese Assembly, Elections (1946–1952)

	ART (1946)	ART (1951)	ATT (1952)
First College			
French Citizens	6	6	
Second College			
CUT	14	1	9
PTP	1	11	6
UPCN	-	12	15
Independent	9	-	-
Total	30	30	30

Source: Own creation.

Because of the incidents in Agbétiko and Vogan, Governor Digo had a bad reputation with the Overseas Ministry. Following the Agbétiko and Vogan incident, Digo's governorship came to a premature end when disputes between him and the PTP leadership broke the camel's back. The quarrel reportedly centred around John Atayi and Pedro Olympio, who were ousted from the PTP, while Digo wanted them reinstated.[371] The PTP representative Robert Ajavon, in particular, went out of his way to complain to Louis Jaquinot, the Minister of Overseas France, about Digo, who allegedly created the myth of a rift within the PTP in the first place. Ajavon painted Digo's course as a danger.

However, in 1954, Pedro Olympio and John Atayi eventually founded the *Mouvement Populaire du Togo* (MPT), which ideologically positioned itself between the CUT (pro-unification) and the PTP (gradual evolution toward self-government within the French Union). Digo's complaint about the PTP on the other hand was likewise an expression of the disappointment of the French administration and the French Overseas Ministry with the PTP regarding its performance vis-à-vis the CUT in the March 1952 elections to the ATT.

As Digo's successor, the Overseas Ministry appointed, of all people, Laurent Pechoux. Pechoux had previously served as a colonial officer in French Togoland but had gained reputations as the governor of the Ivory Coast, where he organized the crackdown on Felix Houphouët-Boigny's *Parti Democratique de la Cote d'Ivoire* and the *Rassemblement Democratique Africain* (RDA) some months earlier.[372]

As the Administering Authorities refused to allow equal representation in the *Joint Council on Togoland Affairs*, the CUT, the Togoland Congress, and the Togoland Union called for a meeting in Lomé on the evening of 6 June 1952. Another meeting was held on 8 June, again in Lomé, where 300 delegates decided to boycott the *Joint Council*. Although

---

371 ANOM (Aix-en-Provence), 1AFFPOL/3297/1, *Affaires politiques*, President of PTP to Minister of Overseas France, 23 April 1952.
372 TNA (London), FCO 141/5026, *Gold Coast: Anglo-French cooperation on security matters in West Africa*, Note of discussion with M. Lefèvre, 28 July 1949.

the unificationist parties participated in the elections to the *Joint Council*, by the third meeting on 5 August 1952, the four British Togoland and the two CUT representatives left the Council in protest to the unequal representation of the two territories in the Council. The remaining Council members, consequently composed only of representatives of the UCPN and the PTP from French Togoland, decided that equal representation should not be introduced, adjourned, and never met again. Instead of participating in the *Joint Council*, where they would be a permanent minority, the unificationist parties decided to approach the UN Visiting Mission, which was scheduled to arrive in the area by August 1952.

Particularly important for the further development of the Togoland unification issue was the regional reorganisation of the Gold Coast in 1952: the southern mostly Ewe-populated part of British Togoland was merged with the Trans-Volta Province of the Gold Coast to form the region of Trans-Volta-Togoland (TVT), that is, the later Volta Region. The newly formed region united the Ewe-speaking areas of the Gold Coast with those of southern Togoland. Thereby, the British cemented the gradual incorporation of British Togoland into the Gold Coast, while making the unification of just French Togoland with British Togoland even less likely. This, of course, reinforced the border that quite accurately divided the Ewe settlement area into one half under French administration and one half under British administration. The TVT, on the one hand, was considered by many unificationist as a step toward Ewe unification,[373] and on the other, it consolidated British efforts to bind British Togoland permanently to the Gold Coast.

As the British trusteeship territory became more intricately linked administratively to the Gold Coast, the reorganisation also affected political developments. Prior to 1951, Togolese were not represented in the Gold Coast Legislative Assembly. The lack of participation in the political institutions of the Gold Coast and the absence of such institutions in British Togoland were, on the one hand, the reason for the strong unification drive of the AEC, the Togoland Union, and the Togoland Congress and, on the other hand, the defence why this stance remained unchallenged.

However, the new institutional interdependence of the two territories enabled the CPP to enter and gain a foothold in Togoland politics. In May 1952, members of the Togoland Congress warned the Gold Coast government in a telegram not to allow Prime Minister Kwame Nkrumah to visit Togoland and interfere in Togoland affairs.[374] In June, the Togoland Congress eventually resolved to set up roadblocks to hinder Nkrumah coming to Togoland. Since the Togoland Congress demanded to reverse the political entanglement of Gold Coast and Togoland territories, it decided to boycott the newly formed legislative body for the TVT Region, the Togoland Council.[375]

It was not only political but also economic reasons that motivated this attitude: Antor was aware that the Gold Coast was obtaining much more revenue from cocoa produced

---

373 TNA (London), FCO 141/5027, *Gold Coast: Anglo-French cooperation on security matters in West Africa*, Copy (without number), 16 August 1953.
374 TNA (London), FCO 141/4997, *Gold Coast: Special Branch Summaries*, Special Branch Supplement No. 40, May 1952.
375 TNA (London), FCO 141/4997, *Gold Coast: Special Branch Summaries*, Special Branch Supplement No. 41, June 1952.

in British Togoland than was being spent in the territory. Therefore, he demanded the break-away from the Cold Coast Cocoa Marketing Boards and the formation of an independent Togoland Cocoa Marketing Board.

The 2nd Visiting Mission (1952)

Above all, it was the security authorities who prepared for the arrival of the UN Visiting Mission in French and British Togoland. In British Togoland, the Permanent Secretary, Michael de Normann Ensor, requested from the SLO Gold Coast, Kirby-Green, and the SLO West Africa, Major Hodson, security relevant material, which MI5 and MI6 had on Ralphe Bunche.[376] A month before the arrival of the UN Visiting Mission, the 1952 June summary of the Special Branch reported for French Togoland:

> "In the Akposso area a Government-sponsored plan is afoot to imprison Theophile MALLY, the leader of the Unite Togolaise in the area, so as to prevent him from contacting the Visiting Mission. Pressure is being brought to bear on village chiefs to concoct a story accusing Mally of collecting their taxes without paying them into the Government chest."[377]

Governor Péchoux ordered the cancellation of a procession by Juvento on 3 July 1952, threatening to break it up with firearms if necessary. The procession of about 2,000 people took place anyway, but informants of the Special Branch stated that many armed police were in the vicinity during the rally. The report concluded that "the French authorities will do their best to prevent Togoland political leaders from contacting the U.N.O. Visiting Mission."[378]

When the four-member Visiting Mission arrived in August 1952, both Administering Authorities frequently drew the attention to the fact that the Mission itself was provoking unrest between political parties. In the hope to claim the Mission's attention, oppositional parties sought to demonstrate their strength and importance by holding mass rallies, which would inevitably clash with each other. This occurred at Jasikan in the cocoa-growing area north of Hohoe, in British Togoland. The Visiting Mission had intended to visit a co-operative but curtailed their itinerary "when it observed that the two rival factions were beginning to demonstrate and grow rowdy."[379] Some days after the Visiting Mission had left, the people of opposing rallies eventually clashed, leading to the arrest of 7 people.[380]

376　TNA (London), FCO 141/5022, *Gold Coast: United Nations Trusteeship Council Visiting Mission to West Africa, 1952; special report on the Ewe and Togoland unification problem, 1952*, Secret Letter OF.176, SLO West Africa to Ministry of Defence & External Affairs, Accra, 26 June 1952.

377　TNA (London), FCO 141/4997, *Gold Coast: Special Branch Summaries*, Special Branch Supplement No. 41, June 1952.

378　TNA (London), FCO 141/4997, *Gold Coast: Special Branch Summaries*, Special Branch Summary No. 42, July 1952, p. 13.

379　TCOR, "13th Session: Visiting Mission 1952 Report on Togoland under United Kingdom Administration" Supplement No. 2 (T/1107) (1954), p. 4.

380　Emphasis added, TCOR, "11th Session: Special report of the United Nations Visiting Mission to Trust Territories in West Africa, 1952, on the Ewe and Togoland unification problem" T/1034 (1952), p. 126.

The news of this clash reached the Visiting Mission when it was in French Togoland. Although explicitly mandated to report on the issue of Togolese reunification, the Visiting Mission had rejected an invitation by the CUT to attend a public meeting organised at the de Souza estate, that is, the main party in French Togoland campaigning for reunification. In fact, the Mission would not attend a single meeting by the unificationists in Togoland under French administration. The French Governor, Laurent Péchoux, had succeeded in persuading the Mission to keep away from those meetings to preserve the peace and public order.[381]

However, it is noteworthy that the mission was divided on this course of action. Like the Council itself, Visiting Missions were equally composed of representatives from Administering and Non-Administering Authorities. This meant that the divide that already existed in the Trusteeship Council between Administering and Non-Administering Authorities extended to the Visiting Mission. The Chinese and Salvadoran member of the mission, that is, members of two Non-Administering Authorities, wanted to meet the CUT, but the Belgian and Australian members of the Mission, that is, the two members of Administering Authorities, did not.[382] Péchoux unabashedly and racially stereotyped the non-Western members of the Visiting Mission:

"Among the non-administering powers is the delegate from El Salvador, who is twenty-eight years old, very inexperienced and light-minded. […] The best way to neutralize him is undoubtedly to offer him distractions to which he is sensitive during this trip. The Chinese delegate, Mr. YANG, is more serious in appearance. Like all Chinese, he is first of all vain. I therefore had the impression that we could more easily get him on this level, by reminding him that he is the representative of an old civilisation, of an intelligent race, free of passions, and that he is therefore naturally the moderating element of this Mission."[383]

Upon the Mission's return, its report explained its decisions on the ground that Governor Péchoux warned the mission that "if it accepted invitations to attend the mass meeting in Lomé organized by the Comité de l'Unité togolaise, the Parti togolais du Progrès could also demonstrate its strength and this could lead to *bloodshed and even 'a state of civil war'*."[384] By employing securitisation tactics, Governor Péchoux successfully persuaded the Visiting Mission to abstain from conducting the investigations explicitly assigned to it.

---

381   ANOM (Aix-en-Provence), 1AFFPOL/3341/2, *Entretiens franco-britanniques sur le Togo-Cameroun*, Péchoux to Ministry of Oveseas France, Cablegram N°416 DS/AP, Séjour au Togo Mission de visite, 28 August 1952, p. 3.

382   ANOM (Aix-en-Provence), 1AFFPOL/3289/4, Affaires Politiques, Secret Cablegram, Péchoux to France Outremer, 21 August 1952.

383   ANOM (Aix-en-Provence), 1AFFPOL/3341/2, *Entretiens franco-britanniques sur le Togo-Cameroun*, Péchoux to Ministry of Oveseas France, Cablegram N°416 DS/AP, Séjour au Togo Mission de visite, 28 August 1952, p. 6.

384   TCOR, "11th Session: Special report of the United Nations Visiting Mission to Trust Territories in West Africa, 1952, on the Ewe and Togoland unification problem" (1952), p. 19.

Photo 12: Chairman of the 1952 UN Visiting Mission (2 September 1952)[385]

Source: UN Photo.

According to Governor Arden-Clarke, the Salvadorian and Chinese member of the Mission

> "had clearly formed an unfavourable impression during the few days they were in Lomé and the two non-Administering Members were contemplating considerable criticism of the French regime in the report. To forestall this Mr. Peachy has written to the Commissaire de la republique in Lome advising him, it is understood, to remove the restrictions which the Mission had formed the impression had been placed on public gatherings."[386]

Regarding the unification issue, the Mission's report confirmed that in the south of the two trusteeship territories the demand for Togoland unification was widespread. Even the PTP and the UCPN were open to unification if it came about under French administration and the CPP was open to unification of French and British Togoland as long as Togoland as a whole would be integrated into the Gold Coast. The problem the Mission found was only that there was no particular form of unification that would be acceptable

---

385   Roy Peachy, Australian Chairman of the Visiting Mission, together with the Chief of Krachi.
386   TNA (London), FCO 141/5022, *Gold Coast: United Nations Trusteeship Council Visiting Mission to West Africa, 1952; special report on the Ewe and Togoland unification problem*, Saving Telegram 1333, Govenor of Cold Coast to Secretary of State, 20 September 1952.

to all parties or a clear majority of the inhabitants of the two trusteeship territories. The Visiting Mission reiterated the view already held by the 1949 Visiting Mission that the border problem was not an economic but a political one. It had received over 2,899 communications calling for the unification of the Togolands under a United Nations administration.[387] The French administration approached the Mission not to publish these statistics in its report.[388] Due to the considerable number of allegations against the French administration made by the unificationists, the Visiting Mission felt compelled to annex them to the report. Again, the Mission was divided on the alleged repression and therefore avoided taking a clear position:

> "Two members find it difficult to express satisfaction on the matter. However, they did not in any way overlook the fact that much of the political tension which gave rise to many complaints about the infringement of human rights and fundamental freedom was largely due to misunderstanding between the Administering Authority and leaders of some of the political parties.
> On the other hand, it appeared to one Member of the Mission that the political atmosphere in Lomé was obviously not as calm as he would have desired it to be, since: [...]
> (b) The Comité de l'Unité which is allegedly *supported by influences foreign to the territory* and which certainly *finds encouragement in the communist press*, had been faced with decreasing power in the last few years and adopts a hostile attitude towards its rival party. In dealing with the latter, it uses *methods of a terroristic and fraudulent character*.
> (c) The Parti togolais de Progrès condemns the platform of the Comité de l'Unité which it considers does not serve the interests of Togoland but is inspired by private interests. The methods used by the CUT against the PTP provoke on the latter's part a certain reaction.
> (d) This situation obliged the Administering Authority to be constantly watchful in order to maintain public order while respecting the right of all. It has never prohibited meetings."[389]

In the end, the allegations of the unificationists were included in the appendix, followed by the official (and expectedly refuting) response of the French administration.

The long-awaited report of the 1952 UN Visiting Mission was received at the end of the Council's prolonged 11th Session (1952).[390] An American-sponsored draft resolution expressed general satisfaction with the report as a basis for further consultations and recommended its forwarding to the General Assembly.[391] The Soviet delegate attacked the report stating that for six years the Ewe had asked for unification. The political importance of Ewe movement had been stressed by the report, but its conclusions failed

---

387 Emphasis added, TCOR, "11th Session: Special report of the United Nations Visiting Mission to Trust Territories in West Africa, 1952, on the Ewe and Togoland unification problem" (1952), p. 18.
388 ANOM (Aix-en-Provence), 1AFFPOL/3289/4, *Affaires Politiques*, Cablegram No. 1961, "Haussaire Yaounde" to "France Outre-Mer", 11 October 1952.
389 TCOR, "13th Session: Visiting Mission 1952 Report on Togoland under French Administration" Supplement No. 3 (1108) (1954), p. 12.
390 TCOR, "11th Session: Special report of the United Nations Visiting Mission to Trust Territories in West Africa, 1952, on the Ewe and Togoland unification problem" (1952).
391 T/L.322 in TCOR, "11th Session: Annexes" (1952).

to contain any proposals to meet the Ewe claims. Therefore, the USSR could not accept the justification in the preamble of the report that no change was desirable in view of the present administrative arrangements. The Chinese representative congratulated the Mission's zeal and thoroughness but regretted that they had not had time to conclude their study and submit concrete proposals. He highlighted from the report that from the 2,899 communications the Mission had received, 2,479 were in favour of some form of unification and that the Visiting Mission had complained that there was not enough time to review and undertake necessary research on important communications.[392]

The closing of ranks between the Administering Authorities was unmissable: On the basis of the new classification scheme for petitions, the Chairman of the Mission, the Australian delegate Roy Peachy, had simply decided that most of these communications should not be considered as petitions but as communications intended for the Mission's own information. Those communications that fell under this classification were therefore not to be examined by the Standing Committee on Petitions. Although the Visiting Mission recommended that the Council should amend its *rules of procedure* for periods of time for future missions to follow up on communications, the Council would not comply with this request. Against this backdrop, the Chinese and El Salvadoran delegations, that is, the two Non-Administering Authorities, which were also represented in the Visiting Mission to Togoland, attempted to highlight the multitude of communications in favour of unification with an amendment to the American draft resolution:

> "[The Trusteeship Council] *Notes* with interest that the majority of the communications received by the Visiting Mission requested immediate unification of the two Territories under United Nations administration."[393]

The Administering Authorities rejected the amendment. They argued that although most communications might have requested unification, they did not exclusively request it 'under United Nations administration.' Furthermore, they argued it cannot be concluded that communications were representative. The New Zealand representative noted that the only way to obtain a clear picture in such circumstances would be to organise a plebiscite, yet this method was already ruled out by the Administering Authorities during the previous sessions of the Council.[394] Finally, the compromise was agreed upon that the Council ...

> "*Notes* that, although no general consultation of the population was made, the majority of the written communications received by the Visiting Mission were in favour of unification and independence."[395]

---

392   United Nations visiting mission to trust territories in West Africa, 1952: report on procedures of visiting mission, T/1044 (March 16, 1953), available from https://digitallibrary.un.org/record/3854062.
393   TCOR, "11th Session" (1952), 458th Meeting, p. 2.
394   TCOR, "11th Session" (1952), p. 3.
395   TCOR, "11th Session" (1952), p. 5.

Before the voting on the draft resolution took place, the Iraqi delegate, Khalidy, announced his abstention since his delegation had long recognised that the "nationalistic clamour of the Ewes was not to be ignored as a danger to peace in West Africa."[396] Khalidy complained that the Council had failed to find a real solution and had given no satisfaction to the Ewes. The conclusions of the Visiting Mission's report were therefore illogical, extraordinary, and baffling.

The final resolution was adopted by five to four votes, with three abstentions and resolved to transmit to the General Assembly the report "as representing not only an objective appraisal of the diverse aspect of this problem but also suggesting the soundest approach to its solution consonant with the present diversity of views of the inhabitants of the two Trust Territories concerned."[397]

6.5.3 Securitising the French "Reign of Terror" (1952)

The securitisation of the Togoland unification issue reached its climax at General Assembly's 7th Session (1952). When the Fourth Committee had received for the second time requests by the leadership of the unification movement to be heard, once again, the colonial powers sought not to have them appear before the Fourth Committee but insisted that petitioners should always be referred to the Council first,[398] since the Council (unlike the Fourth Committee) already had established an official procedure for examining petitions.[399] The anti-colonial members such as the Philippine representative, Victorio D. Carpio, objected to this procedure:

> "the manner in which petitions were dealt with left much to be desired. Petitions were reaching the Trusteeship Council in such numbers that a great deal of the Council's attention during recent sessions had been directed to the formulation of a procedure for dealing with them according to their importance. The Standing Committee on Petitions, [...] classified them; and petitions of a general nature were simply referred back to the Trusteeship Council, which usually decided that, as it had considered similar petitions in the past, no action was required. The chief reason why requests for oral hearings were being addressed to the Fourth Committee was the dissatisfaction of petitioners at the manner in which the Trusteeship Council dealt with petitions; they felt the General Assembly should know what was happening. The Philippine delegation, faithful to its consistent policy of championing the rights of the voiceless millions, would oppose any attempt to postpone the granting of a hearing [...] but the Council was dominated by the Administering Authorities. If the Trusteeship Council did not perform the functions vested in it by the Charter, the General Assembly should exercise some of those functions itself."[400]

---

396 TCOR, "11th Session" (1952), p. 4.
397 See T/L.322 available at TCOR, 11th Session, Annexes (T/11S/Annexes).
398 GAOR, "7th Session: 4th Committee" (1952), pp. 14–16.
399 GAOR, "7th Session: 4th Committee" (1952), p. 102.
400 GAOR, "7th Session: 4th Committee" (1952), pp. 101–2.

The British Council representative, Alan Burns, rebutted snidely that the "Fourth Committee should concern itself with the general progress of those Territories and support, rather than attack the principal organ established under the authority of the General Assembly."[401] Yet, as Burns said himself, the Charter stipulated after all that the Council operated under the authority of the General Assembly, which had the primary right to receive and consider petitions. It was argued therefore that the General Assembly would not be trespassing on the competence of the Council. A Dominican-sponsored draft resolution tried to find a compromise by proposing the elaboration of an appropriate procedure for oral hearings in the Fourth Committee.[402] The British delegation was very comfortable with this proposal, informing the Governor Arden-Clarke that it might be "possible that policy restricting hearings in future will be adopted."[403] Yet, several anti-colonial delegations expressed serious doubts about the silencing effects such a procedure would have and the proposal was eventually withdrawn.[404]

When the news broke that the leadership of the unification movement had arrived, the Philippine delegate prophetically stated that "the Trusteeship Council continued to deal with petitions with so much deference to the views of the Administering Authorities and with so little concern for the petitioners that the Committee was about to see a veritable parade of dissatisfied spokesmen from almost every Trust Territory in Africa."[405] And so it happened.

When the leadership of the unification movement appeared before the Fourth Committee, Olympio stepped up his attacks on the French administration from the previous year by calling the Governor of French Togoland, Laurent Péchoux, a *"specialist of repression"* who allegedly has installed a *"veritable regime of terror."*[406] Allegedly the French administration resorted to intimidation, coercion, and arrests, while unificationists "had been beaten up by the police and gendarmes and others had been forced by threats to resign their membership in the party. Houses have been searched and petitions ready for dispatch to the Visiting Mission been seized."[407] Olympio claimed the French police forces had shielded the Visiting Mission from contact with the unificationists – the main reason why the report of the Visiting Mission denied repression. He criticised the institution of Visiting Missions, by questioning:

"what purpose such an inquiry [by Visiting Missions] served with meetings prohibited, acts of violence against demonstrators, closure of frontiers, and resort to force. He [Olympio] had been reminded in reading the Visiting Mission's report of the usual report of the Trusteeship Council's Standing Committee on Petitions. Any fact put forward by an African was an 'allegation'; the denial made by the Administering Authority was the truth! If acts of violence and the prohibition of popular demonstrations were

---

401 GAOR, "7th Session: 4th Committee" (1952), p. 202.
402 GAOR, "7th Session: 4th Committee" (1952), p. 216.
403 TNA (London), FCO 141/5010, *Gold Coast: the Ewe and Togoland unification problem*, Saving Telegram N° 1126, Secretary of State to Governor, Gold Coast, 26 November 1952.
404 GAOR, "7th Session: 4th Committee" (1952), p. 238.
405 GAOR, "7th Session: 4th Committee" (1952), p. 209.
406 GAOR, "7th Session: 4th Committee" (1952), p. 358.
407 GAOR, "7th Session: 4th Committee" (1952), p. 358.

not to be investigated and if the Visiting Mission was merely to collect petitions and denials, what was the use of leaving New York and going to Togoland? The Mission [...] was a cross-section of the Trusteeship Council and everyone knew by that time the character of the Council."[408]

He declared, the people of Togoland were offended "by the failure of the Council to take their claims seriously, and the fact that it buried all petitions, whether relating to unification or any other matter."[409] Olympio expressed doubts that French Togoland would ever gain independence as long as the final decision rested with the French National Assembly,[410] and proposed direct administration by the United Nations.[411]

Photo 13: Olympio & Antor conversing with Ralph Bunche (1 December 1952)[412]

Source: UN Photo.

Finally, Olympio expressed his profound frustration to the Fourth Committee about how the Administering Authorities managed to silence the unification movement:

"Do you, the United Nations, mean business when you say that we are to have self-government or independence? Do you mean business when you tell us that we are to be allowed to work out our destinies in accordance with our freely expressed wishes? If you mean business, now is the time to show it to us. If you do not, what do you

---

408 GAOR, "7th Session: 4th Committee" (1952), p. 359.
409 GAOR, "7th Session: 4th Committee" (1952), p. 359.
410 GAOR, "7th Session: 4th Committee" (1952), p. 359.
411 GAOR, "7th Session: 4th Committee" (1952), p. 370.
412 Left to right: Benjamin Gerig, Ralph Bunche, Senyo G. Antor, and Sylvanus Olympio.

expect us to do? Shall we follow the examples of other peoples who have felt frustrated in their search for emancipation? For instance, shall we defy the laws, shall we let our hotheads make riots and disturbances? That is what they did in the Gold Coast in 1948 – and the result was that within two years they were making for themselves a constitution giving them something very close to self-government. Do you advise us to follow *that* example? Shall we take up policies of civil disobedience, simply going in our own ways and ignoring the very presence of those who govern us? They did that in other countries – and those countries are independent today. Is that the course of action you would advise for us? Do you expect us to take matters into our own hands, and present you with a *fait accompli* which you will formally recognize and accept? We have seen you do that for other countries, over and over again. But, Mr. Chairman, we in Togoland still put from our minds the thought of using violence to secure our legitimate aspirations. Heaven knows, we have been provoked, but we have kept our faith in the promises of the United Nations Charter perhaps longer than any other people on earth. But the time has come for you to tell us, frankly and honestly, where we stand. We cannot devote the rest of our lives to making these annual trips to New York. We cannot go on wasting away our money and energy in reaffirming the truth for your benefit whenever the Administering Powers try to blacken it."[413]

On a theoretical note, in his securitising effort to secure support from his audience, that is, the Fourth Committee, he strategically crafted a narrative to bolster legitimacy for the unification movement. He underscored the movement's commitment to peace, emphasizing that any inclination towards violence should be seen as a lapse in judiciousness. Consequently, he argued that the responsibility and accountability for such actions ultimately rested with the UN, which must overcome the silencing attempts of the Administering Authorities. Alex Odame (Togoland Congress) struck the same chord, albeit less elaborately:

"During their journey through Togoland under French administration the members of the Mission had seen with their own eyes the *barbarism and brutality* with which the Administering Authority treated the indigenous inhabitants, even in their presence. [....] the people of Togoland were beginning to think that the United Nations was helpless to call a halt to the misrule in the Territories."[414]

Furthermore, the unificationists complained about the conduct of the Visiting Mission: Olympio expounded that the Mission had refused to attend AEC and CUT meetings to which it had been invited. Antor declared representatives of the unificationist movement had not been allowed to contact the Visiting Mission. When at Ho, a representative of the AEC wanted to address the Mission, whereupon the Australian Chairman of the Mission, Roy A. Peachy, had asked the representative of the British administration whether the petitioner should be heard. For Antor, such incidents proved that the Administering

---

413 Emphasis in original, as quoted in Padmore, *The Gold Coast revolution*, pp. 166–67. This direct quote corresponds to the summarized record at GAOR, "7th Session: 4th Committee" (1952), 300th Meeting, p. 360, para. 20–24.
414 Emphasis added, GAOR, "7th Session: 4th Committee" (1952), pp. 361–62.

Authorities had influenced the Visiting Mission.[415] In Togoland under French administration the arrival of the Visiting Mission had been announced only on the eve of that event. The announcement had contained no suggestion as to where petitions should be addressed or how petitioners should contact the Visiting Mission.

Antor continued, that under the terms of the British Trusteeship Agreement, the union with Gold Coast was supposed to be purely administrative, but in fact it has become economic and political, thereby threatening the independence of the trusteeship territory. Olympio therefore reiterated the previously made proposal to hold a plebiscite with the addition that in the meantime Togoland should be governed by a United Nations High Commissioner. The difference with the UCPN and PTP, which Olympio believed were parties created, supported, and maintained by the French authorities, was not the demand for independence but whether it should happen inside or outside the French Union. Olympio concluded his criticism of the Visiting Mission with the claim that "a group of honest, impartial and objective representatives could have realized the violence and intimidation practised against the people of Togoland."[416]

The three unificationists responded at length to questions from members of the Fourth Committee about the alleged repression as well as the electoral and administrative tactics of the Administering Authorities to render unification an impossibility. From the British point of view the Iraqi representative, Awni Khalidy, "asked a series of most malevolent questions."[417] Olympio noted that the representative of France had on several occasions stated that the right of assembly was governed in Togoland by the same law as in France, namely the law of 1881. But under the provisions of the law of 1907, which was also supposed to apply in Togoland, public meetings could be held without prior notice. Yet, despite this legal provision, no meetings were allowed in French Togoland without prior notice. Even when notice had been given and permission received, "a meeting could not be held in a cafe or a cinema and always took place in the presence of armed police who tried to stir up trouble."[418]

The oral hearing had an impact and the subsequent debate in the Fourth Committee was heated. Yet, as before, through strategies of *illocutionary frustration* and *illocutionary disablement*, both Administering Authorities attempted to thwart the petitioners' securitising moves by denying or dismissing the repression as greatly exaggerated, questioned the representativity of the petitioners and in turn accused the unificationists of "incidents often accompanied by bloodshed that had been provoked by that party, which did not hesitate at times to resort to the most violent reprisals against its opponents."[419] The endeavour to enforce *illocutionary disablement*, namely the metaphorical transmission of distortion signals, was further manifested in the concerted efforts of both Administering Authorities to contest the representativeness of the petitioners. For example, the French

---

415 GAOR, "7th Session: 4th Committee" (1952), p. 367.
416 GAOR, "7th Session: 4th Committee" (1952), p. 359.
417 TNA (London), FO 371/101369, *Problems of Trust Territories of British and French Togoland*, 1952, Report on Debate [No° 107], 13th December 1952, para. 4. Khalidy's questioning of the petitioners at GAOR, "7th Session: 4th Committee" (1952), pp. 367–69.
418 GAOR, "7th Session: 4th Committee" (1952), pp. 368–69.
419 GAOR, "7th Session: 4th Committee" (1952), pp. 378–85.

representative, Pignon, voiced that he "did not understand how it was possible to gauge the popularity of a political party by the number of petitions its members presented."[420] The British representative, Alan Burns, accused the unificationists of refusing to participate in the work of the *Joint Council for Togoland Affairs* because they had no chance of finding a majority: "Instead of appealing to the people, they had appealed to the United Nations."[421] He held that British Togolanders had allegedly submitted written communications only on the instructions of the unification parties, "since their normal habit was to convey their ideas orally. Submission of written communications was a device resorted to most frequently by those who had studied the machinery of the United Nations with a view to *exploiting* it for their own political advantage."[422] Last but not least, Burns protested the series of questions Khalidy had posed to the petitioners.[423]

Photo 14: Robert Ajavon addressing the 4th Committee (12 December 1952)

Source: UN Photo.

Robert Ajavon, himself a Togolander who was a member of the French delegation, said the report of the Visiting Mission accurately reflected the different trends of opinion in the area. He claimed that three quarters of the population in French-administered Togoland opposed the unification of the Ewe people and that the UN itself was partly responsible for delaying Togoland's advancement towards independence and self-gov-

---

420 GAOR, "7th Session: 4th Committee" (1952), p. 386.
421 GAOR, "7th Session: 4th Committee" (1952), p. 379.
422 Emphasis added, GAOR, "7th Session: 4th Committee" (1952), p. 378.
423 GAOR, "7th Session: 4th Committee" (1952), p. 379.

ernment. The agitation of the unificationists was artificial, short-lived, and designed to focus world public opinion on a few attention seekers.⁴²⁴

The French delegation was also able to mobilize Simon-Kangni Kpodar (PTP) as a counter-petitioner before the Fourth Committee. Despite several difficult and tendentious questions, Kpodar impressed the Committee by the quality of his statements. Although the *Joint Council for Togoland Affairs* had met only once and not even its entirety, Kpodar declared that its representatives could have raised any issues that they wished, including that of unification. He supported the proportional representation at the *Joint Council for Togoland Affairs* and denied that a different method of election in French Togoland would have produced a different result. Kpodar also described the CUT as a minority voice, but also clarified that the PTP was not fundamentally agitating against reunification.⁴²⁵

Photo 15: Odame, Olympio & Kpodar before 4ᵗʰ Committee (15 December 1952)⁴²⁶

Source: UN Photo.

General Debate

During the general debate, the representatives of Poland⁴²⁷ and Yugoslavia⁴²⁸ strongly condemned the report of the Visiting Mission and the Administering Authorities, claiming that they "put their own interests before those of the indigenous inhabitants,"⁴²⁹ while the Guatemalan delegate found the petitioners' proposal of direct trusteeship by

---

424 GAOR, "7ᵗʰ Session: 4ᵗʰ Committee" (1952), pp. 382–85.
425 GAOR, "7ᵗʰ Session: 4ᵗʰ Committee" (1952), pp. 383–400.
426 Left to right: Alex Odame (Togoland Congress), Rodolfo Muñoz (Chairman of the Fourth Committee), Sylvanus Olympio (AEC) and Simon Kpodar (PTP).
427 GAOR, "7ᵗʰ Session: 4ᵗʰ Committee" (1952), pp. 399–400.
428 GAOR, "7ᵗʰ Session: 4ᵗʰ Committee" (1952), p. 411.
429 GAOR, "7ᵗʰ Session: 4ᵗʰ Committee" (1952), p. 409.

the United Nations worth considering.[430] Most of the representatives of the anti-colonial states consistently argued that the overwhelming majority in the two trusteeship areas wanted unification.

The colonial powers vehemently denounced this as presumptuous, insisting that the entire population of the territories should be allowed to decide freely on a solution, for which the *Joint Council on Togoland Affairs* represented the appropriate body. The representative of United States blamed the UN for the failure of the *Joint Council* because it had been hastily set up only for the Visiting Mission to observe it at work.[431] Therefore, the US tabled a draft resolution calling on France and Britain to merely reconstitute the *Joint Council for Togoland Affairs*.[432]

Yet, after the hearing of Olympio, Antor and Odame, this proposal seemed too truncated for various anti-colonial delegations. The Iraqi representative, Awni Khalidy, made a speech which the Committee members had waited for several days. He criticized that the representatives of various Administering Authorities had protested against a number of the questions which had been put to the petitioners by the Forth Committee: "If such questions had to be approved by the Administering Authorities, the hearing of petitioners would lose all meaning."[433] Khalidy repeated that the "nationalistic clamour of the Ewes was not to be ignored as a danger to peace in West Africa."[434] As the chairperson of the 1949 Visiting Mission to West Africa, he had reported that the majority of Togolanders desired unification of the two trusteeship territories. However, surprisingly, the conclusions of the 1952 Visiting Mission seemed to precisely favour the position of the Administering Authorities on maintaining the status quo. He criticized that it was the 'bounden duty' of the Visiting Mission to attend rallies of the principal parties demanding unification. The argument put forward by the Mission concerning the maintenance of public order was valueless because the Visiting Mission had not heard the African point of view and thus had succumbed to the influence of the Administering Authority. He concluded that the Mission had failed in its duty: "If visiting missions did not fulfil the tasks entrusted to them within the framework of the Trusteeship System, the system should be abolished forthwith."[435]

Various anti-colonial delegations tabled a whole series of amendments to bring the American draft resolution more in line with their views. The amendment by the Guatemalan delegation stated that "the unification of the two Togolands is the manifest aspiration of the majority of the population of both Trust Territories," calling on France and Britain to negotiate a revision of the trusteeship agreements "to make possible the unification of the said territories under a single trusteeship administration."[436] A ten-

---

430   GAOR, "7th Session: 4th Committee" (1952), p. 409.
431   GAOR, "7th Session: 4th Committee" (1952), p. 408.
432   A/C.4/L.256/Rev.1 available at GAOR, 7th Session, Annexes, (A/7/Annexes/Vol.1), *Agenda item 32: The Ewe and Togoland unification problem: special report of the Trusteeship Council*, p. 5.
433   GAOR, "7th Session: 4th Committee" (1952), p. 410.
434   PRAAD (Ho), VRG/AD/1043, *Trusteeship Council and Togoland*, 1953, Saving Telegram 361, 25 November 1952.
435   GAOR, "7th Session: 4th Committee" (1952), p. 411.
436   A/C.4/L.258, available at GAOR, 7th Session, Annexes, (A/7/Annexes/Vol.1), *Agenda item 32: The Ewe and Togoland unification problem: special report of the Trusteeship Council*, p. 8.

power amendment recommended the re-establishment of the *Joint Council of Togoland Affairs* through "direct elections based on universal adult suffrage by secret ballot."[437] In a tedious paragraph-by-paragraph vote, both the draft resolution and the amendments were adopted by the Fourth Committee despite opposition from all Administering Authorities, including the US, which originally sponsored the draft resolution.

The French and British representatives made it clear that their governments would refuse to implement the Fourth Committee's resolution in this form, even if it were adopted in plenary. Thus, in the spirit of compromise, during the plenary debate Argentina and Venezuela therefore proposed a slight amendment to the ten-power motion and a vote was taken on the controversial paragraph, sponsored by Guatemala, which requested France and Britain to enable the establishment of a single trusteeship administration.

Through hallway diplomacy the French and British delegation were able to secure some concessions before the vote was taken in the plenary. It's regrettable for the securitisation historian that there are no records documenting these diplomatic hallway exchanges. Some delegations that had voted for the Guatemalan amendment during the session of the Fourth Committee were persuaded to abstain in plenary, while others that had abstained in the Fourth Committee were persuaded to vote against the amendment in plenary. Finally, the paragraph calling for the establishment of a single administration was rejected by a narrow majority of 22 votes to 18, with 18 abstentions.[438] The thus-pruned resolution was adopted even without opposition from France and Britain, although it still contained the uncomfortable statement that "the unification of the two Togolands is the manifest aspiration of the majority of the population of both Trust Territories."[439]

For the Administering Authorities, the results were better than one would normally have expected.[440] The British and French were off the hook, as they could now argue that the deletion of the Guatemala-sponsored paragraph from the Fourth Committee resolution indicated that the General Assembly rejected the idea of an early unification of the two Togolands under a single administration. Nevertheless, the Venezuelan delegate, Victor Rivas, bolstered the case for unification by securitising the unificationists whilst presenting reunification as a measure to appease them:

> "[...] the negative attitude of the Administering Authority concerned would prevent only a peaceful settlement, but not the solution of the problem itself. [...] the metropolitan government postpones recognition of the capacity of that people to assume full responsibility for self-government, the result is effective clandestine activity, and then violence to achieve what could not be achieved amicably. [...] What

---

437 A/C.4/L.260 sponsored by Brazil, Burma, Egypt, El Salvador, India, Indonesia, Iraq, Liberia, Pakistan and Yugoslavia. Available at GAOR 7th Session, Annexes, (A/7/Annexes/Vol.1), *Agenda item 32: The Ewe and Togoland unification problem: special report of the Trusteeship Council*, p. 6.
438 GAOR, "7th Session: Plenary" (1952), pp. 459–60.
439 Resolution 652 (VII), *The Ewe and Togoland unification problem*, adopted on 20 December 1952.
440 ANOM (Aix-en-Provence), 1AFFPOL/3341/2, *Entretiens franco-britanniques sur le Togo-Cameroun*, without title [compte-rendue], 7 February 1953, p. 5.

should the United Nations do in the face of this threat, which is basically international in character, and in the face of this problem which affects collective security?"[441]

Whilst the 1952 oral hearings of Olympio, Antor, and Odame before the Fourth Committee certainly marked the climax of their efforts to securitise Togoland unification, the resolution adopted by the General Assembly most certainly did not go as far as they had hoped. But they expressed their frustration to such an extent that it was unequivocally heard by delegations from states of the Global South as well as the Eastern Bloc, who were more than content to denounce the colonial policies of the Western powers anyway. Although the two Administering Authorities of Togoland got off lightly, they had to fear that the unificationists now had the attention of the world public opinion altogether.

Thus, to limit future declarations, such as Olympio's "reign of terror"-speech before the Fourth Committee during the General Assembly's 7th Session (1952), the colonial powers sought to extend the Trusteeship Council's restrictive *rules of procedure* to the General Assembly. During Anglo-French conversations on colonial issues related to the United Nations on 4 and 5 February 1953, the French delegation argued forcibly that hearings of oral petitioners by the Fourth Committee represented...

> "[...] a dangerous tendency, which should be resisted by all means. They [the French] pointed out that the hearing of witnesses by the Assembly encouraged extremist movements in the territories from which they came, inflated the petitioners' own importance in the territories, and established a most undesirable direct contact between vociferous agitators from the territories and certain delegations in New York. The British delegation while paying tribute to the efficacy of the French counter-petitioners at the 1952 Session, agreed that such hearings, if they became general practice, might be severely damaging to the prestige of the Administering Powers in the territories. M. Pignon [442] regarded it as very important that these hearings should be brought under control in 1953, and that petitioners should be heard by the Fourth Committee only after preliminary examination of their petitions by the Trusteeship Council. [...] the United States Government might be persuaded to take the initiative in the matter. [...] hearing of petitioners from non-self-governing territories could in no circumstances be permitted, and the British delegation reaffirmed that this was one of our 'sticking points'."[443]

6.5.4 A Spectre haunts Africa – the Spectre of the "Red Menace" (1953)

Marc Michel summarizes the year 1953 as "a year of anticipation, preparation, and consultation with parties, associations, chiefs, and notables in both Togos regarding the eventual reconstitution of a [Joined] Council, this time elected by universal suffrage."[444]

---

441 GAOR, "7th Session: Plenary" (1952), p. 458.
442 Léon Pignon was the head of the political department in the Ministry of Overseas France.
443 TNA (London), CO 554/665, *Togoland*, Anglo/French Conversations on Colonial Questions in the United Nations: 4th and 5th February, 1953, p. 2.
444 Michel, "The Independence of Togo," p. 307.

But far from the public eye, much more happened, since 1953 marked a series of changes in the colonial security and intelligence services in British Togoland and the Gold Coast.

A considerable impetus, as Rathbone holds, consisted in London's fear of communist infiltration, which it considered ubiquitous in the structures of the colonial administrations. In March 1953, the Security Liaison Officer for West Africa, Philip M. Kirby Green, for instance, drafted a circular on how to respond best to suspected acts of sabotage and eavesdropping by the Soviet Union in West Africa.[445]

Not even a month later, in late April 1953, the Permanent Under-Secretary of State for the Colonies, Thomas Lloyd, reminded Governor Arden-Clarke that "It is not true that a communist threat exists only where there is an organised communist party, or where there are apparent contacts with overseas."[446] Lloyd found the information-gathering procedures inadequate and emphasised the routinisation of security- and intelligence-related work, which should not just take place during emergencies: "In normal Colonial circumstances [...] It is important that the machinery for assessing and reporting on intelligence should be systematic and regular, and that such reporting should not take place only when there appears to be some particular problem to investigate."[447] Despite the lessons already drawn from the Accra Riots, the Colonial Office held the view that the intelligence services needed to focus their activities on *externally* induced threats. While Lloyd insisted on scrutinizing communist influence in the colonies, Governor Arden-Clarke considered that Westminster's insistence on the 'red menace' had little substance and never took the Special Branch's evidence of Soviet infiltration very seriously.[448] Yet, Governor Arden-Clarke bent to London's will, prompting the *Local Intelligence Committee* (LIC), chaired by the Permanent Secretary for the Ministry of Defence, Reginald Saloway, to get the ball rolling.[449]

The LIC identified the most important sources that could pose a threat to public order and stability in labour unrest ("from natural causes [!], e. g. economic pressure [...] or artificially fomented, e.g. by communist-inspired organisations"), opposition to taxation, political parties and "so-called Youth Organisations inspired with communist ideology and methods."[450] Accordingly, most of the work of the Special Branch was therefore concentrated on the activities of organised trade unions and political parties in the urban centres of the territories.[451] Not only were Special Branch officers required to keep in

---

445 TNA (London), FCO 141/4999, *Gold Coast: security and political intelligence; policy*, Secret Letter SF. 1310, 31 March 1953.
446 TNA (London), FCO 141/4999, *Gold Coast: security and political intelligence; policy*, T.I.K. Lloyd to Charles Arden-Clarke, *Securtiy and Political Intelligence* (without number), 29 April 1953, p. 3.
447 TNA (London), FCO 141/4999, *Gold Coast: security and political intelligence; policy*, T.I.K. Lloyd to Charles Arden-Clarke, Securtiy and Political Intelligence (without number), 29 April 1953, p. 2.
448 TNA (London), FCO 141/4999, *Gold Coast: security and political intelligence; policy*, Arden-Clarke, Secret Letter, 17 August 1953.
449 TNA (London), FCO 141/4999, *Gold Coast: security and political intelligence; policy*, Local Intelligence Committee, Notes of a Meeting held on 23 May.
450 TNA (London), FCO 141/4999, *Gold Coast: security and political intelligence; policy*, Local Intelligence Committee, Notes of a Meeting held on 23 May.
451 TNA (London), FCO 141/4999, *Gold Coast: security and political intelligence; policy*, Pol.F.200. Vol.VI, Reporting of Information of Security Interest by All ranks, 5 June 1953, p. 2.

close touch with large businesses, such as mining companies, but also with local government officers in their areas. A remarkable feature was the division of tasks in intelligence work: the police's Special Branch collected intelligence, but it was mainly up to the colonial District Officers, that is, a *political* administrator and not a security professional, to assess its content. This aspect was subject of discussion of the LIC, which divided intelligence into two categories: *security intelligence* "i.e. intelligence of threats to public order and stability" and *political intelligence* "i.e. intelligence of developments which might lead to breaches of public order and stability."[452] That is, for LIC, it was the 'hard facts' of current circumstances that constituted 'security,' while the assessment of contingencies seemingly constituted the 'political' element of intelligence work. In fact, the Secretary of State for the Colonies, Lennox-Boyd, who constituted the terminus for all security and intelligence reports from the British Empire, would later admit the indistinguishability of 'security intelligence' and 'political intelligence':

> "As regards the collection of information, it is in practice impossible and indeed wrong, whether 'security' or 'political' purposes are in view, to draw a distinction. [...] All intelligence in varying degrees has a 'political' bearing; while, on the other hand, intelligence derived from a 'political' source may have just as much bearing on internal security as that derived from a 'security' source. [...] The term [political intelligence] was originally used in 1948 to make plain that the Secretary of State did not desire a new series of reports dealing simply with the 'security' aspects of administration. What was required was a regular and comprehensive collation of all important information, including inter alia matters of 'security' concern such as the activities of nationalist movements, local societies and organisations and in particular Communist activities."[453]

For this reason, Lennox-Boyd thought it better to have the governors abandon the distinction in the monthly reports to be submitted to him, but remarkably by abandoning the term 'political intelligence' rather than 'security intelligence.' One cannot help suspecting that Lennox-Boyd issued these instructions with the intention of interpreting his function under the neutral light that 'security intelligence' casts, rather than the indicative one that 'political intelligence' casts.

By May 1953, Special Branch grew sevenfold to a total strength of 73. Yet, more importantly, the network of paid informants on which the Special Branch relied also grew. Due to source protection, exact figures are not available but by June 1953, Governor Arden-Clarke was "satisfied with the arrangements the Police have made for penetrating potentially subversive organisations. I am advised that it is comparatively simple to make such arrangements on a financial basis."[454]

---

452 TNA (London), FCO 141/4999, *Gold Coast: security and political intelligence; policy*
453 TNA (London), FCO 141/5000, *Gold Coast: security and political intelligence; policy*, Alan Lennox-Boyd, *Organisation of Intelligence* (Circular No. 458/56), 28 May 1956, pp. 1–2.
454 TNA (London), FCO 141/4999, *Gold Coast: security and political intelligence; policy*, Charles Arden-Clarke, *Security and Political Intelligence* (G/2250), p. 2 [100], 8 June 1953

According to Rathbone, it was London that "was far more convinced about the communist menace in the Gold Coast than the 'men on the spot'."[455] In fact, for these 'men on the spot' intelligence gathering was more of a nuisance. In May 1953, instructions were given that, in addition to Special Branch officers of the police, the Regional Officers of the colonial administration should now also contribute to the *Weekly Intelligence Reports* (WIR) for CenSeC and LIC.[456] The Chief Regional Officer of the Cape Coast, A.J. Loveridge, made his frustration about the instructions known to Secretary of Defence, Saloway:

> "The country abounds in quarrels and I don't think they are more or less than they were before [...] Government Agents spend their lives dealing with these things and the only difference between now and former days is that there is a Minister now who gets to hear of them and a Ministry that gets alarmed."[457]

Saloway saw himself compelled to reprimand the Regional Officer, insisting that he should simply comply with the instruction.[458] In response to the new instructions, the Regional Commissioner for Trans-Volta-Togoland, George Sinclair, saw himself incapable of providing the LIC with intelligence information. He complained about the inadequacy of intelligence gathered in British Togoland, since only one Special Branch officer was responsible for Trans-Volta Togoland. This very officer also had to devote his time to the Eastern Province in the Gold Coast. Sinclair therefore complained:

> "There is no 'Branch' in this area. [...] It often happens that the information contained in these [intelligence] reports comes not from the region but from French territory or from Accra where some of the political parties operating in this region have their headquarters. At present the Regional Officer has no access."[459]

Sinclair recommended therefore the establishment of a *Regional Intelligence Committee* (RIC) for Southern Togoland. Ironically, just five days earlier, LIC discussed and rejected such an idea, since it was concluded that information must reach the central committees as quickly as possible, and a multiplicity of committees might cause delay. There was also the danger of security information leaking out if too many people knew about it.[460] Yet, Arden-Clarke gave Sinclair a free hand and allowed him to create such a Regional Intelligence Committee at his own discretion. Consequently, Sinclair hoped to receive copies of all Special Brand reports, which were of concern to the TVT region but issued

---

455   Rathbone, "Police intelligence in Ghana in the late 1940s and 1950s," p. 114.
456   TNA (London), FCO 141/4999, *Gold Coast: security and political intelligence; policy*, Secret Letter No. 539, 28 May 1953.
457   TNA (London), FCO 141/4999, *Gold Coast: security and political intelligence; policy*, Secret Letter No. 385/SF9, Loveridge to Saloway, 12 June 1953.
458   TNA (London), FCO 141/4999, *Gold Coast: security and political intelligence; policy*, Secret Letter No. 539, Saloway to Loveridge, 27 June 1953.
459   TNA (London), FCO 141/4999, *Gold Coast: security and political intelligence; policy*, Secret Letter 0038/SF7/3, Political Intelligence in Trans Volta Togoland, 28 May 1953.
460   TNA (London), FCO 141/4999, *Gold Coast: security and political intelligence; policy*, Local Intelligence Committee, Notes of a Meeting held on 23rd May, p. 3.

in Accra. However, the Superintendent of Police in Accra was not willing to have the Special Branch Officer in charge of Togoland and the Eastern Region of the Gold Coast send the Special Branch reports to Sinclair.[461] Sinclair, who had already taken over SLO Robin Stephens' duties on a transitional basis in 1949–1950 after tangling with the latter, refused to be swayed. The dispute over responsibilities went through several government officials, reaching once again Governor Arden-Clarke, who had to put his foot down. Finally, it was decided that only clippings pertaining to the Trans-Volta-Togoland Region would be allowed to be forwarded to Chief Regional Officer Sinclair.[462]

Three months after the order has been passed to the Regional Officers, in September 1953, the Gold Coast's Under-Secretary of Defence, P.H. Canham, complained that none of the Regional Commissioners provided him at all with 'security intelligence' or 'political intelligence' and that he was therefore constantly put in an embarrassing situation during the weekly LIC meetings.[463] Six months later, the given order was again a topic during a CenSeC meeting, since only one report had been submitted. In the end, on recommendation by SLO Kirby Green, CenSeC decided to implement Sinclair's idea of establishing territory-wide Regional Intelligence Committees.[464]

These episodes show that there was at times rivalry and nuisance concerning responsibilities between local government officials and security officers. The communication about the intelligence reports from the regions is revealing. Apparently, a recurring concern was the work that went into the reports, how they circulated, who was allowed to read which reports, how much information was duplicated, etc. Ultimately, the colonial security and intelligence apparatus, including the Special Branch, was a bureaucracy machine, which was by no means well-oiled.

Governor Arden-Clarke, for his part, went beyond Arthur Young's recommendation to Africanise the Special Branch and planned to have the new African ministers, especially Nkrumah, slowly be integrated into the security concerns of the Gold Coast by furnishing them the Special Branch's *Weekly Intelligence Reports*. However, much was concealed from African ministers since different versions of the reports were produced for the British and the African Ministers. Nonetheless, African participation in LIC meetings changed the style of communication within the security apparatus. Given its focus on trade unions, this concerned especially the African Minister of Labour, who was henceforth invited to attend the meetings of the LIC. The Colonial Office found Arden-Clarke's plan "bold and shrewd" yet wished him success with this "imaginative experiment."[465] The

---

461 TNA (London), FCO 141/4999, *Gold Coast: security and political intelligence; policy*, Secret Letter, Regional Intelligence Committees, 6 July 1953.
462 TNA (London), FCO 141/4999, *Gold Coast: security and political intelligence; policy*, Secret Notes 539, 22 July 1953.
463 TNA (London), FCO 141/4999, *Gold Coast: security and political intelligence; policy*, Secret Note No. 539, P.H. Canham, 8 September 1953.
464 TNA (London), FCO 141/5000, *Gold Coast: security and political intelligence; policy*, Exctract from CENSEC Agenda Meeting, 1 April 1954.
465 TNA (London), FCO 141/4999, *Gold Coast: security and political intelligence; policy*, Secret Letter from C.Y. Carstairs to Arden-Clarke, 2 June 1953.

SLO, Philip Kirby-Green, on the other hand, was less pleased and considered this move an entry "into a danger zone."[466]

The SLO's concerns were soon to be confirmed, putting an abrupt end to Arden-Clarke's experiment. When in August 1953 it became known that a "Most Secret" document had been stolen from Nkrumah's office, Arden-Clarke's staff insisted that the African Ministers should not see the *Weekly Intelligence Reports*. Though Arden-Clarke felt that Nkrumah, who was Prime Minister after all, should see the reports in the interest of the "Security of the State,"[467] he was surprised by Nkrumah's reaction to them:

> "He [Nkrumah] has expressed to me his reluctance to read them [the Weekly Intelligence Reports]. He went so far as to tell me that he would prefer not to have access to them, and it is only because of my insistence that he continues to receive them. I am not sure why this should be, but think that it is largely due to his dislike of facing unpleasant facts which do not accord with the wishful thinking in which he is prone to indulge. I shall learn more about this in due course."[468]

The SLO later argued that Arden-Clarke's wishes to integrate Nkrumah could no longer be followed so as not to leak intelligence reports and compromise Special Branch informants.[469] When he told the Minister of Defence and Foreign Affairs, E. Norton-Jones, of his reluctance to entrust Nkrumah with the reports, the racist undertone of his reasoning came to light:

> "It is admittedly extremely difficult for any Special branch to obtain reliable information in any Colony in which 'nationalism' is the basis of all political activity. It is also admitted that of all races the African is the most difficult for a Special Branch to handle when it comes to dealing with informants. It is therefore very much to the credit of the very small Gold Coast Special Branch that they have been able to acquire and to control one or two informants in key positions. By 'key positions' I mean that these informants are in a position to produce the type of intelligence which is required by those who have the responsibility for administering the Colony. Obviously no Special Branch can ever guarantee complete coverage of the security and political field all the time, and certainly this cannot be done in the Gold Coast. The fact remains that the Special Branch have today one or two extremely well-placed informants and the very fact that they are 'well-placed' makes their position one of extreme delicacy. It is on these few informants that Special Branch largely relay for their ability to perform their duties in supplying for His Excellency the Governor the intelligence which His Excellency requires, and if for any reason Special Branch were to lose control of these informants they would not be able thereafter to fulfil their obligation, and what is more they would not be able to replace those informants by any others. It has taken

---

466 TNA (London), FCO 141/4997, *Gold Coast: Special Branch Summaries*, Philip Kirby Green to Chairman Local Intelligence Committee, 20 July 1953.
467 TNA (London), FCO 141/4999, *Gold Coast: security and political intelligence; policy*, File No. 539, Personal Note, 10 September 1953.
468 TNA (London), FCO 141/4999, *Gold Coast: security and political intelligence; policy*
469 TNA (London), FCO 141/4997, *Gold Coast: Special Branch Summaries*, Philip Kirby Green to Norton-Jones, 9 September 1953.

a long time and a good deal of public money to acquire control of these individuals and there are no alternative sources.⁴⁷⁰

A day later, a letter from the Superintendent of Police, argued along the same lines.⁴⁷¹ As Arnold holds, such instances show how the heads of the security services willingly "defied the authority of the Governor and threatened the stability of diarchy because of its views of Kwame Nkrumah."⁴⁷² The described episodes of disunity within the British security and intelligence apparatus show that the Ministry of Defence, the Regional Commissioners, the SLOs – in short, all the security professionals involved – feared that the constitutional changes would lead to serving two masters and ultimately to conflicts of authority and loyalty. The disunity in the security apparatus was not only symptomatic of the approaching decolonisation but rather symptomatic of the lack of an agreed colonial order.

Accounting for "Most Secret" (1953)

The "Most Secret" document, which was stolen from Nkrumah's office, was titled "The Future of Togoland under United Kingdom Trusteeship." The classification of the authorless document as "Most Secret" does not correspond to the usually used "Top Secret" of British government papers. Therefore, it can be assumed that the document did not originate from within the Colonial Office or the colonial administration of the Gold Coast.

However, in June 1953, the Colonial Office obtained a copy of said document, which according to the Colonial Under-Secretary, William Gorell Barnes, displayed the author's detailed knowledge about the intricacies of "charterology and U.N. tactics."⁴⁷³ According to Gorell Barnes the document was written in the UN Secretariat, possibly (though not certainly) by the original founder of the Ewe Newsletter and Ewe unification movement, that is, Daniel A. Chapman, who by then had already decamped the Ewe unification cause and joined the faction of Kwame Nkrumah for the sake of an early independence of the Gold Coast. Thus, coined by Governor Arden-Clarke as "Chapman's memorandum,"⁴⁷⁴ the "Most Secret" document analyses the strength of the CPP in Togoland and suggests steps to increase its influence. Most importantly it lays out a plan on how to satisfy the UN that Togoland will be integrated into the Gold Coast⁴⁷⁵: "Undoubtedly the safest and best way of persuading UNO is to arrange for UNO to be bombarded by a broadside of petitions which demand the integration of British Togoland into the Gold Coast [...] A plebiscite, however, would not be acceptable because the opposition to be expected from

---

470   Emphasis in original, TNA (London), FCO 141/4999, *Gold Coast: security and political intelligence; policy*
471   TNA (London), FCO 141/4997, *Gold Coast: Special Branch Summaries*, Security Intelligence, Superintendent of Police, 10 September 1953.
472   Arnold, "'The Cat's Paw of Dictatorship": Police Intelligence and Self-Rule in the Gold Coast, 1948–1952," p. 175.
473   TNA (London), CO 554/668, *Togoland under UN Trusteeship: future policy*, Secret & Personal Letter, WAF 262/177/02 Annex, 3 July 1953, para. 4.
474   TNA (London), CO 554/668, *Togoland under UN Trusteeship: future policy*, Inward Telegram, Secret & Personal (No. 73), Arden-Clarke to Secretary of State for the Colonies, 29 June 1953, p. 1.
475   GAOR, "8th Session: 4th Committee" (1953), p. 323.

the French would serve to delay it."⁴⁷⁶ If Chapman was indeed the author of the document, it would mean that the former founder of the AEC has conspired against the remnants of the movement he helped to create.

Shortly after Nkrumah made his "Motion of Destiny" speech in the Gold Coast Legislative Assembly on 10 July 1953, asking the British government to set a date for self-government, the disaster that "Most Secret" would unleash took its course: less than six weeks after the Colonial Office itself first got to see the document, a petition from the AEC was received in Accra, announcing that the "Most Secret" document will be send to the Trusteeship Council for circulation. It is unclear how the memorandum exactly came into the hands of the unificationists. Governor Arden-Clarke assumes that Nkrumah himself, in an attempt to persuade Sylvanus Olympio to integrate all of Togoland into the Gold Coast, handed the memorandum to Olympio, with the result that it was rapidly reproduced and a summary of it appeared in the local press.⁴⁷⁷ If this was the case, the plan backfired: since "Most Secret" revealed the CPP's plans to integrate British Togoland, a rift occurred between Nkrumah and Olympio as well. Other archival sources speak of a theft from Nkrumah's office,⁴⁷⁸ such as a telegram by the SLO, Philip Kirby-Green, stating that the plans were stolen from Kwame Nkrumah's office and, by a roundabout route, ended up in the hands of Antor and the Togoland Congress.⁴⁷⁹

Attempts to stop the circulation of "Most Secret"

When the news broke, the British Permanent Representative to the Trusteeship Council, Alan Burns, attempted to persuade Secretary-General Dag Hammarskjöld that petitions containing classified information illegally obtained by petitioners should not be circulated, but the latter refused since no "grave damage to the security of the state is involved."⁴⁸⁰ The publication of "Most Secret" was a disaster for the British as it confirmed, from the French point of view, their suspicion that the British's long-term plan was to annex French territory.⁴⁸¹

The last possibility for the British was to suppress the hearing of petitioners. At the beginning of the Assembly's 8th Session (1953), the Fourth Committee had again several requests for oral hearings before it and, as had happened in the previous two years, the

---

476 Senyo G. Antor, *"Most secret" politics in Togoland: the British government's attempt to annex Togoland to the Gold Coast* (New York: Comtemporary Press, 1954), p. 11.
477 TNA (London), CO 554/668, *Togoland under UN Trusteeship: future policy*, Arden-Clarke to Gorell Barnes, Secret Letter 571/7, 4 August 1953, p. 1.
478 TNA (London), FCO 141/4999, *Gold Coast: security and political intelligence; policy*, handwritten note, 18 August 1953, [125] p 1.
479 TNA (London), FCO 141/4999, *Gold Coast: security and political intelligence; policy*, Telegram (Pol. F.21/1), 10 August 1953, P.M. Kirby Green to Chairman L.I.C.
480 TNA (London), CO 554/668, *Togoland under UN Trusteeship: future policy*, Secret Letter, W.A.C. Mathieson to John Martin, 30 July 1953.
481 TNA (London), CO 554/668, *Togoland under UN Trusteeship: future policy*, Secret Letter, W.A.C. Mathieson to John Martin, 30 July 1953; ANT (Lomé), 2APA Kloto/23, *Affaires Politiques*, Examen du Plan Secret du Gouvernement du Gold-Coast Relatif à l'Annexion du Togo sous Tutelle Britannique – Divulgué en Juillet 1953 – Traduction in extenso (without number), without date, p. 2 and 5.

Administering Authorities troubled the Fourth Committee with a debate on the admissibility of oral hearings. The colonial powers were unwilling to grant these hearings but were expectedly outvoted by the anti-colonial majority.

As agreed during Anglo-French conversations of February 1953,[482] the British delegation thereupon proposed the establishment of a sub-committee to make recommendations on the adoption of rules of procedure for oral hearings in the Fourth Committee. The proposal established that out of its eight members of the sub-committee, four should consist of members of the Trusteeship Council (two administering and two non-administering).[483] Once the proposal was made, the French delegation argued "to postpone consideration of any requests for oral hearings until the sub-committee had completed its work."[484] Suspiciously specific, the British representative expressed that the British's intention was not to restrict the right of petition and was solely in the interests of orderly procedure.[485] The French delegation supported the proposal arguing that the right to petition might be misused by petitioners forming "the advance guard of communism in Africa."[486]

The Yugoslav representative, Josip Djerdja, questioned the French and British intentions:

> "one of the basic elements of the International Trusteeship System was the right to petition. It was the United Nations' right and duty to examine petitions and recommend measures to be taken to eliminate grievances. The petitions system was a means of establishing close contact between the United Nations and the Trust Territories. The value of the assistance to be given to the inhabitants of those Territories, and their confidence in the United Nations, would depend largely on whether or not petitions and oral hearings were given thorough consideration. Some of the statements made in the course of the discussion could only be interpreted as attempts to restrict the rights of the inhabitants of the Trust Territories, which were guaranteed by the Charter."[487]

Most of the anti-colonial state representatives found the British proposal to establish a sub-committee to develop rules of procedure for oral hearings "tantamount to transferring competence to a body which was not essentially answerable to the Fourth Committee."[488] They did not believe that the number of requests for oral hearings warranted rules of procedure for the Fourth Committee anyway. For them, petitioners should not only have direct access to the General Assembly, but hearing petitioners should assist the Assembly in considering the issues before it. Thus, the British proposal was rejected.[489]

---

482 TNA (London), CO 554/665, *Togoland*, Anglo/French Conversations on Colonial Questions in the United Nations: 4th and 5th February, 1953, p. 2.
483 A/C.4/L.271, available at GAOR 8th Session, Annexes, (A/8/Annexes), *Agenda item 13: Requests for oral hearings-United Kingdom of Great Britain and Northern Ireland: draft resolution*, p. 1.
484 GAOR, "8th Session: 4th Committee" (1953), p. 10.
485 GAOR, "8th Session: 4th Committee" (1953), p. 10.
486 GAOR, "8th Session: 4th Committee" (1953), p. 17.
487 GAOR, "8th Session: 4th Committee" (1953), p. 20.
488 GAOR, "8th Session: 4th Committee" (1953), p. 59.
489 GAOR, "8th Session: 4th Committee" (1953), p. 28.

Thullen holds that the Togoland unification question reached its peak at the Assembly's 8th Session (1953). 13 out of 82 sessions of the Fourth Committee dealt exclusively with this question, clearly showing the importance attached to it. France also attached significant importance to this session as the French Foreign Minister, Georges Bidault, noted just a week before the discussion on the Togoland problem to the French Overseas Minister: "It is undeniable that in Black Africa, Togo has served and is serving as a starting point for the work of disintegration of the opponents of our imperial vocation."[490] There is a certain historical irony behind this assertion, considering that less than two years earlier, Antor prophesied to the General Assembly the opposite result, that is, "the loss of Togoland would lead sooner or later to the disintegration of the whole French Union."[491]

Oral Hearing

When in November 1953, the delegation of the Togoland unificationists appeared again for an oral hearing before the Fourth Committee, their attacks had it in spades. First Alex Odame attacked the Trusteeship Council and the 1952 UN Visiting Mission to West Africa, both of which allegedly "had joined the Administering Authorities in a concerted and ingeniously planned policy to defeat the basic guarantees, rights and protections accorded to those peoples under the Charter."[492] Thereupon Antor claimed that instead of working toward the establishment of the *Joint Council on Togoland Affairs*, the British government had done its utmost to integrate Togoland into the Gold Coast. He said the "Most Secret" document now before the Fourth Committee served as evidence of the methods employed by the British government. He called for the Trusteeship Agreement to be amended so that a UN Special Commissioner could draft a constitution for a unified and free Togoland.

Knowing that after his last hearing before the Fourth Committee he almost succeeded in having the General Assembly punish France and Britain with an embarrassing resolution, Olympio stepped up his securitising attacks by maintaining that in French Togoland:

> "increasingly repressive measures had been taken to make it impossible for his party [the CUT] to hold meetings or to pursue any normal political activities. The police and gendarmes had even entered private houses to break up private meetings and arrest those responsible for organizing them. In Lomé public meeting places were cordoned off a few hours before the meetings were to start and all those who wished to attend were forcibly driven away. Several peaceful citizens had suffered bodily injuries in that way, although they had committed no offence. Members of parties furthering unification and independence were treated almost as outlaws; if they were attacked, they could expect no help from the police. They were dismissed from the government services and business houses on flimsy pretexts."[493]

---

490 MAE (La Courneuve), 77QO-2, *Politique intérieure*, Le Ministre des Affaires Étrangères à Monsieur le Ministre de la France d'Outre-Mer, 5 November 1953, p. 4.
491 GAOR, "6th Session: 4th Committee" (1951), p. 163.
492 GAOR, "8th Session: 4th Committee" (1953), p. 320.
493 GAOR, "8th Session: 4th Committee" (1953), p. 326.

Photo 16: Petitioners of Togoland Congress (17 November 1953)[494]

Source: UN Photo.

Olympio expressed the urgency to liberate French Togoland from the clutches of the French Union where it would be "deprived of any hope of ever attaining self-government or independence."[495] Olympio dedicated a lot of time to highlight the repression by the French administration, its police violence, the banning of meetings and the harassment in the issuing of visas.[496] Finally, Olympio called for elections held under UN supervision.

Whilst Frederick Brenner (PTP) disputed most of the points put forth by the unificationists, Robert Ajavon (PTP) attacked the UN since in recent years the abuses of the right to petition had been increasingly corrupting the very principle:

"The Trusteeship Council and the Fourth Committee, through their indiscriminate acceptance of all petitions and their desire to discredit a colonial Power, had been induced six years previously to acknowledge the reality of a problem which they knew to be insoluble because it did not rest on a serious foundation. The Fourth Committee had ultimately convinced itself of the insolubility of the problem of Ewe unification, but meanwhile vain hopes had been aroused in the minds of certain Togolanders, social unrest had been stirred up, and the development of Togoland had been considerably retarded. Togoland unification was a convenient way out for the Committee. But the problem was almost impossible of solution; procrastination was therefore indicated."[497]

---

494 This photograph shows the three representatives of the Joint Togoland Congress (seated, left to right): R.E.G. Armattoe, Alex K. Odame, and Senyo G. Antor. Standing behind them is Theodore O. Asare, a Togoland-born New York lawyer.
495 GAOR, "8th Session: 4th Committee" (1953), p. 326.
496 GAOR, "8th Session: 4th Committee" (1953), pp. 327–37.
497 GAOR, "8th Session: 4th Committee" (1953), p. 360.

The British representative, W.A.C. Mathieson, strongly objected to the securitising language used by the unificationists. He criticized that Armattoe "had spoken with a lack of restraint which was particularly indefensible when coming from a man of such wide education and persuasive or rather elusive eloquence."[498] Likewise he criticized Odame, who "had claimed that a reign of terror existed in Togoland under British administration. Those words were generally used to describe a situation characterized by murder, public disorder and violation of human rights. The visiting missions had pointed out in their reports on the Territory [...] that the freedom of speech, movement and assembly was fully respected in Togoland under British administration."[499]

Yet, the accusations of the unificationist caught on with anti-colonial state representatives, such as the Polish representative, Joseph Winiewicz, who held:

"The representatives of the different Togoland organizations had clearly shown what methods were being used by the Administering Authorities to reach their ends, and how the interests of the peoples under trusteeship were being neglected. [...] Political meetings were cynically banned, and persons who dared to show the slightest opposition to the government were subjected to police terror and imprisonment."[500]

General Debate

Unsurprisingly, the following debate was heated and resulted in the consideration of three draft resolutions. The first draft resolution reaffirmed the basic premises of the unificationists, stating that "the unification of the two parts of Togoland is the manifest aspiration of the majority of the population of the two Trust Territories" and recommended the re-establishment of the *Joint Council on Togoland Affairs*, but this time with the power to consider and make recommendations on the question of unification and on all other matters affecting the two territories.[501]

The second draft resolution called on the Administering Authorities "immediately" to review electoral eligibility in the territories and to introduce a system of voter registration based on personal identification to ensure universal, direct, and secret suffrage.[502] Both the French and the British delegates considered the draft to be completely unrealistic. The French delegate, Léon Pignon, voiced: "The French Government was of course in favour of universal suffrage, and in practice the system had no political disadvantage but many advantages. However, at the present stage of development in Togoland, and in dark

---

498 GAOR, "8th Session: 4th Committee" (1953), p. 365.
499 GAOR, "8th Session: 4th Committee" (1953), p. 366.
500 GAOR, "8th Session: 4th Committee" (1953), p. 369.
501 GAOR, "8th Session: 4th Committee" (1953), p. 408. The draft resolution A/C.4/L.308, available at GAOR, 8th Session, Annexes, (A/8/Annexes), *Agenda Item 13*, 6, was approved by the Fourth Committee by 44 votes to 0, with 8 abstentions (including U.K. and France) and later approved in plenary as General Assembly resolution 750 A (VIII), *The Togoland unification problem*, A/RES/750(VIII)[A] (8 December 1953), available from digitallibrary.un.org/record/666076.
502 The draft resolution A/C.4/L.309 was approved by the Fourth Committee by 48 to 1 (Belgium), with 3 abstentions (U.K., France, and Canada) and later approved in plenary as General Assembly resolution 750 B (VIII), *The Togoland unification problem*, A/RES/750(VIII)[B] (8 December 1953), available from digitallibrary.un.org/record/666078.

Africa generally, the problem of universal suffrage was not a political but a social problem."[503] Pignon basically argued that Africans themselves were not ready yet to fully accept democratic elections to ensure representation. Nevertheless, France abstained and did not vote against the resolution after the word "immediately" was deleted from the resolution.

The third draft resolution, which was aimed at preventing the integration of British Togoland into the Gold Coast under any circumstances, was the most controversial.[504] The draft resolution considered that further amendments to the Gold Coast Constitution would require a revision of the Trusteeship Agreement as far as the administrative union was concerned and stated:

> "Any revision of the trusteeship agreement [...] with a view to the integration or annexation of the territory, or any part of it to the Gold Coast would be contrary to the principles and purposes of the international trusteeship system."[505]

In response to sharp criticism from the Administering Authorities and a few Western delegations, the initiators of the draft amended the text so as not to exclude the possibility of eventual integration once both territories have achieved self-government or independence.[506] Britain insisted that Article 76 of the Charter did not require self-government or independence of a trusteeship territory as a separate entity, and that the third draft resolution therefore denied the future of a British Togoland in which the people freely chose integration with a self-governing Gold Coast.[507] The British delegation therefore submitted an alternative text:

> "The integration of Togoland under British administration, or any part of it, to the Gold Coast can only be accepted as a satisfactory termination of the trusteeship agreement if the prior agreement of the General Assembly is obtained by the administering authority in the light of the principles and purposes of the international trusteeship system."[508]

However, this was unacceptable to the anti-colonial majority, which continued to insist that the Charter did not allow for the transformation of an *administrative* union into a *political* union under any circumstances. Following a paragraph-by-paragraph vote, the

---

503 GAOR, "8th Session: 4th Committee" (1953), p. 391.
504 See GAOR, "8th Session: 4th Committee" (1953), p. 409. The draft resolution A/C.4/L.310 was approved the Fourth Committee by 33 to 8 (including U.K. and France), with 12 abstentions.
505 A/C.4/L.310, paragraph 3 available at GAOR 8th Session, Annex (A/8/Annexes), *Agenda item 31*, p. 7.
506 A/C.4/L.310/Rev.1 "Considers further that the integration of Togoland under British administration, or any part of it, to the Gold Coast before both territories have attained self-government or independence, would be contrary to the principles and purposes of the international trusteeship system."
507 GAOR, "8th Session: 4th Committee" (1953), p. 407.
508 A/C.4/L.317 see GAOR 8th Session, Annex (A/8/Annexes), Agenda item 31, p. 10.

Committee rejected the amendments by the Administering Authorities and adopted the original texts.[509]

Although the Fourth Committee adopted the resolution, it still had to go through the plenary. Again, the British delegation was successful in its strenuous effort of hallway diplomacy to secure a rejection of the controversial third paragraph in plenary by taking advantage of the Assembly's two-thirds voting rule.[510] Once more, the now pruned resolution then passed with little opposition.[511]

Thullen notes that the UN's failure to find a mutually acceptable solution to the unification question was partly due to the extreme complexity of the issue, but also because the second UN Visiting Mission (1952), through its more than ambiguous report, failed to live up to its proper function as the eyes and ears of the UN.[512] Therefore, the Fourth Committee was confronted with a situation in which anti-colonial petitioners demanded an immediate solution in line with their own interpretations. The colonial powers, on the other hand, merely willing to set up various bodies to study the problem and facilitate contacts between the two territories, categorically rejected the solutions favoured by the General Assembly. Thus, the unificationists' securitising moves resonated with most representatives of the anti-colonial states, partly because they could identify with the petitioners due to their own colonial past. In consequence, most of the anti-colonial state representatives tended to distrust the statements of the colonial powers since they were more justificatory than explanatory. There was much truth to the remark by the Syrian delegate, Abdul Aziz Allouni, made at the end of the Assembly's 8th Session, that there was...

> "[...] a tendency for the machinery [of petitioning] to become an automatic device into which petitions were fed at one end, together with the explanations of the Administering Authorities, and highly polished resolutions came out at the other end. Under the pressure of mass production there was a danger that those resolutions would tend to show a standardization of thought and action."[513]

6.6 Turning the Tides I: British Togoland (1954-1957)

At the Trusteeship Council's 13th Session (1954), as usual the Council members were divided between the Administering Authorities who praised the political advancement of the Gold Coast in which British Togoland participated and the non-Administering Council members who feared that integration might prevent Togoland unification.[514] How-

---

509 GAOR, "8th Session: 4th Committee" (1953), pp. 408–9.
510 TNA (London), FCO 141/5027, *Gold Coast: Anglo-French cooperation on security matters in West Africa*, Secretary of State to Governor of Gold Coast, 30 November 1953.
511 GAOR, "8th Session: Plenary" (1953), 440. The third paragraph was rejected by 28 to 17, with 3 abstentions. See Resolution 750 C (VIII), *The Togoland unification problem*, A/RES/750(VIII)[C] (8 December 1953), available from digitallibrary.un.org/record/666079.
512 Thullen, *Problems of the Trusteeship System*, p. 148.
513 GAOR, "8th Session: 4th Committee" (1953), p. 461.
514 TCOR, "13th Session" (1954), pp. 135–37.

ever, what was new was that India, of all states, until recently a British colony, began to withdraw from its former insistence on unification and support the British position. The Indian representative considered that British Togoland's continued association with the Gold Coast might prove more profitable than union with French Togoland, which was not making as much progress in political institutions as the Gold Coast.[515]

The British representative, Alan Burns, announced that the British Government was negotiating the revision of the existing constitution of the Gold Coast. Once these were concluded, new general elections would take place. As a by-product of these elections, so to speak, the British government hoped to obtain useful supplementary information on the wishes of the people concerning association with the Gold Coast and would take that information into consideration in its final consultations with the French.[516] The French representative, Léon Pignon, reported that consultations in French Togoland revealed that the majority of the people were opposed to the re-constitution of the *Joint Council* and considered that the time was past when the *Joint Council* could serve any useful purpose in solving problems common to the two territories.[517]

Integrationists before the Trusteeship Council (1954)

The Trusteeship Council's 13th Session (1954) represented a novum in as much the Council heard for the very first-time oral petitions from British Togolanders supporting integration with the Gold Coast: Solomon Togbe Fleku, from the CPP's Southern Togoland Section, Jacob Kwadwo Mensah, representative of the Buem-Krachi District Council, and Joseph Henry Allassani, of the Dagomba District Council in Northern Togoland.

Fleku indicated that…

> "[a]s an Ewe, he had felt keenly the sufferings endured by the Ewes in Togoland under French administration and the difficulties of communicating with them. His party had supported the Ewe unification movement but it had never envisaged Ewe unification except in association with the Gold Coast where so many Ewes lived. [… The CPP] prepared to consider any political proposals which would endanger the present unity of most of the Ewes, at least until final integration had been achieved through the ending of the Trusteeship Agreement."[518]

As long as integration was assured, British Togoland would be prepared to participate in a Joint Council, but it was not prepared to take part in a *Joint Council*, which might jeopardize Togoland's future in association with the Gold Coast. Allassani said the peoples, whose homeland stretches over the Gold Coast and Northern Togoland, did not want to be split again by a possible unification of the Togolands.[519] Mensah said the independence of British Togoland could be achieved more promptly by its complete integration with the Gold Coast, which was far more advanced on the road of independence.[520]

---

515   TCOR, "13th Session" (1954), p. 138.
516   TCOR, "13th Session" (1954), pp. 184–85.
517   TCOR, "13th Session" (1954), p. 185.
518   TCOR, "13th Session" (1954), p. 186.
519   TCOR, "13th Session" (1954), pp. 187–88.
520   TCOR, "13th Session" (1954), pp. 188–89.

Photo 17: Oral Hearing of Integrationists (1 March 1954)[521]

Source: UN Photo/Albert Fox.

The British representative, Alan Burns, requested to adjourn the discussion hoping that in the light of the forthcoming elections in the Gold Coast the British Government would be able to submit concrete proposals for the Togoland issue.[522] Although the Council agreed to this proposal, it was strongly opposed by the Soviet representative, Semyon K. Tsarapkin, who considered it another tactic to frustrate the unification movement. He accused that France and Britain (who were ostensibly supporting General Assembly and Trusteeship Council decisions) had done all in their power to prevent their implementation. He referred to the "Most Secret" document that outlined that the Trusteeship Council was to be "bombarded" with petitions, followed by the personal appearance of selected spokesmen of the CPP. There was striking proof that was exactly what the Council was now witnessing. Furthermore, Tsarapkin saw through the British adjourning-plan since...

> "The argument that Togoland under British administration could achieve independence in association with the colony of the Gold Coast more easily than by advancing to independence and sovereign statehood under the International Trusteeship System was patently absurd. Obviously, the United Kingdom Government hoped that the so-called constitutional reforms in the Gold Coast and the Trust Territory – on which, incidentally, neither the Council nor the General Assembly had been consulted

---

521 The spokesmen (facing camera, first row) are (left to right): Mensah, Allassani, and Fleku. At left, back to camera: Leslie Knox Munro (New Zealand), President of the Council and, at right, Victor C. Hoo, Assistant Secretary-General of the UN in-charge of the Department of Trusteeship and Information from Non-Self-Governing Territories.
522 TCOR, "13th Session" (1954), p. 193.

– would have come into effect by the next session and that it would be able to confront the Council *a fait accompli.*"[523]

Yet, since the Indian representative no longer considered unification a viable option,[524] the discussion was deferred until after the election.

Meanwhile, in French Togoland, the French increased pressure on the unification movement. The French administration had already tried in 1951 to get Olympio transferred from London to the Paris branch of the United Africa Company. Since he refused the 'promotion,' the French administration tried to eliminate him by other means: On 3 May 1954, he was convicted of a minor technical violation of foreign exchange regulations (signing a sterling check in a franc zone city in 1953), fined 5,000,000 CFA or $25,000, and deprived of his civil rights for the next five years, including the prohibition to run for elective office.

6.6.1 "A New Type of Threat" (1954)

On 29 April 1954, the Gold Coast Government approved the new constitution under which British Togoland also fell. Under the new constitution the Assembly was enlarged, and its members were no longer elected by the District Councils but chosen by direct election. All *ex-officio* cabinet members, including the Minister of Defence and External Affairs, were abolished, thus, establishing a cabinet composed exclusively of African ministers. Yet, internal security, defence, and external relations remained firmly within Governor Arden-Clarke's reserve powers.

Rathbone argued that there was nothing natural about the British's firm grip on internal and external security up to the last days until independence.[525] In hindsight, even Governor Arden-Clarke regretted the decision to leave internal security, defence, and external relations remained firmly within the reserve powers:

> "Then came the time when we had to make another move forward and have a new Constitution. [...] the Governor's reserve powers remained much as before. [...] Defence included internal security, i.e. the control of the police and the measures necessary to deal with any outbreaks of violence and lawlessness within the Gold Coast. I think it is a doubtful proposition whether we were wise in making internal security a reserved subject [...] it would have been better not to reserve internal security but to let it be dealt with by the appropriate Minister [...] a Government which is not responsible for internal security tends to be, and sometimes is, irresponsible in its approach to provocative administrative measures or legislation. It may quite happily enact measures which in certain areas are bound to create trouble and then sit back and watch the Governor trying to deal with the consequent disorders; that is not a satisfactory state of affairs."[526]

---

523 TCOR, "13th Session" (1954), p. 197.
524 TCOR, "13th Session" (1954), pp. 197–99.
525 Rathbone, "Police intelligence in Ghana in the late 1940s and 1950s," p. 125.
526 Arden-Clarke, "Gold Coast Into Ghana," pp. 54–55.

The constitutional development in the Gold Coast coincided with a joint memorandum, which the Security Service and the Colonial Office circulated empire-wide with the goal to reset the focus of the Special Branch. Since the end of World War II, and especially since Thomas Lloyd's circular in 1953, the focus of intelligence services, including the Special Branch, was set on *external threats*, such as Soviet eavesdropping or the spread of communism by outside elements. The 1954 memorandum shifted this focus:

> "The first Security Service posts overseas were established at points of strategic military importance at the instance of the Defence Departments and, initially, the emphasis was on liaison and defence against *external threats* rather than upon internal and mainly indigenous security problems. [...] For a variety of reasons, including increasing political and racial consciousness, the stresses and strains resulting from economic and social change, and the impact of Communist and other external influences, there is now a much increased liability to *internal security threats* in the form of clandestine, violent and, unconstitutional action. [...] The new type of threat necessarily calls for internal security intelligence machinery adapted to deal with it."[527]

The memorandum justified internally the practice of surveillance of unions and political parties by asserting that the new colonial Secret Service...

> "[...] constitutes a means for discharging its necessary task which is consistent with free and democratic political institutions. It is not a 'secret police' [...] The guiding criterion is the *objective one* of 'security risk', and *not subjective* and debatable concepts such as 'loyalty'. The primary concern of the Security Service is with what a man may do, and with what he may think or feel only to the extent that it is a guide to his possible actions."[528]

In other words, the Colonial Office drew on a depoliticized or 'objective' understanding of security and professionalisation to legitimize colonial espionage, convinced that the identification of 'security risks' was not and could not be ideologically motivated.

Yet, unmistakably the memorandum was a reaction to the Mau-Mau rebellion in Kenya, which broke out in the latter half of 1952. Another indication that the Mau-Mau rebellion was a key factor for the shift to 'internal threats' was that the Colonial Office sent Derek Franklin, who at the time was Deputy Inspector General of the Colonial Police working for the Special Branch in Kenya, for a short-term audit tour to the Gold Coast.[529]

While a year earlier, the Colonial Office still had insisted on the importance of *external* security threats, it dawned on the colonial security authorities that they had looked the other way for too long. Now the Colonial Office together with the British Security

---

[527] My emphasis, TNA (London), FCO 141/5000, *Gold Coast: security and political intelligence; policy* May 1954, "The Security Service and the Colonies. Joint Memorandum by the Security Service and the Colonial Office", p. 1

[528] TNA (London), FCO 141/5000, *Gold Coast: security and political intelligence; policy* The Security Service and the Colonies. Joint Memorandum by the Security Service and the Colonial Office, May 1954.

[529] TNA (London), FCO 141/5000, *Gold Coast: security and political intelligence; policy*, Secret and Personal Letter, Franklin to Arden-Clarke, 12 December 1954.

Service planned for the Special Branch to be organized, staffed, and trained accordingly to this new type of *internal* threat. Accordingly, a *Security Intelligence Advisor*, Alex A. MacDonald, was appointed to conduct audit tours and provide special advice in the colonial possessions across the British Empire.

For SLO, Kirby Green, the memorandum merely amounted to a slight reorganization of intelligence. Before he was replaced by the SLO for West Africa, Major Hodson, Kirby Green endeavoured to intensify exchanges with the SLOs of the other British West African colonies, including arrangements with the French intelligence organization "to provide the best possible security intelligence coverage."[530] In October 1954, the British administration revealed the identity of the SLO Kirby Green to Nkrumah – no easy matter for the British, since the SLO's function was primarily directed against Soviet Union influence and Nkrumah harboured open leanings towards communist ideas. Therefore, it was decided that in order to engage with the SLO, Nkrumah had to go through the governor.[531]

As far as Togoland was concerned, the change in threat perceptions proved to be well founded: In August 1954, an informant of the administration in French Togoland came into possession of an usurpation plan authored by the unificationists Anku Morny (Togoland Congress) and Jean Foly (Juvento). The plan stated:

> "Should the General Assembly of the U.N.O. fail to agree to Ewe – Togoland manifest aspiration, there should be organized in all towns and villages of British and French Territories, 'The Peoples Police' [...] to mobilise a strong force of people who will take by force the Government of Togoland. [...] foreign immigrants and natives who do not support unification will be massacred and their houses reduced to ashes."[532]

The adjutant of the French Consulate in Accra, V. Gares, seemed convinced that the group was inspired by the Mau-Mau rebellion in Kenya and on inquiring with the British, the latter were convinced of the authenticity of the project, yet considered it childish and unworkable.[533] For both powers, especially the younger members of the Togoland Congress and Juvento seemed prone to exaggeration.

There was some truth in this assessment: In 1954, Juvento experienced its first split into a Marxist-Leninist wing under Messan Aithson. The Cameroonian-born Aithson had been arrested and imprisoned by the French authorities, and upon his release from prison, been deprived of his citizenship and expelled from Togoland. Aithson sought refuge in the Gold Coast. Having built Juvento, Aihtson wished to see it become the local branch of the militant interterritorial RDA. Thus, in 1954 Aihtson resigned from Juvento, carrying with him some of the more militant members, while Ben Apaloo assumed the

---

530 TNA (London), FCO 141/4990, *Gold Coast: Security Liaison Officer, West Africa*, Secret Letter Pol. F. 8, Kirby Green to Arden-Clarke, 9 August 1954.
531 TNA (London), FCO 141/4990, *Gold Coast: Security Liaison Officer, West Africa*, Secret and Personal Letter Def.240/11/01, Piper to Hadow, 21 September 1954.
532 MAE (La Courneuve), 77QO-5, *Politique intérieure*, Annexe to dépêche 237/SC, Togoland Peoples Police.
533 MAE (La Courneuve), 77QO-5, *Politique intérieure*, Renner to Ministre des Affaires Etrangeres, 27 August 1954.

leadership of the truncated moderate movement in which above all the lawyer Anani Santos stood out.

A case in point was that during the same month of the usurpation plan, under the leadership of Ben Apaloo, Juvento passed a resolution alleging that the French administration was "exerting a dictatorial regime and was the cause of emigration of several French Togolese."[534] It is probable that these accusations had the intention to serve as an attack against the French during the Fourth Committee's upcoming 9th Session (1954). As a provision for this attack, the emigrated French Togolese founded the *Rassemblement Populaire des Refugies du Togo Français* in the Gold Coast.

The British Memorandum to end Trusteeship (1954)

Since the circulation of "Most Secret," Governor Arden-Clarke was the first to acknowledge that it was set in stone that without a referendum the General Assembly would never agree to the integration of British Togoland into the Gold Coast.[535] Yet, the British knew how to make ends meet: The General Elections scheduled after the constitutional changes represented the first time that the Togoland Congress and the CPP contested with one another. Thus, the General Elections for the Assembly were the "first real trial of strength between Government Party and the all-Ewe-Movement,"[536] which functioned as "a species of plebiscite of integration versus unification."[537]

Table 4: 1954 General Elections' results in British Togoland (South)

District	CPP	Togoland Congress
Ho	32%	68%
Kpando	48%	52%
Buem-Krachi	71%	23%
Total Southern Togoland	48,1%	49,5%

Source: Coleman, *Togoland*, p. 77.

Since in the southern section of Togoland, the vote was evenly distributed, the British were now able to calculate that a majority of British Togolanders, taken as a whole, would prefer integration into the Gold Coast. It seemed that for many, the promise of early independence seemed to have a greater appeal than the uncertainty of either Ewe or Togoland reunification. The British produced a statistical analysis, which concluded that if at least

---

534 MAE (La Courneuve), 77QO-5, *Politique intérieure*, Renner to Ministre des Affaires Étrangères, 27 September 1954.
535 TNA (London), CO 554/668, *Togoland under UN Trusteeship: future policy*, Secret Letter No. 571/7, from Arden-Clarke to Gorell Barnes, 4 August 1953, p. 2.
536 In possession of Kudzordzi (private) (Ho), *Kudzordzi Archives*. Cabinet: Togoland under United Kingdom Trusteeship (C.54 169), 19 May 1954, p. 2
537 PRAAD (Accra), RG 3/5/2073, "*Trusteeship Council's Discussions on Togoland T/C.2/SR.227 (10 Feb 1955)*", the Economist: The future of Togoland, 20 November 1954, [p. 2].

40% of the registrable electorate in the Northern Section of British Togoland went to the polls and "independence" as an electoral alternative for British Togoland was not put on vote, a referendum would favour British Togoland's integration into the Gold Coast.[538]

Thus, the time was ripe: not even a week after the Gold Coast's General Elections, during the Trusteeship Council's 14th Session (1954), the British presented a memorandum entitled "The future of the Trust Territory of Togoland under UK Trusteeship," which sought the termination of the Trusteeship Agreement. Due to the to the imminent independence of the Gold Coast and its administrative union with British Togoland, the British made it clear that they were unwilling to continue administering British Togoland after the Gold Coast had attained independence. The memorandum proposed that the regular 1955 Visiting Mission should be tasked with examining the situation in the light of these new developments. Considering the heated debates in the Fourth Committee over the last three years, the memorandum warned "the political destinies of a territory or its peoples cannot be determined to legal texts or the proceedings of the General Assembly."[539] With regard to Togoland unification, the British virtually blackmailed the General Assembly:

> "In Considering 'Togoland unification' [...], the General Assembly must consider whether it is prepared to insist upon a delay in the attainment by the inhabitants of the trust territory of a full measure of self-government in order to experiment with arrangements which may or may not prove workable."[540]

The memorandum suggested that the United Nations should ascertain the wishes of the inhabitants by any means it might deem desirable. The memorandum suggested that the General Assembly, at its upcoming 9th Session (1954), could authorize the Trusteeship Council to formulate recommendations on methods and procedures.

The British representative, Alan Burns, announced that the results of the General Election were regarded by the British government as indicative concerning public opinion on the future status of British Togoland. Therefore, there was no point in continuing discussion on the re-establishment of the *Joint Council* until the British memorandum had been debated by the forthcoming session of the General Assembly.[541] The French representative, Léon Pignon, supported this viewpoint. He asserted that the re-establishment of the *Joint Council* was no longer pertinent. Besides, the great majority of the people in French Togoland allegedly opposed it. The French Government considered it impossible to reconstitute the *Joint Council* merely to satisfy two minority groups in the two Togolands.[542]

---

538 TNA (London), FCO 141/5013, *Gold Coast: the Ewe and Togoland unification problem*, 1955, Analysis of possible voting results in a plebiscite in Togoland under United Kingdom Trusteeship. See also Coleman, *Togoland*, p. 77.
539 TCOR, "14th Session: The Future of the Trust Territory of Togoland under British Administration" A/2660 (1954), para. 29.
540 TCOR, "14th Session: The Future of the Trust Territory of Togoland under British Administration" (1954), para. 49.
541 TCOR, "14th Session" (1954), pp. 224–25.
542 TCOR, "14th Session" (1954), p. 225.

The Syrian representative, Rafik Asha, disagreed that the Gold Coast elections could be regarded as a test between unification and integration since it was not a clear-cut election over the issue of integration and unification.[543] But it was to no avail, since the Trusteeship Council resolved to transfer to the General Assembly the memorandum under the item 'the Togoland Unification Problem'."[544]

Integrationist Wave before the Fourth Committee (1954)

Amenumey chronicled how the unificationists immediately responded to the British memorandum and held meeting after meeting in the months that followed, agreeing on petitions opposing the incorporation of British Togoland into the Gold Coast and calling on the General Assembly to organize a referendum under UN supervision not only in British Togoland but in both territories to ensure self-determination for the people.[545] But being aware of the frustration of written petitions, the unificationists requested to be heard in an oral hearing before the Fourth Committee.

Unsurprisingly, at the Assembly 9th Session (1954), the British memorandum was met with mixed feelings, especially since the Administering Authorities once again refused to grant oral hearings to petitioners on the matter. The French representative, Léon Pignon, once again voiced concern that it was "hardly in the interests of the General Assembly to hear statements by representatives of political parties concerning problems to which there was no immediate solution. Furthermore, by granting such hearings the General Assembly was to a certain extent usurping the functions of the Trusteeship Council, which inevitably led to some confusion."[546] The representative from the Philippines, Victorio Carpio, countered that from "three years' experience, he knew that the procedure to which petitions were subjected in the Council and its committees virtually nullified the right of petition embodied in the Charter."[547] As expected, the overwhelming majority of anti-colonial representatives approved the requests for an oral hearing. 15 petitioners appeared before the Fourth Committee.[548]

Komla Gbedemah (CPP) as well as Liana Asigri (Maprusi District Councils), J.H. Allassani and Mahama Bukhari (Dagomba District Council) supported the idea of integrating British Togoland into the Gold Coast. Allassani stressed that

> "Since the sensible idea of Ewe unification had been overshadowed by the idea of Togoland unification, the peoples in the Northern Section of the Territory had taken steps to make it clear that they were opposed to such unification. The Dagombas, Nanumbas and Mamprusis were opposed to Togoland unification because it would disunite them, cut them away from their blood relations in the Gold Coast and arbi-

---

543 TCOR, "14th Session" (1954), p. 226.
544 TCOR, "14th Session" (1954), p. 227.
545 Amenumey, *The Ewe Unification Movement*, pp. 240–41.
546 GAOR, "9th Session: 4th Committee" (1954), p. 7.
547 GAOR, "9th Session: 4th Committee" (1954), p. 9.
548 Or 17 if one considers that Komla Gbedemah, who was the Co-Founder of the CPP and then Minister of Finance of the Gold Coast Government, was part of the official UK delegation and Nicholas Grunitzky, head of the PTP, was part of the French delegation.

trarily join them to people with whom they had no cultural, social or linguistic relations."[549]

Photo 18: 15 Togoland Petitioners before the 4th Committee (1 December 1954)[550]

Source: UN Photo

Allassani raised attention to the fact, that both integration and unification would result in the division of ethnic groups. He deplored that…

> "the Fourth Committee and the Trusteeship Council had been misled by members of the Togoland Congress Party who had tried to give the impression that they represented the views and wishes of the majority, whereas the evidence showed that only a small fraction of the people of one out of several principal states in the Territory advocated a separate Togoland nation."[551]

---

549   GAOR, "9th Session: 4th Committee" (1954), p. 339.
550   Desk at right (right row, bottom to top): Sylvanus Olympio (AEC), Jacob Mensah (Buem-Krachi District Council), Solomon Togbe Fleku (CPP) and S.W. Kuma (CPP); (left row, bottom to top): J.H. Allassani and Mahama Bukhari (Dagomba District Council); Liana Asigri (Mamprusi District Council); Chief Nana Akompi Firam III (Natural Rulers of the Buem-Krachi District). Desk at left (right row, bottom to top): Senyo Gatror Antor (Togoland Congress); Alasan Chamba and Alex K. Odame (Northern Region and Buem-Krachi Branch of the Togoland Congress respectively); (left row, bottom to top): Anani Ignacio Santos (Juvento), S. Aguereburu (MPT); Frederic Brenner (PTP), Mama Fousseni (UCPN).
551   GAOR, "9th Session: 4th Committee" (1954), p. 339.

Jacob Mensah (Buem Krachi District Council), and Nana Akompi Firam III (Natural Rulers of the Buem-Krachi District), declared that the people of Buem Krachi favoured continued association with the Gold Coast.[552] S. E. Kuma and Solomon Fleku (CPP) opposed the idea of uniting both Togolands and later federating a united Togoland with the Gold Coast. The CPP was against holding a simultaneous plebiscite. Furthermore, unification of the Togolands would break up the Ewe unity achieved so far through the establishment of the TVT region.[553] Fleku said the CPP would "would continue their struggle to liberate Togoland under French administration."[554]

Frederic Brenner (PTP) charged that the CUT was an "anachronistic tribal movement."[555] Brenner said the complexity of the situation could not be put in a simple plebiscite question that is answerable with "yes" and "no."[556] Together with Mama Fousseni (UCPN), he held that there should be no unification outside the French Union.[557] Brenner, too, spoke against a simultaneous plebiscite arguing that the British proposal should not delay advance in French Togoland where a plebiscite would merely give rise to disturbances. The people should be allowed to enjoy new reforms in peace.

Unificationists

S. Aquereburu (MPT) feared the Administering Authorities would crush any movement for unification by fanning discord among the people and the various ethnic groups. He also raised attention to the problem of bribing chiefs. Since the Gold Coast was already self-governing, it was difficult to see why French Togoland did not have comparable rights after thirty-four years of administration by France. The UN should organise a plebiscite whereas a UN Mission should first visit the territory and explain to the chiefs and peoples that they could vote according to their conscience without fear of reprisals either from political parties or the Administering Authorities.[558]

Antor alleged that there was no adequate safeguard for Togoland as a trusteeship territory in the new Gold Coast constitution. This was because although the final word on Togoland affairs rested with the Governor, he acted in accordance with the Cabinet advice: yet there was no Togolander in the Cabinet. He demanded that British Togoland be given a properly constituted body which could represent its views, even if it were in favour of association with the Gold Coast. If such an organ had been created, it could have advocated unification with French Togoland. It was clear that the voice of Togoland would not be heard in whatever government was established in the Gold Coast and that the people would be powerless to demand unification with French Togoland. He too called for a special Commission to visit Togoland.

Alasan Chamba (Togoland Congress) claimed that the chiefs and peoples of the Nanumba, Nawuri, Nanjoro, Konkomba and B'moba tribes in Northern Togoland had

---

552 GAOR, "9th Session: 4th Committee" (1954), pp. 343–44.
553 GAOR, "9th Session: 4th Committee" (1954), pp. 344–46.
554 GAOR, "9th Session: 4th Committee" (1954), p. 390.
555 GAOR, "9th Session: 4th Committee" (1954), p. 364.
556 GAOR, "9th Session: 4th Committee" (1954), p. 365.
557 GAOR, "9th Session: 4th Committee" (1954), pp. 365–66.
558 GAOR, "9th Session: 4th Committee" (1954), pp. 361–62.

unanimously asked him to speak on their behalf, accused government officials in the territory of conducting propaganda on behalf of those who wanted integration, and he argued that the only solution possible was a plebiscite under UN supervision.

Odame pointed out that the programme of the "Most Secret" document was being implemented, as was indicated by the large contingent of CPP petitioners before the Committee.[559] The very presence of Komla Gbedemah as a high official of the new Gold Coast Government in the British delegation (and an Ewe from the Gold Coast, after all) proved that integration was not a spontaneous movement among the Togoland people. He criticized this development by stating that "the Administering Authorities were using Africans against Africans in order to cover a flagrant violation of the Charter and the Trusteeship Agreements."[560] In other words, the Administrative Authorities brought in the African opposition to quell the efforts of those seeking unification by employing tactics that involved *illocutionary disablement* to silence their securitising moves.

Similarly, Sylvanus Olympio noted that the Administering Authorities succeeded in redefining the subject matter as the "The Togoland unification problem" and not, as previously, "The Ewe and Togoland unification problem."[561] Olympio deplored that the political situation in French Togoland had deteriorated. After the last session of the Fourth Committee, in October 1953 "four women members of the *Comité de l'Unité togolaise* from Kpélé had been arrested and subjected to assault and battery while returning from a political meeting at Lomé. Their fathers and husbands had also been arrested, subjected to physical violence and prosecuted for asking members of their party to contribute to the travelling expenses of the women's delegation."[562]

Santos (Juvento) added…

"With regard to political liberties, […] a decision of the Court of First Instance at Lomé, dated 6 May 1953, by which three persons had been sentenced to ten months' imprisonment and a fine of 15,000 francs each for having read to a public meeting a resolution, stating various grievances, addressed to the Chief Sub-Divisional Officer at Tsevie. After serving his sentence, one of the three, who was the Secretary-General of Juvento, had been informed that he was being exiled from the Territory, and was immediately conducted to the frontier. The Court of Appeal at Abidjan had subsequently reversed the verdict, but in the meantime the three Juvento members had undergone ten months of imprisonment, and the Secretary-General's sentence of expulsion had not been withdrawn."[563]

Therefore, Santos announced, that Juvento "no longer doubted the French colonial administration's lack of good will and its systematic opposition to the work of the United Nations."[564] He considered that integration of British Togoland into the Gold Coast would leave France a free hand in French Togoland and bring the idea of unification to naught.

---

559   GAOR, "9th Session: 4th Committee" (1954), p. 358.
560   GAOR, "9th Session: 4th Committee" (1954), p. 359.
561   GAOR, "9th Session: 4th Committee" (1954), p. 359.
562   GAOR, "9th Session: 4th Committee" (1954), p. 359.
563   GAOR, "9th Session: 4th Committee" (1954), p. 363.
564   GAOR, "9th Session: 4th Committee" (1954), p. 363.

Juvento suggested that the General Assembly should appoint a special Visiting Mission to establish a *Joint Council for Togoland Affairs* empowered to study the arrangements for holding a plebiscite in both Togolands. Furthermore, Santos requested the General Assembly to set up direct United Nations trusteeship.[565]

Generally, the unificationists insisted that the plebiscite, now being considered as a popular consultation on the possible "integration" of British Togoland into the Gold Coast, should be held not only in British Togoland but simultaneously in French Togoland.[566] Yet, the unificationists argued that a single referendum in British Togoland would effectively exclude the potential votes for reunification in French Togoland, specifically of the Ewe.[567]

Figure 7: Number of Petitioners before the 4th Committee (1951–1957)

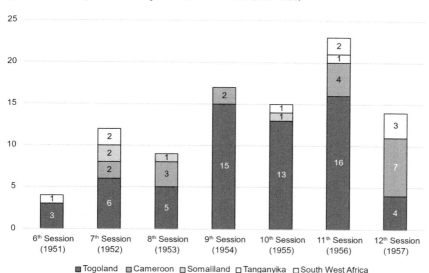

Source: Own creation. Counts based on Verbatim Records of the 4th Committee.[568]

While the unificationists represented a solid front in oral hearings until the Assembly's 8th Session (1953), at the 9th Session (1954), 15 petitioners appeared before the Fourth

---

565 GAOR, "9th Session: 4th Committee" (1954), p. 364.
566 GAOR, "9th Session: 4th Committee" (1954), p. 365.
567 For a detailed account note Heise, "United Nations Colonial Complicity in Decolonization Referenda."
568 Counting does not include pro-Administering Authority petitioners, who came along as official members of the Administering Authorities diplomatic delegation.

Committee,[569] of whom only 5 defended the cause of unification.[570] A similar picture emerged during the 10th Session (1955) and 11th Session (1956).

The petitioners that were brought in by the colonial powers slowly began to change the balance of opinion among anti-colonial delegates in the Fourth Committee.

General Discussion

During the general discussion that followed many delegations welcomed the imminent independence of the Gold Coast and British Togoland's association with it.

The Indian delegation, supporting integration and the British suggestions, took the initiative by submitting a draft resolution recommending that steps be taken to ascertain the wish of the inhabitants of British Togoland and that the Trusteeship Council study the problem and consider what arrangements should be made. For the Indian delegate, Krishna Menon, independence together with the Gold Coast meant "independence, which did not mean isolation. [...] Integration would mean fusion, with independence."[571] Furthermore he argued that: "It was for the British Togolanders to decide and not wait for French Togolanders to be ready to take a comparable decision. Once British Togoland will be independent, France would have great difficulty in refusing to grant the same status to French Togoland."[572]

The following discussion revolved around the Indian resolution. Iraqi and US-American delegations especially supported it. Other delegations were torn between the principle that a trusteeship territory should become fully independent before deciding on its future political relations with other countries and the practical fact that integration of British Togoland into the Gold Coast would result in its imminent independence.

Especially the delegations of Haiti, the Philippines, Greece, Ecuador, the USSR, Poland, and China opposed the Indian proposal. The Haitian representative, Max Dorsinville, cautioned that once the integration of British Togoland into the Gold Coast became an accomplished fact, France would probably "seek to induce the other part of Togoland to join the French Union, by offering it self-government. [...] the elimination of Togoland under British administration would herald the end of Togoland as a whole and also that of the International Trusteeship System, the purposes of which would have been betrayed."[573] He securitised that "the policy being pursued by the United Kingdom Government was a danger to the International Trusteeship System."[574] The Philippine delegate, Gonzalez, argued that a plebiscite would be premature because of the "backward" situation in the Northern Section of the trusteeship territory.[575] For the Ecuadorian delegate the British memorandum "showed clearly that the administrative

---

569 Or 17 if one considers that Komla Gbedemah, who was the Co-Founder of the CPP and then Minister of Finance of the Gold Coast Government, was part of the official UK delegation and Nicholas Grunitzky, head of the PTP, was part of the French delegation.
570 These were Olympio, Antor, Santos, Odame, and Chamba.
571 GAOR, "9th Session: 4th Committee" (1954), p. 412.
572 GAOR, "9th Session: 4th Committee" (1954), p. 412.
573 GAOR, "9th Session: 4th Committee" (1954), p. 418.
574 GAOR, "9th Session: 4th Committee" (1954), p. 467.
575 GAOR, "9th Session: 4th Committee" (1954), p. 435.

union established by the United Kingdom for Togoland had developed into a means of political annexation."[576]

While several amendments to the Indian draft resolution were submitted and considered, the French representative was campaigning for separating the issue of British Togoland's future from that of French Togoland. He claimed that "for substantial physical reasons it was impossible at that time to organize a plebiscite in French Togoland. An agreement must first be reached on a number of points including the principal and subsidiary questions to be raised."[577]

Thullen holds that although discussion of the Indian draft resolution was marked by bitterness and animosity, there was never serious question of it being defeated. The amended draft resolution, product of laborious behind-the-scenes negotiations, was adopted both in the Fourth Committee,[578] and in plenary.[579] In the end, it all came down in favour of ascertaining the wishes of the people in British Togoland without prejudging the outcome by insistence on either unification or integration. Finally, a majority of the Fourth Committee agreed to a proposal that the British administration should find out the 'true' wishes of the people in Togoland. Significantly, it also accepted the thesis that the future of British Togoland should be dealt with separately from that of French Togoland, although this acceptance was preceded by a bitter controversy.

The course of the debate revealed that the unificationists did not exert sufficient effort to securitise their demand for unification. While the unificationists argued that the British memorandum amounted to a form of 'annexation in disguise,' their mentions of political liberty violations primarily focused on the conditions in French Togoland and were thus not directly related to the British proposal. Moreover, a significant symbolic setback for the unification movement occurred when the Indian delegation, and notably the Iraqi delegate Awni Khalidy – previously an early supporter of the unification movement – turned their backs on the unification parties aligned with Olympio and Antor.

1st Togo Statute

In view of the constitutional development in the Gold Coast and in British Togoland, on 16 March 1955, the French proclaimed a new statute for Togoland. This first Togo statute is considered the precursor of the reforms that would take shape a year later in the *loi-cadre* (framework law) for the whole of French Africa.

The statute expanded the authority of the *Assemblé Territoriale du Togo* (ATT) and gave French Togoland a governing body (*Conseil de Gouvernement*). But this was at most the embryo of an executive: The French Governor not only chaired the *Conseil de Gouvernement* but also appointed four of its members. The ATT elected the five other members. These quasi-ministers had only the right to 'inform and investigate,' that is, they had no say. The 1955 statute also meant that the ATT did not yet become a true legislature, but (only) participated in the exercise of legislative and regulatory power, the focus of which, as before, lay with the colonial administration. When elections for the newly created ATT

---

576 GAOR, "9th Session: 4th Committee" (1954), p. 437.
577 GAOR, "9th Session: 4th Committee" (1954), p. 453.
578 GAOR, "9th Session: 4th Committee" (1954), pp. 465–66.
579 GAOR, "9th Session: Plenary" (1954), p. 501, Resolution 860 (IX).

were held in July 1955, Olympio was not eligible since his conviction on 3 March 1954. Not that it would have mattered because the elections were boycotted by the CUT. Apart from the fact that suffrage was still restricted, the *Conseil de Gouvernement* did neither have a truly representative character nor powers that would have made it a real government. As such, the pro-French parties, UCPN and PTP, won all of the 30 seats.

On 4 July 1955, the new ATT adopted a motion of the PTP, which affirmed to continue the development of the territory in close cooperation with France and to end the trusteeship over the territory. The French government therefore officially declared that it felt obliged to take the request into account and to respond to it by directly consulting the wishes of the population.[580]

6.6.2 Action Plan & Internal Security Updates (1955)

Following the Mau-Mau rebellion, Derek Franklin, sent from Kenya by the Colonial Office to assess the Special Branch of the Gold Coast, observed a malfunctioning exchange of security and intelligence reports between Regional Commissioners and Special Branch officers. This issue was particularly pronounced in Togoland:

> "Until very lately he [the officer in charge of Special Branch] has not had an officer of his own in T.V.T. Consequently, he has not had much information to go on from that region. The officer just appointed is young and not very experienced in that type of work. It would therefore be of great help if a copy of the [Chief Regional Officer]'s report went to the Special Branch officer."[581]

But not even a month later, a delicate document was to surface in TVT. In January 1955, a British Togoland border officer received a "Final Liberation Plan" and was told "that arms and ammunition dumps have secretly been built," one on the French and another on the British side.[582] Allegedly rifles and other weapons were being manufactured at the two places by French-trained Africans. Furthermore, the conspirators have allegedly met with members of the Ashanti and National Liberation Movement (NLM), which was formed in 1954 by disaffected Ashanti members of the CPP, that opposed the process of centralisation whilst supporting a continuing role for traditional leaders. The so-called 'Action Plan' stated that the "1954 Togoland Unification delegation to the United Nations is the last one. It must be realised that the UNO is a marionette organisation and willing to placate the British and French administering authorities in Togoland."[583] The plan considered the kidnapping of members of the Gold Coast Legislative Assembly, as well as blowing up bridges and cutting telephone wires. The idea was to create tension in Togoland to force the UN to send a mission tasked with transferring power.

---

580 See *The future of£ Togoland under French administration* (T/1274/Rev.1), p. 12.
581 TNA (London), FCO 141/5000, *Gold Coast: security and political intelligence; policy*, Secret and Personal Letter, Franklin to Arden-Clarke, 12 December 1954.
582 MAE (La Courneuve), 77QO-5, *Politique intérieure*, Confidential Letter, Liberation Movement, 28 January 1955.
583 MAE (La Courneuve), 77QO-5, *Politique intérieure*, Action Plan 1955.

Again, the British saw Juvento's Marxist-Leninist splinter group around Mensah Aihtson and Anku Morny behind the plans for armed insurrection.[584] Until then, the French had as well been convinced of the non-violent attitude of the unificationists, especially the AEC, but the French Consul General in Accra, Charles Renner, was now convinced that the divergence in the unification movement was manifesting itself between those around Olympio, who wanted to take the diplomatic route, and those frustrated unificationists around Anku Morny or Alex Odame, who increasingly stressed that the independence and reunification of Togoland could only be achieved by 'direct action' and, if necessary, by violence.[585]

The authenticity of the *Action Plan* was officially confirmed in 1958, when Major Benjamin Awhaitey was court-martialled on suspicion of receiving arms from Mathias K. Apaloo and R. R. Amponsah (both Togoland Congress) to stage a coup. The majority report of the Commission of Inquiry indicated that Antor had plotted with Joe Appiah and Victor Owusu (both former members of the NLM) to install Kofi Busia, the leader of the oppositional *Ghana Congress Party*, as Nkrumah's successor.[586] Faced with the likelihood that British Togoland would become part of an independent Ghana with a unitary constitution, before the arrival of the 3rd UN Visiting Mission, Antor sought to establish ties with opposition parties in the Gold Coast that opposed the CPP's plans for a unitary constitution, especially the NLM. In July 1955, Antor attended a conference in Ashanti's capital, Kumasi, held by 'movements and parties other than the CPP.' There he had signed a document entitled 'Proposals for an Independent Gold Coast and Togoland,' which called for a federal constitution instead of a unitary constitution.[587]

The fact that the *Action Plan* did not come to the attention of the British neither by the Special Branch officer nor the Chief Regional Officer of TVT gave rise to yet another complaint on the executive level, that the information to the CenSeC and LIC from TVT was disappointing and lacking.[588] Twice complaints were raised that the Chief Regional Commissioner in the TVT had not sent a single intelligence report from the time the order was first issued in May 1953 until January 1956.[589]

The *Action Plan* was likely taken as an opportunity, by the successor of SLO Kirby Green, Major Hodson, to continue the former's intensification of Anglo-French security cooperation by organizing yet another Anglo-French security conference in Accra for

---

584 MAE (La Courneuve), 77QO-5, *Politique intérieure*, Letter No. 29/TC, Renner to Ministre des Affairs Etrangeres, 15 February 1955.

585 MAE (La Courneuve), 77QO-5, *Politique intérieure*, Letter No. 62/SC, Renner to Ministre des Affaires Etrangeres, 3 March 1955.

586 Government of Ghana, "Report: Enquiry into matters disclosed at the trial of Captain Benjamin Awhaitey held on the 20th and 21st January 1959, before a court-martial convened at Giffard Camp, Accra, and the surrounding circumstances," Government White Paper 10 (Accra, 1959).

587 Jean Marie Allman, *The quills of the porcupine: Asante nationalism in an emergent Ghana* (Madison: University of Wisconsin Press, 1993), pp. 113–14.

588 TNA (London), FCO 141/5000, *Gold Coast: security and political intelligence; policy*, Secret Letter No. Pol.F.302.Vol.II., Headquarters Gold Coast Police to Russel, 8 March 1955.

589 TNA (London), FCO 141/5000, *Gold Coast: security and political intelligence; policy*, Monthly Intelligence Reports from Regions. List of Reports received from Regions until 1.7.1955; TNA (London), FCO 141/5000, *Gold Coast: security and political intelligence; policy*, Note File No. 539 Vol II, G.S., p. 2.

March 1955.⁵⁹⁰ Even if the French had doubts about the authenticity of the documents (there was speculation that the unificationists disseminated them deliberately to alarm the Administering Authorities), the alarm must have sounded: France was already deeply involved in the unrest in Algeria, and in May 1955 the unrest in the other trusteeship territory, Cameroon, seemed to be a sign of how things were slipping out of the hands of the French trusteeship power.

Security Intelligence Advisor

Coinciding with the Visiting Mission, the *Security Intelligence Advisor*, Alex MacDonald, arrived after several stops in British colonial possessions around the world in September 1955 for his audit tour of the Gold Coast. Aware that he would be advising a territory on security and intelligence matters that would be independent in the foreseeable future, by October, MacDonald reported that there was a great "need to provide an adequate number of Special Branch officers, particularly African officers capable of maintaining an efficient intelligence organisation in a future self-governing territory."⁵⁹¹ The territory's Special Branch was handicapped by the fact that it was losing experienced personnel either by retirement or by transfer just at a time when their services were most required.⁵⁹² Moreover the Special Branch did not comprise a single senior African officer.⁵⁹³ The entire makeup of the Special Branch for 1955–56 consisted of merely 70 officers, only two of whom were African officers, and eight of whom were stationed in TVT. Regarding the latter, MacDonald noted that:

> "Meanwhile the Colony may in the near future be faced with a general election and a plebiscite in Togoland. There is growing dissention between the Convention Peoples Party and the National Liberation Movement and there can be little doubt that during the present transition period accurate intelligence will be of the first importance."⁵⁹⁴

MacDonald's report commented on the significant aspect of what safeguards were to be provided to ensure that a future Gold Coast Government would not use the Special Branch as a political weapon. MacDonald was not optimistic:

> "There can, of course, be no effective safeguard. As in other Colonies advancing towards full independence we can only try to educate Ministers in the tradition of an independent *non-political* Special Branch and to maintain the link with the Security

---

590 TNA (London), FCO 141/4990, *Gold Coast: Security Liaison Officer, West Africa*, Secret Letter Pol.F.17/1, SLO Gold Coast, 4 February 1955.
591 TNA (London), FCO 141/5000, *Gold Coast: security and political intelligence; policy*, Intelligence Organisation in the Gold Coast.
592 TNA (London), FCO 141/5000, *Gold Coast: security and political intelligence; policy*, Intelligence Organisation in the Gold Coast.
593 TNA (London), FCO 141/4992, *Gold Coast: Special Branch; security and training*, Gold Coast Dispatch No. 2, Governor, 19 January 1956.
594 TNA (London), FCO 141/5000, *Gold Coast: security and political intelligence; policy*, Intelligence Organisation in the Gold Coast, p. 1.

Service which by assisting with training and advice can do much to keep the territory within the Commonwealth intelligence."[595]

Lastly, MacDonald noted like all his predecessors the failure of the Regional Commissioners to provide intelligence reports and, on the other hand, pointed out that before full self-government was achieved there was the need for Special Branch records to be "weeded."[596] Promptly the Ministry of Interior reprimanded the lapsus of submitting intelligence reports by Regional Commissioners who in turn "felt 'nothing was done about' such reports."[597] On the other hand, it was proposed to set up a committee to devise for the disposal of delicate records.[598] Although not proposed by MacDonald, as a further measure, both the CenSeC and the LIC were immediately placed under the newly formed Defense Committee in November 1955 to assist the Governor in carrying out his responsibilities for the security of the Gold Coast.[599]

6.6.3 The 3rd Visiting Mission (1955)

The 3rd Visiting Mission arrived in Accra in mid-August 1955 and spent six weeks in the two Togolands until the end of September. A novelty, however, was that for the first time a member of the UN Secretariat, namely the Undersecretary for Trusteeship and Information from the Non-Self-Governing Territories, Benjamin Cohen, went along. The membership of the Visiting Mission comprised a representative of the US, Australia, Syria, and India, that is, already of most state representatives whose governments saw favourably towards the integration of British Togoland into the Gold Coast. The Visiting Mission adopted its special report and transmitted it to the Secretary General on 18 October 1955.

The Visiting Mission had received over 200,000 communications,[600] out of which 100,000 spoke out in favour of unification and immediate independence. However, due to the rules of procedure, the Visiting Mission considered less than 100 of these communications as petitions and the remainder simply for its own information.[601]

Yet, overall, the Visiting Mission was presented with two main points of view in British Togoland. On the one hand, the CPP and its affiliated groups, especially the tra-

---

595 TNA (London), FCO 141/5000, *Gold Coast: security and political intelligence; policy*, Intelligence Organisation in the Gold Coast, p. 2.
596 TNA (London), FCO 141/5000, *Gold Coast: security and political intelligence; policy*, Intelligence Organisation in the Gold Coast, p. 3.
597 TNA (London), FCO 141/5000, *Gold Coast: security and political intelligence; policy*, Intelligence Reports [Ref. 908/17/2], from Secretary CenSec to Regional Officers, 23 May 1957.
598 TNA (London), FCO 141/4992, *Gold Coast: Special Branch; security and training*, Secret Letter (without title), PMC, 7 January 1956.
599 TNA (London), FCO 141/5000, *Gold Coast: security and political intelligence; policy*, Organisation of Intelligence, 27 June 1956.
600 These communications contained for the most part slogans and expressions of views favouring the political alternatives concerning Togoland unification and the future of the Trust Territory of Togoland under British administration.
601 United Nations, "Art. 87," in United Nations (UN) *Repertory of Practice of United Nations Organs*, Vol. Vol. II. Also see T/1/Rev.3, Rule 84, para. 2.

ditional chiefs in the northern part, called for the integration of British Togoland once the Gold Coast would become independent. On the other hand, the Togoland Congress, the AEC, and their affiliated groups, especially the traditional chiefs in the southern part, demanded that British Togoland be kept separate from the Gold Coast for the time being. In this way, the people of British Togoland could be given the choice of merging with the latter or uniting with an independent French Togoland so that Togoland in its entirety could eventually be merged with the Gold Coast.

As foreseen and whished by the British administration, the mission endorsed a plebiscite as "the most democratic, direct and specific method of ascertaining the true wishes of the people," and recommended specifically that the following questions be put at the plebiscite:

> "(a) Do you want the integration of Togoland under British administration with an independent Gold Coast?
> (b) Do you want the separation of Togoland under British administration from the Gold Coast and its continuance under trusteeship pending the ultimate determination of its political future?"

The mission proposed that four separate voting districts should be considered where the "future of each of these four units should be determined by the majority vote in each case."[602] In the north and south, preferences seemed to be clearly distributed: In the north, most of the population was clearly in favour of integration with the Gold Coast. In the southernmost districts of Kpando and Ho, with a large Ewe population, the mission had found a majority in favour of separation. Located between these two strongholds, the Buem-Krachi district was home to people of diverse ethnic composition and linguistic characteristics. Within this district, the mission found that public opinion in the northern parts was strongly in favour of integration with the Gold Coast, while in the southern parts opinion was divided between integration and reunification. The Visiting Mission therefore recommended that Buem-Krachi should be divided into two separate areas to meet the wishes of the population as much as possible. In sum, the mission recommended that the results of the plebiscite be determined separately by the respective majority decision in the following four areas (see Map 8):[603]

1) Northern section of British Togoland
2) Buem-Krachi (North)
3) Buem-Krachi (South)
4) Kpando and Ho districts (together as one unit)

In other words, the Visiting Mission appears to have put forth the following rationale: They suggested that North Togoland as a whole should constitute Plebiscite Unit 1,

---

602 TCOR, "5th Special Session: Special Report on the Togoland Unification problem and the future of the Trust Territory of Togoland under British Administration" Supplement No. 2 (T/1218) (1955), pp. 15–16.

603 TCOR, "5th Special Session: Special Report on the Togoland Unification problem and the future of the Trust Territory of Togoland under British Administration" (1955), p. 16.

given the assured support for integration in this region. However, the scenario in South Togoland was different. The Visiting Mission subdivided the region into three Plebiscite Units. It was anticipated that Plebiscite Unit 2, encompassing Buem-Krachi (North), would overwhelmingly favor integration, while Plebiscite Unit 4, covering the Kpando and Ho districts, was expected to lean strongly towards separation. Only in Plebiscite Unit 3, comprising Buem-Krachi (South), did the vote appear to be evenly balanced.

Map 8: Voting Districts as Recommended by Visiting Mission (1955)

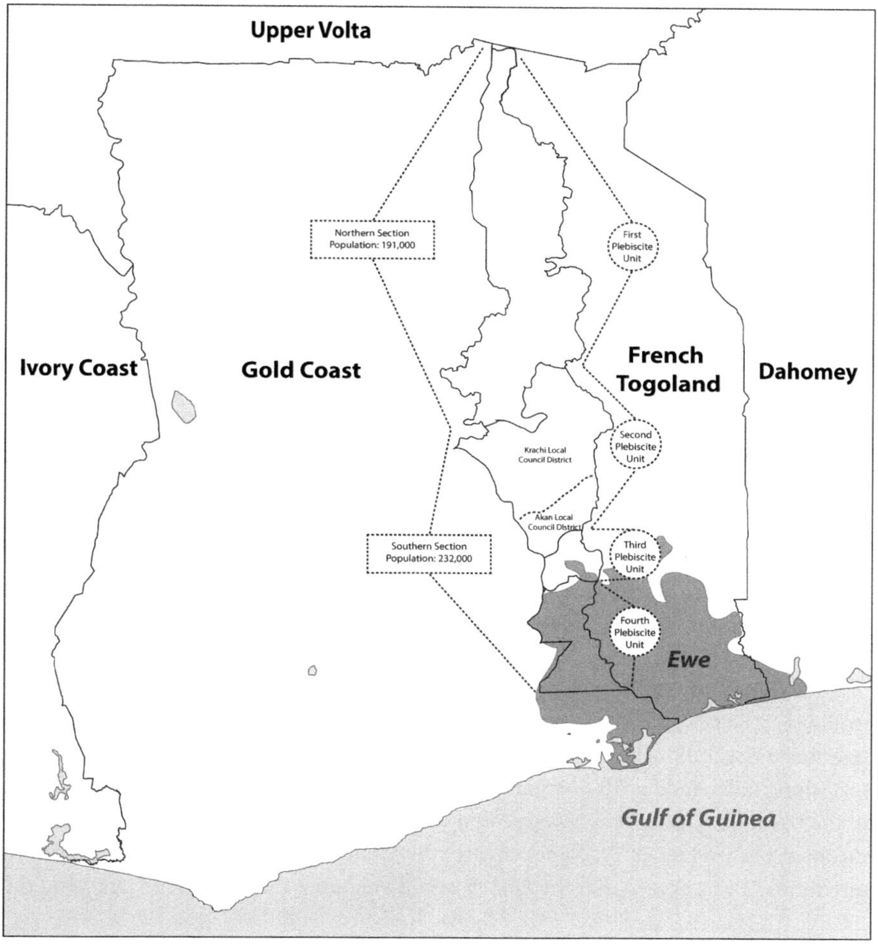

Source: Own creation. Based on TCOR 1955, 5th Special Session: Special Report on the Togoland Unification problem and the future of the Trust Territory of Togoland under British Administration, p. 60.

It is of noteworthy importance that, due to the recent motion of the newly constituted ATT, the French authorities informed the Visiting Mission that they also intended to hold a consultation in a few years to clarify the termination of trusteeship and Togoland's potential incorporation into the French Union.[604]

6.6.4 Anglo-French Arrangements for the Togoland Referenda (1955)

On 14 November 1955, one week before the Trusteeship Council would meet for its 5th Special Session to consider the report of the Visiting Mission, the British Secretary of State for the Colonies, Alan Lennox-Boyd and the French Overseas Minister, Henri Teitgen convened a meeting on the Visiting Mission's proposals and discussed how the proposed plebiscite in British Togoland could be favourable for both powers. Teitgen maintained that the procedure in British Togoland should be treated as an exception and not a "dangerous" and "regrettable"[605] precedent for all remaining trusteeship territories and colonial possessions. Teitgen's concern that Togoland would set a dangerous precedent is understandable in light of international developments: from 18 to 24 April 1955, the Bandung Conference was held and gave new momentum to the tide of anti-colonialism. In the same year, it became clear that what had begun in Algeria in November 1954 had become a national revolutionary war. With the approaching independence of Morocco on 2 March 1956 and Tunisia on 20 March 1956, the definitive detachment of the Maghreb from the French grip seemed destined. Given these developments, what was to become of French *Afrique Noire*?

Thus, Teitgen stressed "the powers of the UNO […] do not give it any right to organize a plebiscite in a territory under trusteeship, regardless whosoever it is, but just to supervise it."[606] Furthermore, Teitgen was against the establishment of the four voting districts that the Visiting Mission had recommended because they would "prejudge the results of the vote" and lead to the "balkanization of Africa."[607] Eventually Lennox-Boyd and Teitgen agreed to organize two separate referenda in British and French Togoland, whereas the latter would decide upon French Togoland's permanent inclusion into the French Union.

The French were under time pressure: announcing the French referendum too early would risk the UN linking the future of British and French Togoland; announcing it too late would risk linking it with the Gold Coast's nearing independence, which would lead to a young independent African state, whose anticolonial voice would have great weight in the UN. In any case, Teitgen expressed concerns about Nkrumah's annexationist demeanour toward French Togoland. Thus, to thwart demands for equal treatment of both territories, it was agreed that the French would announce their plebiscite only after the

---

604 TCOR, "5th Special Session: Special Report on the Togoland Unification problem and the future of the Trust Territory of Togoland under British Administration" (1955), p. 17.
605 ANOM (Aix-en-Provence), 1AFFPOL/3340/1, *Entretiens franco-britaniques sur le Togo-Cameroun*, Note (without number), without date, p. 2
606 ANOM (Aix-en-Provence), 1AFFPOL/2182/2, *Royaume-Uni*, Procès-Verbal (without number), 14 November 1955, p. 1
607 ANOM (Aix-en-Provence), 1AFFPOL/2182/2, *Royaume-Uni*, Procès-Verbal (without number), 14 November 1955, p. 1

British referendum was over. Teitgen solicited the assurance from his British counterpart "that the questions asked during the plebiscite in British Togoland did not refer, even indirectly, to the fate of French Togoland."[608] A possible reference to Togoland reunification or independence outside the Commonwealth or the French Union had to be rejected at all costs.

As settled by Teitgen and Lennox-Boyd, at the Trusteeship Council's 5th Special Session (1955) and the General Assembly's 10th Session (1955), the British representative agreed with the main recommendation of the Visiting Mission to hold a plebiscite under the auspices of the UN but rejected the recommendation regarding the four voting districts because it would prejudice the results of the plebiscite itself:

"the will of the majority should determine the overall outcome, and the minority should loyally abide by the result, whatever it may be. [...] If there was to be a process of fragmentation whenever there was a test of public opinion under the United Nations similar to that now proposed for Togoland under British administration, the prospect was indeed disturbing."[609]

General Assembly's 10th Session (1955)

As was by now well established, the Fourth Committee's 10th Session (1955) began with yet another debate whether to grant request for oral hearings by petitioners of trusteeship territories. Yet, this time it was the Israeli delegation that proposed to establish a five-member sub-committee to study merely the advisability of establishing procedures for the acceptance and examination of petitions by the Committee.[610] Besides Denmark, it was of course the Administering Authorities that lent approval to the proposal. Only the Belgian delegate, Pierre Ryckmans, went further in his opinion about oral representations before the Fourth Committee. He would vote even against the Israeli proposal because "he was convinced that an objective and impartial study could lead to only one conclusion: that it served no useful purpose for the Fourth Committee to hear oral petitions."[611]

Most of the anti-colonial state representatives were apprehensive as well. The fear was stated that any recommended rules of procedure would effectively transfer any petitioner back to the Trusteeship Council. The most notorious comment came from the Indonesian representative saying, "any procedures advocated by the proposed sub-committee would be restrictive in effect and deprive the petitioners of their last court of appeal – the General Assembly."[612] After a US amendment had been accepted by Israel, the draft resolution, as amended, was rejected by 26 votes to 15, with 9 abstentions.[613]

---

608 Ibd. Original : « il serait d'autre part préférable que les questions posées lors du plébiscite au Togo britannique ne se réfèrent pas, même indirectement, au sort du Togo français."
609 TCOR, "5th Special Session" (1955), pp. 3–4.
610 A/C.4/L.390 "Acceptance and examination of petitions concerning Trust Territories—Israel: draft resolution", 14 October 1955.
611 GAOR, "10th Session: 4th Committee" (1955), p. 125.
612 GAOR, "10th Session: 4th Committee" (1955), p. 121.
613 GAOR, "10th Session: 4th Committee" (1955), p. 125.

When discussion of the 1955 Visiting Mission's report began, seven political organizations from Togoland made oral statements. During the discussion of the Fourth Committee, Antor stressed the importance of the Volta River project,[614] which would not be conducted if British Togoland remained a trusteeship territory or was separated from the Gold Coast.[615] He criticized the Mission's recommendation to hold a referendum in British Togoland, but not in French Togoland. He also found the wording of the referendum question proposed by the Visiting Mission unacceptable. He suggested that the choice should be independence first and integration second.[616]

Photo 19: Togoland Unificationists before 4th Committee (1 December 1955)[617]

Source: UN Photo.

Odame added that given the serious political crisis in the Gold Coast between the CPP government and the NLM it was "unlikely that the best interests of world peace and of the inhabitants of Togoland under British administration would be served by authorizing the integration of Togoland into the Gold Coast in the existing circumstances."[618]

Olympio generally agreed with the Visiting Mission's recommendation to hold a plebiscite under UN supervision. However, given that he himself first called for a plebiscite on Ewe unification in late 1947, it came as no surprise when he protested that

---

614   Completed in 1965, the project involved constructing the Akosombo Dam in Ghana. This hydroelectric initiative aimed to generate power for domestic and industrial use, leading to the formation of Lake Volta, one of the world's largest artificial reservoirs. The dam remains a key element in Ghana's energy infrastructure.
615   GAOR, "10th Session: 4th Committee" (1955), p. 336.
616   GAOR, "10th Session: 4th Committee" (1955), p. 338.
617   At left are (left to right): Alex Odame, A Chamba, and Senyo Gatror Antor (Togoland Congress). Across the desk from them are Mr. Anani Santos (left), representing Juvento, and Sylvanus Olympio (AEC).
618   GAOR, "10th Session: 4th Committee" (1955), p. 340.

he "knew no reason why the plebiscite could not be held in 1957 in both Togolands."[619] He held: "If there was any difference between the two plebiscites proposed by the Mission, it was only a difference in timing."[620] He also regretted that in recent discussions in the Trusteeship Council there seemed to be a tendency to apply the report of the Visiting Mission only to the question of the future of British Togoland. He warned that once British Togoland became part of the Gold Coast, the two Togolands could never be united. The reunification of Togoland already seemed to be off the table. He found it indicative that "an effective argument in favour of the reforms for Togoland had been that they should be regarded as a means of hastening the Trust Territory's removal from what Mr. Ajavon, speaking in the French Parliament, had called the 'intolerable meddling of the United Nations' and its integration into the French Republic."[621]

The CPP representatives, Mensah, Asare, and Fleku, opposed the continuation of trusteeship over any part of British Togoland after the attainment of Gold Coast independence and any delay in holding the 1956 plebiscite. Mama Fousseni (UCPN) and Robert Ajavon (PTP) reiterated their arguments that the complete and immediate independence of French Togoland was a fantasy since the territory still needed French help for economic and social advancement.[622]

General Debate

During the general discussion, India supported the views put forward by the British representative. The Indian representative, Krishna Menon, could not agree with the attempt to use the Ewe in French Togoland to decide the fate of the Ewe in British Togoland and the Gold Coast. The draft resolution that his delegation introduced was divided into two sections: "The future of Togoland under British administration" and "The future of Togoland under French administration."[623] In this way, the draft resolution avoided to mention the unification of Togoland and the future of each territory was dealt with separately. The first part of the draft approved the Visiting Mission's recommendations for a plebiscite in British Togoland under United Nations supervision and recommended its immediate implementation. The second part endorsed the Visiting Mission's conclusions on the need for a similar plebiscite in French Togoland and asked the French to submit programs for political reform and their recommendations for holding a plebiscite.

Liberia tabled a number of amendments, the essence of which was to remove the separation of the "future of British and French Togoland" in the two sections of the Indian draft, so as to include unification as a possibility in the referendum question, and to allow an immediate referendum in French Togoland as well. Finally, a revised version of the Indian draft resolution expressed that the referendum should ascertain a majority in

---

619 GAOR, "10th Session: 4th Committee" (1955), p. 352.
620 GAOR, "10th Session: 4th Committee" (1955), p. 349.
621 United Nations, "UN Yearbook 1955" (1955), p. 351.
622 GAOR, "10th Session: 4th Committee" (1955), p. 354.
623 A/C.4/L.428/Rev.1 available at GAOR, 10th Session, Annexes, (A/10/Annexes), *Agenda item 35: The Togoland unification problem and the future of the Trust Territory of Togoland under British administration: report of the Trusteeship Council*, p. 5.

regard to form a union with an independent Gold Coast. The term 'union,' which was proposed in the referendum question (a core component on which the separatist discourse of the HSGF is built on today) was, according to the Indian delegate, Jaipal, merely meant that it "would leave open the question of the nature of the union of Togoland with an independent Gold Coast."[624]

The French, British, and Indian delegation opposed the Visiting Mission's proposal that the results in the four proposed voting districts should be considered separately. Yet, the Dutch delegate noted that the Visiting Mission had in a way prejudged the issue by presenting alternatives for which the Togolanders should have an opportunity through the plebiscite to indicate their preference.[625] The Guatemalan representative dispelled the disagreement over the four-unit formula: following the plebiscite, the General Assembly could decide at its 11th Session (1956) whether the peoples' wishes could best be met by looking at the results as a whole or by considering each voting district separately. Oddly, the fact that leaving this question open could influence the voters' decision was not contested by any delegation.

The General Assembly was divided. For many anti-colonial states the early sealing of the first independence of an African colony trumped the unification of Togoland. In the end, the Liberian amendments favouring the pro-unification position were defeated, albeit narrowly.[626] In the plenary session, the draft resolution was adopted without change.[627] Mexico's representative, Espinosa Y. Prieto, was elected UN plebiscite commissioner.

Ultimately, the questions were formulated in such a way that France and Britain could hope for a confirmation of their agenda. The people in British Togoland could vote for

a) "the union [integration][628] of Togoland under British Administration with an independent Gold Coast," or
b) "the separation of Togoland under British Administration from the Gold Coast and its continuance under Trusteeship, pending the ultimate determination of its political future."

Thus, the people in British Togoland could choose between either independence or the status quo. Skinner assesses that the "framing of the plebiscite question reflects the extent to which the reunificationists had lost – or had been excluded from – control of the mechanisms through which the future of the trust territory would be decided."[629]

---

624 GAOR, "10th Session: 4th Committee" (1955), p. 437.
625 GAOR, "10th Session: 4th Committee" (1955), p. 420.
626 GAOR, "10th Session: 4th Committee" (1955), pp. 461–63.
627 General Assembly Resolution 944(X), adopted on 15 December 1955.
628 Today's confusion around the HSGF's claims concerning the "union" between Ghana and Togoland can be traced back to the Indian draft resolution, which changed the wording of the ballot from "integration" to "union" because it sounded less aggressive and "would leave open the question of the nature of the union of Togoland with an independent Gold Coast", GAOR, "10th Session: 4th Committee" (1955), p. 437.
629 Skinner, *The Fruits of Freedom in British Togoland*, pp. 153–54.

6.6.5 The British Togoland Referendum (1956)

Three major political parties engaged in the plebiscite campaign: the Togoland Congress, the CPP and the Northern People's Party (NPP). The Togoland Congress, which campaigned for the reunification of Togoland, promoted the separation of British Togoland from the Gold Coast, while the NPP and the CPP, although opponents in Gold Coast politics, took the same position regarding the referendum and campaigned for the integration of British Togoland.

Photo 20: Voting Campaign in Southern Togoland (April 1956)

Source: Information Services Department (Accra), R-2832-5. Photo: J.T. Ocansey.

In its campaign, the Togoland Congress naturally endeavoured to securitize the issue at hand, spreading the message that integration would mean "slavery."[630] The people of British Togoland would lose their culture, identity, and personality as well as surrender the people of French Togoland to the French with no prospect of reunification. Separation from the Gold Coast, on the other hand, would mean that the people would remain free people forever; the road to unification, independence and eventually federation would be open. These ideas were also spread on posters and banners.

---

630 As quoted in Amenumey, *The Ewe Unification Movement*, p. 264.

Photo 21: March organised by Togoland Congress, Ho (6 May 1956)

Photo 22: Alex Odame addressing a gathering, Jasikan (April 1956)

Source: UN Photo.

Photo 23: Referendum Day, Logba Adzakoe (9 May 1956)[631]

Source: UN Photo.

Amenumey quotes an election poster of the Togoland Congress, which securitises the electoral choice by calling upon the Togolanders to "demonstrate our patriotism, our sympathy for our suffering of our brothers under French administration […] can you the

---

631   Voting scene on plebiscite in the village of Logba Adzakoe as voters line up at the polling station..

Southern Togolanders forsake your kinsmen under the French perpetually?"[632] As the report of the 1955 Visiting Mission showed, with few exceptions, the debate on integration and unification was conducted along ethnic lines,[633] with a majority of Ewe in favour the status quo and a majority of non-Ewe in favour of integration. However, the British willingly left open the question of whether British Togoland would gain independence as a federal state of Ghana or be subsumed under a unitary constitution. As calculated by the British statistical analysis of the 1954 General Election, the question divided many unificationists and dominated much of the campaign.

The referendum was held on 9 May 1956 in an "atmosphere of absolute freedom, impartiality and fairness."[634] The overall result was 54,785 votes for integration to 43,976 for separation, that is a clear majority of 58% voted in favour of integration (see Map 9).

Map 9: British Togoland Referendum (1956)

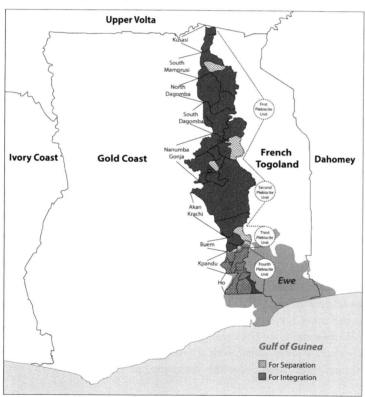

Source: Own creation.

---

632 As quoted in Amenumey, *The Ewe Unification Movement*, p. 264.
633 Nugent's (2002) analysis of the referendum, however, concludes that ethnicity played only a minor role in the referendum.
634 GAOR, "Report of the United Nations Plebiscite Commissioner" A/3173 (United Nations (UN), 1956), p. 467.

While the north of British Togoland, sparsely populated mainly by Dagomba and Mamprusi, clearly favoured integration into the Gold Coast for the sake of their territorial unity, the south, densely populated by Ewe but ethnically far more heterogeneous, was more in favour of separation for the sake reunifying French and British Togoland. As predicted, the northern section voted overwhelmingly for integration, whilst in the southern section, the vote was divided between the Guans and Akans, opting for integration, and the Ewes, opting for separation. Especially many Ewes in the Ho and Kpando district voted against integration because they feared to be degraded to an ethnic minority within Akan-dominated Ghana and to be further removed from the Ewes in neighbouring French Togoland.

6.7 Turning the Tides II: French Togoland (1956-1960)

6.7.1 Loi-Cadre & the Autonomous Republic of Togoland (1956)

Despite the understanding reached between Teitgen and Lennox-Boyd, concerns arose within the French Overseas Ministry arose that the matter of the southern section of British Togoland might be deferred until the referendum in French Togoland.[635] The reason being that international developments caught up with France and put the Overseas Ministry under time pressure to implement reforms: Morocco and Tunisia had already achieved independence in March 1956, revolutionary war was raging in Algeria, fuelling nationalist sentiment in other colonial territories, and the already-imminent independence of the Gold Coast was considered a threating spark that could soon spread to French sub-Saharan Africa. Thus, to avoid another catastrophe in *Afrique Noire* and the possible disintegration of the French Union, the Minister of Overseas France, Gaston Defferre, prepared the *loi-cadre* (framework law) to grant more autonomy to the French overseas territories. When on 23 June 1956 the French National Assembly passed the 'framework law', it gave Defferre in essence the power to fill the 'framework' with decrees, thus, enabling the rapid introduction of Territorial Assemblies and universal suffrage in French overseas territories. Strictly speaking, the framework law (including the decrees) did not bring autonomy to the overseas territories, but rather 'decentralization' or half-autonomy since the administration of the overseas territories was split: while the territorial authorities would now fall under the administration of the newly introduced territorial assemblies, including (limited) budgetary authority, the security-related areas of the *Service d'État*, such as foreign policy, defence, gendarmerie, and the areas' criminal police, remained within the reserve powers of the Ministry of Overseas France.

Without doubt, the *loi-cadre* can be considered a securitisation measure straight out of the Copenhagen School's playbook: The background to its adoption was the danger of a disintegration of the French Union. Its purpose was to circumvent the impossibility to get all the individual measures through the legislative mills at the usual bureaucratic

---

635 ANOM (Aix-en-Provence), 1AFFPOL/2182/3, *Royaume-Uni*, Procès-Verbal des entretiens franco-britannique des Directeurs, 17–18 May 1956, p. 2 [8].

pace. Not only the decrees, but the framework law itself has been whipped through the French National Assembly with unprecedented speed, so that Ansprenger felt compelled to coin it a "parliamentary lightning campaign."[636]

On 29 February 1956, the French Council of Ministers approved the draft for submission to the French National Assembly. The following day, in a speech to the *Cercle de la France d'outre-mer*, Defferre securitised the quick adoption of the law: "If we act quickly, we will not be caught up in the tow of events."[637] In less than two weeks, on 13 March, the report of the *Assemblée de l'Union Française* was already available and a week later, on 22 March, the first reading of the draft law took place in the French National Assembly. On 12 June the Council of the Republic approved the draft with slight changes and a week later, on 19 June, the second reading took place in French National Assembly. During the final debate, Defferre called out to the Conservative Member of Parliament, Guy Petit: "In Black Africa there is still time to do something; in a few months it may be too late!"[638] Without seriously examining the well-founded objections to the constitutionality of the framework law (it violated Articles 74, 77 and 78 of the 1946 Constitution), the majority of the National Assembly followed Defferre with 470 votes to 105. The framework law was promulgated four days later. The existential threat, which nationalist movements posed to the French Union, seemed to dominate the concerns of French parliamentarians. In any case, the changes were welcomed in the French overseas territories so that the adoption caused little resistance.

With regards to French Togoland, time was pressing because of the imminent independence of the Gold Coast. France had a very tight schedule to keep, which meant making concessions to its political interests: the *loi-cadre* authorized the Minister of Overseas France, Gaston Defferre, to draw up a second statute for French Togoland, a sort-of-constitution, which gave more powers to French Togoland's political institutions, such as budgetary powers, making it an Autonomous Republic. Yet, the statute provided that the most important political areas, such as defence, foreign affairs, justice, security, and public liberty, remained with the central organs of the French Republic.[639] As mentioned before, it was not ultimately a matter of granting autonomy, but merely of decentralizing power from the French Republic. For example, French Togoland's Prime Minister, Nicholas Grunitzky, was appointed by the French Governor and only had to be confirmed by French Togoland's Legislative Assembly.[640] In the Togolese cabinet itself, only two members, the Prime Minister and the Minister of Information and Press, were members of the Legislative Assembly. The other members were either civil servants, French citizens, or French nationals, none of whom had been elected. At the same time, the statute was intended to definitively integrate the territory into the French Union.

---

636 Ansprenger, *Politik im Schwarzen Afrika*, p. 244.
637 As cited in Ansprenger, *Politik im Schwarzen Afrika*.
638 As cited in Ansprenger, *Politik im Schwarzen Afrika*, p. 244.
639 ANOM (Aix-en-Provence), DPCT59, *Organisation*, Décret n° 56–847 du 24 août 1956 portant statut du Togo, Titre V – De la répartition des compétences, Art. 27.
640 ANOM (Aix-en-Provence), DPCT59, *Organisation*, Décret n° 56–847 du 24 août 1956 portant statut du Togo, Titre III – Du conseil des ministres du Togo, Art. 15.

In terms of security, the Statute established that a core function of the *gendarmerie* was to assure the re-establishment of public order in case of serious disturbances.[641] In this regard, the *gendarmerie* was under the sole authority of the French Governor, the so-called High Commissioner, and that only he or authorities to whom he has delegated his powers may make requisitions for its intervention, though he could only intervene in the maintenance of internal public order at the request or with the agreement of the Togoland Government. The High Commissioner could decide on the use of general security forces at his disposal and call upon land, sea and air forces stationed in Togoland under conditions provided by laws and decrees. In case of external threat or if disorders fomented by foreign elements, the High Commissioner could intervene in liaison with the Togoland Government and had the power to requisition Togoland police and security forces. In short, as was already becoming apparent in the Gold Coast, the Togo Statute put the gendarmes before the dilemma of serving two masters, which in turn evoked a clash of loyalty.

The statute was supposed to be adopted after the adoption of the *loi-cadre* but before the implementation of the decrees for the rest of French Africa. The idea was that the framework law foresaw to ratify this move by referendum through which the people of French Togoland could choose between the new statute or the continuation of trusteeship. The decision was thus either for the French Union or a simple step backwards. Thus, the *loi-cadre* is evidence of the two-referendum agreement that Teitgen and Lennox-Boyd had reached six months earlier, for it was passed by the French National Assembly just one month after the British Togoland referendum. In terms of the official narrative, it is hard to imagine that these considerations only came about after the result of the referendum in British Togoland. The first versions of the law, including the provisions for French Togoland, were drawn up in March 1956, just three months after the French told the Trusteeship Council that they ruled out a soon-to-be-held referendum in French Togoland and two months before the British Togoland referendum. France played too casually with its credibility.

Endorsement for Ending Trusteeship in British Togoland

On 13 July 1956, the British delegation to the United Nations submitted a memorandum on the referendum.[642] It considered that the plebiscite showed a clear majority in the territory in favour of union with the Gold Coast. The only districts in which there had been a majority vote in favour of separation comprised approximately one seventh of the whole territory. The memorandum argued that the separation of this small territory as a separate political entity would be detrimental to the long-term interests of its residents. The Trusteeship Council and the General Assembly should therefore view the overall result of the referendum as a clear sign to prepare for the termination of the Trusteeship Agreement and the union of the territory with the Gold Coast. Moreover, in the General Election, held in July 1956, that is, two months after the referendum, the CPP, that is, the

---

641 ANOM (Aix-en-Provence), DPCT59, *Organisation*, Décret n° 56–847 du 24 août 1956 portant statut du Togo, Titre III – Du conseil des ministres du Togo, Art. 13.

642 HMG, "The future of Togoland under British administration: memorandum by the Administering Authority" T/1270 (1956).

party advocating integration and unitary government won 8% more votes in Southern Togoland than in the referendum, thus securing a majority of 52.6% in the region.

When during its 18th Session (1956), the Trusteeship Council considered the future of British Togoland, it had before it the report of the UN plebiscite commissioner, the report of the British plebiscite administrator, the memorandum of the British government, and the results of the General Election held in July. The US, Italy and India declared that they were unwilling to support the fragmentation of the territory by considering the vote in the Ho and Kpando districts separately. The US representative declared that he could...

> "not support any action liable to nullify the wishes of the huge majorities in the north which had voted for unification with the Gold Coast. Nor could it support the separation of the southern minority from the rest of the Territory, for that, by setting a precedent for fragmentation in other Trust Territories in Africa, would inevitably delay their progress towards self-government or independence."[643]

Non-Administering Authorities, such as Guatemala and Haiti, accepted the plebiscite results, yet disapproved of the process which had led to these outcomes, namely the administrative union of British Togoland with the Gold Coast.[644] Nevertheless, on 31 July 1956 the Trusteeship Council adopted, by overwhelming majority,[645] an Indian draft proposal endorsing the British memorandum that the General Assembly should take the necessary steps to lift trusteeship.[646]

No Supervision for the French Referendum

In the next meeting, on 2 August 1956, the Council considered an urgent request by the French delegation, inviting the UN to supervise the referendum, which the *loi-cadre* foresaw for French Togoland.[647] Given that the French delegation argued during the Council's 17th Session (1956), that is, right before the referendum in British Togoland, that due to the state of development of French Togoland, a plebiscite in the foreseeable future was not possible,[648] the request came as a surprise. The Council rejected the French request in a 7:7 tie vote.[649]

The Suez crisis, the war in Algeria, and the unificationists' past accusations of election rigging gave the Trusteeship Council much reason for its decision. The Trusteeship Council might have agreed to oversee the referendum if France would have agreed to revise the outdated electoral list, but the non-Administering members of the Trusteeship

---

643 TCOR, "18th Session" (1956), p. 282.
644 TCOR, "18th Session" (1956), p. 291.
645 All in favour except Guatemala, which abstained.
646 TCOR, "18th Session" (1956), p. 294.
647 TCOR, "18th Session" (1956), p. 299. Document T/1274/Rev.I.
648 TCOR, "17th Session" (1956), 60, 75, 94.
649 The seven Administering Authorities (Australia, Belgium, France, Great Britain, Italy, New Zealand, and the United States) supported the proposal; the seven non-Administering Authorities (Burma, China, Guatemala, Haiti, India, Syria, and the Union of Soviet Socialist Republics) opposed it. The distribution of votes is not mentioned but can be deduced from the speeches of the Council members, TCOR, "18th Session" (1956), p. 343.

Council based their opposition to the proposal on several grounds: While in the case of British Togoland independence had been offered as one of the alternatives, in the case of French Togoland there was no such choice. Autonomy, as envisaged by the French, did not equate with self-government or independence as envisaged in the Trusteeship Agreement. While autonomy did not equate independence, sending United Nations observers could be seen as an endorsement of the referendum's results. Moreover, the referendum did not offer the possibility of independence outside the French Union, and no mention was made of a possible agreement that would allow reunification with British Togoland. Bottom line: the Council did not have enough time to consider the question, nor had it been authorised by the General Assembly to supervise any referendum for the purpose of terminating the Trusteeship Agreement. Instead, the Council decided to forward the French memorandum and the records of the Council's deliberations to the General Assembly, which was to consider the matter.

After the Council's decision, the French representative, Robert Bargues, stated that "France refused to be a party to any procedure which would delay the consultation. It refused to share the responsibility which the Council had just assumed of delaying the accession of Togoland to self-government. The referendum would therefore take place at the appointed time and under the conditions envisaged but in the absence of United Nations observers."[650] Since the referendum was already cast into law passed by the French National Assembly, the French were legally bound to proceed with the referendum anyhow.

6.7.2 The French Togoland Referendum (1956)

Amenumey holds that "Over the succeeding months it became clear that the [French] Government tended to conduct this popular consultation in such a manner as to achieve the particular results it wanted."[651] Guy Périer de Feral, a member of the French Council of State, was charged with supervising the referendum and was independent of the local French administration (yet, not entirely impartial). The French thought that abstention from the referendum will be weak.[652]

Despite the French administration's certainty about the insignificance of the unification parties and the outcome of the vote, peace was apparently not trusted and preparations were made for the worst case scenario: in preparation for the referendum, the *journal de mobilisation* was ordered from the *Commandant de Cercle* in Dapango to serve as a template for the entire territory.[653] The archival documents are not unambiguous, but it appears that the military bureau of the French administration wanted to have ready-made call-up lists in case political tensions arose in the course of the referendum. For perspective: In 1956, about 1,500 African soldiers were supposed to ensure the security

---

650 TCOR, "7th Special Session: Report of the United Nations Commission on Togoland under French Administration" Supplement No. 2 (T/1343) (1958), p. 8.
651 Amenumey, *The Ewe Unification Movement*, p. 286.
652 ANOM (Aix-en-Provence), 1AFFPOL/2182/4, *Royaume-Uni*, Le Referendum du 28 Octobre 1956 au Togo.
653 ANT (Lomé), 2APA Dapango/77, *Affaires Militaires*, Secret Letter No. 156/S, Pateul to Commandant de Cercle Dapango, 20 July 1956.

of French Togoland, an area with a population of just under two million, including only 1,200 Europeans.⁶⁵⁴ Administratively, French Togoland was a miniature state whose security forces disproportionately outnumbered even the staff of the colonial administration. Amenumey describes in detail how the pro-French PTP and UCPN once again collaborated with the administration and chiefs to disrupt the CUT and Juvento protest campaign in the run-up to the referendum.⁶⁵⁵

Since the unificationist parties were not allowed to participate in the committee revising the electoral lists, they again called for an electoral boycott. Of the total population, 41% had been registered as voters and of these, 77% participated in the referendum; 71.5% of the registered electorate voted for the Statute of the Autonomous Republic and 5% for continuance of trusteeship. Therefore, the referendum led unsurprisingly to a landslide victory in favour of the new statute and a "puppet government" under the new Togolese Prime Minister, Nicholas Grunitzky (PTP). ⁶⁵⁶

Protesting the Plebiscites (1956)

In the months following the referendum in British Togoland, over a hundred petitions were sent to the UN by a wide variety of organizations in the Gold Coast, British Togoland, and French Togoland.

Some petitions from pro-unificationists attempted to securitise what they referred to as a potentially dangerous misinterpretation of the referendum's results. A cablegram by Alex Odame implored the UN as the "world peace organization" to disregard the results and to press for unification, otherwise "serious unrest" and "ultimate war" might ensue.⁶⁵⁷ Another petition by the Kumasi-based *Ewe & All-Togoland-Congress* pursued a similar strategy: First, the UN was hailed as a peace-making organisation, congratulating it on its ability to avoid open warfare in the Suez conflict. Now, "Togoland [...] requires the same positive action, to settle it at once and for all, unless we are to believe that it is only when blood is shed that you (U.N.O.) will step in."⁶⁵⁸ A letter from one of the few female unificationist petitioners even compared the proposed union of British Togoland with the Gold Coast to a forced marriage, which "will lead us to destruction, lamentation and various kinds of misery and finally civil war. If your aims are really the Protection of Human Rights and justice, please, save us."⁶⁵⁹ A petition of the Jasikan Ex-Servicemen Union demanded the separation and independence of British Togoland, pleading that the United Nations "must not force introduction of GESTAPO methods."⁶⁶⁰ Petitions from the integrationist camp, such as the CPP, welcomed the referendum result and warned the United Nations to ignore the protest of the unification parties.

The referendum in French Togoland was also a subject of several petitions. A petition by Ben Apaloo, president of Juvento, described how the French administration banned

---

654 *New York Times*, "Togoland Facing Divergent Pulls," 14 August 1956.
655 Amenumey, *The Ewe Unification Movement*, pp. 295–96.
656 MAE (La Courneuve), 77QO-4, *Politique intérieure*, Annexe a la dépêche d'Accra No. 329/SC.
657 UN ARMS (New York), S-0443-0030-0006-00006, *T/PET.6/L.73*, 01 July 1956.
658 UN ARMS (New York), S-0443-0030-0004-00019, *T/PET.6&7/L67*, 14 November 1956.
659 UN ARMS (New York), S-0443-0030-0004-00017, *T/PET.6&7/L65*, 01 November 1956.
660 UN ARMS (New York), S-0443-0030-0006-00017, *T/PET.6/L.84*, 04 December 1956.

a Juvento rally in Aného. Since Juvento held it anyway, the police came to the scene with a "demonstration of force" and stormed in with beatings. A police officer from the French administration allegedly threatened Anani Santo's life in the process. According to Apaloo's petition, the entire incident showed how a "climate of insecurity" had existed in the run-up to the referendum in French Togoland.[661] Another petitioner from French Togoland put it briefly: "Give unification or we perish. [...] We are drowning, U.N., save us."[662] In turn, a PTP-petition shared some of the electoral posters for the referendum, stating that Olympio and Santos "want to leave the chains of trusteeship on the hands of the people."[663]

Yet, it was all in vain. Of the petitions that were on the agenda of the Council's 18th Session (1956), 263 were postponed to the 19th Session (1957).[664] When at the opening of the Council's 19th Session in March 1957, the Council was informed of the receipt of 4,508 communications, particularly from French and British Cameroon. Still, about 87 petitions originated from French and British Togoland. Because of the impending independence of British Togoland in 1957, the Trusteeship Council resolved not to process any pending petitions from British Togoland.[665] Hundreds of petitions were thereby silenced.

To deal with the remaining volume of incoming communications, at its 20th Session (1957) the Council established in addition to its Standing Committee on Petitions a two-member Committee on Classification.[666] Despite Soviet protests that the Committee on Classification was being used to eliminate thousands of petitions, it was decided that this procedure should be applied retroactively to the enormous number of pending petitions still awaiting examination, including the petitions that protested against the conduct of the referendum in French Togoland. The 'successes' of the Committee on Classification led to its annual renewal. As such, between 1958 and 1961, the Trusteeship Council dealt in a few resolutions with a staggering 17,014 petitions (14,411 from the Cameroon alone). Yet, the number of written petitions did not matter anymore. As a result, the Standing Committee on Petitions was dissolved and the Council itself dealt with a total of only 30 petitions until its dissolution in 1994.

Oral Hearing (British Togoland)

After both referendums had been held several political parties were heard during the Fourth Committee's 11th Session (1956). At the beginning of the discussion, the British representative informed the Fourth Committee that, subject to parliamentary approval, the Gold Coast would become independent on 6 March 1957.[667] Antor, Odame, Ametowobla, and Asamany spoke on behalf of the Togoland Congress, whilst Asare and

---

661 UN ARMS (New York), S-0443-0031-0002-00015, T/PET.7/L29, 12 November 1956.
662 UN ARMS (New York), S-0443-0031-0002-00016, T/PET.7/L.30, 20 September 1956.
663 UN ARMS (New York), S-0443-0031-0002-00008, T/PET.7/L22, 16 October 1956.
664 United Nations, "UN Yearbook 1956" (1956), p. 316.
665 TCOR, "19th Session" (1957), pp. 3–4.
666 Including a member of an Administering and a Non-Administering Authority. Trusteeship Council Resolution 1713, *Review of procedures regarding petitions*, T/RES/1713(XX) (July 8, 1957), available from https://digitallibrary.un.org/record/218825.
667 GAOR, "11th Session: 4th Committee" (1956), p. 8.

Kumah appeared for the CPP, and Olympio, Santos, and Akakpo spoke for the AEC, Juvento and MPT, respectively.

Photo 24: Togoland Congress and CPP before 4th Committee (ca. November 1956)[668]

Source: UN Photo.

The unificationists generally agreed with the report of the UN electoral observation mission that the referendum in British Togoland was impartial, yet they argued that the results were not interpreted correctly. Odame voiced his dissatisfaction drastically:

"The plebiscite had, however, been held simply because the United Kingdom, having discovered a new kind of colonialism – the colonialism of the Commonwealth Club – wanted the Gold Coast to join that club as a larger, wealthier, and more desirable member than it would be were Togoland under British administration not integrated with it. In 1946, when the Trusteeship Agreement had been signed, the people of Togoland under British administration had already been under United Kingdom administration for thirty-two years. At no time during that period had it been suggested that they should be called upon to decide their own fate, the reason being that Togoland was a peaceful country. [...] If for thirty-two years Togoland under British administration had not been qualified to decide its own fate, it might be asked by what miracle it had been transformed within two years into a country fully qualified to express freely the wish to be self-governing. The truth was that in 1948 the people of the Gold Coast

---

668 From top to bottom, at left: Regina Asamany (Togoland Congress), Francis R. Ametowobla (Togoland Congress), S. W. Kumah (CPP). At right: Alex K. Odame (Togoland Congress), Senyo G. Antor (Togoland Congress), Francis Y. Asare (CPP).

had successfully carried out a revolution to free themselves from British colonial rule and Togoland was therefore to be sacrificed to satisfy the requirements of the new colonialism of the United Kingdom and France."[669]

Odame thus echoed the widely held view among unificationists that the referendum was the British response to the violent riots in Accra in 1948. Asamany found even more drastic words:

"World morality was at stake. Not only the people of Togoland, but all the Members of the United Nations and all the people of the world, were being cheated of justice. The matter involved profound moral, ethical, political and economic decisions which would affect all those who took part, and to overlook those facts and join the United Kingdom and France because they were world Powers and had mighty allies would be a step in the direction of a war in which mankind might be destroyed. [...] The people of Togoland and Africa had faith and confidence in the peaceful, just and democratic peoples of the United States, the United Kingdom, France and the Western bloc generally. They trusted those peoples to put an end to the flagrant violations of international agreements being practised by the United Kingdom and France."[670]

Odame and Asamany argued that the results of the referendum should be invalidated because a decision on the important constitutional or political question of changing the status of a trusteeship territory should require a two-thirds majority.[671] Ametowobla raised the question of the future character of statehood, as the population could not agree on a unified or federal constitutional form in the run-up to the country's independence. While the Northern Territories and Ashanti wanted a federation, only the Coastal Colony favoured a unitary system. But when by now already two of the three regions that made up the Gold Coast thought that their territory could not participate in independence because the present constitution did not protect their interests, one could hardly blame the people of British Togoland for being sceptical about rushing into an indefinite union with the Gold Coast. Thus, without certainty as to the nature of the constitution under which Gold Coast independence was to be granted, the General Assembly should not terminate the Trusteeship Agreement.[672] Antor elaborated on this point but affirmed that the Togoland Congress would consider the possibility of a union on the exclusive condition that Togoland would join the Gold Coast within a federal state, even though the Legislative Assembly had overwhelmingly approved a unitary constitution just two weeks earlier.

The CPP petitioners, Kumah and Asare, replied that the views of the Togoland Congress were those of the losing party. They stressed that the opinion of the majority should be respected, and the Trusteeship Agreement should be terminated. Kumah also maintained that integration would bring about at least partial unification of the Ewe people.

---

669 GAOR, "11th Session: 4th Committee" (1956), pp. 17–18.
670 GAOR, "11th Session: 4th Committee" (1956), p. 19.
671 GAOR, "11th Session: 4th Committee" (1956), pp. 18–19.
672 GAOR, "11th Session: 4th Committee" (1956), pp. 20–21.

Olympio argued like the Togoland Congress. He argued that the result of the referendum should be interpreted to mean that the population of northern British Togoland tended not to vote for integration within a unitary Gold Coast, but rather to favour 'union' with the Gold Coast's northern territories, the latter of which in turn did not want to join such a unitary state either. Nor did the overwhelming majority of Southern Togolanders who voted against integration in any way imply a complete rejection of integration with the Gold Coast. Voters in the south were much more in favour of a form of union that would, however, preserve Togoland's identity and not exclude a possible association of French Togoland with the future state.[673] Santos addressed the replacement of the term 'integration' by the term 'union' in reference to the future of Togoland under British administration. Far from being a simple matter of terminology, that substitution involved the whole question of the future of Togoland and, in his opinion, the responsibility of the United Nations.[674]

Santos and Akakpo then took on developments in French Togoland. Santos questioned whether 70% had really voted for the Autonomous Republic and the end of trusteeship, that is, for quasi-annexation by France. He further argued that rather than for true self-government there was no question that the *loi-cadre*, the Togo Statute, and the referendum in French Togoland were devised for decentralization of power "to strengthen the role of the population in the overseas territories, by which was meant a carefully selected *elite*."[675] He maintained that "Every possible means had been used to bring about the annexation: the good old colonial methods of corruption and pressure, ambiguity, deprivation of freedoms of all kinds, and intimidation, or even repression, of the mass of the people; the modern technique of manipulation of electoral lists and voting papers."[676] Akakpo made a similar point concerning the electoral practices in French Togoland: "During the election itself, intimidation and pressure had frequently been used by the Administration. [...] it's easy to imagine what could happen in the bush, where the *commandants de cercle* were monarchs, where autocratic chiefs abused their power with impunity and where the people were afraid to complain of the irregularities."[677]

General Debate

In the general debate, three camps were emerging. A draft resolution was introduced jointly by eleven countries expressing approval of the union of British Togoland with the Gold Coast. Another camp contended a union might render impossible the unification of Togoland, a course which had been advocated by the General Assembly in the past.

The referendum in British Togoland was inconclusive because, on the one hand, the overwhelming majority in the southern part was against integration and, on the other hand, it was not clear whether the people wanted to live in a united Gold Coast with a unitary or a federal state. It was argued that it would be premature to agree to the integration of the British Togoland into the Gold Coast until there is an agreed constitution

---

673 GAOR, "11th Session: 4th Committee" (1956), p. 25.
674 GAOR, "11th Session: 4th Committee" (1956), p. 28.
675 GAOR, "11th Session: 4th Committee" (1956), p. 29.
676 GAOR, "11th Session: 4th Committee" (1956), p. 28.
677 GAOR, "11th Session: 4th Committee" (1956), p. 30.

setting out the future form of statehood. For example, the Guatemalan delegate, Rolz Bennett, pointed out "the development of Trust Territories might give rise to de facto situations which neither the peoples of those Territories nor the United Nations could undo."[678]

The third group of delegations sat more or less between the two camps. While it shared some of these reservations and fears, it took the view that integration British Togoland into the Gold Coast was the only practicable way by which the people of British Togoland could achieve independence without delay. Although the constitution of the independent Gold Coast had not yet been formalised, the Gold Coast government had already informed the Committee Fourth of the most important provisions. In any case, it would be better if the representatives of the peoples of the two countries, rather than the Fourth Committee, decided on it. Accordingly, the Fourth Committee adopted an amended version of the eleven-nation draft resolution by fifty-eight votes to none with eleven abstentions,[679] thereby approving the union of British Togoland with an independent Gold Coast and on the day of independence the Trusteeship Agreement should no longer be in force.

French Memorandum to End Trusteeship (1956)

During the Trusteeship Council's 6th Special Session (1956), that is, exactly one day after the Fourth Committee had approved the integration of British Togoland into the Gold Coast, the French government presented a memorandum,[680] declaring that since the people in French Togoland had voted for political autonomy within the French Union, it wished to end trusteeship and rejected any other solution for its future.[681]

Yet, the non-Administering Council members were not persuaded, especially since the French representative, Robert Bargues, explained that "external affairs and defence, the currency and foreign exchange system and the other matters enumerated [...] would depend on laws to be adopted by the French Parliament."[682] However, the representative of Guatemala proposed that all documents relating to the referendum in French Togoland be transmitted to the General Assembly. All the non-Administering Council members supported this proposal, as well as the United States. They held that the Trusteeship Council could not take a decision without hearing from the petitioners and representatives of the new Togolese government, all of whom had appeared before the Fourth Committee and since the Fourth Committee was meeting at the same time, it did not have the information available to the Council. The remaining colonial powers, of course, considered this proposal an affront and protested that it was yet another of the many manoeuvres directed against them to increase General Assembly pressure on the Administering

---

678 GAOR, "11th Session: 4th Committee" (1956), p. 64.
679 GAOR, "11th Session: 4th Committee" (1956), p. 90.
680 TCOR, "The future of the Trust Territory of Togoland under French Administration: memorandum by the Administering Authority" (T/1290), available from https://digitallibrary.un.org/record/1653395.
681 TCOR, "6th Special Session" (1956), p. 1.
682 TCOR, "6th Special Session" (1956), p. 6.

Authorities and to weaken the constitutional position of the Trusteeship Council "by depriving it of the safeguard provided for it in the Council's parity of membership."[683] Nevertheless, with the vote of the United States' representative, Mason Sears, who regarded French Togoland's autonomy as incomplete,[684] the proposal passed by eight votes to six.

The French representative, Robert Bargues, was furious about the "non-administering powers' lack of objectivity"[685] and the decision of his American colleague.[686] Bargues feared the worst for French reputation and complained that Sears apparently "makes no secret of its desire to join, at every available opportunity, the bloc of non-administrating Nations."[687] In the midst of a debate of colonial nature, it was obvious that the American Government found itself in great embarrassment. The Americans advised the French against their desire to terminate Trusteeship but offered support through other arrangements. They were not *per se* against integration of French Togoland into the French Union, yet, held "If in the current case we proceed too fast, it might prejudice future cases and weaken the possibility of maintaining European administration in areas that are no ready for self-government."[688] The problem was not even the manner in which the referendum was held, since the US Government did "not believe that the views of the local population are necessarily decisive since they may not be necessarily prepared to express their views properly, and the United Nations should conduct investigations to ascertain if the various peoples are in fact ready to divest the United Nations trusteeship."[689] Seldom do instances of racist mindsets and expressions of illocutionary disablement, through the abandonment of democratic principles and the silencing of the entire population's voice, manifest with such stark clarity in archival records. The US delegation warned the French delegation to continue its demand to lift trusteeship before the Fourth Committee, which constituted the "worst possible forum" for them and advised to seek a compromise resolution.[690]

Oral Hearing (French Togoland)

The Fourth Committee was already in its 11th Session (1956–57), when Gaston Defferre, Minister for Overseas France, Georges Apedo-Amah, the Minister of Finance of the Autonomous Republic of Togoland and Guy Perier de Feral, the referendum's administrator,

---

683 TCOR, "6th Special Session" (1956), p. 8.
684 MAE (La Courneuve), 77QO-10, *Nouvel examen de la question togolaise par la 4ème Commission de l'Assemblée générale des Nations Unies*, Telegram 3115, 13 December 1956, p. 3.
685 MAE (La Courneuve), 77QO-10, *Nouvel examen de la question togolaise par la 4ème Commission de l'Assemblée générale des Nations Unies*, Circulare N°110, 24 December 1956, p. 3.
686 MAE (La Courneuve), 77QO-11, *Nouvel examen de la question togolaise par la 4ème Commission de l'Assemblée générale des Nations Unies*, Secrétariat des Conférences, Note, 10 January 1957.
687 MAE (La Courneuve), 77QO-10, *Nouvel examen de la question togolaise par la 4ème Commission de l'Assemblée générale des Nations Unies*, Telegram N°3346/47, 22 December 1956, p. 1.
688 MAE (La Courneuve), 77QO-10, *Nouvel examen de la question togolaise par la 4ème Commission de l'Assemblée générale des Nations Unies*, Telegram N° 14682/88, 28 December 1956, p. 2.
689 MAE (La Courneuve), 77QO-10, *Nouvel examen de la question togolaise par la 4ème Commission de l'Assemblée générale des Nations Unies*, Telegram N° 14682/88, 28 December 1956, p. 2.
690 MAE (La Courneuve), 77QO-10, *Nouvel examen de la question togolaise par la 4ème Commission de l'Assemblée générale des Nations Unies*, Telegram N° 14682/88, 28 December 1956, p. 2.

appeared as members of the official French delegation. Against the advice of the US delegation, Defferre called for the Trusteeship Agreement to be ended and to that effect a memorandum by the Togoland Government was circulated to members of the Committee.[691]

Representatives of the PTP and UCPN endeavoured to argue that the statute granted the territory extensive internal self-government. Only Nanamale Gbegbeni (UCPN) used a more drastic tone when stating that "the sole aim of the so-called nationalists was to turn Togoland into a vassal of the independent Gold Coast. The chiefs and people of the North did not share that desire. [...] They did not want their country to be exploited by colonialists of their own race, to the detriment of its interests."[692]

Photo 25: Pro-French Counter-Petitioners before 4th Committee (3 January 1957)[693]

Source: UN Photo.

Since the General Assembly had already passed a resolution contrary to the unification of French and British Togoland, Olympio (CUT), Santos (Juvento) and Akakpo (MPT) appeared no longer as embodiments of the unification movement but 'merely' as representatives of the opposition in French Togoland. They appealed to the Fourth Committee not to terminate trusteeship on the grounds that self-government granted by the statute was illusory, and that the referendum had been conducted in an atmosphere of repression and irregularities.

---

691 GAOR, "11th Session: 4th Committee" (1956), pp. 173–75.
692 GAOR, "11th Session: 4th Committee" (1956), p. 177.
693 From left to right: Victor Atakpamey (PTP); Michael Ayassou (Traditional Chiefs of the South); Nanamale Gbegbeni (UCPN); and Sambiani Mateyendou (Traditional Chiefs of the North).

Photo 26: Akakpo, Santos & Olympio before 4ᵗʰ Committee (03 January 1957)[694]

Source: UN Photo.

Once more, they securitised the threat to political liberties in French Togoland. Akakpo maintained that in French Togoland "political liberties did not exist. In the past political meetings had often been prevented by the police. A new tactic had now been adopted: it was the village and cantonal chiefs who, with the protection of the police, prevented the opposition parties from holding meetings in their villages."[695] Santos reiterated that independence for French Togoland was a hypothesis formally excluded in advance by the referendum. Regarding the political campaigning, he added that…

> "leaders of the Parti togolais du progrès and other sympathizers of the Administering Authority had been allowed to prevent the Comite de l'Unite togolaise, by threats of force, from holding political meetings; that Mr. Olympio, of the All-Ewe Conference, had been attacked by anti-Ewe elements who had gone unpunished […] Such partiality for sympathizers of the Administering Authority was an old story and had been the subject of numerous petitions."[696]

Olympio pointed out that the Trusteeship Council had already expressed on two occasions that it did not agree with the French demand to terminate the Trusteeship Agreement. It was only because of this that the French Senator for Togoland, Robert Ajavon, threatened that Togoland would sever all ties with the United Nations if the French plan was not accepted. The CUT, in contrast, would do all in its power to ensure that any change in relations between the trusteeship territory and the United Nations was af-

---

694 At left (profile): André Akakpo (MPT), Anani Santos (Juvento), Sylvanus Olympio (AEC). At the rostrum, Angie Brooks (Liberia), Benjamin Cohen, Under-Secretary of the U.N., Enrique de Karobena (Dominican Republic) Heinrich A. Wieschhoff, Committee Secretary.
695 GAOR, "11ᵗʰ Session: 4ᵗʰ Committee" (1956), p. 179.
696 GAOR, "11ᵗʰ Session: 4ᵗʰ Committee" (1956), pp. 180–81.

fected peacefully and in accordance with the Charter.[697] He expounded how "his own party for instance, because it stood for independence, had been systematically intimidated and persecuted. By a variety of improper practices, the political atmosphere had been so falsified as to make it appear that only a minority desired independence and unification."[698]

Olympio asserted that the CUT would eventually cooperate on condition that the idea of ending trusteeship be abandoned and that new elections be held to the Legislative Assembly to make it a truly democratic and representative body. In this sense, it would be able to amend the statute so that it would be transformed into a constitution allowing for true self-government as a precursor to independence.

General Debate

Once again, the opposition petitioners made quite an impression on the anti-colonial state representatives of the Fourth Committee. Haiti's representative, Max Dorsinville, accused France of missing the alternative of independence in the referendum, which made the whole operation suspect in the eyes of the majority,[699] and Yugoslavia's representative, Bozovic, accused France of holding the referendum in undue haste after assuring the General Assembly immediately before the referendum that the decision on the future of French Togoland would take years. Had France followed the United Kingdom's example and organized and conducted the referendum in cooperation with the United Nations, the Fourth Committee would have been obliged to approve the results, even if they had not pleased all delegations.[700]

During the debate, the Indian delegation introduced a draft resolution that proposed that the General Assembly appoint a commission and send it to French Togoland to investigate the entire situation in the territory and report back. A similar draft resolution was made by five-powers and resubmitted in the form of amendments to the Indian draft resolution.[701] The course of the discussion signalled that the Fourth Committee would go no further and that the plan of the French Overseas Minister, Gaston Defferre, was bound to fail. The French should have listened to the warnings of the Americans.

Therefore, Apedo-Amah informed the Fourth Committee that "the Government of the Autonomous Republic of Togoland would be happy to welcome a United Nations information mission to observe at first-hand how Togoland's institutions were functioning and how the Statute was being applied."[702] Defferre stated that the French Government, which was responsible for Togoland's foreign relations, associated itself with that request and confirmed France's willingness to abandon its request to terminate trusteeship in 1957 "if the further course of discussion and the substance of the resolution adopted were

---

697 GAOR, "11th Session: 4th Committee" (1956), p. 183.
698 GAOR, "11th Session: 4th Committee" (1956), p. 183.
699 TCOR, "11th Session" (1952), pp. 207–8.
700 TCOR, "11th Session" (1952), p. 219.
701 Canada, Denmark, the Dominican Republic, Liberia, and Peru.
702 GAOR, "11th Session: 4th Committee" (1956), p. 196.

acceptable to France."[703] This new, more conciliatory attitude took much of the edge off subsequent discussions.

With the amendments, the Fourth Committee explicitly noted that the new statute had been approved by a substantial majority of the population of the Territory and considered it a significant step toward achieving the objectives of Article 76 of the Charter and the Trusteeship Agreement. The soon-to-be-dispatched United Nations Commission was to examine the situation in the Territory only regarding "the practical application of the new statute and the conditions under which it is applied."[704] A Philippine amendment recommended that French Togoland's Legislative Assembly should be constituted as soon as possible by elections based on universal adult suffrage. Based on equitable geographical distribution, the President of the General Assembly nominated on 20 February 1957, members for the 'Commission on the Future of Togoland under French Administration' under the Liberian chairmanship of Charles King.

Photo 27: The "King-Commission" (3 May 1957)[705]

Source: UN Photo.

For the unification movement, the 11th Session of the General Assembly (1956–57) marked both a defeat and a triumph. A defeat for the Togoland Congress, since the decision had been sealed to incorporate British Togoland into the Gold Coast – and a triumph, since the opposition parties of French Togoland were able to inflict another defeat on France and the door to genuine independence (and possible reunification with neighbouring territories) had not yet been slammed shut.

---

703   GAOR, "11th Session: 4th Committee" (1956), p. 213.
704   See GAOR, "11th Session" (1956), Annexes (A/12/Annexes, Item 39, p. 59.
705   Briefing on details of the commission's organization (1.to r.): G. Makovsky (Interpreter), E. Meihnstorp (Denmark), Karl I. Eskelund, (Denmark); J. L. Delisle (Canada); J. A. Correa (Principal Secretary); Charles T. O. King (Liberia); Jose Rolz Bennett (Guatemala), Victorio D. Carpio (Philippines), Aleksandar Bozovic (Yugoslavia), Ian E. Berendsen (Asst. Secretary), and Richard W. Wathen (Asst. Secretary).

6.8 The Independence of British & French Togoland

Transitional Security

With the approaching independence of Ghana, that is, not just the independence of the first British colony in Africa, but virtually the first handover of power to an African country ever, London faced the problem of its own reservations about giving up security competences. The aim of the Secretary of the Colonies, Lennox-Boyd, for the territories that were (still) under British control (and the whole idea behind sending *Security Intelligence Advisor*, Alex MacDonald, on audit tours across the Empire) was not only to create a professional intelligence service that could stand on its own feet and meet the territories' intelligence needs once they achieved self-government, but ultimately to create intelligence services with which the British Security Service could continue to operate within the network of the Commonwealth of Nations. This is an indication that the massive buildup of the Gold Coast's security and intelligence structures,[706] despite their imminent handover to the Nkrumah government, was therefore not an altruistic act but an act in the service of Britain's global security architecture.

The irony of transitional security during decolonisation was that as independence approached, and with it the relinquishing of colonial security responsibilities, the security apparatus was ever more expanded and intelligence gathering intensified. By February 1956, the Gold Coast police force comprised 6,000 men with an intended increase of 10,000 more men.[707] As recommended by the report of *Security Intelligence Advisor*, Alex MacDonald, the Colonial Office and Governor Arden-Clarke agreed that the Africanization of the Special Branch needed to get underway as soon as possible. Yet, a training school financed solely by Gold Coast funds was considered too costly.[708] The idea was to establish a regional training school where African police officers from all over West Africa would be trained for Special Branch tasks in courses such as "Communism and the Colonial Question."[709] The Colonial Office proposed that the training school for West Africa be established in Nigeria, since "Nigerian Ministers were very touchy about prestige considerations involved in the proposal that a joint Army Training School should continue in the Gold Coast territory."[710] For his part, however, Nkrumah also seemed to have a prestige problem with a police training school in Nigeria. Arden-Clarke tried to dissuade

---

706 The Special Branch cost £44,000 per annum in 1957, TNA (London), FCO 141/5001, *Gold Coast: security and political intelligence; policy*, Memorandum, Post-Independence Intelligence Organisation, p. 3.
707 TNA (London), FCO 141/4992, *Gold Coast: Special Branch; security and training*, Memorandum by the Minister responsible for the Interior.
708 TNA (London), FCO 141/4992, *Gold Coast: Special Branch; security and training*, Minutes, 5 January 1956.
709 TNA (London), FCO 141/4992, *Gold Coast: Special Branch; security and training*, Circular 1280/55, Lennox-Boyd, 20 December 1955, Annex Subjects for Inclusion in a Course for Colonial Pohce Offlcera who have already attended a Regional School; TNA (London), FCO 141/5000, *Gold Coast: security and political intelligence; policy*, Minutes (No. 539), 21 March 1956.
710 TNA (London), FCO 141/4992, *Gold Coast: Special Branch; security and training*, Cablegram 510, Arden-Clarke to Nkrumah, 1 February 1956.

Nkrumah from his tentative refusal to co-operate in the regional police training school, but he was unsuccessful since Nkrumah and his ministers sought their own.[711]

After the referendum of 9 May 1956 confirmed that British Togoland would also become independent together with the Gold Coast, the Gold Coast's Ministry of Interior set to work to prepare the entire territory for the period of transition. The Ministry considered that in case of emergencies during the delicate transition process, the normal Cabinet procedures would be too slow. Therefore, there was a need for standing instructions.[712] Yet, the Ministry's main difficulty has been "to devise a formula whereby the responsibility for Internal Security will remain ultimately with the Cabinet [...] and to preserve the essential independence of the LIC so that it may submit unbiased reports."[713] Thus, it was agreed to draft an *Internal Security Scheme*, which pointed out that the two most important principles of internal security are, first, speed in conducting operations so that, second, the use of force may be kept to a minimum. The *Internal Security Scheme* also served as a template for an *Internal Security Scheme* written specifically for Trans-Volta-Togoland, which came into force less than two months after the referendum in British Togoland.[714] While the Regional Commissioner for Trans-Volta-Togoland, Geroge Sinclair, had complained a few years earlier that the only Special Branch officer in charge of Trans-Volta-Togoland had to divide his valuable time to cover the Eastern Region as well, by July 1956 Trans-Volta-Togoland already comprised nine Special Branch officers and a total of 253 police officers[715] – not much considering the area to be covered, but still a lot considering the quasi-nonexistence of the Special Branch in the years before.

On 25 September 1956, an Advisory Committee on Defence and External Affairs considered the *Internal Security Scheme* prepared by Governor Arden-Clarke's Secretary, who at the same time was chairing the LIC and dealt with the control of *internal* security measures after independence.[716] After its consideration, the Ministry of Interior submitted also a carefully crafted version of this scheme to Prime Minister Nkrumah. Reading between the lines, it appears that based on MacDonald's report, the Ministry was still concerned how the Nkrumah-government would use the internal security apparatus. In a reminiscent tone the memorandum pointed out that "the persons against whom internal security operations are directed are not 'enemies.'"[717] Yet, because the records were

---

711 TNA (London), FCO 141/4992, *Gold Coast: Special Branch; security and training*, Cablegram SRC.0055/52, Nkrumah to Arden-Clarke, 8 February 1956.
712 TNA (London), FCO 141/5000, *Gold Coast: security and political intelligence; policy*, Draft: Control of Internal Security Matters after Independence, p. 5.
713 TNA (London), FCO 141/5000, *Gold Coast: security and political intelligence; policy*, Secret Letter (SCR. 909), Ministry of Interior to T. Hindle, 8 August 1956.
714 PRAAD (Ho), VRG/AD/1043, *Trusteeship Council and Togoland*, No. 28, Trans-Volta Togoland Internal Security Scheme 1956, 1 July 1956.
715 PRAAD (Ho), VRG/AD/1043, *Trusteeship Council and Togoland*, Appendix B, Gold Coast Police Forces, Strength of Personel.
716 TNA (London), FCO 141/5000, *Gold Coast: security and political intelligence; policy*, Memorandum for the Secretary of Defense AC 32(56)
717 TNA (London), FCO 141/5000, *Gold Coast: security and political intelligence; policy*, Draft: Control of Internal Security Matters after Independence, p. 2.

'weeded,' the archives reveal little about how the administration and Nkrumah negotiated security and intelligence.

Yet, in December 1956, that is, just three months before independence, the Local Intelligence Committee considered the (albeit unlikely) possibility of an outbreak of guerilla warfare in Ashanti as a result of the declared intention of the Asanteman Council and the National Liberation Movement (NLM) to secede from the colony on independence.[718] For CenSeC's deliberation, the Secretary of LIC drafted a memorandum following the principle of 'hope for the best, but plan for the worst.' The memorandum encompassed preparations for potential jungle warfare, the establishment of field security units to enhance intelligence gathering, specifically focusing on Ashanti guerrilla tactics, and also contemplated the potential use of starvation as a strategic weapon.[719] Though, the latter was ruled out by CenSeC.[720]

Nkrumah seemed to have taken this meeting as an impetus to indicate the wish of reforming the Special Branch after independence. Nkrumah suggested that an African police officer should also belong to the LIC. However, he was given to understand that membership depended on 'office' rather than 'characteristics.'[721] Certainly, this was a flimsy pretext, considering that despite the intended Africanisation, key positions within the security apparatus, including the Commissioner of Police, continued to be held by British officers for a period after independence. Consequently, the LIC remained predominantly white.

Furthermore, Nkrumah suggested that the intelligence service should report directly to the Prime Minister.[722] Due to the imminent transfer of powers, it would have been futile for the Ministry of Interior to disregard this aspiration and at best it could influence it by working towards its fulfilment through its own version. Thus, the question of the desirability of a separate Special Branch organization after independence was raised, that is, whether the Special Branch and the police should be separate identities rather than one entity. The question led to a dispute between secretaries of the Ministry of the Interior and the Ministry of Defence over which ministry should have control of the Special Branch. The Under-Secretary of the Ministry of Interior and Commissioner of the Gold Coast Police, Matthew Collens, referred to the experience in Ceylon, where the separation of the Special Branch from the police forces and its establishment as a separate organization was apparently a misadventure. Collens insisted that after independence he should have access to Nkrumah on all matters of intelligence and internal security. Collens was concerned that Nkrumah had access to information from the Security Commissioner

---

718 PRAAD (Ho), not indexed by PRAAD [No. 38/SF.8-10], CENSEC [Central Security Committee] & Ghana Intelligence Commitee – General, 1957, Memorandum by Secretary, Local Intelligence Committee
719 PRAAD (Ho), not indexed by PRAAD [No. 38/SF.8-10], CENSEC [Central Security Committee] & Ghana Intelligence Commitee – General, Memorandum by Secretary, Local Intelligence Committee
720 PRAAD (Ho), not indexed by PRAAD [No. 38/SF.8-10], CENSEC [Central Security Committee] & Ghana Intelligence Commitee – General, CENSEC, Recommendations by the Local Intelligence Committee on certain proposals concerning the Establishment of a Joint Planning staff.
721 TNA (London), FCO 141/5001, Gold Coast: security and political intelligence; policy, Note on Terms of Reference etcetera of the Intelligence Committee, February 1957.
722 TNA (London), FCO 141/4992, Gold Coast: Special Branch; security and training, Top Secret Letter Ref. 0158, John Duncan, 28 December 1956.

and the Commonwealth pool of security, which gave him a very large trove of accumulated security information that was seen only with reluctance in the hands of an avowed sympathizer of communism.[723] Thus, weighing whether the Special Branch should come under Nkrumah's direct control, it was considered that "There would be a greater – and very dangerous – tendency to provide only information judged palatable to the Prime Minister and to suppress or ignore information which it was considered to be unwelcome."[724] As Arden-Clarke indicated as early as 1953, among the British administrators Nkrumah had earned a reputation for not responding too well to information contrary to his 'wishful thinking.' Furthermore, it was considered that as soon as the existence of such a separate service became known, as it inevitably would eventually, allegations of the creation of 'political spies' would immediately be made. Therefore, it was decided that the intelligence service should remain integrated with the police. Thus, in February 1957, it was finally decided that the Special Branch should remain under the control of the Ministry of Interior. It was also decided that the chairmanship of the LIC would be transferred to the Permanent Secretary in the Ministry of the Interior, who would report directly to Nkrumah and the Minister of the Interior, just as the Chairman of the LIC had until then reported to Governor Arden-Clarke.

History sometimes plays strange games since of all people it was Daniel A. Chapman, the founder of the *Ewe Newsletter* and alleged author of the *Most Secret* document, who was recalled from his ambassadorial post in Washington to become Nkrumah's personal secretary and chair of the future Ghana Intelligence Committee.[725]

Independence Disturbances

Immediately after the resolution on British Togoland's integration into the Gold Coast was passed, the Jasikan branch of the Togoland Congress passed a motion calling on all Togolanders to boycott the independence celebrations. In early January 1957, Antor declared at a meeting of the Togoland Congress that if the Gold Coast government accepted his constitutional proposals for the unification of British Togoland with the Gold Coast, the unification of the two territories would take place in peace; otherwise, any attempt at unification would be met with violence. On 16 February 1957, Antor handed over the resolution, which had been signed by several chiefs, to the Regional Commissioner in Ho, Thomas Mead, protesting against the integration of British Togoland into Ghana as part of TVT and demanded that the southern part of British Togoland alone should form its own region. Mead had adopted a conciliatory approach, promising that although "any attempt […] to interfere with peaceful celebrations in the region would be quickly and firmly dealt with […] he would [also] do his best to ensure that persons celebrating independence offered no unnecessary provocation."[726]

---

723 TNA (London), FCO 141/4992, *Gold Coast: Special Branch; security and training*, Secret & Personal Letter [Pol. F. 202], Collens to Hindle, 12 January 1957, p. 2.
724 TNA (London), FCO 141/5001, *Gold Coast: security and political intelligence; policy*, Memorandum: Post-Independence Intelligence Organisation, 28 January 1957.
725 TNA (London), FCO 141/5001, *Gold Coast: security and political intelligence; policy*, Letter N° No. SCR.0158, D. Chapman to Permanent Secretary, Ministry of Interior, 11 February 1957.
726 Daily Graphic, 20 December 1956, p. 16.

On 23 February 1957, that is, two weeks before Ghana's independence, the leadership of the Togoland Congress assembled some 45 chiefs at a cocoa farm at Logba Alakpeti, where it was decided to establish paramilitary training camps in Hodzo and Alavanyo, near Kpando. Apparently, by attacking offices, facilities, and forces, the conspirators hoped to attract the attention of the United Nations and thus obtain the repeal of the 'union resolution.' However, the Special Branch had its informants on the scene and believed Reverent Francis Ametowobla to be the main instigator of the usurpation plan.[727]

As a response, Governor Arden-Clarke signed two *Peace Preservation Orders*, which required the inhabitants of Alavanyo and Hodzo to give up all unlicensed weapons and ammunition. When on 1 March 1957, the local police found evidence that telephone wires had been cut. Two hundred extra police were sent to the area whilst three companies of the Ghana Regiment were dispatched to British Togoland and stationed at Ho, Hohoe, and Kpando in order to function as 'reserve security forces.'[728] The large-scale movement of troops and the implementation of a Peace Preservation Order in effect placed parts of southern British Togoland under martial law. The two camps, with small cachés of weapons and evidence of recent occupation, were discovered. Most of the usurpers escaped by fleeing into the nearby forest. Sixteen individuals were arrested for refusing to give up their weapons. The preparations for transitional security and intelligence had obviously been justified.

In the days leading up to independence, minor incidents occurred in the strongholds of the unification parties in Southern Togoland. Yet, on the Independence Day itself, 6 March 1957, a major incident occurred at Kpando-Konda. A platoon of police reserves, leaving the town by lorry, was surrounded, and fired upon. Reinforcements of police arrived, and in the ensuing riot, three unificationists were killed and six were wounded by shotgun pellets. About 100 arrests were made, and a curfew was imposed on Ho.

According to the *Ashanti Pioneer* the Nkrumah-government insisted that "troops were 'at no time ... engaged in operations' and had simply been posted to the region to demonstrate that reinforcements were available in the event of any serious insurrection."[729] The Ashanti Pioneer, however, likened the posting of troops to southern Togoland to the approach of the colonial government to the servicemen's riots of 1948:

"If, therefore, Mr Nkrumah's Government, after ousting the imperialist government, now wants so cheerfully to go the way of the imperialists, then it has far too soon betrayed the very struggle for independence. In the sacred name of independent Ghana, will the Government please put the army in its true place in a true democracy, by dis-

---

727 MAE (La Courneuve), 77QO-5, *Politique intérieure*, Secret Letter, Renner to Ministre des Affaires Etrangeres, 14 March 1957, p. 4.
728 Government of Ghana, "Report: Enquiry into matters disclosed at the trial of Captain Benjamin Awhaitey held on the 20th and 21st January 1959, before a court-martial convened at Giffard Camp, Accra, and the surrounding circumstances" (Accra, 1959), Statement by the Government, pp. 24–25.
729 As cited in Skinner, *The Fruits of Freedom in British Togoland*, p. 167.

couraging it from vying with the police in its inalienable role of maintaining law and order."[730]

The criticism foreshadowed what later became reality. The leaders of the Togoland Congress, first of all Antor, publicly disassociated themselves from the troublemakers and none of them, during this period of unrest, showed an attitude that would confirm the suspicions of men like Ametowobla, Ayeke, and Kofi Dumoga, who are believed to be the instigators of the uprising. Too late for Antor. In October 1957, Nkrumah declared that he was convinced that the incidents had been planned and carried out by "irresponsible politicians who cared only for their own selfish ambitions."[731] In November Antor and Kojo Ayeke, both Members of the Legislative Assembly, and nine others were accused of complicity in the incidents which were "aimed at insurrection against the incorporation of Togoland into Ghana."[732]

The independence disturbances served as a basis for the passage of the *Avoidance of Discrimination Act* on new year's eve "to prohibit organizations using or engaging in tribal, regional, racial and religious propaganda to the detriment of any community or securing the election of persons on the account of their tribal, regional or religious affiliations and for other purposely connected thereto."[733] The law mainly targeted the Asante separatists around the NLM, but due to its clear regional reference, the Togoland Congress also fell under the purview of the act and, although it had been represented in Parliament since the 1954 elections, thus became illegal virtually overnight. In January 1958, to avoid a party ban, the NLM, the Togoland Congress, and other parties were forced to merge to form the *United Party*. Nevertheless, Antor and Ayeke were brought to trial for their alleged implication in the independence disturbances and in March 1958 were sentenced to six years imprisonment with hard labour "for conspiring to attack with armed force persons within Ghana."[734] Although they were subsequently acquitted on appeal since the judge had misdirected the jury, by July 1958, Nkrumah's CPP passed a *Preventive Detention Act*, which gave the government the power to detain an individual for up to five years without the right of appeal.

In November 1957, just one month before the enactment of the Avoidance of Discrimination Act, of all people, Charles H. Chapman, the brother of the founder of the Ewe unification movement, Daniel A. Chapman, and himself a former member of the AEC, was appointed Regional Commissioner of Trans-Volta Togoland, who enforced the *Preventive Detention Act* to quell unrest in Trans-Volta-Togoland. The Nkrumah government proceeded to arrest parliamentarians who were representing the former Togoland Congress. As an increasing number of arrests were made throughout Ghana, including

---

730 *Ashanti Pioneer*, "Police or Army," 14 March 1957, p. 4.
731 *West Africa*, 2 November 1957, p. 1047.
732 *The Times*, "Ghana Minister's Warning on Emergency Powers Bill," 03 December 1957; *Sunday Times*, "Ghana M.P.S Arrested," 01 December 1957.
733 Avoidance of Discrimination Act (31.12.1957)
734 TNA (London), DO 35/9279, *Political affairs in Togoland*, confidential Note [10].

in the territory of the former British Togoland, Togoland unificationists, such as Francis Ametowobla, began to flee across the border into French Togoland to avoid detention.[735]

As a result of the independence disturbances, Nkrumah wanted to take direct responsibility for security and intelligence matters after independence,[736] so in 1958, Daniel Chapman, was released from his position as chairman of the Ghana Intelligence Committee and demoted to principal of the Achimota College, for which he nursed a bitter grievance. At Achimota College it soon became an open secret that he bore strong resentment towards Nkrumah and his government. Chapman in turn was accused of indulging in "tribalism" and of passing on secrets to the Republic of Togo.[737] The former chairman of the Ghana Intelligence Committee was informed eventually that he himself was under surveillance by the Ghana Intelligence Service, which had emerged from the Special Branch. Judging by the wording, it was someone close to the nucleus of power who informed him, possibly the Principal Secretary of Ghana's African Affairs Secretariat, Michael Dei-Anang.[738] Chapman's trajectory is imbued with bitter irony: to achieve Ewe unification, Chapman had sided with Nkrumah in the early 1950s and, after Ghana's independence, he even chaired the Ghana Intelligence Committee that would later prosecute unificationists. Now Chapman had become a victim of his own politics, as his unification aspirations were stigmatized as "tribalism" and rendered remote.

6.8.1 Securitising the Independence of French Togoland (1957)

In March 1957, the French government enacted a slight amendment to the statute, thereby adhering to the General Assembly and wishes, which the Togolese Legislative Assembly pronounced on 8 December 1956 and 13 February 1957 concerning an enlargement of autonomy over public liberties and the protection of their exercise. This change did not satisfy the nationalists, so that in April 1957, during the Trusteeship Council's 19th Session (1957), Sylvanus Olympio appeared in an oral hearing before the Trusteeship Council. After appearing only before the Fourth Committee for nearly six years, it was the first time since the summer of 1950 that he had decided to address that body. As he had noted earlier, when pointing out that the Trusteeship Council had already dealt France a serious setback twice (the refusal to supervise the referendum and the transmission of the subsequent memorandum to the General Assembly), he seemed to have hoped that the balance of opinion in the Council had shifted to France's disadvantage.

---

735   By October 1961, 5,700 Ghanaians (belonging to various ethnic groups and also Togoland-unrelated opposition parties) had taken refuge in francophone Togo.
736   PRAAD, 038/SF12 [old signature], *Field Intelligence Organisation*.
737   PRAAD (Accra), RG 17/1/224, *Daniel Chapman*, The Activities of the Headmaster of Achimota College, Mr. D.A. Chapman, 2 September 1960.
738   PRAAD (Accra), RG 17/1/224, *Daniel Chapman*, Personal and Confidential Letter (without number), 3 September 1960.

Photo 28: Sylvanus Olympio before Trusteeship Council (17 April 1957)

Source: UN Photo.

Olympio appealed for not terminating the Trusteeship Agreement over French Togoland merely because of the statute, and, since the current Legislative Assembly was not elected by universal suffrage, he called for new and free elections. Olympio maintained that there was a "total absence of democratic liberties in Togoland under French administration."[739] He pointed out that in late March 1957, the French administration used the independence unrest in Ghana as a pretext to ban mass meetings near the Togo-Ghana border. Suspiciously, the decision had been delayed a full two weeks after the disturbances, that is, until the eve of a scheduled CUT meeting. In another incident in Atakpamé, the French authorities allegedly made use of armed peace-breakers to give the French administration a pretext to intervene and break up a rally organized by the CUT. Olympio remarked "Those recent events had confirmed in him the belief that there was a real danger of the establishment of a self-perpetuating autocracy rather than a democratic State in Togoland."[740] Olympio interpreted the French representative's response, asserting that it was the business of the Togoland Assembly itself and that the Administering Authority had no power to intervene, as "an invitation to dictatorship in Togoland, which now had a one-party Assembly supporting a one-party Government."[741] The French representative, Robert Bargues, played down the incident at Atakpamé and replied that the meeting had been banned for the protection of the people assembled there. Olympio rebutted that the CUT did not need protection.[742]

General Debate

After the hearing, the French representatives, Robert Bargues, requested to postpone the debate on the hearing, the statute, and the trusteeship territory in general until the United Nations Commission had returned and submitted its report.[743] At first, the request was ignored and the anti-colonial Council members dwelt at length on the politi-

---

739 TCOR, "19th Session" (1957), p. 194.
740 TCOR, "19th Session" (1957), p. 194.
741 TCOR, "19th Session" (1957), p. 195.
742 TCOR, "19th Session" (1957), p. 198.
743 TCOR, "19th Session" (1957), p. 202.

cal situation in French Togoland.[744] The Syrian delegate accused that the French "Administering Authority had tried to remove the Trust Territory from United Nations supervision"[745] by requesting termination of trusteeship on the basis of a statute that "could only be described as a farce,"[746] inappropriate as an instrument leading to self-government or independence. New elections, in accordance with the previous General Assembly's resolution, were considered essential. The Council adopted a Belgian proposal to defer establishing a drafting committee on French Togoland and to abstain from passing any resolution on the issue until the return of the United Nations commission.[747] Yet, the Indian and Syrian delegations subsequently claimed that the decision applied only to a drafting committee, whereas resolutions which the Council itself might want to adopt were still admissible. The Syrian Council President, Asha, upheld their interpretation. The Syrian and Indian delegation thus submitted a draft resolution requesting France to establish a new Legislative Assembly by free elections based on universal suffrage.[748] The colonial powers opposed the draft on the ground that it was inconsistent with the spirit of compromise which characterised the General Assembly resolution. The Italian delegate formulated "it would be wrong for the Council to reopen the matter at that stage with a draft resolution which was based on the testimony of a single petitioner, and which did not even take the Administering Authority's views into consideration. [The Italian delegation] saw no need for prodding the Administering Authority constantly and systematically."[749] The Indo-Syrian draft resolution was then rejected by two tie-votes.[750] Once again, the Council frustrated Olympio's request.

The '4th Visiting Mission'

Although the UN Visiting Commission was a sort of fourth, special Visiting Mission, it is important to remember that it differed significantly from the three previous regular Visiting Missions. It was not dispatched by the Trusteeship Council, but by the General Assembly, and therefore not subject to the Trusteeship Council's restrictive *rules of procedure* such as parity between Administering and non-Administering Authorities (in fact, not a single Administering Authority was represented on the Visiting Commission). Although it did not have a mandate to receive written petitions (this was still the prerogative of the Council), it was not prevented from investigating freely upon claims from the opposition parties. This was facilitated through its significantly larger membership, in contrast to the usual four-member composition of regular Visiting Missions. For this very reason, its report was much more significant than those of earlier regular Visiting Missions.

The Visiting Commission spent the entire month of June 1957 in French Togoland. Independence demonstrations and calls for new elections accompanied its stay in Lomé.

---

744 TCOR, "19th Session" (1957), pp. 226–34.
745 TCOR, "19th Session" (1957), p. 232.
746 TCOR, "19th Session" (1957), p. 232.
747 TCOR, "19th Session" (1957), p. 245.
748 See T/L.754, "Togoland under French administration – India and United States of America: draft resolution," available at TCOR 19th Session, Annex (T/19S/Annexes, *Agenda Item 3*, p. 50.
749 TCOR, "19th Session" (1957), p. 259.
750 TCOR, "19th Session" (1957), p. 262.

In Lomé, echoing the successful approach of former Governor Péchoux, Prime Minister Nicholas Grunitzky sought to securitise his efforts to dissuade the Commission's attendance at rallies of the opposition. He argued that, given the proximity to the frontier, "public order might be seriously threatened."[751] The Commission prevailed upon the Prime Minister not to insist upon his objections, and in the event no disorder whatsoever occurred.

On the day when the Commission attended the Legislative Assembly, the Government took considerable security measures to prevent the possibility of disturbances. Some representatives of the press were even excluded, and only a limited number of persons were permitted to attend the meeting. There were heavy police patrols in the town, but no serious incidents occurred. In general, the forces of order were present in reasonable numbers during the Commission's tour. In the halls of the Assembly itself, Robert Ajavon, President of the Legislative Assembly, expressed to the members of the UN Commission that the Legislative Assembly, then exclusively comprising members of pro-French parties, unanimously whished that the Assembly should not be dissolved and renewed, not so much out of fear of not being re-elected but out of "a desire to see the new Government and the new Legislative Assembly continue with their task in good circumstances and in social peace and security."[752] The Commission noted that these arguments "were repeated [...] by supporters of the Government throughout the country, not only in doubtful constituencies, but also in areas where there appeared to be a virtual certainty that the present members would be returned in a new election."[753] In other words, the pro-French parties tried to prevent new elections by securitising them. Ajavon elaborated that...

> "For a dependent country, gentlemen, there are two ways to win its independence: the one, brutal, bloody, destructive; the other, peaceful, based on patient negotiation in an atmosphere of good will and mutual understanding. We preferred the latter. And no one can blame us for that."[754]

But Ajavon's statements were soon to be overshadowed. On 20 June 1957, in Mango, in northern French Togoland, fisticuffs broke out between young supporters of a pro-government chief and a pro-opposition chief after the latter returned from a meeting with the Commission. As the conflict transitioned to the town's market square, supporters of the pro-government chief shot at the group of opposition members, killing one and seriously injuring four.[755] Two days later, on 22 June 1957, another regrettable incident

---

751 TCOR, "7th Special Session: Report of the United Nations Commission on Togoland under French Administration" (1958), p. 53.
752 TCOR, "7th Special Session: Report of the United Nations Commission on Togoland under French Administration" (1958), p. 56.
753 TCOR, "7th Special Session: Report of the United Nations Commission on Togoland under French Administration" (1958), p. 56.
754 TCOR, "7th Special Session: Report of the United Nations Commission on Togoland under French Administration" (1958), p. 76.
755 ANT (Lomé), 2APA Mango – 48, *Administration Générale et Politique*, 1957, Letter N°27/c, Commandant de Cercle to Prime Minister, 21 June 1957, p. 3; TCOR, "7th Special Session: Report of the United

occurred in northern Togoland, at Pya-Hodo, in the *cercle* of Lama-Kara, as the result of which at least seven people lost their lives. According to the representatives of the Lama-Kara branches of Juvento and the CUT, the *commandant de cercle* of Lama-Kara had threatened reprisals against nationalists who refused to take part in the manifestations organized by the local authorities. Juvento and CUT supporters responded by rioting, erecting road barricades, and throwing stones. The auxiliary police and a squad of local militia arrived on the scene. When by nightfall the *commandant de cercle* tried to clear the barricades and have the rioters arrested, he was hit by an arrow and the order was given to shoot. The estimates of casualties range from an official figure of seven to unofficial reports of 14 killed, and 10 seriously wounded.[756] Several members of Juvento and CUT were arrested and detained.

Two deputies representing the Kabré people of Lama-Kara as well as a report by the Prime Minister, Grunitzky, attributed the incident to local leaders of the CUT and Juvento, who, so it was claimed, had attempted to organize an insurrection against the local Government authorities.[757] CUT and Juvento, of course, made use of the incidents by casting a bad light on the French Administering Authority, who in turn tried to argue that the presence of Visiting Missions was often a cause of violence between competing parties and should therefore be scaled back.

It was no use. In the section of the report on political freedoms, the Commission noted that "the relationship between opposing parties is marked by a certain bitterness and that in consequence the political situation in the Territory is somewhat tense."[758] The Commission held the view that "in many areas opposition parties do not enjoy the same measure of political freedom of expression and assembly as do the pro-government parties. This is particularly so in the north of the Territory, where the opposition must reckon with the well-known objections and often public condemnations of traditional chiefs."[759] Furthermore, the Commission considered that the presence of the armed forces and *gendarmerie* under French control was a substantial limitation on the autonomy enjoyed by Togoland. Clearly, the Commission was not convinced of the continued necessity of reserve powers possessed by the French High Commissioner.[760]

Beyond the question of political liberties, the Commission's report casted grave doubts on the French administration's liberalism on the voter registration and polling

---

Nations Commission on Togoland under French Administration" (1958), p. 72; ILRM (New York Public Library), b. 12, *Togoland*, Daily Graphic, "Unificationists demonstrate in French Togoland", 27 June 1957.

756 Albert Menveyinoyu Alidou Djafalo commanded the platoon that perpetrated the Pya-Hodo massacre that would be commemorated by General Eyadema fifteen years later. After independence, Alidou Djafalo became one of Eyadema's closest friends and most trusted lieutenants – a key figure in the new military regime installed after the 1967 coup.

757 TCOR, "7th Special Session: Report of the United Nations Commission on Togoland under French Administration" (1958), pp. 71–72.

758 TCOR, "7th Special Session: Report of the United Nations Commission on Togoland under French Administration" (1958), p. 59.

759 TCOR, "7th Special Session: Report of the United Nations Commission on Togoland under French Administration" (1958), p. 59.

760 TCOR, "7th Special Session: Report of the United Nations Commission on Togoland under French Administration" (1958), p. 58.

procedure. The Commission therefore followed Olympio's demand that new elections to the "representative organs in Togoland on the basis of universal suffrage would represent the implementation of an important democratic principle embodied in the Statute and might contribute towards the creation of a more favourable political atmosphere."[761]

Overall the Commission concluded that the statute "represents a very significant step in the achievement of the objectives of Article 76 of the Charter and of the Trusteeship Agreement, has been broadly interpreted and liberally applied, and that in consequence Togoland possesses a large measure of internal autonomy or self- government."[762] On the other hand the Commission found that "there are still important restrictions by virtue of the retention of certain specified powers and competences."[763] It was felt that "a trend of events had been set in motion which makes inevitable further broadening of the degree of autonomy achieved by towards full autonomy."[764]

The French for their part were furious with the report, which in their eyes…

> "[…] would not miss discussing on the tribune not only the aspects of a conflict between the French Government and the Togolese but also the protests of the opposition, which would thus find the permanence of its means of complaint to an international body. A similar procedure was not foreseen in the incorporation of British Togo into Ghana, in order to preserve the hypothesis that the former British Togolese would no longer be willing to continue their life in a unitary state, and it is difficult to see the reasons for the adoption of a discriminatory measure against us in its very principle." [765]

The French grudgingly considered the admission of international arbitration and thus interference in what they considered an 'internal domain' to be a serious precedent, not only for trusteeship territories but also for territories that were in the process of gaining autonomy. French Togoland was by no means an isolated case and had to be considered in the context of all territories that were not yet fully self-governing.[766]

The Trusteeship Council's 7th Special Session

When the Trusteeship Council met at its 7th Special Session (1957) to discuss the Commission's report, the French delegate, Jacques Kosczuisko-Morizet, opened with a statement that the Statute would not enshrine the relationship between France and the Autonomous Republic of Togoland in an unalterable manner, but would remain fully evolutionary in character.[767] Accordingly further amendments to the statute would be put into

---

761 TCOR, "7th Special Session: Report of the United Nations Commission on Togoland under French Administration" (1958), p. 59.
762 TCOR, "7th Special Session: Report of the United Nations Commission on Togoland under French Administration" (1958), p. 58.
763 TCOR, "7th Special Session: Report of the United Nations Commission on Togoland under French Administration" (1958), p. 58.
764 TCOR, "7th Special Session: Report of the United Nations Commission on Togoland under French Administration" (1958), p. 58.
765 ANOM (Aix-en-Provence), 1AFFPOL/2182/5, *Royaume-Uni*, Commission d'Information, p. 2.
766 ANOM (Aix-en-Provence), 1AFFPOL/2182/5, *Royaume-Uni*, Commission d'Information, p. 1.
767 TCOR, "7th Special Session" (1957), p. 2.

effect as soon as the Trusteeship Agreement was terminated. French Togoland's Minister of Finance, Georges Apedo-Amah, who came along as a member of the French delegation, added that "the residual powers still held by France had been transferred to Togoland, or in other words, as soon as the statute had come into full effect, the mission of the present Legislative Assembly could be regarded as completed."[768] Therefore elections to it would be possible before the statutory date of renewal.

Photo 29: Apedo-Amah & Koscziusko-Morizet (12 September 1957)

Source: UN Photo.

After a lengthy wrangling over wording and amendments, the Council adopted an US resolution based primarily on the idea of an early general elections to establish a Legislative Assembly fully qualified to express its views on the future of the territory. The report of the Commission together with the work of the Council was transmitted to the General Assembly.

Fourth Committee Hearing (1957)

During the Fourth Committee's 12th Session (1957), Robert Ajavon, President of the Togoland Legislative Assembly and Georges Apedo-Amah, Togolese Minister of Finance, both appeared as members of the French delegation. Together with the French representative, Jacques Koscziusko-Morizet, they expressed satisfaction with the Visiting Commission's report. They felt the time had come to complete Togoland's self-government by transferring the residual powers still vested in France and renewed the request to terminate the Trusteeship Agreement. Ajavon stressed that "Togoland would need France's

---

768   TCOR, "7th Special Session" (1957), pp. 19–20.

economic and financial aid for several more years. The Government of Togoland realized that political independence without economic independence would be illusory and that premature independence could be harmful to the social structure of a country and detrimental to its development."[769] Ajavon proclaimed that the Togolese government was prepared to hold elections before the end of 1958 if the statute, that had been modified in March 1957, would be accepted fully and trusteeship be lifted automatically when the newly elected Legislative Assembly would meet for the first time.[770] Ajavon thus indicated that the Togolese government was at least prepared to suspend the demand for a termination of trusteeship until 1958. Yet, the French representative, Jacques Kosczeiusko-Morizet, on the other hand, continued to demand the immediate termination of the Trusteeship Agreement. He appealed to the members of the Committee...

> "to consider the facts dispassionately and to cast aside out-dated ideas of colonialism and anticolonialism and of the arbitrary opposition of the so-called Administering Authorities to the so-called non-administering Powers. The problem to be settled was a human problem. The resolution to be adopted would affect human beings who had faith in the impartiality of the United Nations and would influence the future of a people. To a certain extent the prestige and influence of the United Nations were at stake when a decision was to be taken on so serious a subject."[771]

Photo 30: Akakpo & Ohin before 4th Committee (8 November 1957)[772]

Source: UN Photo.

---

769 GAOR, "12th Session: 4th Committee" (1957), p. 231.
770 GAOR, "12th Session: 4th Committee" (1957), p. 232.
771 GAOR, "12th Session: 4th Committee" (1957), p. 235.
772 André Akakpo (left, speaking), and Alexandre John Orin.

In the following, the Committee listened to the opposition: Alexandre John Ohin (MPT), André Akakpo (MPT), Anani Santos (Juvento) and Sylvanus Olympio (AEC). Santos went first. In his tame lawyerly style, he reiterated the plea for new elections and a rejection of the French proposal. Santos maintained that although the UN Commission had been dispatched at the invitation of the French Government, the latter appeared reluctant to accept its conclusions. He warned that the slight increase in autonomy granted in March 1957 was merely "to induce the United Nations to agree to the termination of the Trusteeship Agreement."[773]

Both Ohin and Akakpo expressed that continued trusteeship under the auspices of the United Nations was the only way for French Togoland to achieve 'true' independence and that the Trusteeship Agreement should therefore not be terminated before this goal was achieved.

Ohin proclaimed that the people of northern Togoland "were being deceived. The sanguinary incidents at Mango and Lama-Kara in June 1957 were sacrifices which only a desperate people would be willing to make."[774] He claimed that the opposition had refused to take part in the Government because "No true patriot could accept a post under a government whose deputies represented, not the majority of the people, but a minority upheld by a régime of intimidation, persecution and electoral fraud."[775] Accordingly the "question was not one of being pro- or anti-French, or even pro- or anti-colonialist: the question was whether a people which had reached maturity had the right to manage their own affairs, both domestic and foreign, and to give free expression to their views without fear of brutal oppression."[776] Akakpo protested against the premature termination of trusteeship and the referendum in French Togoland, which had not been supervised by the United Nations and had been marked by fraud and gerrymandering. He securitised the future statehood of Togo:

> "[Under the new statute] Togoland still could not freely determine its domestic policies or its policy with regard to France and as it still participated, through representatives, in the functioning of the central organs of the French Republic, the danger of integration [into the French Republic] remained. The achievement of the goals of trusteeship was thus threatened [...] The members of the Government and the Togoland Legislative Assembly, who had not been elected by universal suffrage, were setting up a virtually dictatorial system in the Territory."[777]

He described the difficulties in organising political meetings, as the authorities ordered the local chiefs to disrupt the opposition parties in their organisation, whereupon the *commandants de cercle* had these banned.[778]

---

773   GAOR, "12th Session: 4th Committee" (1957), p. 236.
774   GAOR, "12th Session: 4th Committee" (1957), p. 238.
775   GAOR, "12th Session: 4th Committee" (1957), p. 238.
776   GAOR, "12th Session: 4th Committee" (1957), p. 238.
777   GAOR, "12th Session: 4th Committee" (1957), p. 239.
778   GAOR, "12th Session: 4th Committee" (1957), p. 240.

Olympio maintained that "France had offered Togoland only a substitute for independence."[779] He claimed that:

"attempts on the part of political parties [...] to organise political rallies have met so far with the sternest of repressive measures, such as imprisonment, deportation and shooting down in cold blood. Some of these measures were taken directly by the French officers of the administration or indirectly through the African Chiefs who are Government Agents."[780]

Photo 31: Santos & Olympio before 4th Committee (8 November 1957)

Source: UN Photo.

Olympio pointed out that the Commission reported that opposition rallies were held in private locations away from the city centre, while pro-French party rallies were mostly held in central public streets or squares. He demanded that political freedom should be restored, and all political parties should be enabled to exercise their right to freedom of expression, assembly, and movement. He also referred to the repressive measures in the wake of the shootings in Lama-Kara and Mango, in which, according to him, a total of 19 people died, whereafter "a reign of terror was unleashed in this otherwise peaceful district"[781] and several hundred were imprisoned as a result of the incident.

He pre-empted a retort by the French delegation, which would probably argue that the French Government was no longer responsible for the internal security of the country. Yet, Olympio underlined that "the Trusteeship Agreement was still in force."[782] He deemed it inconceivable why Togolanders should "settle for anything less than indepen-

---

779 GAOR, "12th Session: 4th Committee" (1957), p. 240.
780 GAOR, "12th Session: 4th Committee" (1957), "Circulated statement by Sylvanus Olympio", p. 6.
781 GAOR, "12th Session: 4th Committee" (1957), "Circulated statement by Sylvanus Olympio", p. 7.
782 GAOR, "12th Session: 4th Committee" (1957), p. 240.

dence when their blood brothers and neighbours [in British Togoland] had attained it?"[783] Therefore, the Fourth Committee should not accept Ajavon's proposal to agree to the election of a new Legislative Assembly on the condition that all amendments to the Statute would have to be approved by the present Legislative Assembly, since this would defeat the very purpose of new elections.

The question-and-answer session that followed shows how the representatives of the Fourth Committee, especially those from the anti-colonial states, were drawn into the opposition's securitising moves. The petitioners and the representatives engaged in a considerable number of brief exchanges on the disruption of political activities and on political persecution, violence, and imprisonment in French Togoland.[784] It was obvious that the petitioners of the opposition parties made quite an impression on the representatives of the Fourth Committee. Yet, in one instance Santos expressed his disappointment in the exchanges at the UN:

> "The only course open to the opposition, since it had renounced force or violence, was to appeal to the United Nations to organize free democratic elections under United Nations supervision. Those requests had been the object of various General Assembly resolutions, but as the desired result had not been obtained, they were renewed each year."[785]

The Indonesian representative, Imam Abikusno, was interested in probing the securitisation move undertaken by Olympio and raised the question whether the agitation of the opposition parties had been deliberately fomented before the arrival of the UN Visiting Commission to create the impression that there was no peace and order in French Togoland. Olympio countered that his party had never agreed with the French authorities' claim that visits by UN missions led to unrest. Rather, it had been the policy of the French authorities to discourage members of the Visiting Missions from attending rallies, on the (securitised) pretext that violence would occur. It was to the credit of the composition of the recent UN Visiting Commission, which unlike the regular Visiting Missions did not reflect a cross-section of the Trusteeship Council but of the Fourth Committee, that it had not been deterred by such threats and had participated in rallies without any disturbances.[786]

As foreseen by Olympio, at the end of the oral hearing, the French representative, Jacques Koscziusko-Morizet, put the blame regarding the excessive use of repression on new government of the Autonomous Republic as he stated that "France did not wish to intervene in purely Togoland affairs."[787] Koscziusko-Morizet insisted that...

> "the opposition which the petitioners represented was only a minority, and if the opposition in every country represented in the United Nations was invited to address the Committee he was sure that its remarks would often be more severely critical than

---

783 GAOR, "12th Session: 4th Committee" (1957), p. 241.
784 GAOR, "12th Session: 4th Committee" (1957), pp. 242–55.
785 GAOR, "12th Session: 4th Committee" (1957), p. 249.
786 GAOR, "12th Session: 4th Committee" (1957), p. 251.
787 GAOR, "12th Session: 4th Committee" (1957), p. 259.

those of the petitioners. It was not the function of the United Nations to help an opposition or a minority to gain power with the aid of the democratic system, but to promote the advancement of all territories."[788]

The Syrian representative, Jawdat Mufti, responded to this statement by paying tribute to the petitioners. He regretted that there had been attempts to discredit them and thus interfere with the right to petition enshrined in the Charter.[789]

General Debate

In the general debate, it became clear that many anti-colonial representatives suspected that France's stance was dictated by the intention to preserve the possibility of incorporating Togoland into the French Union after the termination of the Trusteeship Agreement. Yet, as a condition for this, the anti-colonial representatives insisted on new elections to the Legislative Assembly. The majority of the Fourth Committee agreed that terminating the Trusteeship Agreement before its objectives had been fully achieved was unacceptable and therefore considered Ajavon's condition that the Trusteeship Agreement be terminated automatically an ultimatum.[790] Aware that the two-thirds majority required to lift the Trusteeship Agreement could not be obtained, France was forced to concede and declared in the Assembly that it would transfer all powers to the Togolese government except for defence, foreign policy and currency, and that the Legislative Assembly should be re-elected by universal adult suffrage in 1958, while the government of the Autonomous Republic invited the UN to supervise these elections.

Following this concession, the Fourth Committee quickly adopted an amended version of a five-power draft resolution that free UN-supervised elections would clarify the domestic political situation in Togoland and resolve the issues of statute revision as well as the termination of trusteeship.[791] Finally, the Haitian representative, Max Dorsinville, was elected as Commissioner for the supervision of the 1958 elections to the Togolese Legislative Assembly.

For once, both the unificationists and the French and Togolese governments were somewhat satisfied with the compromise which had been achieved at the UN. For the time being, the unificationists had succeeded in stopping the attempt to integrate Togoland into the French Union, and thus the door for genuine independence and reunification of the Ewe people had been pushed open again. The UN-supervised elections would provide the first opportunity since 1952 to demonstrate the real strength of their electorate.

On the other hand, the General Assembly resolution meant that the UN practically recognized the institutions of the Statute and was now finally committed to terminating the Trusteeship Agreement within a year, and France was quite confident that her protégé parties would return to power.

---

788   GAOR, "12th Session: 4th Committee" (1957), p. 259.
789   GAOR, "12th Session: 4th Committee" (1957), p. 260.
790   GAOR, "12th Session: 4th Committee" (1957), p. 232.
791   A/C.4/L.508, submitted jointly by Canada, Colombia, Denmark, Ireland and Liberia. GAOR, "12th Session: 4th Committee" (1957), p. 335; GAOR, "12th Session: Plenary" (1957), pp. 554–57.

6.8.2 The Parliamentary Election in French Togoland (1958)

In 1958, for the second time ever in its long-lasting history of election observation, the United Nations was to oversee another election, and again in Togoland. The Haitian head of the mission, Max Dorsinville, left for Lomé on 28 February 1958 and was followed by his staff of 21 observers in early March. Initially, many misunderstood the role, which the Mission was to play in the elections, thinking that it was to organize the elections rather than the ruling pro-French authorities.

Photo 32: Bureau of UN Observation Mission (25 March 1958)[792]

Source: UN Photo.

Nonetheless, the mission not only oversaw and reported on the organisation of the elections, but also actively intervened in their conduct. One of Dorsinville's most important measures was the expansion of the electoral lists, which was virtually completed before the UN Commission arrived. Composed by the pro-French authorities, the electoral lists left out a considerable number of people, many of them were suspected supporters of the opposition who met all the electoral requirements. Accordingly, the CUT and Juvento complained to Dorsinville not to permit the use of the existing voter lists. Their request to compile a new electoral list was opposed by the pro-French Government. Since the

---

792 UN Commissioner Max Dorsinville (centre, hand in pocket), meets with local leaders of the opposition parties. Third from left is Mr. Dessou (in white robe), President of the Aného district of the CUT.

whole matter was pressed for time, Dorsinville resorted as a remedy to the procedure of "emergency registration,"[793] whereby individuals could register themselves with the local magistrate.

Photo 33: Emergency registration, Hall of Justice, Lomé (7 April 1958)

Source: UN Photo.

Thereupon, the unificationist parties conducted an effective campaign to encourage their supporters to register and vote. Amenumey has made an insightful quantitative evaluation of this process.[794] A total of 79,917 applications were submitted, of which 76,624, or nearly 96%, came from the Ewe-populated south from members of the opposition parties.[795] The majority of applications were from women. The total number of emergency registrations constituted about 20% of the voters already registered. Of the applications, 46,102 or about 58% were successful. Dorsinville attested that if more time had been available, many more potential voters likely would have been registered.[796] As 29,322

---

793   TCOR, "Report of the United Nations Commissioner for the Supervision of the Elections in Togoland under French Administration" T/1392 (1958), p. 20. para. 155.
794   Amenumey, *The Ewe Unification Movement*, p. 315.
795   TCOR, "Report of the United Nations Commissioner for the Supervision of the Elections in Togoland under French Administration" (1958), p. 17. para. 133–134.
796   TCOR, "Report of the United Nations Commissioner for the Supervision of the Elections in Togoland under French Administration" (1958), para. 141–142.

or 91% of the total 32,000 rejection notices were issued in the final two weeks preceding the election, suspicions arose those officials in charge of voter registration had intentionally neglected their duties. In response, the Togolese trade union federation threatened a general strike just days before the election. The pro-French Grunitzky-Government considered the threat a maneuver by the opposition and asked Dorsinville to intervene with the Union and avert the strike. The strike was eventually called off, and 490,796 voters, or 44% of an estimated total population of 1,111,068 were registered.

The 1958 election campaign was basically fought on the same issue as the 1956 referendum. The PTP, UCPN and their ancillary parties supported the Statute, close association with France and called for an immediate termination of trusteeship, which they argued was incompatible with the regime established by the Statute. The CUT and Juvento, on the other hand, advocated for the continuation of trusteeship until full independence was achieved. Remarkably, the reunification of the Ewe or the two Togolands was not at the forefront of their campaign. The already completed incorporation of British Togoland into Ghana had given the chances of reunification a different spin, although in some of the villages, posters in favour of unification were constantly to be seen.

Nevertheless, the election campaign was vigorous, and the presence of United Nations observers has not encouraged either the ruling or opposition parties to exercise restraint. As usual, the CUT and Juvento were not able to use the same public facilities as the pro-French parties. Furthermore, they were facing the hostility of chiefs previously appointed by the French administration and subject to administrative harassment such as verification of permits by their police, the so-called *gardes-cercle*. At the request of the Togolese Government, three platoons of French West African auxiliaries were requested from the High Commissioner in Dakar. One platoon was stationed at Mango and the other two at Lomé.[797]

In the capital city of Lomé, an organised gang of 50–200 opposition supporters, who were armed with pocket-knives, apparently aimed to provoke disturbances and bloodshed whenever members of the PTP and UCPN organised a public meeting. The French accused the CUT of electoral intimidation: "Not content with holding conferences in major centres and tackling them not only in the Togolese Government but also in France, the CUT leaders have undertaken a real campaign of intimidation threatening to retaliate against those who would vote for Progress [PTP]."[798]

For the French, the elections represented a test by which world opinion would judge French politics in Africa.[799] Although the French assumed that their protégés parties would win the election, they helped matters along by adopting older ploys. Already before the arrival of Max Dorsinville in February 1958, the Juvento newspaper *Denyigba* was banned.[800] According to Joël Glasman, the Jacques Foccart's archives also show how the

---

797   MAE (La Courneuve), 77QO-13, *Élections de 1958, travaux du Conseil de Tutelle*, Borderau N° 83, April 1958, p. 4.

798   MAE (La Courneuve), 77QO-13, *Élections de 1958, travaux du Conseil de Tutelle*, Minister of Overseas France to Minister of External Affairs, 9 April 1958, p. 3.

799   MAE (La Courneuve), 77QO-13, *Élections de 1958, travaux du Conseil de Tutelle*, Cablegram, de la part de Kosczuisko-Morizet, 14 Feburary 1958.

800   Amenumey, "The General Elections in the 'Autonomous Republic of Togo', April 1958," p. 58.

French tried to rig the elections by paying money from secret funds to chiefs and notables to encourage voters to make the 'right choice.' A letter from the High Commissioner regarding the 1958 elections, which reported on the amount of money paid, stated that "it would be very desirable that this report be burned."[801] In an issue of newspaper *Pravda* the former Daily Telegraph correspondent, Russell Howe, quotes an UN observer that "This election [...] is so crooked you could walk along it without going in the same direction twice."[802] Furthermore, the authorities closed the border with Ghana several days before election day, so that several hundred vehicles were stuck on the Ghanaian side of the border. Especially for French-Togolese unification supporters, it was not uncommon to live on the other side of the border. Many of them were prevented from voting. On the other hand, 45 vehicles from Dahomey, transporting voters on behalf of Nicholas Grunitzky, entered the area on election day. Thus, despite the presence of UN observers, both the CUT and Juvento were critical of the way in which the pre-electoral proceedings had been conducted.

Photo 34: Line-up during election day, Agabadelogan (27 April 1958)

Source: UN Photo.

But the election turned out differently than everyone had predicted. Overall, the result was a landslide victory for CUT and Juvento. With 64% of the 311,019 votes cast, they won a total of 29 seats, or nearly two-thirds of the total 45 seats in the Legislative Assembly.

The results confirmed the CUT and Juvento's claims that they indeed represented the majority opinion in the country and not the French protégé parties. The French had hoped that the elections would confirm the results of the 1956 referendum on the Statute and the incorporation of Togoland into the French Union, but now the results called them into question. The result furthermore questioned the validity of the elections in the

---

801   Glasman, *Les corps habillés au Togo.*, p. 228, footnote 43.
802   MAE (La Courneuve), 77QO-5, *Politique intérieure*, p. 226.

trusteeship territory of French Cameroon, and led to suspicions regarding the representativeness of Legislative Assemblies in French colonial territories in general. The Ashanti Pioneer even went as far as to consider the parliamentary election in French Togoland as the precedent in the undoing of French colonial policy at large.[803] Furthermore, the French feared that with the help of the Ghanaian Ewes the new Togolese government could reach an agreement with Ghana of mutual, economic, and military support. An independent Togo would probably ask to join the zone of the pound sterling.

Photo 35: CUT and Juvento supporters celebrating, Lomé (1 May 1958)

Source: UN Photo.

The French High Commissioner, Georges Spénale, was expressively contemplative:

"It is probably too early to fully analyse the causes of the government's defeat and all its consequences – even considering only TOGO. First of all, it must be noted that everyone was wrong: the Government, the Heads of Constituency, the UN Observers, the mission leaders, the opposition itself."[804]

---

803 *Ashanti Pioneer*, "French Policy on Test," 30 April 1958
804 Translation of MAE (La Courneuve), 77QO-13, *Élections de 1958, travaux du Conseil de Tutelle*, Secret Letter 312/CAB, Spénale to Ministre de la France d'Outre-Mer, 28 April 1959, pp. 1–2.

Map 10: French Togoland Parliamentary Elections (1958)

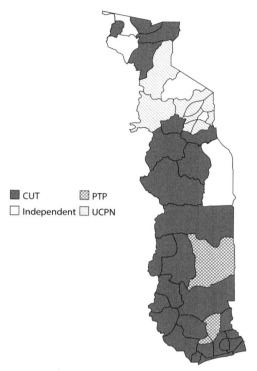

Source: Gayibor (2005), p. 656.

For the French, the result was completely incomprehensible. Not even Spénale was able to recognize that the French administration's repressive and electorally exclusionary policies of recent years were self-blinding:

> "Africans – and at least Togolese – even those in the most remote parts of the bush, are now able to radically change their political feelings without any administrative, customary, governmental or opposition observers being able to take off the scale of these changes. The fact that such surprises from one end of the Territory to the other show that the phenomenon is widespread: a large number of African voters have learned to hide their political feelings to the polls."[805]

Ginette Kponton pointed out that one of the reasons for the surprise during the 1958 Legislative Assembly election was probably the female vote. Due to the traditional division of labour in Togoland, women engaged in a disproportionately high number of activities as market traders. Due to economic interest, female traders favoured open borders

---

805   MAE (La Courneuve), 77QO-13, *Élections de 1958, travaux du Conseil de Tutelle*, Secret Letter 312/CAB, Spénale to Ministre de la France d'Outre-Mer, 28 April 1959, p. 6.

with the Western neighbour or even better: unification. In a society based on orality, like Togoland, markets were hubs of slogans, where CUT and Juvento political propaganda was spread through informal conversations with neighbouring market women.[806] The majority of market women, who spread political word and ideas, saw no gain from the administrative clique of the pro-French PTP or UCPN.

Photo 36: *Juventists singing party song on election eve (26 April 1958)*

Source: UN Photo.

The French were not aware of this development because during past elections in French Togoland a large number of female voters followed Juvento's and CUT's call for boycott. It was not until the 1958 elections that the boycott was lifted due to UN election monitoring and the floodgates of female CUT and Juvento supporters were opened.

In this present study, which is devoted to a history of silence, it should not be omitted that in the unification movement, too, it was primarily men who as petitioners, political actors, and negotiators, elbowed their way into the foreground of historiography. Nevertheless, the CUT and Sylvanus Olympio owe their rise to electoral power largely to women, who thus also set the course of Togo's historical rise to independent statehood.

6.8.3 Termination of Trusteeship & Independence

Since Olympio's conviction in May 1954, he was prohibited from running for elective office. Yet, the Statute did not stipulate that the Prime Minister must be a member of the

---

806 Ginette A. Kponton, "La Femme Dans La Lutte Pour La Décolonisation (1946–1960)," in Gayibor, *Les Togolais Face À La Colonisation*, Vol, pp. 218–19.

Legislative Assembly. Thus, after the election results were announced, the French High Commissioner, Spénale, auditioned the leader of the new parliamentary majority party, that is, Olympio, and appointed him Prime Minister, who was unanimously confirmed by the Legislative Assembly. Jonathan Savi de Tové, founding member of the CUT, was elected President of the Chamber.

Olympio did not consider upsetting the French. In his inauguration speech on 16 May 1958, he declared that: "In an independent Togo, France will be the most favoured nation, and my government will endeavour to improve the opportunities for real co-operation between the two countries".[807]

In August 1958, the Legislative Assembly (now renamed Chamber of Deputies) adopted a motion authorizing the Togolese Government to open negotiations with the French Government on the future modifications to the Statute. Two things were of import: First, after the 1958 elections, it was not the Ministry for Overseas France anymore that was responsible for Togoland affairs, but the Foreign Ministry took the helm of Franco-Togolese relations. This took a lot of colonial clings out of the negotiations. Second, the April 1958 elections virtually coincided with de Gaulle's return to power and the impending establishment of the Fifth Republic. This new French government had much less to do with the period of repressive measures against the CUT and Juvento. It approved the main amendments to the statute, including Togo's independence in 1960 and the consequent termination of the Trusteeship Agreement. On 23 October 1958, Togo's Chamber of Deputies adopted a resolution proclaiming the decision in favour of complete independence. The resolution proposed 1960 as the year for its fulfilment and requested the UN General Assembly to maintain trusteeship until that date.

When in October, the Trusteeship Council met for its 8th Special Session (1958) to examine the results of the parliamentary elections in French Togoland, the chairman of the UN electoral observation mission, Max Dorsinville, felt justified in saying that "the mere presence of the United Nations mission had helped to create circumstances favourable to the free expression of the people's will."[808] The French representative, Jacques Kosciusko-Morizet, lay out the transfer of power and the inauguration of the CUT under the leadership of the new Prime Minister, Sylvanus Olympio, and the decision that the trusteeship territory would become independent in 1960.[809] On 17 October 1958, the Council unanimously recommended to the General Assembly to take steps to terminate the Trusteeship Agreement in 1960 upon the attainment of independence by Togo.[810]

A month later, in November 1958, Olympio reappeared solemnly before Fourth Committee (no longer as a petitioner but as the incarnation of his country), where ("avec plaisir"[811]) he accepted the invitation to sit on the benches of the French delegation – just like the pro-French anti-unificationists before him.

---

807 Togo Legislative Assembly, "2nd Legislature: Debats" (1958).
808 TCOR, "8th Special Session" (1958), p. 1.
809 TCOR, "8th Special Session" (1958), pp. 2–3.
810 TCOR, "8th Special Session" (1958), p. 9.
811 GAOR, "13th Session: Plenary" (1958), p. 437.

Photo 37: Olympio (with nameplate of France), 4th Committee (3 November 1958)

Source: UN Photo.

On 14 November 1958, the UN General Assembly approved the joint proposal of France and Togo to proclaim independence on 27 April 1960,[812] that is, exactly two years after the electoral victory of the CUT.

With the independence of the "Republic of Togo" a subsidiary aim of the unificationists was achieved. Two main factors were responsible for this success. On the one hand, it was the determination and constant securitising efforts by the unificationist petitioners, above all Sylvanus Olympio, and on the other hand, the attitude of their audience – the anti-colonial states in the General Assembly of the United Nations, which resisted the French plan to declare trusteeship over.

The April 1958 elections came just before de Gaulle's return to power and the establishment of the Fifth Republic. It was thus also the temporally coincidental change in French colonial policy that contributed to Togo's genuine independence because the fall of the Fourth Republic and de Gaulle's reoriented 'decolonisation' policy radically modified French policies and motives in colonial matters. In the hope of peace in Algeria, the French Union was reshaped. While a first phase of the French Union's assimilation policy established at the Brazzaville Conference created territorial assemblies in Overseas France, this was abandoned in favour of a second phase of autonomy policy. The *loi-cadre* was intended to allow territories to establish their own local administrations. France's new Constitution of 1958 replaced the French Union with the French Community. However, the French Community dissolved amid the Algerian War, almost all other African colonies were granted independence in 1960 after local referendums. Yet, Togo's independence left unresolved the efforts of some Togoland and Ewe unificationists. The problem of unifying the Ewe remained: Only the UN, whose goodwill Olympio wanted to maintain at all costs, could enable him to fulfil his wishes in this matter.

---

812   GAOR, "13th Session: Plenary" (1958), p. 437.

6.9 Post-Independence Conflict

For Nkrumah, the last and only obstacle for complete Ghana-Togoland unification were seemingly the French. With Olympio's electoral victory, after all a leader of the unification movement, and (French) Togoland's imminent independence, this obstacle seemed to be overcome in due course. Thus, Nkrumah congratulated Olympio on his electoral success and announced his intention to maintain good relations with the new Togolese government, hoping to solve the division of the Ewe by removing the "'irksome custom barriers' and frontier tribal problems."[813] Yet, ever since Nkrumah embarked on a relentless 'Africa must unite' campaign against what he called 'tribalism,' it was clear that he was not so much interested in uniting the Ewe as in expanding Ghana's territory under a unitary constitution.

Nkrumah's interest in African unity was based on the view that African states could not prevail individually and should unite to protect themselves against 'balkanization.' He, thus, adopted the securitising argument that had been advanced by the British and French colonial powers since the establishment of the Trusteeship System to argue *against* Ewe and Togoland unification. It was clear, then, that Nkrumah was using the Ewe unification argument only as a pretext to press on French Togoland's integration into Ghana. Besides, since the leaking of *Most Secret*, among the unificationists at least, Nkrumah carried a reputation of undertaking a sort of "black imperialism."[814]

Olympio, in turn, whose reputation as a nationalist leader was built in opposition to French policy, reconsidered his attitude toward France and within days of his electoral victory in 1958, issued statements expressing his desire to cooperate with the trusteeship power, while proposing Nkrumah to establish merely a customs union between the two countries for the time being.

As Amenumey remarked, clearly, after the unificationists' long and bitter struggle against the French, the CUT leadership was not ready to give up its sovereignty before it had a taste of it.[815] For the readership of the American *Foreign Affairs* magazine, Olympio put his stance towards Nkrumah's pan-African aspirations this way:

"Achieved at great sacrifice, such a reward [(independence)] is not to be cast away lightly; nor should the national will, once unified, be diluted by the formation of nebulous political units. [...] Furthermore, few serious governments would be willing to relinquish their hard-won seats in international councils, seats which permit them to be heard and which grant them *the moral security provided by access to world opinion*."[816]

This assessment was undoubtedly grounded in his own experience of campaigning before the UN Trusteeship Council and the General Assembly, in which the unificationists felt abandoned by Nkrumah's CPP.

---

813   *The Times*, "Telegrams in Brief," 27 May 1958.
814   TNA (London), CO 554/667, *Togoland Administration*, Confidential Letter [334], Mathieson to Wilson, 14 December 1953, p. 2.
815   Amenumey, *The Ewe Unification Movement*, p. 338.
816   Emphasis added, Sylvanus E. Olympio, "African Problems and the Cold War," *Foreign Affairs* 40, no. 1 (1961): 51.

Thus, on the surface, it seemed as if the tables had turned: the former unificationist, Olympio, opposed Nkrumah's versions of African Unity, and Nkrumah, who had hampered Ewe and Togoland unification once pursued by Olympio, now vigorously advocated it. Yet, it soon became apparent that the Togoland-Ghana border no longer separated two currencies and two administrations, it separated two regimes and two ambitions: on the one hand, in Togoland, the 'Brazilian' elite, that is, a bourgeois oligarchy that adhered to economic liberalism, and on the other, in Ghana, a government that made blatant territorial claims and was on its way to socialist rule and an authoritarian regime.

While Olympio favoured merely a loose customs union, Nkrumah rejected the idea of anything less than Togo-Ghana unification in a unitary state. Nkrumah extended an invitation to a joint meeting between the two heads of state on 17 July 1958 in Sogakofe, halfway between Lomé and Accra, to clarify the differences in opinion. Yet, when Olympio did not show up, Nkrumah's relationship with Olympio soured dramatically.[817]

As mentioned previously, at the beginning of 1958, the Nkrumah government already took arbitrary measures against former unificationists, some of which appeared together with Olympio before the UN General Assembly. First, the *Avoidance of Discrimination Act* banned political organizations of regional and ethnic orientation, forcing the Togoland Congress and the All-Ewe Conference in a political union within the *United Party*. Then, the passing of the *Preventive Detention Act* in July 1958 enabled the arrest of members of the former Togoland Congress and the All-Ewe Conference.[818] The Togolese Government granted asylum to a number of individuals, who Nkrumah considered enemies of Ghana, including Ametowobla, Antor, and Ayeke, all of whom petitioned for Togoland unification side by side with Olympio before the General Assembly.

Yet, the trickle of refugees across the border has been a two-way one. After the electoral victory of April 1958, many CUT and Juvento supporters vented their desire for retribution for the past years of oppression. In one instance, the local CUT leader of Kpalimé, Chief Kofi Apetor II, organised gangs that called themselves "Ablodé Sodzawo" (Freedom Soldiers) – in Kpalimé itself and in the entire Kloto District – to beat members of the PTP, break their houses and cause damages on their farms. For example, Adassou Bernabé was one of those PTP members that was instated by the French government as Divisional Chief of Akata Agame, Kloto District. Following the April 1958 election, Bernabé sought refuge in Ghana stating to the Ghanaian authorities:

> "On 2nd May 1958, [...] the terrorists summoned me to appear before them, at the meeting they ordered me to kneel down and to prostrate under a mat on which a white flag was spread out. I carried out their orders. They then declared that from that day I have become their slave and that the elections had proved it. [...] As it became clear that the Government of the Republic of Togoland itself was the author of these irregularites and therefore could not take steps to stop them, I was obliged to fly [sic!] to Ghana that night with my wife, to seek refuge."[819]

---

817 MAE (La Courneuve), 77QO-5, *Politique intérieure*, Paul Henry, 1 August 1985.

818 By 1961, 5,700 unificationists were thereby forced to flee to independent French Togo to avoid imprisonment. Skinner, *The Fruits of Freedom in British Togoland*, p. 170.

819 PRAAD (Ho), D-DA-368, *Frontier Incidents Ghana / Togoland*, 1958, Bernabe to District Commissioner Ho,

Bernabé and other PTP refugees appealed to the new Regional Commissioner for Ghana-Eweland for whom the Ghanaian government appointed of all people Krobo Edusei, until recently the Ghanaian Minister of Interior.[820] Consequently, the Ghanaian authorities viewed the PTP refugees as collaborators with the French colonial power and had little sympathy for them. Rather, the local administrators viewed them suspiciously as a threat:

> "I don't think we can do anything in this matter since they are non-Ghanaians, other than to acknowledge receipt of their letters and to express our sympathy. But if in the interest of security, you wish to know more about the trouble in the Kloto area i.e. in the neighbourhood of Kpedze, you might invite them to your office to give them audience. [...] the question of their repatriation and their homes was a matter they have to take up with the French Ambassador in Ghana. Whilst they remain in Ghana they would be under very close observation. To be on the safe side, I think that the R.C. [Regional Commissioner, Krobo Edusei] should be informed that such persons are residing in the district and that he should take any security precautions he might think necessary."[821]

Relations between the Nkrumah- and Olympio-government did not improve when in October 1958, during a tour of Trans-Volta-Togoland (TVT), Edusei accused the Togolese authorities of subversive activities in former British Togoland and threatened with severe prison sentences any Ghanaian who travelled to French Togoland for political contacts or was found in possession of a photograph of Olympio or CUT membership cards.[822] The measures were clearly directed against former Ewe-unificationists and allies of Olympio.

Trouble at Home

Olympio, meanwhile, showed himself to be unimpressed by the measures, stating several times that he did not believe that Ghana would attempt military annexation. Moreover, during the same time, his government was struggling at home and the French were trying to convince Olympio that it was much more likely that the Togolese government would be overthrown through subversive means.

Olympio's government had inherited an explosive social question from the French. In the 1958 parliamentary elections, the pro-French PTP and UCPN were also voted out of office because many people hoped that with the CUT in power things would change quickly, namely more employment and better pay. Yet, for an experienced businessman like Olympio, after the hard struggle for Togo's political independence, it was only natural that he did not want Togo to fall back into economic dependence on France right away. Since the CFA franc was difficult to convert, Togo was forced to sell all Togolese products to France and in return to buy all imports from there. Olympio therefore intended to join the pound sterling zone in order to be able to buy goods anywhere on the world market

---

820 TNA (London), CO 554/667, *Togoland Administration*, Notes by Mr. T. G. Brierly, 31 December 1958, p. 2.
821 PRAAD (Ho), D-DA-368, *Frontier Incidents Ghana / Togoland*, handwritten note VRG /2/119, p. 1.
822 TNA (London), FO 371/138262, *Internal political situation in Togoland. Code JF file 1019*, 1959, Notes by Mr. T. G. Brierly, p. 2.

and truly retain Togo's independence. Thus, in order to ensure economic independence and not have to rely too much on French FIDES credits, Olympio's government had to adopt a strict policy of austerity, including severe budget cuts and a raise of taxes.

While the British were impressed by Olympio's "remarkable housekeeping",[823] the left-leaning Juvento found Olympio's conservative market-liberal course repugnant and grew disillusioned of Olympio's close political collaboration with the trusteeship power and his non-alignment with Nkrumah's' pan-African movement. In December 1958, informants of the French Embassy in Ghana reported that the Juvento section, which was linked to the CPP and supportive of Nkrumah's demand for complete Togo-Ghana integration, was preparing a coup against Olympio's government in early January 1959. In the absence of Nkrumah, the conspirators were reportedly received by the Ghanaian Minister of Foreign Affairs, Kodjo Botsio, who discouraged his interlocutors and refused to provide them with the arms, which they asked for. The British High Commissioner in Accra, Arthur Wendell Snelling, was impressed that French "sources of information on what goes on along the border are extremely good – so good as to be a source of annoyance to the Ghanaians."[824] The French diplomats did not take the plot serious and considered the would-be-insurgents to be dreamers.

Yet, when the French SDECE officer reported the plot to the High Commissioner of French Togoland, Georges Spénale, the security-intelligence agent must have laid on too much since Spénale considered the conspiracy more serious than the diplomats at the French embassy in Accra that received originally the intelligence. Within days, Spénale mobilized a company of paratroopers from Cotonou of neighbouring French Dahomey, bringing the Togolese government to a "war footing."[825]

Though, in the end, nothing occurred on the suspected day of the plot, the incident was a minor media disaster for the French trusteeship power. An article of the *Times Magazine* insinuated that despite French Togoland's impending independence, the French Administering Authority was moving troops there without consulting Togoland's Prime Minister, Olympio. Ben Apaloo, the Juvento leader, accused the French of faking the news of a plot to topple the Togolese government, using it as a pretext to play up the threat of subversion and the need of close association with France.[826] From the perspective of the Paris School of Critical Security Studies, this was clearly a security theatre. But Olympio did not resist the security measures in any way.[827]

Unity among the nationalists was already showing cracks but Olympio's approval of the deployment of the paratroopers was one of the last straws that broke the camel's back. In May 1959, Anani Santos, a major Juvento figurehead and former companion

---

823   TNA (London), DO 35/9278, *Future of Togoland*, 1960, Watson to Ewart-Biggs, 24 March 1960.
824   TNA (London), FO 371/138262, *Internal political situation in Togoland*. Code JF file 1019, Secret Letter, Maclennen to Lintott, 15 Januar 1959, p. 1.
825   MAE (La Courneuve), 77QO-5, *Politique intérieure*, Letter, Ambasade de France au Ghana, 21 January 1959, pp. 1–3.
826   ILRM (New York Public Library), b. 4, *Togoland*, Motion adoptée par le bureau directeur de la "Juvento", 12 January 1959.
827   MAE (La Courneuve), 77QO-5, *Politique intérieure*, Letter, Ambasade de France au Ghana, 21 January 1959, pp. 1–3.

of Olympio, resigned as Minister of Public Works, Mines, Transport and Communication. Two months later, Juvento broke with the CUT. By December 1959, Anani Santos and Firmin Abalo were excluded from the CUT parliamentary group.[828] Olympio's former political companions were now political opponents. Juvento made a tactical alliance with the northern-based opposition, *the Union Démocratique des Peuples Togolais* (UDPT), itself a merger of PTP and UCPN, to form under the leadership of Ben Apaloo the *Mouvement Nationaliste Togolais-Juvento*.

Looking for Security Alliances

In August 1959, the Nkrumah government changed the name of Trans-Volta-Togoland (TVT) simply to "Volta Region," thereby eliminating the name "Togoland" altogether, vindicating those unificationists, who argued that British Togoland would be deprived of its identity. The renaming of the region was only a foretaste of Nkrumah's public declaration in October 1959 at a public meeting in Ho, the capital of what was now the Volta Region, that (French) Togoland in turn would now become "the seventh province of Ghana."[829]

It was then, that Olympio seriously began to look for an insurance of Togo's security and integrity. Olympio took the opportunity of the visit by UN Secretary-General, Dag Hammarskjöld, to Lomé at the end of December 1959, calling for assurances that Togo would never be annexed by Ghana.[830] Hammarskjöld reportedly assured that the Security Council would meet within 72 hours of an invasion, and that a United Nations force would be on its way within the week.[831]

But only a few weeks before the scheduled independence of the Republic of Togo, Ghanaian ministers intensified their threats. On 5 March 1960, the Ghanaian Minister of Finance (and former AEC member), Komla Gbedemah, declared at Aflao, just a stone's throw away from Lomé, that Togo will be integrated with Ghana "whether it likes it or not."[832] On the same occasion, Nathaniel Welbeck, the Ghanaian Minister of State, exclaimed "Togoland, Togoland, your days are numbered; people of Lomé, unless you act at once, Mr. Olympio will lead you into slavery."[833] Two days later, on 7 March 1960, the Ghanaian Government revealed a pamphlet entitled *Government Proposals for a Republican Constitution*, which was allegedly "designed to enable peoples who are at present outside Ghana but who are linked by family and historical connexion, with Ghanaian peoples to join them in one integrated State."[834] Another three days later, on 10 March 1960, the Ghanaian government sent a memorandum to the French embassy in Accra, claiming

---

828 ANF (Pierrefitte-sur-Seine), AG/5(F)/1209, *Dossiers de C. Rostain*, Situation hebdomadaire N°3, Semaine du 5 au 11 décembre; MAE (La Courneuve), 77QO-5, *Politique intérieure*, Prime Minister to Minister of Foreign Affairs, 9 September 1959.
829 As cited in Welch, *Dream of Unity*, p. 142.
830 Michel, "The Independence of Togo," p. 316.
831 Warren Howe, "Togo: Four Years of Military Rule," p. 9.
832 TNA (London), DO 35/9278, *Future of Togoland*, Russel Howe to Lord Home, 2 May 1960, p. 1.
833 TNA (London), FO 371/146938, *Dispute about Togoland between France and Ghana*, 1960, Bérard and Kosczius ko-Morizet to UN Secretary-General, 24 March 1960, p. 2.
834 TNA (London), FO 371/146938, *Dispute about Togoland between France and Ghana*, bérard and Kosczius ko-Morizet to UN Secretary-General, 24 March 1960, p. 2.

that it came into the possession of a draft constitution for the future independent Republic of Togo, which allegedly claimed the former British Togoland as part of its territory. The Nkrumah-Government accused the Olympio-government of preparing military measures, including the training of refugees for armed incursions into the territory of Ghana.[835] The French responded perplexed that the revised Togo Statute was still in force and a draft constitution hasn't even been negotiated yet. Nonetheless, the French were seriously worried. As the Trusteeship Agreement was still in force, France, as Administering Authority, was still responsible for the peace and security in French Togoland – after all, the primary objective of the Trusteeship System – and involved the UN Secretary-General.[836]

After these verbal attacks and made-up accusations, the Olympio-government deliberated with the leaders of the short-lived Federation of Mali whether to organize the former French colonies in Africa into a defence pact under which a military attack on one member state would be considered an attack on all, that is, Olympio imagined an African equivalent of the NATO and the Warsaw Pact.[837] Olympio regarded such an alliance as an insurance against any military adventure by Ghana into a neighbouring francophone African state. Such a possibility did not seem that unlikely anymore, when Nkrumah ordered the Ghanaian army to hold its annual exercises from 22 to 28 March 1960 in the Volta Region, merely sixteen kilometres from the Togoland-Ghana border and only a month from Togo's independence.

Thus, on the eve of Togo's independence, the atmosphere was tense. Ghanaian police reports show that in the middle of March 1960, Olympio, his ministers, and the French seriously anticipated that Ghana was preparing to launch a military attack on Togoland and annex it. The French moved sizable bodies of troops from Dahomey and other parts of West Africa into French Togoland, reinforcing the garrison at Lomé. These troop movements were apparently inspired by the Ghanaian security measures at the frontier and by the military exercises in the Volta Region. Fortunately, tension relaxed when it became clear that after the military maneuver the Ghanaian Army returned to the barracks and by the end of the month most of the French reinforcements returned to Dahomey.[838]

Nonetheless, on the advice of Jaques Foccart, the French government proposed a Defence Agreement to Olympio.[839] Previously, Olympio had made it clear that he was not prepared to bind himself too closely the French as a protection against Ghana. Indeed, since no coup took place a year earlier, he was aware that the French have done their best to play this threat up to him.[840] Despite his reservations about a too strong French influence, Olympio felt compelled to conclude a military agreement with France. If Nkrumah

---

835 TNA (London), FO 371/146938, *Dispute about Togoland between France and Ghana*, Annex I, Ministry of Foreign Affairs, 10 March 1960, pp. 1–3.
836 TNA (London), FO 371/146938, *Dispute about Togoland between France and Ghana*, Bérard and Koscziusko-Morizet to UN Secretary-General, 24 March 1960, p. 2.
837 *New York Times*, "Alliance Is Aired in French Africa," 12 March 1960
838 TNA (London), DO 35/9278, *Future of Togoland*, Secret Letter (ACC.80/42/5), 4 April 1960, p. 2.
839 ANF (Pierrefitte-sur-Seine), AG/5(F)/1209, *Dossiers de C. Rostain*, Rendu du Conseil restreint, 11 April 1960.
840 TNA (London), DO 35/9278, *Future of Togoland*, Telegram N° 48 Saving, 4 May 1960.

had gone over to enforcing his ideas militarily, the small state of Togo, whose foreign policy orientation was based on neutrality and whose troop strength amounted to 120 men, would have had no way of defending itself against the superior strength of the Ghanaian army.

Table 5: Togolese Security Personnel after Independence[841]

Togolese Gendarmerie	65
Gendarmerie (French Community)	45
AOF Forces (from outside Togo)	250
French Military Personnel	50
Togolese Guard (distributed throughout Togo)	655
Total Security Forces	1.065

Source: TNA (London), FO 371/147612, Internal political situation, 1960, Togoland Affairs, p. 2.

Hence, the only option was to lean on France for defence. Thus, as relations with Ghana continued to deteriorate, Olympio declared shortly before independence that an independent Togo would consider some sort of pact with France in light of Nkrumah's expansionist threats. Though, the defence agreement with France was not to be concluded until late 1961, after an exchange of letters on defence in May 1960, Olympio declared, "for the moment this agreement is in force and we can say, as the English say, that 'it takes care of the defence.'"[842]

Olympio's Security-Independence-Dilemma

For Olympio, however, this arrangement created the problem that even after Togo's former independence, issues of external defence and security remained the responsibility of and depended on the former trusteeship power, France. Olympio faced a dilemma: on the one hand, he wanted an army that was trained to the best available standards to safeguard Togo from a Ghanaian attack, but on the other hand he wanted this army to be a national one. While Olympio sought independence from France, the entire security system (standards, equipment, personnel, and management) was modelled after the French army, and Togo lacked qualified personnel to replace the French specialized advisors.[843]

Needless to say, an independent Togo needed forces of order. Upon his electoral victory in 1958, Olympio established a large Ministry of Interior (including Information and Press), which he entrusted to Paulin Freitas (1958–1960) and after independence to

---

841 TNA (London), FO 371/147612, *Internal political situation*, 1960, Togoland Affairs, p. 2.
842 ANF (Pierrefitte-sur-Seine), AG/5(F)/1887, *Contexte politique des relations bilatérales*, Accords Franco-Togolais (1963), July 1963.
843 Sylvanus E. Olympio, "Allocution Mensuelle Du Président Olympio: 24 Novembre 1961," in *Quelques Discours Importants du Président Sylvanus Olympio en 1961*, ed. Republique Togolaise (Lomé, 1962), pp. 50–52.

Théophile Mally (1960–1963).[844] Nonetheless, Olympio wanted to send a clear signal that he wanted to break with French colonial policy, civilianize the formerly oppressive security forces and, thus, show that the police forces under his government were different from the colonial forces of order. In June 1959, Olympio announced that the whole police force should be re-organised, beginning with the establishment of a police school with qualified and able instructors to train higher school certificate holders as police officers.[845] Yet, in order to implement its budget plans, the number of state employees had to be reduced. Since the forces of order made up one-third of the state workforce, they suffered particularly from the downsizing. In June 1960, Olympio created the *Sûreté National Togolaise*,[846] thereby dissolving the *gardes-cercles*, who were composed of former riflemen of the *Battalion Autonome du Dahomey*, a unit of the French colonial infantry troops, who, despite their lack of education, were thus able to make a good living. Olympio thought that the uneducated were easier enlisted for the repressions of the French colonial policy. Therefore, Olympio envisaged "an intellectual police,"[847] giving preference to teachers for the recruitment of the police and the armed forces and recruitment was done more and more systematically through written selection procedures. Those *gardes-cercle* that were over 37 years of age, did not speak enough French, or were not approved by the Ministry of Interior, were, thus, not integrated into the new security structure and found themselves unemployed. For quite a few, this effectively closed off one of the few opportunities to make a good living despite a lack of education. Olympio's rapid reform of the security sector continued a policy of bureaucratization, thereby devaluing martial capital which caused growl among the former forces of order as they found themselves with less perspective of employment.

After independence, he placed Kleber Dadjo, the commander of the Togolese Guard, a military unit, not under the authority of the Ministry of Defence but directly under the authority of the new Minister of Interior, Théophile Mally. Following the French model, the infantry and the Gendarmerie were under the authority of the Ministry of Defence, yet the National Security and the Togolese Guard were controlled by the Ministry of Interior.

6.9.1 Repressive Tit-For-Tat (1960-1962)

While the Ghanaian Government spiked the security situation with the pronouncement of threats on the eve of Togo's independence, its attempt to frighten the neighbour into giving up sovereignty only served to heighten the latter's sense of national identity. This seemed to bring Nkrumah "to realise that mere Hitlerian shouting would not achieve his object."[848] So he did an unusual about-face: On 11 June 1960, six weeks after Togo's inde-

---

844 Decalo, *Historical dictionary of Togo*, p. 138.
845 Johnson Adjei, "Togo Prepares for the Big Day," *Daily Graphic*, 23 June 1959; in MAE (La Courneuve), 77QO-4, *Politique intérieure*.
846 ANT (Lomé), 2APA Kloto – 108, *Sûreté Nationale*, Decrée N° 60–58, 18 June 1960.
847 Glasman, *Les corps habillés au Togo*, p. 279.
848 TNA (London), FO 371/155660, *Political relations: Commonwealth countries.*, 1961, Confidential Letter WA 10/158/2, High Commissioner in Ghana to Secretary of State, p. 1.

pendence, Nkrumah made a private surprise visit by car to Lomé to ameliorate relations between Ghana and Togo.

Photo 38: Prime Ministers Olympio & Nkrumah, Lomé (11 June 1960)

Source: Republique Togolaise, *Quelques Discours Importants du Président Sylvanus Olympio en 1961* (Lomé, 1962).

According to the Ghanaian version of the meeting, Nkrumah proposed a political union between Ghana and Togo, to which Olympio replied that it would be wiser to start with economic cooperation. It was agreed that Olympio would table definite proposals for closer economic ties between the two countries. Yet, no proposals were forthcoming, and when Olympio was reminded of his promise at the beginning of August 1960, he replied that he preferred to wait until Nigeria achieved independence and then have a three-nation meeting.[849] This rebuff made Nkrumah reputedly so enraged that in the following month, in September 1960, the Ghanaian Government had the Ghana-Togo bor-

---

849   TNA (London), FO 371/155660, *Political relations: Commonwealth countries.*, Confidential Letter WA 10/158/2, High Commissioner in Ghana to Secretary of State, p. 1.

der closed entirely. On both sides of the frontier, this measure certainly caused hardship to the many people who were dependent upon the trade across it. Furthermore, all civil servants in Ghana of Togolese nationality or descent were requested to declare themselves citizens of Ghana or citizens of Togo in which latter case they had to take an Oath of Allegiance. At first no explanation had been given to these measures, but on 19 December 1960, Nkrumah stated publicly that they had been imposed…

> "to bring home clearly and unmistakably, that the union of Ghana and Togo is natural and inevitable […] This action has brought home as forcibly no other action could, the hardships and absurdity involved in maintaining an artificial frontier between us, and in proving to Premier Sylvanus Olympio that Togo and Ghana are one, and that no amount of lies and deception to the people of Togo can disprove this fact."[850]

The irony of this statement lies in the fact that, because of Nkrumah's escalation of the conflict, the 'artificial frontier' became more pronounced after independence than it was during colonial times.

Olympio retaliates

In the meantime, the Olympio government had drafted a constitution that would finally replace the French Togoland Statute of 1956 and turn the country into a Presidential Republic. For this purpose, a constitutional referendum was held in Togo on 9 April 1961 alongside general elections.

Prior to the April 1961 elections, Juvento made a tactical alliance with the *Union Démocratique des Peuples Togolais* (UDPT), itself a merger of the electorally mauled and disintegrated PTP and its former ally, the UCPN. Together they formed the *Mouvement Nationaliste Togolais-Juvento*. In March 1961, however, the formation was disqualified. The Olympio government was apparently still resentful of Juvento's split just a year earlier and used the merger of the parties to kill two birds with one stone by cracking down on the opposition as a whole. Olympio declared that a country as small and poor as Togo could not afford any opposition at all.[851] As Olympio eliminated the opposition, he was unsurprisingly confirmed president in the election that resulted in 99% of all votes for his party. Only one year after independence, Togo became de facto an authoritarian one-party state.

The pro-Government *Ghanaian Times* described the elections as "fake and a mockery of democratic practices."[852] Although the Nkrumah government also cracked down on the opposition, it is also true that opposition candidates were allowed to run in all elections, even though the dice were cast against them in various ways. Needless to say, the Togolese authoritarianism inevitably resulted in the growth of discontentment. In May 1961, the Togolese Minister of Interior, Théophile Mally, had accused the former PTP

---

850   TNA (London), FO 371/155660, *Political relations: Commonwealth countries.*, Confidential Letter WA 10/158/2, High Commissioner in Ghana to Secretary of State, p. 2.

851   Munzinger, "Olympio, Sylvanus," Munzinger, available from http://www.munzinger.de/document/00000009107..

852   As cited by Snelling TNA (London), FO 371/155660, *Political relations: Commonwealth countries.*, WA 10/158/2, Ghana: Relations with Togoland, 17 May 1961, p. 2.

member, Simon Kpodar, of receiving Czech-made pistols through Ghana for an assassination attempt on Olympio.[853] The Olympio government cracked down on critics by tightening the reins: As the Nkrumah government had done a year earlier, the Olympio government amended the Togolese citizenship law in August 1961, including the penal code, which empowered the government "to take measures to remove, intern or expel people who posed a threat to public order and the security of the state."[854]

The Olympio-government grew tired of being harassed by Nkrumah and decided to take the initiative and harass Nkrumah. After Olympio joined the so-called Monrovia Group at the Monrovia Conference in May 1961 to counterbalance the Ghana-Guinea alliance of the Casablanca Group, he immediately flew on to France to finalize negotiations of the defence agreement with the French Government.[855] Armed with these two assurances in his pocket, upon his return, Olympio declared in a speech on 7 July 1961 that the "former territory of British Togoland indisputably belongs to the Republic of Togo."[856] On 2 September 1961, the Chamber of Deputies endorsed his declaration and called for the unification of the Togolese nation.[857] On 23 September 1961, a demonstration of over 10,000 participants, organised by Olympio's party, made a tour of all the foreign embassies presenting at each a petition calling for the unification of former British and French Togoland.[858]

Photo 39: March for the re-unification of Togoland, Lomé (23 September 1961)

Photo 40: "The Togo that we want," Lomé (23 September 196)

Source: TNA (London), FO 371/155660, *Political relations: Commonwealth countries.*

Source: ANT (Lomé), Photographic Archive.

---

853 See Skinner, "West Africa's First Coup," p. 24, endnote 21.
854 ANT (Lomé), 2APA Sokodé/212Add, *Loi Nationalité Togolaise*
855 TNA (London), FO 371/155660, *Political relations: Commonwealth countries.*, Confidential Letter ACC.203/278/3, 25 July 1961, p. 2.
856 Translated from French, TNA (London), FO 371/155660, *Political relations: Commonwealth countries.*, Resolution pour la reunification des 2 Togos, 23 September 1961.
857 TNA (London), FO 371/155660, *Political relations: Commonwealth countries.*, Resolution pour la reunification des 2 Togos, 23 September 1961.
858 TNA (London), FO 371/155660, *Political relations: Commonwealth countries.*, Confidential Letter C.4931, D.A. Roberts, 28 September, p. 1.

The petition came as a bit of a fright to the British Foreign Office, fearing that the issue of the 1956 referendum in British Togoland would be re-opened.[859] The British acknowledged that the Togolese had some justice in their contention that the referendum should have been counted separately in the Northern and Southern regions as was suggested by the 1955 UN Visiting Mission and actually done in the recent UN-supervised referendum in British Cameroon.[860] The British Foreign Office agreed that, if it had been put to a vote, a considerable part of the population would have favoured reunification with French Togoland if the French wouldn't have protracted the latter's independence until after 1956.

Now, it seemed that both Togo and Ghana blamed the imperialist division of the Ewe as a pretext for territorial demands and attributed the others' attitude to the instigation of a Western power. Although the British rumoured that the Togolese Foreign Minister, Paulin Freitas, intended to raise the issue before the General Assembly, Olympio appeared more pliant to the British. During private talks, Olympio assured that the claim to former British Togoland was put forward rather as an answer to Nkrumah's public expression to make Togo the seventh province of a unitary Ghana.[861]

However, Olympio's claims to British Togoland coincided with wildcat strikes that broke out amongst railway workers of Sekondi-Takoradi, Ghana, who purportedly protested the high taxes and the imposition of a development levy. The strike spread quickly to Accra and Kumasi and lasted seventeen days. Yet, Nkrumah attributed the unrest to political sabotage and under the pretext of the *Preventive Detention Act* commenced detention of virtually all prominent members of the opposition. This approach didn't sit well with the Minister of Finance and former AEC member, Komla Gbedemah, who was considering the overthrow of Nkrumah. He is quoted saying: "I would be sorry to have to do it, but the country has had enough of Nkrumah's arrogance, whims and madness."[862] In the same month of the strike, Nkrumah called for the resignation of Gbedemah, who, together with Kofi Busia, leader of the oppositional *United Party*, sought refuge in Togo.[863]

The Olympio government finally intended to raise the issue of Ghanaian refugees, already amounting to 6,000 people, before the General Assembly's Third Committee,

---

859 TNA (London), FO 371/155660, *Political relations: Commonwealth countries.*, Minutes by B. Miller JW 1061/11, Ghana/Togo Relations, 18 November 1961, p. 2.

860 On 11 February 1961, voters of British Trusteeship Territory of Cameroon were given the choice of joining either the newly independent Federation of Nigeria or the Republic of Cameroon. Although the framework resembled the British Togoland referendum of 1956 (even the British referendum administrator, John Dring, participated in both referendums), in accordance with the United Nations position, the vote of the Northern and Southern parts of British Cameroon were assessed separately so that each territory could decide independently on its future: The northern part of British Cameroon voted for incorporation into Nigeria, while the southern part of British Cameroon voted for incorporation into the Republic (formerly French) of Cameroon.

861 TNA (London), FO 371/155660, *Political relations: Commonwealth countries.*, Telegram N° 83, 19 December 1961.

862 "Foreign Relations, 1961–1963, Africa," Released by the Office of the Historian, accessed 23 January 2023, available from https://2001-2009.state.gov/r/pa/ho/frus/kennedyjf/50758.htm..

863 PRAAD (Accra), RG 17/1/281, *Special Committee – Togoland Affairs*, Ivory Coast and Togo Affairs, Dei-Anang to Prime Minister, 12 December 1961.

which deals with human rights and humanitarian affairs, to canvass for the idea of a resolution accusing Ghana of creating a refugee problem in the border area.[864] With the alleged intent to securitise the situation of the Ghanaian refugees in Togo, Olympio once again seemed to hope "to internationalize his quarrel with Nkrumah."[865] This move was certainly based on Olympio's long experience before the Fourth Committee. Yet, the move had only a slight success as at the end of October 1961, the United Nations High Commissioner for Refugees sent a mission to study the situation in Togo.[866]

More importantly, however, in October and November 1961, the Olympio government signed various cooperation treaties with France, including the finalized defence agreement. Therefore, on 3 November 1961, the Togolese National Army was created, whereby the French ceded control of the armed forces and the gendarmerie to the Togolese government (yet, the French Commander of the Togolese Gendarmerie, Georges Maîtrier, remained in place). During the negotiations Olympio showed the French a cold shoulder as he intended to adhere strictly to an open-door regime. Olympio did not grant any privileges, even indirectly, to French exporters and even refused the technical assistance staff in the cooperation agreement that had been signed the previous year.[867] Olympio, as an Anglophile, had his eye on international assistance from the British and Americans. He was aware that London and Washington became increasingly wary of Nkrumah's shift to the left. They desired the survival of both Togo and the Olympio regime as a valuable counterweight, who would provide a link between the moderate Nigerian leaders and the French-speaking states.[868] Moreover, the British considered it unlikely that Nkrumah will take an early aggressive action against French Togo and tried to dissuade him,[869] especially since a large proportion of the trained troops of the Ghanaian army were involved in the United Nations Operation in the Congo at the time.

Bombings

On 5 November 1961, that is, just five days before Queen Elizabeth's trip to Ghana, bombs went off in the capital city of Accra. A statue of Nkrumah was hit, showing symbolically that the president was a target. Concerns were heightened about the Queen becoming collateral damage while with him,[870] and Commonwealth Secretary, Duncan Sands, flew to Ghana to examine the security arrangements for the Queen's visit in view of the recent bomb incidents.

A month after the bombings, on 2 December 1961, the Togolese Government allegedly uncovered a plot to overthrow the Olympio-government by killing Olympio and some

---

864 GAOR, "16th Session: 3rd Committee" (1961), pp. 271–72.
865 Skinner, *The Fruits of Freedom in British Togoland*, p. 202.
866 Shortly before the mission submitted its preliminary report in July 1962, the Olympio government decided in May 1962 to establish a National Refugee Committee in Togo. But relations between Ghana and Togo had deteriorated.
867 ANF (Pierrefitte-sur-Seine), AG/5(F)/1887, *Contexte politique des relations bilatérales*, Telegram N° 7/8 by Mazoyer, 3 January 1963.
868 TNA (London), DO 195/75, *Problems of disaffected Ghanaians seeking refuge in Togo*, Togo Annual Review for 1960, Watson to Foreign Office, 23 January 1961.
869 TNA (London), DO 35/9278, *Future of Togoland*, Note (without number).
870 *The Times*, "Accra Shaken by Another Explosion," 07 November 1961, p. 12.

Ministers. According to the Minister of the Interior, Théophile Mally, interrogation of those captured in the night of 1–2 December revealed that since 1959 the plot had been prepared at a camp in the Volta Region and financed by the Nkrumah-government.[871] Allegedly, about 600 young Togolese and Ghanaians were undergoing weapon training with tear gas bombs and pistols. Implicated were the principle Togolese pro-French leaders, such as Grunitzky, Meatchi, Ajavon, Ayassou and above all Simon Kpodar, but also the former allies of Olympio's unification campaign, such as Apaloo and Aihtson, that is, the leaders of both Juvento wings.[872]

On 4 December 1961, two days after the abortive attempt to overthrow the Togolese government, Olympio left for the independence celebrations of the former trusteeship territory of Tanganyika. He is reported saying that the men involved had been trained in Ghana. During the independence celebrations in Tanganyika, on 9 December 1961, Olympio was quoted that in the event of military attacks on Togo by Ghana, Togo would "invoke its pact with France and Ghana would lose its independence."[873] The December 1961 'conspiracy' prompted Théophile Mally, Minister of the Interior, to take into detention 50 to 80 members of the opposition,[874] including the Juventists Ben Apaloo, Firmin Abalo, and Anani Santos, who were arrested, trialled for the alleged assassination attempt organized from Ghana and imprisoned under harsh conditions in Sansanné-Mango in the far north.[875] Juventists appealed to the New York-based *International League for the Rights of Man* (ILRM), to whose director Olympio responded "At the same time, you might agree with me that exceptional measure are necessary in exceptional circumstances."[876]

The Juvento case showed that the Togolese opposition was already being trained in Ghana. Each time, Olympio blamed Nkrumah. The uncovered plot was used by Olympio to securitise and thus justify the banning of the *Mouvement Nationaliste Togolais-Juvento* and the silencing of oppositional newspapers such as the *Togo Observateur*.[877] Since Olympio adopted an increasingly authoritarian course, many opposition members fled to Ghana. The regime was consequently led to break its promises of democracy by arresting its opponents and restricting liberties, thus finalizing its relapse into presidential and single-party rule.

On 11 December 1961, the Ghanaian government issued a White Paper in which the government justified its arrest and incarceration of leading members of the opposition for instigating the labour strike by unionized workers three months earlier. The White Paper accused Olympio by name of supporting members of the Ghanaian opposition, the *United Party*, and some disaffected members of the CPP in exchange for "a promise of

---

871   ANT (Lomé), 2APA Tsevié/64Add, *Affaires Politiques*, 1962, procés verbal, 11 April 1962.
872   TNA (London), FO 371/155660, *Political relations: Commonwealth countries.*, J.W.S. Corbett, Summary of Recent Togolese Statements, as reported in Lomé in the official daily bulletin, 16 December 1961.
873   ANF (Pierrefitte-sur-Seine), AG/5(F)/1887, *Contexte politique des relations bilatérales*, Accords Franco-Togolais, July 1963.
874   ILRM (New York Public Library), b. 28, *Togo*, Cablegram N° 308, Olympio to Baldwin, 6 March 1962.
875   ILRM (New York Public Library), b. 28, *Togo*, Note by RNB, 9 February 1962.
876   ILRM (New York Public Library), b. 28, *Togo*, Letter N° 308, Olympio to Baldwin, 5 March 1962.
877   ANT (Lomé), 2APA Dapango – 18, *Affaires Politiques*, Decree N°628, 13 January 1962.

ceding to Togo the Volta region of Ghana."[878] Olympio had allegedly supported these men in their attempt to overthrow the Nkrumah government through the September strikes and bomb explosions just before Queen Elizabeth's visit.

The day after the publishing of the White Paper, the Principal Secretary of Ghana's African Affairs Secretariat, Michael Dei-Anang, called for a "stronger, firmer line" towards Togo and proposed the creation of a special 'Committee of Togoland Affairs', which Nkrumah ordered two days later,[879] "to make concrete suggestions as to how best reciprocal repressive measures could be taken against Togoland."[880] Olympio in turn, had expressed repeatedly that he merely whished that Nkrumah leave Togo alone and did not want to quarrel but merely "to diminish the importance of the border."[881] The irony was perfect: Olympio, who had built his reputation as a political leader by campaigning against the hardship and the division of the border, wanted it to remain but now followed the same argumentative line, which the French used since 1947 to hamstring Ewe unification.

Due to the unrelenting threats from Ghana, Olympio increased the search radius for allies. In January 1962, 20 African heads of state met at the unofficial study conference in Lagos, the successor to the Monrovia Conference, where they discussed, among other things, how to keep the Cold War out of Africa and what to do about Pan-Africanism. It is noteworthy that the countries of the Casablanca Group did not participate. Although there was the widely held view that Pan-Africanism was the only way to keep the Cold War out of Africa, which would have obliged the new African states to take sides against each other in the event of hostilities, the Lagos Charter, which was rallied around by eighteen African countries, recommended that members should support each other in the event of an attack, implying Ghana as a principal addressee. Skinner notes that Olympio had furthermore secured from the Nigerian Foreign Minister, Jaja Wachuku, a commitment to defend Togo against any Ghanaian attempt at annexation.[882]

But Olympio also sought out more powerful allies. During his visit to the US in March 1962, the US Government had offered their help in intelligence and security training countering Nkrumah's intention to annex Togo.[883] An American Police Mission was sent to Togo, studied its security forces, and recommended that the Army, the *Garde Togolaise*, and the Gendarmerie, should all be amalgamated into one single force of gendarmerie – a measure which the French Commander of the Togolese Gendarmerie, Georges

---

878 Government of Ghana, "Statement by the government on the recent conspiracy," White Paper no. 7 of 1961, 41, p. illus. (Ministry of Information and Broadcasting on beahlf of the President, Accra, 1961).

879 PRAAD (Accra), RG 17/1/281, *Special Commitee – Togoland Affairs*, Dei-Anang to Minister of Foreign Affairs, 14 December 1961.

880 PRAAD (Accra), RG 17/1/281, *Special Commitee – Togoland Affairs*, Notes of the First Session of the Special Committee for Togoland Affairs, p. 2.

881 TNA (London), FO 371/155660, *Political relations: Commonwealth countries.*, Telegram N° 83, Watson to Foreign Office, 19 December 1961.

882 Skinner, "West Africa's First Coup," p. 389.

883 TNA (London), DO 195/75, *Problems of disaffected Ghanaians seeking refuge in Togo*, Ghana-Togo Relations [N°101], Oliver Kemp to K.M. Wilford, 21 April 1961.

Maîtrier, recommended as well.[884] Olympio, still attached to his policy to demilitarize and decolonise the security forces, decided, however, to maintain the separation of the army and the police.

The Togo-Ghana relations, already at a low point, deteriorated even further when a series of bombings rocked Ghana in the second half of 1962. On 1 August 1962, a grenade attack on Nkrumah occurred in Kulungugu, a village in northern Ghana, killing several people and leaving Nkrumah with a shrapnel wound in his back. On 9 September 1962, about 200 yards from Nkrumah's official residence, at Flagstaff House, a bomb exploded, killing 3 and injuring 60.[885] On 20 September 1962, two bombs exploded in Accra, killing 3 and injuring 100.[886] On 6 November 1962, in Chorkor, Accra, two explosions were caused by grenades, which according to the Ghanaian investigation were of French manufacturing.

The Ghanaian Government drew up an official note of protest, accusing Togo to harbour the men whose attacks have caused up to that point 21 deaths and 385 injured people. Yet, since the Togo-Ghana relations were so bad, the Nkrumah-Government had to ask the British ambassador in Togo to send the letter to the Togolese Government. Yet, the latter did not accept the letter, stating that the Ghanaian Government must direct itself to the French embassy – the official representation of Togo in Ghana at the time.[887] On 7 January 1963, another bomb exploded in Accra, which according to the Ghanaian authorities was supposedly of "French origin, and of a type supplied to a neighbouring territory in West Africa."[888]

6.9.2 Assassination of Olympio (1963)

At this point, the Americans, the British, and even the French were seriously concerned about Olympio's security and had been trying for some time to persuade him to take better security measures for his person.[889] Yet, Olympio had never bothered to do so. A fatal mistake that would cost him his life. Three theories circulated in the subsequent period about those behind the murder of Olympio and the exact course of events. Since Skinner has already discussed these theories in detail, they will only be repeated very briefly here.[890]

The first, on which subsequent political events developed, emphasised the role of disaffected but essentially apolitical Togolese ex-soldiers, who overthrew the Olympio

---

884 TNA (London), FO 371/161755, *Army and police remain separate*, 1962, Confidential Letter, O. Kemp to Barbara Miller, 5 October 1962.
885 *The Times*, "News in Brief," 11 September 1962
886 *The Times*, "100 Injured in Accra," 21 September 1962
887 PRAAD (Accra), RG 17/1/325, *Note of Protest to the Govt of Togo*, de Freitas to Nkrumah, 7 December 1962.
888 *The Times*, "Four Killed by Accra Bomb," 10 January 1963, p. 7.
889 TNA (London), FO 371/167647, *Assassination of President Olympio: coup de'etat*, 1963, Secret Letter 0214/24/1G, British Embassy, Abidjan, to FO, 24 January 1963, p. 2; TNA (London), FO 371/155660, *Political relations: Commonwealth countries.*, Confidential Letter ACC.203/278/4, B.A. Flack to H.R.E. Brown, 20 June 1961, p. 2.
890 Skinner, "West Africa's First Coup"

regime to secure better terms with an intimidated and therefore more accommodating successor government. The second theory, popularised by the publication of François Verschave's *Françafrique*,[891] assumes complicity of the French Ambassador Henri Mazoyer and the French Commander of the Togolese Gendarmerie, Georges Maîtrier, in the ex-soldiers' actions, and invokes France's longstanding and actual preference for a government under Nicholas Grunitzky over Olympio. The third theory placed the blame squarely on Ghana. Supporters of this theory cited the hostile public communication between the two presidents and Nkrumah's statement that Togo could become Ghana's seventh region. Skinner, however, opposes a Ghana-centric approach to historical research on the 1963 coup, for regardless of whether the 'military/unideological' explanation was valid or accurate, it seemed compelling for most stakeholders at the time and therefore formed the basis for the future development of the region. Without emphasizing the 'military/unideological' theory as more valid than the others, purely from the interest of the security-focused perspective applied here, the developments relevant in this explanation shall be portrayed.

The return of the soldiers

With the end of the Algerian war, the French colonial armies and legionnaires were demobilized. Yet, even before Togo's independence, it was clear that returning veterans would pose a problem. When a veterans organization was to be formed in 1958, Olympio argued that the returnees should fall under the care of the French and not his government because, after all, they had fought in Algeria and Indochina for France and not for Togo.[892] The veterans, on the other hand, demanded to be recruited into the Togolese army, which Olympio refused in view of the scarce state resources and the promised UN intervention in the event of a conflict with neighbouring Ghana. On the one hand, Olympio did not want to employ the veterans, because in his eyes they were fighting against peoples who wanted exactly the same thing as Togo: independence. On the other hand, Olympio's austerity policy did not allow for any further burden on the state budget one way or another. With the defence agreements in mind, Olympio declined to tax Togo's limited resources by absorbing the unemployed veterans into the military establishment. The disruption of the important trade with Ghana coming on top of Olympio's budget balancing, deflationary policy, and the reduction of French subsidies led to unemployment and hardship. Similar to the conditions leading up to the Accra riots in 1948, the Olympio-government earned the indignation of the former soldiers, who would later take Olympio's life.

The mercenaries of Togolese origin returning from the Algerian war, who had been discharged from the French army, were recruited mainly from the northern Kabré population group, including the 26-year-old Étienne Gnassingbé, who saw action in Indochina (1953–55) and Algeria (1956–61). He repatriated to Lomé in September 1962. History is unlikely to remember the mercenaries with sympathy, but they were a desperate body of men sitting around unemployed. The Togolese military leaders, Seargent Emmanuel Bodjollé and the Commander of the Togolese Guard, Kléber Dadjo, repeatedly

---

891   Verschave, *La Françafrique*.
892   ANOM (Aix-en-Provence), 1AFFPOL/2217/8-B, *Anciens combattants*, Letter N°720/RI, Governor of Overseas France to High Commissioner of the French Republic, 3 December 1958, p. 1.

tried to persuade Olympio to increase the budget so as to recruit more former soldiers of the French army returning to the country.[893] He was eventually persuaded by Maîtrier to add 100 men to the army, but even then, he planned to bypass the French Army contingent. He told the Bodjollé delegation: "I shall use unemployed school-leavers, or people who fought for independence and not you mercenaries who were killing our Algerian friends when we were fighting for independence."[894] On 24 September 1962, Olympio refused the personal request of Étienne Gnassingbé to join the Togolese military.[895] On 7 January 1963, Dadjo again submitted a written request of former soldiers to join the Togolese Army,[896] which Olympio reportedly tore up.[897] The veterans of the 1963 coup were essentially non-political – a reason why Olympio underrated the threat they posed.[898] Despite the alleged uncovering of various conspiracies by the Ghanaian Government, the Olympio-government thought a military coup not likely. In the end, it was barely 30 soldiers who mutinied under Seargent Bodjollé's command.

The Night of the Coup

It was only a few days after this tongue-lashing that Olympio's house was surrounded. Since a presidential guard did not yet exist and Olympio did not consider it necessary to increase his personal security, only two police officers guarded the house. The putschists tried to force their way into the house through the front door. Since the residence directly bordered the terrain of the US Embassy in the rear, Olympio escaped out the back of the house and jumped over the wall into the compound of the US Embassy, where he hid in or under a car. The putschists did not venture onto the property, but apparently observed it closely from the wall. As day dawned, Olympio left his hiding place to escape into the door of the US embassy, which was only 4 to 5 meters away. However, he found the door locked and was shot by the coup plotters. It is still a mystery and a wide field for speculation, who exactly fired the fatal shots. At the time, there was general agreement in Lomé that it was ex-sergeant Etienne Eyadema, who shot the six bullets into the President in the early morning of 13 January 1963.[899]

Bodjollé announced that the politically inexperienced junta would employ a civilian titular as head of state. In the end, Bodjollé appointed Grunitzky, who had the experience the junta needed and also the backing of the French, and to whom the veterans conveniently owed nothing.[900]

Several African countries condemned the attack and doubted the version of non-political military coup plotters. Due to the preceding conflict between Olympio and Nkrumah, the latter's government was suspected of being involved in the coup and

---

893 Kenneth W. Grundy, "The Negative Image of Africa's Military," *The Review of Politics* 30, no. 4 (1968): 437, https://doi.org/10.1017/S003467050002516X.
894 Warren Howe, "Togo: Four Years of Military Rule"
895 J. A. Lukas, "Olympio Doomed by Own Letter: Sergent Whose Job Appeal Failed Slew Togo Head," *New York Times*, 22 January 1963, p. 3.
896 Lukas, "Olympio Doomed by Own Letter: Sergent whose job appeal failed slew Togo Head," p. 3.
897 Grundy, "The Negative Image of Africa's Military," p. 437.
898 Warren Howe, "Togo: Four Years of Military Rule," p. 9.
899 Warren Howe, "Togo: Four Years of Military Rule," p. 9.
900 Warren Howe, "Togo: Four Years of Military Rule," p. 10.

assassination. The Nigerian Foreign Minister, Jaja Wachuku, hinted at such things immediately after the coup and made it clear that Nigeria would intervene if Ghanaian troops invaded Togo during the state crisis. Other accounts conflated the distinct versions of the coup. For example, the fugitive Minister of Interior, Théophile Mally, claimed in a letter to Secretary General U Thant that the French ambassador, Henri Mazoyer, and the French Commander of the Gendarmerie, Georges Maîtrier, had been accomplices in the coup, which was primarily organised by Ghana. Mally pleaded for a United Nations fact-finding mission and United Nations peacekeepers to maintain order.[901] Yet, despite the many assurances previously given to Olympio, this did not come to pass while the version of the coup by non-political veterans had gained the widest acceptance. Olympio's mistake was to put too much faith in his defence agreements and incur the wrath of the military.

6.9.3 Aftermath: Rise & Demise of The Togoland Liberation Movement

The assassination of Sylvanus Olympio, Togo's first president and former supporter of Ewe and Togoland reunification, in 1963, and the subsequent coup by Ghanaian security forces against Nkrumah, Ghana's first President, in 1966, were the first military coups in the newly independent states of the former French and British territories of West Africa. Both coups led to a period of instability in the region: After Olympio's assassination, the successor government under Nicholas Grunitzky was marked by instability, prompting another coup in 1967, which brought Gnassingbé Eyadéma to power. When two years later, in 1969, the National Liberation Council brought Kofi Busia to power in Ghana, he appointed none other than Senyo G. Antor, the former mouthpiece of the Togoland unification movement, as Ghana's ambassador to Togo from April 1970 to January 1972. When once again the Busia government was overthrown in 1972, Antor, together with Alex Odame and Kofi Dumoga, found themselves in exile in Togo.

Thus, it was no coincidence that in the same year, Togoland and Ewe nationalism revived as activists of the *Togoland Liberation Movement* (TOLIMO) attracted much attention. Since the unification movement had been refining its strategies of influencing international opinion for decades by now, in 1972, TOLIMO petitioned the Organisation for African Union for support in reversing the 1956 plebiscite that accorded British Togoland to Ghana, citing the fact that in Ghana the Ewe were among the poorer classes in the country, while in Togo they were the leaders in economic life.[902] Also, in 1976, TOLIMO sent a delegation to the United Nations General Assembly to inform international opinion on the latest developments regarding Togoland unification.[903] The Eyadéma-regime supported TOLIMO, on the one hand, to prevent political unrest among the Ewe population and, on the other hand, because reunification would have promoted

---

901 UN ARMS (New York), S-0884-0021-11-00001, *Togo*, Cablegram ACR6/CT1460, Mally to Secretary-General, 31 January 1963.
902 Brown, "Borderline Politics in Ghana"
903 National Liberation Movement of Western Togoland, "Movement of Western Togoland (NLMWT)," *New York Times*, 15 October 1976

economic growth, especially by incorporating the Volta River electricity project.[904] In turn, Ghana, then under military rule, cracked down on TOLIMO, banning it in 1976 through the passing of the *Prohibited Organisations Act*, while the decreasing support by the Eyadéma-regime resulted in the movement entering a phase of lethargy. The most prominent figurehead of Togoland unification, Senyo G. Antor, died in exile, Lomé, in 1986 at the age of 80.

A series of scholars, such as Brown,[905] Nugent,[906] or Asamoah,[907] considered that the with unravelling of TOLIMO in the late 1970's, "Western Togoland nationalism seemingly quietly folded, once again, into the pages of the history books."[908] Yet, Togoland nationalism experienced a comeback with the appearance of the Homeland Study Group Foundation in 1994.

---

904 Brown, "Borderline Politics in Ghana," pp. 586–89.
905 Brown, "Borderline Politics in Ghana"
906 Nugent, *Smugglers, secessionists & loyal citizens on the Ghana-Togo frontier*.
907 Asamoah, *The political history of Ghana (1950–2013)*.
908 Bulgarelli, "Togoland's lingering legacy," p. 225.

7. Conclusion

> "It is easy to lose one's way in the 'Togoland question.' There are so many actors in the drama, like a Dostoyevsky novel."[1]

7.1 General Summary

The introductory part of this study was devoted to the resurgent conflict over 'Western Togoland' and one of its most pronounced spokesmen, the late Charles Kwame Kudzordzi. Since September 2020, the conflict has turned violent, including kidnappings and exchanges of gunfire. The subsequent crackdown *by* and overhaul *of* the Ghanaian security and intelligence sector exemplifies how serious the Ghanaian government considered the precariousness of national security. Representatives of the Ghanaian state and the secessionists point out that the roots of the conflict lie in the region's history of decolonisation: the contested integration of the United Nations trusteeship territory of British Togoland into the Gold Coast.

Driven by the purposes of peace and conflict research, the aim of the analysis was to find out why during the period of decolonisation, despite the resources made available under the special conditions of the United Nations Trusteeship System, the then immensely active Ewe and Togoland unification movement was unable to realise its *Dream of Unity*, resulting in British Togoland's integration into the Gold Coast, thus, allowing the seeds of conflict to grow.

The literature review revealed, on the one hand, that the debate on international state-building and peace-building missions recently underscored an increased desideratum of historical work with a special interest in its historical precedents during the era of trusteeship and decolonisation. On the other hand, while previous work by historians and Africanists on the trusteeship territory of Togoland has tended to address the origins and persistence of ethnic and territorial identities, there have been few theory-based explanations of the strategies and ultimate failure of the Ewe and Togoland unification

---

1 Thomas Hodgkin [1956] as cited in Nugent, *Smugglers, secessionists & loyal citizens on the Ghana-Togo frontier*, p. 197.

movement. Thus, trusteeship-related literature that can inform the desideratum of intervention, state-building, and security scholarship, remained limited.

A theoretical framework was designed that adapted theories of International Relations, foremost the Copenhagen School's securitisation framework with a conceptual addendum of postcolonial theory, to grasp securitisation efforts as well as their silencing during the historical context of decolonisation. The Ewe and Togoland unification movement's campaign before the United Nations was thus examined with this postcolonial reading of securitisation, which allowed to analyse under what conditions and with what effects and consequences seeming 'subaltern actors' may or may not (de)securitise.

It has been argued that long before the establishment of the Trusteeship System, not only the unification movement itself, but also the petition and securitisation campaign it ran, drew on antecedents from the period when Togoland was administered under German rule and the Mandates System. Through the opportunities that were opened by the Trusteeship System after World War II, the first Ewe petitioners made their plea known to the Trusteeship Council. However, the two main trusteeship powers, France and Britain, sought to integrate French and British Togoland into the French Union and the Commonwealth of Nations, respectively. They did everything in their power to silence the petition campaign of the Ewe unification movement at the United Nations level and have its leadership closely surveilled by the ever-expanding security and intelligence apparatus in the trusteeship territories. The investigation aimed to understand how the insecuritisation by security agencies influenced discussions at the international level. It delved into the formation of the respective intelligence and security apparatuses, that is, the Special Branch in British Togoland and the Service de Sûreté in French Togoland. Particularly in French Togoland, significant repression by the Administering Authority targeted unificationists

From 1951 onwards, Ewe unificationists formed a tactical alliance with Togoland unificationists and increasingly used a securitising language to present their case not to the Trusteeship Council but to a new audience, the Fourth Committee of the General Assembly. While the Fourth Committee was dismayed by allegations of repressive measures and favourably disposed to the securitised unification argument, the Administering Authorities employed various techniques to silence the petitions of the unificationists, such as by obstructing their consideration (*locutionary silencing*), disrupting oral hearings by mobilising counter-petitioners or presenting counter-securitising arguments (*illocutionary frustration*), or by discrediting the unificationists and by expanding their often civilizational reasoning towards undecided delegations (*illocutionary disablement*).

Albeit the movement's relentless petitioning campaign, the United Nations eventually resolved the integration of the trusteeship territory of British Togoland into the Gold Coast. Exactly ten years after the commencement of the British Trusteeship Agreement for Togoland, Ghana's independence on 6 March 1957 sealed the partition of Ewe- as well as French and British Togoland once and for all, effectively frustrating the securitisation efforts, which the movements had undertaking during this decade. The northern integration-favouring part of British Togoland eventually became the Northern Region of Ghana, while the southern separation-favouring and predominantly Ewe-inhabited Trans-Volta-Togoland became the Volta Region.

After Togo's and Ghana's independence, the region's territorial allocation led to a conflict between the two successor states, which used the security and intelligence services developed by the trusteeship powers to eliminate political opponents. Following growing discontent that led to coups by the security services in both countries, the region entered a period of instability, during which sub-nationalist tendencies seemed extinguished once and for all.

7.2 Key Findings and Conclusion

The methodological and theoretical approaches form the basis to answer the main research question "How did constructions of threat and (in)security influence the decolonisation of Togoland?" including the sub-questions, broken down along the focus on the main actors within the trilateral constellation of the Trusteeship System, that is, the United Nations, the Administering Authorities, and the unificationist petitioners.

7.2.1 Sub-Question 1: (In)Securitisation by the Administering Authorities

The first sub-question focused on the French and British trusteeship powers, their (de)securitising and silencing moves before the United Nations, and the organisation of the colonial security apparatus in French and British Togoland. The theoretical framework was based equally on postcolonial readings of the Copenhagen and Paris Schools. For the conclusion, the analysis of the negotiations at the UN is based primarily on a Copenhagen-School-focused reading, while the analysis of the security and intelligence agencies in Togoland is based primarily on a Paris-School-focused reading.

Insecuritisation by the Administrations of French & British Togoland
The Lomé riots of 1933 initiated the emergence of the *Service de Police et de Sûreté* in French Togoland and the Accra riots of 1948 the *Special Branch* in British Togoland. Both agencies were established in response to anti-colonial discontent. Equally, both agencies equated a broadening and continuous reform of the police, the security command structure, and intelligence gathering, amounting to the demilitarisation, bureaucratisation and increased routinisation of security practises. Via surveillance, the violence of early colonialism was supplemented by more subtle methods of population control, turning the territories into a Foucauldian panopticon.

By infiltrating secret informants at the meetings of the unificationists, the French and British trusteeship administrations were well informed about their strategies, declarations, power struggles, travel plans, etc. Both the Special Branch and the Service de Sûreté were in this respect a type of repository of knowledge from which colonial administrators drew to construct their threat assessments. Thus, as 'knowledge institutions,' both these security and intelligence agencies played a key role in discursively constructing the 'unease,' which the Administering Authorities harboured vis-à-vis the unificationists. Among themselves, the Administering Authorities were not only aware of these structures and developments, but in order to thwart the unificationists, the French and British Administering Authorities even cooperated on security and intelligence matters, albeit to a limited extent. It is noteworthy that while the Special Branch's contributions were relatively modest, the Service de Sûreté played a more significant role in this regard.

Besides the Anglo-French rivalry in colonial matters, the hesitance of the French and British to cooperate on security and intelligence issues can be attributed to the different threat perceptions of the French and British colonial orders. The different national colonial approaches, that is, French *assimilation* versus British *indirect rule*, led to different views of what exactly constituted a threat and how this threat had to be dealt with. While the British *indirect rule* allowed for a colonial state that was not only able to integrate a certain degree of self-government, but indeed even depended on it, the pronounced French colonial policy of *assimilation* could not avoid but to consider demands of self-government by any nationalist movement as a threat. Therefore, nationalist movements, such as the Ewe and Togoland unifications, were much more likely to be perceived as a threat to the assimilationist French Union than, for example, nationalist movements such as the CPP in the British Gold Coast, where the latter was soon introduced and integrated into the security and intelligence architecture. This aspect is further evidenced by the fact that in the oral hearings before the Fourth Commission, France was more often on the defensive than Britain and in the years following decolonisation, intervention in the former British colonies remained limited while intervention in the former French colonies was extensive. In short, since France defined the constraints of its *assimilation* policy and the French Union much more narrowly, the more drastic the measure of its 'management of unease,' that is, the *in*securitisation, means and measures of its security apparatus, had to be.

British unease, on the other hand, stemmed primarily from a different source. In London, that is, the metropolis of liberalism, much more attention was drawn to the 'red menace.' Yet, regarding colonial possessions, London and the Governor of British Togoland diverged widely on the communist threat. The latter was convinced that London was seeing threats where there were none. It seemed that in its intelligence-driven search to clearly predict upcoming threats, the British Special Branch was blinded by London's own insecuritisation. The same applies to French Togoland: The Service de Sûreté that insecuritised and repressed the unification movement was, in a way, a victim of its own success, that is, it was structurally self-blinded as evidenced by the fact that Governor Spénale had no explanation for the 1958 elections that brought Sylvanus Olympio to electoral power.

So, how has the routinised insecuritisation (Paris School) at the level of the territorial administrations informed the securitization dynamics in New York (Copenhagen School)? The British archival materials provide more comprehensive insights into the activities and threat constructions of the Special Branch compared to the scarcity of information in the French archival materials on the Service de Sûreté. Consequently, a direct comparison is hindered by the limited availability of French archival materials. Nonetheless, the repressive behaviour of the French administration suggests a significantly stronger insecuritisation within the Service de Sûreté. Whether this heightened insecuritisation substantially influenced the negotiations in New York, however, can be deemed limited in its impact. Therefore, it can be assumed that the administration-internal insecuritisations of the unificationists had little direct influence on the negotiations in New York. In conclusion, a definitive answer to the question remains elusive though.

Of course, unlike in French Togoland, security policy for British Togoland was mainly determined by the more pressing developments in the Gold Coast. Although in British Togoland the colonial administration was aware of the political activities of the unificationists, their statements at meetings, travel plans, et cetera, the archives indicate that only after the lessons of the Mau-Mau rebellion the colonial administrators realised its dissatisfaction with the intelligence and security arrangements in British Togoland and never really resolved them until independence. After decades of routinized colonial administration, reforms of the security and intelligence apparatus had to be carried out in great haste.

Furthermore, the analysis revealed a profoundly divided security and intelligence service in the Gold Coast and British Togoland. The insistence of London regarding intelligence acquisition often led to conflicts of authority between various levels of the colonial administration. The involved were profoundly divided on matters of the organisation of colonial security. The internal struggles among the various levels of administration remain a neglected topic in studies of decolonisation and clearly show that there was no agreed colonial order. This is also evident in the transfer of power and the resulting conflicts of loyalty over serving two masters: the colonial administration or Nkrumah. Various times the fear was expressed that after independence the latter would gain latent power over his opponents (a fear that was ultimately confirmed).

This problem of loyalty, that is, the dichotomy of serving two masters, also existed in the transition process in French Togoland: according to the Togo Statute, the gendarmerie, responsible for maintaining internal security, was subject to the orders of the Autonomous Government. However, according to the Togo Statute, when the gendarmes acted as auxiliaries to the French forces of law and order, they were subject to the orders of the French High Commissioner. Thus, in French Togoland, too, there seemed to be a reluctance to relinquish control over security functions. Even after Togo's independence, the Togolese Gendarmerie was led by a French Commander – a circumstance without which the theories about the involvement of the French in Olympio's murder would probably not have arisen. Certainly, the conclusion cannot be generalized, but the comparison suggests that this loyalty problem seems to be a fundamental one in processes of power transfers.

The archival record is too scarce for French Togoland, but the post-independence developments of Ghana and Togo suggest that in French Togoland there was a similar problem as in British Togoland. In the final phase of the transition, the question arose as to how internal security and intelligence could be ensured most effectively without being misused as a political weapon. Eventually, the French and British left the successor governments the colonial structures of their security and intelligence agencies without legislative control. In the following, Nkrumah's and Olympio's government became increasingly repressive until they were eventually overthrown by their own security forces.

(De)Securitisation at the United Nations

However, developments in surveillance and security structures remained (and as is usual with intelligence agencies, were supposed to remain) invisible to international monitoring bodies. When it came to answering to others than themselves, that is, to the General Assembly of the United Nations, the Administering Authorities portrayed the territory's path to self-government as a completely normal and orderly process. Instead, the intelligence-driven reform of the security sector was rendered invisible. The annual reports of the Administering Authorities did not indicate the establishment of these agencies. Statistical data on the configuration and size of the police force, especially in French Togoland, were displayed dazzlingly opaque. Considering these secrecy-attempts as a turnout or repertoire of (de)securitisation, the conclusion can be drawn that the struggle of the national movements was desecuritised vis-à-vis the international audience, but *de facto* insecuritised at the places of the colonial power, foremost within metropolitan ministries, the colonial administration, and police stations.

Between 1947 and 1950, that is, since Sylvanus Olympio's first appearance before the Trusteeship Council, France and Britain resolved to frustrate the unification movement. Using the simple expedient of *locutionary silencing*, they proposed ever stricter procedural rules for anonymous petitions, postponed the examination of petitions, agreed on vague resolution, and deliberately refrained from undoing the overburdening of the petition system through which residents of the territories could submit complaints to the United Nations. During tours of Visiting Missions, Administering Authorities exploited the relentless opposition of political parties to securitise potential clashes and, thus, dissuade Visiting Missions from meeting the unificationists.

Conceptualised as *locutionary silencing*, a review of the Trusteeship System's petition examination procedure, thus, shows that the way petitions were examined gave the United Nations the least insight into the conditions of the trusteeship territories. Although the rules of procedure allowed a certain degree of politicising petitions, they systematically excluded securitising petitions. Purposefully, written petitions were prevented from leading to extraordinary measures or even a bending of rules. The opposite is rather true: the steady adoption of ever more restrictive rules of procedure, especially concerning anonymous petitions, led to the bureaucratic marginalisation of written petitions. The result: the right to petition, that is, the very instrument that was supposed to provide a means to bring grievances to the attention of the United Nations, was effectively used to contain these efforts.

The attempts at *locutionary silencing* are, of course, only the result of *illocutionary frustration*, that is, the records show that the Administering Authorities understood and acknowledged the securitising arguments of the unificationists very well but chose not to address and eventually thwart them. Whether or not this happened because the Administering Authorities did not believe in their substance is a matter of *illocutionary disablement*. On many occasions, the Administering Authorities argued (and were quite convinced themselves) that the unificationists were representing a minority demand, which they were only very vocal about. Whether this was the case cannot be answered definitively, because the two referenda of 1956 and the 1958 Legislative Assembly Election only provided limited clarity about the majority situation. A referendum on the unification of Ewe or Togoland, which would have been held simultaneously in British and French Togoland and would have settled the question once and for all, was successfully thwarted by the British and French. In the framework of the present work, however, this is of secondary importance, because if the French and British assertion was true, this would underline the prominence of the securitisation of a vocal minority before the United Nations. If it was false, that is, a majority really championed unification, then the silencing of the unificationists' securitisation efforts by the Administering Authorities should be regarded as even more significant.

Statements in the archival records do not make it easy to always distinguish clearly between *illocutionary frustration* and *illocutionary disablement*, that is, whether actors within the colonial administrators understood the petitioners' securitisation moves but deliberately frustrated them (*illocutionary frustration*), or whether the disabling frames of their colonial mindsets did not allow them to understand the petitioners' securitised demands at all (*illocutionary disablement*). None of this would have mattered to the unificationists, however, because in practice it made no difference whether the trusteeship powers acted in good faith or bad faith. Yet, on a theoretical side, it would substantiate, on the one hand, the need for a context-focused, that is, *perlocution*-focused approach that considers the consequences and effects of securitisation and, on the other hand, that the subaltern can indeed securitise if colonial power structures such as *disabling frames* are sufficiently eroded.

The Administering Authorities certainly made use of these *illocutionary disabling frames*. Figuratively speaking, the Administering Authorities emitted jamming signals to disrupt the expressed securitising arguments of the unificationists. The Administering Authorities tried to discredit the unificationists by portraying them as troublemakers, who used overly radical language. Complaints were regularly made about the language of the unificationists and about their mobilization methods, which allegedly threatened public order in the territories. Furthermore, the Administering Authorities sought to securitise their policy not only as a warranty of peace and order in the trusteeship territories, but also as responsibility for the post-trusteeship period, arguing that meeting the demands of the unification movement would lead to a possible domino effect in other colonial territories, threatening a balkanization of the African continent, which could not be in the interest of the United Nations. The Administrative Authorities did not succeed in misleading the Fourth Committee in general with these *disabling frames*, but at key moments during the negotiations over resolutions they were certainly able to wrest strategically important concessions by their use.

7.2.2 Sub-Question 2: Securitisation by the Petitioners

In 1956, James Coleman noted: "The Togolands have not commanded the international spotlight because of their size or international importance. They are among the smaller of the eleven areas under trusteeship, and they are geographically rather far removed from any direct involvement in the 'cold war.' Nor has the 'colonial crisis' been more acute there than elsewhere."[2] In deciding to achieve its goals by peaceful and largely constitutional means, the unification movement limited its only chance of success by persuading the bodies with the necessary power, namely the British and French governments and the United Nations, through petitions. Notably, Togolese unificationists commanded the international spotlight because they were the first who appeared before the new 'world organisation' and, by imbuing early debates with a securitising language, they were able to ensure for more than a decade that the reunification of Togoland remained the only

---

2   Coleman, *Togoland*, p. 3.

concrete item on the agenda of the Trusteeship System. It was the remarkable perseverance of the AEC, the CUT, and the Togoland Congress, led by men like Sylvanus Olympio and Senyo G. Antor, that had kept unification alive. The United Nations provided the unificationists with a platform. Initially still restrained from 1951 onwards the unification parties dragged their case before the General Assembly, using it not only as a stage to make their case heard internationally but to securitise their demands and thus influence world opinion.

In their endeavour to achieve unification, they securitised the Administering Authorities' reluctance to unify Ewe and Togoland, presenting it as a threat to the territory's identity. Moreover, they securised that the way popular consultations were conducted threatened not only democratic principles but ultimately the principles of trusteeship itself. Also, the harsh repression of the French administration was securitised to discredit the French regime's fitness to rule and its intentions to integrate French Togoland into the French Union. While it may have been somewhat daring, the unificationists, upon their appearance before the General Assembly, progressively employed securitisation as appeasement, strategically emphasizing the risk of violent escalation. It is worth noting how in their attempts at securitisation the petitioners showcased themselves, the residents of the territories, and the United Nations, always emphasizing that they basically wanted to pursue a peaceful agenda. The recourse to violence would not be a result of deliberate planned action but rather of a 'loss of levelheadedness.'

Notably, petitioners from other trusteeship territories followed suit. For example, Ruben Um Nyobe, the figurehead of the Cameroon independence movement, never appeared before the Trusteeship Council, but like the unificationists from Togoland two years earlier, he appeared directly before the Fourth Committee of the General Assembly. The Togolese thus set an example for other trusteeship territories.

For over a decade, almost a hundred appearances in oral hearings before the Trusteeship Council and the Fourth Committee, including 1,015 officially recorded written petitions,[3] kept the unification issue as the only concrete item on the agenda of the Trusteeship System. The hearings before the Trusteeship Council and the Fourth Committee, the enquiries made by the Visiting Missions, the 'pressure' exerted by the General Assembly on the Administering Authorities, in short, all the attention given to the movement greatly encouraged it. In this respect the movement was vocal. James Coleman assesses this performance as follows:

> "One of the striking features of the Trusteeship System – characteristic perhaps of other systems of supervision – is that aggrieved elements not only command special attention; they also tend to become endowed with a higher legitimacy than those elements which are *silent*, indifferent, or content with the status quo. Of course, in any political situation recognition and rewards accrue to the activists. Moreover, in situations of doubt, there is frequently the presumption that articulate elements are genuinely representative of the inarticulate, at least until the contrary is proved."[4]

---

3   United Nations, "Art. 87," in *Repertory of Practice of United Nations Organs, 1955–1959*, Vol. III, ed. United Nations (UN), 333–48 Supplement No. 2, available from legal.un.org/repertory/art87/english/rep_supp2_vol3_art87.pdf, p. 345.

4   Coleman, *Togoland*, p. 49.

Does that conclude that the unificationists have broken through the silence dilemma developed in this work? It is worth recalling Sarah Bertrand's pointedly formulated consideration that one can be silent while screaming loudly. Thus, since unification never came about, the answer seems to be an obvious 'no.' The unification movement had achieved at best a partial success: the Administering Authorities never intended to hold referenda in the territories. The petitioner's securitization of the "Most Secret" document played a pivotal role in compelling the Administering Authorities to acknowledge that without a referendum the General Assembly would vehemently oppose the termination of the Trusteeship Agreement. But unificationists failed to ensure that the referenda would be held under the conditions they saw fit. However, the 1958 UN-supervised Legislative Assembly elections brought the unificationists back to electoral power. In this way, the petitioners not only contributed to French Togoland's accession to full independence outside the French Union, but also to the latter's disintegration.

Yet, after independence, the unification issue took on a new character as it was subsumed under the conflictual relations between the Nkrumah-government and the Olympio-government, which were increasingly hostile to each other. The latter's desire to preserve the newly won independence and the reluctance to form a Togo-Ghana union exemplifies that the demand for unification was ultimately (though not only, but certainly also) an argument to merely oust the colonial powers.

7.2.3 Sub-Question 3: The United Nations as an Audience of Securitisation

Was the United Nations able to bend the Administering Authorities under the influence of world opinion? As mentioned before, since Ewe and Togoland unification was not achieved and the destiny of French and British Togoland went separate ways, the obvious answer is 'no.'

The reason dates to the creation of the Trusteeship System. At the San Francisco and London negotiations, the future Administering Authorities would not have agreed to United Nations supervision without the power to limit it. The United Nations was forced to respect the sovereignty of its member states and without being given any real means of sanctions, the United Nations could do little to prevent the Administering Authorities from treating their trusteeship territories as they saw fit. To most member states it was clear that the Trusteeship System was voluntary and accepting a flawed Trusteeship System was better than none.

Thus, given the composition of the Trusteeship Council, an Administering Authority could for the most part rely on the solidarity of the other Administering Authorities. That is why in 1951 the Ewe and Togoland unificationists dragged their case before the Fourth Committee of the General Assembly and increasingly resorted to a securitising language. Since the Trusteeship System was a window through which the General Assembly, and extension, world opinion could see whether the interests of the inhabitants of the trusteeship territories were not being violated (thus, representing the colonial powers' greater responsibility towards the inhabitants the other so-called Non-Self-Governing Territories), the colonial powers did their utmost to prevent the General Assembly from becoming a 'court of appeal.' Yet, before the Fourth Committee they were ultimately obliged to justify and account for their own attitudes and policies.

However, the Fourth Committee, and in extension, world opinion had negligible effect on the basic policy of France and Britain. Although the General Assembly formally had authority over the Trusteeship System, it lacked the necessary powers to satisfy the unificationists' demands. Under the aspects of securitisation analysis, the Fourth Committee did not represent the *relevant audience*, because it lacked the necessary powers. The only support the unificationists could expect from the Fourth Committee was a suggestion to the Trusteeship Council or the Administering Authority. When they declined to oblige, the General Assembly could only condemn the latter. Without serious sanction and accountability mechanisms, United Nations supervision was thereby effectively limited to observation.

Nevertheless, the General Assembly was not without influence. Only the General Assembly had the power to change and to terminate the Trusteeship Agreement and thus to determine the conditions under which it would occur. In a sense, this competence was the only sanctioning and accountability tool the General Assembly had.

In theory, the General Assembly would have been in a position that in return for the lifting of the Trusteeship Agreement, the four-unit formula recommended by the 1955 Visiting Mission must be applied for the 1956 referendum in British Togoland. Had the four-unit formula been applied, the majority Ewe-populated Ho and Kpando districts, considered one unit, would have separated from the Gold Coast, and remained under trusteeship. But the General Assembly would then have been faced with the problem that the administration of only these areas would have been even more impracticable. The British played their cards right and, in the end, the General Assembly's eventual rejection of the four-unit proposal sealed the future course of the Togo-Ghana border, which cut right through the heart of Eweland.

However, the clause that only the General Assembly has the power to terminate the Trusteeship Agreement caused the French a headache. The United Nations refused to supervise the 1956 referendum in French Togoland and consider the French Togoland Statute as grounds for terminating the Trusteeship Agreement. For the latter to be granted, the General Assembly demanded that the Legislative Assembly be re-elected on the basis of universal adult suffrage. That is to say, the Fourth Committee ultimately exercised direct trusteeship functions, including the hearing of petitioners, deciding upon referenda (1956) and parliamentary election (1958), and sending its own Visiting Mission (1957). Thereby, the Fourth Committee bypassed the Trusteeship Council, reducing it to one of its own subsidiaries. In this way the trustees were not only accountable to themselves, that is, to the clique of Administering Authorities that constituted the Trusteeship Council.

On the other hand, this made future participation in the Trusteeship System increasingly unlikely: although, under the terms of the United Nations Charter, the Trusteeship System was open to the inclusion of further dependent territories, none other than the original eleven territories were ever included in the circle of trusteeship territories. Although most of the 72 so-called Non-Self-Governing Territories to which the Charter applied in 1946 have become independent anyway, 17 Non-Self-Governing Territories still remain under the purview of the Fourth Committee.

Yet, since constitutional reforms were introduced earlier in French Togoland than in other parts of French Africa, James Coleman surmises that the United Nations involvement must have exerted some influence on the progressive development of the trusteeship territories. Here, the archives to which Coleman did not have access reveal that it would be premature to claim that reforms were induced by pressure from the United Nations or the Administering Authority's desire to satisfy its demands.

As Sylvanus Olympio remarked during his outburst before the Fourth Committee in 1952, constitutional progress in the Gold Coast was brought about by the Accra Riots. Thus, the pressure for reform came from considerations of threats to the British colonial order. In French Togoland, on the other hand, reforms came much more hesitantly. Rather, constitutional reform in the Gold Coast increased pressure on the regime in French Togoland, which felt compelled to enter the race of constitutional development to take the wind out of the unificationist sails.

7.2.4 General Conclusion

Thus, how have constructions of threat and (in)security influenced the decolonisation of Togoland? One could argue that the constructions of (in)security had a negligible impact because unification did not materialize and Togoland's path to independence would not have been drastically different if the unificationists had refrained from securitising their cause altogether.

However, the interweaving of the three previous answers indicates a more nuanced assessment, that is, the independence of Togoland, as a general example of decolonisation in Africa and as a particular case under international supervision, was indeed influenced by constructions of (in)security. It should not be overlooked that it took ten long years for the unificationists' failure to make itself evident – ten years in which constructions of (in)security guided the direction that the decolonisation of Togoland would take. No other movement from a trusteeship territory has dominated the agenda of the Trusteeship System as long and as intensely as the Ewe and Togoland unification movement.

What does this imply for peace and conflict studies? In comparative terms, the trusteeship territory of Togoland, where the transfer of state control occurred largely peacefully, is often likened to the trusteeship territory of Cameroon,[5] where the transfer of power, however, was accompanied by violence.[6] The claims that the political contexts of the two territories were completely different have already been rejected as unfounded.[7] The present work indicates that a key difference lies in the fact that, other than the movements of the remaining trusteeship territories, the Ewe and Togoland unification movement pursued its strategy of intervening in international opinion at a very early stage and in a greatly capable manner. Yet, as evidenced by statements made at rallies, as well as various action plans, and the riots during Ghana's Independence Day, some elements of the unification movement did not completely reject the idea of using violence to achieve the long-sought objective of unification. Hence, the unification movement did not decide on a petition campaign because they were completely averse

---

5 Digre, "Ethnic Loyalties, National Choices, and International Oversight"
6 Ketzmerick, *Staat, Sicherheit und Gewalt in Kamerun*.
7 Michel, "The Independence of Togo," p. 317.

to violence, but because it represented a viable alternative for violence to achieve their goals. Furthermore, they strategically utilized the potential for violence by not explicitly ruling it out, all while expressing a steadfast commitment to a peaceful approach. This approach can be seen as employing the prospect of violence within the framework of a 'securitization as appeasement' strategy.

However, from the course of events it can also be deduced that the more their petition campaign was frustrated, the more likely the unificationists were considering resorting to violence. For what stands out: armed conflict only seemed to become a real possibility after the trusteeship powers withdrew. This had less to do with the fact that the trusteeship powers repressed the movement (which they did) and violence only broke its way when the former left. In British Togoland for example, even after the Togoland unificationists' frustrated disposition to participate in the Consultative Commission or the 1956 referendum in British Togoland, they remained peaceful as long as there was the possibility of making their voices heard before the venues of world opinion. Only when the Togoland Congress and Juvento were deprived of the opportunity to internationalize their quarrels in the venues of the Trusteeship System, they resorted to what Fasakin circumscribed as "the subaltern's use of protests and violence in making securitization moves."[8] Simply put, these actors merely strove for a court of appeal. The disturbances surrounding Ghana's Independence Day on 6 March 1957 were thus an expression of the fact that with the end of the trusteeship status, the United Nations would no longer provide a statutory platform for the internationalisation of the unificationists' cause.

This allows a central theoretical conclusion: the Copenhagen School maintains a normative preference for *de*-securitisation. However, the study shows that unificationists refrained from the use of violence only as long as they had a credible means of securitising their cause. The postcolonial addendum to this study's theoretical framework expands the argument that the Copenhagen School's normative preference for *de*-securitisation is not always beneficial. It advances that actors might remain peaceful as long as there is a credible opportunity to securitise their concerns, and that the Copenhagen School's normative preference for *de*-securitisation may lead subaltern actors to become *frustrated* and drive them to resort to violence.

Was the ending of trusteeship thus premature? Nkrumah's annexation threats, the repression of the first years under the Olympio-Government, refugees on both sides of the Togo-Ghana border, and Olympio's assassination – all these events indicate that in terms of maintenance of peace and security, trusteeship proved to be a failure. Yet, if disappointment with the performance of the African state spread rapidly after decolonisation through trusteeship, one must wonder how it is that from the 1990s onwards so many voices called for recourse to the same trusteeship principles as a means of overcoming that disappointment. Rather, it is premature to conclude that the trustees should have pursued Eurocentric statebuilding even longer and more rigorously. They should have taken seriously the concerns expressed before the international fora, instead of establishing political orders serving their own interests. To understand why the unification movement failed, the silencing of securitisation moves is key, since by means of the latter

---

8   Fasakin, *Subaltern Securitization*, p. 93.

the petitioners challenged the Administering Authorities, who in turn employed securitising references to potential threats to negotiate the transfer of power and ultimately the maintenance of *their* established political order.

Separatism in Ghana: Western Togoland

Finally, to what extent is the recent conflict over the attempted secession of 'Western Togoland' rooted in constructions of threat and (in)security from the time of trusteeship?

It is undeniable that the HSGF has been shaped by the history and the securitising rhetoric of Western Togoland nationalists, especially by those of the Togoland Congress and TOLIMO. However, given the inaction of Western Togoland nationalists since the mid-1970s, the HSGF has been accused of not being directly involved in the earlier political struggle of British Togoland seeking its way to separate statehood. The HSGF's historic references to the trusteeship period are often inaccurate. Its recourse to securitise 'Western Togoland's' identity and history is therefore considered a mere gambit or placeholder to lend historical legitimacy to its secessionist claims, which otherwise encompass at present 'only' alleged anti-Ewe sentiment and the relative underdevelopment of the Volta Region.[9] Nonetheless, this work is careful not to claim, as other authors have done, that Western Togoland nationalism will disappear back into the history books, because already twice the spectre of Western Togoland nationalism has jumped right back out of the history books: in the 1970s, TOLIMO, and most recently the HSGF. At least judicially, the threat of Western Togoland separatism was addressed in foresight through the Prohibited Organisations Act. However, whether it is democratic to criminalize this political standpoint, even if it is a secessionist one, is another question.

Finally, I would like to end with a remark on the Togoland question and security in historical perspective. Mark Twain is credited with the phrase "History never repeats itself, but it does often rhyme."[10] This would seem to be the case at least with the recent interplay of the Western Togoland question and developments in the Ghanaian security apparatus. The WTRF attacks took the security apparatus by surprise, just as the Accra riots of 1948 did. Then, as now, the criticism was that the police had increasingly taken on civilian tasks. The increasing militarisation of police practices and the expansion of the intelligence structures of the police apparatus were part of the "management of unease" that the surprising moment of the attacks triggered. Back then it was the institution of the Special Branch, today the National Intelligence Bureau (NIB). Another rhyme of security history are continuities of the colonial intelligence and security command structures, such as the RegSeCs and DisSeCs. Hopefully, at the very least, the Ghanaian state's new approach of including human security and civil society in the authorities' security measures will defuse the conflict rather than exacerbate it.[11]

---

9   Kwawukume, "Revisiting the Road to Secession Agitation in the Volta Region."
10 The attribution is probably incorrect, as there is no reference to it in Twain's work.
11 Mensah Agbenou, "Ghana: Cinq Militants Du Togoland Occidental Emprisonnés," *iciLome*, 23 March 2023

7.3 Potentials, Limits, Outlook

This thesis applied theories of International Relations to the study of history and equally related a historiographical perspective to current problems in International Relations. It is precisely at this point of intersection that the selected case falls on fertile ground.

In the spirit of Frederick Cooper's call to focus on reclaiming paths not taken in history,[12] the recent conflict over Western Togoland invited to a study with theories of International Relations to revisit and rethink the history of the Togoland question. As a historical case, the Togoland question offers insights into blind spots of Critical Security Studies, namely what can be learned from failed securitization.[13] In the process, a key aim of the study was to showcase the potential of postcolonial approaches for Critical Security Studies in general and theories of securitisation in particular. A postcolonial perspective was taken to examine subjectivities and standpoints of actors vis-à-vis the colonial structures and power dynamics in international organizations. There is undoubtedly still a lot of need and potential to bring perspectives from the Global South more strongly into Western knowledge production, even if this is ultimately hampered by publishing practices. To test the developed theoretical framework of a postcolonial perspective on security in other contexts as well, a comparative design would be further useful. The latter could refer to other trusteeship territories, the most similar of which is Cameroon, but also to other cases, including the Global North.

Thus, it should be emphasized that the postcolonial-inspired analysis of security speech not only provided the impetus to look more closely at the Trusteeship System's petitioning system in the first place, but also to examine the practice more critically for counterintuitive silencing effects. It has been shown that the accountability mechanisms, which are provided by international organizations as an instrument to securitize grievances can be intentionally silenced by *locutionary silencing* and *illocutionary frustration*, or unintentionally silenced by *illocutionary disablement* – all three of which need to be highlighted by a decolonising critique. A limitation in the developed theoretical framework of a postcolonial perspective on security is the problem that disabling frames are difficult to grasp empirically. They can be interpreted in the data material, but rarely clearly identified.

Unfortunately, this work has not been able to analyse the debates and discussions within the Standing Committee on Petitions, as Cowan, Pedersen, or van Ginneken have done regarding the League of Nations' petitioning system.[14] The present study dealt only with the 'products' of the Standing Committee. Since the Standing Committee on Petitions, where petitions were first examined, was composed in parity by Administering and non-Administering Authorities, an analysis of the Committee's verbatim records would likely shed light on the fault lines and silencing effects, which securitising petitions were exposed to.

---

12 Frederick Cooper, "Possibility and Constraint," *The Journal of African History* 49, no. 2 (2008): 196
13 Ruzicka, "Failed Securitization"
14 Cowan, "Who's Afraid of Violent Language?"; Pedersen, *The guardians*, pp. 77–95; van Ginneken, "Volkenbondsvoogdij"

It has also been shown that not only the historiography of international organizations, but also the discussion of theories of international relations benefit from the much-underutilized methods of historical and archival research. Archival research can inform debates of International Relations, both in relation to the debate on statebuilding and in the theoretical dimension, that is, the theories of Critical Security Studies, insofar as it can encourage interrogation of concepts and foster a more contextualised understanding of security dynamics in decolonising contexts. Yet, the theorized arguments remain, as usual in qualitative studies, limited to the situational context. Even though extensive material was collected, the conclusions must remain strongly case specific. Documents from seven archives were used, but mainly the colonial and not the anti-colonial point of view was expressed. It remains to be hoped that with the eventual opening of the French archival holdings, a more detailed picture will emerge.

Bibliography

"100 Injured In Accra." *The Times*, 21 September 1962. No. 55502.

"17 members of separatist group rounded up in dawn swoop." *My Joy Online*, 24 December 2019. Accessed January 6, 2020. https://www.myjoyonline.com/news/2019/december-24th/17-members-of-separatist-group-rounded-in-dawn-swoop.php.

Abubakar, Dauda. "The Role of Foreign Actors in African Security." In *African Security in the Anthropocene*. Vol. 36. Edited by Hussein Solomon and Jude Cocodia, 125–43. The Anthropocene: Politik—Economics—Society—Science. Cham: Springer Nature Switzerland, 2023.

"Accra Shaken By Another Explosion." *The Times*, 07 November 1961. No. 55232.

Acharya, Amitav. "The Periphery as the Core: The Third World and Security Studies." In Krause; Williams, *Critical Security Studies*, 299–328.

Acharya, Amitav, and Barry Buzan. "Why is there no non-Western international relations theory? An introduction." *International Relations of the Asia-Pacific* 7, no. 3 (2007): 287–312. https://doi.org/10.1093/irap/lcm012.

Acheampong, Kwame. "Deal with Western Togoland security 'training' reports – Adam Bonaa to Akufo-Addo." *Starr FM Online*, 18 December 2019. Accessed 18.12.219. https://starrfm.com.gh/2019/12/deal-with-western-togoland-security-training-reports-adam-bonaa-to-akufo-addo/.

Adamson, Fiona B. "Pushing the Boundaries: Can We "Decolonize" Security Studies?" *Journal of Global Security Studies* 5, no. 1 (2020): 129–35. https://doi.org/10.1093/jogss/ogz057.

Adjei, Johnson. "Togo prepares for the big day." *Daily Graphic*, 23 June 1959.

Adjei Sarfo, Samuel. "The secession of the Togolanders." *GhanaWeb*, 26 September 2020. Accessed September 29, 2020. https://www.ghanaweb.com/GhanaHomePage/features/The-secession-of-the-Togolanders-1070176.

Agbenorsi, Justice. "Court discharges 20 suspected Western Togoland secessionists." *Graphic Online*, 04 April 2020. Accessed March 26, 2020. https://www.graphic.com.gh/news/general-news/court-discharges-20-suspected-western-togoland-secessionists.html.

Agbenou, Mensah. "Ghana: Cinq militants du Togoland occidental emprisonnés." ici-Lome, 23 March 2023. Accessed March 28, 2023. https://icilome.com/2023/03/ghana-cinq-militants-du-togoland-occidental-emprisonnes/.

Aklama, Benjamin. "Separatist movement declares independence for Western Togoland." *Citi Newsroom*, 17 November 2019. Accessed April 29, 2020. https://citinewsroom.com/2019/11/separatist-movement-declares-independence-for-western-togoland/.

Akumatey, Samuel. "Hohoe and Buem youth clash at hearing on new region." *Ghana News Agency*, 20 January 2018. Accessed December 6, 2019. https://www.ghananewsagency.org/social/hohoe-and-buem-youth-clash-at-hearing-on-new-region-127667.

Alabira, Mohammed. "18 suspected Western Togoland separatists arrested in Bimbilla." *Citi Newsroom*, 30 December 2019. Accessed January 6, 2020. https://www.ghanaweb.com/GhanaHomePage/NewsArchive/18-suspected-Western-Togoland-separatists-arrested-in-Bimbilla-826081.

Alence, Rod. "Colonial Government, Social Conflict and State Involvement in Africas Open Economies: The Origins of the Ghana Cocoa Marketing Board, 1939–46." *The Journal of African History* 42, no. 3 (2001): 397–416.

Alexandre, Pierre, pseud. Praetor Africanus. "Vers une Federation Franco-Africaine: Naissance de la République Togolaise." *L'Afrique et l'asie* 11, no. 36 (1956).

Aligwekwe, Iwuoha Edozie. "The Ewe and Togoland problem: a case study in the paradoxes and problems of political transition in West Africa." Dissertation, Ohio State University, 1960. Accessed June 7, 2021. http://rave.ohiolink.edu/etdc/view?acc_num=osu1486478713870084.

"Alliance is aired in French Africa: Togoland Premier Projects Grouping for Joint Step to Meet Any Attack." *New York Times*, 12 March 1960. Accessed January 16, 2023. https://www.nytimes.com/1960/03/12/archives/alliance-is-aired-in-french-africa-togoland-premier-projects.html.

Allman, Jean Marie. *The quills of the porcupine: Asante nationalism in an emergent Ghana*. Madison: University of Wisconsin Press, 1993.

Alozie, Bright C. "Female Voices on Ink: The Sexual Politics of Petitions in Colonial Igboland, 1892–1960." *The Journal of the Middle East and Africa* 10, no. 4 (2019): 343–66. https://doi.org/10.1080/21520844.2019.1684719.

Alsheimer, Rainer. *Zwischen Sklaverei und christlicher Ethnogenese: Die vorkoloniale Missionierung der Ewe in Westafrika (1847 – ca. 1890)*. Münster: Waxmann, 2007. http://www.waxmann.com/kat/inhalt/1764.pdf.

Amenumey, D. E. K. "The Pre-1947 Background to the Ewe Unification Question: A Preliminary Sketch." *Transactions of the Historical Society of Ghana* 10 (1969): 65–85. https://www.jstor.org/stable/41406350.

Amenumey, D. E. K. "The General Elections in the 'Autonomous Republic of Togo', April 1958: Background and Information." *Transactions of the Historical Society of Ghana* 16, no. 1 (1975): 47–65. http://www.jstor.org/stable/41406580.

Amenumey, D. E. K. *The Ewe Unification Movement: A political history*. Accra: Ghana University Press, 1989. Ph.D. Thesis.

Amenumey, D. E. K. "The brouhaha over Togoland Plebiscite. The historical fact." *GhanaWeb*, 03 September 2016. Accessed July 28, 2020. https://www.ghanaweb.com

/GhanaHomePage/features/The-brouhaha-over-Togoland-Plebiscite-The-historic al-fact-467248.
Amenyo, Kofi. "Deutschland uber alles – what if Germany had not lost its colonies in Africa?" *GhanaWeb*, 06 March 2017. Accessed April 2, 2020. https://www.ghanaweb.com/GhanaHomePage/features/Deutschland-uber-alles-what-if-Germany-had-no t-lost-its-colonies-in-Africa-516088.
Amnesty International. "Ghana: Forced evictions in the Digya national park area must stop." News release. April 19, 2006. Accessed June 10, 2019. https://www.amnesty.or g/download/Documents/68000/afr280012006en.pdf.
Amoako Bahh, Richard. "The UN document on the Ghana and 'Western Togoland' unionization." *GhanaWeb*, 06 October 2020. https://www.ghanaweb.com/GhanaHo mePage/NewsArchive/The-UN-document-on-the-Ghana-and-Western-Togoland-unionization-1078846.
Amoakwa, Kobina Andoh. "Statement by former President Rawlings on deployment of security agencies in Volta, Oti Regions." News release. July 29, 2020. Accessed October 27, 2021. https://twitter.com/officeofJJR/status/1277480313070006272/photo/.
Amos, Alcione M. "Afro-Brazilians in Togo: The Case of the Olympio Family, 1882–1945." *Cahiers d'études africaines* 41, no. 162 (2001): 293–314. https://doi.org/10.4000/etudesa fricaines.88.
Andersen, Louise. "Outsiders Inside the State: Post-Conflict Liberia between Trusteeship and Partnership." *Journal of Intervention and Statebuilding* 4, no. 2 (2010): 129–52. https ://doi.org/10.1080/17502970903533660.
Anderson, Benedict. *Imagined Communities: Reflections on the Origin and Spread of Nationalism*. London, New York: Verso, [1983] 2006. http://hdl.handle.net/2027/heb.01609.0 001.001.
ANF (Pierrefitte-sur-Seine), AG/5(F)/1887, *Contexte politique des relations bilatérales*.
ANF (Pierrefitte-sur-Seine), 72AJ/537, *Henri Laurentie*.
ANF (Pierrefitte-sur-Seine), AG/5(F)/1209, *Dossiers de C. Rostain*.
Anim-Appau, Felix. "Western Togoland brouhaha is recipe for tribal war – Antwi-Danso warns." *My Joy Online*, 26 November 2019. Accessed December 2, 2019. https://www. myjoyonline.com/politics/2019/November-26th/western-togoland-brouhaha-is-a-recipe-for-tribal-war-dr-antwi-danso-warns.php.
Annan, Kofi. "In larger freedom: towards development, security and human rights for all." A/59/2005, 2005.
ANOM (Aix-en-Provence), 1AFFPOL/3289/4, *Affaires Politiques*.
ANOM (Aix-en-Provence), 1AFFPOL/3284/1, *Affaire Ewe*.
ANOM (Aix-en-Provence), 1AFFPOL/3284/2, *Affaire Ewe*.
ANOM (Aix-en-Provence), 1AFFPOL/3284/3, *Affaire Ewe*.
ANOM (Aix-en-Provence), 1AFFPOL/2115/1, *Dossiers généraux*.
ANOM (Aix-en-Provence), 1AFFPOL/3297/1, *Affaires politiques*.
ANOM (Aix-en-Provence), 1AFFPOL/2217/8-B, *Anciens combattants*.
ANOM (Aix-en-Provence), 1AFFPOL/2182/2, *Royaume-Uni*.
ANOM (Aix-en-Provence), 1AFFPOL/2182/3, *Royaume-Uni*.
ANOM (Aix-en-Provence), 1AFFPOL/2182/4, *Royaume-Uni*.
ANOM (Aix-en-Provence), 1AFFPOL/2182/5, *Royaume-Uni*.

ANOM (Aix-en-Provence), 1AFFPOL/3316/3, *Affaire Ewe*.
ANOM (Aix-en-Provence), 1AFFPOL/3283/4, *Affaire Ewe*.
ANOM (Aix-en-Provence), 1AFFPOL/3341/2, *Entretiens franco-britanniques sur le Togo-Cameroun*.
ANOM (Aix-en-Provence), 1AFFPOL/3340/1, *Entretiens franco-britaniques sur le Togo-Cameroun*.
ANOM (Aix-en-Provence), DPCT59, *Organisation*.
Ansprenger, Franz. *Politik im Schwarzen Afrika: Die modernen politischen Bewegungen im Afrika französischer Prägung*. Wiesbaden: Verlag für Sozialwissenschaften, 1961. https://doi.org/10.1007/978-3-322-98464-7.
ANT (Lomé), 2APA Dapango/77, *Affaires Militaires*.
ANT (Lomé), 2APA Kloto – 108, *Sûreté Nationale*.
ANT (Lomé), 2APA Kloto/23, *Affaires Politiques*.
ANT (Lomé), 2APA Aného/71Add, *Affaires Politiques*.
ANT (Lomé), 2APA Dapango – 18, *Affaires Politiques*.
ANT (Lomé), 2APA Mango – 48, *Administration Générale et Politique*.
ANT (Lomé), 2APA Sokodé/212Add, *Loi Nationalité Togolaise*.
ANT (Lomé), 2APA Tsevié/64Add, *Affaires Politiques*.
Antor, Senyo G. "*Most secret*" politics in Togoland: the British government's attempt to annex Togoland to the Gold Coast. New York: Comtemporary Press, 1954.
Appeltshauser, Laura. "African In/Security and Colonial Rule: Security Studies' Neglect of Complexity." In *Globalizing International Relations*. Edited by Ingo Peters and Wiebke Wemheuer-Vogelaar, 239–64. London: Palgrave Macmillan, 2016.
Aradau, Claudia. "From securitization theory to critical approaches to (in)security." *European Journal of International Security* 3, no. 3 (2018): 300–305. https://doi.org/10.1017/eis.2018.14.
Aradau, Claudia, and Jef Huysmans. "Critical methods in International Relations: The politics of techniques, devices and acts." *European Journal of International Relations* 20, no. 3 (2014): 596–619. https://doi.org/10.1177/1354066112474479.
Aradau, Claudia, Jef Huysmans, Andrew W. Neal, and Nadine Voelkner, eds. *Critical security methods: New frameworks for analysis*. New international relations. London, New York: Routledge, 2015.
Arden-Clarke, Charles. "Gold Coast Into Ghana: Some Problems of Transition." *International Affairs* 34, no. 1 (1958): 49–56.
Arnold, Chase. ""The Cat's Paw of Dictatorship": Police Intelligence and Self-Rule in the Gold Coast, 1948–1952." *The Journal of the Middle East and Africa* 11, no. 2 (2020): 161–77. https://doi.org/10.1080/21520844.2020.1756604.
Asamoah, Obed Y. *The political history of Ghana (1950–2013): The experience of a non-conformist*. Bloomington, IN, USA: AuthorHouse, 2014.
Asare, Fred Quame. "Peace Council moves to address allegations of ethnic identity-based discrimination, marginalization by Ewes." *My Joy Online*, 30.11.20222. Accessed January 30, 2023. https://www.myjoyonline.com/peace-council-moves-to-address-allegations-of-ethnic-identity-based-discrimination-marginalization-by-ewes/.
Asare, Fred Quame. "Update: Military invades 'secessionist' training camp, arrests 21 trainees." *My Joy Online*, 17 February 2020. Accessed February 23, 2020. https://www.

myjoyonline.com/news/2020/February-17th/military-invades-secessionist-training-camp-arrests-20-trainees.php.

Asare, Fred Quame. "Western Togoland: 14 suspected secessionists arrested at Kpando Aziavi." *My Joy Online*, 30 May 2020. Accessed June 2, 2020. https://www.myjoyonline.com/news/regional/western-togoland-14-suspected-secessionists-arrested-at-kpando-aziavi/.

Ashon, Enimil. "Western Togoland: Blame UK and UN, not Ghana." *Graphic Online*, 22 November 2019. Accessed January 15, 2020. https://www.graphic.com.gh/features/features/western-togoland-blame-uk-un-not-ghana.html.

Ashon, Enimil. "West Togoland: Let's go to UN." *My Joy Online*, 05 October 2020. Accessed October 14, 2020. https://www.myjoyonline.com/opinion/enimil-ashon-west-togoland-lets-go-to-un/.

Asogli State Council. "Oti Region Referendum: Entire Region Must Vote." News release. October 3, 2018. Accessed February 24, 2020. https://starrfm.com.gh/2018/10/oti-region-referedum-entire-region-must-vote-asogli-state/.

Association of Volta Youth. "Petition: Justice Brobbey's commission of enquiry into the creation of new regions is preparing the grounds for yet another fraudulent plebiscite in the Volta Region of Ghana." Accessed March 22, 2021. https://www.modernghana.com/news/828252/volta-group-in-the-usa-petitions-un-over-split.html.

Atsu Ahianyo, Peter. "New Separatist Group Pops-Up In Volta Region." *Modern Ghana*, 19 August 2019. Accessed June 21, 2021. https://www.modernghana.com/news/950799/new-separatist-group-pops-up-in-volta-region.html.

Atsu Ahianyo, Peter. "Secessionist Armed Conflict Looms In Ghana As The World Is Silent." *Modern Ghana*, 23 December 2019. Accessed January 6, 2020. https://www.modernghana.com/news/975321/secessionist-armed-conflict-looms-in-ghana-as.html.

Atta-Asamamoah, Andres. "Are Africa's borders sacrosanct? Ghana's Western Togoland crisis." Accessed December 11, 2020. https://issafrica.org/iss-today/are-africas-borders-sacrosanct-ghanas-western-togoland-crisis.

"Attempts to cede Volta Region from Ghana misguided – Prez Akufo-Addo." *Modern Ghana*, 09 June 2021. Accessed June 21, 2021. https://www.modernghana.com/news/1086863/attempts-to-cede-volta-region-from-ghana-misguided.html.

Austin, Dennis. "The Uncertain Frontier: Ghana-Togo." 1, no. 2 (1963): 139–45. Accessed December 13, 2019. https://www.jstor.org/stable/159025.

Austin, John Langshaw. *How to do things with words*. London: Oxford University Press, 1962.

Avoidance of Discrimination Act. 38. December 31, 1957.

Ayamga, Emmanuel. "National Security confirms operations of Western Togoland militia group; goes after them." *Pulse GH*, 18 December 2019. Accessed January 9, 2020. https://www.pulse.com.gh/news/local/national-security-confirms-operations-of-western-togoland-militia-group-goes-after/8k3ccrw.

Ayoob, Mohammed. "Defining Security: A Subaltern Realist Perspective." In Krause; Williams, *Critical Security Studies*, 121–46.

Bagayoko, Niagale, Eboe Hutchful, and Robin Luckham. "Hybrid security governance in Africa: rethinking the foundations of security, justice and legitimate public authority." *Conflict, Security & Development* 16, no. 1 (2016): 1–32. https://doi.org/10.1080/1467 8802.2016.1136137.

Bahceci, Sergen. "Universal Security/Emancipation: A Critique of Ken Booth." *E-International Relations*, 23.03.2015. Accessed December 13, 2020. https://www.e-ir.info/2015/03/23/universal-securityemancipation-a-critique-of-ken-booth/.

Bain, William. *Between anarchy and society: Trusteeship and the obligations of power*. Oxford: Oxford University Press, 2003.

Bain, William. "Saving failed states: Trusteeship as an arrangement of security." In *The empire of security and the safety of the people*. Edited by William Bain, 188–205. Routledge advances in international relations and global politics 45. London, New York: Routledge, 2006.

Balzacq, Thierry. "The Three Faces of Securitization: Political Agency, Audience and Context." *European Journal of International Relations* 11, no. 2 (2005): 171–201. https://doi.org/10.1177/1354066105052960.

Balzacq, Thierry, ed. *How Security Problems Emerge and Dissolve*. London: Routledge, 2011.

Balzacq, Thierry, ed. *Securitization theory: How security problems emerge and dissolve*. PRIO new security studies. New York: Routledge, 2011.

Balzacq, Thierry, and Stefano Guzzini. "Introduction: 'What Kind of Theory – If Any– Is Securitization?'." In Balzacq et al., *What Kind of Theory – If Any – Is Securitization?*, 2–8.

Balzacq, Thierry, Stefano Guzzini, Michael C. Williams, Ole Wæver, and Heikki Patomäki, eds. *What kind of theory – if any – is securitization?* 29., 2015.

Barkawi, Tarak, and Mark Laffey. "The Imperial Peace." *European Journal of International Relations* 5, no. 4 (1999): 403–34. https://doi.org/10.1177/1354066199005004001.

Barkawi, Tarak, and Mark Laffey. "The postcolonial moment in security studies." *Review of International Studies* 32, no. 02 (2006): 329. https://doi.org/10.1017/S0260210506007054.

Bat, Jean-Pierre, Olivier Forcade, and Sylvain Mary. *Jacques Foccart: Archives ouvertes (1958–1974) la politique, l'Afrique et le monde*. Mondes contemporains. Paris: Presses de l'Université Paris-Sorbonne, 2017.

Bayart, Jean-François. *L'État en Afrique: La politique du ventre*. L'espace du politique. Paris: Fayard, 1989.

Baynham, Simon. "Quis Custodiet Ipsos Custodes? The Case of Nkrumah's National Security Service." *The Journal of Modern African Studies* 23, no. 1 (1985): 87–103. https://www.jstor.org/stable/160465.

Beauvais, Joel C. "Benevolent Despotism: A Critique of U.N. State-Building in East Timor." *New York University Journal of International Law and Politics*, no. 33 (2001): 1101–78.

Beck, Teresa Koloma, and Tobias Werron. "Gewaltwettbewerbe: >Gewalt< in globalen Konkurrenzen um Aufmerksamkeit und Legitimität." In *Ordnung und Wandel in der Weltpolitik: Konturen einer Soziologie der internationalen Beziehungen*. Edited by Stephan Stetter. 1st ed., 249–77. Leviathan Sonderband 28. Baden-Baden: Nomos, 2013.

Bening, R. Bagulo. "The Ghana-Togo boundary, 1914–1982." *Africa-Spectrum* 18, no. 2 (1983): 191–209.

Berda, Yael. "Managing Dangerous Populations: Colonial Legacies of Security and Surveillance." *Sociological Form* 28, no. 3 (2013): 627–30. https://www.jstor.org/stable/43653901.

Berdal, Mats, and Richard Caplan. "The Politics of International Administration." *Global Governance* 10, no. 1 (2004): 1–5.

Berger, Mark T. *From Nation-Building to State-Building*. ThirdWorlds. Hoboken: Taylor and Francis, 2013.

Bertrand, Sarah. "Can the subaltern (in)securitize? A rejoinder to Claudia Aradau." *European Journal of International Security* 3, no. 03 (2018): 306–9. https://doi.org/10.1017/eis.2018.15.

Bertrand, Sarah. "Can the subaltern securitize? Postcolonial perspectives on securitization theory and its critics." *European Journal of International Security* 3, no. 03 (2018): 281–99. https://doi.org/10.1017/eis.2018.3.

Bhambra, Gurminder K., Yolande Bouka, Randolph B. Persaud, Olivia U. Rutazibwa, Vineet Thakur, Duncan Bell, Smith, Karen, Haastrup, Toni, and Seifudein Adem. "Why Is Mainstream International Relations Blind to Racism?" *Foreign Policy*, 03 July 2020. Accessed August 28, 2020. https://foreignpolicy.com/2020/07/03/why-is-mainstream-international-relations-ir-blind-to-racism-colonialism/.

Bigo, Didier. "When two become one: Internal and external securitisations in Europe." In *International relations theory and the politics of European integration: Power, security, and community*. Edited by Morten Kelstrup and Michael C. Williams, 171–204. London: Routledge, 2000.

Bigo, Didier. "Security and Immigration: Toward a Critique of the Governmentality of Unease." *Alternatives: Global, Local, Political* 27, Special Issue (2002): 63–92. https://doi.org/10.1177/03043754020270S105.

Bigo, Didier, and Anastassia Tsoukala. *Terror, insecurity and liberty: Illiberal practices of liberal regimes after 9/11*. Routledge studies in liberty and security. London, New York: Routledge, 2008.

Bilgin, Pinar. "The 'Western-Centrism' of Security Studies: 'Blind Spot' or Constitutive Practice?" *Security Dialogue* 41, no. 6 (2010): 615–22. https://doi.org/10.1177/0967010610388208.

Bilgin, Pinar. "The politics of studying securitization? The Copenhagen School in Turkey." *Security Dialogue* 42, 4–5 (2011): 399–412. https://doi.org/10.1177/0967010611418711.

Blanchard, Emmanuel. "French Colonial Police." In *Encyclopedia of Criminology and Criminal Justice*. Edited by Gerben Bruinsma and David Weisburd, 1836–46. New York, NY: Springer, 2014.

Bliesemann de Guevara, Berit. *Statebuilding and state-formation: The political sociology of intervention*. Routledge studies in intervention and statebuilding. Abingdon, Oxon, New York: Routledge, 2012.

Bliesemann de Guevara, Berit, and Florian P. Kühn. *Illusion Statebuilding: Warum sich der westliche Staat so schwer exportieren lässt*. Hamburg: Ed. Körber-Stiftung, 2010.

Bonacker, Thorsten. "Internationales Statebuilding und die liberale Politik des Schutzes." In *Vorsicht Sicherheit! Legitimationsprobleme der Ordnung von Freiheit*. Edited by Gabriele Abels, 177–98. Nomos eLibrary Politikwissenschaft. Baden-Baden: Nomos, 2016.

Bonacker, Thorsten. "'Wann werden die Vereinten Nationen Truppen nach Kalifornien senden?': Human Security aus nicht-westlichen Perspektiven." In *Menschliche Sicherheit und gerechter Frieden*. Edited by Ines-Jacqueline Werkner and Bernd Oberdorfer, 49–76. Gerechter Frieden Politisch-ethische Herausforderungen 4. Wiesbaden: Springer, 2019.

Bonacker, Thorsten. "Situierte Sicherheit: Für einen methodologischen Situationismus in den Critical Security Studies." *Zeitschrift für Internationale Beziehungen* 28, no. 1 (2021): 5–34. https://doi.org/10.5771/0946-7165-2021-1-5.

Bonacker, Thorsten, Werner Distler, and Maria Ketzmerick, eds. *Securitization in Statebuilding and Intervention*. 1st ed. Politiken der Sicherheit 1. Baden-Baden: Nomos, 2017.

Bonacker, Thorsten, Werner Distler, and Maria Ketzmerick. "Securitisation and Desecuritisation of Violence in Trusteeship Statebuilding." *Civil Wars* 20, no. 4 (2018): 477–99. https://doi.org/10.1080/13698249.2018.1525675.

Bonacker, Thorsten, Maria Ketzmerick, and Werner Distler. "Introduction: Securitization in Statebuilding and Intervention." In Bonacker; Distler; Ketzmerick, *Securitization in Statebuilding and Intervention*, 9–27.

Booth, Ken. *Theory of world security*. Cambridge: Cambridge University Press, 2007.

Bourdieu, Pierre. *Distinction: A social critique of the judgement of taste*. London: Routledge & Kegan Paul, 1984.

Bourdieu, Pierre. *Language and symbolic power*. Edited by John B. Thompson. Cambridge, MA: Harvard University Press, 1991.

Boutros-Ghali, Boutrous. "An Agenda for Peace: Preventive Diplomacy, Peacemaking and Peace-Keeping." New York, 1992.

Boutros-Ghali, Boutrous. "Supplement to An Agenda for Peace." New York, 1995.

Brand, Paul. "Petitions and Parliament in the Reign of Edward I." *Parliamentary History* 23, no. 1 (2004): 14–38. https://doi.org/10.1111/j.1750-0206.2004.tb00718.x.

Brobbey, Appiah. "Opinion: History of Trans Volta Togoland." *My Joy Online*, 28 November 2019. Accessed December 2, 2019. https://www.myjoyonline.com/opinion/2019/november-28th/opinion-history-of-trans-volta-togoland.php.

Brogden, Mike. "The emergence of the police: The colonial dimension." *British Journal of Criminology* 27, no. 1 (1987): 4–14.

Brown, David. "Borderline Politics in Ghana: The National Liberation Movement of Western Togoland." *The Journal of Modern African Studies* 18, no. 4 (1980): 575–609.

Brown, David. "Sieges and Scapegoats: The Politics of Pluralism in Ghana and Togo." *The Journal of Modern African Studies* 21, no. 3 (1983): 431–60.

Browning, Christopher S., and Pertti Joenniemi. "Ontological security, self-articulation and the securitization of identity." *Cooperation and Conflict* 52, no. 1 (2017): 31–47. https://doi.org/10.1177/0010836716653161.

Bruce, Emanuel G. Kodjo. "Vom kolonialen zum unabhängigen Afrika: Memoiren." Unpublished manuscript, 2007. PDF.

Buell, Raymond Leslie. *The Native Problem in Africa* 2. New York: Macmillan, 1928.

Bulgarelli, Ashley. "Togoland's lingering legacy: the case of the demarcation of the Volta Region in Ghana and the revival of competing nationalisms." *Australasian Review of*

African Studies 39, no. 2 (2018): 222–38. https://doi.org/10.22160/22035184/ARAS-2018-39-2/222-238.

Burke, Edmund. *The Works of the Right Honourable Edmund Burke* 2. Boston: Little, Brown, and Company, 1899.

Burke, Edmund. *Miscellaneous writings*. Edited by Francis Canavan. Select works of Edmund Burke a new imprint of the Payne edition 4. Indianapolis, Ind.: Liberty Fund, 1999.

Burke, Roland. *Decolonization and the evolution of international human rights*. Pennsylvania studies in human rights. Philadelphia: University of Pennsylvania Press, 2010.

Burns, Alan. *In defence of colonies: British colonial territories in international affairs*. London: Allen & Unwin, 1957.

Buttner, Thea, ed. "Leadership and National Liberation Movement in Africa." Special issue, *Asia, Africa, Latin America*, no. 7 (1980).

Buur, Lars, Steffen Jensen, and Finn Stepputat. *The security-development nexus: Expressions of sovereignty and securitization in Southern Africa*. Uppsala, Cape Town: Nordiska Afrikainstitutet; HSRC, 2007.

Buzan, Barry, and George Lawson. *The global transformation: History, modernity and the making of international relations*. Cambridge studies in international relations. Cambridge: Cambridge University Press, 2015. https://doi.org/10.1017/CBO9781139565073.

Buzan, Barry, and Ole Wæver. "Macrosecuritisation and security constellations: Reconsidering scale in securitisation theory." *Review of International Studies* 35, no. 02 (2009): 253.

Buzan, Barry, Ole Wæver, and Jaap de Wilde. *Security: A new framework for analysis*. Boulder, London: Lynne Rienner Publishers, 1998.

Callahan, Michael Dennis. *A sacred trust: The League of Nations and Africa, 1929–1946*. Brighton: Sussex Academic Press, 2004.

Canefe, Nergis. "Turkish Nationalism and the Kurdish Question: Nation, State and Securitization of Communal Identities in a Regional Context." *South European Society & Politics*, no. 3 (2013): 391–98.

Caplan, Richard. *A New Trusteeship? The International Administration of War-torn Territories*. Oxford: Oxford University Press, 2002.

Caplan, Richard. "From collapsing states to neo-trusteeship: The limits to solving the problem of 'precarious statehood' in the 21st century." *Third World Quarterly* 28, no. 2 (2007): 231–44. https://doi.org/10.1080/01436590601153622.

Carr, Edward Hallett. *What is history? The George Macaulay Trevelyan lectures delivered in the University of Cambridge, January – March 1961*. 2nd ed. Edited by R. W. Davies. Penguin history. London: Penguin Books, 1990.

Carry, Anthony. "Cary report on release of the colonial administration files." Foreign & Commonwealth Office, 24 February 2011. https://www.gov.uk/government/publications/cary-report-on-release-of-the-colonial-administration-files.

Castryck, Geert, Silke Strickrodt, and Katja Werthmann, eds. *Sources and methods for African history and culture: Essays in honour of Adam Jones*. With the assistance of Adam Jones. Leipzig: Leipziger Universitätsverlag, 2016.

Chakrabarty, Dipesh. *Provincializing Europe: postcolonial thought and historical difference*. Princeton: Princeton University Press, 2000.

Chandler, David. "The uncritical critique of 'liberal peace'." *Review of International Studies* 36, S1 (2010): 137–55. https://doi.org/10.1017/S0260210510000823.

Chandler, David, and Timothy D. Sisk, eds. *Routledge handbook of international statebuilding*. Routledge handbooks. London: Routledge, 2013.

Charter. United Nations. 1945.

Chesterman, Simon. *You, the people: The United Nations, transitional administration, and statebuilding*. Project of the International Peace Academy. Oxford, New York: Oxford University Press, 2004.

Chopra, Jarat. "The UN's Kingdom of East Timor." *Survival* 42, no. 3 (2000): 27–40. https://doi.org/10.1093/survival/42.3.27.

Chowdhry, Geeta. "Edward Said and Contrapuntal Reading: Implications for Critical Interventions in International Relations." *Millennium: Journal of International Studies* 36, no. 1 (2007): 101–16. https://doi.org/10.1177/03058298070360010701.

Chowdhuri, Ramendra Nath. *International Mandates and Trusteeship Systems: A Comparative Study*. Dordrecht: Springer, 1955.

Coggins, Bridget L. "Fragile is the New Failure." *Political Violence at a Glance*, 27 June 2014. https://politicalviolenceataglance.org/2014/06/27/fragile-is-the-new-failure/.

Coleman, James S. *Togoland*. International Conciliaton 509. New York: Carnegie Endowment for International Peace, 1956.

Collective, C.A.S.E. "Critical Approaches to Security in Europe: A Networked Manifesto." *Security Dialogue* 37, no. 4 (2006): 443–87. https://doi.org/10.1177/0967010606073085.

Commission des Affaires Étrangères. "Engagement et diplomatie: quelle doctrine pour nos interventions militaires?." Rapport d'Information 2777, Assemblée Nationale, 20 May 2015. https://www.assemblee-nationale.fr/14/rap-info/i2777.asp#P830_305195.

Conze, Eckart. "Securitization: Gegenwartsdiagnose oder historischer Analyseansatz?" *Geschichte und Gesellschaft* 38, no. 3 (2012): 453–67. https://doi.org/10.13109/gege.2012.38.3.453.

Conze, Eckart. *Geschichte der Sicherheit: Entwicklung – Themen – Perspektiven*. V&R Academic. Göttingen: Vandenhoeck & Ruprecht, 2018.

Cooper, Frederick. "Possibility and constraint: African independence in historical perspective." *The Journal of African History* 49, no. 2 (2008): 167–96.

Cooper, Frederick, and Ann Laura Stoler, eds. *Tensions of empire: Colonial cultures in a bourgeois world*. Berkeley, Calif.: University of California Press, 1997.

Cornevin, Robert. *Histoire du Togo*. Paris: Berger-Levrault, 1959.

Cornevin, Robert. *Le Togo: Nation-Pilote*. Collection Survol du monde. Paris: Nouvelles Éditions latines, 1963.

Cornevin, Robert. "Les militaires au Dahomey et au Togo." *Revue française d'études politiques africaines*, 1968, 65–84.

Côté, Adam. "Agents without agency: Assessing the role of the audience in securitization theory." *Security Dialogue* 47, no. 6 (2016): 541–58. https://doi.org/10.1177/0967010616672150.

Côté-Boucher, Karine, Federica Infantino, and Mark B. Salter. "Border security as practice: An agenda for research." *Security Dialogue* 45, no. 3 (2014): 195–208. https://doi.org/10.1177/0967010614533243.

Cowan, Jane K. "Who's Afraid of Violent Language? Honour, Sovereignty and Claims-Making in the League of Nations." *Anthropological Theory* 3, no. 3 (2003): 271–91. https://doi.org/10.1177/14634996030033002.

Crawford, James. *The creation of states in international law.* 2nd ed. Oxford: Clarendon Press, 2010.

Crawford, Neta. *Argument and change in world politics: Ethics, decolonization, and humanitarian intervention.* Cambridge studies in international relations 81. Cambridge: Cambridge University Press, 2002. https://doi.org/10.1017/CBO9780511491306.

Crawford, Neta. "Decolonization through Trusteeship: The Legacy of Ralph Bunche." In *Trustee for the Human Community: Ralph J. Bunche, the United Nations, and the Decolonization of Africa.* Edited by Robert A. Hill and Edmond J. Keller, 93–115. Athens, OH: Ohio University Press, 2010.

Daase, Christopher. "Sicherheitskultur: Ein Konzept zur interdisziplinären Erforschung politischen und sozialen Wandels." *Sicherheit und Frieden* 29, no. 2 (2011): 59–65.

Daase, Christopher, and Cornelius Friesendorf, eds. *Rethinking security governance: The problem of unintended consequences.* Contemporary security studies. London: Routledge, 2012.

Dafeamekpor, Rockson-Nelson E.K. "Rambo-style arrest of 'Western Togoland' separatists worrying – MP." News release. May 7, 2019. Accessed November 23, 2021. https://www.ghanaweb.com/GhanaHomePage/NewsArchive/Rambo-style-arrest-of-Western-Togoland-separatists-worrying-MP-744471.

Danso, Kwaku, and Kwesi Aning. "African experiences and alternativity in International Relations theorizing about security." *International Affairs* 98, no. 1 (2022): 67–83. https://doi.org/10.1093/ia/iiab204.

Darby, Phillip. "Rolling Back the Frontiers of Empire: Practising the Postcolonial." *International Peacekeeping* 16, no. 5 (2009): 699–716. https://doi.org/10.1080/13533310903303347.

Davis E. Alexander. "An Archival Turn for International Relations: Interrogating India's Diplomatic History from the Postcolonial Archive." ISA Singapore.

de Wilde, Jaap. "Speaking or Doing Human Security?" In *The viability of human security.* Edited by Monica den Boer and Jaap d. Wilde, 225–54. Amsterdam: Amsterdam University Press, 2008.

"Deal with secessionist group-Awoamefia." *Ghana News Agency*, 27 September 2020. Accessed September 29, 2020. https://newsghana.com.gh/deal-with-secessionist-group-awoamefia/.

Decalo, Samuel. *Historical dictionary of Togo.* 3rd ed. African historical dictionaries 9. London: Scarecrow Press, 1996.

Deflem, Mathieu. "Law Enforcement in British Colonial Africa: A Comparative Analysis of Imperial Policing in Nyasaland, the Gold Coast, and Kenya." *Police Studies* 17, no. 1 (1994): 45–68.

Department of State. *The United Nations Conference on International Organization: San Francisco, California, April 25 to June 26.* Conference Series 83. Washington: U.S. Government Printing Office, 1946.

"Detailed account of how Western Togoland group staged successful attacks in Volta Region." *GhanaWeb*, 04 October 2020. Accessed October 14, 2020. https://www.ghan

aweb.com/GhanaHomePage/NewsArchive/Detailed-account-of-how-Western-To goland-group-staged-successful-attacks-in-Volta-Region-1076896.

Devereux, Annemarie. "Searching for clarity: A case study of UNTAET's application of international human rights norms." In *The UN, human rights and post-conflict situations*. Edited by Nigel D. White and Dirk Klaasen, 293–321. Manchester: Manchester University Press, 2005.

Diamond, Larry. "Is the Third Wave Over?" *Journal of Democracy* 7, no. 3 (1996): 20–37.

Digre, Brian Kenneth. "The United Nations, France, and African Independence: A Case Study of Togo." *French Colonial History* 5, no. 1 (2004): 193–205. https://doi.org/10.1353/fch.2004.0003.

Digre, Brian Kenneth. "Ethnic Loyalties, National Choices, and International Oversight: The Politics of Independence in the British Trust Territories of Togoland and the Cameroons, 1955–1961." In *The Histories, Languages, and Cultures of West Africa: Interdisciplinary Essays*. Edited by Akua Sarr, 187–212. Lewiston, NY: Edwin Mellen Press, 2006.

Dillon, Michael, and Julian Reid. *Global governance, liberal peace, and complex emergency*. Contemporary welfare and society., 2000.

Distler, Werner. "Breaking with the Past? Neo-Trusteeship in the 21st Century." In *United Nations Trusteeship System: Legacies, continuities, and change*. Edited by Jan Lüdert, Maria Ketzmerick and Julius Heise. Global Institutions. London: Routledge, 2022.

Djokoto, Vincent. "Eeto and the partitions of Eenyigba." *My Joy Online*, 30 April 2020. Accessed May 28, 2020. https://www.myjoyonline.com/opinion/e%CA%8Beto-and-the-partitions-of-e%CA%8Benyigba/.

Dobbins, James, Seth G. Jones, Crane Keith, and Beth Cole DeGrasse. *The beginner's guide to nation-building*. Santa Monica: Rand, 2007.

Doty, Roxanne Lynn. *Imperial encounters: The politics of representation in North-South relations*. Borderlines 5. Minneapolis: University of Minnesota Press, 1996.

Doyle, Michael W. "Kant, Liberal Legacies, and Foreign Affairs." *Philosophy & Public Affairs* 12, no. 3 (1983). https://www.jstor.org/stable/2265298.

Doyle, Michael W., and Nicholas Sambanis. *Making War and Building Peace: United Nations Peace Operations*. Princeton: Princeton University Press, 2011.

Duffield, Mark. *Global governance and the new wars: The merging of development and security*. Critique, Influence, Change. London: Zed Books, 2001.

Duffield, Mark, and Nicholas Waddell. "Securing Humans in a Dangerous World." *International Politics* 43, no. 1 (2006): 1–23. https://doi.org/10.1057/palgrave.ip.8800129.

Duncan, Jude. "Referendum: Oti residents okay new region with 99% YES vote." *Citi Newsroom*, 26 February 2020. Accessed February 26, 2020. https://citinewsroom.com/2018/12/referendum-oti-residents-okay-new-region-with-99-yes-vote/.

Duodu, Cameron. "The 'Western Togoland' Issue: Can The UN Be Challenged In The Modern World?" *Peace FM Online*, 28 November 2019. Accessed December 2, 2019. https://www.peacefmonline.com/pages/comment/features/201911/396532.php.

Dzamboe, Tim. "Group to declare 'Volta region' independence on May 9, 2017." *Graphic Online*, 17 August 2016. Accessed January 10, 2020. https://www.graphic.com.gh/news/general-news/homeland-group-to-declare-western-togoland-independence-on-may-9-2017.html.

Dzamboe, Tim. "Western Togoland "secessionists" discharged, bonded." *Graphic Online*, 20 July 2017. Accessed July 14, 2020. https://www.graphic.com.gh/news/general-news/volta-secessionists-discharged-bonded-to-good-behaviour.html.

Dzigbodi-Adjimah, Komla. "Oti Region: the First Step Towards the Balkanisation of Volta Region." *Gbi Voice*, 22 March 2017. Accessed February 20, 2020. https://www.gbivoice.com/2017/03/oti-region-first-step-towards.html.

Eckert, Andreas. "Theories of Colonial Rule." *The Journal of African History* 38, no. 2 (1997): 301–58. https://doi.org/10.1017/S0021853797377019.

Eggers, Nicole, Jessica Lynne Pearson, and Aurora Almada e Santos, eds. *The United Nations and decolonization*. Routledge studies in modern history 69. Abingdon, Oxon, New York, NY: Routledge, 2020.

"Election 2020: 'Military siege' of Volta Region creates atmosphere of fear – Mahama." *GhanaWeb*, 04 December 2020. Accessed December 11, 2020. https://www.ghanaweb.com/GhanaHomePage/politics/Election-2020-Military-siege-of-Volta-Region-creates-atmosphere-of-fear-Mahama-1126463.

el-Malik, Shiera S., and Isaac A. Kamola, eds. *Politics of the African anticolonial archive*. Kilombo: International Relations and Colonial Questions. Lanham: Rowman & Littlefield, 2017.

Erbar, Ralph. *Ein" Platz an der Sonne"? Die Verwaltungs- und Wirtschaftsgeschichte der deutschen Kolonie Togo 1884–1914*. Beiträge zur Kolonial- und Überseegeschichte 51. Stuttgart: Steiner, 1991.

Esteva, Gustavo, Salvatore J. Babones, and Philipp Babcicky. *Future of development: A radical manifesto*. Britsol: Policy Press, 2013.

European Commission. "Commission Decision: on the financing of the Annual Action Programme 2020 in favour of the Republic of Ghana." Annex. Annex, 10 September 2020. https://ec.europa.eu/international-partnerships/system/files/ghana_aap_2020-annex.pdf.

Ezeokafor, Edwin, and Christian Kaunert. "Securitization outside of the West: conceptualizing the securitization-neo-patrimonialism nexus in Africa." *Global Discourse* 8, no. 1 (2018): 83–99. https://doi.org/10.1080/23269995.2017.1412619.

Falcón, Sylvanna M. *Power interrupted: Antiracist and feminist activism inside the United Nations*. Decolonizing feminisms. Seattle: University of Washington Press, 2016.

Fasakin, Akinbode. *Subaltern Securitization: The Use of Protest and Violence in Postcolonial Nigeria*. Stockholm Studies in International Relations 2. Stockholm: Department of Economic History and International Relations, Stockholm University, 2022.

Fearon, James D., and David D. Laitin. "Neotrusteeship and the problem of weak states." *International Security* 28, no. 4 (2004): 5–43.

Fieldhouse, David. "British Merchants and French Decolonization: UAC in Francophone Africa, 1945–1960." In *L'Afrique noire française: l'heures des Indépendences*. Edited by Charles R. Ageron and Marc Michel, 489–98. Paris: CNRS Éditions, 1992.

"Foreign Relations, 1961–1963, Africa: Ghana." Released by the Office of the Historian. Accessed January 23, 2023. https://2001-2009.state.gov/r/pa/ho/frus/kennedyjf/50758.htm.

Fortna, Virginia Page. *Does peacekeeping work? Shaping belligerents' choices after civil war*. Princeton, NJ: Princeton Univ. Press, 2008.

"Forum on Race and racism in critical security studies." *Security Dialogue* 52, 1S (2021).

Foucault, Michel. *Society must be defended: lectures at the Collège de France, 1975–1976.* Edited by Mauro Bertani and Alessandro Fontana. Lectures at the Collège de France 3. New York: Picador, 2003.

"Four Killed by Accra Bomb." *The Times*, 10 January 1963. No. 55595.

Frank, Andre Gunder. *Capitalism and Underdevelopment in Latin America: Historical Studies of Chile and Brazil.* The Pelican Latin American library. Harmonsworth: Penguin, 1971.

"French Policy on Test." *Ashanti Pioneer*, 30 April 1958.

Friesendorf, Cornelius, and Jörg Krempel. *Militarized versus civilian policing: Problems of reforming the Afghan National Police.* PRIF reports in English 102. Frankfurt am Main: Peace Research Institute Frankfurt (PRIF), 2011.

Fukuyama, Francis. *The end of history and the last man.* New York: Free Press, 1992.

Fukuyama, Francis. "The Imperative of State-Building." *Journal of Democracy* 15, no. 2 (2004): 17–31. https://doi.org/10.1353/jod.2004.0026.

GAOR. "11th Session: Plenary..".

GAOR. "1st Session: 62nd Plenary Meeting." A/PV.62, 1946.

GAOR. "1st Session (2nd Part): 4th Committee." 1946.

GAOR. "5th Session: 4th Committee." 1950.

GAOR. "6th Session: 4th Committee." 1951.

GAOR. "7th Session: 4th Committee." 1952.

GAOR. "7th Session: Plenary." 1952.

GAOR. "8th Session: 4th Committee." 1953.

GAOR. "9th Session: 4th Committee." 1954.

GAOR. "10th Session: 4th Committee." 1955.

GAOR. "11th Session: 4th Committee." 1956.

GAOR. "Report of the United Nations Plebiscite Commissioner." A/3173, United Nations (UN), 1956.

GAOR. "12th Session: 4th Committee." 1957.

GAOR. "12th Session: Plenary." 1957.

GAOR. "13th Session: Plenary." 1958.

GAOR. "16th Session: 3rd Committee." 1961.

Gayibor, Nicoué Lodjou, ed. *Les Togolais face à la colonisation.* Collection "Patrimoines" 3. Lomé: Presses de l'Université de Bénin, 1994.

Gayibor, Nicoué Lodjou, ed. *Histoire des Togolais: De 1884 à 1960* 2. Lomé: Presses de l'UL, 2005.

Gayibor, Nicoué Lodjou, ed. *de l'histoire des origines à l'histoire des peuplements.* 4 vols. Histoire des Togolais. Des origines aux années 1960 1. Paris, Lomé: Karthala; Presses de l'Université de Lomé, 2011.

Gayibor, Nicoué Lodjou, ed. *du XVIe siècle à l'occupation colonaiale.* 4 vols. Histoire des Togolais. Des origines aux années 1960 2. Paris, Lomé: Karthala; Presses de l'Université de Lomé, 2011.

Gayibor, Nicoué Lodjou, ed. *Le refus de l'ordre colonial.* 4 vols. Histoire des Togolais. Des origines aux années 1960 4. Paris, Lomé: Karthala; Presses de l'Université de Lomé, 2011.

Gayibor, Nicoué Lodjou, ed. *Le Togo sous administration coloniale*. 4 vols. Histoire des Togolais. Des origines aux années 1960 3. Paris, Lomé: Karthala; Presses de l'Université de Lomé, 2011.

Gayibor, Nicoué Lodjou. *Sources orales et histoire africaine: Approches méthodologiques*. With the assistance of Moustapha Gomgnimbou and Komla Etou. Paris: Harmattan, 2011.

Gayibor, Nicoué Lodjou, Dominique Juhé-Beaulaton, and Moustapha Gomgnimbou, eds. *L'écriture de l'histoire en Afrique: L'oralité toujours en question*. Hommes et sociétés. Paris: Karthala, 2013.

Getachew, Adom. *Worldmaking after empire: The rise and fall of self-determination*. Princeton: Princeton University Press, 2019.

Getz, Trevor R. "Connecting Decolonization and the Cold War." 82oL. Accessed December 27, 2023. https://www.oerproject.com/-/media/WHP-1200/PDF/Unit8/WHP-1200-8-1-9-Read---Connecting-Decolonization-and-the-Cold-War---82oL.ashx.

"Ghana doesn't legally exist – Kosi Kedem." *GhanaWeb*, 30 September 2020. Accessed September 30, 2020. https://www.ghanaweb.com/GhanaHomePage/NewsArchive/Ghana-doesn-t-legally-exist-Kosi-Kedem-1072990.

"Ghana M.P.s Arrested." *Sunday Times*, 01 December 1957. No. 7020.

"Ghana Minister's Warning On Emergency Powers Bill." *The Times*, 03 December 1957. No. 54014.

GhanaWeb. "New photos revealing 'military operations' of Western Togolanders pop up." Accessed December 18, 2019. https://www.ghanaweb.com/GhanaHomePage/NewsArchive/New-photos-revealing-military-operations-of-Western-Togolanders-pop-up-818080.

Ghani, Ashraf, and Clare Lockhart. *Fixing failed states: A framework for rebuilding a fractured world*. 1st ed. Oxford: Oxford University Press, 2009.

Giddens, Anthony. *The constitution of society: Outline of the theory of structuration*. Berkeley: University of California Press, 1984.

Gilligan, Michael J., and Ernest J. Sergenti. "Do UN Interventions Cause Peace? Using Matching to Improve Causal Inference." *Quarterly Journal of Political Science* 3, no. 2 (2008): 89–122. https://doi.org/10.1561/100.00007051.

Glasman, Joël. *Les corps habillés au Togo: Genèse coloniale des métiers de police*. Paris: Karthala, 2015.

Go, Julian. "Introduction: Entangling Postcoloniality and Sociological Thought." In *Postcolonial sociology*. Edited by Julian Go. 1st ed., 3–34. Political power and social theory. Bingley: Emerald, 2013.

Go, Julian, ed. *Postcolonial sociology*. 1st ed. Political power and social theory. Bingley: Emerald, 2013.

Go, Julian. *Postcolonial thought and social theory*. New York: Oxford University Press, 2016.

Gomda, A. R. "Manhunt for Papavi as new group emerges." *Daily Guide Network*, 22 November 2019. Accessed December 6, 2019. https://dailyguidenetwork.com/manhunt-for-papavi-as-new-group-emerges/.

Gordon, Ruth E. "Some legal problems with trusteeship." *Cornell international law journal*, 1995.

Gordon, Ruth E. "Saving failed states: Sometimes a neocolonialist notion." *The American University journal of international law and policy*, 1997.

Gouvernement Français. "Rapport Annuel: Togo placé sous la Tutelle de la France." T/221, 1948.

Gouvernement Français. "Rapport Annuel: Togo placé sous la Tutelle de la France." Année 1951 T/994. Année 1951, 1952.

Gouvernement Français. "Rapport Annuel: 1955." T/1300, 1957.

Government of Ghana. "Report: Enquiry into matters disclosed at the trial of Captain Benjamin Awhaitey held on the 20th and 21st January 1959, before a court-martial convened at Giffard Camp, Accra, and the surrounding circumstances." Government White Paper 10, Accra, 1959.

Government of Ghana. "Statement by the government on the recent conspiracy." White Paper no. 7 of 1961, 41, p. illus., Ministry of Information and Broadcasting on beahlf of the President, Accra, 1961.

Government of Ghana. "Report of the Commission of Inquiry into the Creation of New Regions: Equitable Distribution of National Resources for Balanced Development." 26 June 2018.

Greene, Sandra E. "Notsie Narratives: History, Memory, and Meaning in West Africa." *South Atlantic Quarterly* 101, no. 4 (2002): 1015–41. https://doi.org/10.1215/00382876-1 01-4-1015.

Greenwood, Maja Touzari, and Ole Wæver. "Copenhagen–Cairo on a roundtrip: A security theory meets the revolution." *Security Dialogue* 44, 5–6 (2013): 485–506. https://doi.org/10.1177/0967010613502573.

Groom, A. J. R. "The Trusteeship Council: A Successfull Demise." In *The United Nations at the millennium: The principal organs*. Edited by Paul Taylor and A. J. R. Groom. 1st ed., 142–76. London: Continuum, 2000.

Gruffydd Jones, Branwen, ed. *Decolonizing International Relations*. Lanham: Rowman & Littlefield, 2010.

Grundy, Kenneth W. "The Negative Image of Africa's Military." *The Review of Politics* 30, no. 4 (1968): 428–39. https://doi.org/10.1017/S003467050002516X.

Guzzini, Stefano. "Securitization as a causal mechanism." *Security Dialogue* 42, 4–5 (2011): 329–41. https://doi.org/10.1177/0967010611419000.

Guzzini, Stefano. "A dual history of securitization." *DIIS Working Paper*, no. 2 (2015): 1–17. https://www.files.ethz.ch/isn/192491/DIIS_WP_2015_02_A_dual_history_of_Securitisation.pdf.

Guzzini, Stefano, and Dietrich Jung, eds. *Contemporary security analysis and Copenhagen peace research*. The new international relations. London, New York: Routledge, 2004.

Habermas, Rebekka. *Skandal in Togo: Ein Kapitel deutscher Kolonialherrschaft*. Frankfurt/Main: S. Fischer, 2016.

Hagmann, Tobias, and Didier Péclard, eds. *Negotiating Statehood: Dynamics of Power and Domination in Africa*. New York, NY: John Wiley & Sons, 2013.

Hall, H. Duncan. "The British Commonwealth and Trusteeship." *International Affairs* 22, no. 2 (1946): 199–213.

Hall, H. Duncan. *Mandates, Dependencies and Trusteeship*. Studies in the administration of international law and organization 9. Washington: Carnegie Endowment for International Peace, 1948.

Hansen, Lene. "The Little Mermaid's Silent Security Dilemma and the Absence of Gender in the Copenhagen School." *Journal of International Studies* 29, no. 2 (2000): 285–306.

Hansen, Lene. "Reconstructing desecuritisation: The normative-political in the Copenhagen School and directions for how to apply it." *Review of International Studies* 38, no. 03 (2012): 525–46. https://doi.org/10.1017/S0260210511000581.

Hansen, Lene. "Are 'core' feminist critiques of securitization theory racist? A reply to Alison Howell and Melanie Richter-Montpetit." *Security Dialogue*, 2020, 1–8. https://doi.org/10.1177/0967010620907198.

Heise, Julius. "United Nations Colonial Complicity in Decolonization Referenda: UN-Supervision of the 1956 Referendum in Western Togoland." *Topos*, no. 1 (2021): 107–24. journals.ehu.lt/index.php/topos/article/view/1048.

Hellberg, Uliana. "Securitization as a modern strategy of constructing identity 'negative proof identity' in the European Union." http://muep.mau.se/handle/2043/14368.

Helman, Gerald B., and Steven R. Ratner. "Saving Failed States." *Foreign Policy*, no. 89 (1992): 3.

His/Her Majesty's Stationery Office. "Report of the Commission of Enquiry into Disturbances in the Gold Coast." Colonial Reports 231.

HMG. "Togoland under United Kingdom Administration: Report for the Year 1947." Colonial Reports 225, 1948.

HMG. "Togoland under United Kingdom Administration: Report for the Year 1948." Colonial Reports 243, 1949.

HMG. "The future of Togoland under British administration: memorandum by the Administering Authority." T/1270, 16 July 1956.

Hobson, John M. *The Eurocentric conception of world politics: Western international theory, 1760–2010*. Cambridge: Cambridge University Press, 2012.

Hobson, John M. "Unmasking the racism of orthodox international relations/international political economy theory." *Security Dialogue* 53, no. 1 (2022): 3–20. https://doi.org/10.1177/09670106211061084.

Hobson, John M. "Un-Veiling the Racist Foundations of Modern Realist and Liberal IR Theory." In *Globalizing International Theory: The Problem with Western IR Theory and How to Overcome It*. Edited by A. Layug and John M. Hobson, 54–71. Worlding Beyond the West Ser. Milton: Taylor & Francis Group, 2022.

Hodder, Bramwell William. "The Ewe Problem: A Reassessment." In *Essays in Political Geography*. Edited by Charles A. Fisher, 271–83. London: Methuen, 1968.

Holbraad, Martin, and Morten Axel Pedersen. "Revolutionary securitization: an anthropological extension of securitization theory." *International Theory* 4, no. 2 (2012): 165–97. https://doi.org/10.1017/S1752971912000061.

Holmes, James. "Mahan, a "Place in the Sun," and Germany's Quest for Sea Power." *Comparative Strategy* 23, no. 1 (2004): 27–61. https://doi.org/10.1080/01495930490274490.

Hönke, Jana, and Markus-Michael Müller. "Governing (in)security in a postcolonial world: Transnational entanglements and the worldliness of 'local' practice." *Security Dialogue* 43, no. 5 (2012): 383–401. https://doi.org/10.1177/0967010612458337.

Hönke, Jana, and Markus-Michael Müller, eds. *The global making of policing: Postcolonial perspectives*. Interventions. London, New York: Routledge, 2016.

Houngnikpo, Mathurin C. "The military and democratization in Africa: A comparative study of Benin and Togo." *Journal of Political and Military Sociology* 28, no. 2 (2000): 210–29.

Howell, Alison, and Melanie Richter-Montpetit. "Is securitization theory racist? Civilizationism, methodological whiteness, and antiblack thought in the Copenhagen School." *Security Dialogue* 26, no. 22 (2019): 1–22.

Hughes, Bryn W., Charles T. Hunt, and Boris Kondoch, eds. *Making sense of peace and capacity-building operations: Rethinking policing and beyond*. Leiden: Martinus Nijhoff Publishers, 2010.

Hultman, Lisa, Kathman Jacob D., and Megan Shannon. "United Nations peacekeeping dynamics and the duration of post-civil conflict peace." *Conflict Management and Peace Science* 33, no. 3 (2016): 231–49.

Huysmans, Jef. *The European Union and the securitization of migration.*, 2000.

Huysmans, Jef. "Agency and the politics of protection: Implications for security studies." In *The politics of protection: Sites of insecurity and political agency*. Edited by Jef Huysmans, Andrew Dobson and Raia Prokhovnik. 1st ed., 1–18. Routledge advances in international relations and global politics. New York, N.Y: Routledge, 2006.

"I'll be angry with God if my dream for Western Togoland is not realized – Papavi." *MyNewsGH*, 26 September 2021. Accessed September 28, 2021. https://www.mynewsgh.com/ill-be-angry-with-god-if-my-dream-for-western-togoland-is-not-realized-papavi/.

ICISS. *The responsibility to protect: Report of the International Commission on Intervention and State Sovereignty*. Ottawa: International Development Research Centre, 2001.

Ignatieff, Michael. "Empire lite." *Prospect*, 2003.

ILRM (New York Public Library), b. 12, *Togoland*.

ILRM (New York Public Library), b. 4, *Togoland*.

ILRM (New York Public Library), b. 28, *Togo*.

Imray, Colin. *Policeman in Africa*. Lewes: Book Guild, 1997.

Istrefi, Remzije. "Should the United Nations create an independent human rights body in a transitional administration? The case of the United Nations Interim Administration Mission in Kosovo (UNMIK)." In *Accountability for human rights violations by international organisations*. Edited by Jan Wouters et al., 355–72. Antwerpen: Intersentia, 2010.

"It is our responsibility to prevent violent extremism – National Security." *Ghana News Agency*, 01 September 2021. Accessed September 24, 2021. https://newsghana.com.gh/it-is-our-responsibility-to-prevent-violent-extremism-national-security/.

Ivarsson, Søren, and Søren Rud. "Rethinking the Colonial State: Configurations of Power, Violence, and Agency." In *Rethinking the colonial state*. Edited by Søren Rud and Søren Ivarsson, 1–20. Political power and social theory 33. Bingley: Emerald Publishing, 2017.

Jabri, Vivienne, and Oliver P. Richmond. "Critical Theory and the Politics of Peace." In Richmond; Visoka, *The Oxford Handbook of Peacebuilding, Statebuilding, and Peace Formation*, 91–106.

Jackson, Nicole J. "International Organizations, Security Dichotomies and the Trafficking of Persons and Narcotics in Post-Soviet Central Asia: A Critique of the Securitization Framework." *Security Dialogue*, 2006.

Jackson, Paul. *Reconstructing security after conflict: Security sector reform in Sierra Leone*. New security challenges series. Basingstoke, England: Palgrave Macmillan, 2011. http://site.ebrary.com/lib/alltitles/docDetail.action?docID=10445769.

Jackson, Paul, ed. *Handbook of International Security and Development*. Cheltenham: Edward Elgar Publishing, 2015.

Jackson, Robert H. *Quasi-states: Sovereignty, international relations, and the Third World*. Cambridge studies in international relations 12. Cambridge: Cambridge University Press, 1990.

Jackson, Robert H., and Carl G. Rosberg. "Why Africa's Weak States Persist: The Empirical and the Juridical in Statehood." *World Politics* 35, no. 1 (1982): 1–24. https://www.jstor.org/stable/2010277.

Jackson, Robert H., and Carl G. Rosberg. "Sovereignty and Underdevelopment: Juridical Statehood in the African Crisis." *The Journal of Modern African Studies* 24, no. 1 (1986): 1–31. https://www.jstor.org/stable/160511.

Jahn, Beate. "Liberal Internationalism." In Richmond; Visoka, *The Oxford Handbook of Peacebuilding, Statebuilding, and Peace Formation*, 31–41.

Jessee, Erin. "The Limits of Oral History: Ethics and Methodology Amid Highly Politicized Research Settings." *The Oral History Review* 38, no. 2 (2011): 287–307. https://www.jstor.org/stable/41440904.

"Journalists barred from covering Oti referendum." *Starr FM Online*, 27 December 2018. Accessed July 30, 2020. https://starrfm.com.gh/2018/12/journalists-barred-from-covering-oti-referendum/.

Jutila, Matti. "Securitization, history, and identity: some conceptual clarifications and examples from politics of Finnish war history." *Nationalities Papers* 43, no. 6 (2015): 927–43. https://doi.org/10.1080/00905992.2015.1065402.

Kafui Kanyi, A. B. "Police arrest Volta secessionist group leaders." *Modern Ghana*, 08 March 2017. Accessed January 10, 2020. https://www.modernghana.com/news/760197/police-arrest-volta-secessionist-group-leaders.html.

"Kan Dapaah must resign – Adib Sani on Western Togoland brouhaha." *Happy Ghana*, 29 September 2020. Accessed November 26, 2021. https://www.ghanaweb.com/GhanaHomePage/NewsArchive/Kan-Dapaah-must-resign-Adib-Sani-on-Western-Togoland-brouhaha-1071829.

"Kan Dapaah's attack on security analysts laughable – Adib Saani." *My Joy Online*, 12 February 2020. Accessed February 22, 2021. https://www.myjoyonline.com/kan-dapaahs-attack-on-security-analysts-laughable-adib-saani/.

Kapur, Saloni, and Simon Mabon. "The Copenhagen School goes global: securitisation in the Non-West." *Global Discourse* 8, no. 1 (2018): 1–4. https://doi.org/10.1080/23269995.2018.1424686.

Kedem, Kosi. "Why there is urgent need to talk about the British Togoland question." *Ghanaian Times*, 15 June 2022. https://www.ghanaiantimes.com.gh/why-there-is-urgent-need-to-talk-about-the-british-togoland-question/.

"Keep quiet and let experts speak – Information Minister chided over Western Togoland comments." *Happy Ghana*, 30 September 2020. Accessed November 26, 2021. https://www.ghanaweb.com/GhanaHomePage/NewsArchive/Keep-quiet-and-let-experts-speak-Information-Minister-chided-over-Western-Togoland-comments-1073740.

Keese, Alexander. "Rigged Elections? Democracy and Manipulation in the Late Colonial State in French West Africa and Togo, 1944–1958." In *The French Colonial Mind: Mental Maps of Empire and Colonial Encounters*. Vol. 1. Edited by Martin Thomas. 2 vols., 324–45. France Overseas: Studies in Empire and Decolonization Series 1. Lincoln: University of Nebraska Press, 2011.

Keese, Alexander. *Ethnicity and the Colonial State*. Studies in global social history 22. Boston: Brill, 2016. https://doi.org/10.1163/9789004307353.

Kelle, Udo, and Susann Kluge. *Vom Einzelfall zum Typus: Fallvergleich und Fallkontrastierung in der qualitativen Sozialforschung*. 2nd ed. Qualitative Sozialforschung 15. Wiesbaden: Verlag für Sozialwissenschaften, 2010.

Kelly, John D., and Martha Kaplan. "Nation and decolonization: Toward a new anthropology of nationalism." *Anthropological Theory* 1, no. 4 (2001): 419–37. https://doi.org/10.1177/14634990122228818.

Kent, John. "The Ewe Question: Origins and Impact, 1945–1949." In *The Internationalization of Colonialism*. Edited by John Kent, 214–38. Oxford University Press, 1992.

Kent, John. "The Ewe Question 1945–56: French and British Reactions to Nationalism in West Africa." In *Imperialism, the State, and the Third World*. Edited by Michael Twaddle, 183–206. London: British Academic Press, 1992.

Ketzmerick, Maria. *Staat, Sicherheit und Gewalt in Kamerun: Postkoloniale Perspektiven auf den Dekolonisierungsprozess unter französischer UN-Treuhandverwaltung*. Postcolonial studies 36. Bielefeld: transcript, 2019.

Ketzmerick, Maria, and Werner Distler. "The 'Politics of Protection' and Elections in Trusteeship and International Administration. The Cases of Cameroun and Kosovo." In Bonacker; Distler; Ketzmerick, *Securitization in Statebuilding and Intervention*, 127–54.

"Kill All Ewes in The Ashanti Region – Kennedy Agyapong." *GhanaWeb*, 16 April 2012. Accessed October 27, 2021. https://www.ghanaweb.com/GhanaHomePage/NewsArchive/Kill-All-Ewes-in-The-Ashanti-Region-Kennedy-Agyapong-236095.

Killingray, David. "Soldiers, Ex-Servicemen, and Politics in the Gold Coast, 1939–50." *The Journal of Modern African Studies* 21, no. 3 (1983): 534.

Killingray, David. "Guarding the Extending Frontier: Policing the Gold Coast, 1865–1913." In *Policing the empire: Government, authority and control, 1830–1940*. Edited by David Anderson and David Killingray, 106–25. Studies in imperialism. Manchester: Manchester University Press, 1991.

Knoll, Arthur J. *Togo under Imperial Germany 1884–1914: a case study in colonial rule*. Hoover colonial studies 190. Stanford: Hoover Inst. Press, 1978.

Knoll, Bernhard. "Legitimacy and UN-Administration of Territory." *German Law Journal* 8, no. 1 (2007): 39–56. https://doi.org/10.1017/S207183220000540X.

Koddenbrock, Kai. "Recipes for intervention: Western policy papers imagine the Congo." *International Peacekeeping* 19, no. 5 (2012): 549–64. https://doi.org/10.1080/13533312.2012.721987.

Korhonen, Outi. ""Post" As Justification: International Law and Democracy-Building after Iraq." *German Law Journal* 4, no. 7 (2003): 709–23. https://doi.org/10.1017/S2071832200016357.

Kponton, Ginette Ayélé. "La femme dans la lutte pour la décolonisation (1946–1960)." In Gayibor, *Les Togolais Face À La Colonisation*, 213–24.

Kponton, Ginette Ayélé. "Réactions populaires au pouvoir colonial: Agbetiko, Vogan et Mango (1951)." In Gayibor, *Les Togolais Face À La Colonisation*, 173–93.

Krasner, Stephen D., and Carlos Pascual. "Addressing State Failure." *Foreign Affairs*, July/August (2005): 153–63.

Krause, Keith, and Michael C. Williams, eds. *Critical Security Studies: Concepts and Cases*. Abingdon, Oxon: Routledge, 1997.

Krauthammer, Charles. "Trusteeship for Somalia: An Old-Colonial-Idea Whose Time Has Come Again." *Washington Post*, 09 October 1992.

Kreijen, Gerard. *State failure, sovereignty and effectiveness: Legal lessons from the decolonization of Sub-Saharan Africa*. Leiden, Great Britain: Martinus Nijhoff Publishers, 2004.

Kudzordzi (Ho), *Kudzordzi Archives*.

Kudzordzi, Charles Kwami. *A history of Eweland: A Resource Document for Ewe Socio-Political Studies*. Ho: E.P. Church Publishing Ltd., n.d.

Kudzordzi, Charles Kwami. *A Stolen Nation and Her Deprived Nationals: (Franco-British Atrocities in Togoland). An Irredentist Nationalism*. Ho: Win I.C.T. Centre, 2016.

Kudzordzi, Charles Kwami. Interview by Julius Heise. November 19, 2018. Ho, Ghana.

Kudzordzi, Charles Kwami. Interview by Julius Heise. November 21, 2018. Ho, Ghana.

Kudzordzi, Charles Kwami. *Founder of Western Togoland Papavi sends "Love Note" to President Akufo-Addo*. GhanaNews TV, 2019. YouTube. Accessed June 15, 2021. https://www.youtube.com/watch?v=P5phVqGsO9A.

Kurz, Christof P. "What You See is What You Get: Analytical Lenses and the Limitations of Post-Conflict Statebuilding in Sierra Leone." *Journal of Intervention and Statebuilding* 4, no. 2 (2010): 205–36. https://doi.org/10.1080/17502970903533702.

Kwawukume, Andy C.K. "Revisiting the Road to Secession Agitation in the Volta Region." *Modern Ghana*, 08 December 2019. Accessed December 9, 2019. https://www.modernghana.com/news/972331/revisiting-the-road-to-secession-agitation-in.html.

Kwon, Heonik. *The other Cold War*. Columbia studies in international and global history. New York: Columbia University Press, 2010. https://search.ebscohost.com/login.aspx?direct=true&scope=site&db=nlebk&db=nlabk&AN=982234.

"La France transmet des archives aux avocats de la famille." *L'Alternative*, 15 October 2021. No. 978. Accessed October 20, 2021.

Lake, David A. *The Statebuilder's Dilemma*. Cornell University Press, 2016. https://doi.org/10.7591/9781501703836.

Lake, David A. "Coercion and Trusteeship." In *The Oxford handbook of governance and limited statehood*. Edited by Thomas Risse, Tanja A. Börzel and Anke Draude. 1st ed., 293–311. Oxford handbooks. Oxford, New York: Oxford University Press, 2018.

Lake, David A., and Christopher J. Fariss. "Why International Trusteeship Fails: The Politics of External Authority in Areas of Limited Statehood." *Governance* 27, no. 4 (2014): 569–87. https://doi.org/10.1111/gove.12066.

Landwehr, Achim. *Historische Diskursanalyse*. 2nd ed. Historische Einführungen 4. Frankfurt/Main: Campus, 2009.

Lansing, Robert. *The Peace Negotiations: A Personal Narrative*. Boston, New York: The University Press Cambridge, 1921.

Lartey, Nii Larte. "Ohene, Elizabeth asks: Who speaks for Ewes?" *Citi Newsroom*, 02 November 2018. Accessed February 14, 2020. https://citinewsroom.com/2018/11/elizabeth-ohene-asks-who-speaks-for-the-ewes/.

Lartey, Nii Larte. "NCA shuts down Radio Tongu over national security concerns." *Citi Newsroom*, 12 February 2020. Accessed February 16, 2020. https://citinewsroom.com/2020/02/nca-shuts-down-radio-tongu-over-national-security-concerns/.

Latham, Michael E. *Modernization as ideology: American social science and "nation building" in the Kennedy era*. 2nd impr. The new Cold War history. Chapel Hill: University of North Carolina Press, 2006.

Laumann, Dennis. "A historiography of German Togoland, or the rise and fall of a "model colony."" *History in Africa* 30 (2003): 195–211.

Lawrance, Benjamin Nicholas. *Locality, Mobility, and "Nation": Periurban colonialism in Togo's Eweland, 1900–1960*. Rochester studies in African history and the diaspora. Rochester, NY: University of Rochester Press, 2007.

Lawrance, Benjamin Nicholas, Emily Lynn Osborn, and Richard L. Roberts, eds. *Intermediaries, interpreters, and clerks: African employees in the making of colonial Africa*. Africa and the diaspora: history, politics, culture. Madison: University of Wisconsin Press, 2006.

League of Nations. *The Mandate system: origin, principles, application*. Series of League of Nations Publications. Geneva.

League of Nations. *Official Journal.*, 1923 *League of Nations Official Journal* 4, no. 3.

League of Nations. Covenant. 1919. avalon.law.yale.edu/20th_century/leagcov.asp.

Lellouche, Pierre, and Dominique Moisi. "French Policy in Africa: A Lonely Battle against Destabilization." *International Security* 3, no. 4 (1979): 108. https://doi.org/10.2307/2626765.

Lemay-Hébert, Nicolas. "Statebuilding without Nation-building? Legitimacy, State Failure and the Limits of the Institutionalist Approach." *Journal of Intervention and Statebuilding* 3, no. 1 (2009): 21–45. https://doi.org/10.1080/17502970802608159.

Lemay-Hébert, Nicolas. "Rethinking Weberian approaches to statebuilding." In Chandler; Sisk, *Routledge Handbook of International Statebuilding*, 3–14.

Leonard, S., and Christian Kaunert. "Reconceptualising the Audience in Securitization Theory." In *How Security Problems Emerge and Dissolve*. Edited by Thierry Balzacq, 56–73. London: Routledge, 2011.

"Letsa Warns Media Promoting Secessionists." *Daily Guide Network*, 10 January 2020. Accessed January 15, 2020. https://dailyguidenetwork.com/letsa-warns-media-promoting-secessionists/.

Limon, Marc. *Reform of the UN Human Rights Petitions System: An assessment of the UN human rights communications procedures and proposals for a single integrated system.*, 2018.

Lobo-Guerrero, Luis. "Archives." In *Research methods in critical security studies: An introduction*. Edited by Mark B. Salter and Can E. Mutlu, 121–25. London, NewYork: Routledge, 2013.

Logan, Rayford. "The System of International Trusteeship." *The Journal of Negro Education* 15, no. 3 (1946): 408–19.

Lohrmann, Ullrich. *Voices from Tanganyika: Great Britain, the United Nations and the decolonization of a Trust Territory, 1946–1961*. Europa-Übersee 16. Berlin, London: Lit; Global, 2008.

Lottholz, Philipp, and Nicolas Lemay-Hébert. "Re-reading Weber, re-conceptualizing state-building: from neo-Weberian to post-Weberian approaches to state, legitimacy and state-building." *Cambridge Review of International Affairs* 29, no. 4 (2016): 1467–85. https://doi.org/10.1080/09557571.2016.1230588.

Luca, Stephen M. de. "The Gulf Crisis and Collective Security under the United Nations Charter." 3, no. 1 (1991): 267–307.

Luchaire, François. *Du Togo français sous tutelle à la République autonome du Togo*. Paris: Librairie générale de droit et de jurisprudence, 1957.

Lugard, Frederick Dealtry. *The Dual Mandate in British Tropical Africa*. 3rd ed. Blackwood, 1926.

Lukas, J. Anthony. "Olympio Doomed by Own Letter: Sergent whose job appeal failed slew Togo Head." *New York Times*, 22 January 1963.

Lyon, Peter. "The rise and fall and possible revival of international trusteeship." *The Journal of Commonwealth & Comparative Politics* 31, no. 1 (1993): 96–110. https://doi.org/10.1080/14662049308447651.

Mac Ginty, Roger. *International peacebuilding and local resistance: Hybrid forms of peace*. Rethinking peace and conflict studies. New York: Palgrave Macmillan, 2011. http://site.ebrary.com/lib/alltitles/docDetail.action?docID=10481693.

Mac Ginty, Roger, and Oliver P. Richmond. "The Local Turn in Peace Building:: a critical agenda for peace." *Third World Quarterly* 34, no. 5 (2013): 763–83. https://doi.org/10.1080/01436597.2013.800750.

MacKenzie, Megan H. *Female soldiers in Sierra Leone: Sex, security, and post-conflict development*. Gender and political violence series. New York: New York University Press, 2016.

MAE (La Courneuve), 77QO-5, *Politique intérieure*.

MAE (La Courneuve), 77QO-2, *Politique intérieure*.

MAE (La Courneuve), 77QO-4, *Politique intérieure*.

MAE (La Courneuve), 77QO-10, *Nouvel examen de la question togolaise par la 4ème Commission de l'Assemblée générale des Nations Unies*.

MAE (La Courneuve), 77QO-11, *Nouvel examen de la question togolaise par la 4ème Commission de l'Assemblée générale des Nations Unies*.

MAE (La Courneuve), 77QO-13, *Élections de 1958, travaux du Conseil de Tutelle*.

Mann, Gregory. "What was the Indigénat? The 'Empire of Law' in French West Africa." *Journal of African History* 50, no. 3 (2009): 331–53. https://doi.org/10.1017/S0021853709990090.

Marauhn, Thilo, and Michael Bothe. "UN Administration of Kosovo and East Timor: Concept, Legality and Limitations of Security Council-Mandated Trusteeship Administration." In *Kosovo and the international community: A legal assessment*. Edited by Christian Tomuschat, S. 217–242. The Hague: Den Haag; Kluwer Law International, 2002.

Marquette, Heather, and Danielle Beswick. "State Building, Security and Development: state building as a new development paradigm?" *Third World Quarterly* 32, no. 10 (2011): 1703–14. https://doi.org/10.1080/01436597.2011.610565.

Mawunyah, Nicholas. "The complexities of the Western Togoland problem." *My Joy Online*, 26 September 2020. Accessed September 30, 2020. https://www.myjoyonline.com/opinion/nicholas-mawunyah-the-complexities-of-the-western-togoland-problem/.

Mayall, James, and Ricardo Soares de Oliveira. *The new protectorates: International tutelage and the making of liberal states*. New York: Columbia University Press, 2011.

Mayring, Philipp. *Qualitative content analysis: theoretical foundation, basic procedures and software solution*. Klagenfurt, 2014. http://nbn-resolving.de/urn:nbn:de:0168-ssoar-395173.

Mazower, Mark. *No Enchanted Palace: The End of Empire and the Ideological Origins of the United Nations*. Lawrence Stone lectures. Princeton: Princeton University Press, 2009.

Mazower, Mark. *Governing the world: The history of an idea*. London: Lane, 2012.

Mazrui, Ali. "Decaying Parts of Africa Need Benign Colonization." *International Herald Tribune*, 04 August 1994.

McHendry, George F. "The politics and poetics of airport (in)security rhetoric: Materialism, affect, and the Transportation Security Administration." Dissertation, Department of Communication, University of Utah, 2013. https://core.ac.uk/download/pdf/276265588.pdf.

McSweeney, Bill. "Identity and Security: Buzan and the Copenhagen School." *Review of International Studies* 22, no. 1 (1996): 81–93. https://www.jstor.org/stable/20097432.

Mégret, Frédéric, and Florian Hoffmann. "The UN as a Human Rights Violator? Some Reflections on the United Nations Changing Human Rights Responsibilities." *Human Rights Quarterly* 25, no. 2 (2003): 314–42.

Mensah, Mary. "Suspected secessionists charged for conspiring to commit treason felony." *Graphic Online*, 08 May 2019. Accessed November 23, 2021. https://www.graphic.com.gh/news/general-news/ghana-news-suspected-secessionists-charged-they-conspire-to-commit-treason-felony.html.

Michel, Marc. "The Independence of Togo." In *Decolonization and African Independence: The transfer of power, 1960–1980*. Edited by Prosser Gifford, 295–319. New Haven: Yale University Press, 1988.

Michels, Stefanie. "Koloniale Beutekunst: Andauerndes Verstecken hinter rechtlichen Konzepten." *Forum Recht*, no. 3 (2011): 78–79.

Mifetu, Seth. "Why Western Togoland Restoration Struggle Is Lawful." *Modern Ghana*, 27 November 2019. Accessed March 26, 2020. https://www.modernghana.com/news/970111/why-western-togoland-restoration-struggle-is-lawfu.html.

Mifetu, Seth. "How divine Odonkor saved Ghana from torrential encumbrances." *Modern Ghana*, 08 August 2020. Accessed September 14, 2020. https://www.modernghana.com/news/1021684/how-divine-odonkor-saved-ghana-from-torrential.html.

Mignolo, Walter D., and Catherine E. Walsh, eds. *On decoloniality: Concepts, analytics, and praxis*. On decoloniality. Durham, London: Duke University Press, 2018.

Milliken, Jennifer, ed. *State failure, collapse and reconstruction*. Development and change book series. Malden, MA: Blackwell, 2003.

Moberly, F. J. *Military operations: Togoland and the Cameroons, 1914–1916*. London: H.M.S.O., 1931.

Moffette, David, and Shaira Vadasaria. "Uninhibited violence: race and the securitization of immigration." *Critical Studies on Security* 4, no. 3 (2016): 291–305. https://doi.org/10.1080/21624887.2016.1256365.

Momirov, Aleksandar. *Accountability of International Territorial Administrations: A Public Law Approach*. The Hague: Eleven International Publishing.

Momirov, Aleksandar. "The Individual Right to Petition in Internationalized Territories: From Progressive Thought to an Abandoned Practice." *Journal of the History of International Law* 9, no. 2 (2007): 203–31. https://doi.org/10.1163/138819907X237174.

Morlang, Thomas. *Askari und Fitafita: "Farbige" Söldner in den deutschen Kolonien*. Berlin: Ch. Links, 2008.

Morrell, W. Gordon. "A Higher Stage of Imperialism? The Big Three, the UN Trusteeship Council, and the Early Cold War." In *Imperialism on trial: International oversight of colonial rule in historical perspective*. Edited by R. M. Douglas, Michael D. Callahan and Elizabeth Bishop, 111–37. Lanham, Md.: Lexington Books, 2006.

Mortimer, Edward. "The Politics of International Administration." *Global Governance* 10, no. 1 (2004): 7–14. https://www.jstor.org/stable/27800505.

Moss, Michael S., and David Thomas, eds. *Archival silences: Missing, lost and, uncreated archives*. London, New York: Routledge, 2021.

Mubarik, Abu. "Over 1000 security personnel deployed for Oti Region referendum." *Pulse GH*, 26 December 2018. Accessed December 6, 2019. https://www.pulse.com.gh/news/local/over-1000-security-personnel-deployed-for-oti-referendum/r8nf32m.

Munzinger. "Olympio, Sylvanus." http://www.munzinger.de/document/00000009107.

Murray, Christopher. "Imperial dialectics and epistemic mapping: From decolonisation to anti-Eurocentric IR." *European Journal of International Relations* 26, no. 2 (2020): 419–42. https://doi.org/10.1177/1354066119873030.

Nartey, Kabu. "Our independence is not complete without Western Togoland." *My Joy Online*, 04 December 2019. Accessed December 5, 2019. https://www.myjoyonline.com/opinion/2019/December-4th/kabu-nartey-writes-our-independence-is-not-complete-without-western-togoland.php.

National Liberation Movement of Western Togoland. "Movement of Western Togoland (NLMWT): On The Question of Liberation of Western Togoland And The Reunification Of Togo At The Headquraters of The UNO In New York On Octover 12, 1976." *New York Times*, 15 October 1976.

Nay, Olivier. "Fragile and failed states: Critical perspectives on conceptual hybrids." *International Political Science Review* 34, no. 3 (2013): 326–41. https://doi.org/10.1177/0192512113480054.

"NCCE calls for peaceful co-existence." *Business Ghana*, 24 August 2021. Accessed September 2, 2021. http://www.businessghana.com/site/news/politics/244863/NCCE-calls-for-peaceful-co-existence.

"NCCE cautions security against threats of vigilantism, fundamentalism and secessionism." *Ghana News Agency*, 09 May 2021. Accessed May 11, 2021. https://newsghana.com.gh/ncce-cautions-security-against-threats-of-vigilantism-fundamentalism-and-secessionism/.

Newman, Edward. "The violence of statebuilding in historical perspective: Implications for peacebuilding." *Peacebuilding* 1, no. 1 (2013): 141–57. https://doi.org/10.1080/21647259.2013.756281.

"News in Brief: Two More Die After Ghana Explosion." *The Times*, 11 September 1962. No. 55493.

Nexon, Dan, and Patrick Thaddeus Jackson, writers, "It Isn't Just About Wæver and Buzan." aired May 27, 2020. https://www.duckofminerva.com/2020/05/it-isnt-just-about-waever-and-buzan.html.

"No amount of arrest will stop us – Citizens of Western Togoland." *Rainbow Radio*, 18 September 2020. Accessed September 21, 2020. https://www.rainbowradioonline.com/no-amount-of-arrest-will-stop-us-citizens-of-western-togoland/.

Nugent, Paul. *Smugglers, secessionists & loyal citizens on the Ghana-Togo frontier: The lie of the borderlands since 1914*. Western African studies. Athens: Ohio University Press, 2002.

Nugent, Paul. "Putting the History Back into Ethnicity: Enslavement, Religion, and Cultural Brokerage in the Construction of Mandinka/Jola and Ewe/Agotime Identities in West Africa, c. 1650–1930." *Comparative Studies in Society and History* 50, no. 4 (2008): 920–48. https://www.jstor.org/stable/27563713.

Nugent, Paul. *Boundaries, communities, and state-making in West Africa: The centrality of the margins*. African Studies 144. Cambridge, United Kingdom, New York: Cambridge University Press, 2019.

Nugent, Paul, and Carola Lentz, eds. *Ethnicity in Ghana: The Limits of Invention*. London: Palgrave Macmillan, 2016.

Nyabor, Jonas. "Eight arrested for trying to declare Volta Region an independent state." *Citi Newsroom*, 06 May 2019. Accessed July 30, 2020. https://citinewsroom.com/2019/05/eight-arrested-for-trying-to-declare-volta-region-an-independent-state/.

Nyabor, Jonas. "Clamp down on Western Togoland 'militia group' – Security analyst to government." *Citi Newsroom*, 18 December 2019. Accessed December 18, 2019. https://citinewsroom.com/2019/12/clamp-down-on-western-togoland-militia-group-security-analyst-to-govt/.

Obuobi, Patrick Peprah. "Evaluating Ghana's Intelligence Oversight Regime." *International Journal of Intelligence and CounterIntelligence* 31, no. 2 (2018): 312–41. https://doi.org/10.1080/08850607.2017.1375841.

Okoampa-Ahoofe, Kwame, JR. "Let Us Settle the Western Togoland Problem Once and for All." *Modern Ghana*, 08 December 2019. Accessed December 9, 2019. https://www.modernghana.com/news/972367/let-us-settle-the-western-togoland-problem-once.html.

Olympio, Sylvanus E. "African Problems and the Cold War." *Foreign Affairs* 40, no. 1 (1961): 50.

Olympio, Sylvanus E. "Allocution mensuelle du Président Olympio: 24 Novembre 1961." In *Quelques Discours Importants du Président Sylvanus Olympio en 1961*. Edited by Republique Togolaise, 50–54. Lomé, 1962.

O'Reilly, K. P. "Perceiving Rogue States: The Use of the "Rogue State" Concept by U.S. Foreign Policy Elites." *Foreign Policy Analysis* 3, no. 4 (2007): 295–315. https://doi.org/10.1111/j.1743-8594.2007.00052.x.

Orford, Anne. *International Authority and the Responsibility to Protect*. Cambridge: Cambridge University Press, 2011. https://doi.org/10.1017/CBO9780511973574.

Orwell, George. *Politics and the English Language*. London: Pinguin Books UK, 2013 [1946].

Osei, Leticia. "Police to charge Volta 'separatist' group members with Treason." *Ultimate FM online*, 08 March 2017. Accessed July 14, 2020. https://web.archive.org/web/20180212055652/http://ultimatefmonline.com/2017/03/08/police-charge-volta-separatist-group-members-treason/.

Osei-Hwedie, Kwaku, T. Galvin, and H. Shinoda, eds. *Indigenous methods of peacebuilding*. Hiroshima: Institute for Peace Science Hiroshima University, 2012.

"Our 4000-man army Dragons'll re-claim 'the motherland' in 21 days – Togolanders warn Amewu, Letsa, Ablakwa." *Class FM online*, 14 October 2020. Accessed June 16, 2021. https://www.classfmonline.com/news/politics/Our-4000-man-army-Dragons-ll-re-claim-the-motherland-in-21-days-Togolanders-warn-Amewu-Letsa-Ablakwa-19360.

Padmore, George Arthur. *The Gold Coast revolution: The struggle of an African people from slavery to freedom*. London: Dennis Dobson Ltd, 1953.

Paliwal, Avinash. "Colonial Sinews of Postcolonial Espionage: India and the Making of Ghana's External Intelligence Agency, 1958–61." *The International History Review*, 2021, 1–21. https://doi.org/10.1080/07075332.2021.1888768.

Paliwal, Avinash. "Ghana's national security ministry ignites old fears after fracas over photos." *The Conversation*, 30 May 2021. Accessed June 16, 2021. https://theconversation.com/ghanas-national-security-ministry-ignites-old-fears-after-fracas-over-photos-161663.

"Papavi's death should not be viewed as end of Western Togoland separatists – Security analyst warns." *GhanaWeb*, 18 October 2021. Accessed October 22, 2021. https://www.ghanaweb.com/GhanaHomePage/NewsArchive/Papavi-s-death-should-not-be-viewed-as-end-of-Western-Togoland-separatists-Security-analyst-warns-1382563.

Paris, Roland. "Peacebuilding and the Limits of Liberal Internationalism." *International Security* 22, no. 2 (1997): 54. https://doi.org/10.2307/2539367.

Paris, Roland. "Human Security: Paradigm Shift or Hot Air?" *International Security* 26, no. 2 (2001): 87–102.

Paris, Roland. *At war's end: Building peace after civil conflict*. Cambridge: Cambridge University Press, 2004. https://doi.org/10.1017/CBO9780511790836.

Paris, Roland. "Saving liberal peacebuilding." *Review of International Studies* 36, no. 2 (2010): 337–65. https://doi.org/10.1017/S0260210510000057.

Paris, Roland, and Timothy D. Sisk, eds. *The dilemmas of statebuilding: Confronting the contradictions of postwar peace operations*. Security and governance series. London: Routledge, 2010.

Parker, Tom. *The Ultimate Intervention: Revitalising the UN Trusteeship Council for the 21st Century*. Sandvika, 2003. Accessed July 29, 2019. www.bi.edu/globalassets/forskning/centre-for-european-and-asian-studies/pdf/03-03the_ultimate_intervention.pdf.

"Parliament discusses Security and Intelligence Agencies Bill, 2020." *Ghana News Agency*, 12 August 2020. Accessed February 22, 2021. newsghana.com.gh/parliament-discusses-security-and-intelligence-agencies-bill-2020/.

Pauvert, Jean-Claude. "L'évolution politique des Ewés." *Cahiers d'études africaines*, no. 2 (1960): 161–92.

Pearson, Jessica Lynne. "Defending Empire at the United Nations: The Politics of International Colonial Oversight in the Era of Decolonisation." *The Journal of Imperial and Commonwealth History* 45, no. 3 (2017): 525–49. https://doi.org/10.1080/03086534.2017.1332133.

Pedersen, Susan. *The guardians: The League of Nations and the crisis of empire*. New York, NY: Oxford University Press, 2015.

Peoples, Columba, and Nick Vaughan-Williams. *Critical Security Studies: An Introduction*. London: Routledge, 2010.

Perritt, Henry H. "Structures and Standards for Political Trusteeship." *Journal of International Law and Foreign Affairs* 8, no. 2 (2003): 385–472.

Perritt, Henry H. "Providing Judicial Review for Decisions by Political Trustees." *Duke Journal of Comparative & International Law* 15, no. 1 (2004): 1–74.

Pfaff, William. "A New Colonialism? Europe Must Go Back into Africa." *Foreign Affairs* 74, no. 1 (1995): 2–6. https://doi.org/10.2307/20047013.

Pigeaud, Fanny. "La famille du président du Togo tué en 1963 réclame l'accès aux archives françaises." *Mediapart*, 21 June 2021. Accessed October 20, 2021. https://www.mediapart.fr/journal/international/210621/la-famille-du-president-du-togo-tue-en-1963-reclame-l-acces-aux-archives-francaises.

"Police or Army." *Ashanti Pioneer*, 14 March 1957.

Popper, Karl R. *Conjectures and Refutations: The growth of scientific knowledge*. London: Routledge, 1963.

Powell, Nathaniel K. "Battling Instability? The Recurring Logic of French Military Interventions in Africa." *African Security* 10, no. 1 (2017): 47–72. https://doi.org/10.1080/19392206.2016.1270141.

PRAAD (Accra), ADM 39/1/339, *Unification of Ewe speaking Peoples*.

PRAAD (Accra), ADM 39/1/676, *Standing Consultative Commission for Togoland*.

PRAAD (Accra), ADM 39/1/677, *Agenda notes and minutes of the Standing Consultative Commission for Togoland*.

PRAAD (Ho), VRG/AD/250, *Standing Consultative Commission for Togoland*.

PRAAD (Ho), VRG/AD/1027, *Standing Consultative Commission for Togoland*.

PRAAD (Accra), ADM 39/1/651, *Togoland Union and Togoland Association for the United Nation Association Statement subject and reasons etc*.

PRAAD (Accra), ADM 39/1/105, *United Nations Organisation Visiting Mission – Petitions*.

PRAAD (Accra), ADM 39/1/94, *Administration of Southern Togoland*.

PRAAD (Ho), VRG/AD/1185, *Trusteeship Council 6th Session June 1950*.

PRAAD (Ho), D/DA/376, *Togo Union*.

PRAAD (Ho), VRG/AD/1043, *Trusteeship Council and Togoland*.

PRAAD (Accra), RG 3/5/2073, *"Trusteeship Council's Discussions on Togoland T/C.2/SR.227 (10 Feb 1955)"*.

PRAAD (Ho), not indexed by PRAAD [No. 38/SF.8-10], *CENSEC [Central Security Committee] & Ghana Intelligence Comitee – General*.

PRAAD, 038/SF12 [old signature], *Field Intelligence Organisation*.

PRAAD (Ho), D-DA-368, *Frontier Incidents Ghana / Togoland*.

PRAAD (Accra), RG 17/1/224, *Daniel Chapman.*
PRAAD (Accra), RG 17/1/281, *Special Commitee – Togoland Affairs.*
PRAAD (Accra), RG 17/1/325, *Note of Protest to the Govt of Togo.*
Prohibited Organisations Act. Supreme Military Council Decree 20. 1976. Accessed March 22, 2023. https://lawsghana.com/pre_1992_legislation/SMC%20Decree/PROHIBITED%20ORGANISATIONS%20ACT,%201976%20(SMCD%2020)/118.
Pugh, Michael. "Protectorates and Spoils of Peace: Political Economy in South-East Europe." In *Shadow globalization, ethnic conflicts and new wars: A political economy of intrastate war.* Edited by Dietrich Jung, 47–69. The new international relations series. London: Routledge, 2003.
Pugh, Michael. "The Political Economy of Peacebuilding: A Critical Theory Perspective." *International Journal of Peace Studies* 10, no. 2 (2005): 23–42. Accessed February 8, 2022. https://www.jstor.org/stable/41852928.
Pugh, Michael, Neil Cooper, and Mandy Turner. *Whose Peace? Critical Perspectives on the Political Economy of Peacebuilding.* New Security Challenges. London: Palgrave Macmillan, 2008. https://doi.org/10.1057/9780230228740.
Quaison-Sackey, Alex. *Africa unbound: Reflections of an African statesman.* New York: Praeger, 1963.
"Radio Tongu broadcaster suspended, director arrested in Ghana." *Committee to Protect Journalists*, 11 March 2020. Accessed November 27, 2021. https://cpj.org/2020/03/radio-tongu-broadcaster-suspended-director-arreste/.
Rajagopal, Balakrishnan. *International law from below: Development, social movements, and Third World resistance.* Cambridge, U.K, New York: Cambridge University Press, 2003. https://search.ebscohost.com/login.aspx?direct=true&scope=site&db=nlebk&db=nlabk&AN=120466.
Rathbone, Richard. "The Government of the Gold Coast after the Second World War." *African Affairs* 67, no. 268 (1968): 209–18. https://www.jstor.org/stable/719904.
Rathbone, Richard. "Police intelligence in Ghana in the late 1940s and 1950s." *The Journal of Imperial and Commonwealth History* 21, no. 3 (1993): 107–28. https://doi.org/10.1080/03086539308582909.
Rathbone, Richard. "West Africa: Modernity & Modernization." In *African modernities entangled meanings in current debate.* Edited by Heike Schmidt and Jan-Georg Deutsch, 18–30. Portsmouth, NH: Heinemann, 2002.
Raunet Robert-Nicoud, Nathalie. "Elections and borderlands in Ghana." *African Affairs* 118, no. 473 (2019): 672–91. https://doi.org/10.1093/afraf/adz002.
Republique Togolaise, ed. *Quelques Discours Importants du Président Sylvanus Olympio en 1961.* Lomé, 1962; Olympio, Sylvanus E.
Reychler, Luc. "Peacemaking, Peacekeeping, and Peacebuilding." *Oxford Research Encyclopedia of International Studies*, 2017. Accessed October 12, 2021. https://doi.org/10.1093/acrefore/9780190846626.013.274. https://oxfordre.com/internationalstudies/view/10.1093/acrefore/9780190846626.001.0001/acrefore-9780190846626-e-274.
Richardson, Henry J. ""Failed states," self-determination, and preventive diplomacy: Colonialist nostalgia and democratic expextations." *Temple international and comparative law journal*, 1996.

Richmond, Oliver P. "A post-liberal peace: Eirenism and the everyday." *Review of International Studies* 35, no. 3 (2009): 557–80. https://doi.org/10.1017/S0260210509008651.

Richmond, Oliver P. *A post-liberal peace*. Routledge studies in peace and conflict resolution. London: Routledge, 2011.

Richmond, Oliver P. *Failed statebuilding: Intervention, the state, and the dynamics of peace formation*. New Haven: Yale University Press, 2014. http://search.ebscohost.com/login.aspx?direct=true&scope=site&db=nlebk&db=nlabk&AN=861313.

Richmond, Oliver P. "Rescuing Peacebuilding? Anthropology and Peace Formation." *Global Society* 32, no. 2 (2018): 221–39. https://doi.org/10.1080/13600826.2018.1451828.

Richmond, Oliver P., and Gëzim Visoka, eds. *The Oxford Handbook of Peacebuilding, Statebuilding, and Peace Formation*. Oxford University Press, 2021.

Richmond, Oliver P. P. *Hybrid Forms of Peace: From Everyday Agency to Post-Liberalism*. Rethinking peace and conflict studies. Basingstoke: Palgrave Macmillan, 2011. http://gbv.eblib.com/patron/FullRecord.aspx?p=931736.

Risse, Thomas. *Governance Without a State: Policies and Politics in Areas of Limited Statehood*. New York: Columbia University Press, 2011.

Roe, Paul. "The Intrastate Security Dilemma: Ethnic Conflict as a 'Tragedy'?" *Journal of Peace Research* 36, no. 2 (1999): 183–202.

Rotberg, Robert I. "Failed States in a World of Terror." *Foreign Affairs* 81, no. 4 (2002): 127. https://doi.org/10.2307/20033245.

Rubin, Barnett. "Peace Building and State-Building in Afghanistan: Constructing Sovereignity for Whose Security?" *Third World Quarterly* 27, no. 1 (2006): 175–85.

Rubinstein, Robert A. "Peacekeeping and the Return of Imperial Policing." *International Peacekeeping* 17, no. 4 (2010): 457–70. https://doi.org/10.1080/13533312.2010.516652.

Ruby, Sigrid, and Anja Krause, eds. *Sicherheit und Differenz in historischer Perspektive*. 1st edition. Politiken der Sicherheit 10. Baden-Baden: Nomos, 2022.

Ruzicka, Jan. "Failed Securitization: Why It Matters." *Polity* 51, no. 2 (2019): 365–77. https://doi.org/10.1086/702213.

Sabaratnam, Meera. "IR in Dialogue ... but Can We Change the Subjects? A Typology of Decolonising Strategies for the Study of World Politics." *Millennium: Journal of International Studies* 39, no. 3 (2011): 781–803. https://doi.org/10.1177/0305829811404270.

Sabaratnam, Meera. "History repeating? Colonial, socialist, and liberal statebuilding in Mozambique." In Chandler; Sisk, *Routledge Handbook of International Statebuilding*, 106–17.

Sabaratnam, Meera. *Decolonising intervention: International statebuilding in Mozambique*. Kilombo: International Relations and Colonial Questions. London, Lanham, Maryland: Rowman & Littlefield, 2017.

Scartozzi, Cesare Marco. "Decolonizing One Petition at the Time: A Review of the Practice of Accepting Petitions and Granting Oral Hearings in the Fourth Committee." *Politikon: IAPSS Journal of Political Science* 34 (2017): 49–67. https://doi.org/10.22151/politikon.34.4.

Schlichte, Klaus. *Der Staat in der Weltgesellschaft: Politische Herrschaft in Asien, Afrika und Lateinamerika*. Frankfurt/Main, New York: Campus, 2005.

Schneider, Robert A., ed. "AHR Forum: Entangled Empires in the Atlantic World." Special issue, *The American Historical Review* 112, no. 3 (2007). https://www.jstor.org/stable/i40000361.

Schou Tjalve, Vibeke. "Designing (de)security: European exceptionalism, Atlantic republicanism and the 'public sphere'." *Security Dialogue* 42, 4–5 (2011): 441–52. https://doi.org/10.1177/0967010611418715.

SCRBC (New York). Bunche, Ralph Johnson, b. 12 f. 5, *Doctoral Thesis "French Administration in Togoland and Dahomey"*.

SCRBC (New York). Bunche, Ralph Johnson, b. 45 f. 16, *Proposed Agreement: French Togoland*.

Sebald, Peter. *Togo 1884–1914. Eine Geschichte der deutschen „Musterkolonie" auf der Grundlage amtlicher Quellen*. De Gruyter, 1987. https://doi.org/10.1515/9783112472583.

Sebald, Peter. *Die deutsche Kolonie Togo 1884 – 1914: Auswirkungen einer Fremdherrschaft*. Schlaglichter der Kolonialgeschichte 14. Berlin: Links, 2013.

Seckinelgin, Hakan, and Joseph Bigirumwami. "Securitization of HIV/AIDS in Context: Gendered Vulnerability in Burundi." *Security Dialogue* 41, no. 5 (2010): 515–35.

"Separatist movement intended to destabilize Volta Reg. ahead of polls – MP." *Starr FM Online*, 30 September 2020. Accessed September 30, 2020. https://starrfm.com.gh/2020/09/separatist-movement-intended-to-destabilize-volta-reg-ahead-of-polls-mp/.

Shilliam, Robbie. *International relations and non-Western thought: Imperialism, colonialism and investigations of global modernity*. London: Routledge, 2012.

Silva, Marta. "Securitization as a nation-building instrument." *Politikon: IAPSS Journal of Political Science* 29 (2016): 201–14. https://doi.org/10.22151/politikon.29.12.

Sinclair, Georgina. *At the end of the line: Colonial policing and the imperial endgame, 1945–80*. Studies in imperialism. Manchester: Manchester University Press, 2010.

Sinclair, Georgina, and Chris A. Williams. "'Home and Away': The Cross-Fertilisation between 'Colonial' and 'British' Policing, 1921–85." *The Journal of Imperial and Commonwealth History* 35, no. 2 (2007): 221–38. https://doi.org/10.1080/03086530701337567.

Skinner, Kate. "Local Historians and Strangers with Big Eyes: The Politics of Ewe History in Ghana and Its Global Diaspora." *History in Africa* 37 (2010): 125–58. https://doi.org/10.1353/hia.2010.0022.

Skinner, Kate. *The Fruits of Freedom in British Togoland: Literacy, Politics and Nationalism, 1914–2014*. African Studies 132. New York: Cambridge University Press, 2015.

Skinner, Kate. "West Africa's First Coup: Neo-Colonial and Pan-African Projects in Togo's "Shadow Archives."" *African Studies Review* 63, no. 2 (2019): 375–98. https://doi.org/10.1017/asr.2019.39.

Smith, Shirley B. "The formation and functioning of the Trusteeship Council procedure for examining petitions." Master's Thesis, Boston University, 1957. Accessed February 3, 2020. hdl.handle.net/2144/22520.

Smuts, Jan Christiaan. *The basis of trusteeship in African native policy*. New Africa pamphlet 2. Johannesburg: R. L. Esson, 1942.

Snetkov, Aglaya. "Theories, methods and practices: a longitudinal spatial analysis of the (de)securitization of the insurgency threat in Russia." *Security Dialogue* 48, no. 3 (2017): 259–75. https://doi.org/10.1177/0967010617701676.

Spieth, Andreas Jakob. *Die Ewe-Stämme: Material zur Kunde des Ewe-Volkes in Deutsch-Togo*. Berlin: Reimer, 1906. https://archive.org/stream/dieewestmmematoospie#page/n9/mode/2up.

Spivak, Gayatri Chakravorty. "Can the subaltern speak?" In *Colonial discourse and postcolonial theory: A reader*. Edited by Patrick Williams, 66–111. New York, NY: Harvester Wheatsheaf, 1993. http://planetarities.web.unc.edu/files/2015/01/spivak-subaltern-speak.pdf.

Stoler, Ann Laura. *Along the archival grain: Epistemic anxieties and colonial common sense*. Princeton, NJ: Princeton University Press, 2009.

Streets-Salter, Heather, and Trevor R. Getz. *Empires and colonies in the modern world: A global perspective*. New York: Oxford University Press, 2016.

Stritzel, Holger. "Towards a Theory of Securitization: Copenhagen and Beyond." *European Journal of International Relations* 13, no. 3 (2007): 357–83. https://doi.org/10.1177/1354066107080128.

Stritzel, Holger, and Sean C. Chang. "Securitization and counter-securitization in Afghanistan." *Security Dialogue* 46, no. 6 (2015): 548–67. https://doi.org/10.1177/0967010615588725.

Suissa, Rachel. "The Scientific Status of New Security Studies: A Critical Search for Epistemic Identity of Homeland and Civil Security Research." In *Cross-disciplinary Perspectives on Homeland and Civil Security: A Research-Based Introduction*. Edited by Alexander Siedschlag, 231–45. New York: Peter Lang Inc., International Academic Publishers, 2016.

TCOR. "The future of the Trust Territory of Togoland under French Administration: memorandum by the Administering Authority." T/1290. https://digitallibrary.un.org/record/1653395.

TCOR. "1st Session." 1947.

TCOR. "2nd Session." 1947.

TCOR. "Memorandum on the Petition of the All Ewe Conference to the United Nations." T/58, 1947.

TCOR. "Trusteeship Agreements." T/8, 1947.

TCOR. "3rd Session." 1948.

TCOR. "4th Session." 1949.

TCOR. "5th Session." 1949.

TCOR. "6th Session." 1950.

TCOR. "6th Session: Special Report of the first Visiting Mission to the Trust Territories of Togoland under British Administration and under French Administration on the Ewe Problem." T/463, 1950. digitallibrary.un.org/record/794632.

TCOR. "7th Session." 1950.

TCOR. "3rd Special Session." 1951.

TCOR. "7th Session: Reports of the United Nations Visiting Mission to Trust Territories in West Africa." Supplement No.2 (T/793), 1951.

TCOR. "8th Session." 1951.

TCOR. "9th Session." 1951.

TCOR. "10th Session." 1952.

TCOR. "11th Session." 1952.

TCOR. "11th Session: Special report of the United Nations Visiting Mission to Trust Territories in West Africa, 1952, on the Ewe and Togoland unification problem." T/1034, 1952.
TCOR. "13th Session." 1954.
TCOR. "13th Session: Visiting Mission 1952 Report on Togoland under French Administration." Supplement No. 3 (1108), 1954.
TCOR. "13th Session: Visiting Mission 1952 Report on Togoland under United Kingdom Administration." Supplement No. 2 (T/1107), 1954.
TCOR. "14th Session." 1954.
TCOR. "14th Session: The Future of the Trust Territory of Togoland under British Administration." A/2660, 21 June 1954.
TCOR. "5th Special Session." 1955.
TCOR. "5th Special Session: Special Report on the Togoland Unification problem and the future of the Trust Territory of Togoland under British Administration." Supplement No. 2 (T/1218), 1955.
TCOR. "17th Session." 1956.
TCOR. "18th Session." 1956.
TCOR. "6th Special Session." 1956.
TCOR. "19th Session." 1957.
TCOR. "7th Special Session." 1957.
TCOR. "7th Special Session: Report of the United Nations Commission on Togoland under French Administration." Supplement No. 2 (T/1343), 1958.
TCOR. "8th Special Session." 1958.
TCOR. "Report of the United Nations Commissioner for the Supervision of the Elections in Togoland under French Administration." T/1392, 30 June 1958.
"Telegrams in Brief: Commonwealth, Accra." *The Times*, 27 May 1958. No. 54161.
Terretta, Meredith. ""We Had Been Fooled into Thinking that the UN Watches over the Entire World": Human Rights, UN Trust Territories, and Africa's Decolonization." *Human Rights Quarterly* 34, no. 2 (2012): 329–60. https://doi.org/10.1353/hrq.2012.0022.
Terretta, Meredith. *Petitioning for our rights, fighting for our nation: The history of the Democratic Union of Cameroonian Women, 1949–1960*. Bamenda, Cameroon: Langaa Research & Publishing, 2013. URL http://afrika.proxy.fid-lizenzen.de/fid/abc-ebooks/publikationen.ub.uni-frankfurt.de/frontdoor/index/index/docId/60341.
Terretta, Meredith. *Nation of outlaws, state of violence: Nationalism, Grassfields tradition, and state building in Cameroon*. New African histories. Athens, Ohio: Ohio University Press, 2014.
Tété-Adjalogo, Têtêvi Godwin. *Histoire du Togo: Le regime et l'assassinat de Sylvanus Olympio 1960–1963*. Histoire du Togo 3. Paris: NM7 Editions, 2002.
"The Trust Territory of Togoland: An International Precedent." *The International Law Quarterly* 2, no. 2 (1948): 257–60; Editorial Notes. www.jstor.org/stable/763176.
Thomas, Martin, ed. *The French Colonial Mind: Mental Maps of Empire and Colonial Encounters*. 2 vols. France Overseas: Studies in Empire and Decolonization Series 1. Lincoln: University of Nebraska Press, 2011.

Thomas, Martin. *Violence and colonial order: Police, workers and protest in the European colonial empires, 1918–1940*. 1st ed. Critical perspectives on empire. Cambridge: Cambridge University Press, 2012.

Thompson, Willard Scott. *Ghana's Foreign Policy, 1957–1966: Diplomacy Ideology, and the New State*. Princeton Legacy Library. Princeton: Princeton University Press, 1969.

Thullen, George. *Problems of the Trusteeship System: A Study of Political Behavior in the United Nations*. Travaux de droit d'économie, de sociologie et de sciences politiques 24. Genève: E. Droz, 1964.

Tickner, Judith Ann. *Gender in international relations: Feminist perspectives on achieving global security*. New directions in world politics. New York, NY: Columbia Univ. Press, 1992.

Tilly, Charles, ed. *The formation of national states in Western Europe*. Studies in political development 8. Princeton, N.J.: Princeton University Press, 1975.

Tilly, Charles. *Coercion, capital, and European states, AD 990–1990*. Studies in social discontinuity. Cambridge, MA: Blackwell, 1990.

TNA. "Foreign and Commonwealth Office and predecessors: Records of Former Colonial Administrations: Migrated Archives." Accessed April 3, 2023. https://discovery.natio nalarchives.gov.uk/details/r/C12269323.

TNA (London), FO 341/1, *Protocols and the General Act of the West African Conference*.

TNA (London), FO 371/7051, *League of Nations*.

TNA (London), FCO 141/4990, *Gold Coast: Security Liaison Officer, West Africa*.

TNA (London), CO 537/2037, *Problem of the Ewe people in British and French Togoland*.

TNA (London), FO 371/67718, *Problem of the unification of the EWE ethnic group in Togoland (under British and French trusteeship)*.

TNA (London), FCO 141/5026, *Gold Coast: Anglo-French cooperation on security matters in West Africa*.

TNA (London), FCO 141/4992, *Gold Coast: Special Branch; security and training*.

TNA (London), FCO 141/5027, *Gold Coast: Anglo-French cooperation on security matters in West Africa*.

TNA (London), FCO 141/5028, *Gold Coast: security reports from the French*.

TNA (London), FCO 141/5004, *Gold Coast: the Ewe and Togoland unification problem*.

TNA (London), FCO 141/4999, *Gold Coast: security and political intelligence; policy*.

TNA (London), FCO 141/4997, *Gold Coast: Special Branch Summaries*.

TNA (London), CO 554/668, *Togoland under UN Trusteeship: future policy*.

TNA (London), FCO 141/5010, *Gold Coast: the Ewe and Togoland unification problem*.

TNA (London), FCO 141/5022, *Gold Coast: United Nations Trusteeship Council Visiting Mission to West Africa, 1952; special report on the Ewe and Togoland unification problem*.

TNA (London), FO 371/101369, *Problems of Trust Territories of British and French Togoland*.

TNA (London), CO 554/665, *Togoland*.

TNA (London), CO 554/667, *Togoland Administration*.

TNA (London), FCO 141/5000, *Gold Coast: security and political intelligence; policy*.

TNA (London), FCO 141/5013, *Gold Coast: the Ewe and Togoland unification problem*.

TNA (London), FCO 141/5001, *Gold Coast: security and political intelligence; policy*.

TNA (London), DO 35/9279, *Political affairs in Togoland*.

TNA (London), FO 371/138270, *Foreign policy of Togoland*.

TNA (London), FO 371/138262, *Internal political situation in Togoland*. Code JF file 1019.

TNA (London), FO 371/146938, *Dispute about Togoland between France and Ghana*.
TNA (London), DO 35/9278, *Future of Togoland*.
TNA (London), FO 371/147612, *Internal political situation*.
TNA (London), FO 371/155660, *Political relations: Commonwealth countries*.
TNA (London), DO 195/75, *Problems of disaffected Ghanaians seeking refuge in Togo*.
TNA (London), FO 371/161755, *Army and police remain separate*.
TNA (London), FO 371/167647, *Assassination of President Olympio: coup de'etat*.
Togo Legislative Assembly. "2nd Legislature: Debats." 16 May 1958.
"Togoland Facing Divergent Pulls." *New York Times*, 14 August 1956.
Toulabor, Comi M. "Togo." In *Challenges of security sector governance in West Africa*. Edited by Alan Bryden, Boubacar N'Diaye and Funmi Olonisakin, 303–21. Wien, Zürich, Berlin, Münster: Lit, 2008.
Trotha, Trutz von. *Koloniale Herrschaft: Zur soziologischen Theorie der Staatsentstehung am Beispiel des "Schutzgebietes Togo"*. Tübingen: Mohr, 1994.
Trumann, Harry. "Inaugural Address." https://www.presidency.ucsb.edu/documents/inaugural-address-4.
UN ARMS (New York), S-0504-0004-0001-00001, *Committee on Rules of Procedure (1–11th Meeting (Conference Papers Nos. 1–10)*.
UN ARMS (New York), S-0504-0004-0001-00003, *Committee on Rules of Procedure (1–11th Meeting (Conference Papers Nos. 1–10)*.
UN ARMS (New York), S-1554-0000-0003, *Africa – Cameroon and Togoland - Visiting Mission*.
UN ARMS (New York), S-1554-0000-0004, *Africa – Togoland – Visiting Mission – Petitions and Communications*.
UN ARMS, T/Pet.7/287, *Petition*.
UN ARMS (New York), S-0443-0030-0006-00006, *T/PET.6/L.73*.
UN ARMS (New York), S-0443-0031-0002-00016, *T/PET.7/L.30*.
UN ARMS (New York), S-0443-0031-0002-00008, *T/PET.7/L22*.
UN ARMS (New York), S-0443-0030-0004-00017, *T/PET.6&7/L65*.
UN ARMS (New York), S-0443-0031-0002-00015, *T/PET.7/L29*.
UN ARMS (New York), S-0443-0030-0004-00019, *T/PET.6&7/L67*.
UN ARMS (New York), S-0443-0030-0006-00017, *T/PET.6/L.84*.
UN ARMS (New York), S-0884-0021-11-00001, *Togo*.
"UN Trusteeship Council Chamber reopens with new hopes for the future, Ban says." *UN News*, 26 April 2013. https://news.un.org/en/story/2013/04/438172-un-trusteeship-council-chamber-reopens-new-hopes-future-ban-says.
UNDP. "Human Development Report." New York, 1994.
United Nations (Geneva), R20/1/4900/3099, *Letter protesting against the present division of Togoland*.
United Nations. "Report to the Preparatory Commission of the United Nations." PC/EX/113/Rev.1, 1945. https://digitallibrary.un.org/record/703121.
United Nations. "Art. 87." In *Repertory of Practice of United Nations Organs, 1945–1954*. Vol. VI, 425–399. legal.un.org/repertory/art87/english/rep_orig_vol4_art87.pdf.
United Nations. "UN Yearbook 1955." 1955.
United Nations. "UN Yearbook 1956." 1956.

United Nations. "Art. 85." In *Repertory of Practice of United Nations Organs*, 1954–1955. Vol. II. Edited by United Nations (UN), 245–63 Supplement No. 1. legal.un.org/repertory/art85/english/rep_supp1_vol2_art85.pdf.

United Nations. "Art. 87." In *Repertory of Practice of United Nations Organs*, 1954–1955. Vol. II. Edited by United Nations (UN), 276–91 Supplement No. 1. legal.un.org/repertory/art87/english/rep_supp1_vol2_art87.pdf.

United Nations. "Repertory of Practice of United Nations Organs." 1954–1955 Supplement No. 1. 1954–1955, New York, 1958.

United Nations. "Art. 87." In *Repertory of Practice of United Nations Organs*, 1955–1959. Vol. III. Edited by United Nations (UN), 333–48 Supplement No. 2. legal.un.org/repertory/art87/english/rep_supp2_vol3_art87.pdf.

United Nations. "Report of the Panel on United Nations Peace Operations." A/55/405-S/2000/809, New York, 2000.

United Nations. "Opinion No. 47/2022 concerning George Nyakpo (Ghana)." A/HRC/WGAD/2022/47, Human Rights Council, 30 January 2023. https://www.ohchr.org/sites/default/files/documents/issues/detention-wg/opinions/session94/2023-01-30/A-HRC-WGAD-2022-47-Ghana-ADVANCE-EDITED-VERSION.pdf.

UNPO. "Member Profile: Western Togoland." Accessed July 9, 2020. https://unpo.org/downloads/2363.pdf.

UNPO. "Western Togoland: Members of HSGF Systematically Persecuted by Ghanaian Authorities." Accessed July 9, 2020. https://unpo.org/article/21783.

UNPO. "Charles Kormi Kudzorzi, leading figure of Western Togoland's self-determination movement, passes away aged 88." Accessed October 20, 2021. https://unpo.org/article/22162.

UNPO. "UNPO submits complaint to UN on detention of Western Togoland activists." Accessed August 2, 2022. https://www.unpo.org/article/22183.

UNPO. "Western Togoland: UNPO Delivers UPR Submission on Ghana Crackdown of Self-Determination Activists." Accessed August 2, 2022. https://unpo.org/article/22222.

van Evera, Stephen. "Bush Administration, Weak on Terror." *Middle East Policy* 13, no. 4 (2006): 28–38. https://doi.org/10.1111/j.1475-4967.2006.00268.x.

van Ginneken, Antonia Helena Maria. "Volkenbondsvoogdij: Het toezicht van de Volkenbond op het bestuur in mandaatgebieden, 1919–1940." [The League of Nations: The supervision of mandatory authority by the League of Nations 1919–1940]. PhD Dissertation, University of Utrecht, 1992.

Veit, Alex. *Intervention as indirect rule: Civil war and statebuilding in the Democratic Republic of Congo*. Mikropolitik der Gewalt 3. Frankfurt/Main: Campus, 2010.

Verschave, François-Xavier. *La Françafrique: le plus long scandale de la République*. Paris: Stock, 1998.

Vitalis, Robert. *White world order, black power politics: The birth of American international relations*. The United States in the World. Ithaca: Cornell University Press, 2015.

Vitoria, Francisco de. "On the American Indians." In *Political writings*. Edited by Anthony Pagden and Jeremy Lawrance, 231–92. Cambridge texts in the history of political thought. Cambridge: Cambridge University Press, 1991.

Vuori, Juha A. "Illocutionary Logic and Strands of Securitization: Applying the Theory of Securitization to the Study of Non-Democratic Political Orders." *European Journal of International Relations* 14, no. 1 (2008): 65–99. https://doi.org/10.1177/1354066107087767.

Vuori, Juha A. *How to do security with words: A grammar of securitisation in the People's Republic of China.* Turun yliopiston julkaisuja. Sarja B, Humaniora 336. Turku: University of Turku, 2011.

Wæver, Ole. *Security, the Speech Act: Analysing the Politics of a Word.* Jerusalem/Tel Aviv, 1989; 2nd Draft.

Wæver, Ole. "Identity, integration and security: Solving the sovereignty puzzle in E.U. studies." *Journal of International Affairs* 48, no. 2 (1995): 389–431. https://www.jstor.org/stable/24357597.

Wæver, Ole. "Securitization and Desecuritization." In *On security*. Edited by Ronnie D. Lipschutz, 46–86. New directions in world politics. New York: Columbia University Press, 1995.

Wæver, Ole. "The Theory Act: Responsibility and exactitude as seen from securitization." In Balzacq et al., *What Kind of Theory – If Any – Is Securitization?*, 26–34.

Wæver, Ole. "The theory act: Responsibility and exactitude as seen from securitization." *International Relations* 29, no. 1 (2015): 121–27.

Wæver, Ole, and Barry Buzan. "Racism and responsibility: The critical limits of deepfake methodology in security studies." *Security Dialogue* 51, no. 4 (2020): 386–94. https://doi.org/10.1177/0967010620916153.

Wallerstein, Immanuel. *The modern world-system I: The capitalist agriculture and the origins of the European world-economy in the sixteenth century.* Studies in social discontinuity. San Diego: Academic Press, 1974.

Walton, Calder. *Empire of Secrets: British Intelligence, the Cold War, and the Twilight of Empire.* New York: ABRAMS Books, 2014.

Warren Howe, Russell. "Togo: Four Years of Military Rule." *Africa Report* 12, no. 5 (1967): 6–12.

Weinstein, Jeremy, Stuart E. Eizenstat, and John Edward Porter. "Rebuilding Weak States." *Foreign Affairs*, 2005. Accessed November 30, 2021. https://www.foreignaffairs.com/articles/2005-01-01/rebuilding-weak-states.

Weisfeld, Michael, writer. *Sonntagsspaziergang,* "Togo: Wie Der Niederrhein Mit Palmen." aired November 17, 2013, on Deutschlandfunk. https://www.deutschlandfunk.de/togo-wie-der-niederrhein-mit-palmen-100.html.

Welch, Claude E. *Dream of Unity: Pan-Africanism and Political Unification in West Africa.* Ithaca: Cornell University Press, 1967.

Wendt, Alexander. "Anarchy is what States make of it: The Social Construction of Power Politics." *International Organization* 46, no. 2 (1992): 391–425.

Wendt, Alexander. *Social theory of international politics.* Cambridge studies in international relations 67. Cambridge: Cambridge University Press, 1999.

Wesley, Michael. "Toward a Realist Ethics of Intervention." *Ethics & International Affairs* 19, no. 2 (2005): 55–72. https://doi.org/10.1111/j.1747-7093.2005.tb00500.x.

Wesley, Michael Shamim. "The state of the art on the art of state building." *Global Governance* 14, no. 3 (2008): 369–85.

"Western Togoland attacks: Five more arrested for stealing AK 47 rifles." *GhanaWeb*, 04 October 2020. Accessed October 8, 2020. https://www.ghanaweb.com/GhanaHomePage/NewsArchive/Western-Togoland-attacks-Five-more-arrested-for-stealing-AK-47-rifles-1076782.

"Western Togoland Case: High Court sentences 5 secessionists to a total of 25 years in prison." *GhanaWeb*, 22 March 2023. Accessed March 22, 2023. https://www.ghanaweb.com/GhanaHomePage/NewsArchive/Western-Togoland-Case-High-Court-sentences-5-secessionists-to-a-total-of-25-years-in-prison-1734935.

"Western Togoland founder Papavi arrested after months of hiding." *GhanaWeb*, 29 July 2021. Accessed July 30, 2021. https://www.ghanaweb.com/GhanaHomePage/NewsArchive/Western-Togoland-founder-Papavi-arrested-after-months-of-hiding-1319953.

"Western Togoland leader 'Papavi Hogbedetor' laid to rest at Xavi." *GhanaWeb*, 31 October 2022. Accessed November 18, 2022. https://www.ghanaweb.com/GhanaHomePage/NewsArchive/Western-Togoland-leader-Papavi-Hogbedetor-laid-to-rest-at-Xavi-1653353.

"Western Togoland: There was no intelligence failure – Govt." *Starr FM Online*, 27 September 2020. Accessed September 30, 2020. https://starrfm.com.gh/2020/09/western-togoland-there-was-no-intelligence-failure-govt/.

Wilde, Ralph. "Accountability and International Actors in Bosnia and Herzegovina, Kosovo and East Timor." *ILSA Journal of International and Comparative Law* 7, no. 2 (2001): 455–60.

Wilde, Ralph. *International territorial administration: How trusteeship and the civilizing mission never went away*. Oxford: Oxford University Press, 2008.

Wilkinson, Claire. "The Copenhagen School on Tour in Kyrgyzstan: Is Securitization Theory Useable Outside Europe?" *Security Dialogue* 38, no. 1 (2007): 5–25. https://doi.org/10.1177/0967010607075964.

Williams, Edward. ""We have no support for secessionist activities"-Fodome Traditional Council." *Ghana News Agency*, 16 January 2020. Accessed January 20, 2020. https://ghananewsagency.org/politics/-we-have-no-support-for-secessionist-activities-fodome-traditional-council-162628.

Williams, Michael C. "Words, Images, Enemies: Securitization and International Politics." *International Studies Quarterly* 47, no. 4 (2003): 511–31. https://doi.org/10.1046/j.0020-8833.2003.00277.x.

Woodman, Connor. "How British police and intelligence are a product of the Imperial Boomerang Effect." Accessed May 25, 2021. https://www.versobooks.com/blogs/4390-how-british-police-and-intelligence-are-a-product-of-the-imperial-boomerang-effect.

Wright, Quincy. *Mandates under the League of Nations*. Chicago, Ill.: University of Chicago Press, 1930.

Wyss, Marco. *Postcolonial security: Britain, France, and West Africa's Cold War*. First edition. Oxford, New York, NY: Oxford University Press, 2021.

Yagla, Wen'saa Ogma. *L'édification de la Nation Togolaise: Naissance d'une conscience nationale dans un pays africain*. Paris: Harmattan, 1978.

Young, Crawford. *The African Colonial State in Comparative Perspective*. New Haven, CT: Yale University Press, 1994. https://doi.org/10.12987/9780300164473. https://www.degruyter.com/isbn/9780300164473.

Zaum, Dominik. *The sovereignty paradox: The norms and politics of international statebuilding*. Oxford: Oxford University Press, 2007. https://doi.org/10.1093/acprof:oso/9780199207435.001.0001.

Ziai, Aram. *Development Discourse and Global History: From colonialism to the sustainable development goals*. Hoboken: Taylor and Francis, 2015.

Zimmerman, Andrew. *Alabama in Africa: Booker T. Washington, the German empire, and the globalization of the new South*. America in the world. Princeton, N.J: Princeton University Press, 2010. http://site.ebrary.com/lib/alltitles/docDetail.action?docID=1064 0072.

Zimmerman, Andrew. "Decolonizing Decolonization: Review of Adom Getachew's Worldmaking after Empire." Accessed November 8, 2021. https://www.boundary2.org/2020/06/zimmerman-decolonizing-decolonization-review-of-adom-getachews-worldmaking-after-empire/.

Zurstrassen, Bettina. *"Ein Stück deutscher Erde schaffen": Koloniale Beamte in Togo 1884–1914*. Campus Forschung 931. Frankfurt/Main, New York: Campus, 2008.

Editorial

Postcolonial research has brought critical perspectives on colonialism in history and its heritage nowadays into public and scholarly focus. Similarly, postcolonial theorists have shown how deeply European scholarship and education are intertwined with the history and present of colonialism. For quite some time now, this postcolonial critique has triggered important public debates on the colonial past and how it should be remembered. The series **Postcolonial Studies** offers an editorial platform to continue these important discussions in an interdisciplinary framework.

Julius Heise, born in 1989, completed his doctorate at the Center for Conflict Studies (CCS) at Philipps-Universität Marburg and the Collaborative Research Center "Dynamics of Security". His research encompasses post- and decolonial approaches to decolonisation and statebuilding, emphasizing Critical Security Studies within Conflict Studies.